MONET AND VENICE

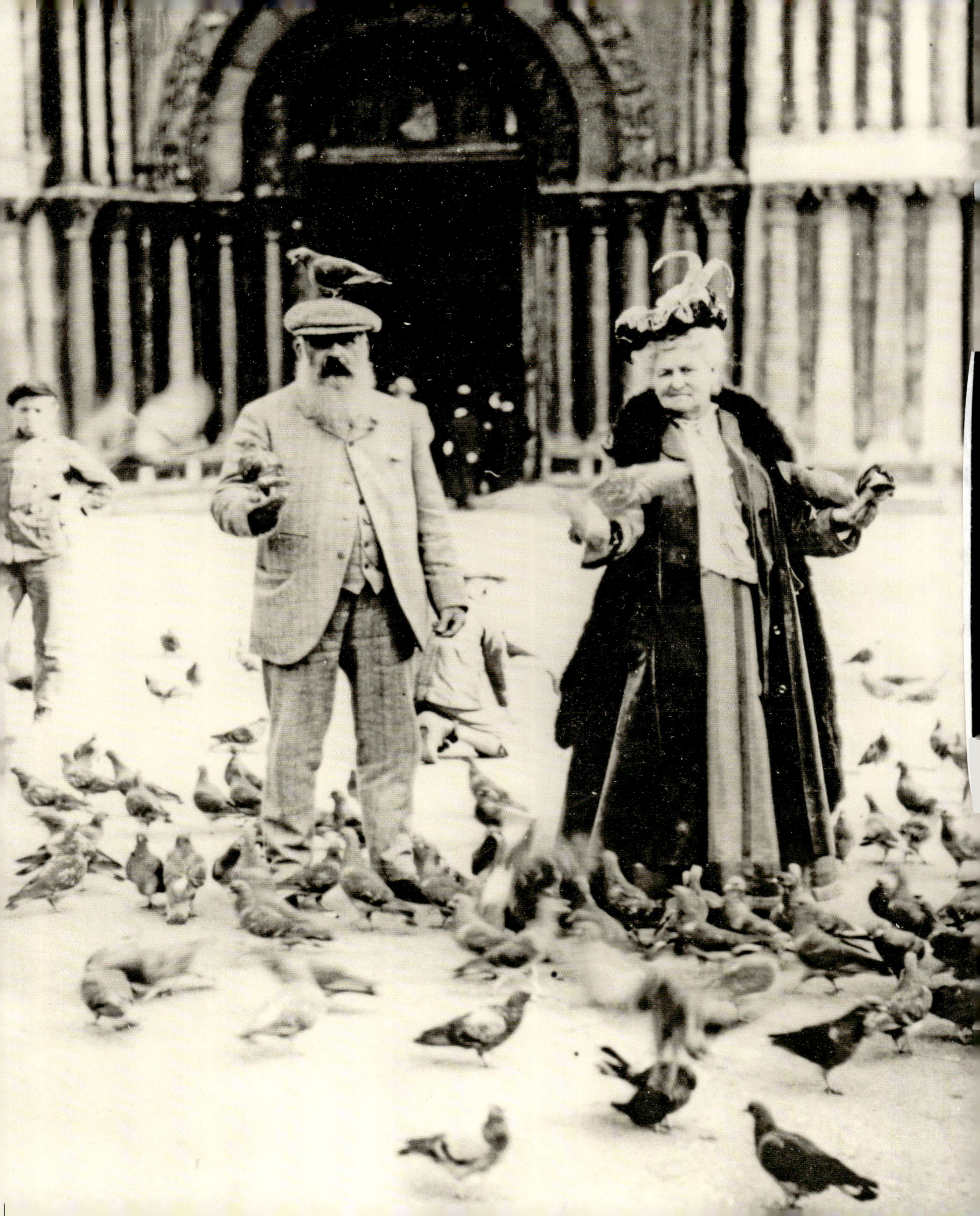

MONET AND VENICE

Rizzoli Electa

BROOKLYN MUSEUM / FINE ARTS MUSEUMS OF SAN FRANCISCO

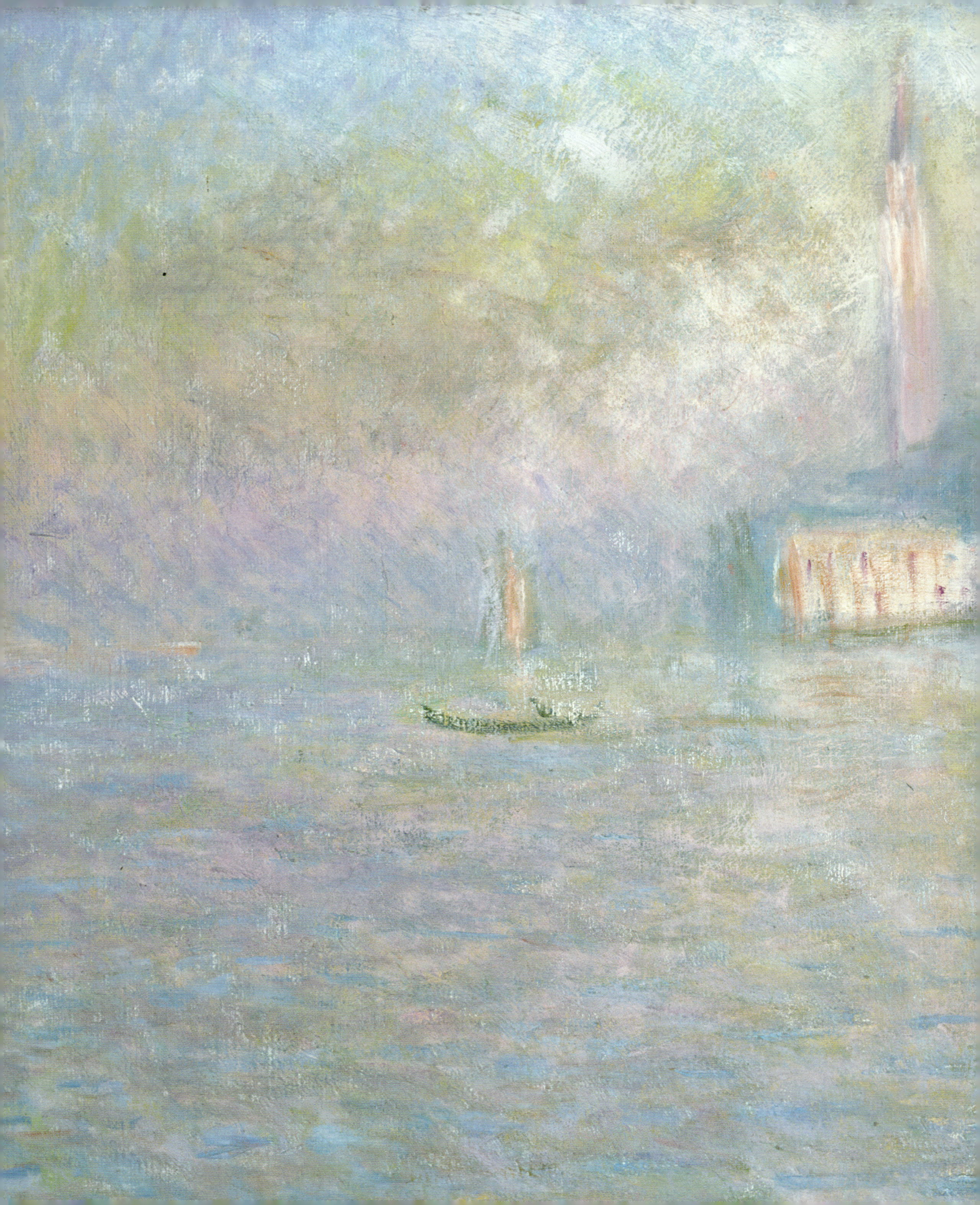

CONTENTS

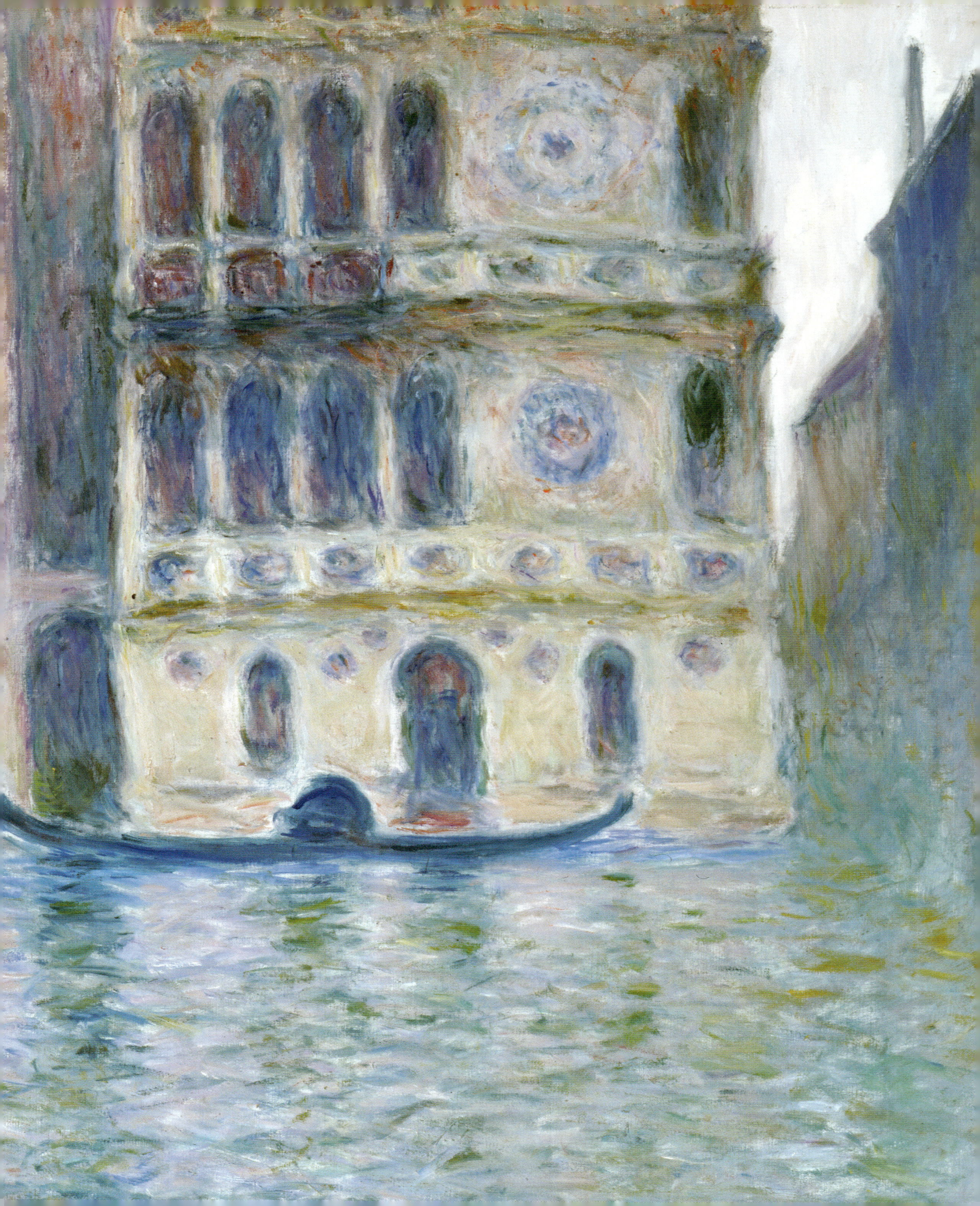

FOREWORD

Anne Pasternak
Thomas P. Campbell

THE BROOKLYN MUSEUM AND THE FINE ARTS MUSEUMS of San Francisco are pleased to present *Monet and Venice*, the first dedicated exploration of the artist's paintings of Venice since their 1912 debut at Galerie Bernheim-Jeune in Paris. Reuniting about twenty of his Venetian views, along with select paintings from key moments across his career and portrayals of the city by other artists such as Canaletto, Édouard Manet, John Singer Sargent, J. M. W. Turner, and Pierre-Auguste Renoir, this exhibition offers audiences a rare opportunity to experience and contextualize Monet's unique vision of La Serenissima.

Monet once remarked that Venice was "too beautiful to be painted," and it is perhaps this very beauty, and the city's fame, that has obscured the significance and daring nature of the works that resulted from his only trip there in 1908. His Venetian paintings are among the most luminous of his oeuvre, yet they are often overshadowed by his iconic depictions of the French landscape, and by his later works that have been linked to the rise of twentieth-century abstraction. It is a great pleasure to explore this significant moment in his career with fresh eyes and insights.

We are particularly proud that our exhibition partnership was inspired by two Monet masterpieces in the respective collections of Brooklyn and San Francisco: *The Palazzo Ducale* and *The Grand Canal, Venice*. Indeed, highlights from each of our rich holdings are featured in *Monet and Venice*, notably San Francisco's magnificent Canaletto, *Venice, the Grand Canal Looking East with Santa Maria della Salute* and Monet's outstanding early Impressionist painting *Sailboats on the Seine at Petit-Gennevilliers*, as well as Brooklyn's group of dazzling Sargent watercolors of Venice and Monet's *Houses of Parliament, Sunlight Effect*, which dates from the years just prior to his Venetian sojourn. Celebrating such significant collection highlights

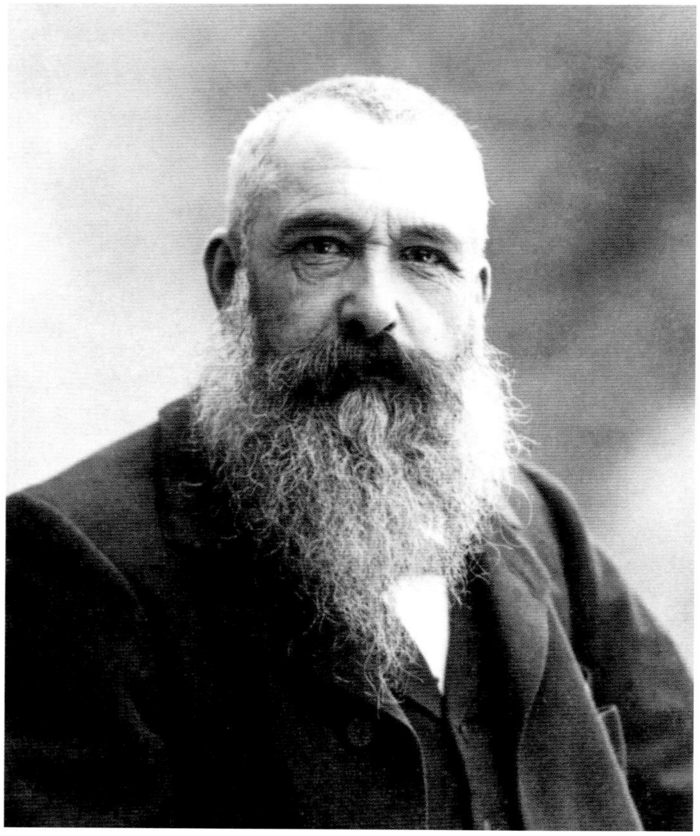

makes this exhibition and publication a rewarding endeavor, as does the fact that both of our museums are in cities that, like Venice, face the challenges and opportunities of being on the water, and that welcome visitors from around the world.

For both museums, *Monet and Venice* represents the latest example of a strong and ongoing commitment to collecting and presenting French art. The Brooklyn Museum has been a trailblazing institution from the start. In 1921, when most U.S. museums still refrained from exhibiting or acquiring modern European art, Brooklyn presented the exhibition *Paintings by Modern French Masters: The Post-Impressionists and Their Predecessors*, which, according to *Art News*, was "the most talked-of art show of the season because . . . it is the first time that a great public museum in this country has taken official cognizance of Modernist art." After visiting the exhibition, no less an expert than Alfred Stieglitz noted, "Brooklyn was stealing a march on its big neighbor in Manhattan." Not long after, the Brooklyn Museum became the first museum in New York City to acquire paintings by Camille Pissarro, Berthe Morisot, Henri de Toulouse-Lautrec, and Claude Monet, whose *Palazzo Ducale* entered our collection in 1920 and is thus emblematic of our bold vision.

Likewise, the Legion of Honor, one of the two museums that make up the Fine Arts Museums of San Francisco, is a three-quarter-scale replica of the Palais de la Légion d'Honneur in Paris—embodying the bonds, both historical and contemporary, between France and San Francisco. The Museums' impressive holdings of eighteenth- and nineteenth-century French decorative arts and paintings distinguish the collection among American peer institutions. Monet's paintings are a particular standout among the Impressionist highlights, which regularly draw enthusiastic visitors to the collections located in Lincoln Park at Lands End. This exhibition, presented in the de Young will add to a strong legacy of Impressionist shows presented by the Fine Arts Museums, including *Monet in Normandy* and the pair of exhibitions *Monet: The Early Years* and *Monet: The Late Years*. Approximately sixty-five years after *The Grand Canal, Venice* was given by San Francisco philanthropist Osgood Hooker, *Monet and Venice* will be the first exhibition to showcase research on Monet's last major international trip and the context in which he painted the lagoon city.

Thanks to support from the Ford Foundation, the Brooklyn Museum's composer-in-residence, Niles Luther, has written an original symphonic score inspired by Monet's Venice paintings. Weaving ambient recordings he made in Venice with melodic themes, Luther has composed a new symphony for the exhibition that sets the stage for the visitor's journey. Just as Monet sought to render Venice's unique atmospheric *enveloppe*—where light, water, and architecture merge into unified sensory impressions—Luther translates these visually dissolving effects into an immersive sonic experience, deepening and enriching the visitor's journey.

An ambitious exhibition like this can be realized only through the contributions and care of a large, talented team. Our cocurators, Lisa Small and Melissa Buron, initiated the project and worked tirelessly and thoughtfully to shape it into an engaging and beautiful experience for our visitors. Creative and dedicated staff at each museum—who are thanked individually in the acknowledgments—joined them to ensure its success at every stage. We are only able to share the moving, fascinating story of Monet's Venice trip with our audiences thanks to the many public institutions and private individuals who have generously agreed to loan their magnificent and precious works of art to us, and we are extraordinarily grateful to all of them. The Fine Arts Museums of San Francisco are grateful to the donors who have supported this project: John A. and Cynthia Fry Gunn, Barbara A. Wolfe, Diane B. Wilsey, Dagmar Dolby, the Henderson Family Foundation, The Herbst Foundation, Inc., The Wollenberg Foundation, Christie's, Gretchen B. Kimball, Annette Alioto, and Lynn and Edward Poole, without whose support our vision for Monet and Venice could not have come to fruition. Finally, we would like to thank the ongoing encouragement and support of our trustees. In Brooklyn, we extend our gratitude to Barbara M. Vogelstein, chair, and to every member of our board. In San Francisco, we extend our thanks to David Hooker Spencer, chair, and Diane B. Wilsey, chair emerita, as well as our trustees. Without the confidence and active engagement of our boards of trustees, it would not be possible for us to pursue and maintain the highest level of exhibition and publication programming that *Monet and Venice* exemplifies.

ANNE PASTERNAK, *Shelby White and Leon Levy Director*
Brooklyn Museum

THOMAS P. CAMPBELL, *Director and CEO*
Fine Arts Museums of San Francisco

LENDERS TO THE EXHIBITION

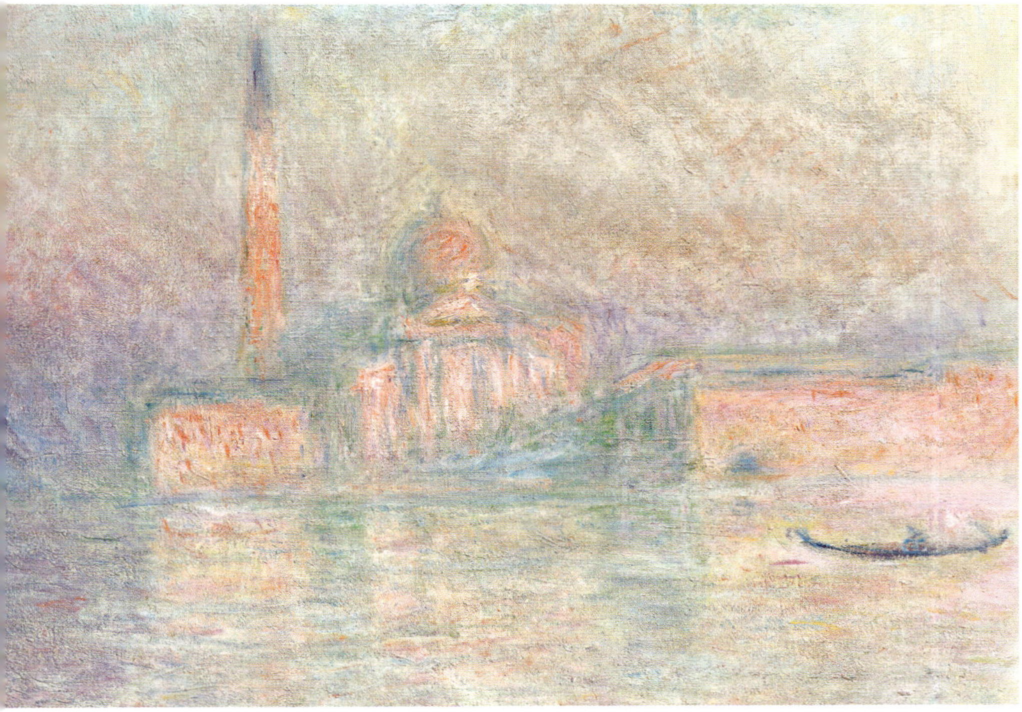

Alon Zakaim Fine Art
Amgueddfa Cymru–Museum Wales
Art Institute of Chicago
Chrysler Museum of Art
Clark Art Institute
Cleveland Museum of Art
Denver Art Museum
The Frick Pittsburgh Museums & Gardens
Galerie Larock-Granoff, Paris
Gallery 19C
Hasso Plattner Collection,
Museum Barberini
Indianapolis Museum of Art at Newfields
Kunsthaus Zürich
Kunstmuseum St. Gallen
La Salle University Art Museum
The Metropolitan Museum of Art
Montreal Museum of Fine Arts
Musée Marmottan Monet
Museum of Fine Arts, Boston
Museum of Fine Arts, Houston
National Gallery of Canada
Philadelphia Museum of Art
Royal Academy of Arts
Solomon R. Guggenheim Museum
Tate
University of Michigan Museum of Art
Victoria and Albert Museum

Mary McClean
Celia Morrissette/Keith Johnson
Bernard and Barbro Osher
Philippe Piguet
Paul Hayes Tucker
Diane B. Wilsey

Private collections, courtesy of Christie's, and other private lenders who wish to remain anonymous

Claude Monet, *San Giorgio Maggiore*, 1908, oil on canvas, 23⅔ × 28 ¾ in., private collection (detail), see pl. 10

ACKNOWLEDGMENTS

Lisa Small
Melissa Buron

IT HAS BEEN AN HONOR and a pleasure to organize *Monet and Venice*, a project we would not have been able to realize successfully without the active participation of many individuals and institutions worldwide. Foremost, we are grateful to Anne Pasternak, Shelby White and Leon Levy Director of the Brooklyn Museum, and Thomas P. Campbell, director and CEO of the Fine Arts Museums of San Francisco, for their leadership and vision.

We in Brooklyn also extend our sincere thanks to the corporate, foundation, and private funders whose crucial support made this exhibition possible, including the Bank of America, The Gladys Krieble Delmas Foundation, Constance L. Christensen, and Mr. and Mrs. Alan Howard.

For generously sharing their exceptional works of art with us and our audiences, we are indebted to the following museum and gallery colleagues: Ben Springett and Alon Zakaim at Alon Zakaim Fine Arts; James Rondeau and Gloria Groom at the Art Institute of Chicago; Erik H. Neil and Mark Castro at the Chrysler Museum of Art; Olivier Meslay and Esther Bell at the Clark Art Institute; William M. Griswold and Heather Lemonedes Brown at the Cleveland Museum of Art; Christoph Heinrich and Angelica Daneo at the Denver Art Museum; Elizabeth Barker and Dawn Brean at the Frick Pittsburgh Museum and Gardens; Edouard Larock and Camille Filaferro at Galerie Larock-Granoff; Eric Weider at Gallery 19C; Mariët Westermann, Richard Armstrong, Megan Fontanella, and Julie Barten at the Guggenheim Museum; Belinda Tate, Colette Pierce Burnette, and Robin Cooper at the Indianapolis Museum of Art at Newfields; Ann Demeester, Philippe Buettner, and Tobias Haupt at the Kunsthaus Zürich; Gianni Jetzer at the Kunstmuseum St.Gallen; Max Hollein and Susan Alyson Stein at the Metropolitan Museum of Art; Stéphane Aquin and Mary-Dailey Desmarais at the Montreal Museum of Fine Arts; Carolyn Greene at the LaSalle University Art Museum; Érik Desmazières, Sylvie Carlier, Aurélie Gavoille, and Marie-Louise Favre at the Musée Marmottan Monet; Hasso Plattner, Ortrud Westheider, Sterre Barentsen, and Daniel Zamani at the Museum Barberini; Matthew Teitelbaum and Katie Hanson at the Museum of Fine Arts, Boston; Helga Aurisch and Gary Tinterow at the Museum of Fine Arts, Houston; Jean-François Bélisle, Anabelle Kienle Poňka, and Hailey Chomos at the National Gallery of Canada; Jane Richardson, Kath Davies, and Andrew Renton at Amgueddfa Cymru–Museum Wales; Sasha Suda, Jennifer Thompson, and Tara Contractor at the Philadelphia Museum of Art; Rebecca Salter, Rebecca Lyons, Ann Dumas, Hannah Higham, and Julien Domercq at the Royal Academy of Arts; Alex Farquharson and Amy Concannon at Tate Britain; Christina Olsen and Corey Gross at the University of Michigan Museum of Art; and Tristram Hunt, Christopher Turner, Jenny Gaschke, Rosalind McKever, Juliet Ceresole, Ruth Hibbard, and Ana Muñoz at the Victoria and Albert Museum. We are grateful to the generous individual collectors who are sharing their works with us, including Keith Johnson and Celia Morrissette, Mary McClean, Bernard and Barbro Osher, Philippe Piguet, Paul Hayes Tucker, and Diane B. Wilsey. We also thank all the individual lenders who wish to remain anonymous.

Our work on this project has also benefited enormously from the collegiality and support of the following individuals, to whom we are grateful: Karen Christenson; Teresa Krasny; Sylvie Patin; Philippe Piguet; Joachim Pissarro; Elizabeth Royer; Karen Serres; Charles Stuckey; Paul Hayes Tucker; Jennifer Gimblett, Elizabeth Gorayeb, and Vitoria Hadba at the Wildenstein Plattner Institute; and Richard Espley, chief librarian, V&A Research Institute, National Art Library and Archives, Victoria and Albert

Museum. We also appreciate the critical assistance provided by various colleagues who helped us secure key loans: Gauri Agarwal; Cyanne Chutkow, Samantha Koslow, and Katherine Mandel at Christie's; and Christy Coombs, Nina del Rio, Sharon H. Kim, and Zoë Zaneteas at Sotheby's.

We extend heartfelt thanks to André Dombrowski, Donato Esposito, Félicie Faizand de Maupeou, Niles Luther, Elena Marchetti, Jonathan P. Ribner, and Richard Thomson, who have enriched this catalogue with their insightful essays. Niles Luther, Brooklyn Museum's composer-in-residence, a position funded by the Ford Foundation, also created a moving and beautiful symphony inspired by Monet's Venice paintings that enhances the exhibition experience in Brooklyn, and we are deeply grateful to him for his unique creative engagement with this project.

For their outstanding work shepherding this publication through its completion, we want to particularly thank Dolores Farrell, the Brooklyn Museum's senior director of exhibitions; Gwen Arriaga, assistant director of exhibitions; Sarah DeSantis, director of digital collections and services; and Taylor Catalana, image licensing specialist. At Rizzoli, we want to thank Loren Olson for producing such a beautiful volume. Our editors Natalie Danford and Richard Slovak were instrumental in finessing the arguments and contents of our essays. Lucinda Hitchcock and Cara Buzzell of 60/40 Projects created the gorgeous design.

The exhibition *Monet and Venice* could not have come to fruition without the hard work and collaborative spirit of our esteemed Brooklyn Museum and Fine Arts Museums of San Francisco colleagues. In Brooklyn, the project was guided and brought into being by an extraordinary team led by Dolores Farrell and Gwen Arriaga, working closely with Paloma Obregón, registrar for exhibitions and loans Katie Welty, senior director of registration and collections care. Lance Singletary, director of exhibition design, and Bob Nardi, manager of time-based media and AV technology, all provided key support. Senior exhibition designer Kyong Kim envisioned and, with the hard work of all our shop teams, executed a dazzling installation, further enhanced by the graphic identity created for it by Adam O'Reilly, director of graphic design, and senior graphic designer Eric Price, and by Sophia Bruneau, who helped craft compelling gallery didactics. Shania Lin, Taylor Maatman, Brooke Baldeschwiler, and our communications and marketing teams did an incredible job creating and spreading excitement for the project. We are grateful to Lisa Bruno, Carol Lee Shen Chief Conservator, Lauren Bradley, associate paintings conservator, Ellen Nigro, assistant paintings conservator, Sara Bone, assistant paper conservator, and art handler/framer Takayuki Umezawa for making Brooklyn's collection works look their very best. Filippo Gentile, senior art handler, led his team in a successful installation. Erika Riches, senior buyer and merchandise manager, Shamilia McBean Tocruray, director of education, and Lauren Zelaya, director of public programs, and their teams spearheaded exciting opportunities to extend and enrich visitor experiences. Sharon Matt Atkins, deputy director for art, provided early and ongoing support for the exhibition and we especially thank her, along with Catherine Futter, curatorial chair and senior curator of decorative arts and design, and Catherine Morris, curatorial chair and Sackler Senior Curator, Elizabeth A. Sackler Center for Feminist Art, for their ongoing intellectual and logistical guidance and encouragement. We are immensely grateful to former and current curatorial assistants Joseph Shaikewitz, Shea Spiller, Talia Shiroma, Michael Gibson-Prugh, and Grace Billingslea for their assistance throughout all stages of this complicated project. Chief development officer Carly Goettel and her team worked tirelessly to secure crucial financial support. We also thank the team at Potion, who, working with videographer Joan Porcel, created a stunning multimedia immersive experience about Venice to welcome visitors to the exhibition in Brooklyn.

The Fine Arts Museums of San Francisco are grateful to the donors who have supported this project: John A. and Cynthia Fry Gunn, Barbara A. Wolfe, Diane B. Wilsey, Dagmar Dolby, the Henderson Family Foundation, The Herbst Foundation, Inc., The Wollenberg Foundation, Christie's, Gretchen B. Kimball, Annette Alioto, and Lynn and Edward Poole.

At the Fine Arts Museums of San Francisco, appreciation is extended to all staff involved in this exhibition across many departments. Foremost and heartfelt thanks are due to Krista Brugnara, chief exhibitions and collections officer, who, along with Anna Wu, senior exhibitions coordinator, was essential in overseeing and organizing the many complex facets of this project for its presentation at the de Young. For their critical efforts in organizing the indemnity and registration of this project, we thank Kimberley Montgomery, director of registration and collections management; Amy Andersson, exhibition registrar; and Julian Drake, senior registrar. For their assistance with the nuanced details of preparing for loans of works on paper from the Achenbach Foundation for Graphic Arts, we thank Cyntia Karnes, head of paper conservation, and Allison Brewer, associate paper conservator. Sincere appreciation is also extended to Furio Rinaldi, curator-in-charge, drawings, prints, photographs, for his collegiality during this collaboration. For their participation in providing information about the many key loans from the collection of European paintings, thanks are extended to Emily A. Beeny, chief curator of the Legion of Honor, Barbara A. Wolfe, curator in charge of European paintings, and Isabella Lores-Chavez, associate curator, as well as Rhiana Ferguson, administrative coordinator in European paintings, and Rachel Sanchez, former curatorial intern. Special appreciation is noted for the supportive collaboration of Danielle St. Germain, chief philanthropy officer, and her team, in fundraising for this exhibition, along with Jason Seifer, chief financial and administrative officer. Thanks are also due to Tricia O'Regan, paintings conservator, and Isaac Messina, assistant paintings conservator, for ensuring the secure condition of the masterpieces in this presentation during their installation. We also thank Tristan Telander, exhibition designer; Alejandro Stein, director of exhibition design; and Ryan Butterfield, director of preparation and installation, and their terrific teams, for realizing the presentation on the museum's walls at the de Young. Isabella Holland, project manager, and Lexi Paulson, former project manager, provided early, enthusiastic, and instrumental support toward this exhibition's development. To anyone else who supported bringing this exhibition to fruition, please know that we are grateful for your contributions.

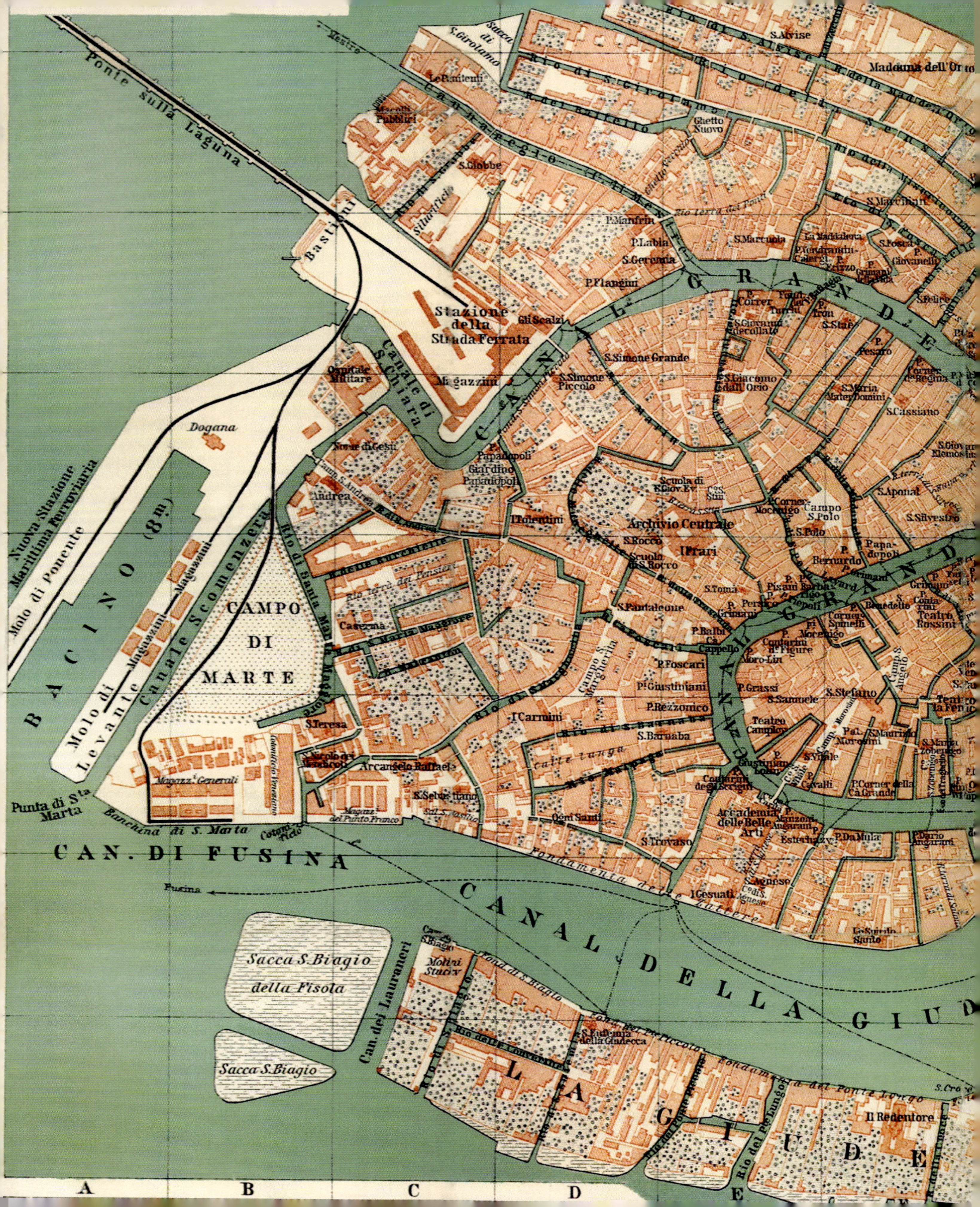

Ponte sulla Laguna
Bastioni
Stazione della Strada Ferrata
Magazzini
Gli Scalzi
Canale di S. Chiara
Ospitale Militare
Dogana
Nuova Stazione Marittima Ferroviaria
Molo di Ponente
BACINO (8m.)
Molo di Levante
Canale Scomenzera
CAMPO DI MARTE
Magazz. Generali
Punta di Sta Marta
Banchina di S. Marta
CAN. DI FUSINA
Fusina
CANAL DELLA GIUD
Sacca S. Biagio della Pisola
Sacca S. Biagio
Can. dei Lauraneri
Mulini Stucky
S. Eufemia della Giudecca
LA GIUDE
Il Redentore
S. Girolamo
Sacca di S. Girolamo
S. Alvise
Madonna dell'Orto
Ghetto Nuovo
S. Giobbe
P. Manfrin
P. Labia
S. Geremia
P. Flangini
S. Marcuola
S. Marciliàn
S. Fosca
CANAL GRANDE
S. Simeone Grande
S. Simeone Piccolo
S. Giacomo dall'Orio
S. Stae
P. Pesaro
S. Cassiano
S. Maria Mater Domini
Papadopoli
Giardino Papadopoli
I Tolentini
Archivio Centrale
I Frari
S. Rocco
Scuola di S. Rocco
S. Polo
Campo S. Polo
S. Aponal
S. Silvestro
S. Toma
S. Pantaleone
Caserma
P. Foscari
P. Giustiniani
P. Rezzonico
I Carmini
S. Barnaba
Calle lunga
S. Teresa
Arcangelo Raffael
S. Sebastiano
Ogni Santi
S. Trovaso
Accademia delle Belle Arti
S. Agnese
I Gesuati
Fondamenta delle Zattere
S. Stefano
S. Samuele
Teatro Camploy
Teatro Rossini
Teatro la Fenice
S. Vitale
P. Corner della Ca Grande
P. Da Mula
La Spirito Santo
A
B
C
D
E

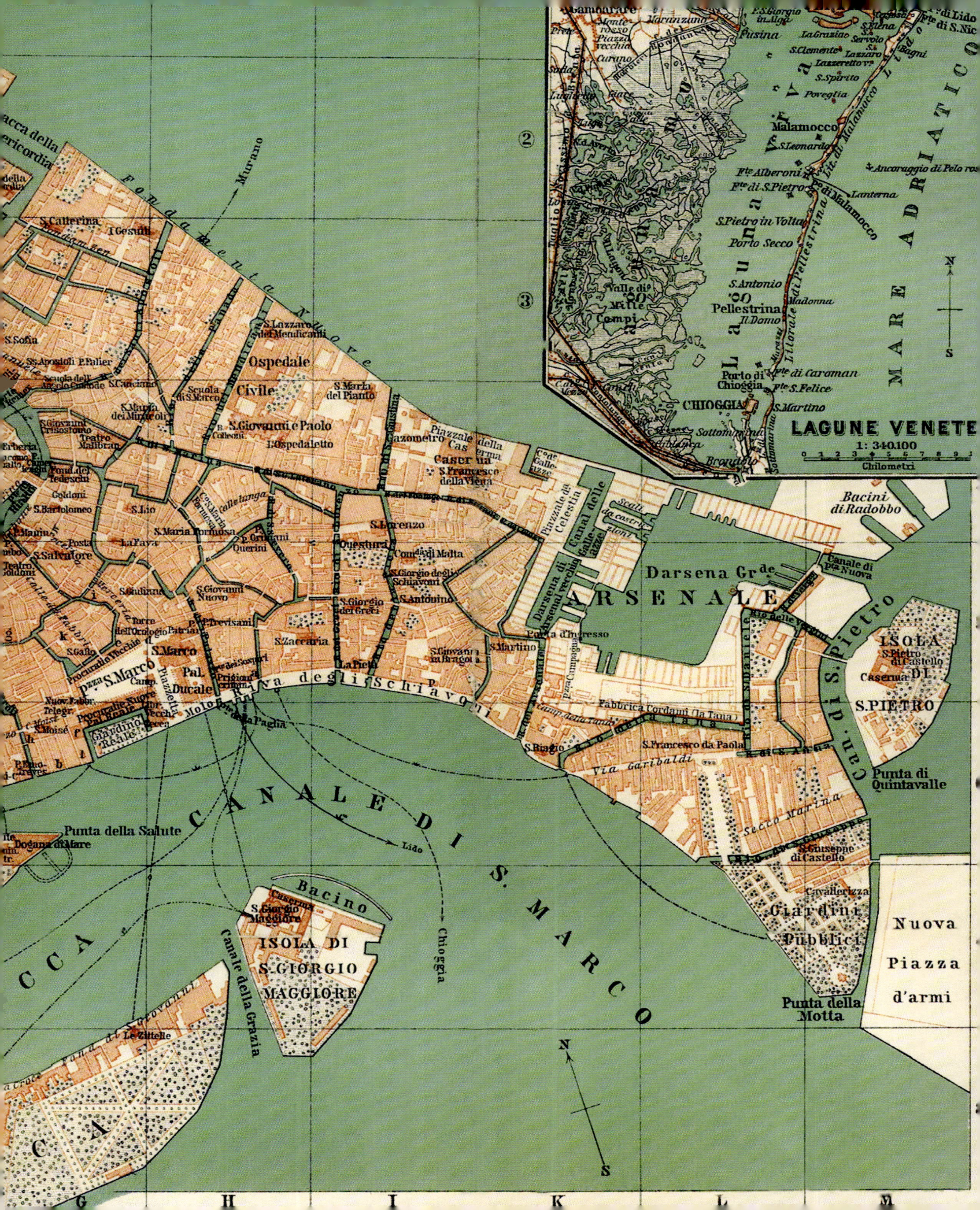

LAGUNE VENETE
1: 340.100
Chilometri
MARE ADRIATICO
Malamocco
S.Leonardo
Fte Alberoni
Fte di S.Pietro
Porto di Malamocco
Lanterna
Ancoraggio di Pelo rosa
S.Pietro in Volta
Porto Secco
S.Antonio
Pellestrina
Il Domo
Madonna
Litorale di Pellestrina
Porto di Chioggia
Fte di Caroman
Fte S.Felice
S.Martino
CHIOGGIA
Sottomarina
Brondolo
Fusina
La Grazia
S.Clemente
S.Servolo
Lazzaretto vo
S.Spirito
Poveglia
Valle di Mille Campi
Murano
Fondamenta Nuove
S.Catterina
I Gesuiti
S.Sofia
SS.Apostoli
S.Canciano
S.Lazzaro dei Mendicanti
Ospedale Civile
Scuola di S.Marco
S.Maria dei Miracoli
S.Giovanni e Paolo
S.Maria del Pianto
L'Ospedaletto
Teatro Malibran
Fond.dei Tedeschi
Goldoni
S.Bartolomeo
S.Lio
S.Maria Formosa
Calle Lunga
Querini
S.Salvatore
S.Zulian
S.Giovanni Nuovo
Torre dell'Orologio
S.Gallo
Procuratie Vecchie
S.Marco
Pal. Ducale
Pzza S.Marco
Piazzetta
Procuratie Nuove
Pal. Reale
Giardino Reale
S.Moisè
Molo
Riva degli Schiavoni
Ponte della Paglia
Prigioni
S.Zaccaria
La Pietà
S.Lorenzo
Questura
Comda di Malta
S.Giorgio degli Schiavoni
S.Giorgio dei Greci
S.Antonino
S.Giovanni in Bragora
S.Martino
Gazometro
Piazzale della Caserma
S.Francesco della Vigna
Piazzale di Celestia
Canal delle Galeazze
Darsena di Arsenal vecchio
Punta d'ingresso
ARSENALE
Darsena Grde
Bacini di Radobbo
Canale di Pta Nuova
Rio delle Vergini
Can. di S.Pietro
ISOLA DI S.PIETRO
S.Pietro di Castello
Caserma
Punta di Quintavalle
Fabbrica Cordami (la Tana)
S.Biagio
S.Francesco da Paola
Via Garibaldi
Secco Marina
S.Giuseppe di Castello
Cavallerizza
Giardini Pubblici
Punta della Motta
Nuova Piazza d'armi
CANALE DI S.MARCO
Punta della Salute
Dogana di Mare
Lido
Chioggia
Bacino
Caserma
S.Giorgio Maggiore
ISOLA DI S.GIORGIO MAGGIORE
Canale della Grazia
Le Zitelle
N
S
G
H
I
K
L
M
2
3

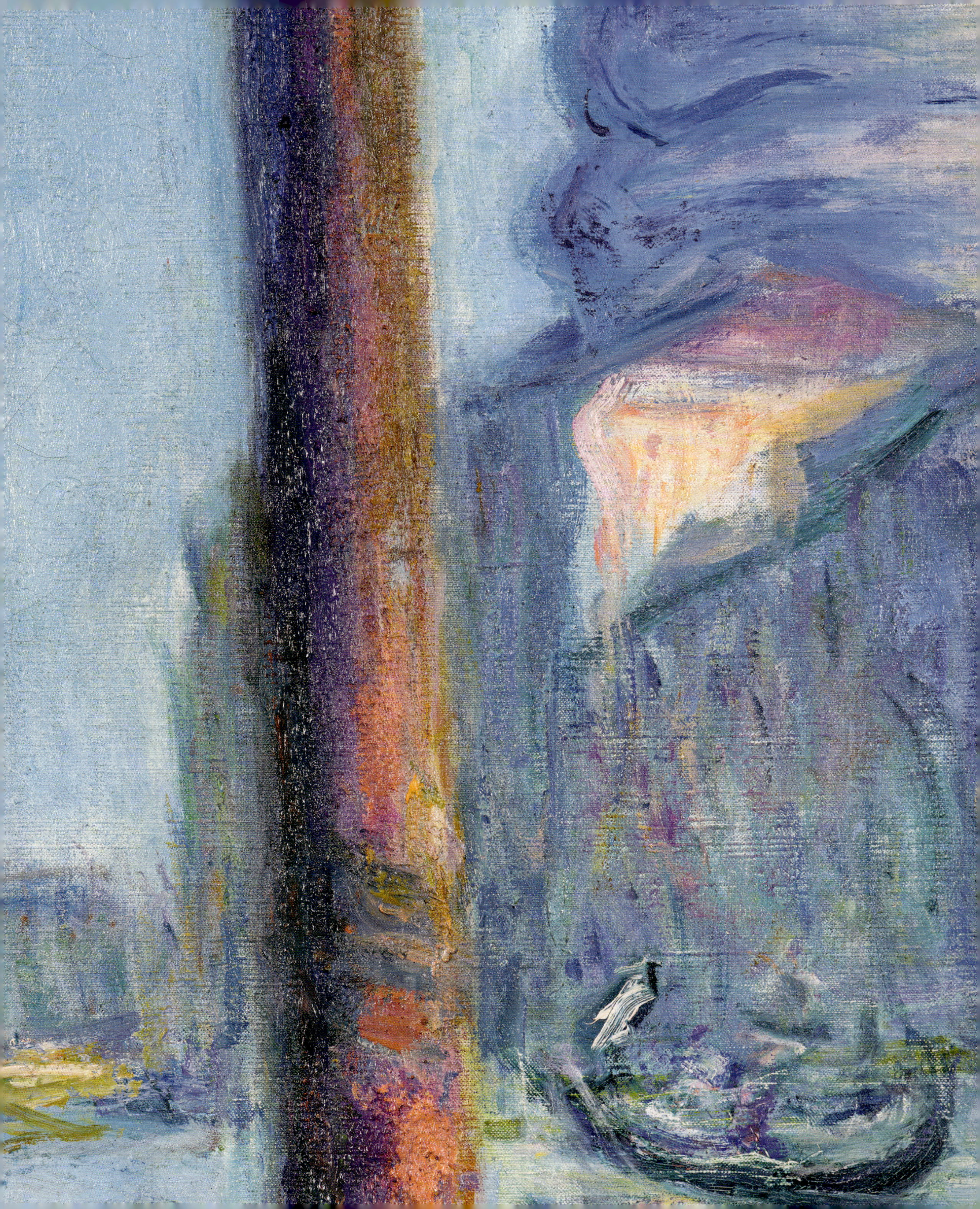

PART ONE

"I WILL NOT GO TO VENICE"

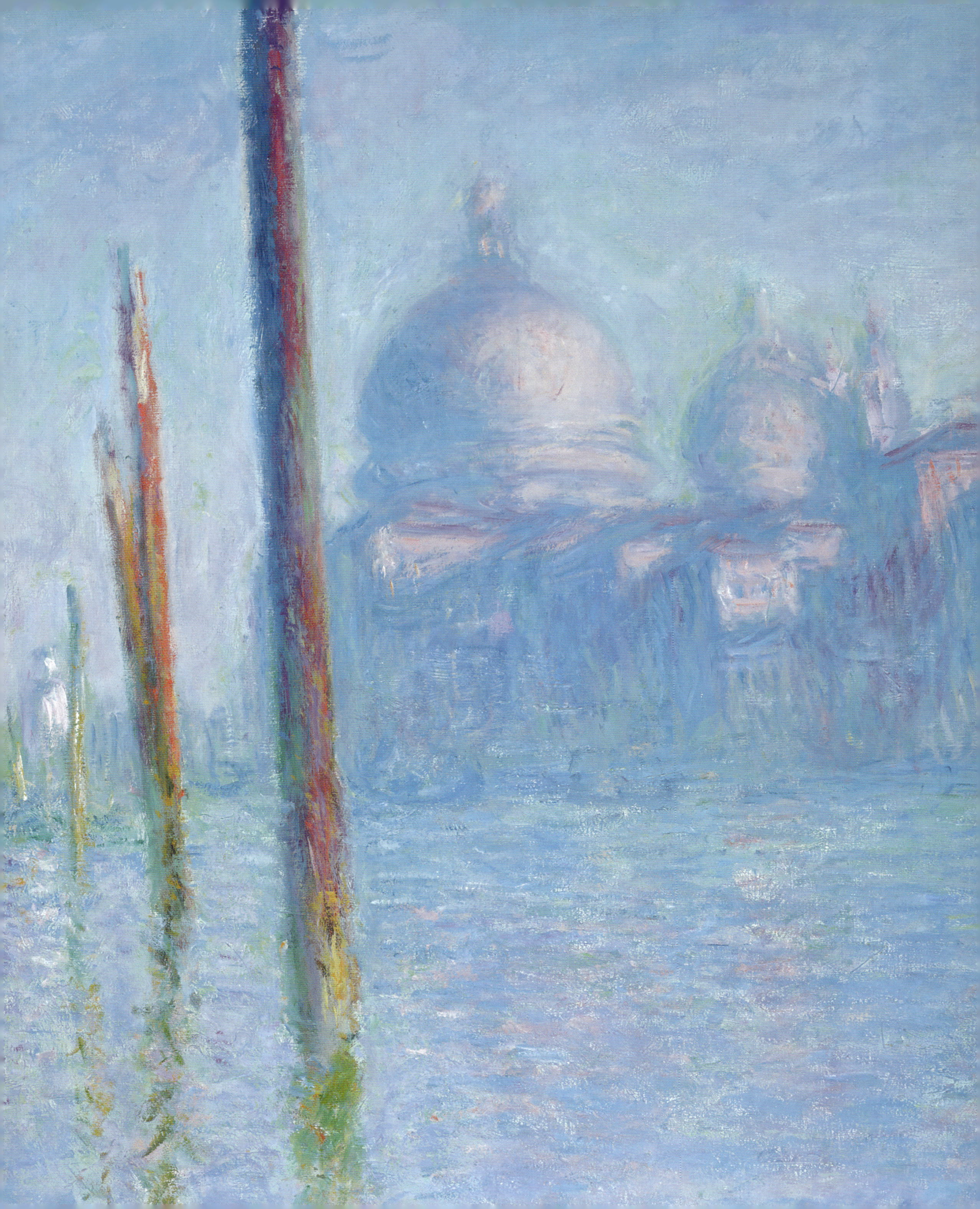

"TOO BEAUTIFUL TO BE PAINTED": MONET AND THE ALLURE OF VENICE

Melissa Buron

MONET AND VENICE, a collaboration between the Brooklyn Museum and the Fine Arts Museums of San Francisco, is the first exhibition devoted to Claude Monet's Venice paintings since 1912, when twenty-nine (out of a total of thirty-seven) made their public debut at the Galerie Bernheim-Jeune in Paris. Through the reunion of approximately twenty of these artworks in Brooklyn and San Francisco, supplemented with additional paintings by Monet and other artists, photographs, prints, and ephemera, and accompanied by the insights presented in this catalogue, *Monet and Venice* sheds new light on the critical role that La Serenissima played in Monet's late oeuvre.

Claude Monet is so closely associated with painting the effects of water and light that his depictions of Venice—a city renowned for these elements—may appear to be a foregone conclusion. Yet Monet's paintings of Venice were not inevitable. If Monet had not faced a crisis of confidence in 1908, ironically over the subject with which he would become synonymous—water lilies—the paintings of Venice by Impressionism's most high-profile acolyte likely would not exist. Credit for his one and only trip to Venice at age sixty-eight is due to two forceful women: his second wife, Alice Monet (fig. 1), and the wealthy English art collector and connoisseur Mary Hunter (née Smyth, fig. 4). Painting in Venice, at their encouragement, reinvigorated Monet's determination to revisit his iconic *Water Lilies*, widely considered his creative grand finale.

Anchoring the exhibition and the catalyst for our partnership are the Brooklyn Museum's *The Palazzo Ducale* (pl. 6) and *The Grand Canal, Venice* (pl. 1) from the Fine Arts Museums of San Francisco. The former left France for America the year after its 1912 debut, when it was purchased from Monet by the sometimes rival dealers Bernheim-Jeune and Durand-Ruel. In

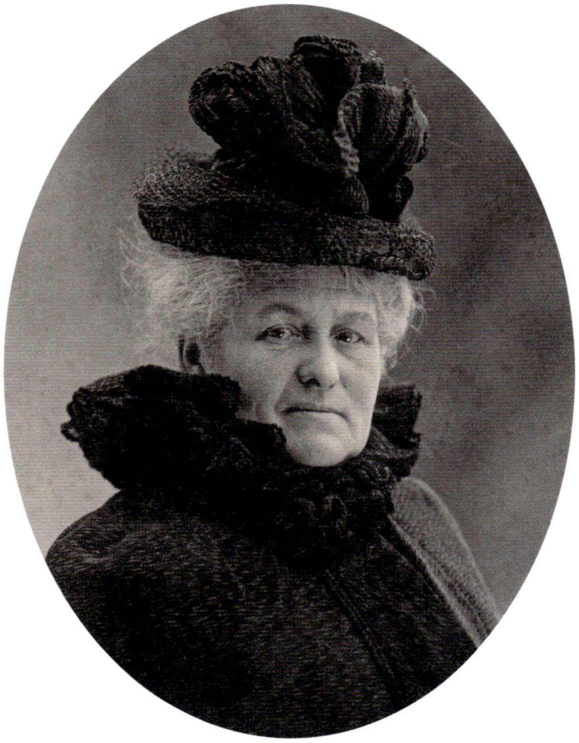

fig. 1—Félix Nadar, portrait of Alice Monet, 1899, silver print, Bridgeman Images

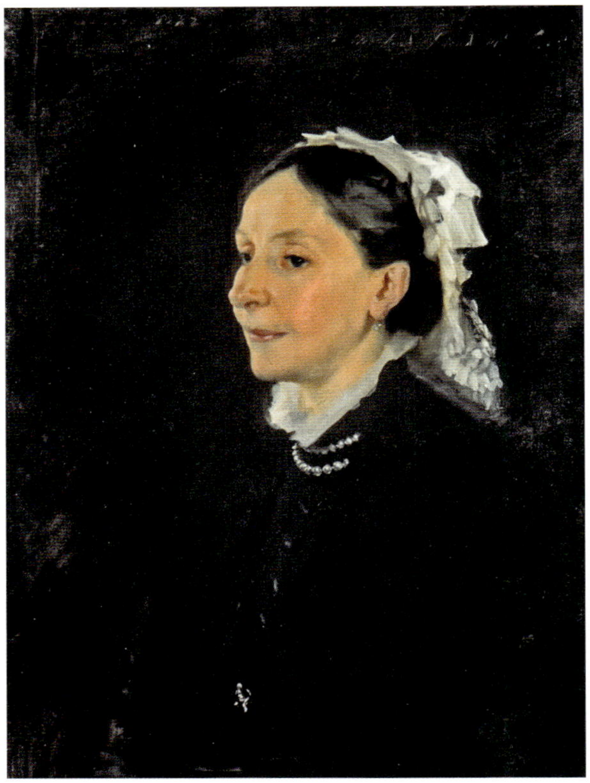

fig. 2—John Singer Sargent, *Portrait of Mrs. Daniel Sargent Curtis*, 1882, oil on canvas, 28×21 in., Spencer Museum of Art

December 1913, they jointly sold it to the American collector Arthur B. Emmons, who already owned *Venice, Palazzo Dario* (pl. 21), purchased in December 1912, as well as *The Palazzo da Mula, Venice* and *The Palazzo Ducale Seen from San Giorgio Maggiore*, both purchased in May 1913 (pl. 29 and pl. 17). *The Palazzo Ducale* was subsequently purchased and donated to the Brooklyn Museum (then the Brooklyn Institute of Arts and Sciences) in 1920 by its president, A. Augustus Healy. It is one of only three focused depictions by Monet of this iconic building, which is among the most emblematic sites in Venice. Moreover, Monet painted it from the perspective of a floating gondola at the intersection of the Grand Canal and the Bacino di San Marco. This mode of transportation refers to the beginning of his career, nearly four decades earlier, when he painted *en plein air* from a floating "studio boat" along the Seine River in Argenteuil, France. In doing so, Monet brought his Impressionist legacy full circle in depicting Venice.

The Grand Canal, Venice took a more circuitous route from the 1912 exhibition in France to America, where it ultimately landed in San Francisco. The wealthy and philanthropic Welsh bachelorette sisters Gwendoline and Margaret Davies purchased multiple canvases from Monet's Venice suite.[1] Margaret's first acquisition from the group and the most expensive Monet Venice purchase made by either of the sisters, *The Grand Canal, Venice* (pl. 1) was also the only painting with a colored illustration in the Bernheim-Jeune catalogue for the 1912 display.[2] Eventually, the sisters owned four (two each) Monet paintings of Venice, three of which (pl. 9, 24, and 33) are currently in the collection of the Amgueddfa Cymru–Museum Wales. In May 1960, Margaret sold *The Grand Canal, Venice* at Sotheby's, where it was purchased by San Francisco architect and philanthropist Osgood Hooker; that same year Hooker gifted it to the California Palace of the Legion of Honor (after 1972 one of the two Fine Arts Museums of San Francisco, along with the de Young Museum, where *Monet and Venice* is presented). Painted from the vantage point of the Palazzo Barbaro, where the Monets initially stayed in Venice, it features a staccato rhythm of *pali* (mooring posts) in the left foreground and the grand dome of the Santa Maria della Salute church, located at the Punta della Dogana in the Dorsoduro district, to the right. Both San Francisco's and Brooklyn's Monet Venice paintings are dominated by shimmering aqueous foregrounds that reinforce Monet's signature captivation with the evanescent effects of water. In each composition, the intrusion of human existence is effectively supplanted by the poetry of the immersive atmosphere that Monet so desperately sought to represent, which he termed the *enveloppe*.

Within two years of the 1912 debut of Monet's Venice pictures, at least eighteen of them were in American collections across the country, including those in Hillsborough, California; St. Louis, Missouri; New York, New York; Newport, Rhode Island; and New Orleans, Louisiana. Eight are in American public museums today. All of these paintings that can be loaned are included in our exhibition, with one exception.[3] Currently, the only Monet Venice painting in a public collection in France is the anomalistic ghostly gondola in the Musée d'Arts de Nantes (fig. 11). There are also two paintings in public collections in Switzerland (pl. 14 and 30). Some of these paintings were last seen together in the

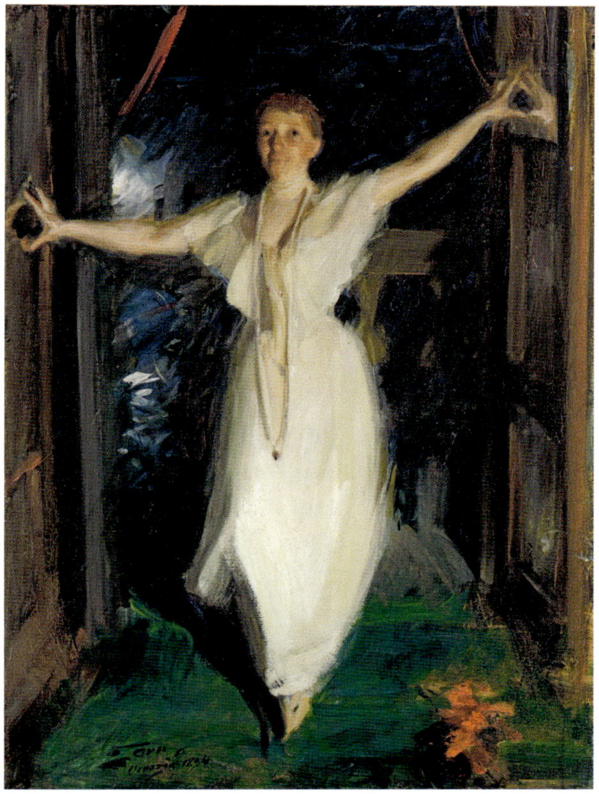

fig. 3—Anders Zorn, *Isabella Stewart Gardner in Venice*, 1894, oil on canvas, 35 13/16 × 26 in., Isabella Stewart Gardner Museum

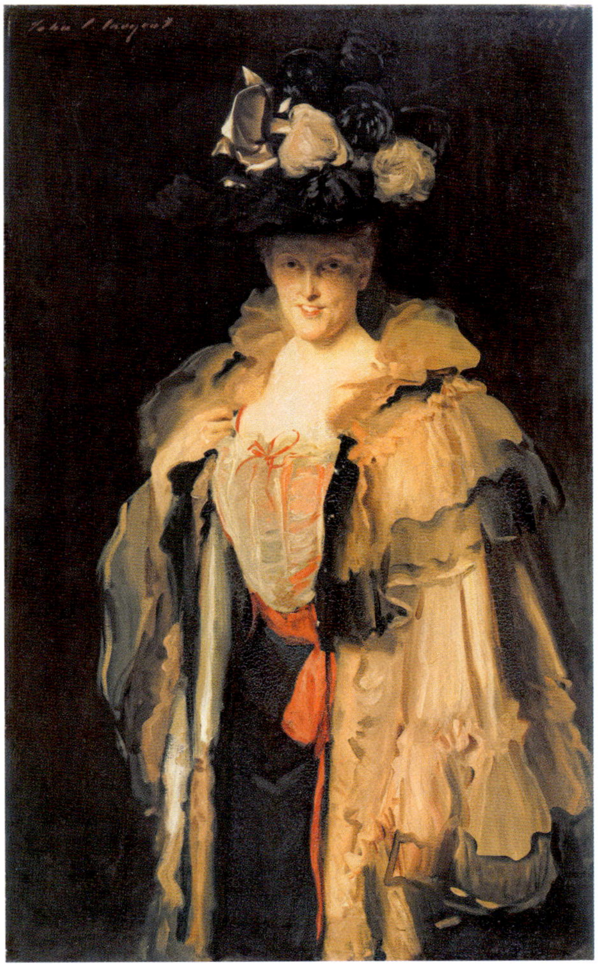

fig. 4—John Singer Sargent, *Mrs. Charles Hunter*, 1898, oil on canvas, 58 ¼ × 35 ¼ in., Tate

United States in the 1997-1998 exhibition *Monet and the Mediterranean*, which focused on works only by Monet and included geographic parameters beyond Venice. In the nearly three decades since, there have been other, smaller groups available for viewing in various exhibitions, most recently nine in *Monet and Architecture* (National Gallery, 2018). But twenty-first-century museum visitors in the United States have never had the opportunity to see and consider Monet's Venice paintings as such a significant group, or in proximity with other paintings of the city by his predecessors and contemporaries.

A challenge to reuniting this set is the fact that approximately half are currently in private collections. Attesting to their historic and modern attraction for connoisseurs, several private collectors have also acquired multiple Monet Venice paintings. In addition to the aforementioned Arthur B. Emmons (who owned four) and the Davies sisters (who owned two each), there was Boston industrialist and former American Bell Telephone director Alexander Cochrane, who bought two (pl. 2 and 10) from the 1912 exhibition. The French pharmacist Henri Canonne, who was a prolific collector of Impressionist paintings—especially by Monet—also owned two (pl. 11 and 27). Three Monet Venice paintings are now in the Hasso Plattner Collection (pl. 20, 25, and 31), where they can be viewed in the Museum Barberini, Potsdam, and another private collection has three (pl. 4, 17, and 28). This exhibition presents six Monet Venice painting loans from private collections, which is a special experience for visitors in Brooklyn and San Francisco.

The reunion of works from private and public collections across the motifs that Monet painted in Venice occasions an opportunity to assess them in a concentrated way for the first time in the twenty-first century. Seeing them together allows viewers to observe their subtle differences: the slight intrusion of steps in the lower left foreground of the paintings featuring the Santa Maria della Salute church, the tonal variations between the palazzo paintings, and the subtle play of light across the facade of the island and church of San Giorgio Maggiore. Unlike Monet's series paintings, where he painted the same subject at different times of day to capture the changing effects of light, in Venice, the artist returned to the same motif at the same time each day to study the subjects from this perspective. Timing in Venice was critical for Monet, and this framework structured his approach to the group of paintings he started there.

The timing of this exhibition is also significant: the year 2026 is the centennial of Monet's death. Although numerous exhibitions in the intervening century have been devoted to the artist, the significant impact of Venice on his late career has not previously been explored fully. Arresting as the Venice pictures might be individually—dispersed among various museums and private collections—their full impact is revealed when they are reunited, which is how Monet originally intended them to be experienced. The harmony of their combined rhythm was of paramount importance to their creator.[4]

Perhaps the wide dispersal of these paintings is at least partially responsible for their relatively low profile. Beyond Cardiff

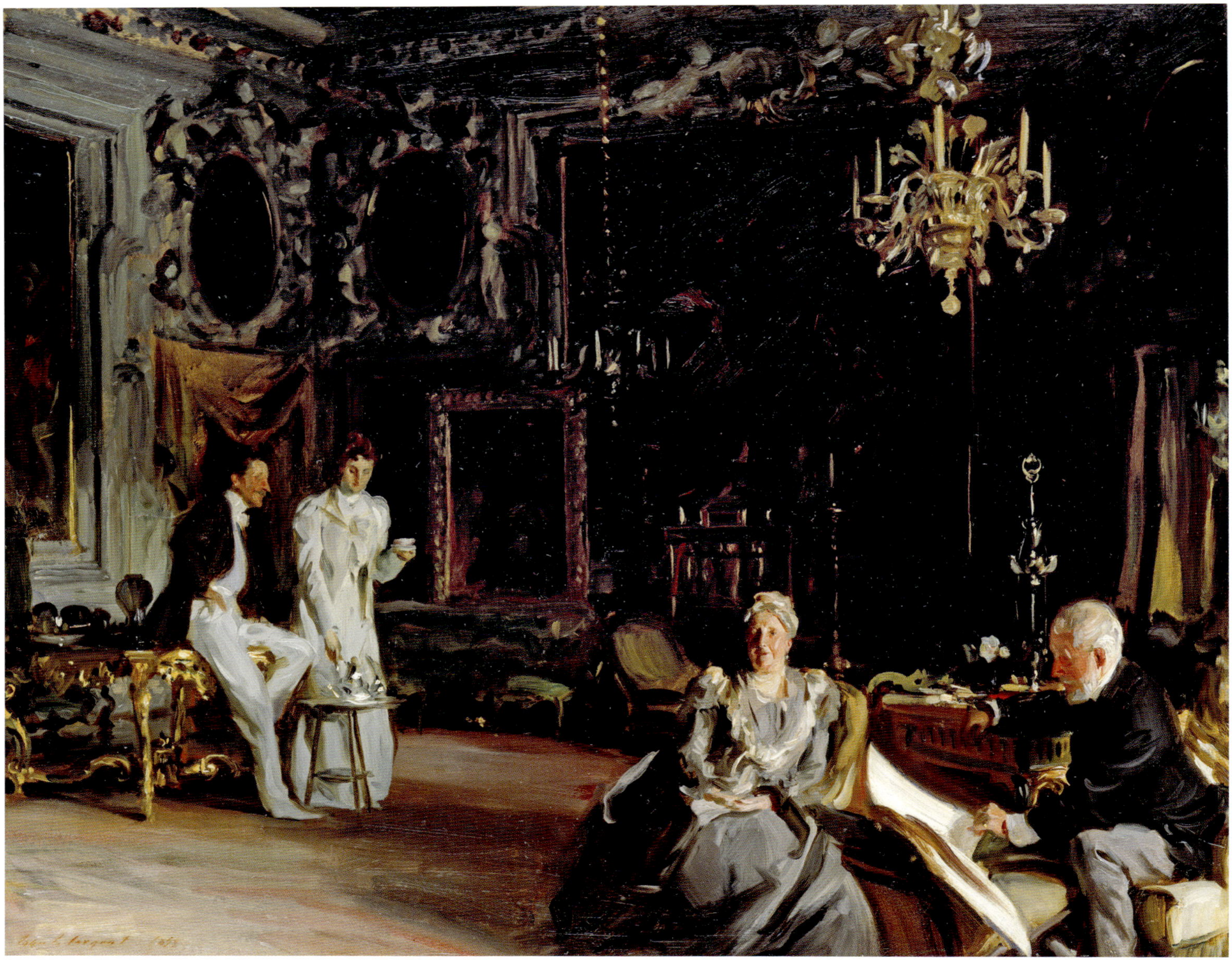

fig. 5—John Singer Sargent, *An Interior in Venice*, 1899, oil on canvas, 26 × 32⁹⁄₁₀ in., Royal Academy of Arts

and Potsdam, visitors cannot see more than one Monet Venice painting at a time in a museum, while it is possible to see multiple *Water Lilies* or views of Rouen Cathedral in the Musée d'Orsay, for example. American museum collections with strengths in Impressionist holdings, such as the Metropolitan Museum of Art, the Museum of Fine Arts, Boston, and the Art Institute of Chicago, also have multiple examples of the now iconic *Water Lilies*, but each has only one Venice painting by Monet. Finally, with thirty-seven extant paintings, the Venice suite is less numerous than the almost one hundred known paintings of the Thames in London, for example.[5]

This exhibition and its accompanying catalogue demonstrate through new scholarship that there remain facets of this well-known artist's career that deserve deeper exploration. The present catalogue gathers a series of essays that further enrich our understanding of Monet's work and times. The essays, in addition to the color plates and contextual figure illustrations,

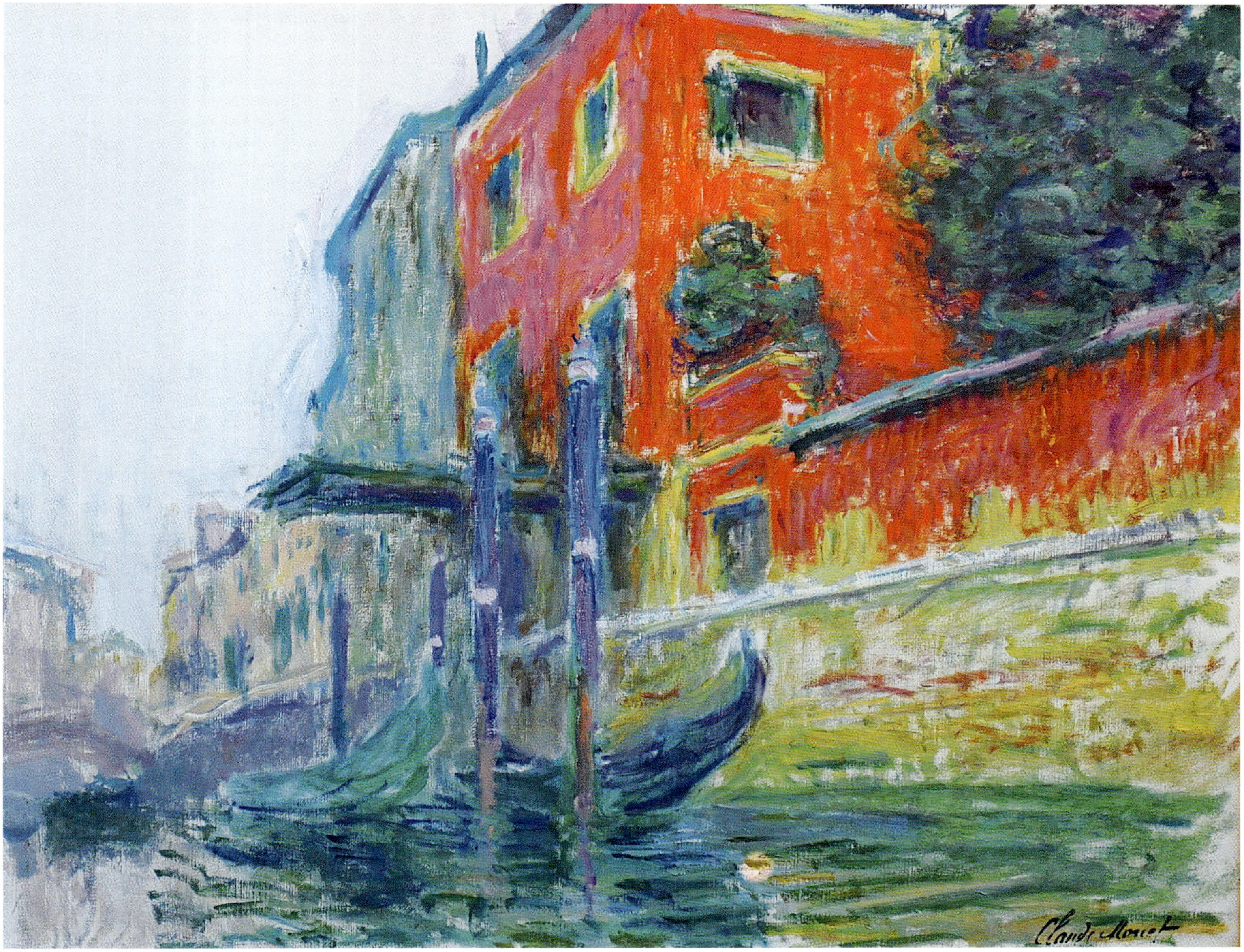

achieve this ambition, and the catalogue also includes an illustrated checklist of all of Monet's thirty-seven Venetian works, including their current locations, if known. In the essays in this volume, Lisa Small, cocurator of the exhibition and senior curator of European art at the Brooklyn Museum, looks at Monet's alternating anxiety over and enchantment with La Serenissima, as well as his relationship to other artists who depicted the city. Elena Marchetti, curator of the Fondazione Musei Civici di Venezia, sets the scene with archival evidence of weather patterns and developments in tourism when Monet was in Venice. André Dombrowski, Frances Shapiro-Weitzenhoffer Associate Professor of Nineteenth-Century European Art at the University of Pennsylvania, considers the meaning and passage of time in the "timeless" city, while Félicie Faizand de Maupeou of the Université Paris Nanterre traces the exhibition history of the Venice paintings, and independent scholar Donato Esposito explores the depictions of Venice Monet might have seen in Paris and

fig. 6—Claude Monet, *The Red House*, 1908, oil on canvas, 25⅔ in. × 31⅘ in., Collection Galerie Larock-Granoff

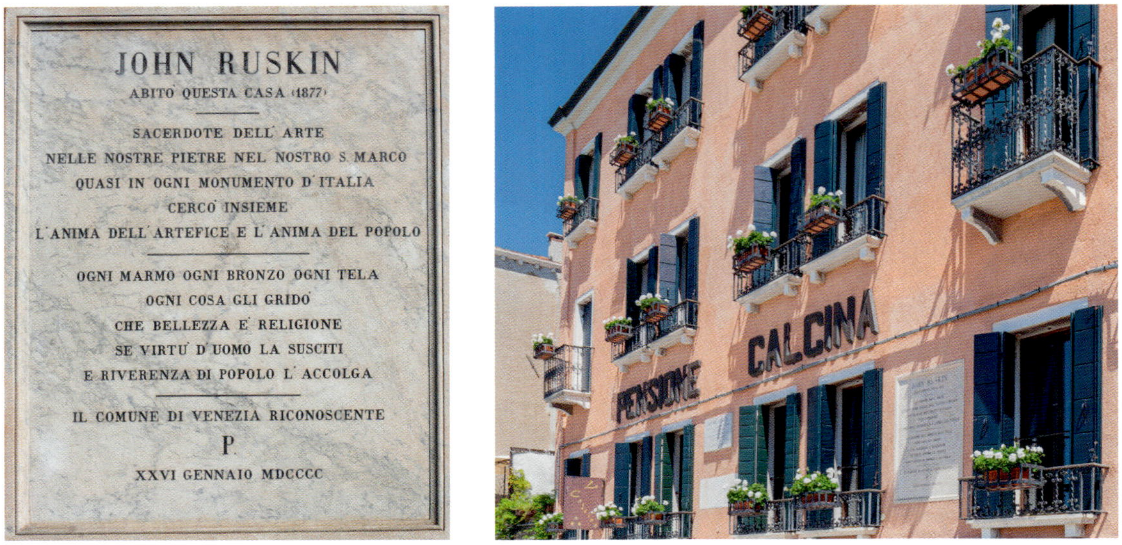

fig. 7—Commemorative plaque to John Ruskin on Pensione Calcina, Dorsoduro, Venice

London. Impressionist scholar Richard Thomson surveys the work of other artists in the period immediately before Monet's visit. Finally, demonstrating the enduring creative stimulation offered by Venice, Niles Luther, composer-in-residence at the Brooklyn Museum, describes his process in crafting symphonic compositions inspired by the paintings—a soundtrack to be enjoyed in tandem with the exhibition.

Since Venice was and remains a source of this kind of inspiration and a popular tourist attraction, Monet painting Venice may seem even more inevitable. Indeed, by the time of his visit in the early twentieth century, Venice as an artistic subject loomed large in the aesthetic vernacular. The great Venetian painters of the Renaissance included illustrious names such as Bellini, Giorgione, Titian, and Tintoretto. Famous artists of the Western canon such as the Venetian painter Canaletto (who is synonymous with the *vedute* tradition—views of cities and towns that emphasize realistic details) and the English artist J. M. W. Turner had famously interpreted the city's majestic views. Two exceptional paintings by Canaletto featuring the subjects depicted by Monet in the Brooklyn Museum's and Fine Arts Museums of San Francisco's paintings, respectively—the Palazzo Ducale and the Santa Maria della Salute church—are included in the exhibition, launching a rich aesthetic dialogue between these artists across several centuries (figs. 32 and 149).

By the time Monet arrived in Venice in autumn 1908, many of his contemporaries had also already visited and rendered their impressions of the city: his mentor, Eugène Boudin, as well as his friends Édouard Manet, Pierre-Auguste Renoir, John Singer Sargent, Paul Signac, and James McNeill Whistler.[6] A noteworthy highlight from this group is a painting by Manet (fig. 184)—one of only two paintings by him of Venice from 1874, just after he spent a summer working alongside Monet on the water at Argenteuil, where he painted the artist in his aforementioned floating studio (fig. 183). The Venetian views by Monet's friends and others offer context to compare with his own impressions of the city.

Venice's very popularity and familiarity was partially responsible for discouraging Monet from approaching it as a subject in his own work. At age sixty-eight and experiencing a lack of faith in his creative abilities, the artist thought he was too old and doubted that he could contribute to an already rich offering of Venetian depictions. Indeed, he had long avoided the iconic Serenissima, confessing to Alice that he thought it was "too beautiful to be painted."[7] But ultimately he would make thirty-seven-oil-on canvas compositions (see page 256) and one pencil sketch (fig. 62), exhibiting in 1912 nine motifs that both became mementoes of his last major international trip and provided critical motivation before he tackled the culmination of his career: a renewed attempt at painting his *Water Lilies* and the *grandes décorations*, which Monet completed months before he died and that can be seen today in two oval rooms in the Musée de l'Orangerie, Paris (fig. 18).

Monet was at a low point when he sojourned in Venice in autumn 1908. He was disheartened by his dealer Paul Durand-Ruel's poor reaction to a series of water lily paintings whose exhibition, originally slated for April 1907, Monet had already delayed several times.[8] Despite having achieved financial and commercial success, at the end of his sixth decade, the artist still relied heavily on the opinions of others. When Durand-Ruel expressed concerns about the marketability of the work, Monet, in the throes of insecurity, renounced the water lily project "once and for all."[9]

By this time, Alice was no stranger to the artist's variable moods. She had met Claude Monet in 1876, when she was still married to the department store owner Ernest Hoschedé, a pioneering collector of Impressionism and Monet's former patron. When Hoschedé went bankrupt in 1877, he and his family, which included six children, moved in with Claude and his first wife, Camille. This unconventional blended family arrangement lasted through Camille's death in 1879 and until Ernest Hoschedé's death in 1891; Claude and Alice married the following year. By 1908, Alice had known Monet for the better

fig. 8—John Ruskin, *The Sound Side of the Basilica of St. Mark, from the Loggia of the Doge's Palace, Venice*, c. 1850–52, watercolor over pencil on paper, heightened with body color, 38 × 18 in., private collection

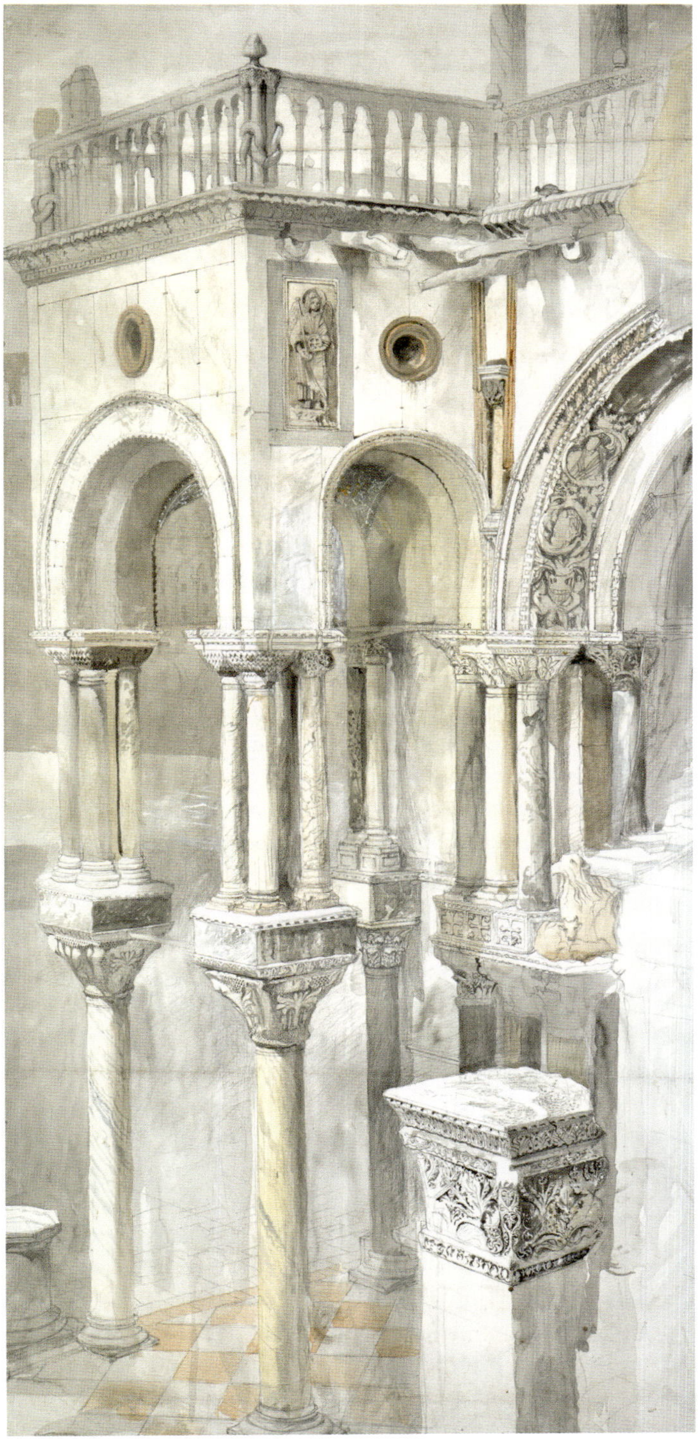

part of three decades, and she recognized that he would benefit from a change of scenery.[10] Still, Monet initially resisted the invitation from Mary Hunter to stay at the famed Palazzo Barbaro on the Grand Canal (fig. 12).

The Monets had met Hunter in London through their mutual friend, the artist John Singer Sargent.[11] Daniel Sargent Curtis, purported to be a distant relative of Sargent's, purchased Palazzo Barbaro in 1885.[12] Sargent had also stayed and worked there: in the palazzo's elegant salon he painted Daniel's wife, Ariana Curtis (fig. 2), and the Curtis family, including Daniel, Ariana, their son Ralph, and their daughter-in-law Lisa (fig. 5).[13] This exceptional loan from London's Royal Academy of Arts demonstrates the elegance of the famed location that lured the Monets to leave Giverny for Venice. There the Curtis family also entertained and hosted cultural luminaries such as English poet Robert Browning (who gave his last public reading there before he died at his son Pen's Ca' Rezzonico in 1899) and the American novelist Edith Wharton. This was the same illustrious location where American novelist Henry James finished *The Aspern Papers* (published in 1888) and where he staged scenes in *The Wings of the Dove* (1902), in which he renamed it Palazzo Leporelli. When the Curtises were away they rented their palazzo to art patrons such as fellow American Isabella Stewart Gardner, with whom James stayed as a guest for several weeks in 1892. A close friend and a patron of Sargent's, Gardner was immortalized in exuberant motion by Anders Zorn on the Palazzo Barbaro balcony (fig. 3).[14] Fortuitously, Palazzo Barbaro was leased to Mary Hunter in the autumn of 1908 at a time when Monet needed creative uplift.[15]

Critic Octave Mirbeau recalled that Monet had once protested, "Venice . . . no . . . I will not go to Venice."[16] But Alice persevered, and Claude finally relented. After a week exploring the fabled city, surrounded by its unique atmospheric conditions of water and light, he could no longer resist its allure. Crates of canvases arrived, and he was ready to start painting on October 7, but weather postponed his start again, and the self-doubt that assailed him throughout his career nearly scuppered his plans.[17] A private concert that evening, performed for Claude and Alice by Ethel Smyth, the eccentric sister of their host, Mary Hunter, buoyed his spirits.[18] Finally, conditions were right and on October 9, 1908, Alice reported that Monet had begun to paint.[19]

In addition to extending the Palazzo Barbaro invitation, Hunter helped Monet with an introduction that facilitated permission for him to paint from a balcony at the Hotel Bucintoro.[20] From there he hoped to paint the island and church of San Giorgio across the Bacino di San Marco.[21] He could also see this view (pl. 9–13) from his room at the Grand Hotel Britannia, where the Monets moved after Hunter departed Palazzo Barbaro for Aix, France (fig. 92). In her letters, Alice praised their new lodgings, but she lamented Hunter's departure: "What regrets to have left Mrs. Hunter and this life where you had only to make a wish for it to be carried out . . . She takes, I think, a part of Venice with her."[22] Monet later gave Hunter a painting of San Giorgio Maggiore (see 31 on page 257) as a token of appreciation for her friendship and her hospitality in Venice.[23]

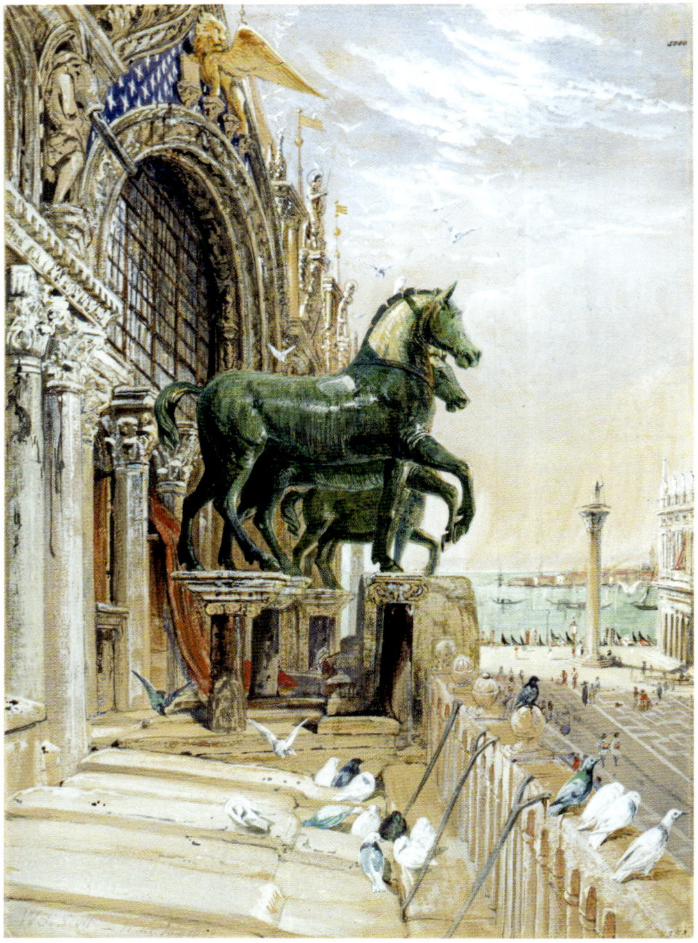

Like Hunter's contribution, John Ruskin's impact on Monet's views of Venice has also been overlooked. The English critic's influential architectural preservationist text, *The Stones of Venice* (published in three volumes between 1851 and 1853), had then recently been translated from English into French. This seminal treatise traces the city's history, art, and architecture while conveying the author's own moralizing views on social and urban progress. Although this title is not recorded in his library inventory, Monet likely would have at least been aware of the well-known text, since he owned a translated copy of Ruskin's *St. Mark's Rest*.[24] Yet Monet's approach to Venice is arguably anti-Ruskinian in its rejection of documenting through a didactic "truth to nature" style, as demonstrated by the more precise renderings in the watercolors of San Marco by Ruskin (fig. 8) and Monet's Scottish predecessor in Venice William Bell Scott (fig. 9). Both works demonstrate a commitment to highly specific details, while for Monet, representing Venice was not about recording and preserving its stones, but rather about evoking the mood and *enveloppe* of its atmosphere.

Compared with the predominantly opalescent palette—pinks, blues, purples, and greens—in Monet's depictions of Venice along the Grand Canal, the blazing scarlet of *The Red House* is more anomalistic (fig. 6). It is also set apart by its perspective from the edge of the Dorsoduro, across from Giudecca, where the Fondamenta Bragadin meets the Giudecca Canal at the Fondamenta delle Zattere. This position was possibly inspired by following in Ruskin's footsteps around Venice.[25] From that vantage point in autumn 1908, Monet could have seen the stone plaque installed in 1900 on the facade of the hotel La Calcina commemorating Ruskin's stay there in the spring of 1877 (fig. 7) after he completed *The Stones of Venice*:

> *JOHN RUSKIN*
> *Lived in this house (1877)*
> *Priest of art*
> *In our stones, in our San Marco*
> *In nearly every landmark in Italy*
> *He searched for both*
> *The soul of the craftsman and the soul of the people*
>
> *Every marble, every bronze, every canvas*
> *Each and every thing proclaimed to him*
> *That beauty is a religion*
> *As man's virtue invokes it*
> *And the people reverently embrace it*
>
> *With grateful acknowledgment, the municipality of Venice*
> *January 26, 1900*

The Red House, one of the last paintings that Monet started in Venice, may reveal his direct confrontation with and ultimate distancing from Ruskin, with whom Venice was closely associated at this time. Monet literally turns his back on Ruskin's view from La Calcina and faces this composition in the direction of the Grand Canal. Moreover, another sign of his rejection of Ruskin may be found in Monet's eight canvases featuring the church of San Giorgio Maggiore (pl. 9–13, 32–33). The church was designed by Andrea Palladio, whom Ruskin called "virtueless and despicable."[26] Ruskin complained about the church that it would be "impossible to conceive a design more gross, more barbarous, more childish in conception, more servile in plagiarism, more insipid in result, more contemptible under every point of rational regard."[27] Monet also never painted the subject closely associated with Ruskin that is most emblematic of Venice itself: the facade of San Marco. By rejecting one of the most famous critics associated with Venice, Monet further established his singular statement on the iconic city. Through representations of glimmering pearlescent light, mesmerically rippling water, and the elusive Venetian *enveloppe*, Monet expressed his own picturesque representation of the city he had once considered beyond his representational capabilities.

Despite the artist's initial resistance to Venice and intermittent weather-related frustrations, Venice was an idyllic respite for the Monets. Shortly after their arrival, they "admired some superb Tintorettos."[28] They may have crossed the (then) iron Accademia Bridge near Palazzo Barbaro to see them in the Gallerie dell'Accademia, or, perhaps, as Elena Marchetti suggests in this volume, they may have seen the temporarily deinstalled *Paradiso* frescoes by Tintoretto in the Palazzo Ducale (fig. 90). They may also have visited the monumental room of Tintoretto paintings

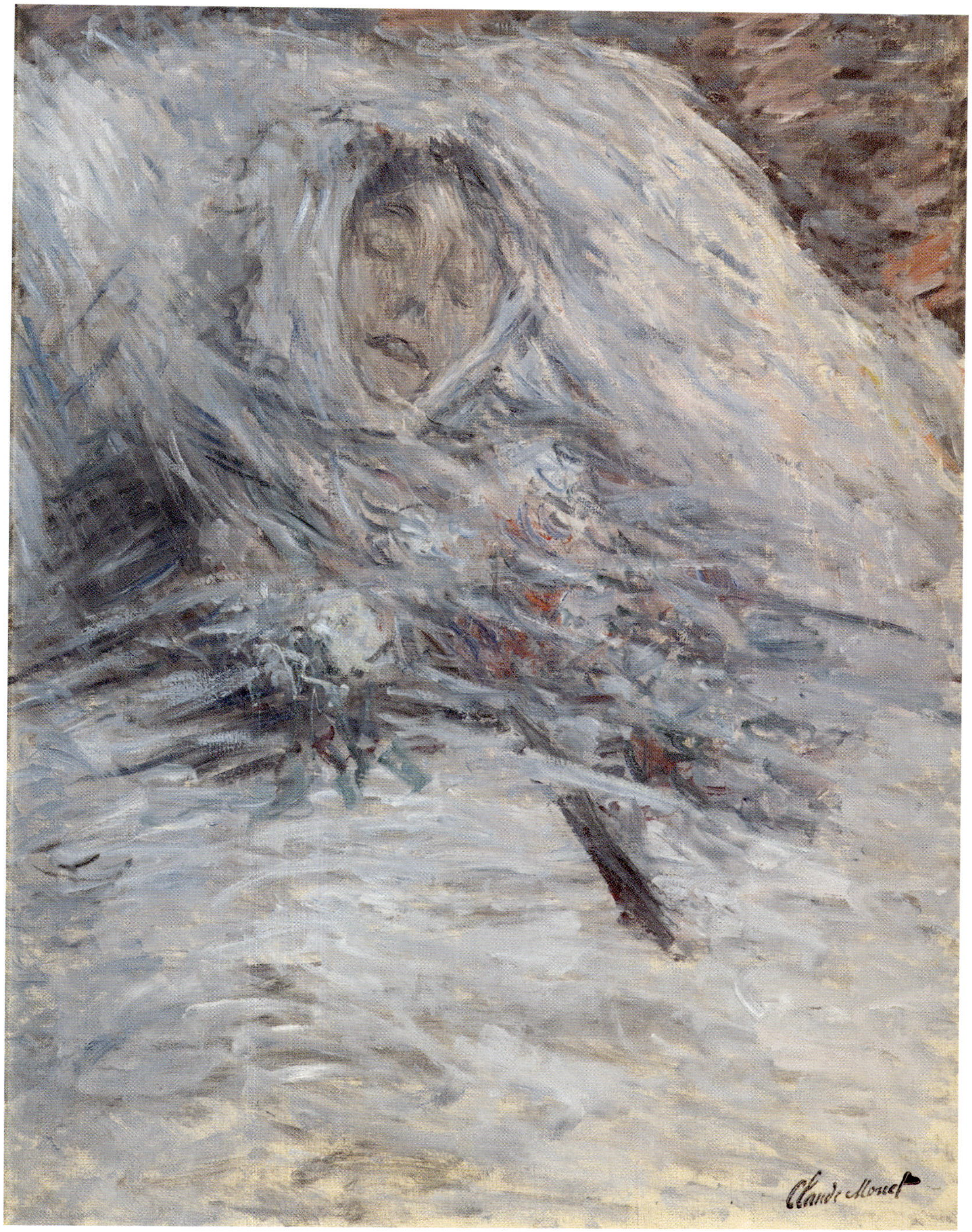

fig. 9—(opposite) William Bell Scott, *Upper Portion of the Facade of St. Mark's, Venice*, 1862, watercolor on paper, $13\frac{9}{10} \times 9\frac{9}{10}$ in., Victoria and Albert Museum

fig. 10—Claude Monet, *Camille on Her Deathbed*, 1879, oil on canvas, $35\frac{1}{2} \times 26\frac{3}{4}$ in., Musée d'Orsay

in the Scuola Grande di San Rocco (fig. 81), perhaps inspiring Monet's immersive *grandes décorations* rooms.[29] The Monets remained in Venice weeks longer than they had anticipated (to continue working outside into the winter, the ill-prepared Monet had to borrow a fur coat from the young American painter Louis Aston Knight, who was also staying at their hotel), and as their inevitable departure drew near, Monet conceded that the city had cast its spell on him.

His intent to return is voiced in a characteristically self-deprecating assessment sent to Durand-Ruel: "I am in awe of Venice; unfortunately, I will not be able to stay here very long.

Therefore, I will not be able to work seriously. I am just doing a few canvases, haphazardly, just to have some record, but I really intend to give it serious time next year."[30] Perhaps with an eye toward another visit, he wrote to Ariana Curtis, his hostess by proxy at Palazzo Barbaro, on the day of their departure, and thanked her profusely: "Without doubt it is thanks to you that I came here. It has been a feast for an artist, a great joy for me."[31] Indeed, when the Monets left Venice on December 7, 1908, they planned to return. It was not to be, however. Their sojourn in Venice would be their last travel adventure together and their final excursion outside France. Monet's pictures would be completed in Giverny, possibly aided by the photographs and postcards the Monets collected in 1908 (figs. 22, 25, 26, 30, 56, 60, 66, 67, and 92).[32] In 1909, Monet also acquired a watercolor by his friend Signac of the Santa Maria Salute church on the Grand Canal (fig. 187). This work remained in the artist's personal collection throughout his life, where it surely evoked memories of Alice and his only visit to Venice.[33]

Alice began exhibiting symptoms of acute myeloid leukemia not long after the pair returned to Giverny, and she died there on May 19, 1911. As Claude Monet finished the Venice pictures after Alice's death, he may have recalled his grief following the fatal illness of his first wife, Camille. The melancholy that tinges the palette of his *Palazzo Dario* paintings recalls the deep violet and cool blue tones in Monet's painting of Camille, on her deathbed at age thirty-two in 1879 (fig. 10). Indeed, Gustave Geffroy highlighted the "melancholic and mysterious aspect" of the Venice suite, and the "luminous veils that envelop it," a description that recalls the veils around Camille in the artist's portrait of her on her deathbed.[34] Rather than similarly painting Alice after she died, her bereaved husband went on to finish his unpopulated Venetian scenes, a metonym for her manifesting in his grief. The paintings of palazzi (pl. 21–24, 28–31) express this poignant mood: there are no signs of quotidian human intervention, only the evocation of a deeply personal view of these iconic Venetian buildings along the Grand Canal. The singular signs of human life in Venice that Monet includes in his compositions from this group are the flicks of dark paint that suggest the curvature of floating gondolas. The vessels held personal symbolism for the artist, who spent hours ferried and floating through Venice beside his wife. Perhaps for this reason, he kept a painting (originally purchased by Bernheim-Jeune and Durand-Ruel in May 1912 and transferred back to Monet in June 1912) of a single empty gondola in front of the Palazzo Dario (pl. 23). It depicts the view that Alice and Claude would have seen across the Grand Canal from Palazzo Barbaro when they first arrived in Venice.[35] A photograph taken around 1920 of Monet's Giverny living room, which he also used as a studio, shows this subject hanging prominently (fig. 82).

Similarly, along with the anomalistic view of *The Red House*, the only extant painting of Venice that Monet seemingly left untouched (and did not include in the 1912 exhibition) is the last picture that he started in Venice on December 3, 1908, mere days before departing. The composition of an empty gondola (fig. 11), rendered in dark swirls of blue and purple paint, suspended above spiraling reflections, and articulated by sketchy brushstrokes, gives a particular impression of the poetic mood that cascades throughout his Venice suite. An hour before their departure, Alice penned a note to her daughter: "Here is a splendid day that gives Monet great regret, it is so beautiful! We just took our last gondola ride. Now we will only go to the [train] station."[36] As a testament to their friendship, Monet gifted this painting to his compatriot, statesman Georges Clemenceau (with whom he would collaborate to bring the *grandes décorations* to fruition). Solidifying their close connection, Clemenceau published a short biography of Monet two years after the artist's death.[37]

Alice's death in 1911 caused Claude to fall into a deep depression. He told Geffroy in July, "No one could know how much I am suffering. I am a lost man, finished, alas!"[38] For months he was unable to paint, and when he resumed the Venice suite in October 1911, three years after their trip in 1908, Alice was on his mind. He wrote to her daughter Germaine, "I do not stop thinking about her while painting."[39] And so the Venice paintings became a testament to Alice and a way of preserving her memory. Finishing them in Giverny also availed the artist of some distance from his subject and perspective to see the group from which he would select the twenty-nine pictures exhibited in 1912. Perhaps he forged ahead pragmatically because he owed the Bernheim-Jeune brothers content for an exhibition, but perhaps he also did so because he remembered Alice encouraging him to persevere, especially in Venice. Without Alice (and a compelling invitation from Mary Hunter), it is unlikely that the Venice trip would have transpired. It is also plausible that the *grandes décorations* would not have manifested with such immersive breadth and ambition without the trip to Venice.

Critically, Monet also intimated that the triumphant, long-delayed completion and 1909 exhibition of his *Water Lilies* owed their existence to Venice. Indeed, he wrote to Durand-Ruel that following his rejuvenation there, he was ready to complete the water lilies from the canceled 1907 exhibition that he had claimed he would abandon forever before the voyage: "My trip to Venice has had the advantage of making me see my [water lily] canvases with a better eye."[40] The year after Venice, Monet exhibited forty-eight water lily paintings (including fig. 16)—the largest group of a single series exhibited to date. Opening May 5, 1909, the exhibition *Les Nymphéas: Séries de Passages d'Eau par Claude Monet* (The Water Lilies: Series of Waterscapes by Claude Monet) was a critical success.[41] Among many words of praise, the art critic Roger Marx declared in the *Gazette des Beaux-Arts*, "For as long as mankind has been around, and for as long as artists have painted, no one has ever painted better than or quite like this."[42] Critics from across the Channel agreed. The Paris correspondent for London's *Burlington Magazine* declared, "The studies of water, lilies, and still water in every possible effective light, and at every hour of the day are beautiful to a degree, which one can hardly express without seeming to exaggerate . . . There is no other living artist who could have given us these marvelous effects of light and shadow, this glorious feast of color."[43] Preeminent Monet scholar Paul Hayes Tucker observes, "Gone is the strident color, the aggressive brushwork,

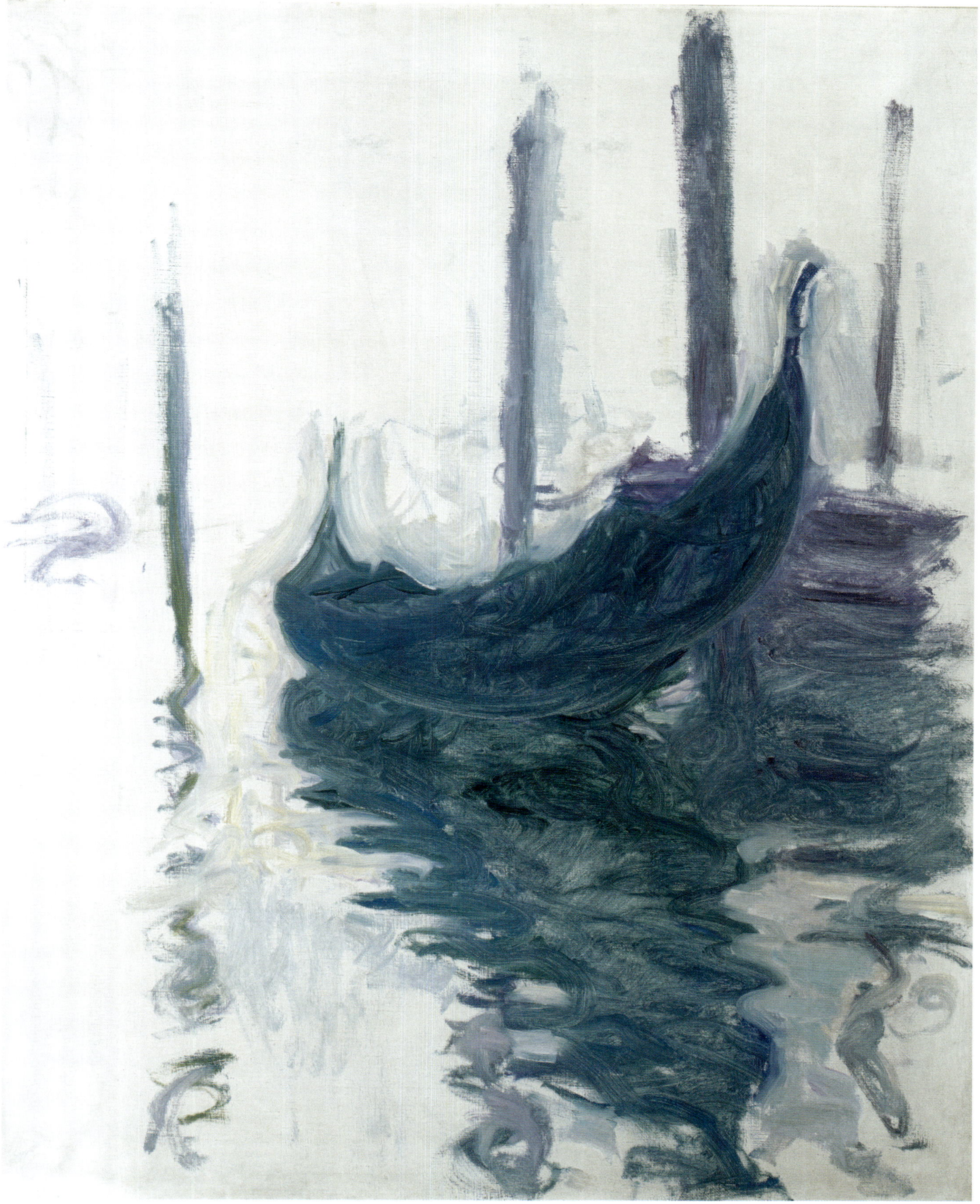

fig. 11—Claude Monet, *Gondola in Venice*, 1908, oil on canvas, 31 9/10 × 25 ½ in., Musée d'Arts de Nantes

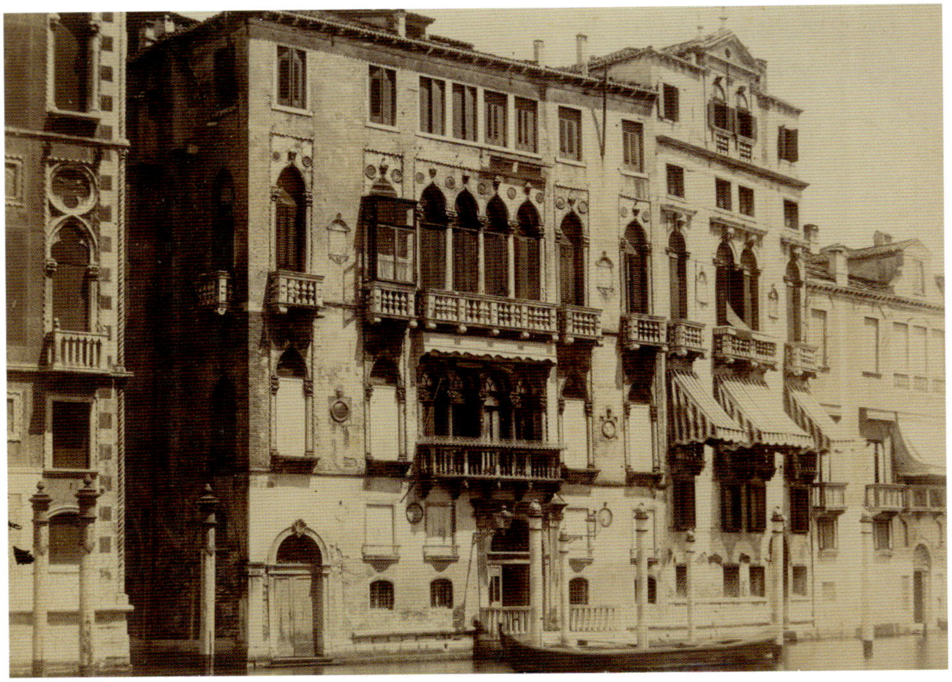

fig. 12 — Paolo Salviati, *Palazzo Barbaro, Grand Canal, Venice*, late 19th c., albumen print, $7\frac{1}{2}$ x $9\frac{13}{16}$ in., Isabella Stewart Gardner Museum

the curious vertical shapes, the tensions between reflections and surface forms, the strong contrast of light and dark, and the sense of surprise and unease."[44]

At age seventy-two, almost four years after visiting Venice, Monet exhibited twenty-nine pictures in *Claude Monet: Venise* at Galerie Bernheim-Jeune (fig. 104). The exhibition was advertised from May 28 to June 8, 1912. The suite received high critical praise and the exhibition was extended until June 15.[45] Like the campanile in Piazza San Marco that toppled in 1902 and was being rebuilt during the Monets' visit, Monet was resurrected from personal ruin to great heights with the *Water Lilies* in 1909 and then the Venice paintings in 1912. Signac wrote to Monet about the Venice pictures, "I admire them as the highest manifestation of your art."[46] Artist Walter Sickert enthused, "Monet's large view of the Ducal Palace and the Piazzetta . . . must remain one of the masterpieces that have been wrung by the painter's art from the city in the sea. None of the painter's predecessors have done just that, or indeed anything at all like it. It is neither the Venice of Canaletto nor that of Byron or Turner."[47] Despite the initial fears that he had nothing of value to contribute in the wake of the artists who came before him, Monet had made his mark on Venice.

Monet's Venice pictures are as much about mood and memory as they are about the atmosphere of the city and the places that represent it. They are tinged with the melancholy of a fragile city in a constant state of decay. Historian Jonathan Keates describes this aspect of Venice as fostering in the nineteenth century "a growing preoccupation among a certain type of northern European visitor with a notion of Venice as a place of decadence, morbidity and death itself."[48] This mood is encapsulated in Thomas Mann's *Death in Venice*, published in 1912, the same year Monet's Venice pictures debuted in Paris. The novella is an ode to Venice as a liberating place where death lurks. This mood reverberates through Monet's paintings, especially the phantasmagorical palazzi paintings, which the critic Jackie Wullschläger describes in her biography of Monet as "voluptuously melancholy... monuments to emptiness" that are "eloquent of tragedy."[49] As Impressionist scholar Joachim Pissarro writes, "There is little wonder, then, that in 1912 Venice... appeared as a testament, the closing link in Monet's oeuvre and perhaps even his life."[50]

This exhibition is presented in Brooklyn and San Francisco, two cities whose characters—like that of Venice—are inextricably tied to their aqueous surroundings; this makes them a perfect backdrop for this exhibition. In it, the evanescent quality of Monet's Venice paintings is revealed. Experienced together in this volume and by the visitors to the exhibition's galleries, they are a moving witness to the power of art as memorial, and proof that creative renewal is possible at any moment and at any stage of life. Although he once contemplated abandoning his water lilies, after time in Venice, Monet courageously rebounded and told Durand-Ruel, "You can absolutely count on me, I will be ready."[51] Without Venice, the work for which Monet is best known today might not have reached the height of its creative expression. Rather than succumbing to the criticism that he once allowed to chip away at his confidence—and even the doubts that he expressed himself when he found Venice "too beautiful to be painted"—Monet, buoyed by close family and friends, found a wellspring of resilience that ultimately resulted in some of his most renowned creative achievements and an indisputably triumphant career comeback.

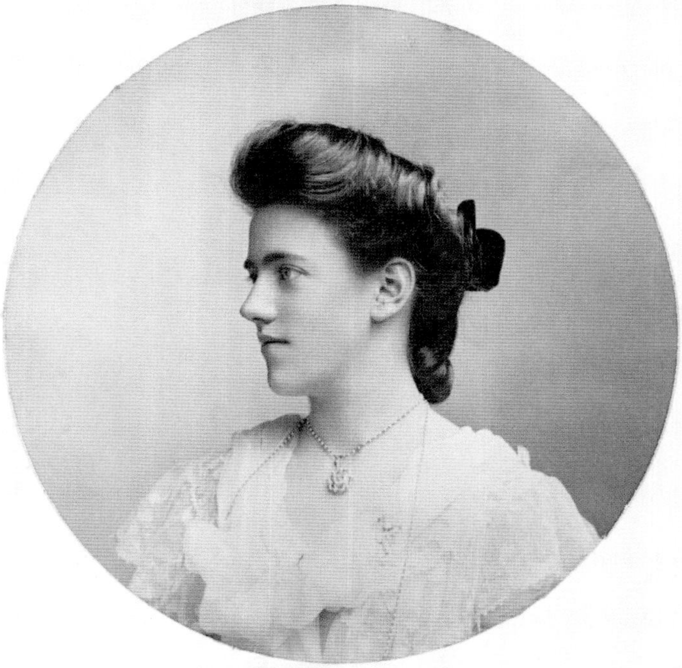

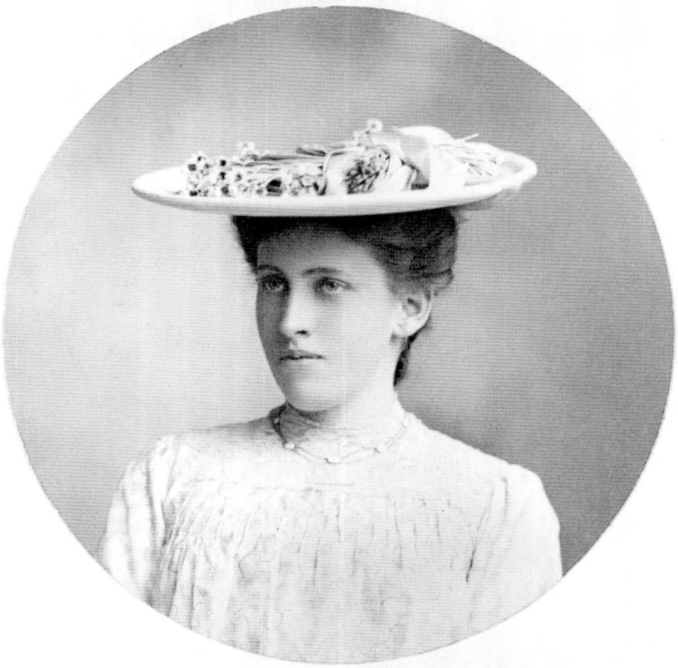

fig. 13—Gwendoline Davies (1884–1963)
fig. 14—Margaret Davies (1882–1951)

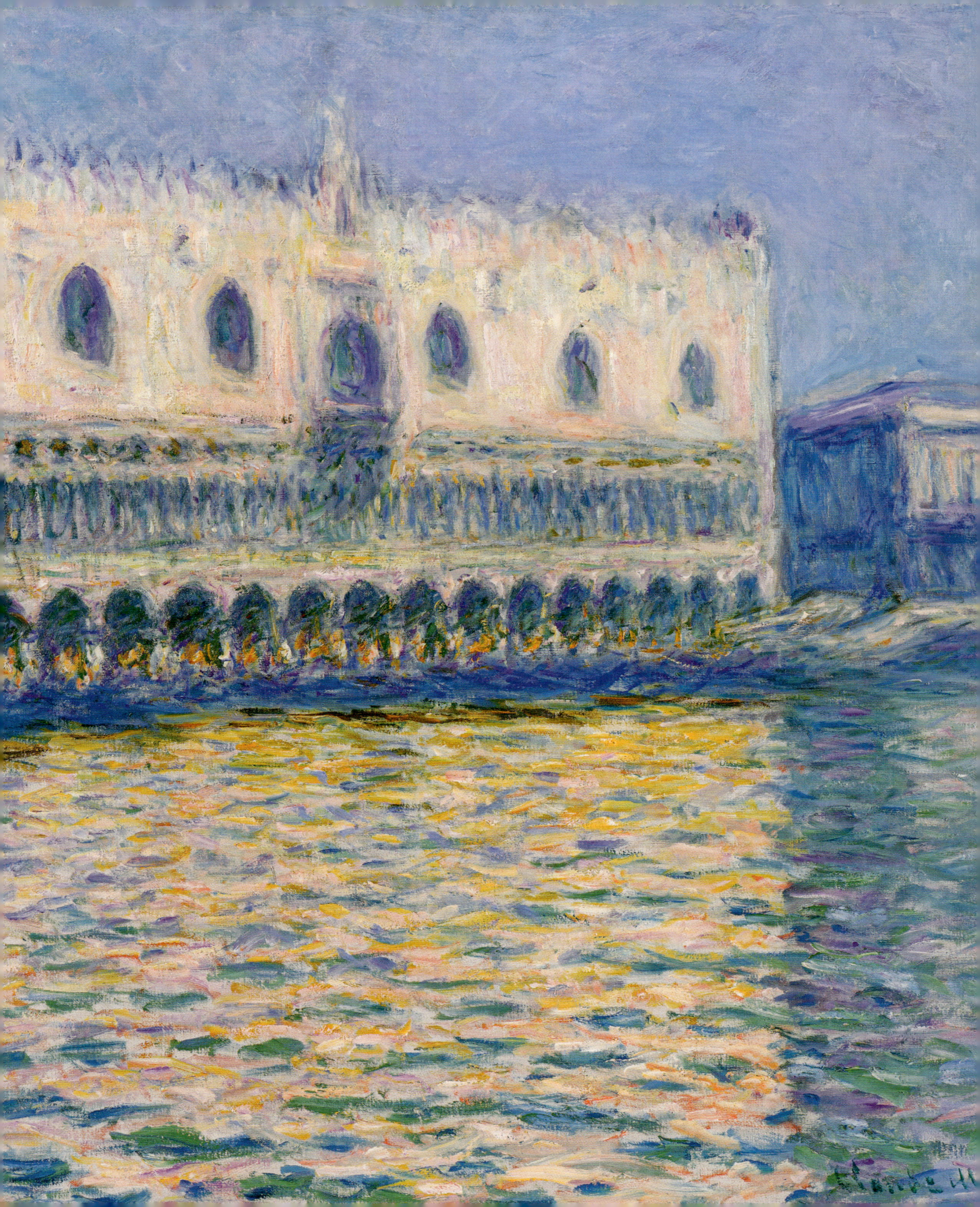

MONET IN VENICE: ANXIETY AND ENCHANTMENT

Lisa Small

CLAUDE MONET TO GEORGES CLEMENCEAU, October 25, 1908
I have been here in raptures for a month, it is wonderful and I'm trying to paint Venice.

ALICE MONET TO GERMAINE SALEROU, November 23, 1908
I am happy here to see Monet so full of ardor, and doing such beautiful things and, between us, other than the endless water lilies, and I believe that it will be a great triumph for him.

CLAUDE MONET TO GUSTAVE GEFFROY, May 2, 1912
I am not getting out of my Venice and am in despair, because the exhibition is irrevocably announced. I have lost the little good there was in these paintings. I feel like a doomed man.

IN OCTOBER 1908, JUST BEFORE turning sixty-eight, Claude Monet traveled to Venice for the first and only time, accompanied by his wife, Alice. The trip was not motivated by a specific desire to work in the city, although his dealer Paul Durand-Ruel, always alert to commercially appealing subjects, wrote to him in 1882 to stress its potential: "I have often mentioned Venice to you."[1] But, as opposed to his friends James McNeill Whistler, John Singer Sargent, Édouard Manet, Pierre-Auguste Renoir, and the many other artists who painted Venice, Monet seems to have been immune—even resistant—to the city's charms. Once there, however, he was enchanted by it, immersing himself in its sites and ambience, and ultimately producing thirty-seven paintings that exemplify the luminous integrated color harmonies and complex textural surfaces of his late works.

Monet painted nature, but he did not always choose specific landscape motifs for their own sake. His fixation, particularly in the 1880s and beyond, was the ephemeral, colored atmosphere that surrounded, unified, and transformed a motif, which he called the *enveloppe*.[2] Everything he painted was also informed by notions of time, whether in registering a fleeting moment in a flick of paint or, as in his later works, meditating on its ceaseless passage in slowly and carefully built-up expanses of color. With his sensitive eye and freely brushed touches of pigment, he conjured *enveloppes* of shifting light and color in towns, villages, and inlets along the Seine; on Normandy's coastline and around the cathedral in Rouen; in Mediterranean seaside towns and tranquil fields near his home in Giverny; as well as in the distinctive environments of London, Norway, and the Netherlands. No matter where he was, Monet wanted to paint "what lies between the motif and me."[3]

In Venice, what lay between him and some of the most fabled of European motifs was glittering water and multihued light; a vaporous marine *enveloppe* that he found both captivating and vexing. The city's special alchemy of celebrated political, social, and aesthetic history; amphibious and labyrinthine topographies; magnificent and idiosyncratic architecture; and the myriad ways it had been described, imagined, envisioned, appropriated, and transformed—all this made the lagoon city a site, sight, and citation unlike any other in Monet's oeuvre. Other locations and motifs of his were identifiable—even potentially symbolic—but arguably none rivaled Venice's unique combination of longstanding global fame and cultural multivalence.[4] The manifold visions of it that came before his own, and the force of the city's legendary seductive beauty, could not help but affect how Monet would perceive Venice, and how his paintings of Venice—a city that seemed unable to be disconnected from its symbolic associations—would be perceived.

Beginning in the 1890s, at his home in Giverny Monet diverted a river, dug a pond, built a bridge, and cultivated colorful flowers "to delight the eye, and also to provide motifs for painting."[5] He created an environment that was, as Marcel Proust described it, "a painting already executed in nature."[6] Nature and art were also entangled in Venice, where centuries of architects and patrons metamorphosed the archipelago of islands and the lagoon into a series of spectacular vistas ready-made to delight the eye (fig. 15). In the years just before his trip there, Monet was preoccupied with the infinite reflective space of the pond he had created as a motif for painting. Frustrated and unsure of his progress, in April 1908 he canceled a planned exhibition of his *Water Lilies* paintings (fig. 16) as he continued to grapple with them, writing to his friend Gustave Geffroy in August that "these landscapes of water and reflections have become an obsession."[7] Two months later, in October 1908, Monet left Giverny and his pond for Venice, the mirage-like city floating on and mirrored in the water. When Monet returned to Giverny, he told Durand-Ruel that he could now move forward with the *Water Lilies* exhibition in 1909, explaining, "I will be ready, for my trip to Venice has had the advantage of making me see my canvases with a better eye."[8]

Alice's recognition of his Venice motifs as a break from the "endless water lilies" thus presciently identified this trip as occurring at a consequential moment in the artist's late career. Twenty-nine of the Venice paintings debuted at the Galerie Bernheim-Jeune in Paris in 1912, and they were celebrated as the latest realization of his consistent artistic vision. Several other paintings by Monet from different points in his career were on view concurrently in Paris in an exhibition of Impressionist works by him and others, enabling a critic to observe, "One can follow the logic of this art from the fogs on the Seine, near Vétheuil, and the pink thaws, and the flowering fogs of London and the blue patches of water under the water lilies, culminating in the fairylike lightness of Venice, which Monet is exhibiting today."[9] Yet, although the Venice paintings were purchased by eager collectors, they have to some extent been treated as anomalous within his career and are not particularly emphasized in the vast Monet art historical literature, especially as compared to his *Grainstacks*, Rouen Cathedral facades, or even the compositionally related London views of 1903 (figs. 58, 97, and 102).[10] Of course, there are important exceptions, most notably Philippe Piguet's 1986 French-language book on Monet and Venice and other considerations in monographic exhibition catalogues by Joachim Pissarro, Paul Hayes Tucker, and Richard Thomson, all of which have greatly informed this project.[11] There are a few possible reasons these paintings have garnered relatively less attention. Chronologically, the Venice paintings count among Monet's

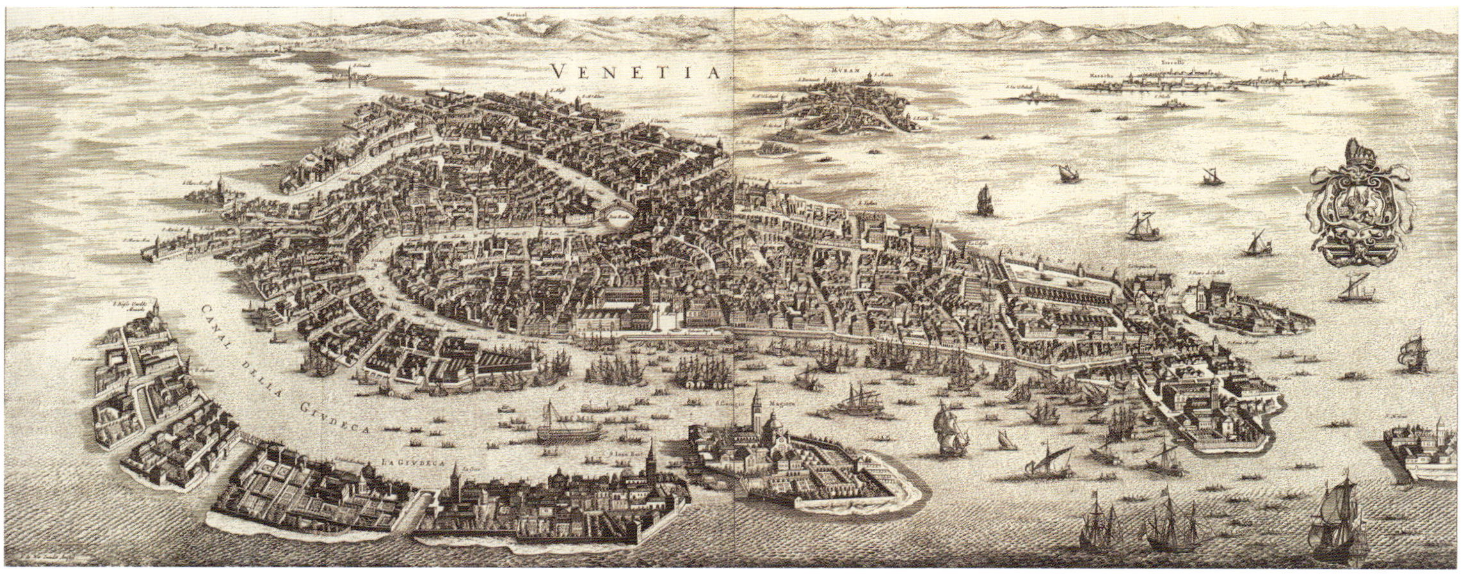

fig. 15—Frederick de Wit, *View of Venice*, late 17th c., engraving on paper, 16×40 in., Victoria and Albert Museum

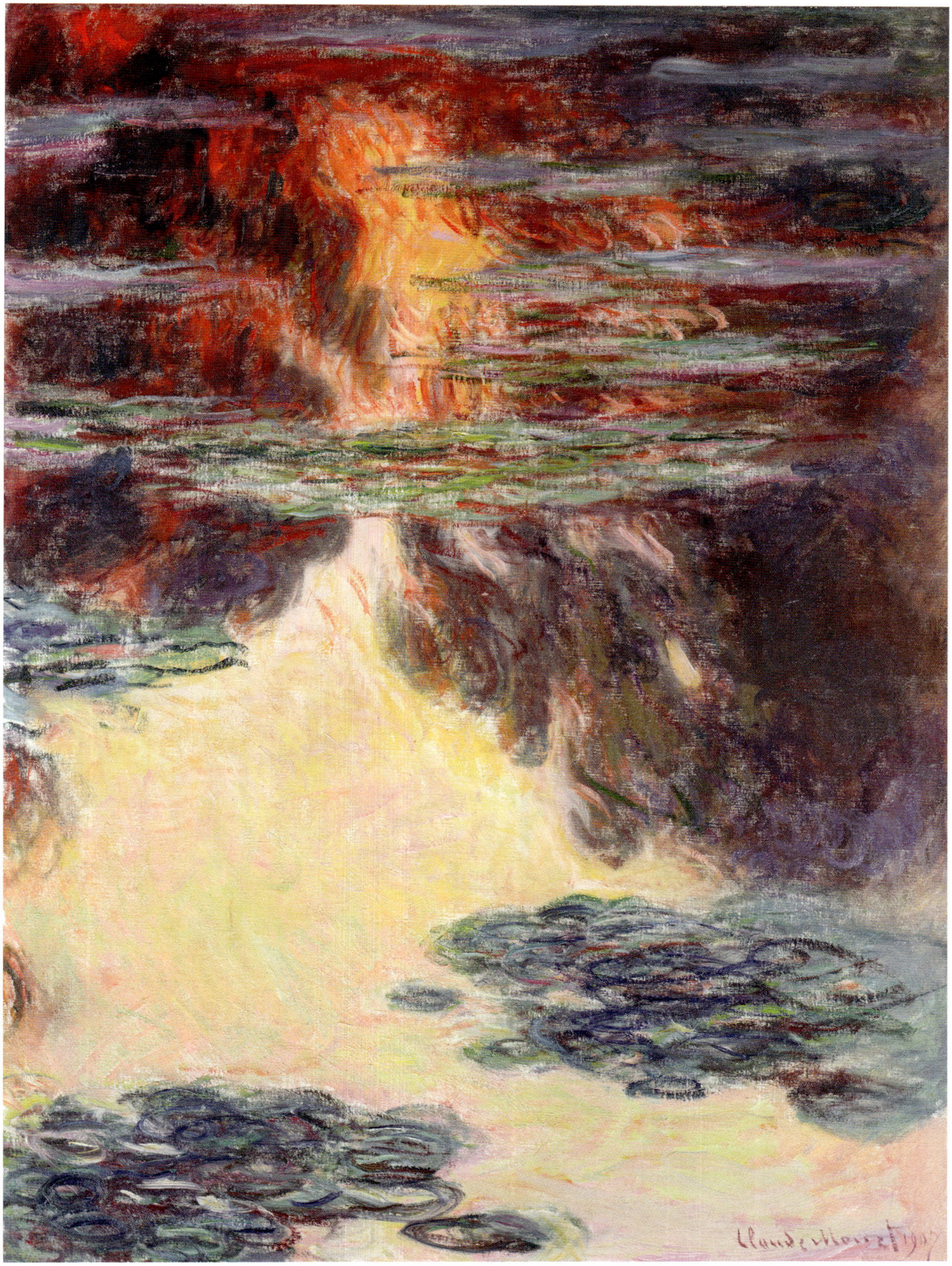

fig. 16—Claude Monet, *Water Lilies*, 1907, oil on canvas, 37⅜ × 28¾ in., Musée Marmottan Monet

twentieth-century "late works." But they are not perceived as belonging to that Monet sub-canon, which is dominated by his *Water Lilies* (figs. 17 and 19), especially the large panoramic group now installed at the Musée de l'Orangerie in Paris—works that, since the mid-twentieth century, some scholars connected to Abstract Expressionism (fig. 18).[12] The motif of Venice—a city famous for its legible, ready-made picturesque qualities—disrupts this prevailing teleological narrative of Monet's path toward modernist abstraction. "Venice" has in many ways become synonymous with "cliché," and as Jennifer Scappettone argues, the city has "represented a rebuke to modernity for artists and intellectuals since the dawn of the Enlightenment.... [It] resists the modern, both formally and symbolically."[13] The city and its perceived excessive devotion to the past caused it to be the target of the 1910 Futurist manifesto *Against Passéist Venice*, nearly eight hundred thousand copies of which Futurist artists, including Filippo Tommaso Marinetti and Umberto Boccioni, dropped from the Clock Tower in Piazza San Marco onto the crowds below. In it, they advocated modernizing the city by burning gondolas and filling the "little reeking canals with the ruins from its leprous and crumbling palaces."[14] Interestingly, the progressive Galerie Bernheim-Jeune presented the first Futurist exhibition in Paris in 1912, just months before Monet's *Venise* exhibition went on view there.

Monet himself contributed to the odd-one-out status of his Venice paintings. By asserting that "there are no series among these views of Venice, but only different motifs repeated once, twice or three times," Monet dissociated them from his most influential conceptual legacy to modern art—seriality—even though the group shares some structural similarities with his other series.[15] Perhaps most significantly, a despondent Monet wrote letters to friends and dealers after Alice's death in May 1911 revealing his struggle to complete the Venice paintings in his studio and his own negative appraisal of them, a judgment that has reverberated through their subsequent art historical reception. Given Monet's feelings about them

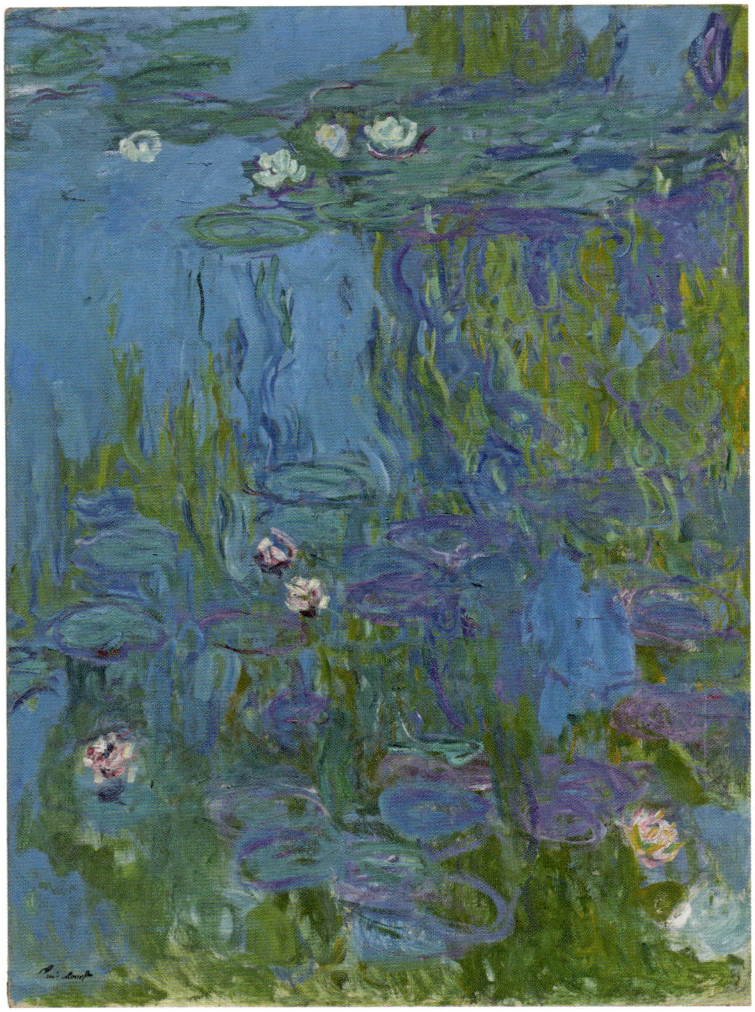

fig. 17—Claude Monet, *Water Lilies*, 1914–17, oil on canvas, 67×48 in., Collection of Diane B. Wilsey

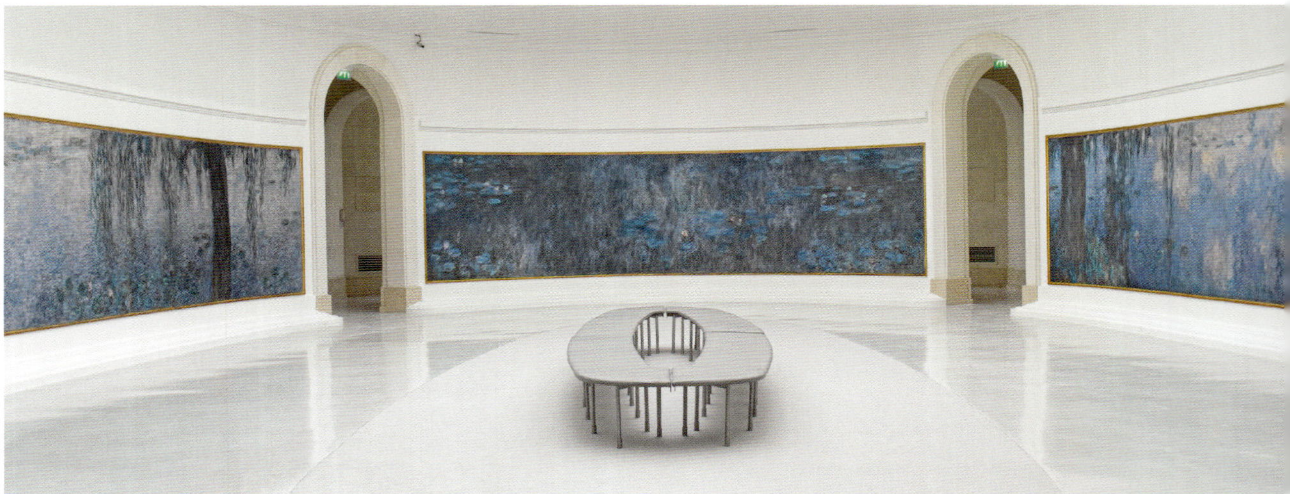

fig. 18—Room two of Claude Monet's *Water Lilies*, 1914–1926, oil "panels" placed on canvas mounted on the wall, Musée de l'Orangerie

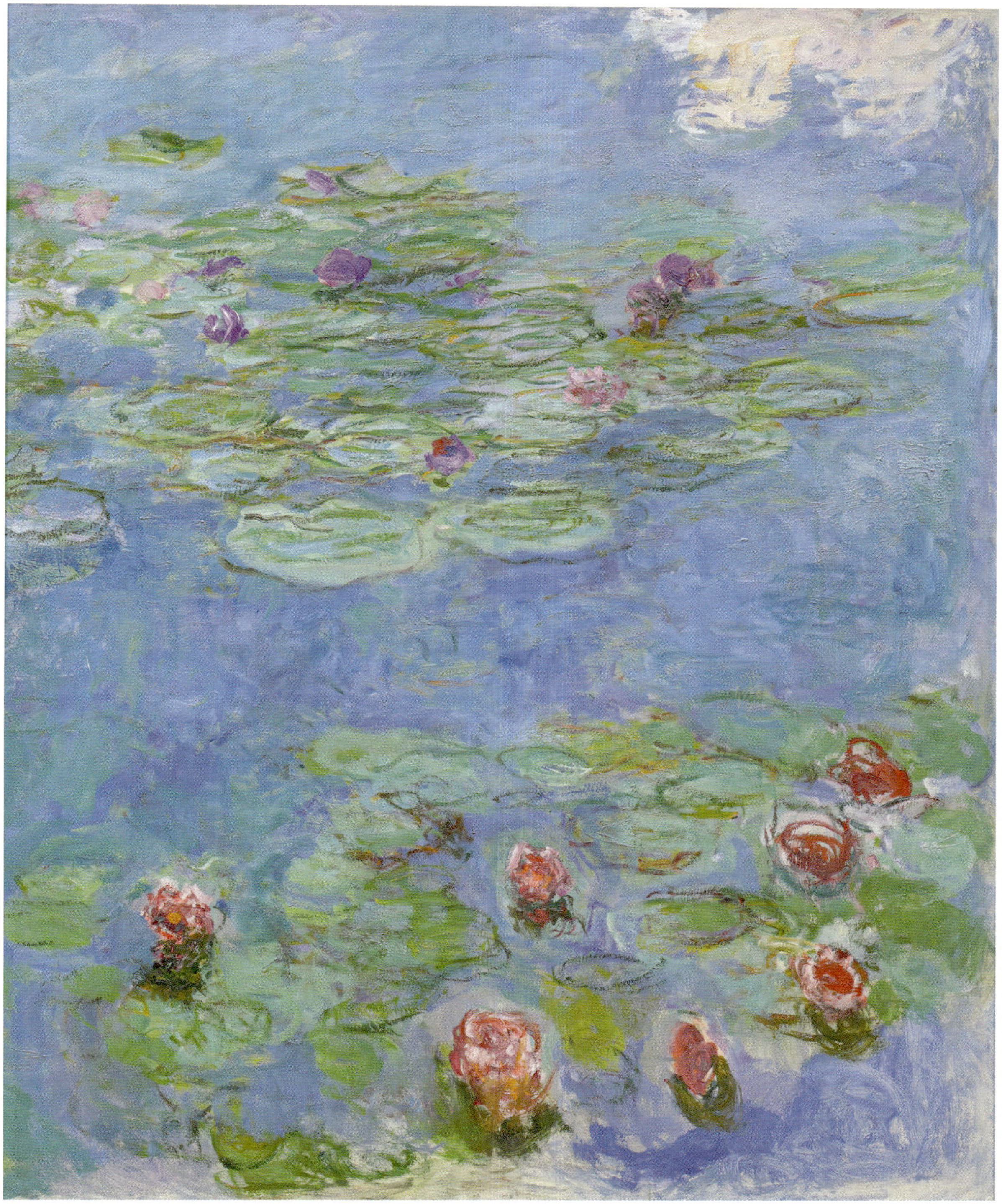

fig. 19—Claude Monet, *Water Lilies*, 1914–17, oil on canvas, 65⅜ × 56 in., Fine Arts Museums of San Francisco

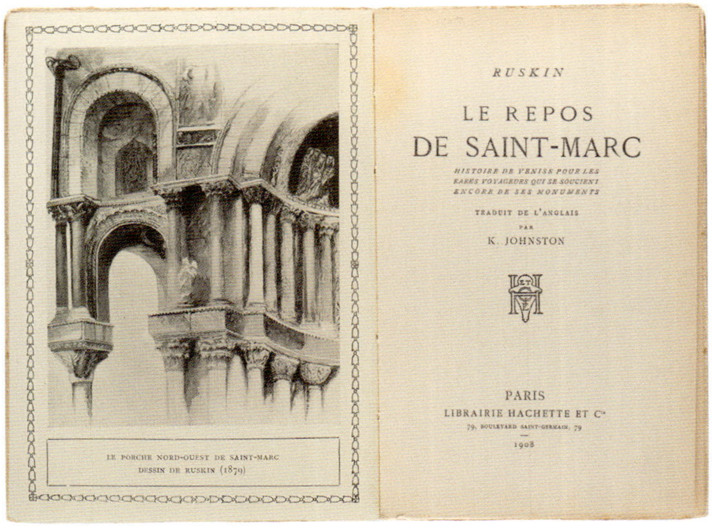

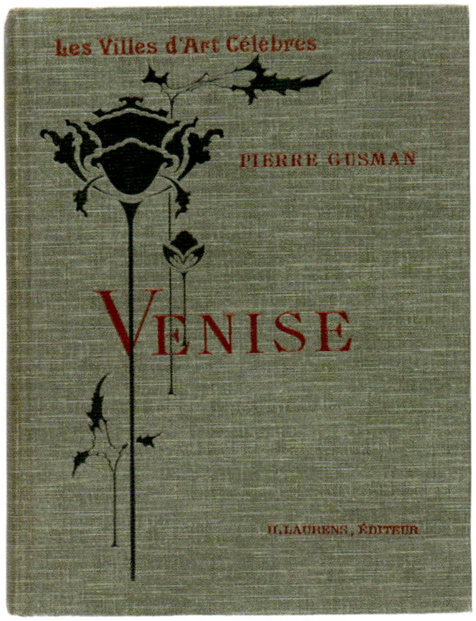

fig. 20—John Ruskin, *Le Repos de Saint-Marc*, bound book, Hachette, 1908, Brooklyn Museum

fig. 21—Pierre Gusman, *Venise*, bound book, Renouard, H. Laurens, 1904, Brooklyn Museum

and after the modernist hegemony of his *Water Lilies* was well established, it is not surprising that there has been a general tendency to regard the Venice paintings as picturesque footnotes or detours along the road to abstraction.[16]

Writing about the Venice paintings as a distinct group in his 1921 book on the artist, the critic Arsène Alexandre recognized that their "extreme delicacy caused the series to be even less understood than some others. But it is likely that it will gain in value over time, and in any case, as a transitional work, it is certain to remain of great interest to those of us who study Monet's work in depth."[17] Taking up this point, and the indispensable existing scholarship on this subject, this exhibition—the first since 1912 to focus on Monet's Venetian sojourn—seeks to reassert and amplify the trip's significance and demonstrate how the evocative paintings that resulted from it resonate within Monet's life and oeuvre. As a place and a motif, Venice was consonant with many of Monet's artistic concerns and challenges. Its spectacular architecture improbably emerging from the lagoon offered a ready-made exemplar of the relationship between art and nature. The fragile city at once symbolized the passage and immobilization of time. Among its defining features is the conjunction and interplay of water, air, stone, and reflections, imagery to which Monet was repeatedly drawn throughout his career. And its iridescent atmosphere was an ideal setting in which to investigate transitory light effects. In a review of the paintings, one critic summed up what the city offered Monet: "The brilliant and glorious painter had to go to Venice, which is all light. Between water and sky, it's liquid, diaphanous. No hardness. The blond light, fluid, purple, glides and turns around palaces and houses. The pink and blue facades seem to float on the water, as if the pearly domes were melting into the sky, which absorbs them, and the water, which reflects them."[18]

The trip to Venice was Monet's last major painting excursion and his final engagement with architectural subject matter. It also generated his last site-specific paintings apart from the *Water Lilies*, which, along with related Giverny garden motifs, were all that he worked on from that point until his death. The only exception was the completion of the Venice paintings themselves in his studio in 1911 and 1912. But perhaps those two motifs have more in common than is typically assumed; after all, in 1907 the philosopher Georg Simmel described the city as "a torn flower borne on the sea."[19] And, as Arsène Alexandre asserted when writing about Monet's Venice paintings, "There's only one step, there and back, from the water lily pond to the lagoon where the colorful palaces bloom."[20]

> I am leaving for Venice with my wife. We have been invited to spend some time there and, my goodness, seeing the weather getting worse and . . . the season almost over, I have decided to leave.
> {Claude Monet to Paul Durand-Ruel, September 25, 1908}

Monet eventually went to Venice because the society hostess Mary Hunter invited him and Alice to be her guests at the opulent fifteenth-century Palazzo Barbaro on the Grand Canal, which she was renting from its owners, Daniel and Ariana Curtis (figs. 12 and 22).[21] The Monets had become friendly with Hunter in London, and Alice was eager to accept the invitation. As the tone of his letter to Durand-Ruel suggests, however, Monet was not particularly enthusiastic about the trip. Alice made this clear in a letter to her daughter Germaine Salerou several days before they left: "As I expected, Monet is very sad to have committed to leaving; the good weather having returned, he cannot decide to abandon his pond and his flowers. Since yesterday, I have heard so much that, really, it spoils the pleasure of the trip."[22]

From the beginning of their relationship, Alice and Claude Monet regularly wrote to each other when he was away on painting trips. They were together in Venice, so it is fortunate that she was an indefatigable correspondent with her daughter during those months. Sitting next to Monet, often in a gondola, she wrote "on my knees, very poorly installed," or "hiding in my little corner," not being able to "do or move anything."[23] Her intimate, casual letters are a crucial source of information about his process, his progress, the weather (upon which so much of Monet's mood always depended), and the daily creative turmoil and emotional upheaval that defined his time there: "How often has he told me to pack our bags and that he'll never touch a brush again, and an hour later he's back at work and has sometimes even started a new canvas."[24] Throughout all, her support and belief in him, her concern for his physical and mental health, her daily encouragement and enjoyment of the time they spent together, and the joy she took in

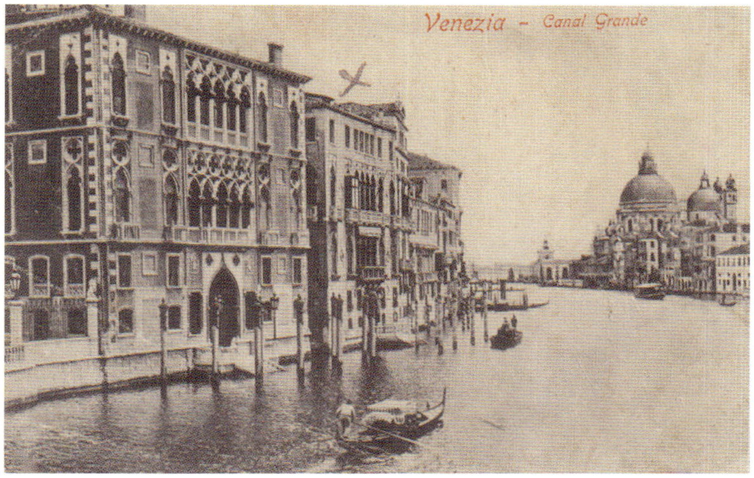

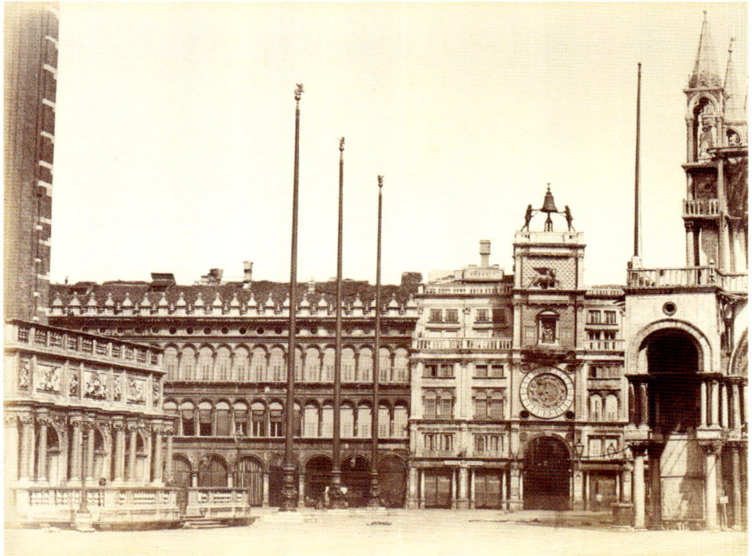

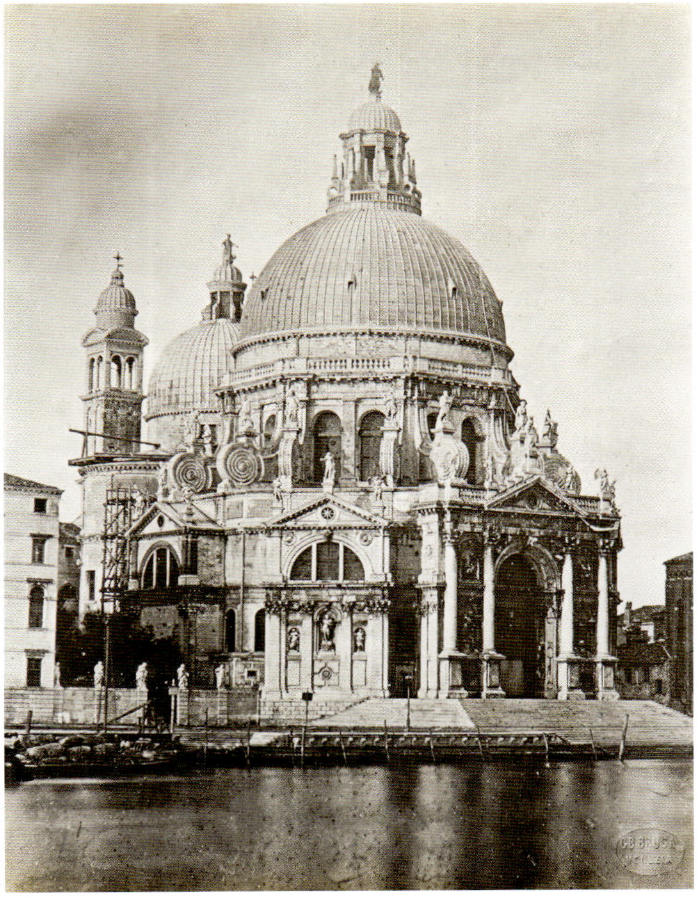

fig. 22—Postcard of Grand Canal with Palazzo Barbaro marked by an X, sent by Alice Monet to her granddaughter Simone Salerou, October 10, 1908, Collection Philippe Piguet

fig. 23—Carlo Naya, *Veduta delle Procuratie Vecchie ed Orologio*, pl. no. 71 from the album *Venezia*, mid-19th c., mounted albumen silver print, 10⅗ × 13¾ in., Fine Arts Museums of San Francisco

fig. 24—*Santa Maria Della Salute*, lantern slide, Brooklyn Museum Libraries and Archives

his work and her admiration of it are clear and unwavering. So too is the toll it took on her own emotional state:

What crazy and sad days I'm going through right now.... Monet who sees that everything changes cannot really tear himself away from his motifs.... You know him, you know the extreme jumps, from the beautiful to the ugly, from the good to the bad and I need... great energy and a good dose of courage because alone like this, it's painful and he has his work, me my thoughts.[25]

Alice immediately fell under La Serenissima's spell and felt as though she were living in a dream or a fairy tale, describing Venice as "magical," "dazzling," and "brilliant," filled with "enchantment," "wonder," and "divine reflections."[26] In the few letters Claude Monet wrote from Venice, he, too, expressed that he was "overcome with admiration for it" and captivated by its "unique light."[27] Although the trip was conceived as a rejuvenating holiday, he still expected to do some painting there, having arranged for canvases and materials to be shipped ahead. But he and Alice spent their first days experiencing the beautiful city together as the tourists they were. Alice wrote of their arrival, "As soon as we landed, Mrs. Hunter was there and, immediately, in a gondola, made us go around the large and small canals and admire the setting sun on Piazza San Marco; all unforgettable."[28] Days later she recounted:

Our day was very busy, I assure you; after our gondola rides, in the morning, we returned on foot to cross the small bridges and typical little rivers, had lunch at 1 p.m. and left at 3 p.m. We visited the interior of San Marco, it is superb, then we went to the Lido — the Venetians' bathing area — and saw the real sea. We returned in the middle of the night with a splendid sunset and finally a divine moonlight. The illuminations of Venice, with their reflections, the gondolas, all of this is wonderful![29]

Like the many thousands of people who visited Venice each year by the early twentieth century, the Monets were enabled by the city's robust tourist infrastructure. They arrived via a two-mile-long railway bridge that since 1846 had carried increasing numbers of vacationers to the island city from the mainland. Their sightseeing itinerary—which included churches and museums—was informed by travel books Monet purchased, such as the 1907 edition of the *Guide Joanne* to Italy, recent French translations of John Ruskin's *St. Mark's Rest* (fig. 20), and Pierre Gusman's *Venise* (fig. 21); in the latter he would have read this pertinent passage describing the city as first seen in the distance: "blooming like an aquatic plant, flower of purple and gold, flower of flesh with luminous petals, vibrant, majestic and magical, it offered itself, full of seduction."[30] The city's flourishing commercial photography industry provided visitors with an endless supply of inexpensive souvenir images. Alice's picture postcards (figs. 22, 25, 26, 30, 56, 60, 66, 67, and 92) might have been among those stocked at Emilio Aickelin's art supply and stationery shop, where Monet bought the sketchbook (fig. 62) that includes his only known drawing of Venice and also some additional canvases.[31] Alice even convinced Monet to participate in one of the most

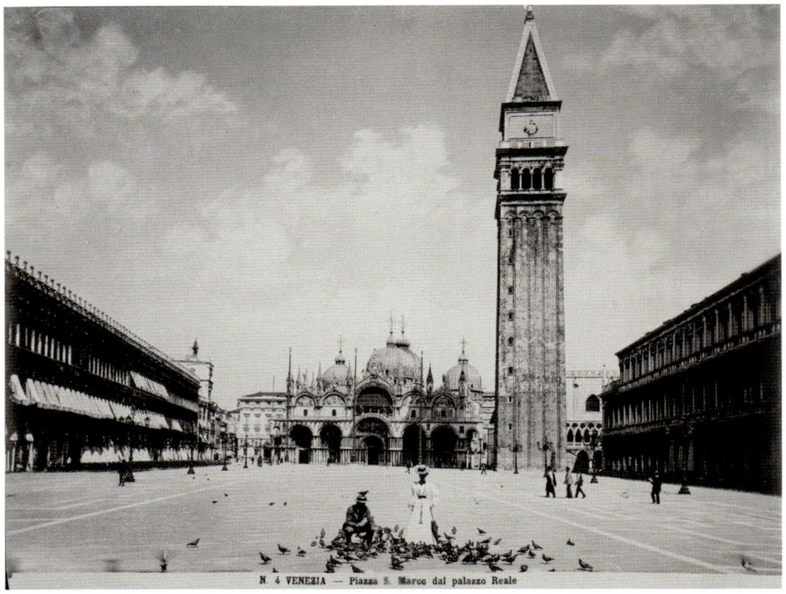

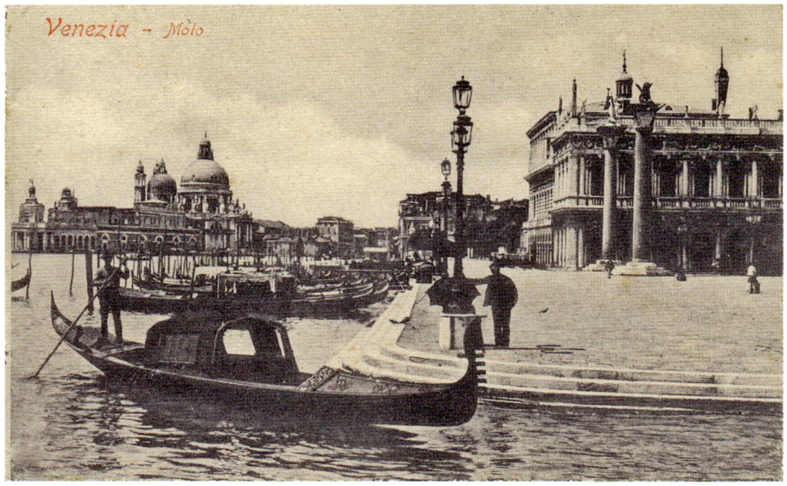

fig. 25—Postcard of Piazza San Marco belonging to Alice Monet (photo taken before 1902), Musée Marmottan Monet

fig. 26—Postcard of the Piazzetta sent by Alice Monet to her granddaughter Alice Butler, October 25, 1908, Collection Philippe Piguet

popular of Venice tourist rituals: they posed for photographs in the Piazza San Marco, their arms and heads covered with the ubiquitous pigeons, about which John Ruskin quipped that "the glory of the creatures is not in being pigeons, but in being Venetians." (fig. 25)[32] Alice made one of these charming photographs into a postcard that delighted Sisi, Germaine's daughter (fig. 27).

By the time Monet arrived there in 1908, Venice—a city long synonymous with the tradition of view painting—was considered an exhausted subject, always already known, sinking under the weight of its artistic cult status and the throngs of tourists who came to "experience" its history. As long ago as 1494, a pilgrim could observe that it was a place "about which so much has been said and written . . . that it appears to me there is nothing left to say."[33] Even Lord Byron, whose poetry would go on to define the city's magical image ("her structures rise / As from the stroke of the enchanter's wand"), wrote in 1816 when newly arrived there: "Of Venice I shall say little. You must have seen many descriptions; and they are most of them like."[34] Author Henry James, for whom Venice was a recurring theme and literary setting, echoed this sentiment in a passage that itself has become a well-known assessment of this well-known city: "Venice has been painted and described many thousands of times, and of all the cities of the world is the easiest to visit without going there. Open the first book and you will find a rhapsody about it; step into the first picture-dealer's and you will find three or four high-coloured 'views' of it. There is notoriously nothing more to be said on the subject. Everyone has been there, and everyone has brought back a collection of photographs."[35]

In his catalogue essay for Monet's 1912 exhibition, Octave Mirbeau recalled that the artist once told him, "Venice . . . no . . . I will not go to Venice."[36] This suggests the anxiety of influence that even an independent artist like Monet might have anticipated experiencing confronted by the city and the glowing colors and bravura brushwork of its sixteenth-century artistic titans, Titian, Tintoretto, and Veronese. Or, indeed, the feelings of disdain evoked by a place that, according to Mirbeau, was no longer a city but merely a decoration, a colored postcard.[37] Upon arrival, Monet lamented to Alice that the city was "too beautiful to be painted" and that he was "too old to paint such beautiful things."[38] He painted Venice nonetheless—its pearly light and humid atmosphere—and, according to one review of the paintings in 1912, successfully demonstrated "that there is no subject, however hackneyed it may seem, that cannot be renewed and magnified by interpretation."[39] No less a critic than Guillaume Apollinaire, progressive champion of Cubism (a style that was already several years old at the time of the *Venise* exhibition), praised the paintings, recognizing that Monet's "new, reserved, almost dull technique" dispelled the city's reputation as a mythical illusion and restored the truth of its "misty aspects."[40] Monet renewed the city by dematerializing its history—in fact, by making it appear ahistorical—reclaiming for it in delicate touches of paint its essential reality: shifting light on stone and water.

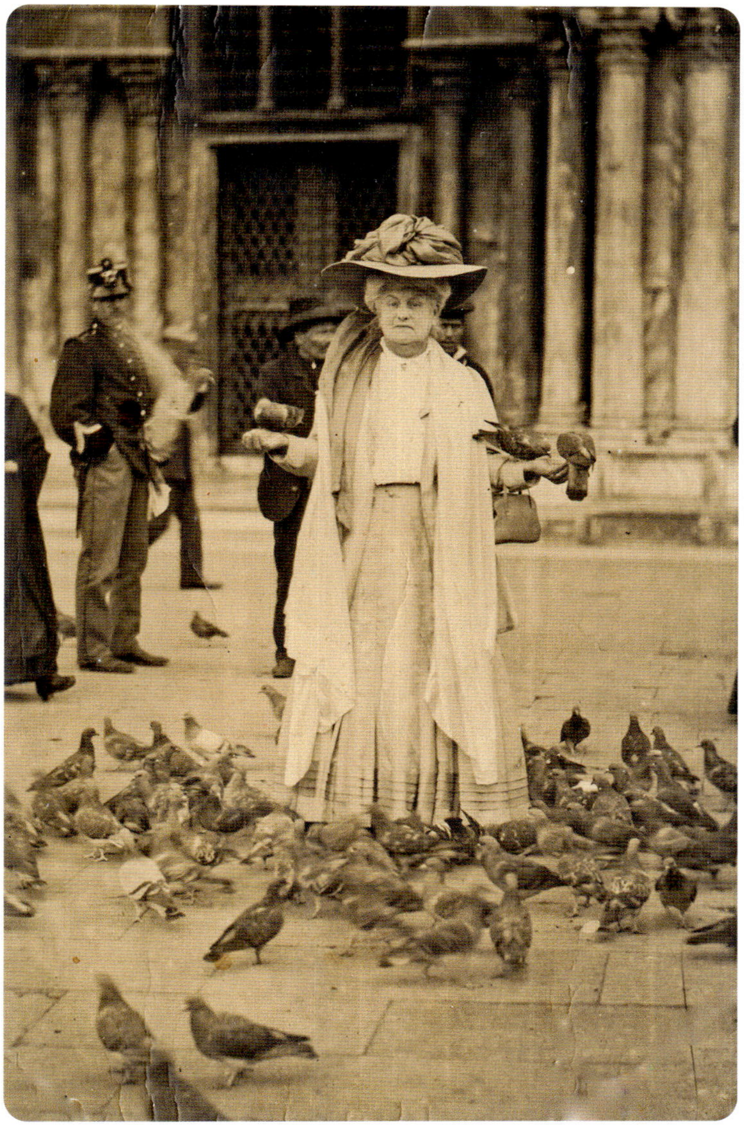

fig. 27—Postcard of Alice Monet in Piazza San Marco belonging to Alice Monet
October 1908, Collection Philippe Piguet

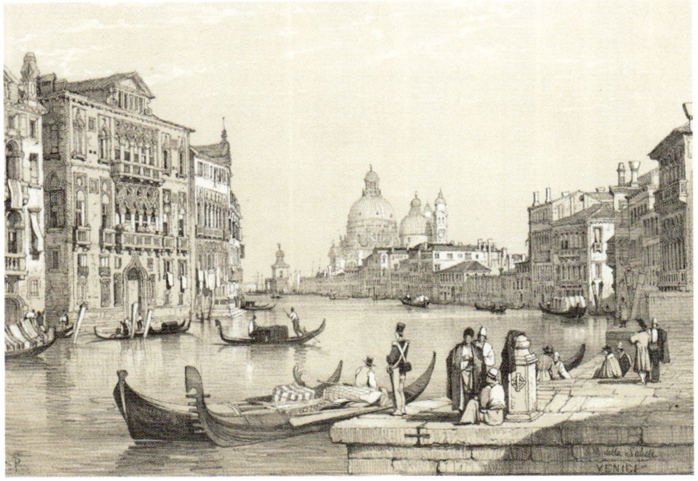

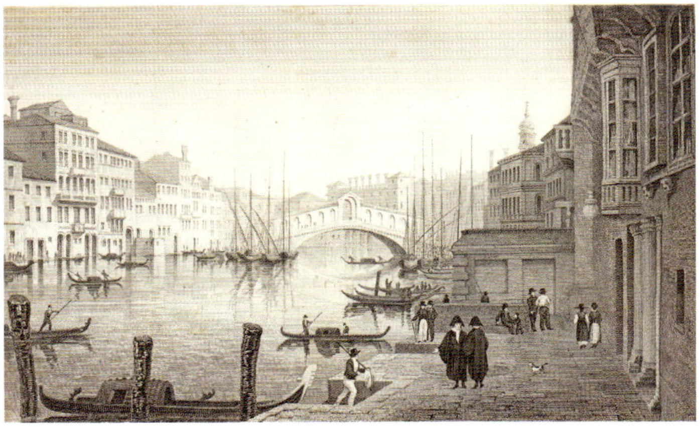

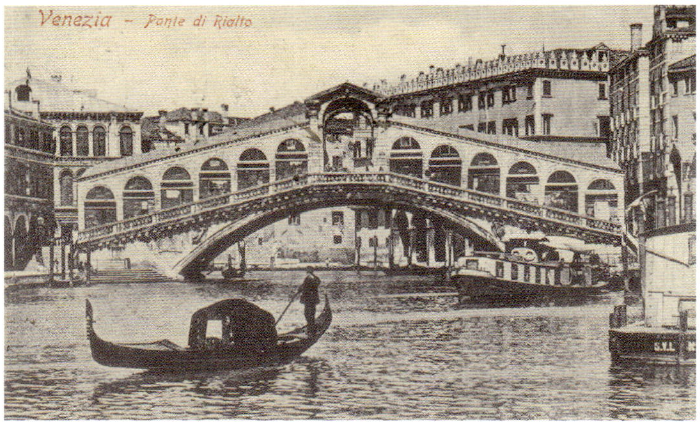

fig. 28—Samuel Prout, *S. M. della Salute,* Pl. No. 20 in *Venice* in *Sketches in France, Switzerland and Italy*, c. 1840, lithograph, 10 9/16 × 14½ in., Fine Arts Museums of San Francisco

fig. 29—*Venice*, engraving after a drawing by Elizabeth Frances Batty, from *Italian Scenery from Drawings* made in 1817 by Miss Batty, 1820, engraving, 6⅓ × 10⅓ in. each, Fine Arts Museums of San Francisco

fig. 30—Postcard showing the Rialto Bridge over the Grand Canal sent by Alice Monet to her granddaughter Alice Butler, October 7, 1908, Collection Philippe Piguet

—

Alas, his canvases do not arrive and I'm afraid that after the first impression of fire and ecstasy, the reflection will cool.
{ Alice Monet to Germaine Salerou, October 6, 1908 }

Monet did not start painting right away because the materials he had sent in advance were delayed. This concerned Alice, who feared that "he won't get to work. I would be so sad."[41] By October 7, he was finally able to begin, but Alice's pleasure swiftly turned into unhappiness in the face of his anxiety and frustration:

Monet goes to work; you know what joy there is for me in this word—but (life always has a but)—the sky, so immutably clear since our arrival, has a few clouds and while I write, at any moment, I go to the window to watch it. What joy for me to see Monet set to work.... Alas! The wind becomes so strong, impossible to work. Monet wanted to, so discouraged, he says he will not even try. It's so sad![42]

In Alice's poignant recounting of Monet's confrontation with Venice and its weather, his mood (and hers) continually fluctuates between bleakness and brightness:

— *Monet... has absolutely given up.*
— *Here, it's always the same wonder and Monet hard at work.*
— *We spent cruel hours in the torrential rain with Monet not wanting to move from this hotel room and not even being able to work through the window.*
— *Monet is working passionately. Venice has got hold of him and won't let go.*
— *Monet back to work, also you can guess with what anxiety I watch the weather.*
— *Monet has returned to work and is making beautiful things.*[43]

Claude Monet painted in Venice for a little more than two months—far longer than he had initially anticipated and despite his almost daily threats to leave whenever it was rainy, windy, or cold. When the weather cooperated, he maintained a highly regimented painting schedule that began early in the morning and ended at sunset. Over the course of the day, he had a two-hour "appointment" with each of his motifs.[44] But unlike his series of Rouen Cathedral paintings, for example, he did not paint the same view at different times of day under different weather and light conditions, but rather the same view at the same time every day (fig. 97). As André Dombrowski discusses in his essay in this volume, Monet strictly managed his own schedule in this "timeless" city, where cultural time was embedded in the architecture and ecological time was registered in the ebb and flow of the sea.

For each appointment, he could have multiple canvases in progress. When he arrived at a location, he chose whichever of his canvases corresponded to the conditions he faced: "I thought that Monet couldn't work, but fortunately he has a palace in gray weather and, sheltered in the gondola, he was able to have

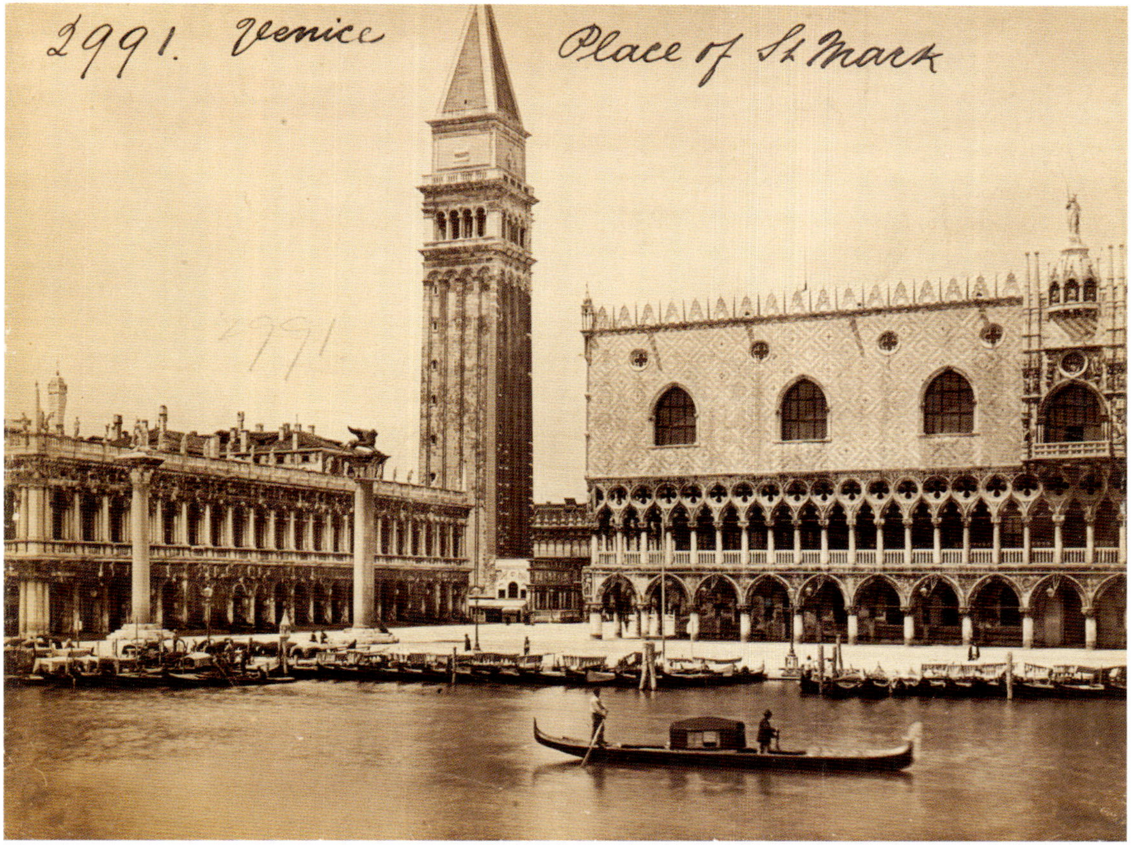

fig. 31—Francis Frith, untitled photograph, Piazza San Marco, 1850s–70s, whole-plate albumen print from wet collodion glass negative, 6½×8 in., Victoria and Albert Museum

a session."[45] There were days when he did no work because he felt he could not render any of his established motifs in that day's atmosphere, and days when the conditions pushed him to start an entirely new canvas: "Yesterday we had a terrible wind that prevented Monet from going to any of his motifs; at first he wanted to leave, then he ordered other canvases and started one—but that doesn't advance the others. This morning there is still bad wind, although the sun is trying to come out; so let's hope that the good weather will return and Monet will work on his motifs."[46]

This complex multi-canvas process had long been overwhelming for the artist. In an 1885 letter to Camille Pissarro from Étretat, he complained, "It was to no avail to set out canvases for all weathers; I do not come to the end of it."[47] John Singer Sargent witnessed him in London grappling with "some ninety canvases—each one the record of a momentary effect of light over the Thames. When the effect was repeated and an opportunity occurred for finishing the picture, the effect had generally passed away before the particular canvas could be found."[48] His practice of working outdoors in changing weather frequently caused him to fall into moods of rage, gloom, frustration, and hopelessness, which he shared in letters to Alice, like this one from 1889 written from Fresselines: "As for work, alas, one day I am full of hope and ardor, and the next I am completely flattened out, and it is that way today.... I am in an atrocious state of enervation and anxiety; it is already so difficult when one has the weather one wishes for.... Yesterday I thought I was safe, it was a beautiful sunny day, and I'd bravely gone back to my canvases

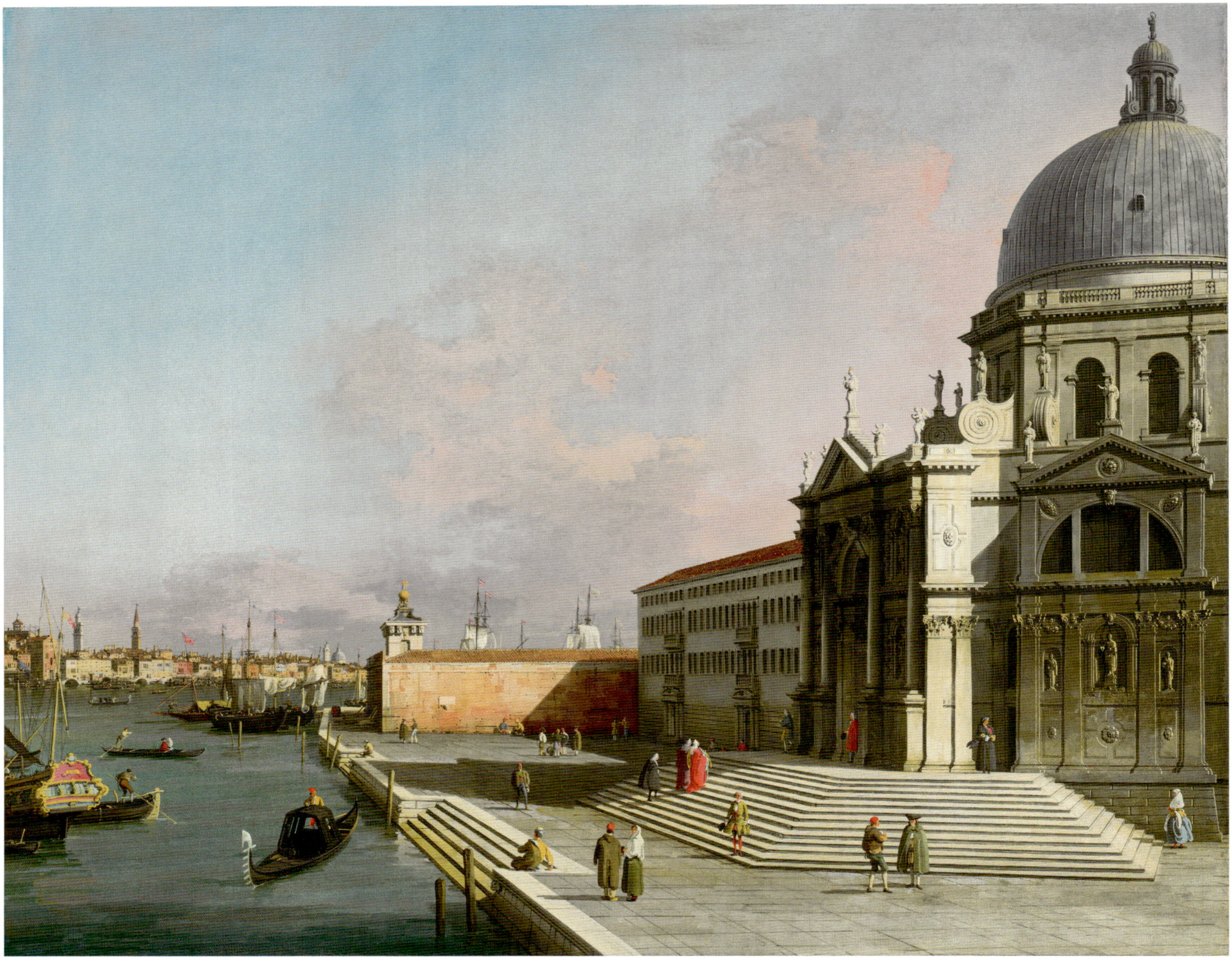

fig. 32—Canaletto, *Venice, the Grand Canal Looking East with Santa Maria della Salute*, 1749–50, oil on canvas, 52 × 64⅞ in., Fine Arts Museums of San Francisco

in sunshine, which I'd considered lost, I was excited, making the changes I wanted, and then, bang, this terrible hurricane that's still going on now. Ah! I'm really worried!"[49] As Mirbeau once admonished him: "To believe you are finished as a painter because it's raining and windy—this is pure madness."[50]

Monet ultimately exhibited nine different Venetian motifs, each treated in as few as three or as many as six canvases.[51] They all focus on some combination of architecture, sky, and water (the latter typically occupying at least half the canvas), and a number were painted from water level. Many of his viewpoints are derived from what might be described as the historical Venice algorithm. They had been painted by his artistic predecessors and illustrated in nineteenth-century travelogues or compendia of picturesque city views (figs. 28 and 29). Most of his motifs would have been familiar to armchair tourists perusing the Venetian offerings of commercial photographic companies

fig. 33—Studio of Canaletto, *Venetian Scene*, mid-18th c., oil on canvas, 27½ × 49½ in., Fine Arts Museums of San Francisco

like Francis Frith & Co. (figs. 31, 57, and 61), and it would not be inconceivable for Monet to have used photographs—perhaps even postcards Alice purchased in Venice—as an aide-mémoire when he was completing the paintings almost four years after he returned to France. When he was finishing his London series in his Giverny studio, he asked Mary Hunter to send a photograph of the Houses of Parliament, writing, with typical anxiety, "With that, I think I could do something, that is, if I am still any good."[52]

That Monet chose such well-established motifs in Venice is not surprising. When painting on the coast of Normandy, he traveled to vantage points recommended in tourist guides because they offered views of that region's natural beauty—views that were then illustrated in those same guides (figs. 32, 33, and 34–54). He understood that such associations helped create a market for paintings of those sites.[53] Although it took him years to heed Durand-Ruel's savvy advice to go to Venice, Monet was aware of the commercial potential of well-known views of a famous place (London had made that clear). The same desire that drove wealthy eighteenth-century Grand Tourists to acquire paintings or sets of engravings (the picture postcards of their day) of the city's prime vistas by Canaletto or other artists as souvenirs was still strong, and Monet was happy to capitalize on it.[54] In the end, however, it was the *enveloppe* that mattered to him. In their mostly rapturous responses to the paintings, critics made it clear they understood that even as he drew from the "traditional repertoire of motifs," the "monuments of Venice do not interest Monet." Instead, they were pretexts through which the artist could explore (and they could poetically describe) his vision of the city:

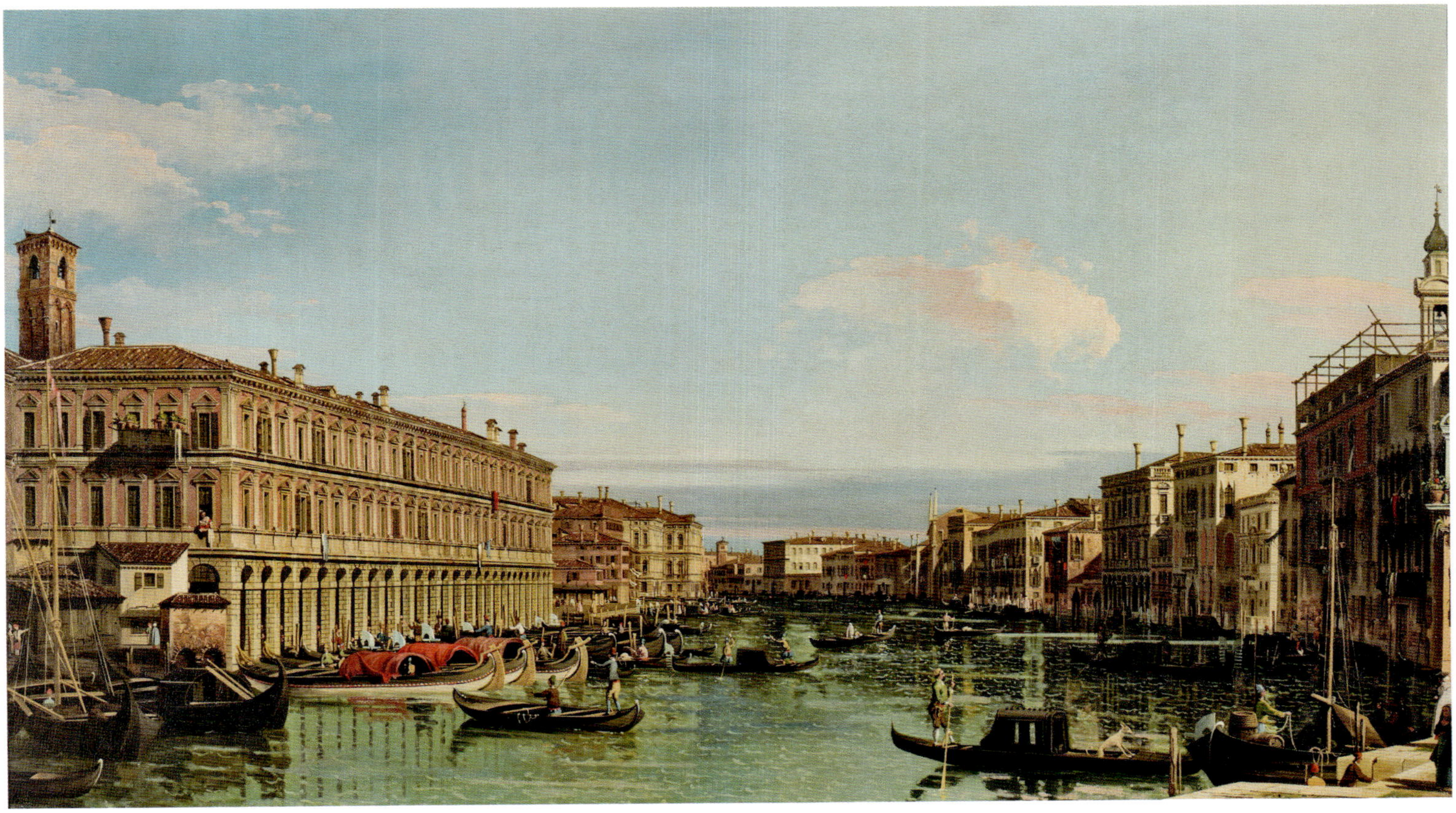

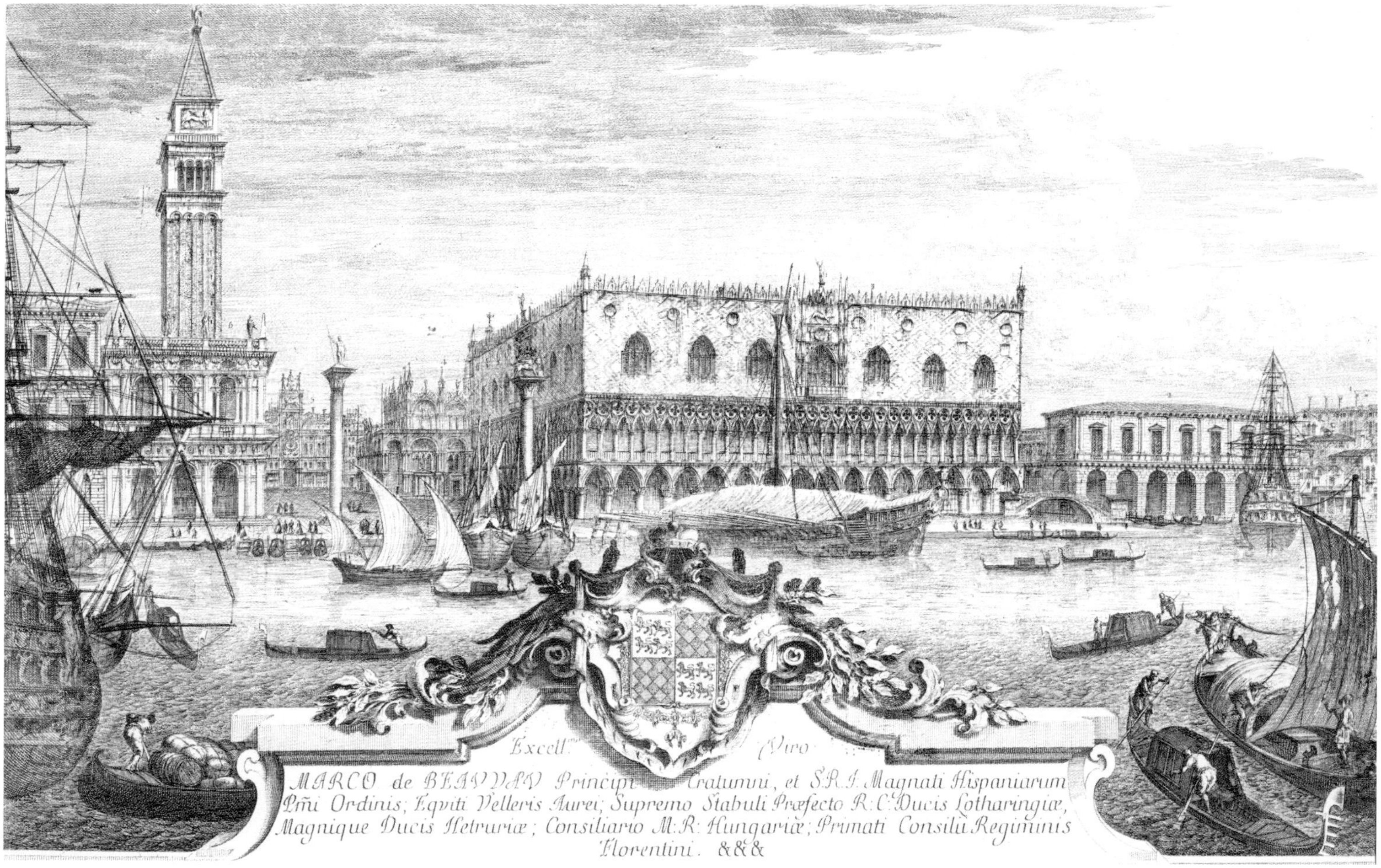

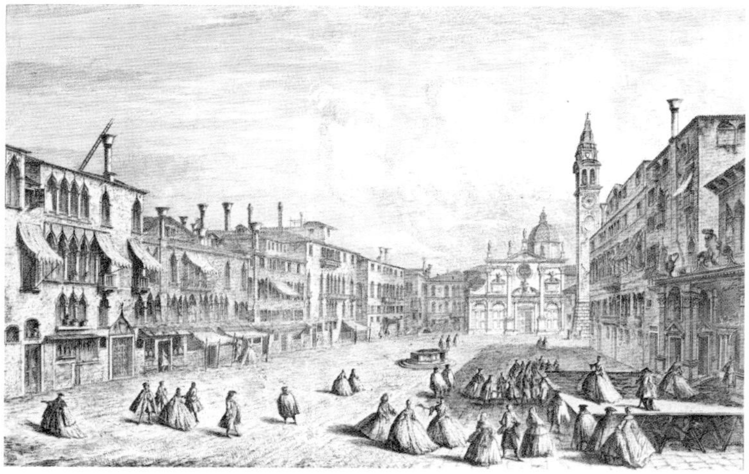

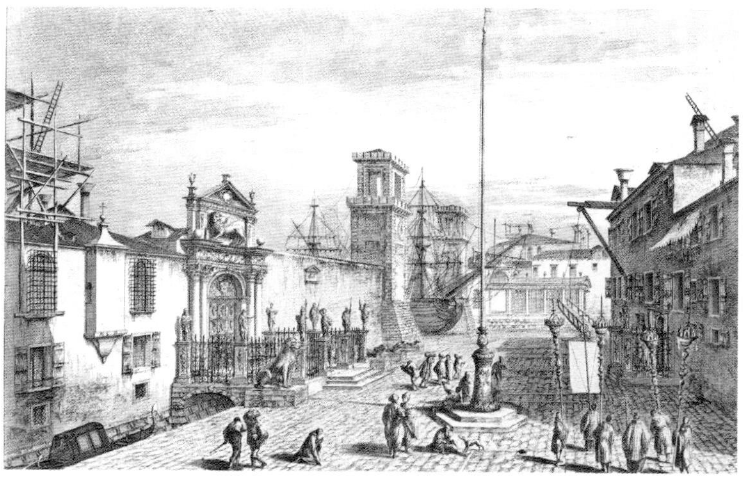

figs. 34–42 (*left to right, top to bottom*): Michele Marieschi, Pl. No. 1–21, *The Piazzetta and Ducal Palace*, *Santa Maria Formosa*, *The Gates of the Arsenal*, *The Basin of St. Mark's*, *The Bridge and Market of the Rialto*, *Santa Chiara*, *Palazzo Pesaro*, *Piazza S. Marco*, *Santa Maria della Salute*, *The Piazzetta*, *Courtyard of the Ducal Palace*, *Campo SS. Giovanni e Paolo*, *Piazzetta S. Basso*, *Cannaregio*, *Canale Grande*, *Campo San Rocco*, *Rialto*, *The Molo and S. Maria della Salute*, *Piazza and Piazzetta*, *Campo dei Frari*, *The Regatta* from the series *Magnificentiores Selectioresque Urbis Venetiarum Prospectus*, 1741, etchings, various sizes, Fine Arts Museums of San Francisco

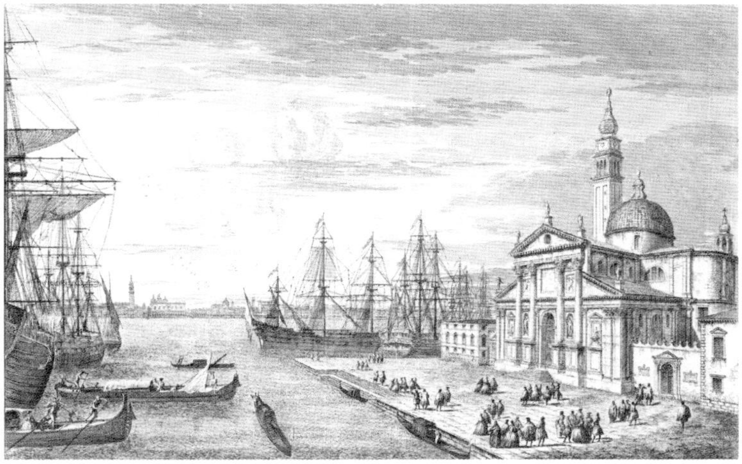
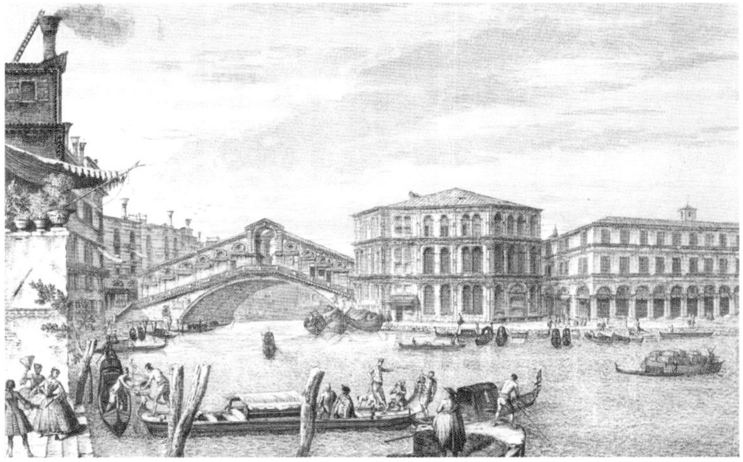
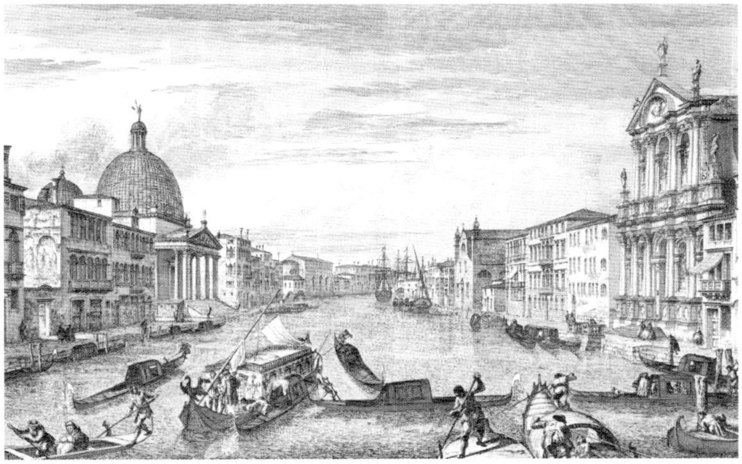
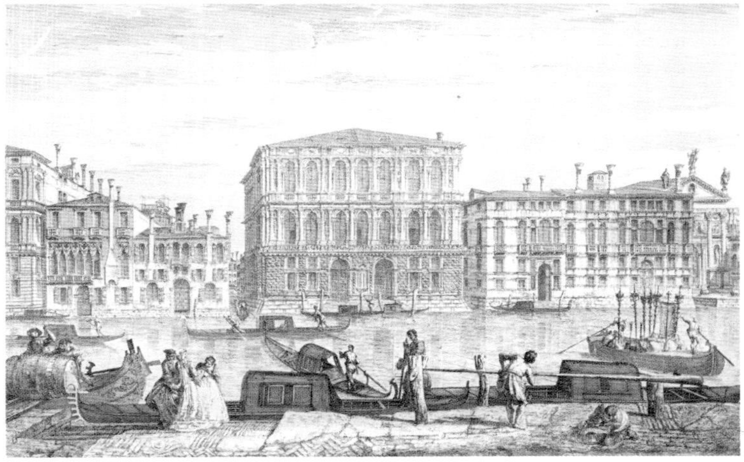
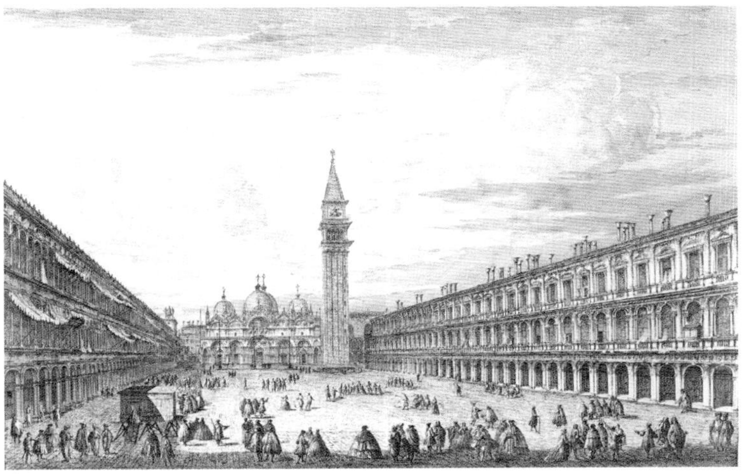
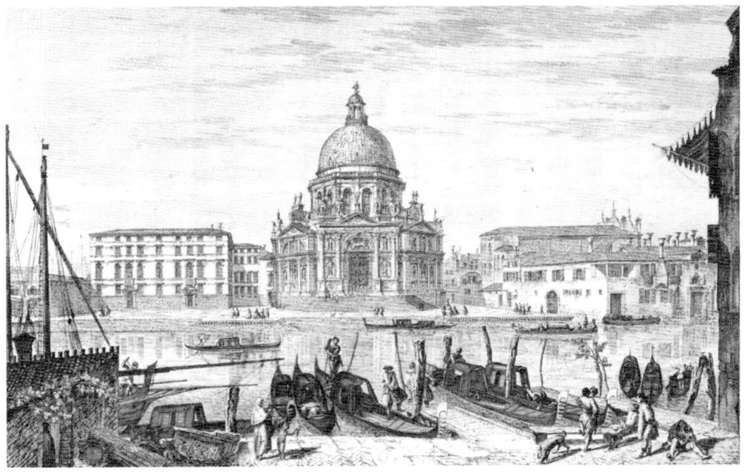

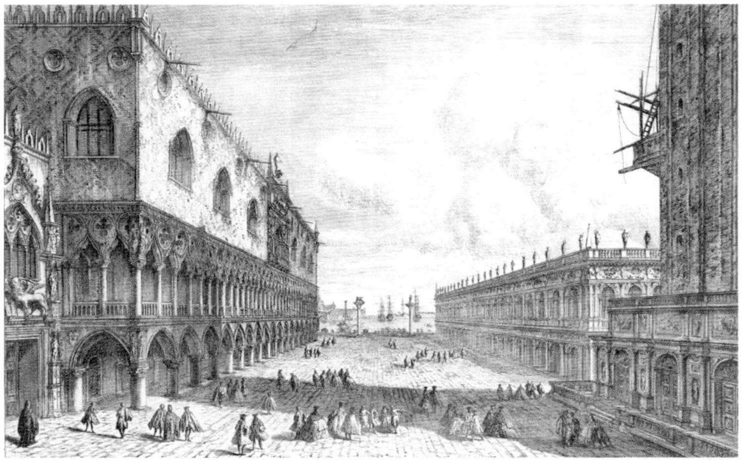
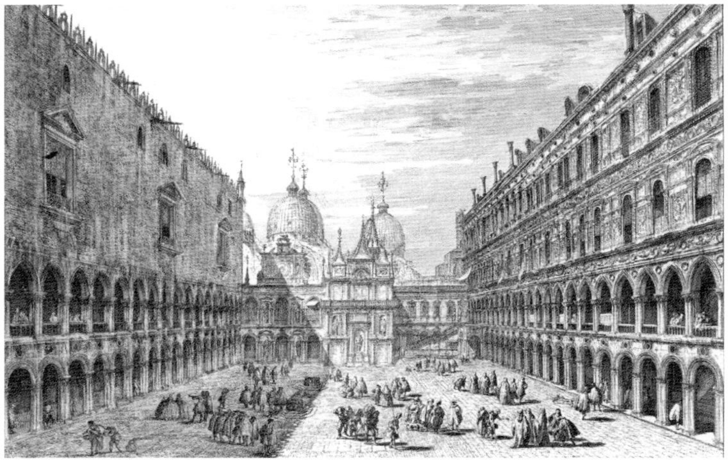
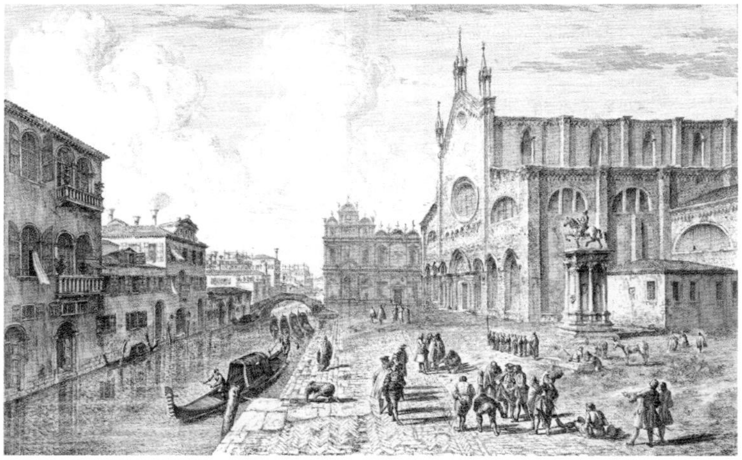
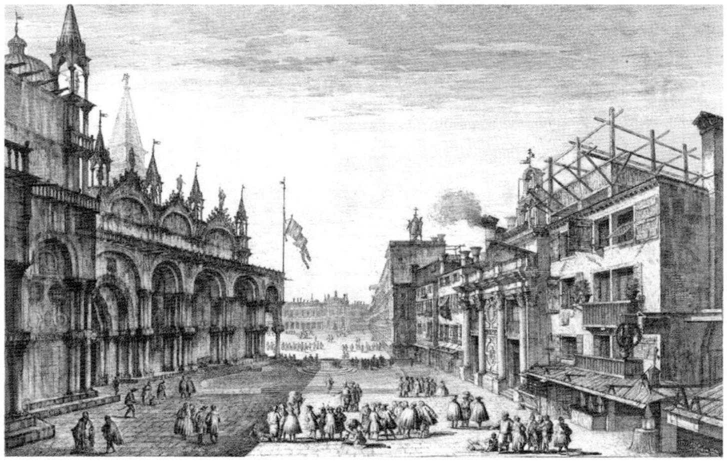
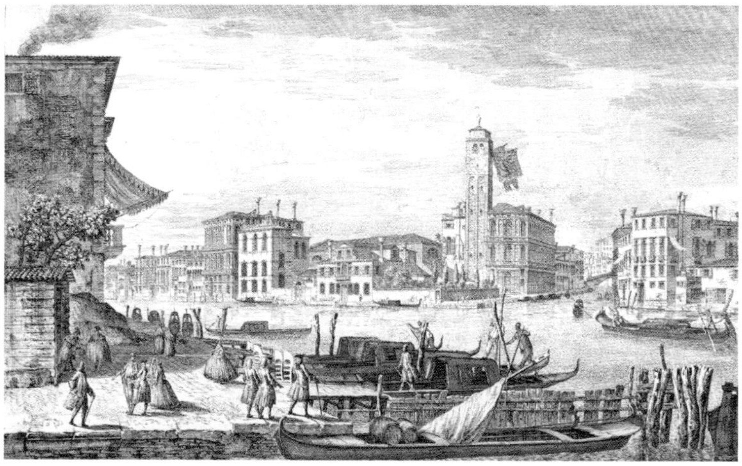
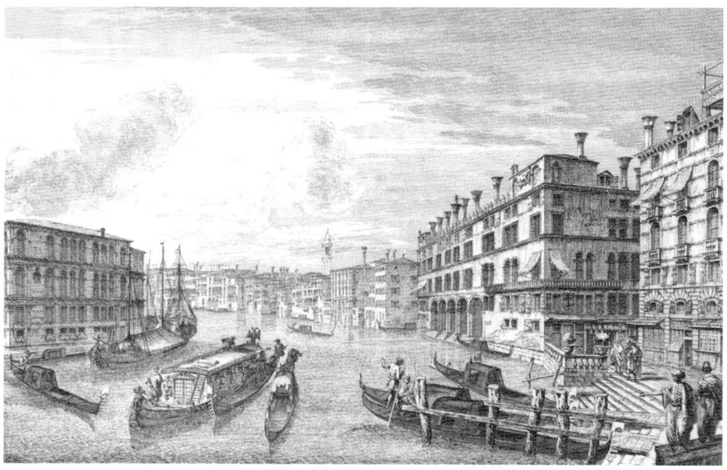

figs. 43–54 (*left to right, top to bottom*): Michele Marieschi, Pl. No. 1–21, *The Piazzetta and Ducal Palace*, *Santa Maria Formosa*, *The Gates of the Arsenal*, *The Basin of St. Mark's*, *The Bridge and Market of the Rialto*, *Santa Chiara*, *Palazzo Pesaro*, *Piazza S. Marco*, *Santa Maria della Salute*, *The Piazzetta*, *Courtyard of the Ducal Palace*, *Campo SS. Giovanni e Paolo*, *Piazzetta S. Basso*, *Cannaregio*, *Canale Grande*, *Campo San Rocco*, *Rialto*, *The Molo and S. Maria della Salute*, *Piazza and Piazzetta*, *Campo dei Frari*, *The Regatta* from the series *Magnificentiores Selectioresque Urbis Venetiarum Prospectus*, 1741, etchings, various sizes, Fine Arts Museums of San Francisco

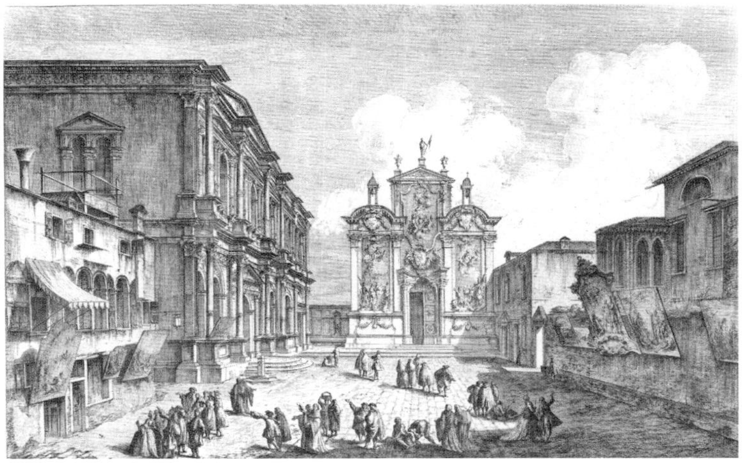
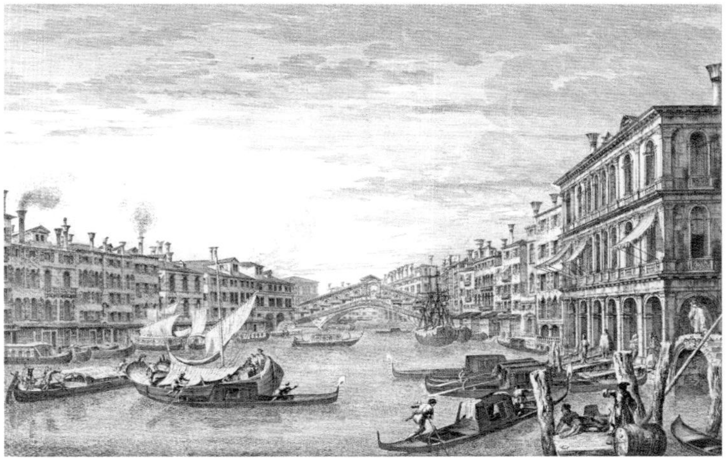
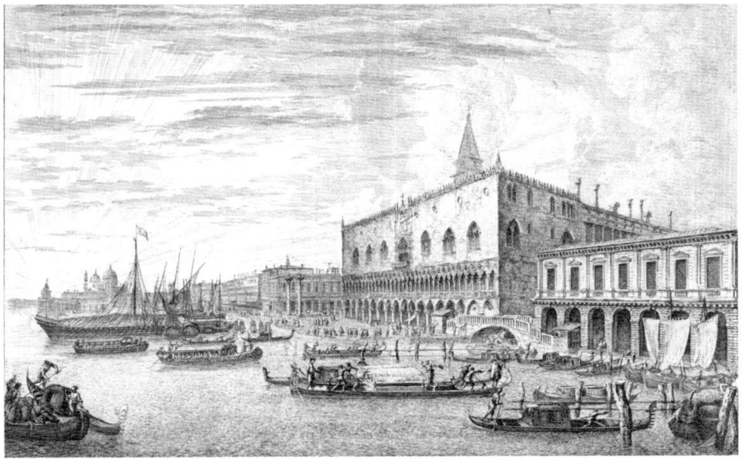
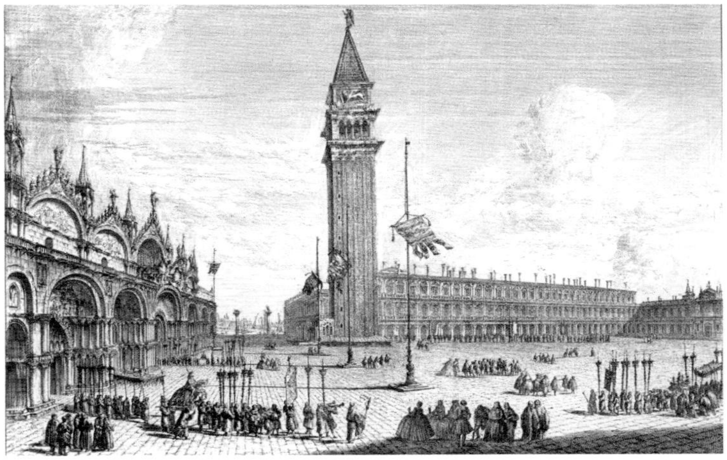
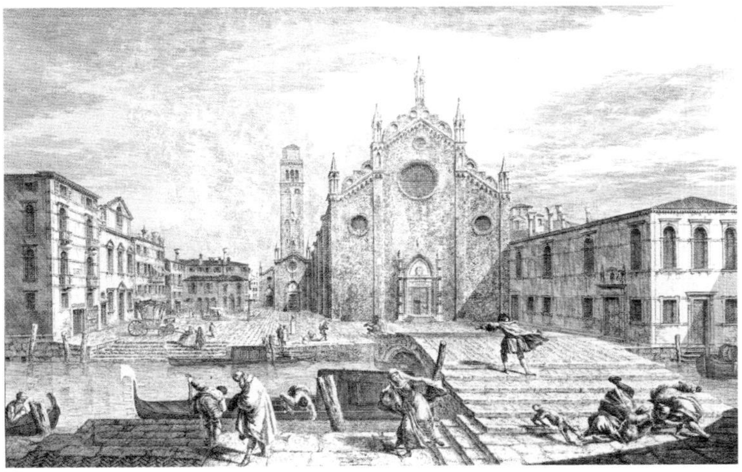
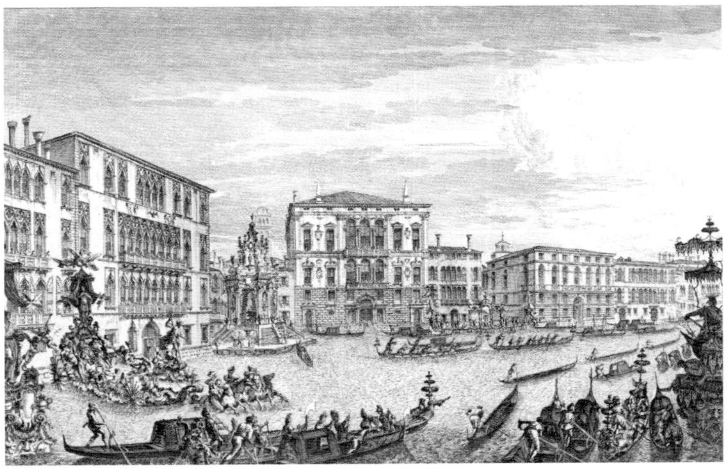

"chimerical," "mirages," "evanescent ghosts," "opalescent incantations," "delicious harmonies," "melancholic lights," "translucent dawns," "vibrations," "transparencies," and "colored mists."[55] For Monet, Venice's famed sites were palimpsests, their rich cultural histories and associations faint amid the layers of colored air that subsumed them.

Six of his paintings depict the Palazzo Ducale seen across the lagoon from the island of San Giorgio, bathed in a pale pink and blue haze (pl. 14–20). It might have been this motif, in which the palace seems to float insubstantially in the distance between sky and sea, that prompted one critic to evoke water lilies in his description of Monet's Venice. The writer encouraged viewers not to see Monet's misty, nebulous images as "a sign of fading or decadence. It is only the decadence of a sick flower of the lagoons, sweet blooms which, like water lilies, participate in the languor of the sky and the waters."[56] These paintings all offer the same frontal view of the palace, except for one that depicts it from a more diagonal, west-facing perspective (pl. 20). This distant Palazzo Ducale motif was likely his first "appointment" most days, since Alice referred to San Giorgio Island as the place where she wrote her letters every morning. Twenty-seven years after Renoir painted from this same spot, Alice echoed an observation he made about its popularity among artists: "It's frightening the number of painters here, in this small square on San Giorgio. There are five of them, plus a woman and Monet."[57] But Renoir saw something Monet now couldn't: the full campanile on the piazza. In Monet's views it is slightly truncated, not yet fully rebuilt after its collapse in 1902 (fig. 87).

All of Monet's paintings of this motif include a visual reference to his own vantage point in the bold form of a geometric slice of the quay at the bottom of the canvas. In one slightly west view, several mooring posts, or *pali*, are also part of the visual field. In this way, Monet grounds the spectator within the space of the image, just as Sargent did by including a segment of his own gondola in some of his watercolors (figs. 179 and 181). The darker quay balances the mist-shrouded architecture, but as a compositional element it bothered Camille Mauclair, who wrote one of the few unfavorable reviews of the 1912 exhibition: "It is impossible, when faced with Monet's paintings, to determine whether this blue or violet plane is a barge deck, a roof, a slab, or a fabric: it is only a layer of color serving as a purely artificial foil."[58]

Another six canvases focus on the church of San Giorgio Maggiore itself (pl. 9–13). Reversing his other vantage point, Monet now depicts the location from which he previously had been painting. The church is seen floating on a distant, sometimes blurred horizon line, merged with the enveloping atmosphere. The poet Rainer Maria Rilke could not yet have seen these paintings, but a phrase in his 1908 poem "Venetian Morning" conjures the image of buildings that almost, but never quite, appear to evaporate in the mist: "the city that perpetually, whenever / a glimpse of sky has met the feel of the sea, / will start becoming without ever being."[59] This motif is by definition a tourist's perspective, likely framed by his own window at the Grand Hotel Britannia, where the Monets moved on October 15 and which had "an even more beautiful view than at the Palazzo" (figs. 55,

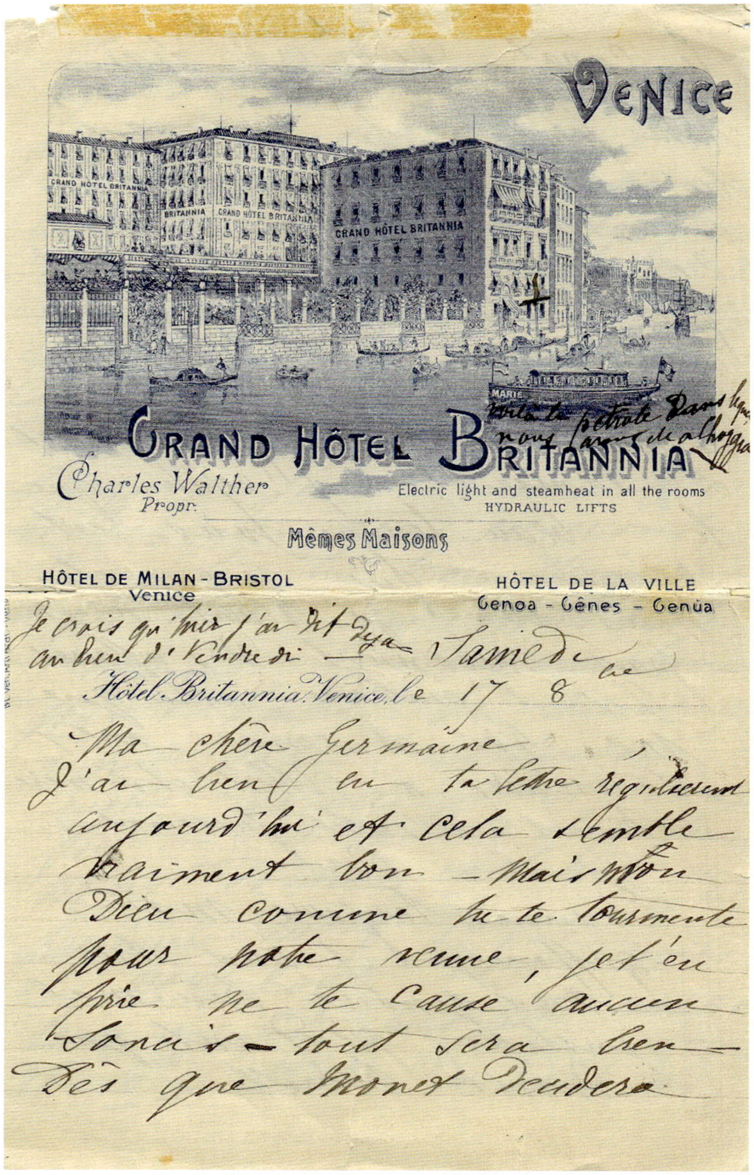
VENICE
GRAND HÔTEL BRITANNIA
Charles Walther Propr.
Electric light and steamheat in all the rooms
HYDRAULIC LIFTS
Mêmes Maisons
HÔTEL DE MILAN - BRISTOL Venice
HÔTEL DE LA VILLE Genoa - Gênes - Genua

Je crois qu'hier j'ai dit il y a au lieu de Vendredi — Samedi
Hôtel Britannia Venice, le 17 8bre

Ma chère Germaine
J'ai bien eu ta lettre régulièrement aujourd'hui et cela semble vraiment bon — Mais mon Dieu comme tu te tourmentes pour notre venue, je t'en prie ne te cause aucun souci — tout sera bien dès que Monet rendera

fig. 55—Letter from Alice Monet to Germaine Salerou on letterhead of the Grand Hotel Britannia, October 17, 1908, Collection Philippe Piguet fig. 56—Postcard of Venice belonging to Alice Monet, Musée Marmottan Monet

fig. 57—Francis Frith, untitled photograph, Island of San Giorgio, 1850s–70s, whole-plate albumen print from wet collodion glass negative, 6½ × 8 in., Victoria and Albert Museum

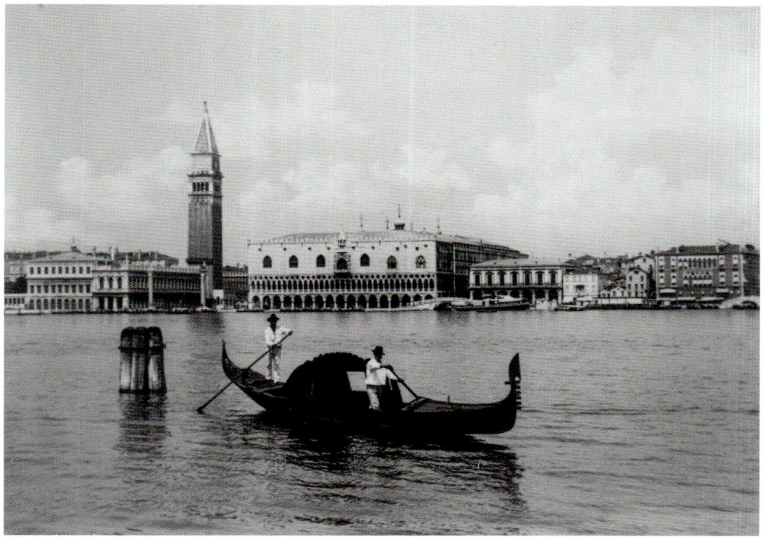

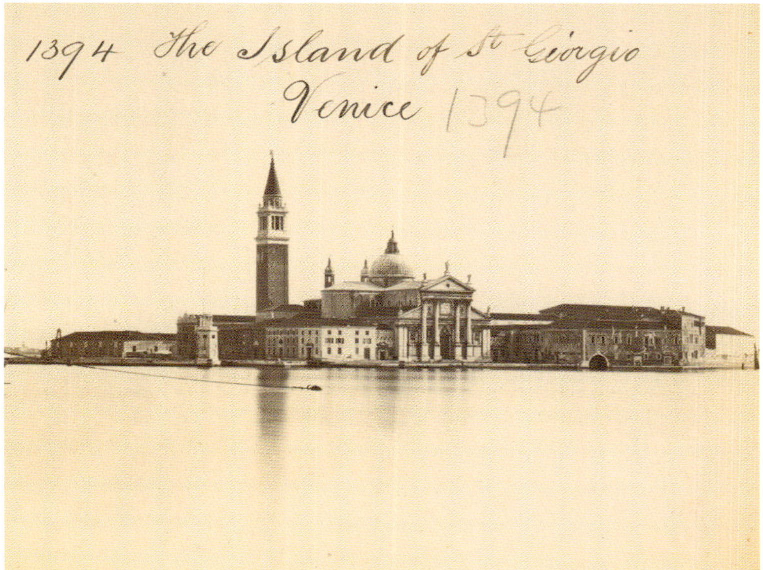

57, and 92).[60] These compositions and their bluish atmospheric veils are like those in many of J. M. W. Turner's watercolors of the same view, some of which he probably made from the window of his own hotel, which was near Monet's (fig. 151). The ethereal, aqueous effects of this motif, as well as its opposite across the lagoon, in which descriptive detail is minimized, recall the ambience Whistler achieved in different impressions of his panoramic lagoon etching *Nocturne*, with its own view of a barely perceptible San Giorgio Maggiore on the horizon (figs. 156, 157).

Two other canvases also feature San Giorgio Maggiore but from a different, closer angle and against a fiery sky (pl 32 and 33), perhaps recalling Monet's many evening excursions with Alice: "Last night we had another wonderful sunset, just the way I'd like you to see it: the sky all red and blue, but so soft, the waves of fire and mother-of-pearl, the crescent moon appearing in the silent lagoons and the two of us, rocked in the gondola."[61] As Jonathan P. Ribner describes in his essay in this volume, the incandescent colors and hazy fogs that Monet recorded in both of these San Giorgio Maggiore motifs suggest the presence and effects of specific atmospheric pollutants in Venice. But the artist's choice of bold, saturated colors may also reveal his response to André Derain's Fauvist paintings of London, which, in turn, were in dialogue with Monet's own 1903 views of that city (figs. 58 and 59).[62]

A closer view of the Palazzo Ducale facade and its reflection on the lagoon is the focus of three other canvases (pl. 6, 7, and 8). At a distance, the palace took on and was absorbed by the lilac hues of the sky, against which its roofline spires are suggested by flicks of paint. In this group, seen close by, the Venetian Gothic palace stands out in a brighter, whitish pink against a blue sky. It is perhaps the city's most iconic structure, and its distinctive patterned stonework, lacy arcades, and grand courtyard spaces are among the most popular and recognizable of motifs, from Canaletto's expansive views to truncated ones by artists such as Sargent, Walter Sickert, Henri Le Sidaner, and Emma Ciardi (figs. 130, 134, 168, 178, and 181). In Monet's composition, the palace's fragmented semblance oscillating on the "shivering liquid mirror" below it is rendered in some of the most vigorously painted passages of his Venice group.[63] Monet made these views from a gondola floating in mid-lagoon—immersed within the *enveloppe*. Trying to find the same spot every day for these sessions was tough, as Alice reported: "For a painting of the Palazzo Ducale where he is working at anchor, the gondoliers, after three times having not been able to find just the right place, he gave up on the session and returned to the hotel absolutely furious and regretful."[64]

The Grand Canal and Santa Maria della Salute, the two-domed seventeenth-century Baroque church prominently sited on the triangular-shaped Punta della Dogana between the Grand and Giudecca Canals, are among the most recognizable views of Venice and together are the subject of another six paintings (pl. 1–5). These are almost identical compositions, except in three of them Monet includes a set of landing steps in the bottom left corner, a difference that has been ascribed to the rise and fall of the tide (pl. 4). It may also be attributed to the shift in what he could see from the door of the Palazzo Barbaro versus what he

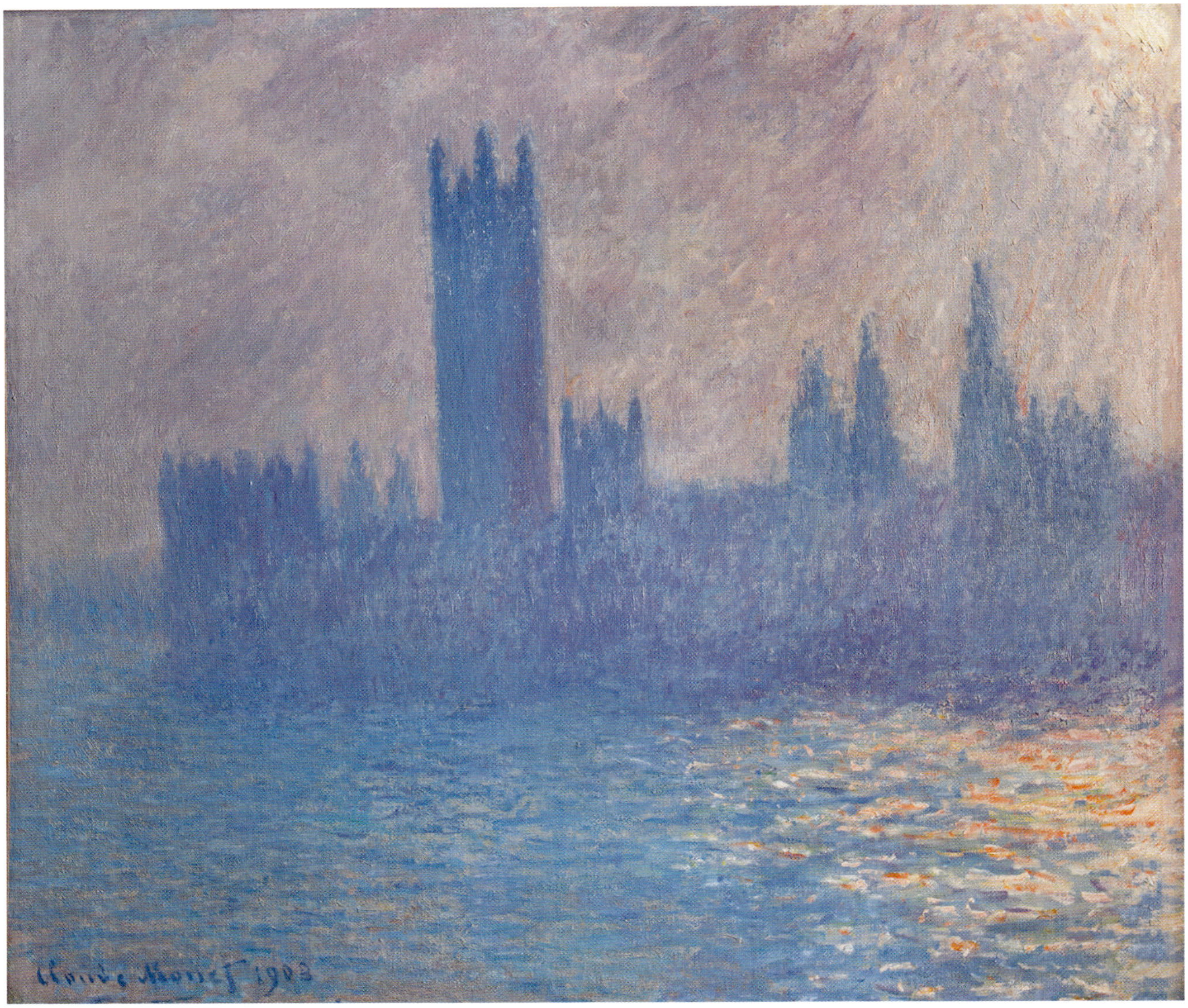

fig. 58—Claude Monet, *Houses of Parliament, Sunlight Effect*, 1903, oil on canvas, 32×36¼ in., Brooklyn Museum

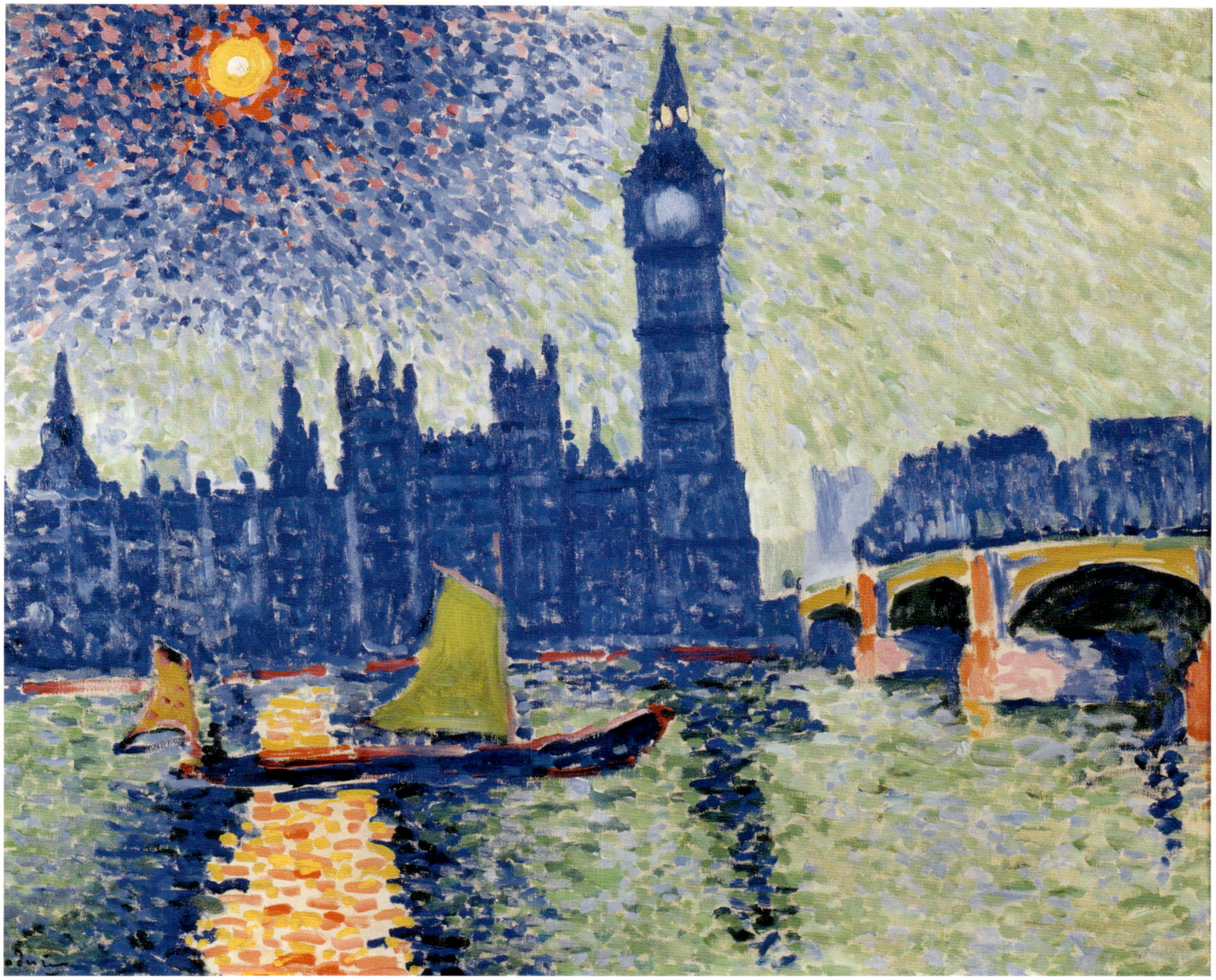

fig. 59—André Derain, *Big Ben*, 1906, oil on canvas, 31 1/10 × 38 3/5 in., Musée d'Art Moderne de la Ville de Paris

could see from his gondola lower in the water when he returned there to work on this motif after leaving to stay at the Grand Hotel Britannia.[65] A group of *pali* that dissolve into touches of color at the point where wood and water meet occupy the left side of each of these compositions. One of the *pali* boldly bisects the canvas just to one side of the church. Corresponding with the picture plane, this post counteracts the sense of space suggested by the other receding *pali*, collapsing near and far in a manner reminiscent of the Japanese woodblock prints Monet so admired (figs. 79 and 80).

Monet devoted eight canvases to the ornamented marble facades of palazzi on the Grand Canal and the flowing water from which they emerge and with which they are chromatically matched in tones of dark blue, rust, and purple. These buildings, which were visible to him across the canal from the gates of the Palazzo Barbaro (from which he could also look down along the Grand Canal to see his Santa Maria della Salute church motif), were frequently the subject of souvenir photographs (fig. 60). Four of Monet's paintings represent the bejeweled Palazzo Dario, also the quickly noted subject of his only drawing in Venice, which appears on the first page of an otherwise empty sketchbook he bought there (pl. 21–24, fig. 62).[66] Another two canvases depict the Palazzo da Mula and two the Palazzo Contarini (pl. 28–31). In these, according to Geffroy, "Fiery or moss-colored facades, doors, windows, balustrades, archways, and pointed arches lengthen or widen in reflections in the movement of passing water."[67] Returning to work on these facades after having left the Palazzo Barbaro had some annoying social consequences for Alice. Ariana Curtis saw them while Monet was working from the Barbaro gate and "she stopped the gondola and invited us to tea. . . . It bothers me, she seems so formal. What a difference from my dear Mary!"[68]

Monet eliminated the sky from most of these shadowy views (a small patch is caught at the top of two of them), its effects sensed only through the variegated tones it bestows on the rippling waters below. Excluding the upper floors of these palazzi confers a looming, enigmatic quality to them, but as with the steps in his Grand Canal paintings, that compositional decision might owe to the cropped view Monet had from beneath his gondola's canopy, or *felze*, which he certainly would have employed on sunny, cold, or otherwise inclement days.[69] Regardless, these motifs, with their partial, frontal views, in which geometric architectural elements and grids of darkened windows and *pali* align with the flat surface of the canvas, are among the most abstracted of Monet's Venetian subjects. Their compositions, dividing building and canal and emphasizing the water's reflective surface, recall modernist photographs taken by Edward Steichen and Alvin Coburn in 1907 and 1906, respectively, though there is no evidence that Monet was aware of them (figs. 63 and 64).[70] Together, Monet's palazzi canvases also call to mind the unfurling view of facades captured on film in 1896 from a boat on the Grand Canal in what is perhaps the first-ever moving camera shot—made by a camera operator working for the Lumière brothers.[71]

Three paintings feature the small Rio della Salute with a rounded stone bridge and the only foliage in any of Monet's Venice

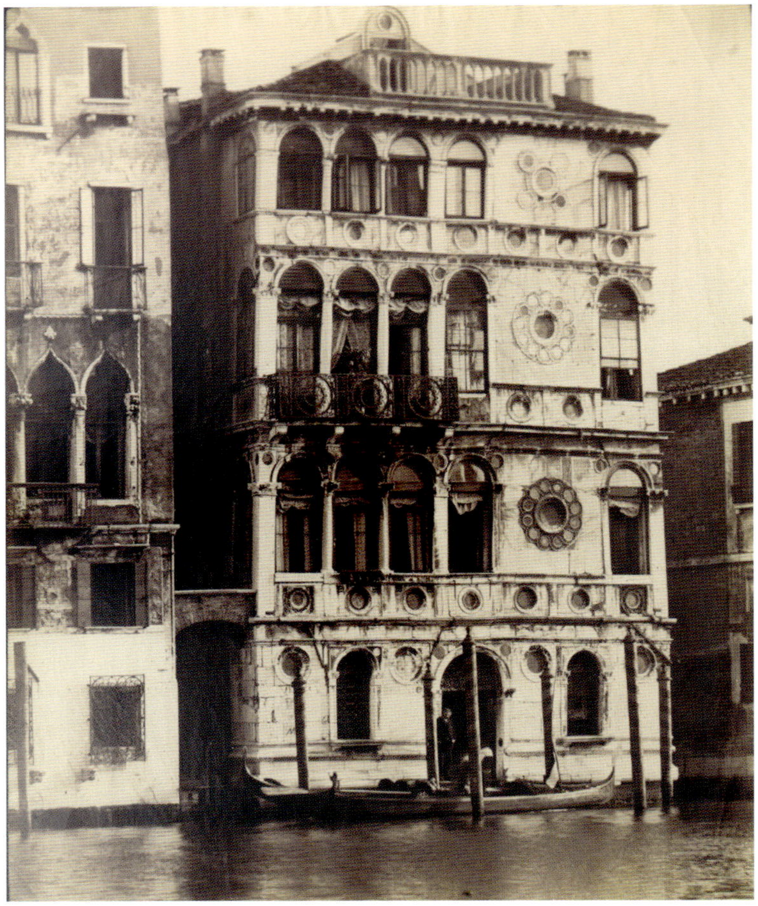

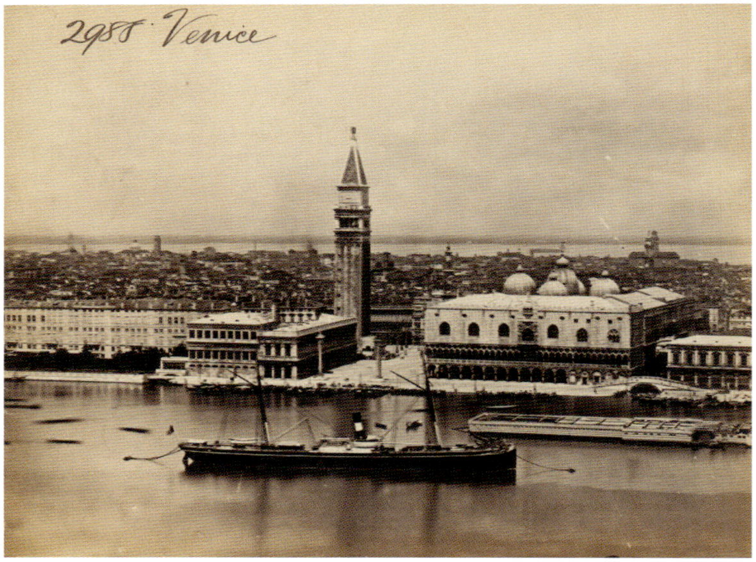

fig. 60—Postcard of Venetian palazzo belonging to Alice Monet, Musée Marmottan Monet

fig. 61—Francis Frith, untitled photograph of Venice from San Giorgio 1850s–70s, whole-plate albumen print from wet collodion glass negative, 6½ × 8 in., Victoria and Albert Museum

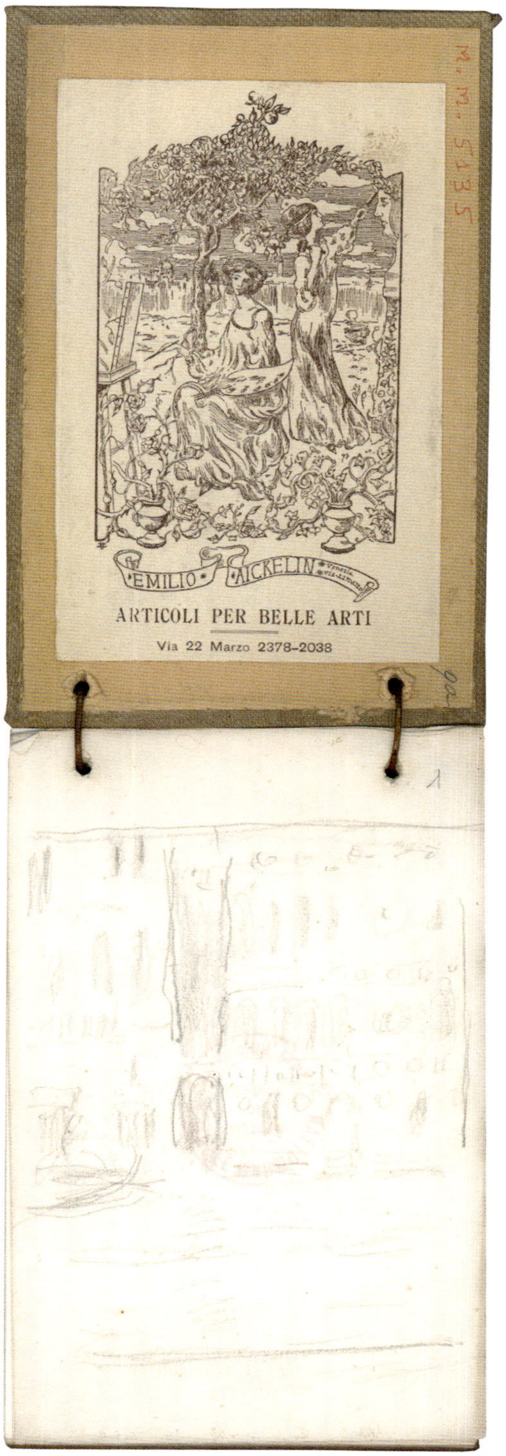

fig. 62—Sketchbook purchased by Monet in Venice. Emilio Aickelin label (top); pencil sketch by Monet of Palazzo Dario (bottom)

imagery; the apse of the church of San Gregorio is just visible in the background (pl 25–27). This is likely the motif Alice described as "a little low in the canal" where Monet worked toward the end of the trip. The blue sky and warm afternoon light belie the conditions the Monets faced one day when there was a "strong east wind so cold it's making my fingernails ache as I write you, and the canal is churning like the sea."[72] Along with a single oil sketch of houses on the Fondamenta Bragadin, an area along the narrow Rio de San Vio, these are the only paintings he made in the smaller, peripheral byways of the city (fig. 6). His final work there, another oil sketch made just a few days before leaving, depicts a moored gondola: "Although there was heavy fog this morning . . . Monet was able to make a sketch of a gondola that is very pretty despite everything; it's really time for him to rest because it's too much work, especially at his age."[73] The last motif he captured in Venice—a boat and its reflection on the water's surface—echoes some of the earliest motifs in his career (fig. 11 and 72).

Venice's buildings, supported by platforms and pilings driven deep into the lagoon centuries ago, attest to human aesthetic interventions within the city's singular environment. Similarly, the marine atmosphere Monet encountered there, which could brighten or dampen the intensity of the city's colors, was partly the result of human-caused air pollution (see the Ribner essay in this volume). But the only sign of human activity or presence in his paintings are distant gondolas on the lagoon or empty ones floating like mute sentinels in front of seemingly uninhabited palazzi. In Monet's Venice, all indications of modernity and its conveniences also have been eliminated. It was something of a challenge to accomplish this: "Yesterday we enjoyed a good cup of tea at Danieli's (a much better hotel than here); we would have stayed there if Monet had found the view to his liking, but there is a flyboat landing in front that spoils everything."[74] From the spectacular regattas of the Venetian Republic's golden age to the early twentieth-century's daily canal traffic, the commercial and ceremonial hubbub of the city's waterways was a popular artistic motif (figs. 61, 65, 68, and 70). But for Monet, such activities were causes for complaint, not composition. Alice, whose postcards (figs. 66, 67, and 69) picture some of these diversions, was perhaps sitting next to him at the window of the Britannia when she described the panorama before them: "Right now, while I'm scribbling these lines and Monet is grumbling and painting, I'm watching a real parade of fishing boats go by, with those marvelous red or blue sails and images of saints, or horses or even the moon. A large three-masted ship is going by, then some real steamers, one of which is docking here to pick up passengers bound for Egypt. What a sight!"[75]

Monet was prevented from working on his evening motifs for three days because of the large wooden bridges ("very curious and completely Japanese") raised under their window at the Britannia as part of a celebration of the Presentation of the Virgin.[76] Special access he was granted to a lagoon-facing building was worthless because its view was compromised: "A ship is almost every day anchored precisely in front of the motif that I wanted to paint."[77] One day, according to Alice, his progress on a "superb motif" was thwarted by "an enormous ship."[78] When his view was blocked another day by oil tankers, he and Alice visited the nearby island of Chioggia instead. Monet shared this dislike of tankers and other signs of contemporary life—like the vaporetto, which first began plying the lagoon waters in 1881—with John Ruskin, who railed against encroachments of his beloved Venetian stones: in place of "the painted sails of the fishing boats... the development of civilization now only brings black steam tugs, to bear the people of Venice to the bathing-machines of Lido, covering their Ducal Palace with soot and consuming its sculptures with sulphurous acid."[79]

The quietude and depopulation of Monet's Venetian imagery were not new. Dwindling since the late 1880s, human figures had essentially disappeared from Monet's landscapes by the late 1890s. At the same time, mysterious and allusive qualities began to be more frequently ascribed to his scenes. His ethereal paintings of Venice particularly lent themselves to subjective responses that were themselves directly or indirectly informed by the pervasive tradition of conjuring Venice as a symbol of melancholy and romantic decay. This was the place where, according to Lord Byron, "silent rows the songless gondolier; / Her palaces are crumbling to the shore, / And music meets not always now the ear: / Those days are gone—but Beauty still is here."[80] Ruskin famously described it as "still left for our beholding in the final period of her decline: a ghost upon the sands of the sea, so weak—so quiet,—so bereft of all but her loveliness, that we might well doubt, as we watched her faint reflection in the mirage of the lagoon, which was the City, and which the Shadow."[81] And for Thomas Mann, whose novella *Death in Venice* was published the same year Monet's Venice paintings debuted in Paris, its black gondolas were like coffins, equated with the finality of "death itself, the bier and solemn rites and last soundless voyage!"[82]

Monet translated the city "in the manner of an inner dream," as a "gloomy environment where the heavy waters eternally reflect in their depths vaporous and distant palaces." He was a poet who "must have felt the very soul of this queen of the Adriatic vibrate within him, mysterious, beautiful, and stinking beneath the jewels in which she dresses."[83] For Geffroy, Monet's lagoon city was a mournful, uninhabited place,

> *where the decor of ten centuries takes on a melancholy and mysterious aspect under the luminous veils that envelop it. The lapping water ebbs and flows, passing back and forth around the palazzi, as if to dissolve these wrecks of history... carrying away and drowning in its reflections all the dead splendors and all the abolished vanity. The serene magnificence of nature reigns alone in those parts of the landscape where the bustling city of pleasure is seen from far enough away that one believes in the enchantment of a dead city under the sun, where nothing is alive except the swift wake of the gondolas, skimming the water like black swallows.*[84]

The painter Walter Sickert also found the emptiness and stillness of Monet's Venice compelling: "It is very modern. The ghost of one gondola hurrying to the traghetto, but the rest, with the marionettes and the bautti [masks] have been put away in their boxes. The modern painter offers us the austere consolation

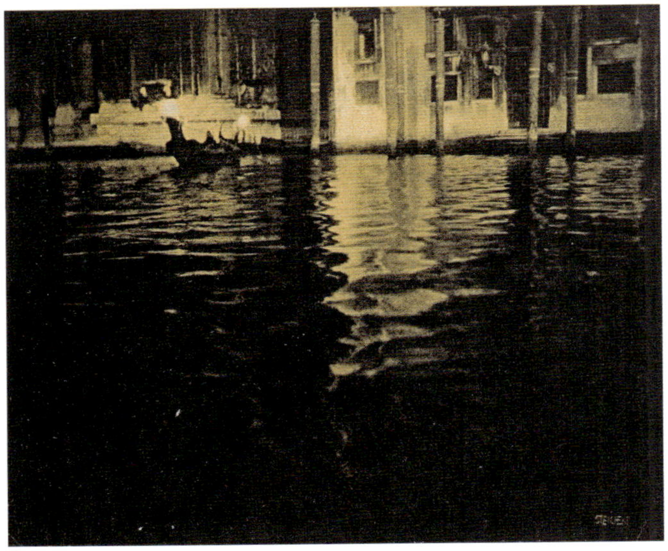

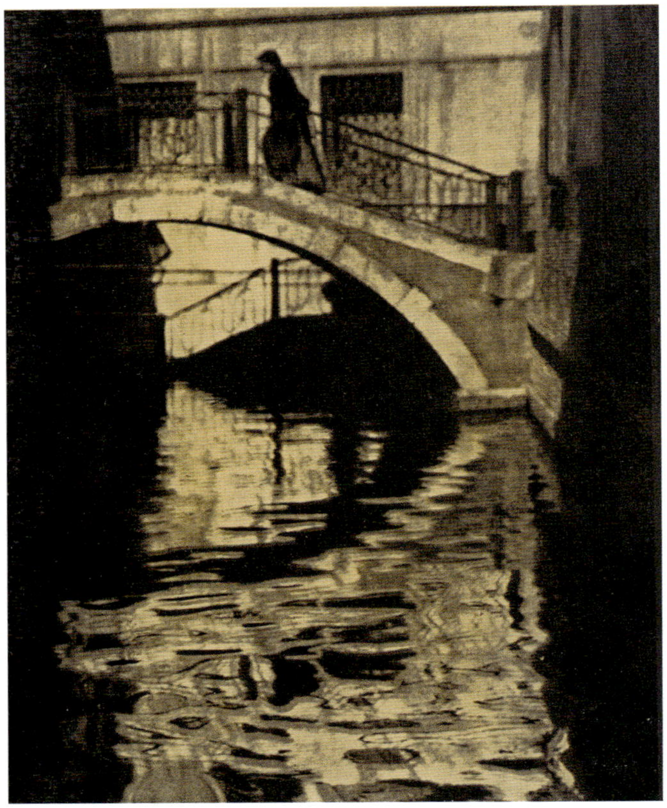

fig. 63—Edward Steichen, *Late Afternoon, Venice*, 1907, published in *Camera Work*, No. 42/43, 1913, photograph, bound volume, Brooklyn Museum Libraries and Archives

fig. 64—Alvin Coburn, *The White Bridge, Venice*, 1906, published in *Camera Work*, No. 21, 1908, photograph, bound volume, Brooklyn Museum Libraries and Archives

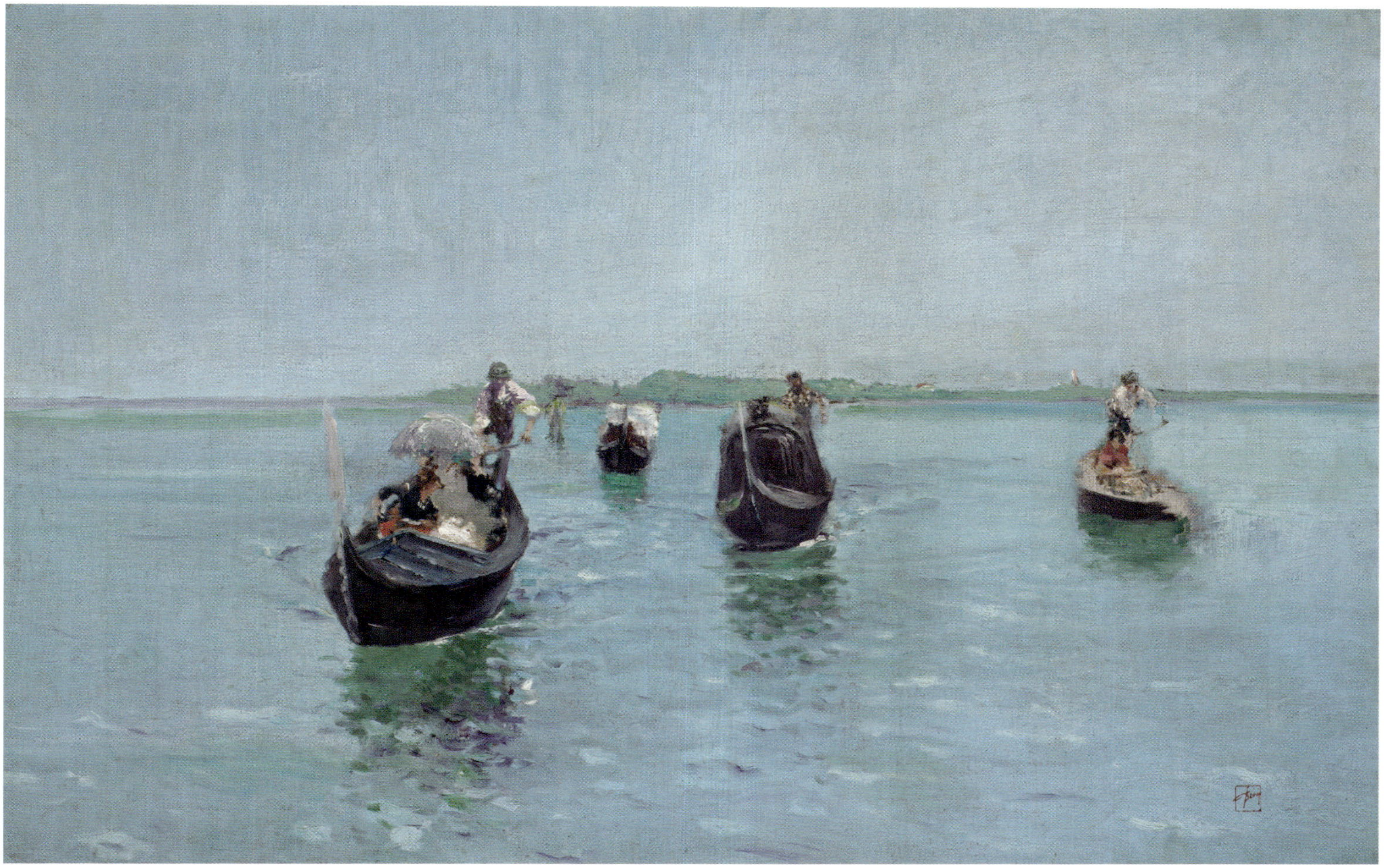

that may be found in the play of light on an empty stage."[85] Mirbeau proclaimed that Monet had "returned Venice to nature," a sentiment Geffroy echoed, casting the artist's view of the city as post-human: "He freed Venice of itself, keeping only its essential form, as if it were deserted, invaded by nature, the steps of its palaces covered with a marine mold emerging from those glaucous waters that create, with the passage of light waves, the only movement of these canvases with dead facades."[86]

In his 1907 poem "Venice," Arthur Symons contemplates the city's hushed mood and self-reflexivity in a way that predictively evokes Monet's paintings of Venice and their correspondence with his *Water Lilies*:

Water and marble and that silentness
Which is not broken by a wheel or hoof;
A city like a water-lily, less
Seen than reflected, palace wall and roof,
In the unfruitful waters motionless,
Without one living grass's green reproof;
A city without joy or weariness,
Itself beholding, from itself aloof.[87]

fig. 65—Robert Blum, *Venetian Gondoliers*, c. 1880–89, oil on canvas, 18⅜ × 28⅝ in., Promised Gift of Bernard and Barbro Osher, Fine Arts Museums of San Francisco

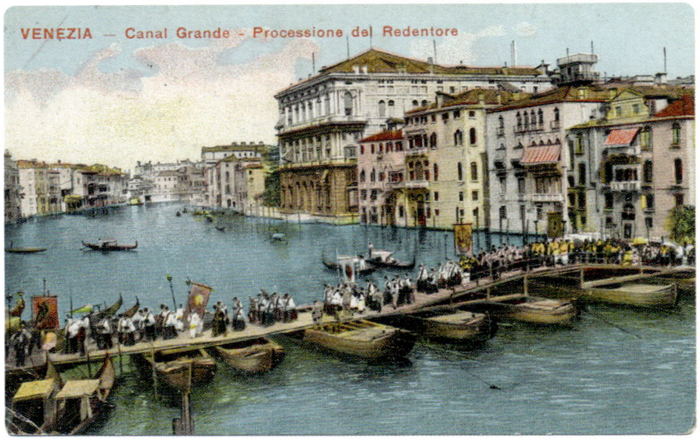

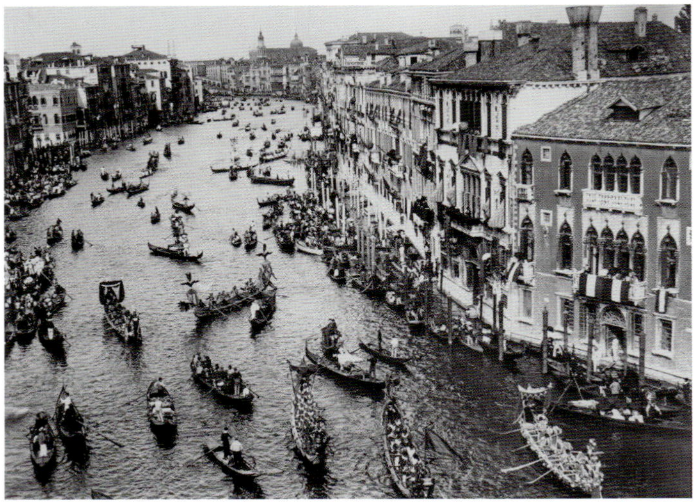

fig. 66—Postcard showing a procession along the Grand Canal sent by Alice Monet to her granddaughter Alice Butler, November 27, 1908, Collection Philippe Piguet

fig. 67—Postcard of Grand Canal with regatta belonging to Alice Monet, Musée Marmottan Monet

—

[Venice] is so beautiful and so made to
tempt you, but who can recreate these marvelous effects?
I see only my Monet who can.
{ Alice Monet to Germaine Salerou, November 6, 1908 }

Despite Monet's initial misgivings, Alice knew he could paint Venice because the *envelope* that surrounded it—glinting water and humidity-softened light—were exactly the kinds of effects he had long pursued and translated into paint. Early in his career, he was hailed among the Impressionists as "the painter of water par excellence," and in his later years, he was called a lifelong "genie of the waters."[88] In 1924, Louis Gillet observed of Monet: "From his childhood spent at Le Havre, and from his first master Eugène Boudin, he retains the nostalgia of the sea, the love of the liquid, multiple, and feminine element, of that which glides, undulates, reflects, sparkles, ruffles and enrages itself; river or ocean, always he loved the nymph or the siren. . . . For an eye like his there is no subject more impassioning than that of this fluid in perpetual metamorphosis."[89]

In Venice, Monet found a new manifestation of this "feminine element." Not a "slut," as he had once described the Atlantic Ocean to Alice, when challenged by its "terrible aspects," but the Adriatic Sea, to which Venice—represented by the doge—had been symbolically betrothed every year for centuries in an elaborate waterborne ceremony dedicated in part to ensuring that the sea remained tranquil (fig 149).[90]

Reviews of the 1912 *Venise* exhibition identified and praised the paintings as the newest expressions of the watery, atmospheric motifs that defined Monet's career:

> *It is with an ever-renewed enchantment that we have seen him show us in famous series, the reflections of sails and boats in the sunny waters of the Seine near the* **Pont d'Argenteuil**, *the hubbub of the* **Gare Saint-Lazare** *in the midst of its lights and smoke, the fields of tulips radiating under the fine light of* **Holland**, *the shock of the waves against the escarpments of* **Belle-Île**, *the mysterious chaos of the rocks of the* **Creuse**, *the vaporous Norman sea seen from the top of the cliffs of* **Pourville** *and* **Varangeville** [sic], *the aspects of the Seine at* **Vétheuil** *in the limpid light of spring or carrying the ice floes under a snowy sky, the* **Grainstacks**, *so diverse in the illumination of the different hours of the day, the* **Poplars** *with their high plumes quivering against the sky, the stones of the* **Cathedrals** *magnificent as jewels,* **London** *with its ghostly architecture in the fog. Here now is* **Venice**, *its great canal, the Palazzo Ducale, San Giorgio Maggiore, the Rio della Salute, in the fluid, subtle, radiant splendor whose atmosphere reveals their domes, their marble facades, in its reality embellished by the magic of light.*[91]

As Philippe Piguet has observed, everything Monet found in Venice "belongs to a memory of his work that was the foundation of his history: water and the light, on the one hand, stone and sky on the other; the liquid and the immaterial, the solid and the ephemeral."[92] In *Sailboats on the Seine at Petit-Gennevilliers*,

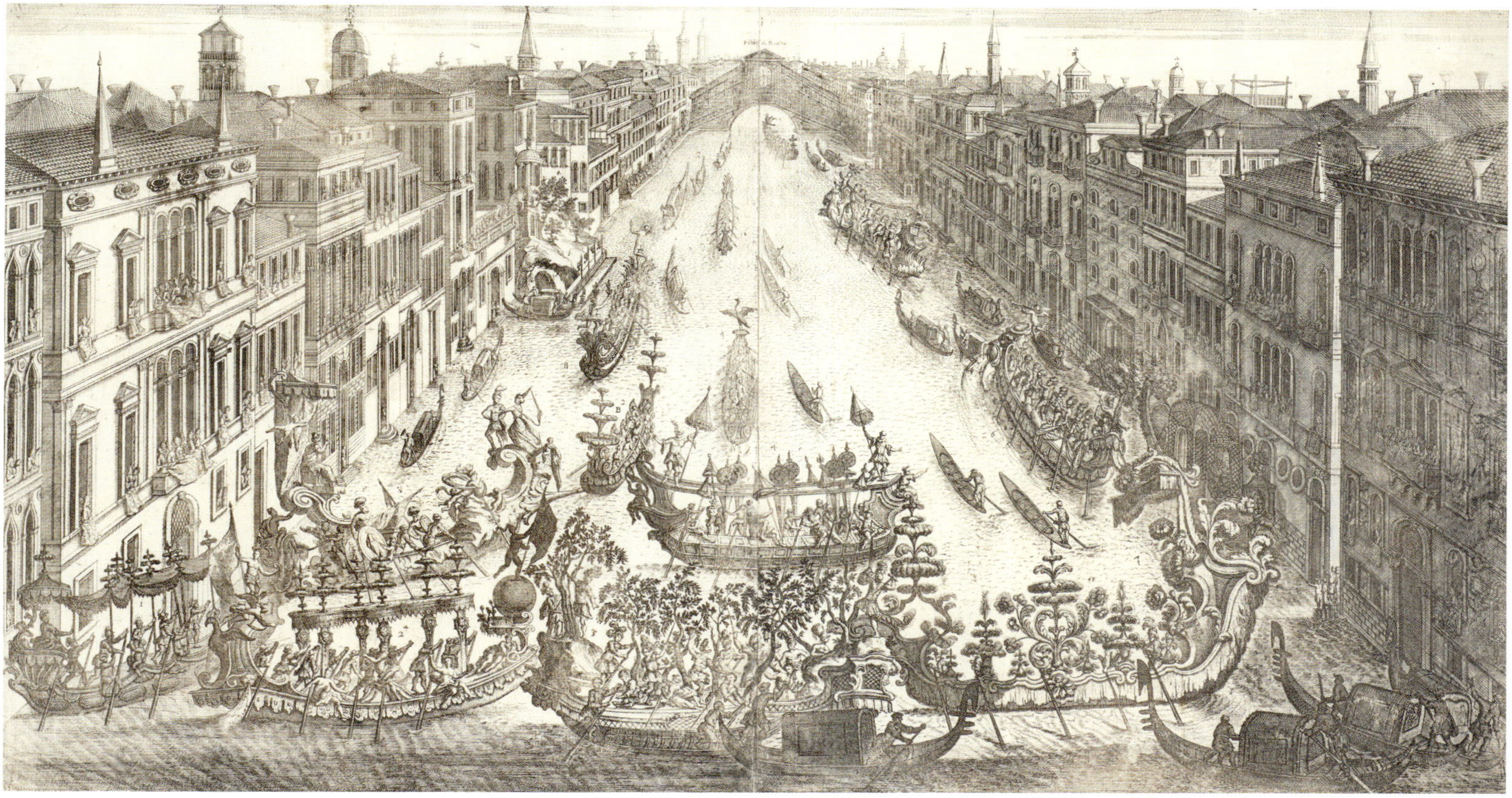

fig. 68—Attributed to Alessandro dalla Via, *Regatta on the Venetian Grand Canal Honoring Ernest Augustus IV of Hanover, Duke of Brunswick-Lüneburg, Presented in 1685 to His Local and Foreign Guests*, 1686, engraving, 20½ × 36¾ in., Fine Arts Museums of San Francisco

boats, trees, and buildings are mirrored in the water, all rendered alike in gestural paint strokes (fig. 72). Twenty years later, he created the same compositional effect in a Rorschach-like painting of his Japanese bridge and its watery echo, and a few years after that, in the mirroring of San Giorgio Maggiore's tower against a vivid sky and lagoon at sunset (fig. 71, pl. 32 and 33). Monet's London and his Venice both feature nebulous, arrhythmic architectural silhouettes set against and amid hazy atmospheres (fig. 58, pl. 32 and 33). Indeed, this description of a Thames painting could as easily refer to one of the Venetian lagoon:

> *Beyond an occasional filmy opalescence in the sky or in the water there is almost no color to be seen. Nevertheless, it is more or less felt. It is as if the painter had put all the glow of the sky above the houses of Parliament, or the myriad lights along Waterloo Bridge, upon his canvas and then covered them with the neutral, ghostly tones of a white mist until only the most brilliant spots of color could be distinguished, and then only as suggestions.... They represent the most subtle handling and an extraordinary gift of making much out of little.*[93]

Monet's San Giorgio Maggiore (pl. 9–13), delicately poised between lagoon and sky, also recalls compositions such as *Banks of the Seine at Lavacourt* (fig. 73), *The Break-up of the Ice* (fig. 75), and especially the misty *The Seine near Giverny* (fig. 74). Despite their different climatic conditions, these earlier riverine scenes, like those of London and Venice, focus on shimmering dissolutions of light and water in air, or on the insubstantial divisions between solid, vapor, and liquid. Objects and their traces interact

fig. 69—Postcard of fishing boat belonging to Alice Monet, Musée Marmottan Monet

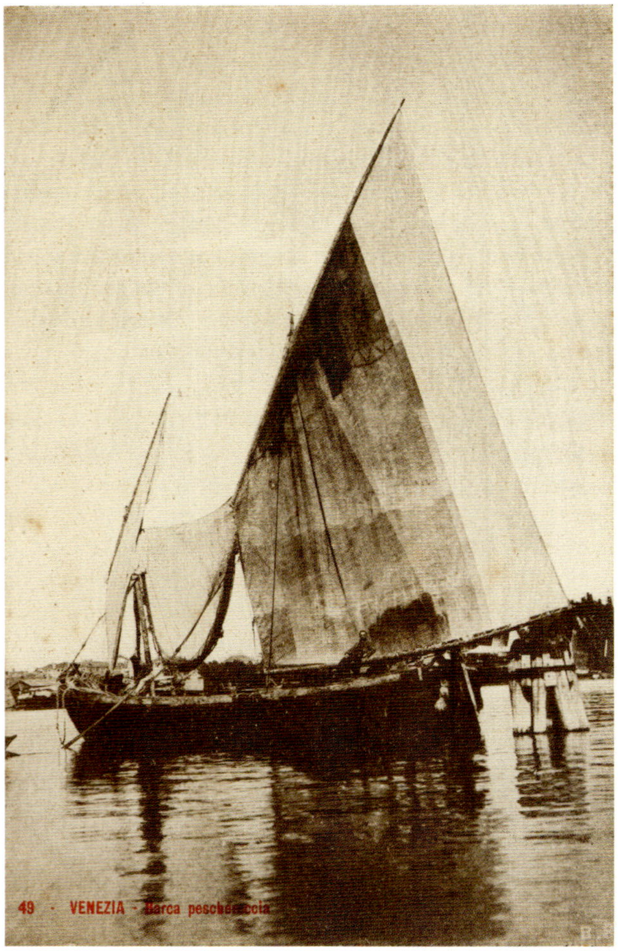

and interpenetrate, the material and immaterial equalized by the painterly touches Monet used to transmute his visual sensations.

Monet's eye was attracted to certain compositions and patterns. Some were based on historical European pictorial strategies that he adopted purposefully or absorbed unconsciously, and others on the unexpected vantage points and jumps in scale he appreciated in Japanese woodblock prints (figs. 78, 79, and 80). He chose motifs and views that corresponded with this preconceived "inner vision," whether they featured geologic formations, bridges, churches, or trees.[94] Writing about Monet's work in 1887, Geffroy used evocative analogies to call attention to these echoes: Monet's cliffs are "massive, like cathedrals, that go off into the distance to fall straight into the sea."[95] Decades later, Geffroy also suggested that, like Proust, who described the Grand Canal's palaces "as a chain of marble cliffs,"[96] Monet saw such parallels in Venice, where the relationship between nature and culture is instantiated in its topography:

> *Claude Monet found himself in front of the Grand Canal, the Palazzo Ducale, San Giorgio Maggiore, the Palazzo Dario, the Palazzo Contarini, in front of this city clad in green and pink marble, scaled in gold, reflected in the mirage of the water, enveloped in clouds heavy with heat, and immediately he saw its monuments, its domes, its spires, its facades, its alleyways, its bridges, as he had seen rocky architecture, hollowed out into caves, ornamental porches, greened with moss.*[97]

In both Normandy and Venice, horizon lines are indistinct and rock formations and palaces face the sea, floating above their own creamy, iridescent reflections in blue, yellow, pink, and green (fig. 77, pl. 6–8). Misty skies above cliffscape and cityscape dissolve into expanses of water, foregrounded planes offer footholds, all harmonized in multihued touches of paint on the canvas's surface (fig. 76, pl. 14–20). Such compositional resemblances and atmospheric reverberations corroborate Monet's frequent assertion that his focus was on effects, not objects. "Other painters paint a bridge, a house, a boat. . . . I want to paint the air in which the bridge, the house, and the boat are to be found—the beauty of the air around them."[98]

More and more enchanted by Venice, but I'm
going to have to leave it behind, alas.
{ Claude Monet to Georges Clemenceau, December 6, 1908 }

Ah, my god, it's so ugly [in Giverny]; not only is it raining,
but it's so sad, so foggy. We're a long way from the brightness
of Venice, but luckily the beloved canvases are here to prove
that it's not a dream and that we'll get back there.
{ Alice Monet to Germaine Salerou, December 18, 1908 }

On December 7, 1908, Claude and Alice Monet left the lagoon city. From the very beginning of the trip, they referred to the canvases he would make there as "beginnings" and "sketches or pochades," and they both wrote about his desire and need to

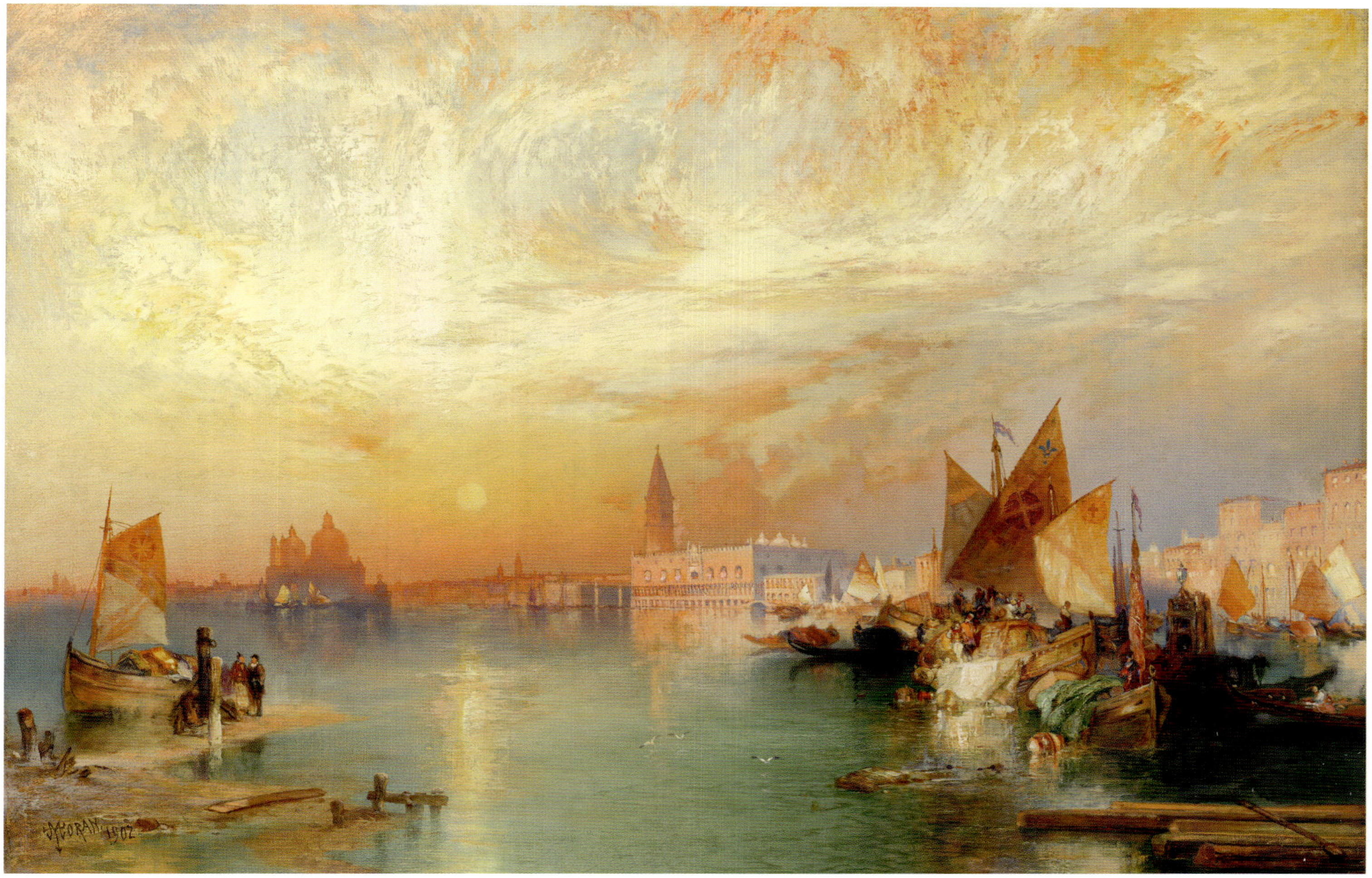

fig. 70—Thomas Moran, *Sunset Santa Maria and the Ducal Palace, Venice*, 1902, oil on canvas, 20¼ × 30 in., Promised Gift of Bernard and Barbro Osher, Fine Arts Museums of San Francisco

return for another painting campaign. Alice was emphatic: "Of course we will come back and I am very happy about it."[99] He made the uncertain status of what he would be able to bring back especially clear to Paul Durand-Ruel and Gaston Bernheim-Jeune, who were vying to purchase the Venice paintings even before Monet returned home.[100] But, as Félicie Faizand de Maupeou recounts in her essay in this volume, a few weeks after returning to Giverny, he agreed to sell the as-yet-unfinished Venice paintings to Galerie Bernheim-Jeune.[101] Back in Giverny, he put those canvases aside and returned to his *Water Lilies*, now seen "with a better eye" and eventually exhibited at Durand-Ruel in May 1909 to great acclaim.

The next several years were an emotional nadir for Monet. He and Alice were not able to return to Venice as planned in the autumn of 1909, as he explained to Geffroy: "You knew my enthusiasm for Venice, well! I had to give up going back there, so ill-disposed and so troubled by my health. For a year now, I have been suffering from terrible headaches, periods of calm with more violent recoveries, which take away my taste for everything."[102] In early 1910, a severe flood damaged Giverny's gardens, sending Monet into a catastrophizing spiral. Alice recounted that his "despair, like the [river] Epte, will not abate.... Monet is unapproachable (everything is lost.... business will never improve, we will have to sell everything, the house, the car...)

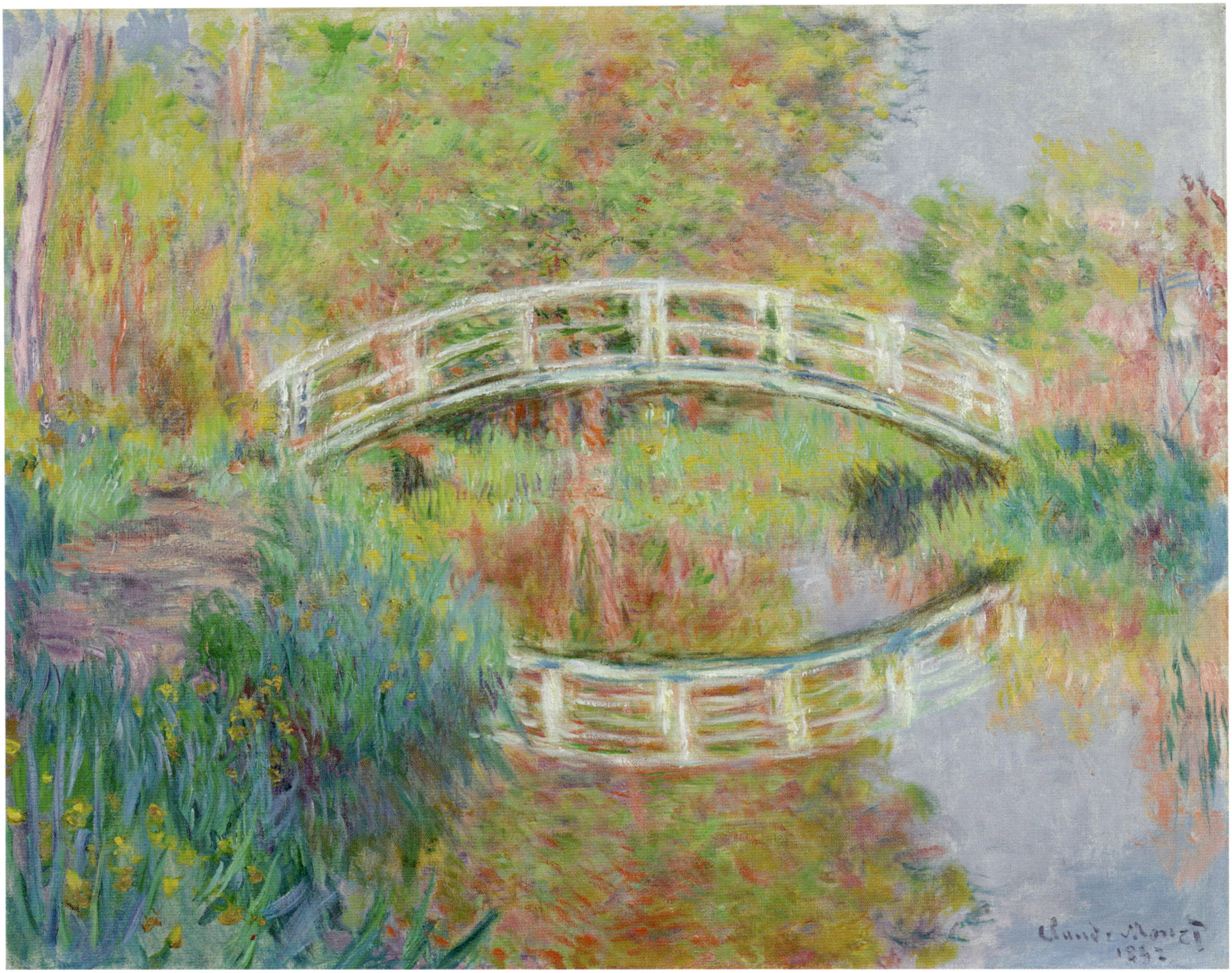

fig. 71—Claude Monet, *Japanese Footbridge, Giverny*, 1895, oil on canvas, 31 × 38½ in., Philadelphia Museum of Art

he is so downhearted and there is nothing I can do."[103] But the worst would begin to unfold in February 1910 when Alice was diagnosed with myeloid leukemia. Only two years earlier, she had written from Venice, "The days slip by, slip by, always in dream and rapture. What a joy to be able to add such luminous hours to the end of one's life."[104] She could not have realized how prophetic her sentiment would prove. After undergoing radiation treatment and experiencing a remission, Alice died at 4 a.m. on May 19, 1911. Monet's great love, confidante, and champion for the past thirty-five years, the person who had been a constant, supportive presence as he painted and prepared for exhibitions and from whom he had sought advice and comfort in anguished letters about battling the weather and his own self-doubt, was now gone, leaving him devastated and unable to work.

Before that, in November 1910, he had told Durand-Ruel that he was thinking about returning to work on some of his Venice paintings.[105] By this point in his career, it was common for

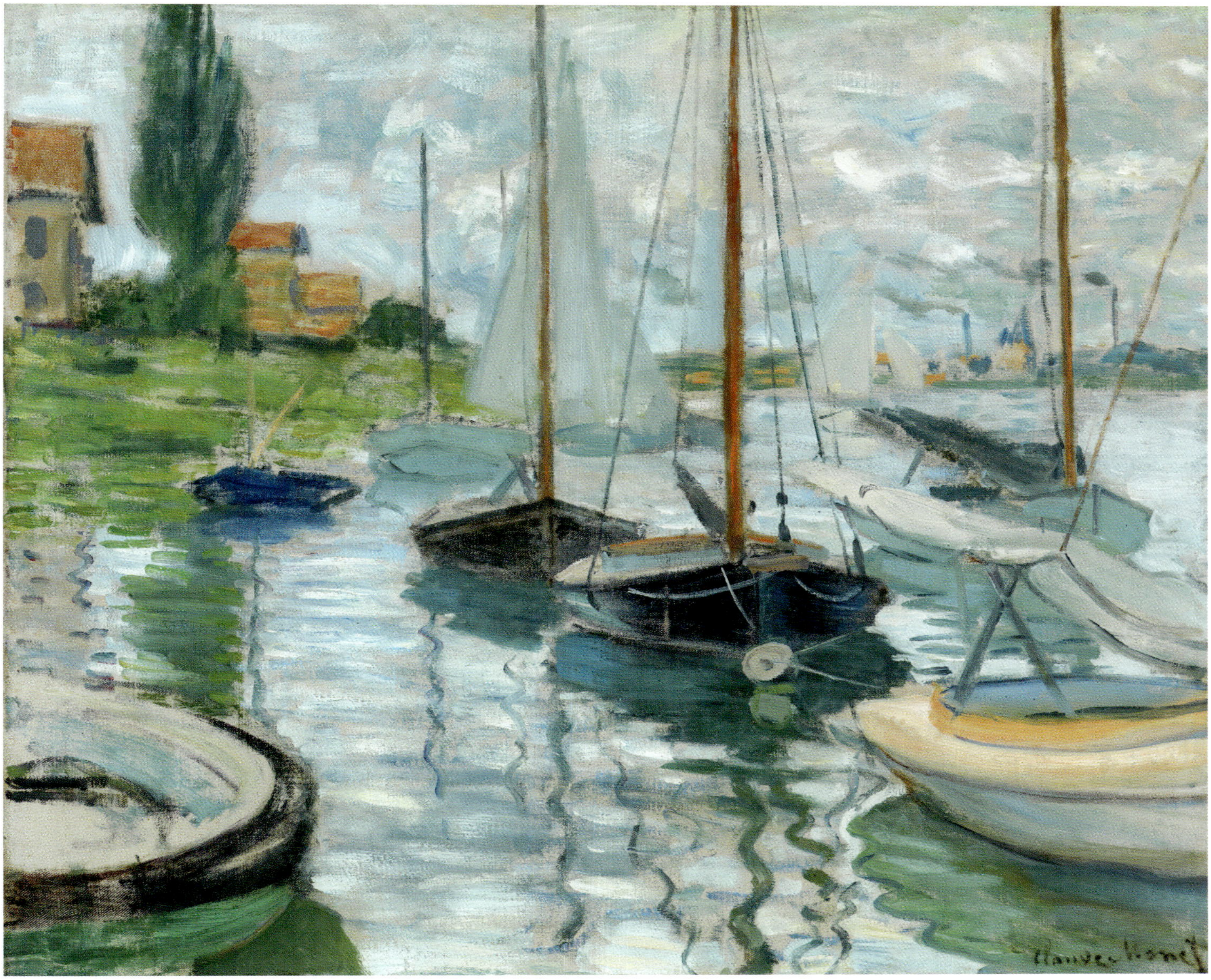

fig. 72—Claude Monet, *Sailboats on the Seine at Petit-Gennevilliers*, 1874, oil on canvas, 21¼ × 25¾ in., Fine Arts Museums of San Francisco

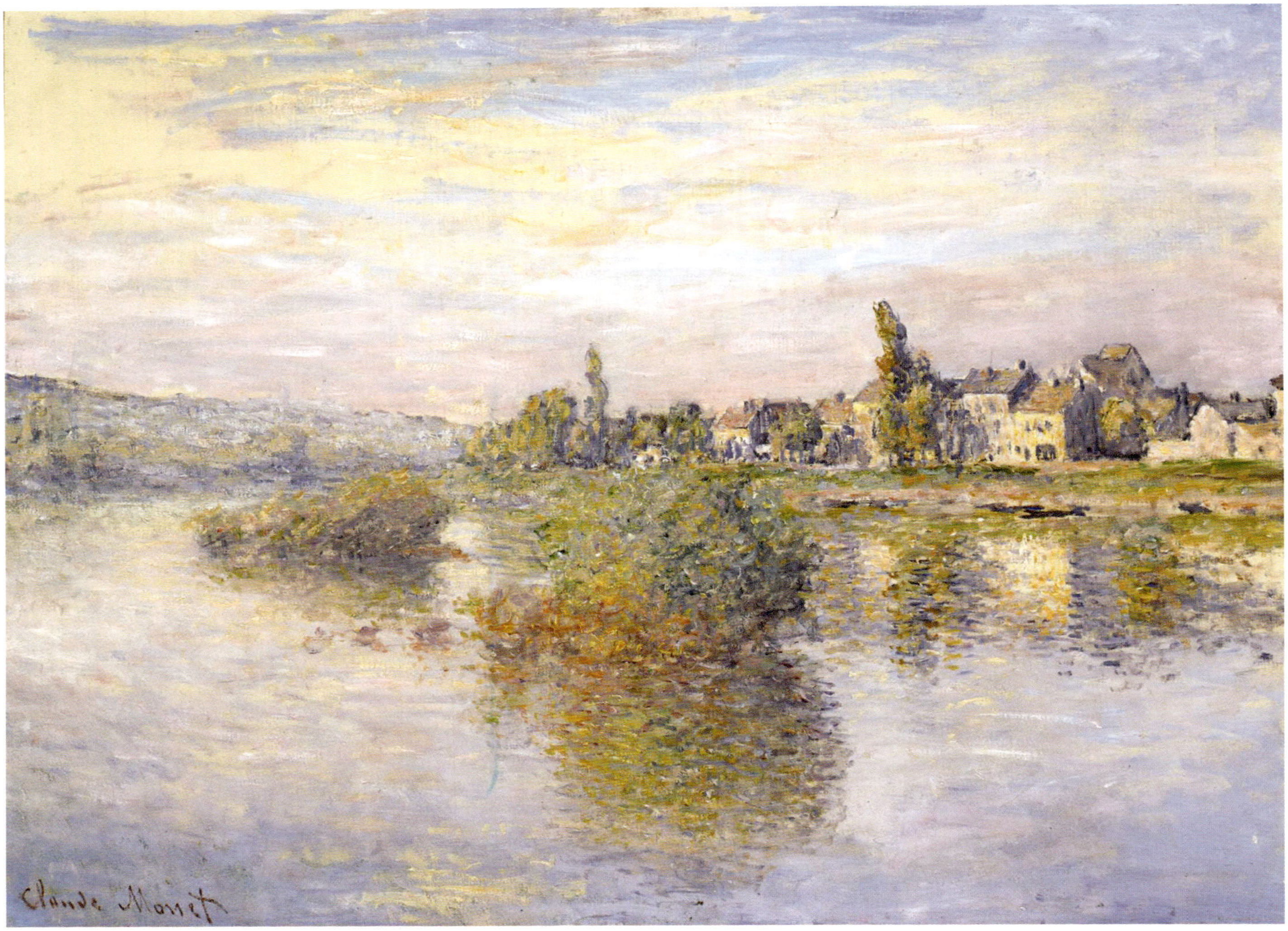

him to refine and complete paintings in his studio (he did this as early as the 1870s and most recently had done so for his London group). This sustained indoor effort, in which he worked to make groups of paintings correspond harmoniously to each other rather than to the individual effects he initially perceived, contradicted the self-perpetuated myth of his working exclusively *en plein air* and having no studio but nature. As one journalist still noted at the time of the *Venise* exhibition, "His studio is in nature, in a gondola in Venice, in his rowboat in Giverny."[106] Regardless, in the aftermath of his wife's death, working on these paintings seemed an insurmountable task. He could not study and finish them in his studio, with Alice "next to me on that poor old sofa," as he had done with past paintings.[107] Not only was he facing the prospect of his first exhibition without her, but it would comprise paintings he had started with her by his side, happy and proud of his hard work.

In October 1911, five months after Alice's death, Monet promised Durand-Ruel and Bernheim-Jeune that in the midst of his immense sadness and pain he would try to pull himself together, pick up his brushes again, and find some consolation in finishing his Venice paintings.[108] But to his stepdaughter Blanche he confided his struggles and unhappiness, an indication that

fig. 73—Claude Monet, *Banks of the Seine at Lavacourt*, 1879, oil on canvas, 22⅞ × 31 ½ in., The Frick Pittsburgh

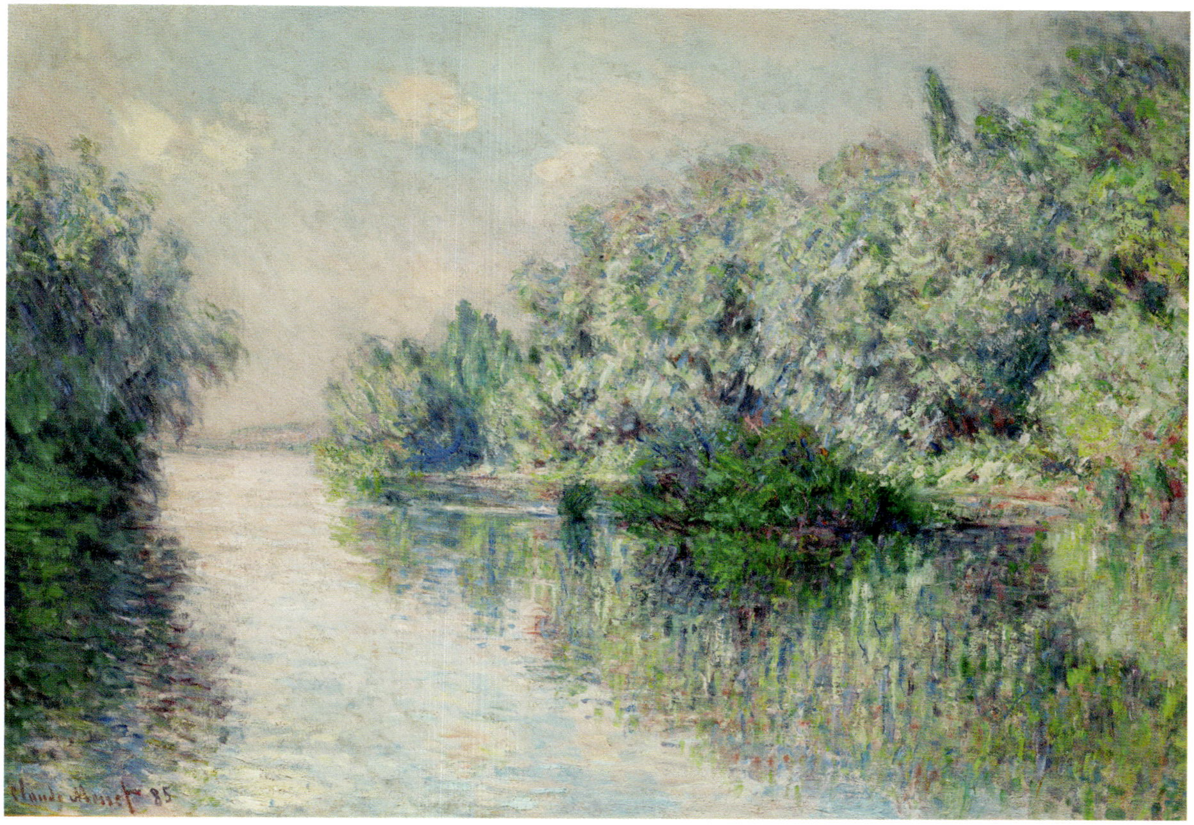

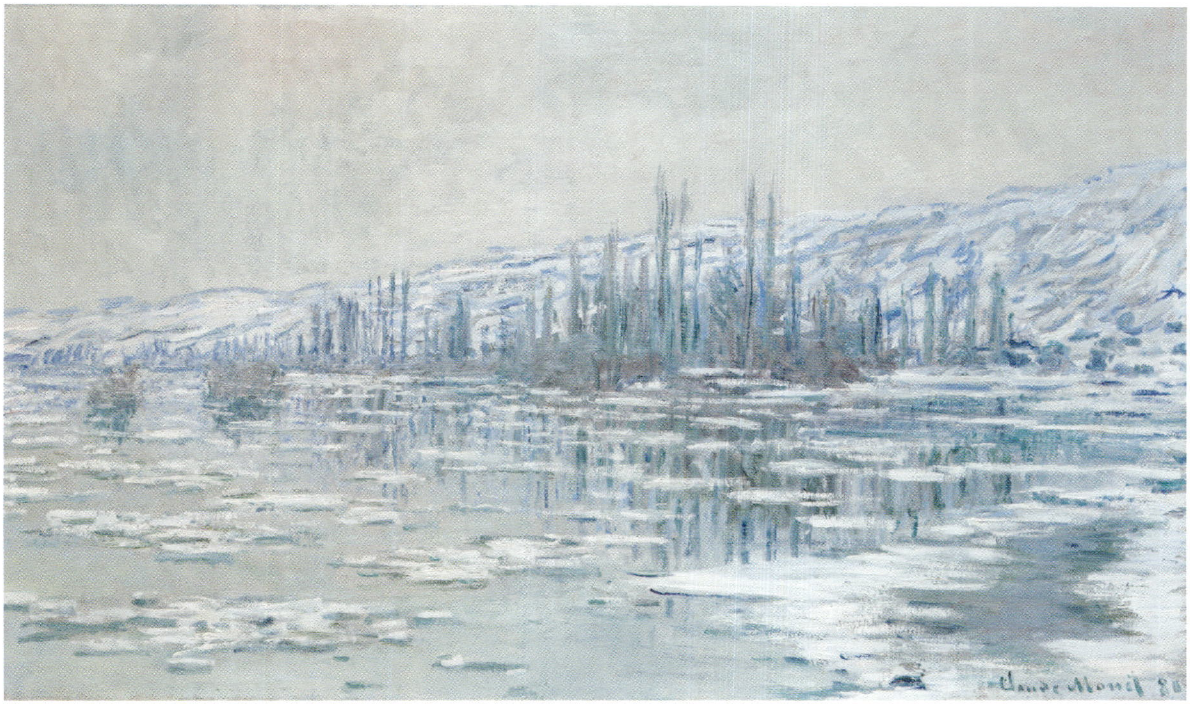

fig. 74—Claude Monet, *The Seine near Giverny*, 1885, oil on canvas, 25⅝ × 36¼ in., Frederic C. Hamilton Collection, Bequeathed to the Denver Art Museum

fig. 75—Claude Monet, *The Break-up of the Ice*, 1880, oil on canvas, 23¾ × 39¼ in., University of Michigan Museum of Art

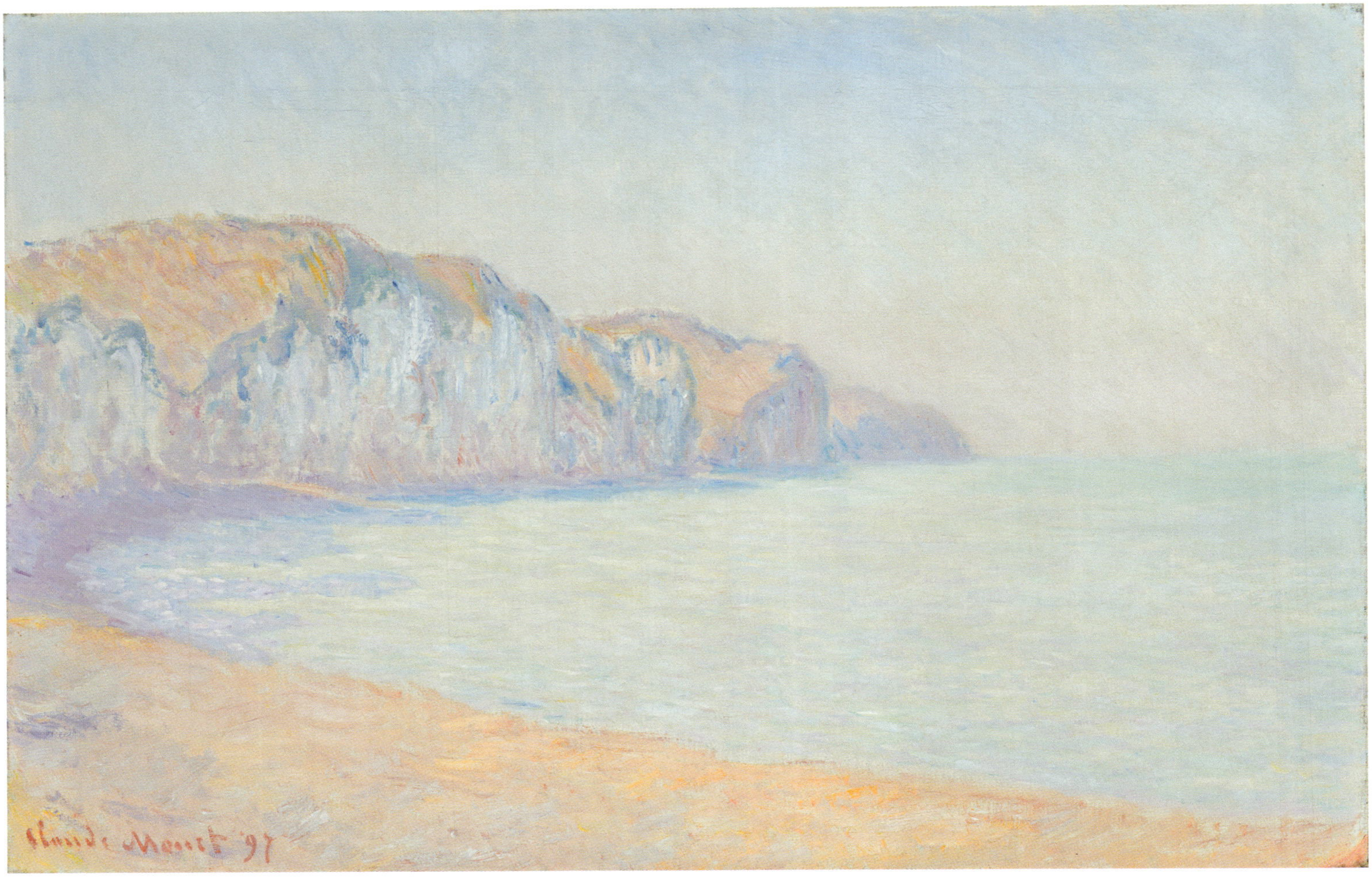

fig. 76—Claude Monet, *A Cliff at Pourville in the Morning*, 1897, oil on canvas, 26 × 39 ½ in., Montreal Museum of Fine Arts

he would only ever be displeased by this group of works: "Painting completely disgusts me and I am going to put away my brushes and colors forever. All I have been able to do recently is to completely spoil several canvases of Venice that I have to destroy, a sad result. I would have done better to keep them as they are, in memory of the happy days spent with my dear Alice."[109] He told the Bernheim-Jeune brothers in February 1912 that the Venice canvases would be ready for exhibition, although he added that he would not be upset if they no longer wanted to present an exhibition so suffused with his despondency:

> *These days of celebrating the renewal of the year have been so painful for me that it has resulted in an increased sadness and complete discouragement. Finally, since there's nothing we can do about the irreparable, I have courageously returned to work, which I had once again completely abandoned, and I think I will very soon have finished my Venice canvases, that is to say those that were worth the effort; therefore an exhibition could be made of them.... However, I am anxious that you should not embarrass yourself with me, should it no longer be convenient for you to follow our agreements. You have always been so friendly and devoted to me that I would be sorry if you felt obliged to follow through on what you would no longer like to do. It's been so long since that return from Venice, when she was so proud of me, I was so excited, and you two were so thrilled.*[110]

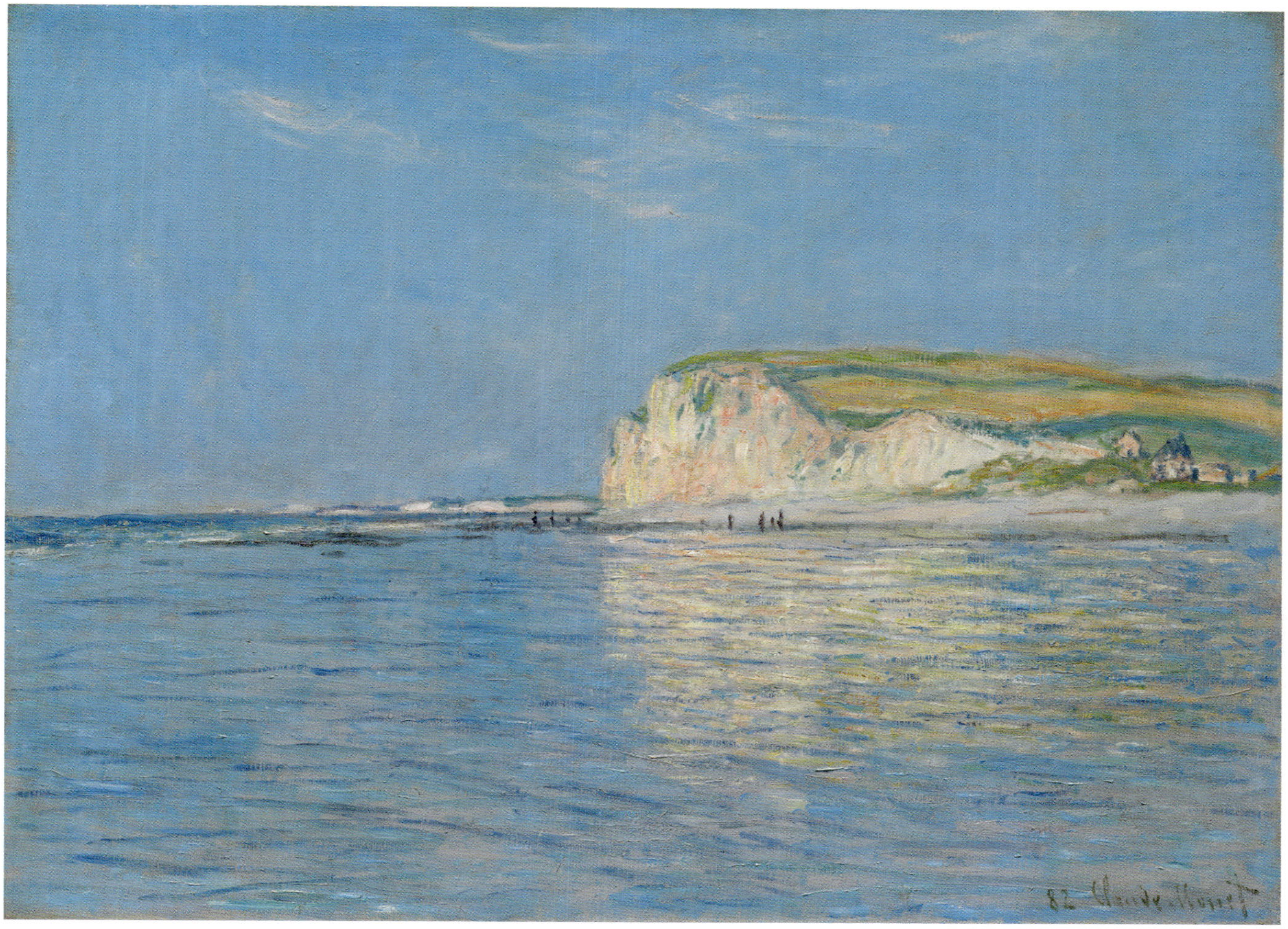

fig. 77—Claude Monet, *Low Tide at Pourville, near Dieppe*, 1882, oil on fabric, 23 9/16 × 32 in., Cleveland Museum of Art

Yet as he worked, he continued to profess his dislike of the paintings: "At the moment not only am I very broken up about my Venetian paintings, which I have managed to turn into horrors, so much so that I am angry and disgusted, but I don't want to repeat my complaints to you. . . . I wouldn't want you to come before I'm completely rid of them within fifteen to twenty days."[111] He even bitterly informed Durand-Ruel, "I know very well in advance that you will find my canvases perfect . . . that they will have great success, but that makes no difference to me since I know they are bad and I am certain of it."[112]

Although he could have, Monet did not cancel the exhibition and Galerie Bernheim-Jeune certainly did not wish to do so either. The exhibition, which included twenty-nine paintings (out of an eventual thirty-seven of Venice), opened at the gallery to widespread critical praise on May 28, 1912; it was scheduled to close on June 8 but was extended and remained on view until June 15.[113] Monet's friend Geffroy published two laudatory reviews, to which Monet was moved to respond:

Heartfelt thanks for your two fine articles of which I am proud. No, I am not a great painter. Neither am I a great poet. I only know that I do what I can to convey what I experience before nature and that most often, in order to succeed in conveying what I feel, I totally forget the

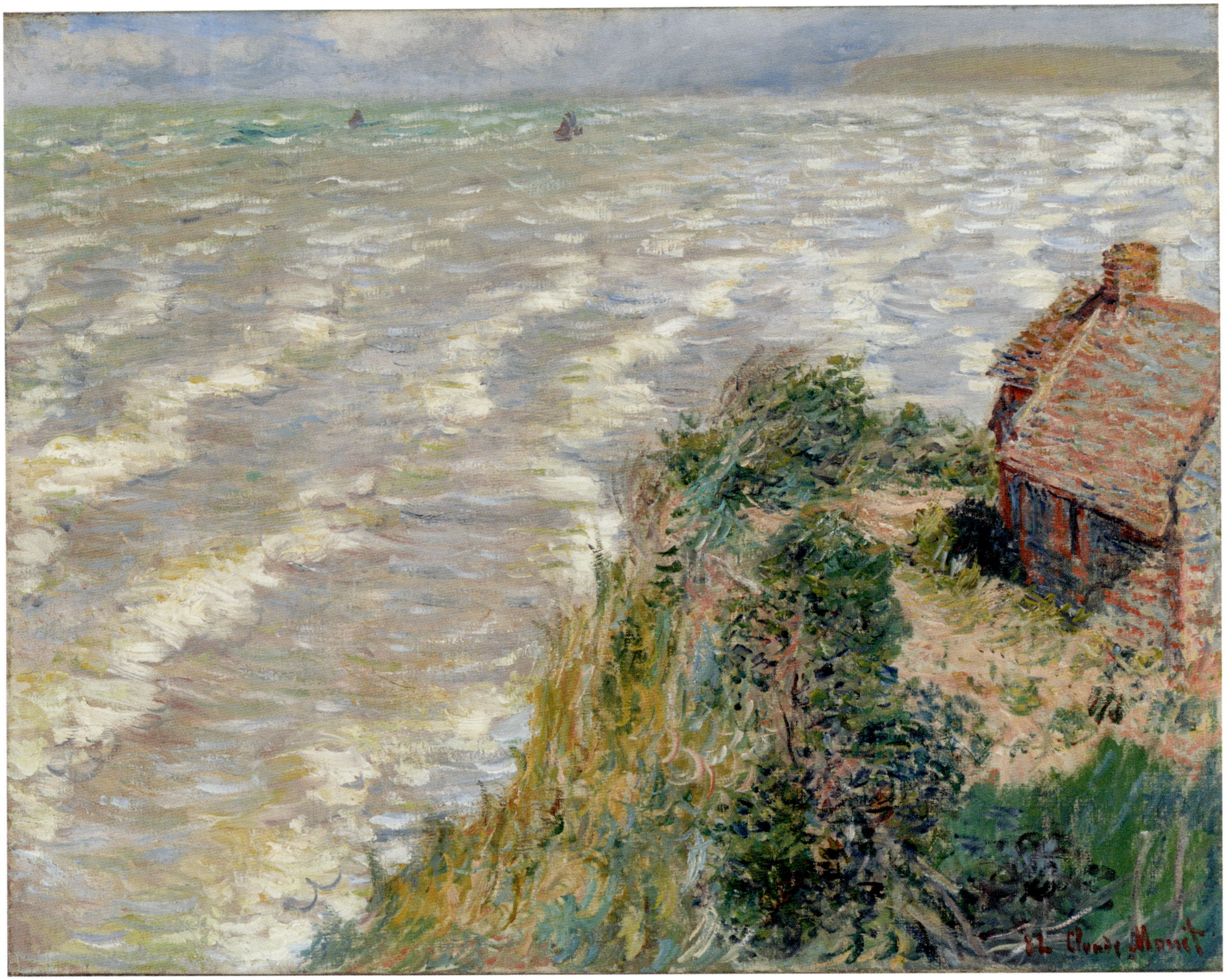

fig. 78—Claude Monet, *Rising Tide at Pourville*, 1882, oil on canvas, 26×32 in., Brooklyn Museum

most elementary rules of painting, if there are any. In short, I let a good many mistakes show through when fixing my sensations. It will always be the same and this is what makes me despair. Thank you for your great and loyal friendship and trust in the no less loyal friendship of your old Claude Monet.[114]

But a month later, Monet insisted to Geffroy, "I was right, despite my good friends: these Venices are pitiful and I would have done better to keep them as a precious souvenir."[115] He did keep at least one—a Palazzo Dario canvas that he requested from the Bernheim-Jeune brothers and which can be seen in photographs at Giverny in 1913 and 1920 (figs. 82 and 106).[116]

Was Monet's assessment of his paintings correct? Should it inform how they are considered today? He offered no specifics and did not criticize any of them individually or compare them unfavorably to other of his works. For him, the Venice paintings represented his tremendous loss and dashed hopes for what might have been if Alice had lived, and they had been able to return together to that enchanted city to revisit the sensations that had so captivated him. One of the many critics who admired the Venetian works acknowledged that Monet "visibly executed these paintings in a state of anxiety."[117] What must be taken into account is not just Monet's opinion of them as paintings, but that he would only ever see them through the *envelope* of his tears.

—

I'm very sad that I'll soon have to leave this unique light.
It is so very beautiful, but we must resign ourselves
to the inevitable.... I comfort myself with the thought that
I'll come back next year... But what a shame I didn't come
here when I was a younger man, when I was full
of daring!... Still... I have spent some delightful hours here,
almost forgetting that I am now an old man.
{ Claude Monet to Gustave Geffroy, December 7, 1908 }

Monet's Venetian sojourn interrupted and replenished the increasingly immersive vision of his *Water Lilies* paintings. But what did he mean when he said that his trip had made him see those canvases "with a better eye"? Along with expanses of scintillating, reflective water, he encountered something else in Venice that may have affected his thinking. The concept of displaying his water lily paintings in a room as a single, encompassing panorama seems to have emerged around 1897 and then become stronger in 1909. He was likely aware of large-scale popular entertainment panorama installations and would have been familiar with the decorated public spaces of Paris.[118] But the encompassing, densely painted architectural settings he encountered in Venice—although entirely different in form and content from his own work—cannot help but have fed his imagination. When the couple first arrived in Venice, they "admired some superb Tintorettos." Alice did not say which ones, but most likely they saw the immense, multipart painting cycles at the Scuola Grande di San Rocco and in the Palazzo Ducale (figs. 81, 89, and 90).[119] In 1924, Marc Elder wrote that Monet recalled seeing in

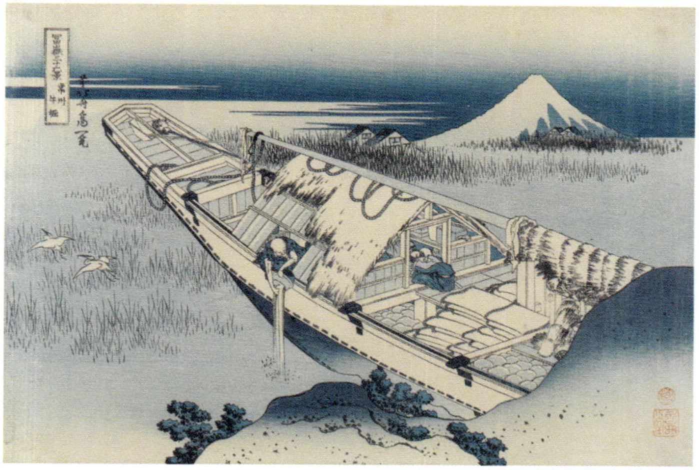

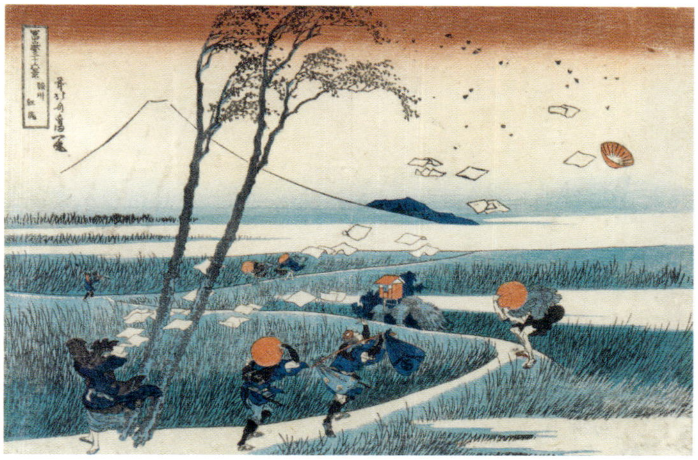

fig. 79—Katsushika Hokusai, *View of Mount Fuji from a Boat at Ushibori* from the series *Thirty-Six Views of Mount Fuji*, 1834, color woodblock print on paper, 10⅜ × 15¼ in., Brooklyn Museum

fig. 80—Katsushika Hokusai, *Ejiri in Suruga Province*, from the series *Thirty-Six Views of Mount Fuji*, c. 1830–31, color woodblock print on paper, 9⁹⁄₁₆ × 14⁵⁄₁₆ in., Brooklyn Museum

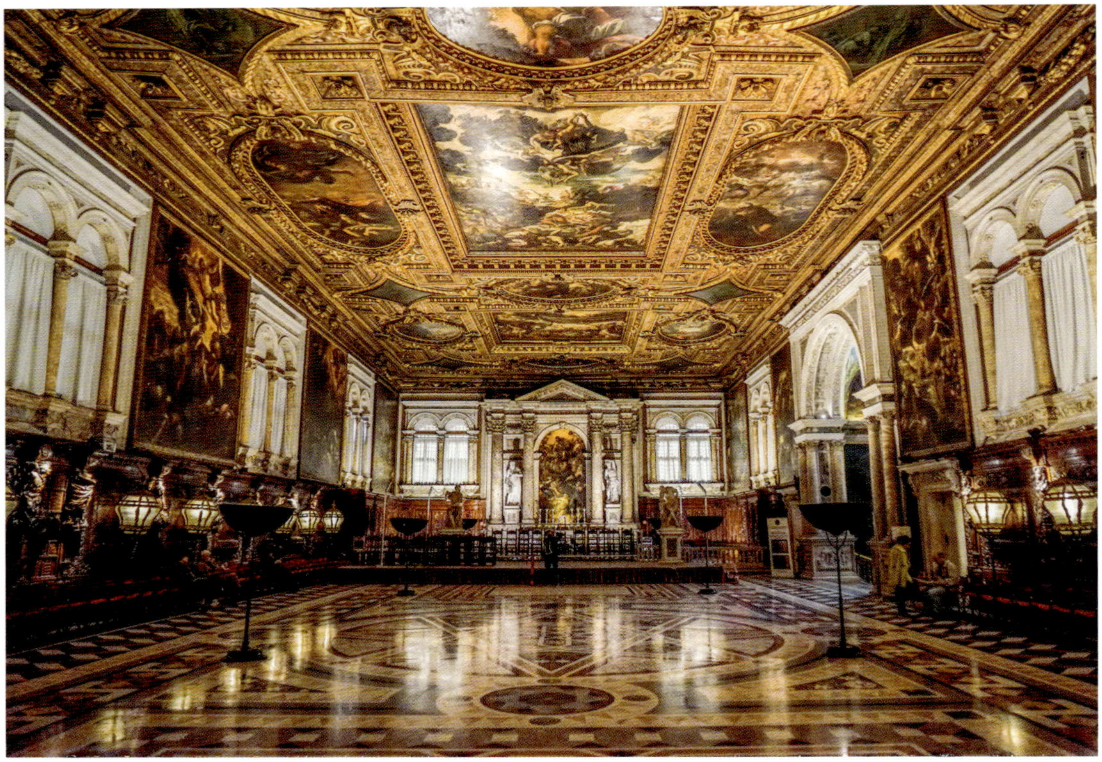

fig. 81—Interior of the Scuola Grande di San Rocco in Venice

Venice "a fragment of Tintoretto, on the floor, there, before my eyes.... Stunning! Each piece gives you a blow to the stomach!"[120] (See Elena Marchetti's essay in this volume and fig. 90.) Indeed, in writing about the *Water Lilies* in 1924, Louis Gillet drew an explicit connection between them and Venice's grand interiors: "What the great Venetians demanded of Olympus, from their ceiling creations, from their populace of neuter and indeterminate divinities seated on clouds on the cornices of the palace of the Doges—that complete representation of experience, that profound humanization of nature, landscape here obtains for the first time."[121]

As Pierre Schneider and Philippe Piguet have suggested, Monet may have felt that before confining himself solely to the reflective surface of his pond, he could, in Venice, confront for the last time not only indisputably "real" motifs, but ones that familiarity had made challenging to see or render afresh. He renewed the image of this famous place by suppressing architectural details and by evacuating the human presence. His Venice is a kind of afterimage, accreted not with history but with layers of paint transmuted into sensation, duration, and memory, both time's stillness and passing made palpable. The "better eye" with which Monet claimed to see his *Water Lilies* may merely have been the result of time away from them; anywhere outside of Giverny would have sufficed to recharge his vision. But it is difficult to dismiss Venice itself as a generative factor, when considering the delicate colors, narrow tonal range, chimerical forms, and emphasis on surface in the *Water Lilies* he continued to develop or rework in the trip's aftermath. Arsène Alexandre posited a reciprocity between the Venice paintings and those of the pond that Monet had already begun and to which he would return:

Whether he wanted to, whether he realized it or not, by the logical force of his temperament and his work... the large surface of water dotted with water lilies could not help but persist in the whole swath of the lagoon, with its solid masses of Oriental masonry and canal paths. However, he would inevitably return from this excursion into the realm of natural similarities and go back to the work he had begun earlier. Indeed, he was already being influenced by the consequences of the experience without foreseeing their full extent.[122]

According to Paul Hayes Tucker, the light, space, and paint of Monet's boundless, mirrored pond "coalesce on the surfaces of the [water lily paintings], suggesting a kind of essential presence, like some enchanting fragrance or the sensed rhythms of silence...remnants of the pictorial, collections of poetically arranged shapes and colors that have their own internal logic."[123] This, too, could describe Monet's immaterial, vestigial Venice, floating and refracted in its aqueous lagoon atmosphere. Endlessly mirroring itself, a place where "the shimmering of the lagoon could evoke the iridescence of the pond," Venice offered Monet the final proof that water and light were all he needed.[124]

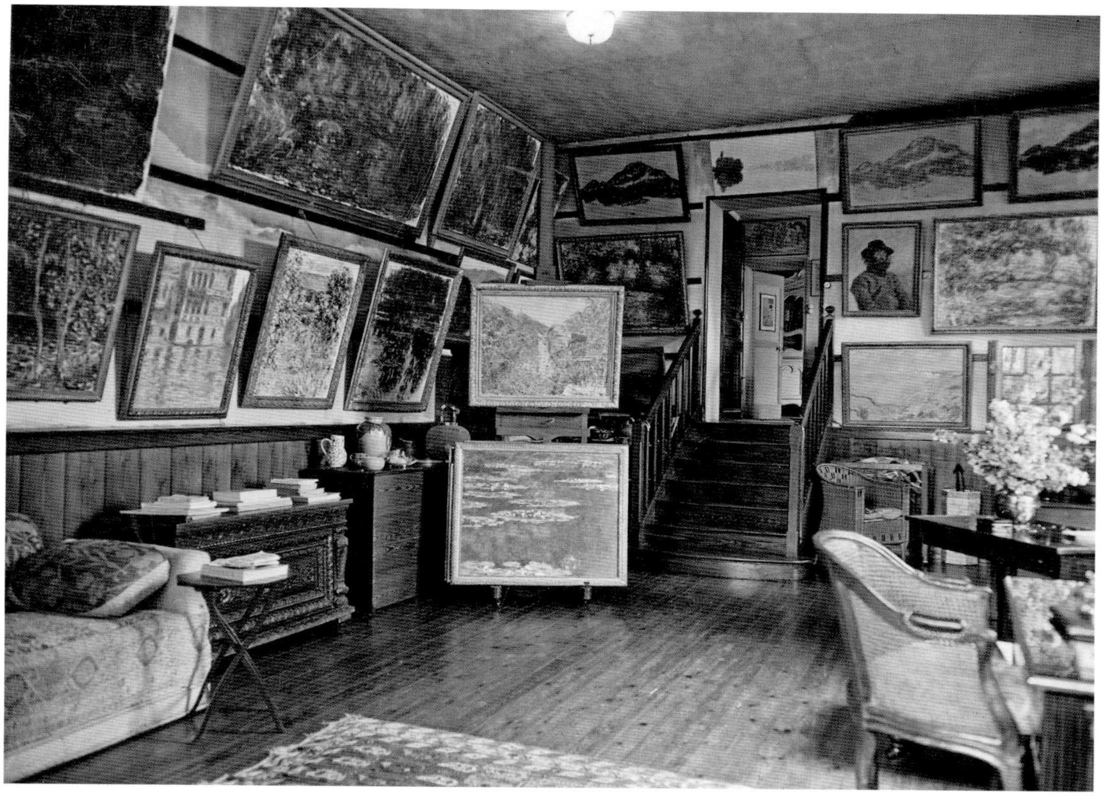

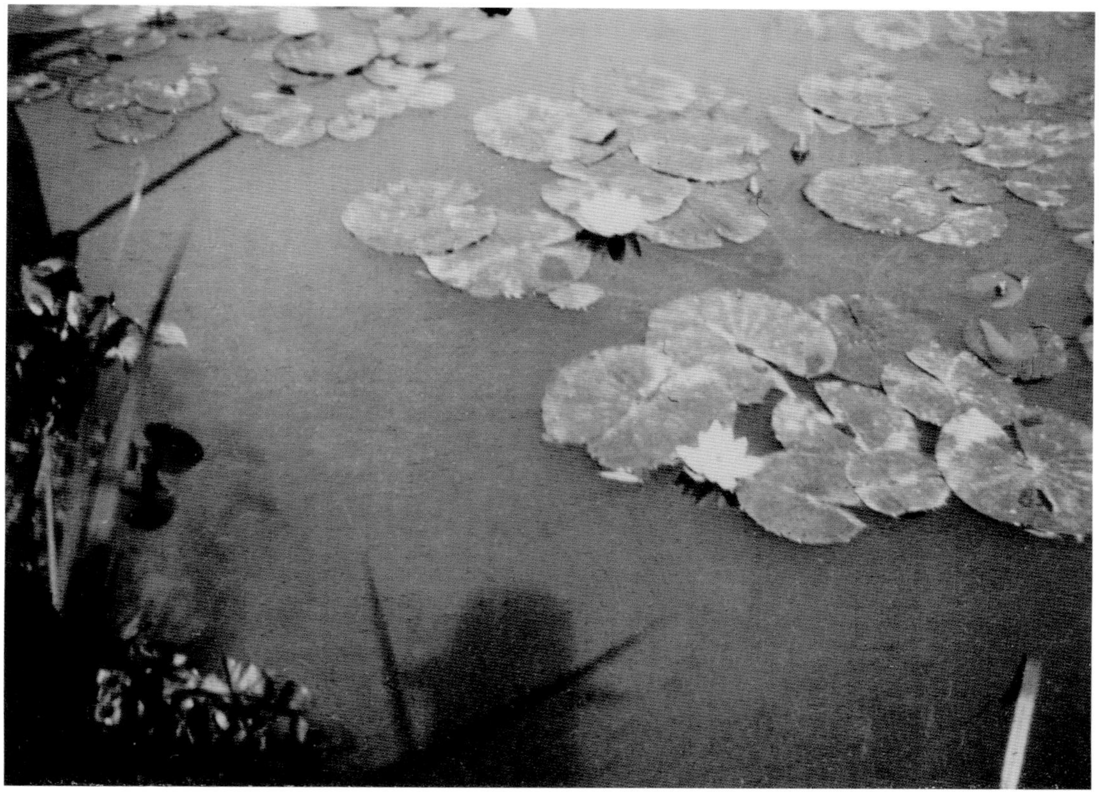

fig. 82—Georges Allié, *Claude Monet's Salon-Studio in Giverny*, c. 1920, Photograph, 6⅓ × 8¹⁄₁₀ in., Collection Philippe Piguet

fig. 83—Claude Monet, *Self-portrait on the Surface of the Lily Pond*, c. 1905, Photograph, 4⅓ × 5 ¾ in., Collection Philippe Piguet

PART TWO

PLATES

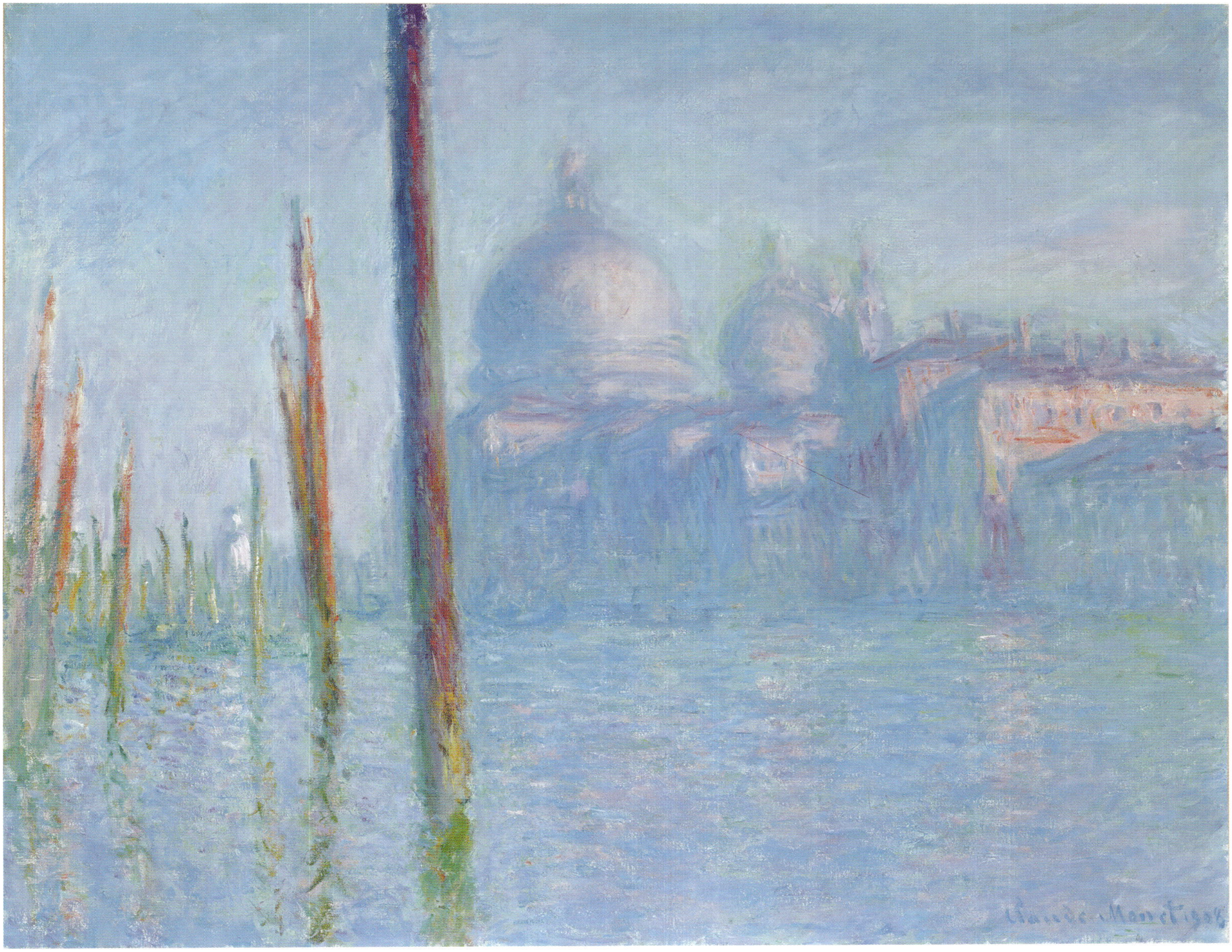

plate 1—Claude Monet, *The Grand Canal, Venice*, 1908, oil on canvas, 28 13/16 × 35 5/16 in., Fine Arts Museums of San Francisco

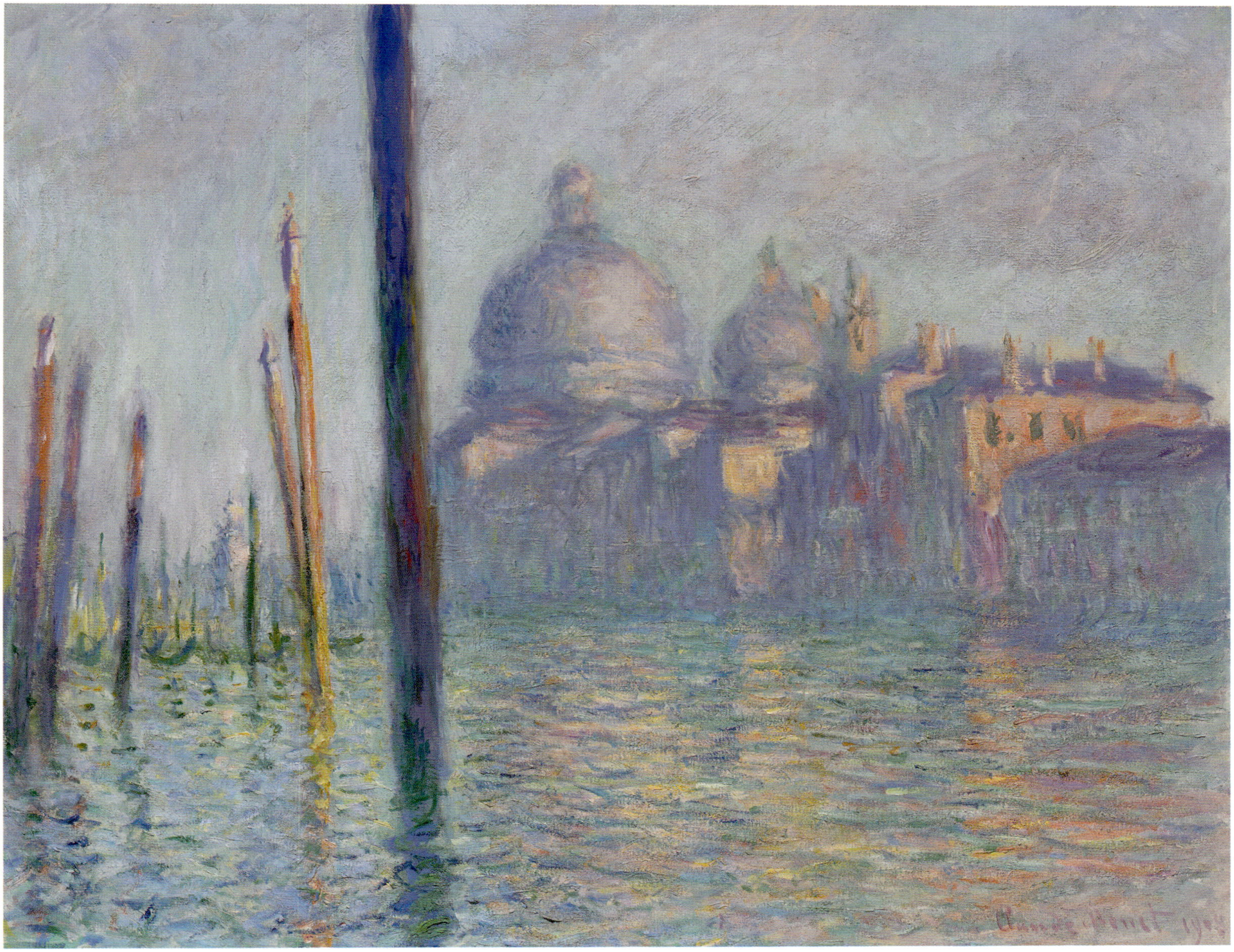

plate 2—Claude Monet, *The Grand Canal, Venice*, 1908, oil on canvas, 29 × 36⅜ in., Museum of Fine Arts, Boston

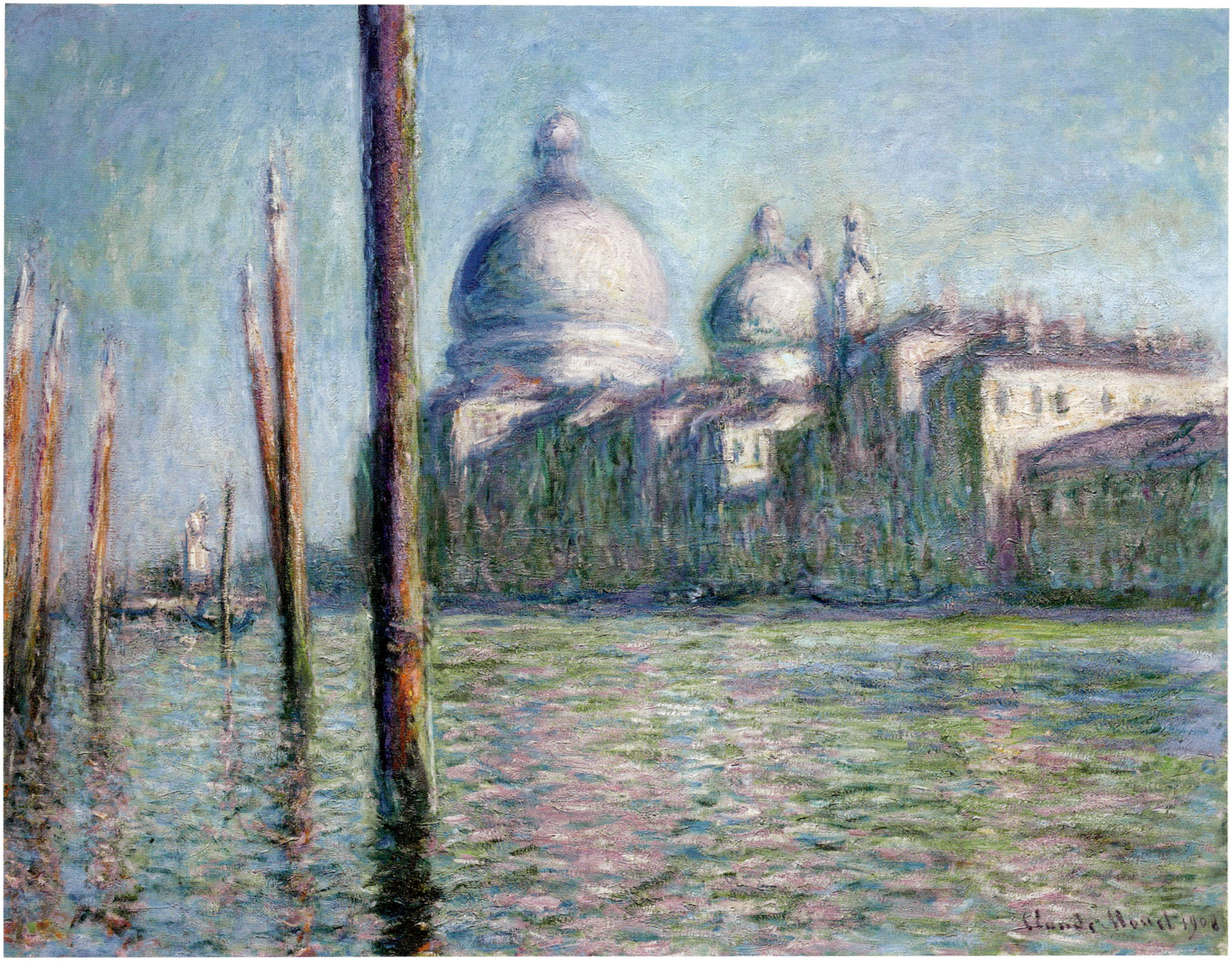

plate 3—Claude Monet, *The Grand Canal*, 1908, oil on canvas, 28 ¾ × 36 ¼ in., private collection

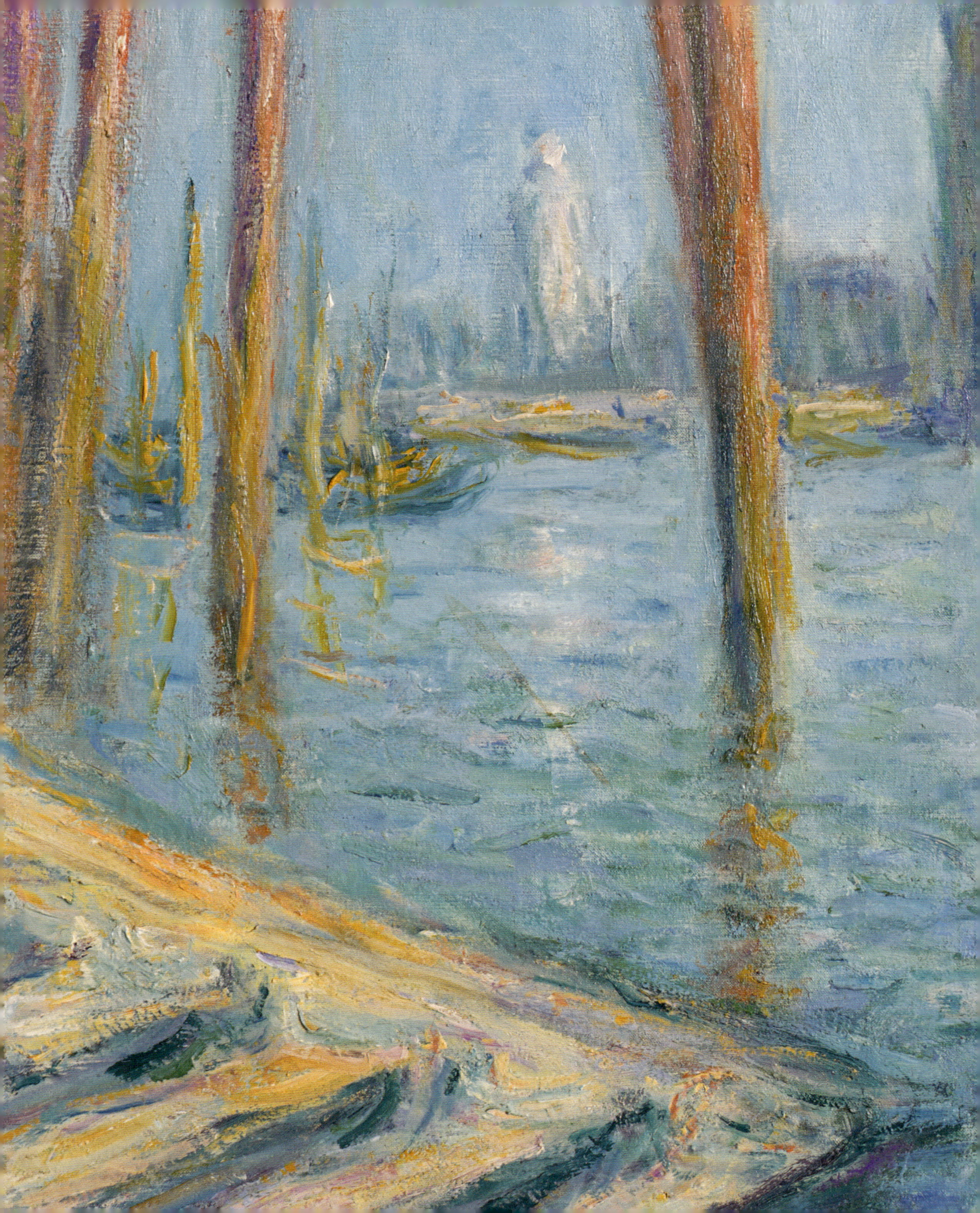

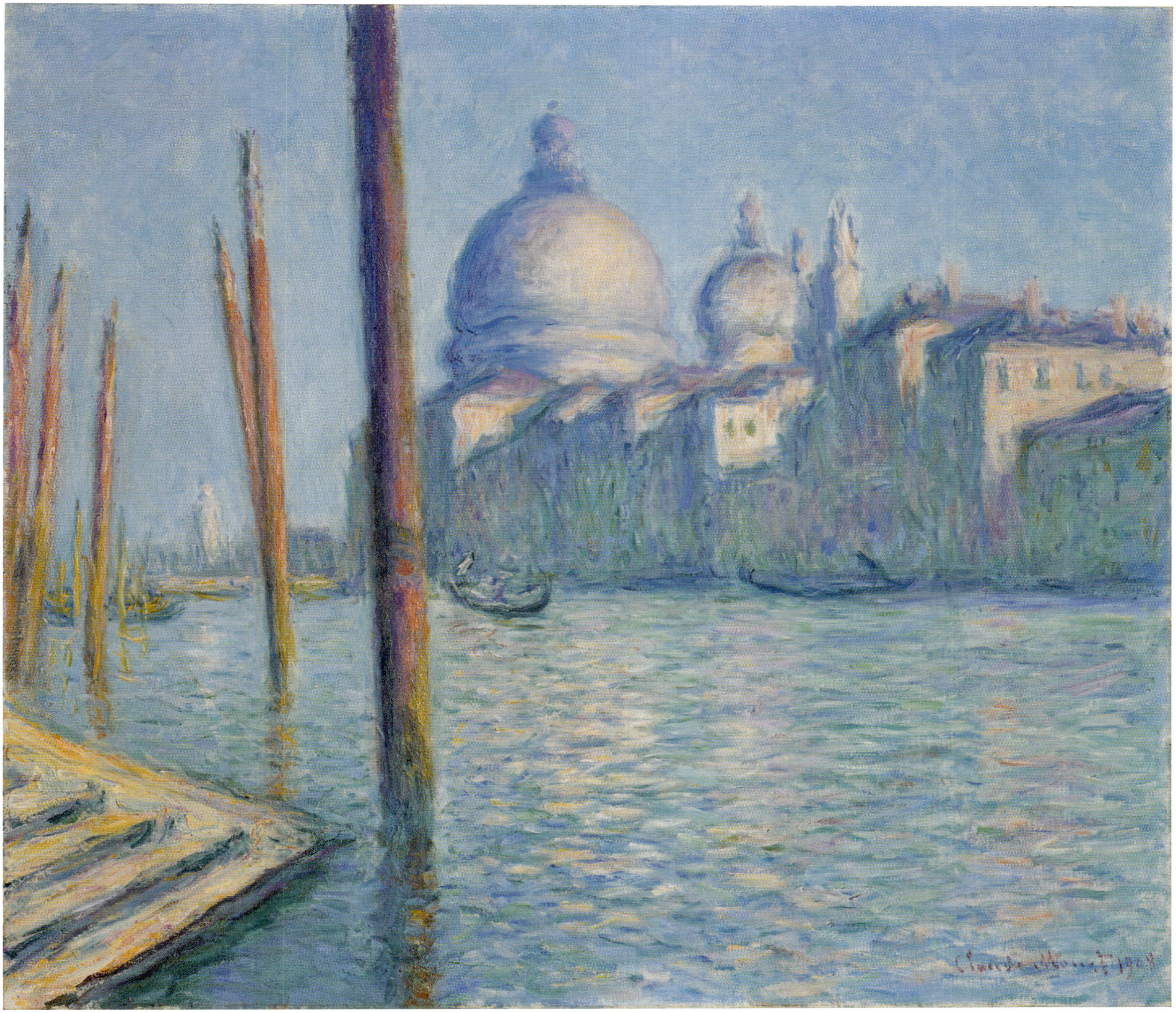

plate 4—Claude Monet, *The Grand Canal*, 1908, oil on canvas, $32\frac{1}{8} \times 36\frac{7}{16}$ in., private collection

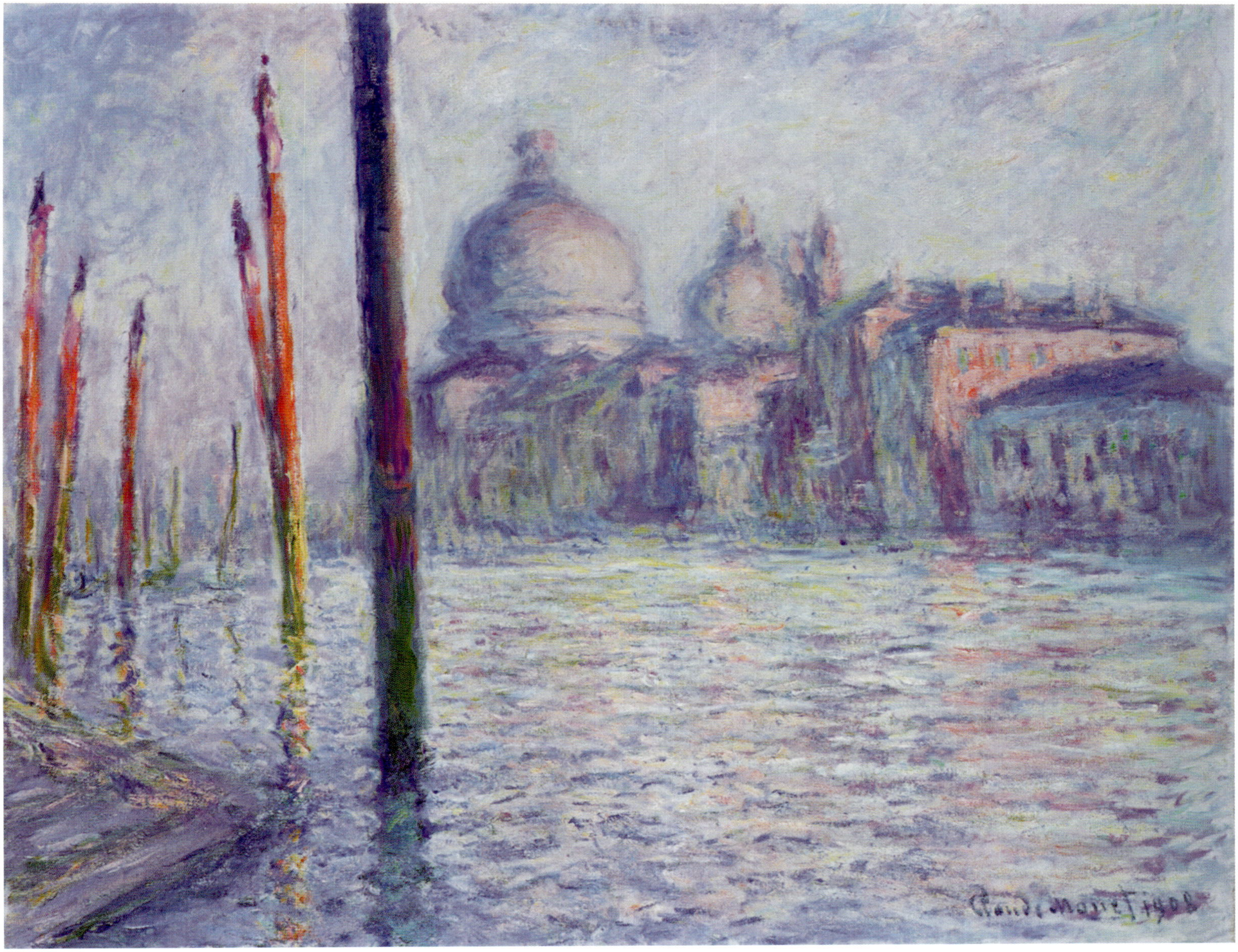

plate 5—Claude Monet, *The Grand Canal*, 1908, oil on canvas, 28 ¾ × 36 ¼ in., private collection

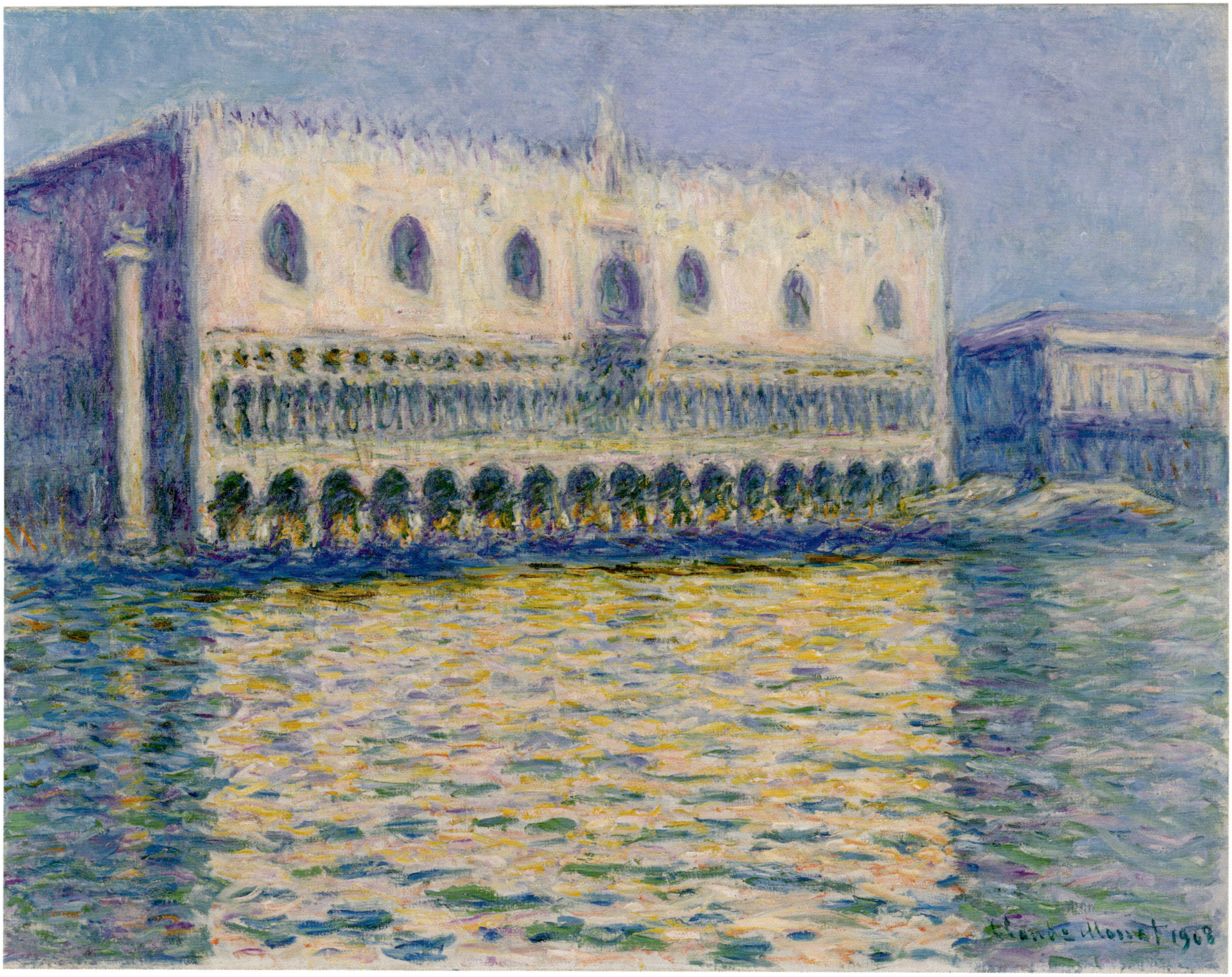

plate 6—Claude Monet, *The Palazzo Ducale*, 1908, oil on canvas, 32 × 39 in., Brooklyn Museum

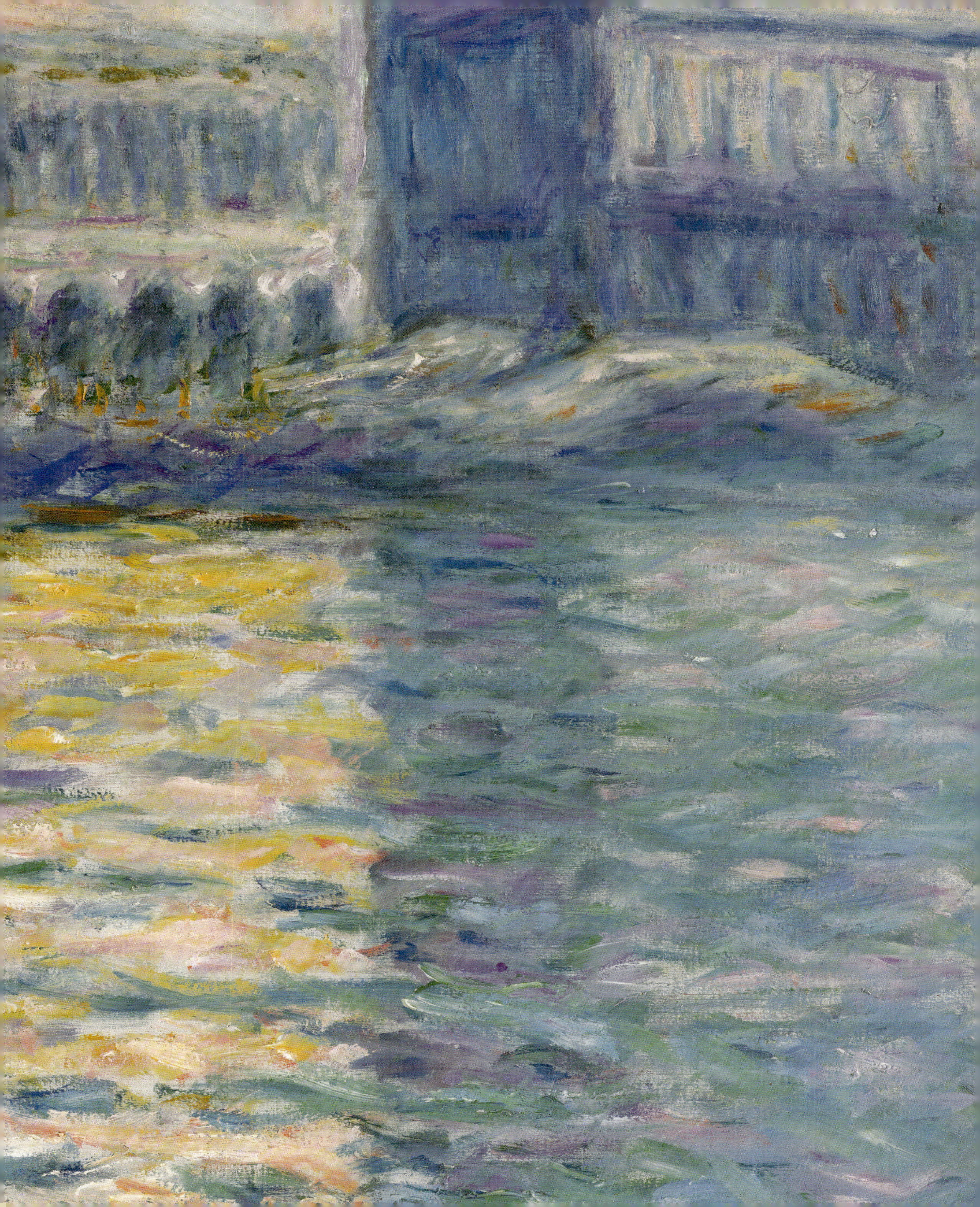

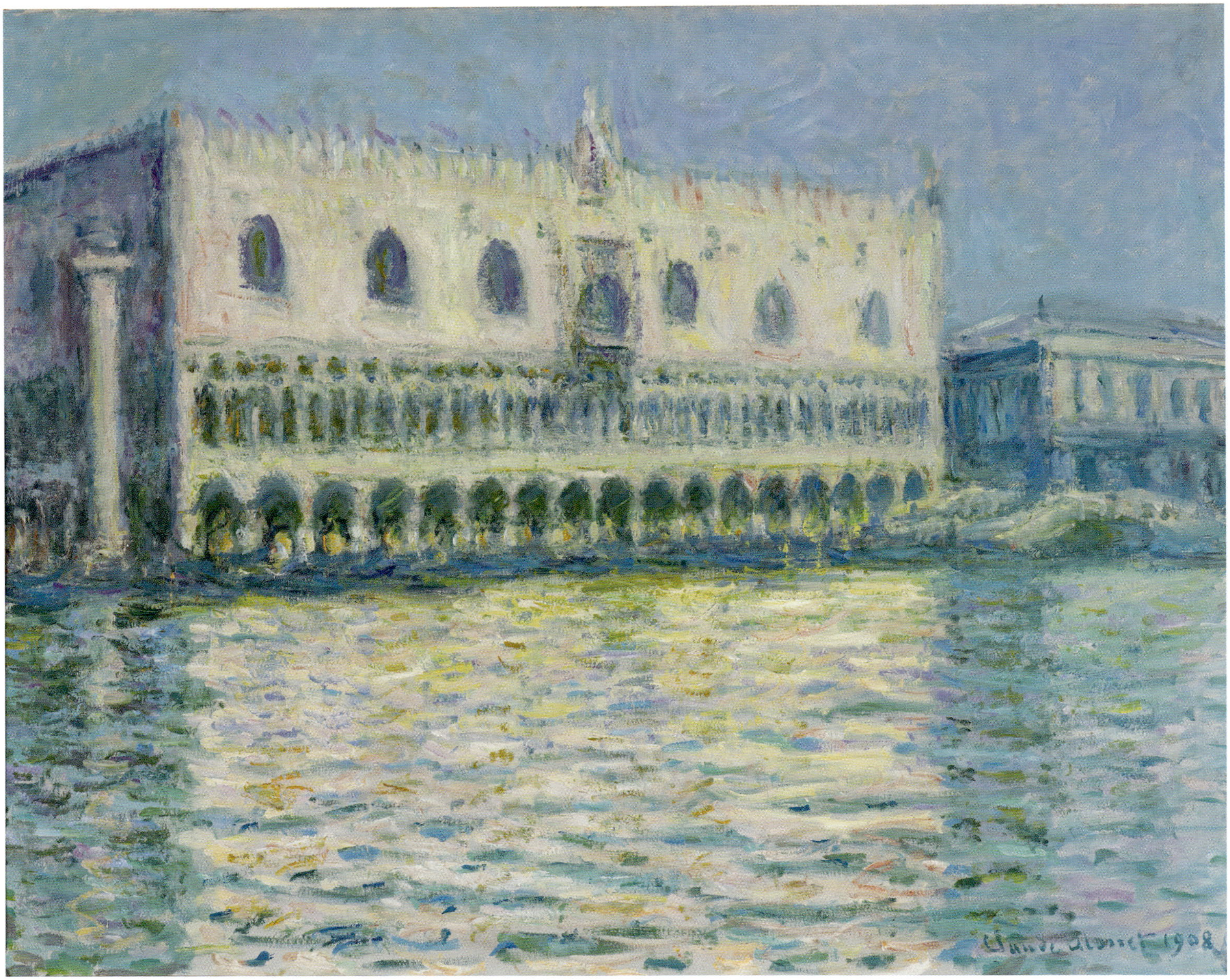

plate 7—Claude Monet, *The Palazzo Ducale*, 1908, oil on canvas, 28 ¾ × 36 ¼ in., private collection

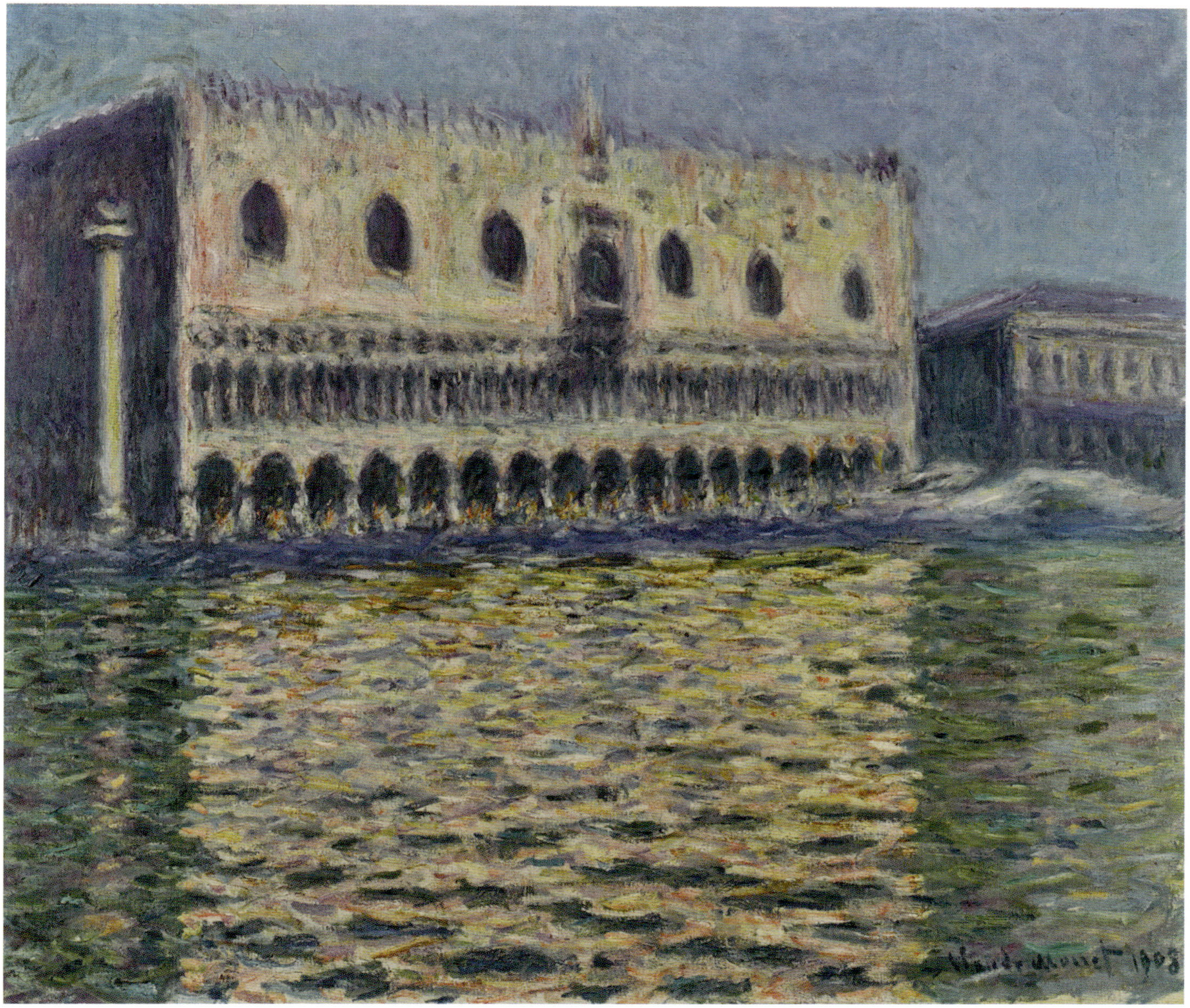

plate 8—Claude Monet, *The Palazzo Ducale, Venice*, 1908, oil on canvas, 31 ½ × 36 ¼ in., private collection

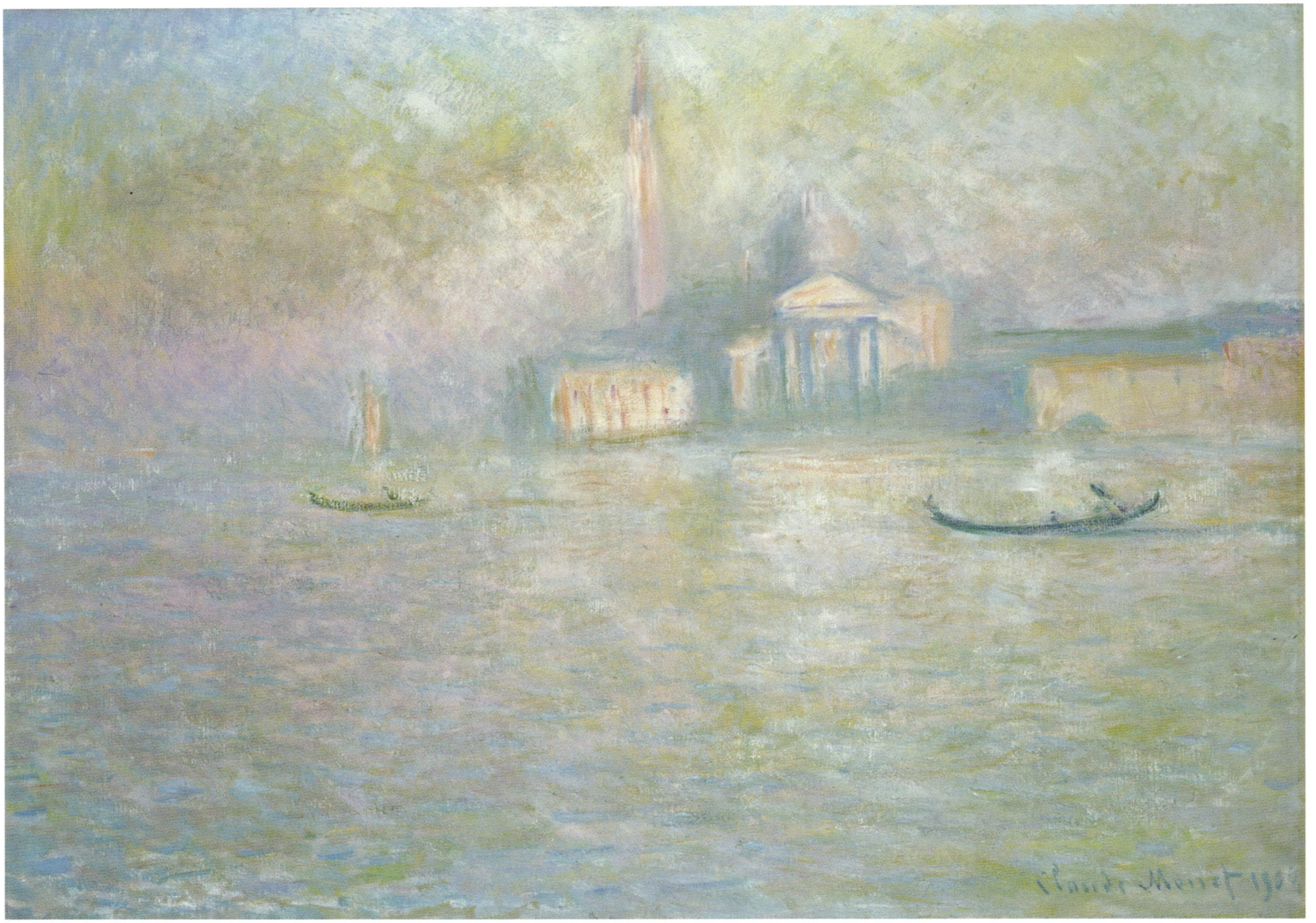

plate 9—Claude Monet, *San Giorgio Maggiore*, 1908, oil on canvas, 23×32 in., Amgueddfa Cymru

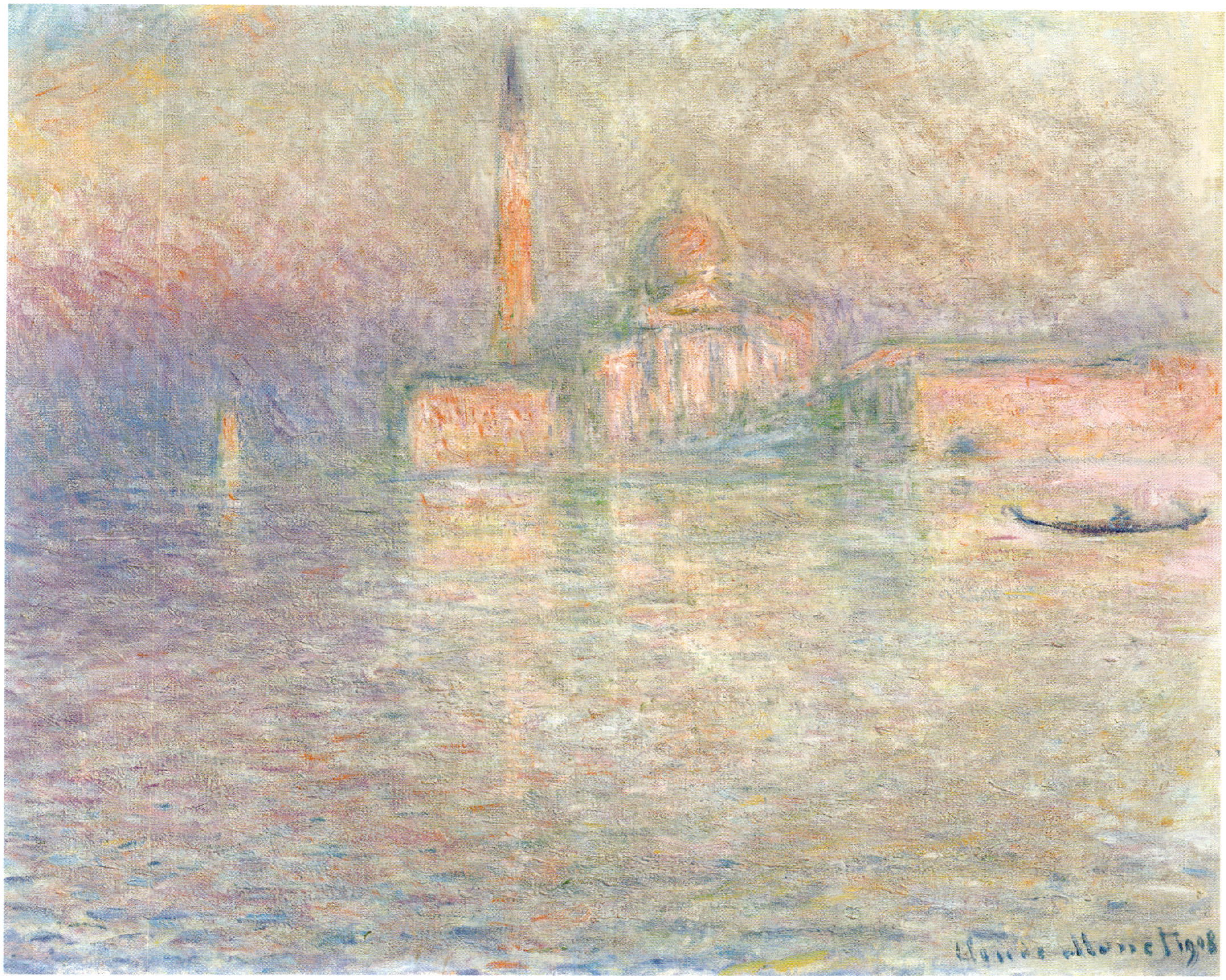

plate 10—Claude Monet, *San Giorgio Maggiore*, 1908, oil on canvas, 23⅔ × 28 ¾ in., private collection

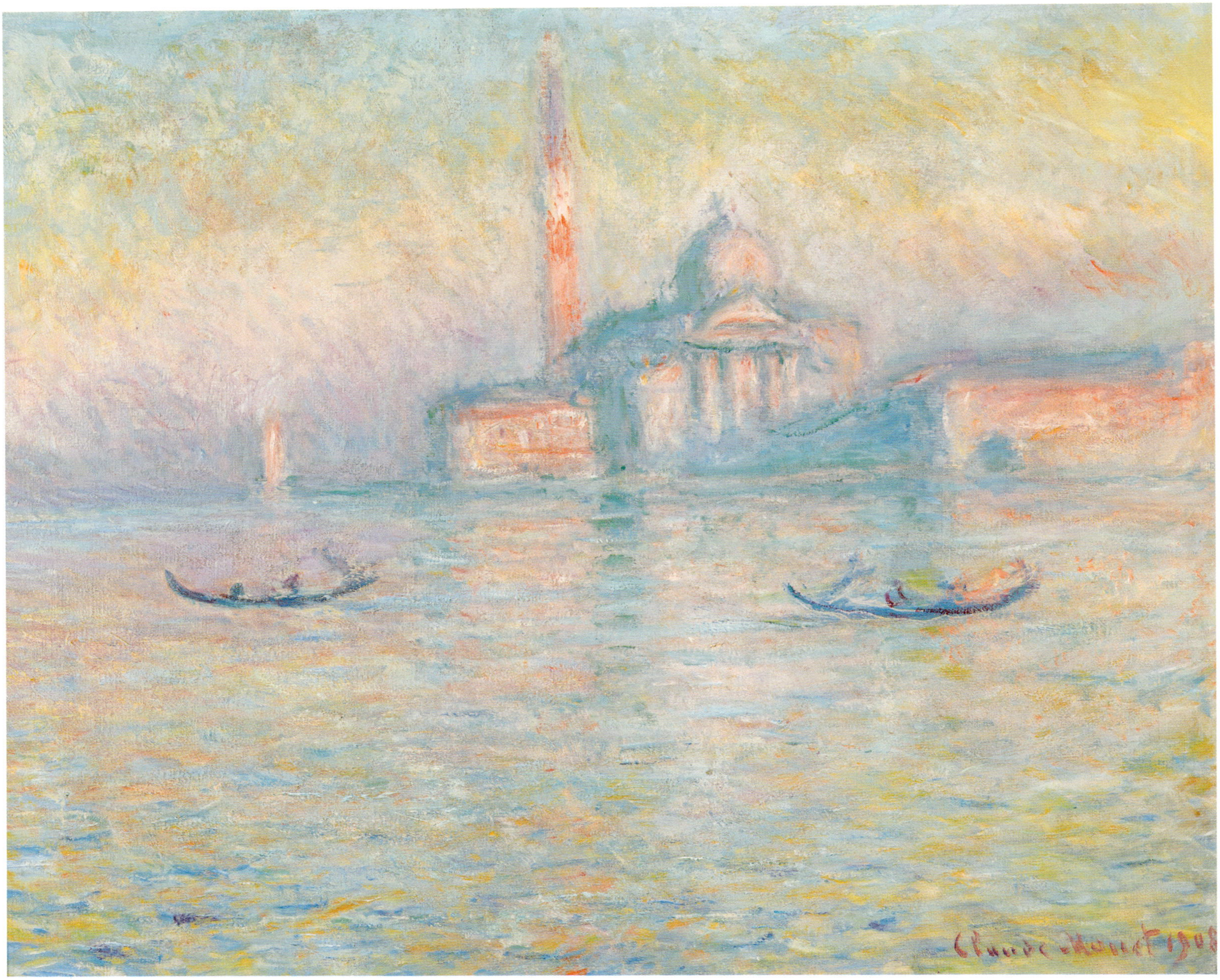

plate 11—Claude Monet, *San Giorgio Maggiore*, 1908, oil on canvas, 23⅔ × 28 ¾ in., private collection, courtesy of Alon Zakaim Fine Art

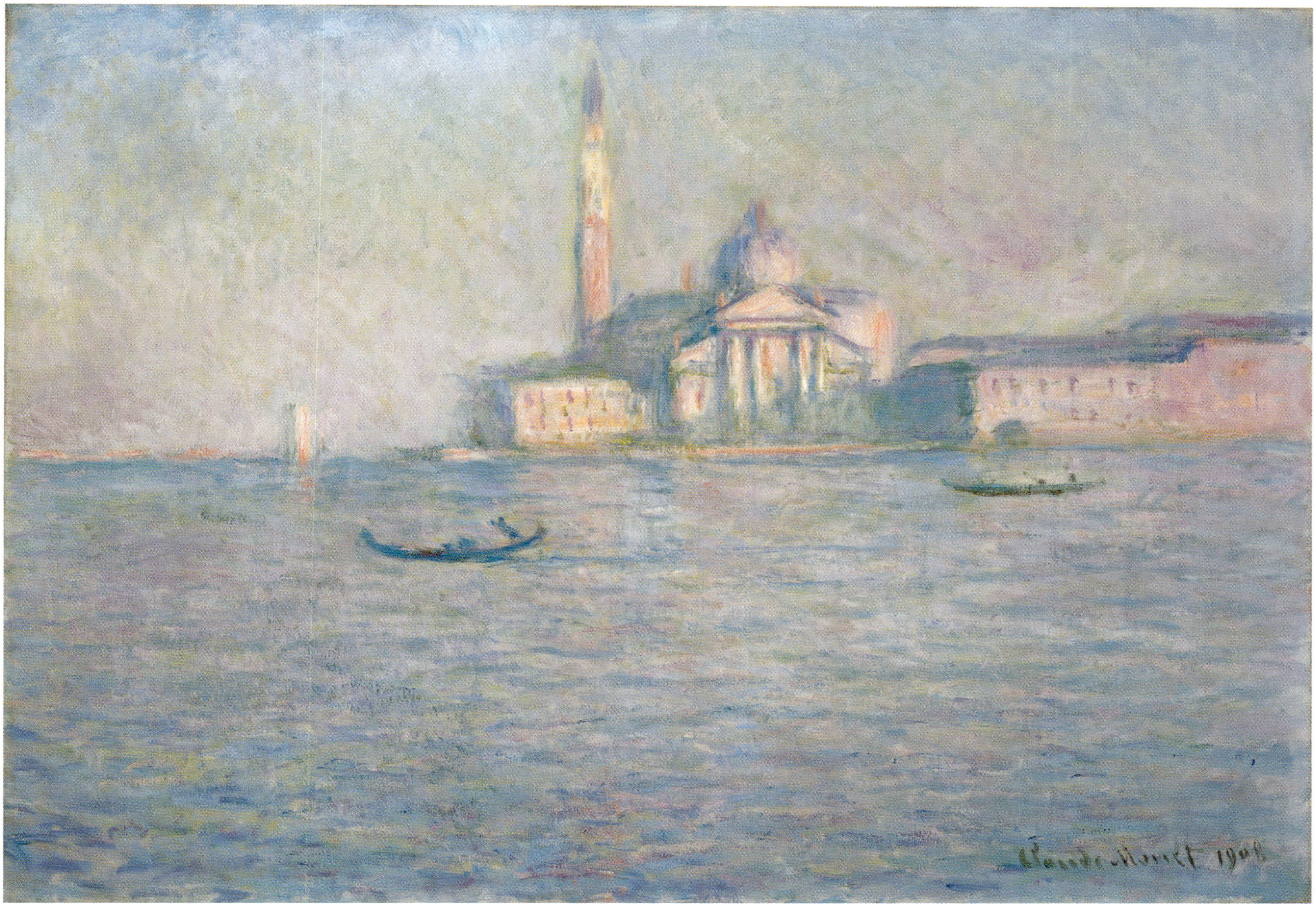

plate 12—Claude Monet, *The Church of San Giorgio Maggiore, Venice*, 1908, oil on canvas, 26⅛ × 36⅞ in., Indianapolis Museum of Art at Newfields

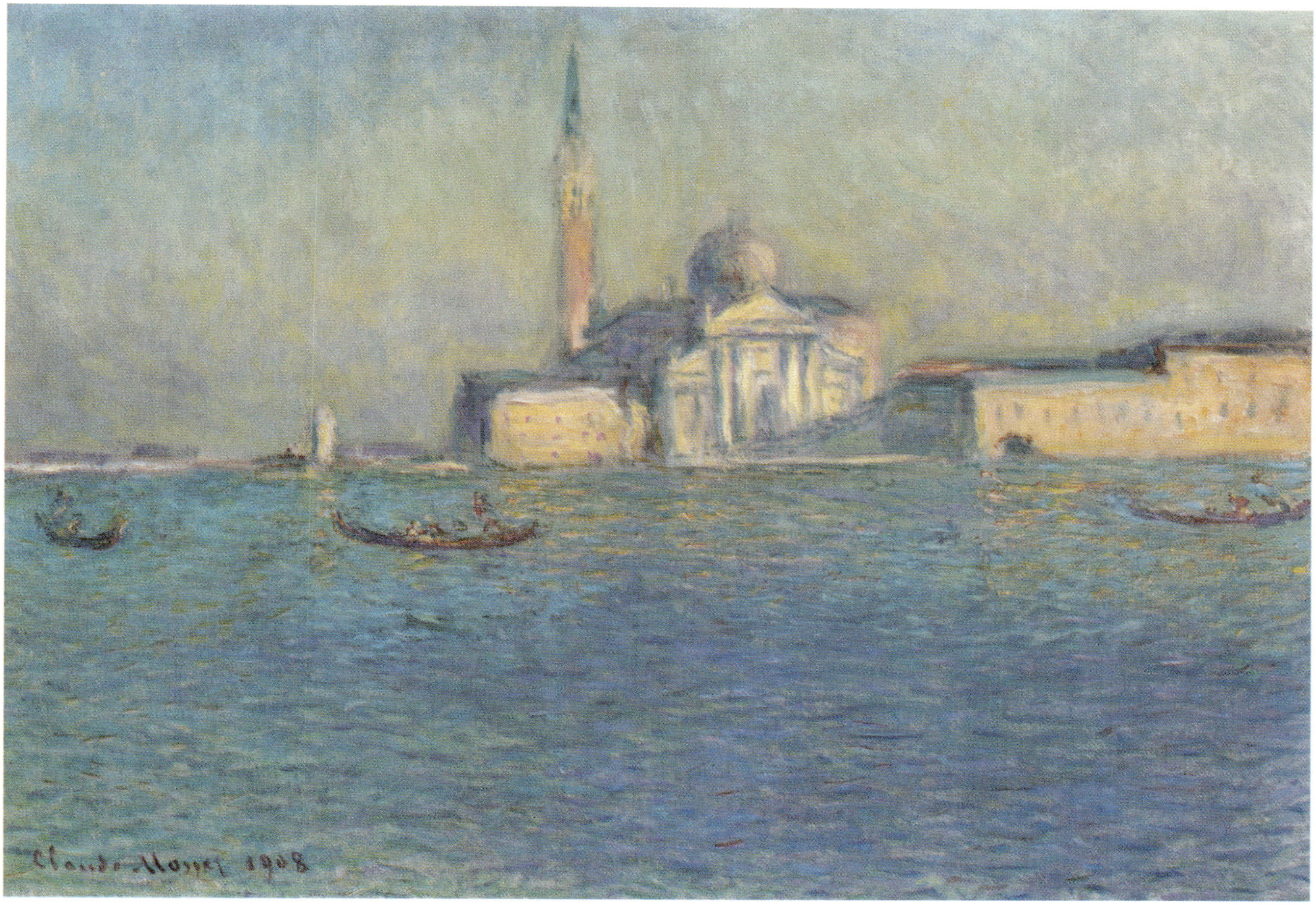

plate 13—Claude Monet, *San Giorgio Maggiore*, 1908, oil on canvas, 25⅗ × 36¼ in., location unknown

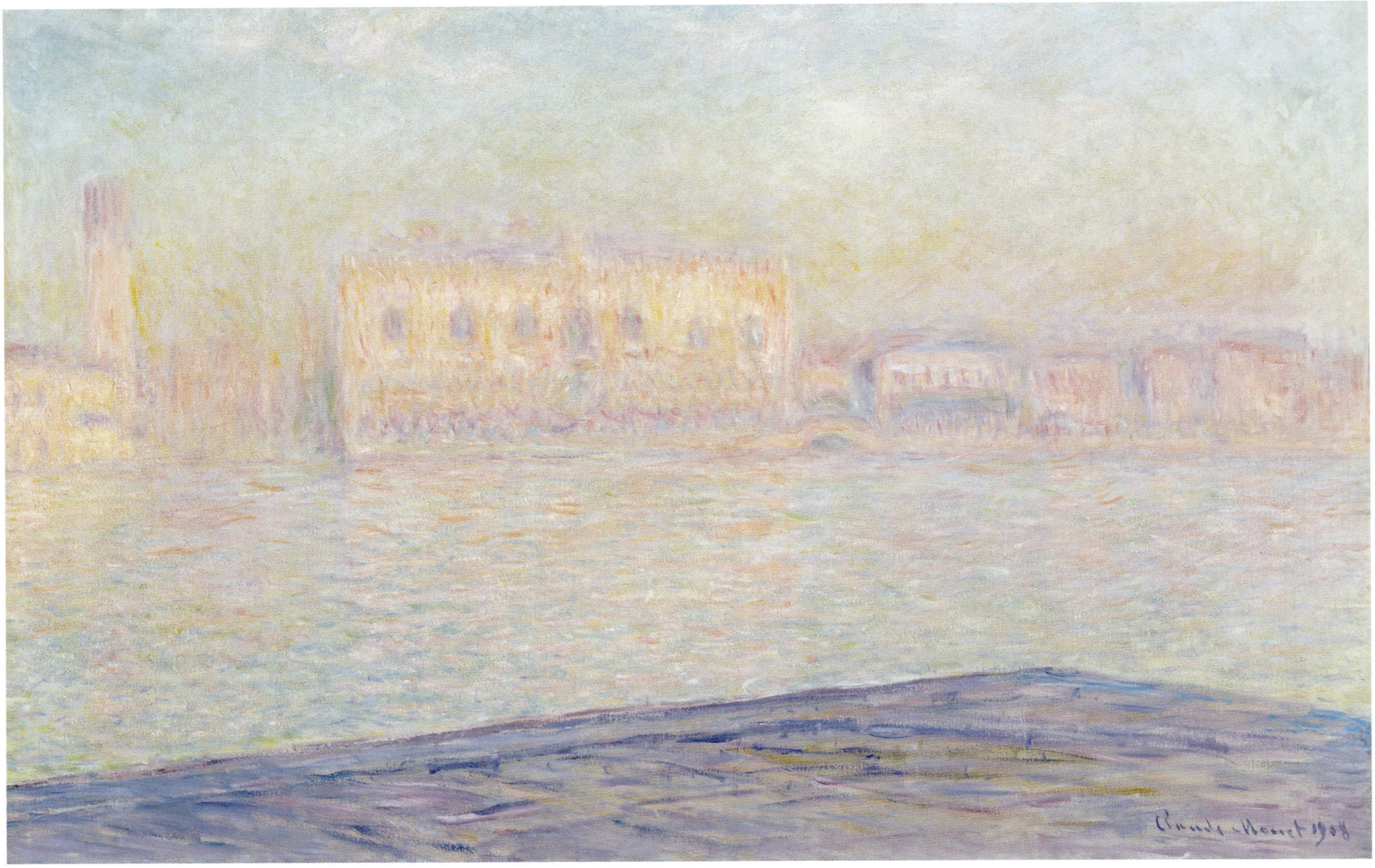

plate 14—Claude Monet, *The Palazzo Ducale Seen from San Giorgio Maggiore*, 1908, oil on canvas, 25⅗ × 39⅓ in., Kunsthaus Zürich

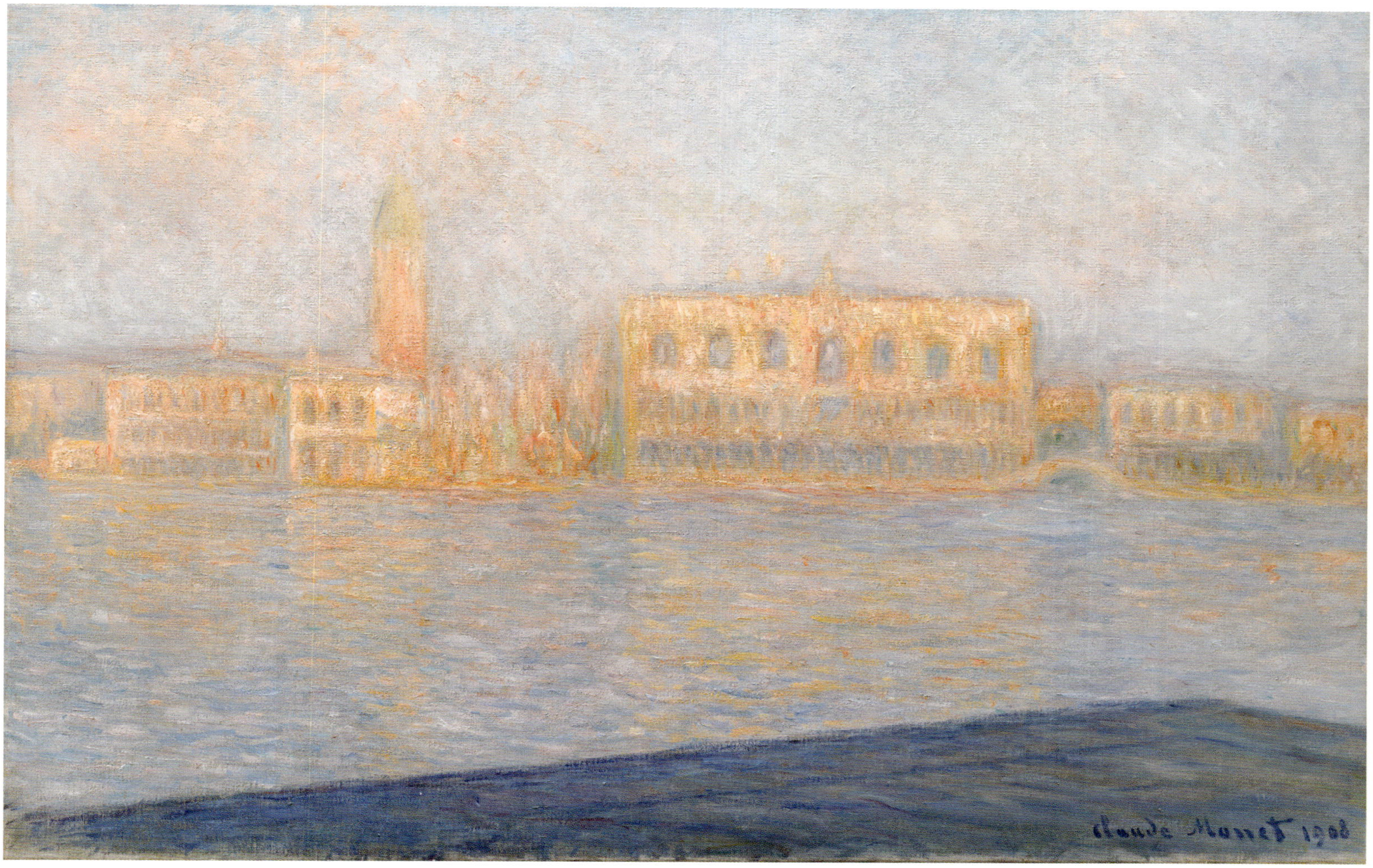

plate 15—Claude Monet, *The Palazzo Ducale, Seen from San Giorgio Maggiore* , 1908, oil on canvas, $25\frac{9}{16} \times 39\frac{9}{16}$ in., Solomon R. Guggenheim Museum

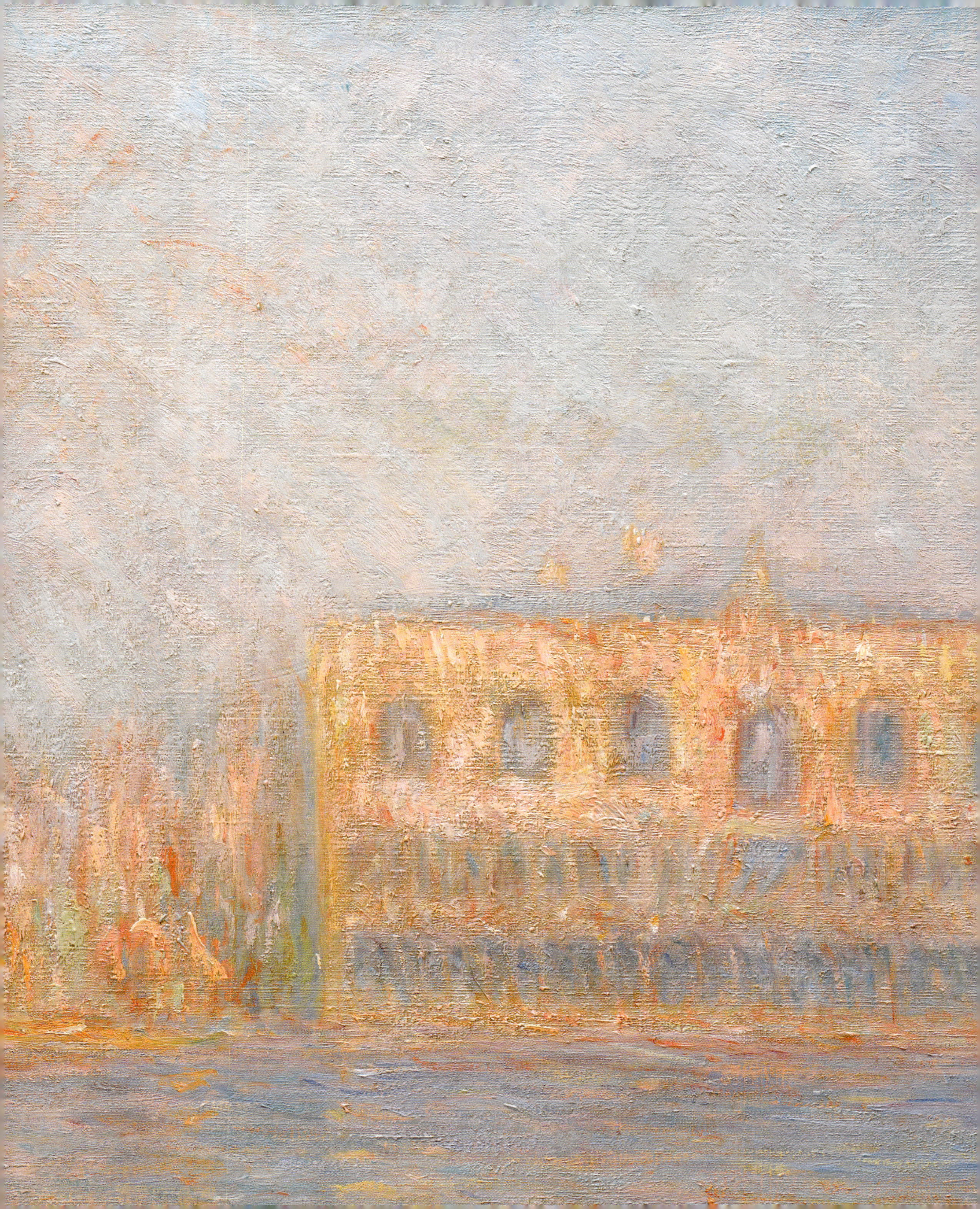

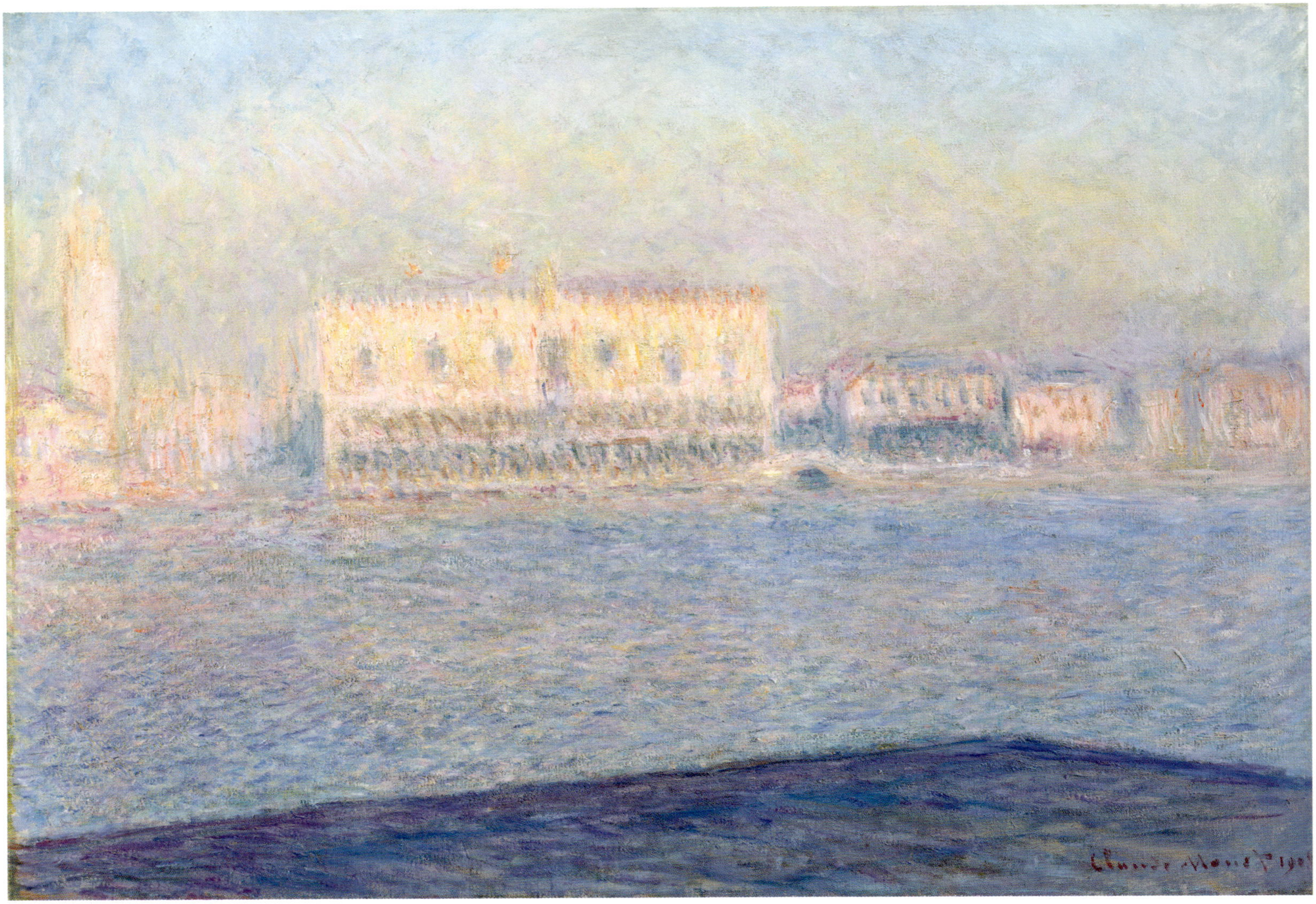

plate 16—Claude Monet, *The Palazzo Ducale Seen from San Giorgio Maggiore*, 1908, oil on canvas, 25¾ × 36½ in., The Metropolitan Museum of Art

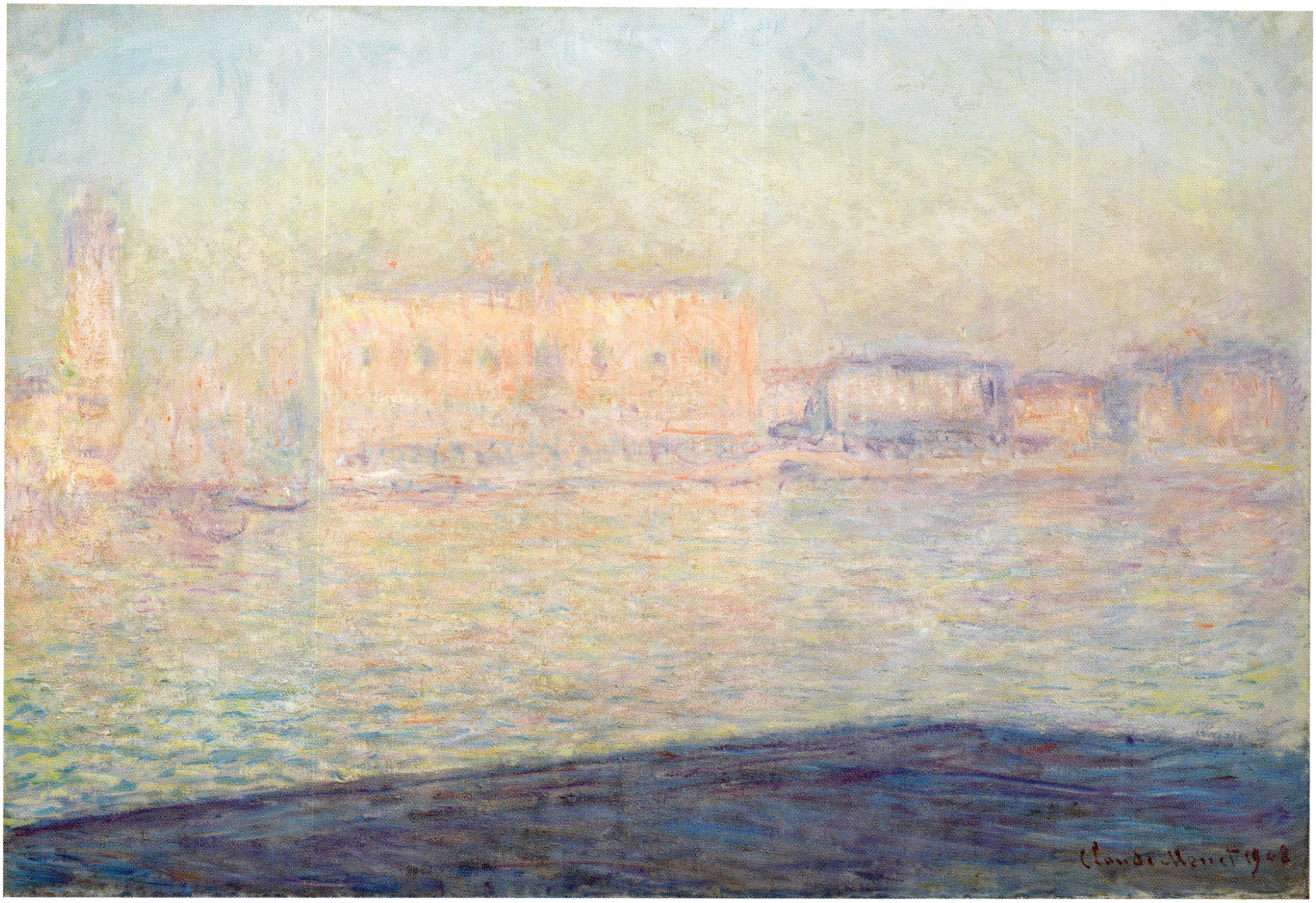

plate 17—Claude Monet, *The Palazzo Ducale Seen from San Giorgio Maggiore*, 1908, oil on canvas, $25\frac{7}{8} \times 36\frac{1}{4}$ in., private collection

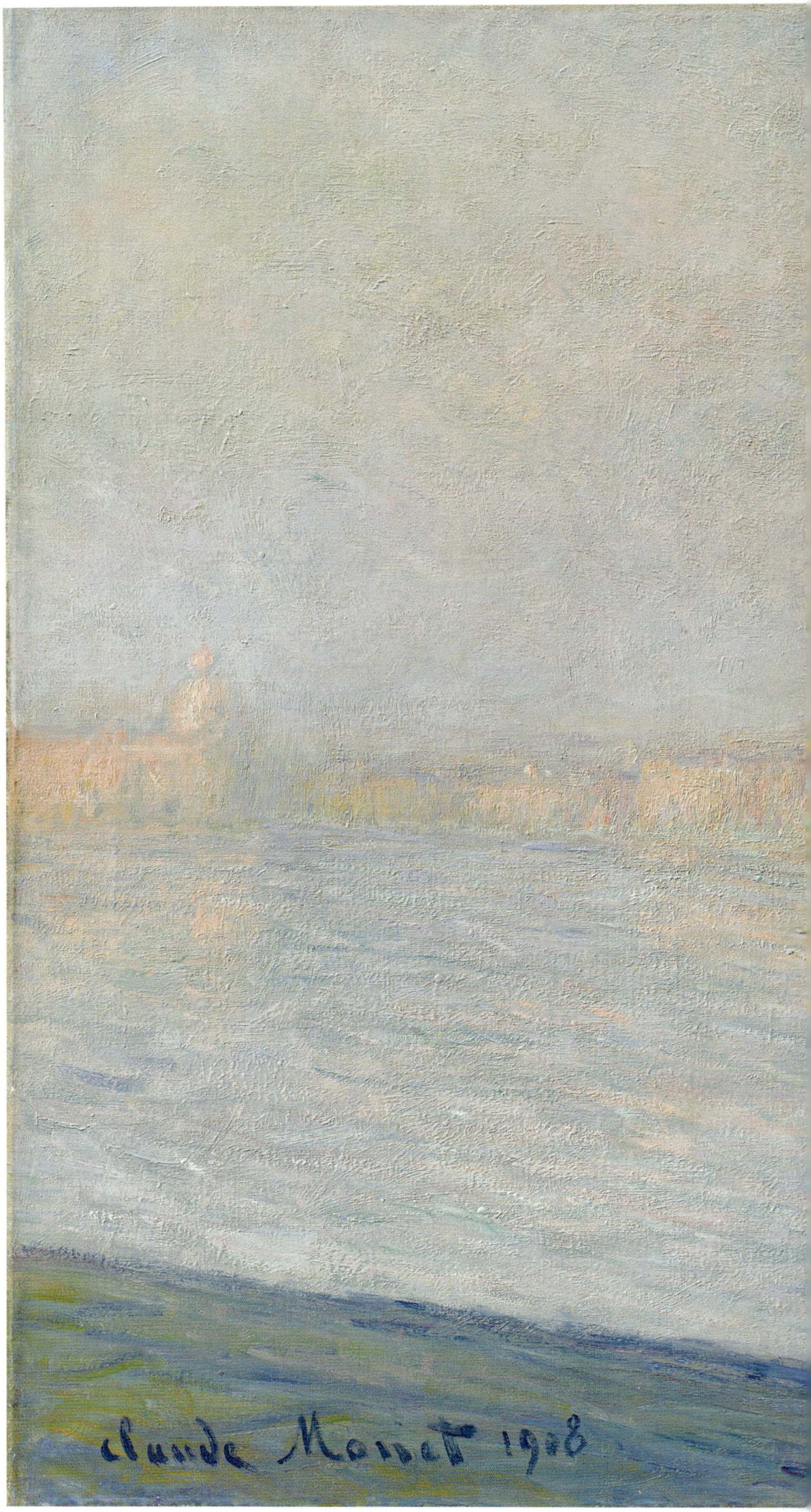
Claude Monet 1908

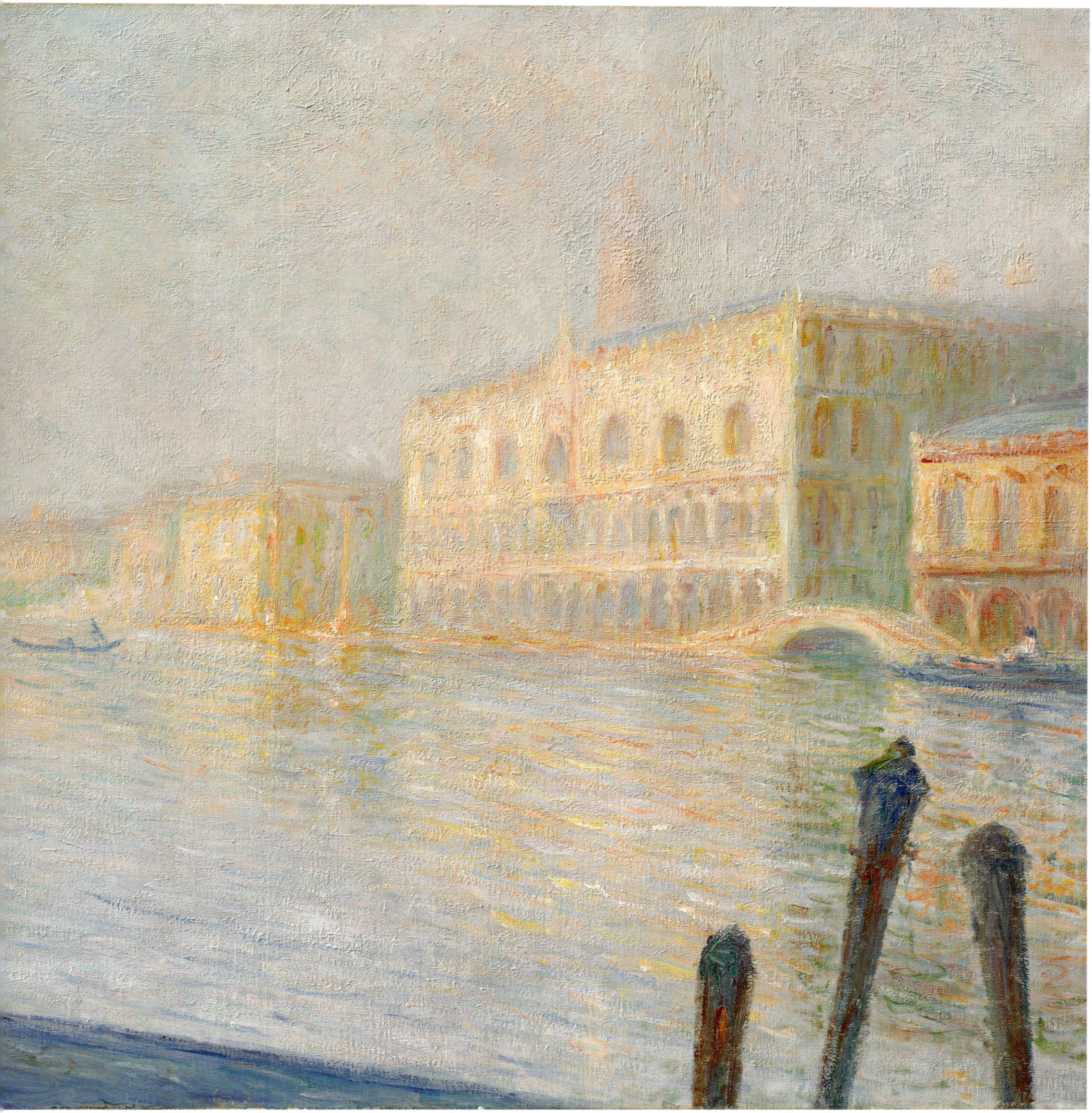

plate 20—Claude Monet, *The Palazzo Ducale*, 1908, oil on canvas, 22⅔ × 36 ¼ in., Hasso Plattner Collection

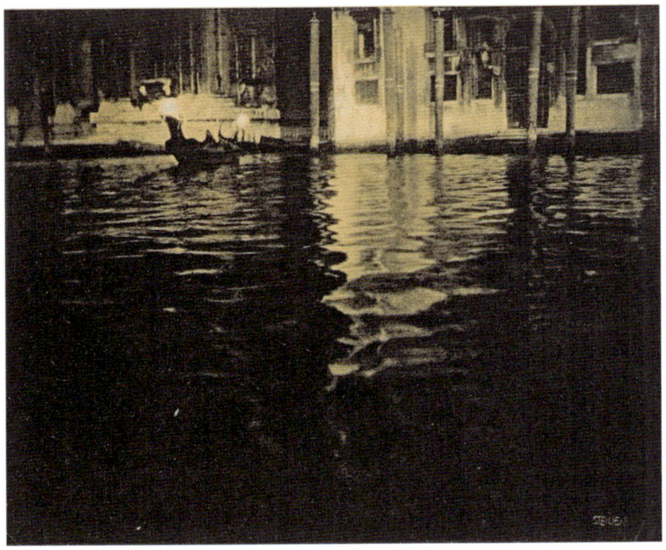

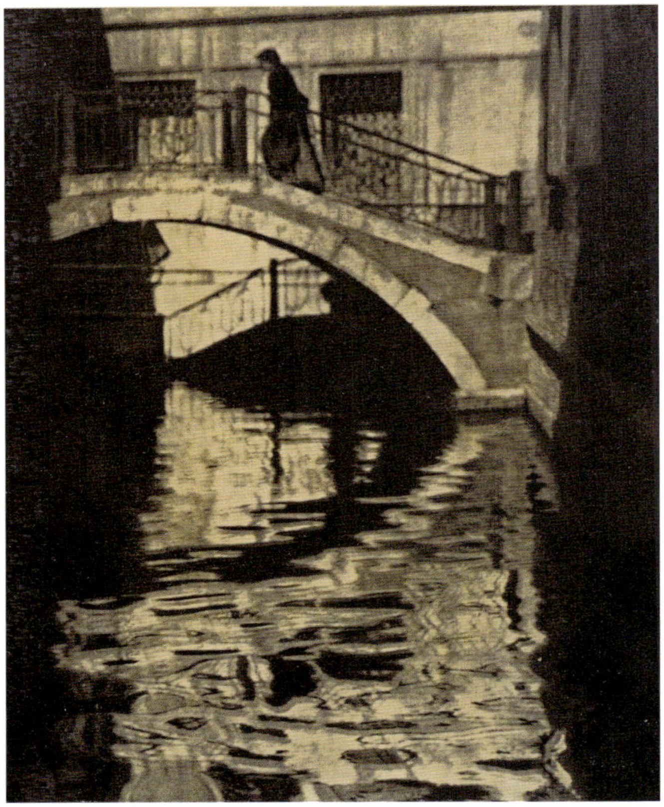

fig. 63—Edward Steichen, *Late Afternoon, Venice*, 1907, published in *Camera Work*, No. 42/43, 1913, photograph, bound volume, Brooklyn Museum Libraries and Archives

fig. 64—Alvin Coburn, *The White Bridge, Venice*, 1906, published in *Camera Work*, No. 21, 1908, photograph, bound volume, Brooklyn Museum Libraries and Archives

blocked another day by oil tankers, he and Alice visited the nearby island of Chioggia instead. Monet shared this dislike of tankers and other signs of contemporary life—like the vaporetto, which first began plying the lagoon waters in 1881—with John Ruskin, who railed against encroachments of his beloved Venetian stones: in place of "the painted sails of the fishing boats... the development of civilization now only brings black steam tugs, to bear the people of Venice to the bathing-machines of Lido, covering their Ducal Palace with soot and consuming its sculptures with sulphurous acid."[79]

The quietude and depopulation of Monet's Venetian imagery were not new. Dwindling since the late 1880s, human figures had essentially disappeared from Monet's landscapes by the late 1890s. At the same time, mysterious and allusive qualities began to be more frequently ascribed to his scenes. His ethereal paintings of Venice particularly lent themselves to subjective responses that were themselves directly or indirectly informed by the pervasive tradition of conjuring Venice as a symbol of melancholy and romantic decay. This was the place where, according to Lord Byron, "silent rows the songless gondolier; / Her palaces are crumbling to the shore, / And music meets not always now the ear: / Those days are gone—but Beauty still is here."[80] Ruskin famously described it as "still left for our beholding in the final period of her decline: a ghost upon the sands of the sea, so weak—so quiet,—so bereft of all but her loveliness, that we might well doubt, as we watched her faint reflection in the mirage of the lagoon, which was the City, and which the Shadow."[81] And for Thomas Mann, whose novella *Death in Venice* was published the same year Monet's Venice paintings debuted in Paris, its black gondolas were like coffins, equated with the finality of "death itself, the bier and solemn rites and last soundless voyage!"[82]

Monet translated the city "in the manner of an inner dream," as a "gloomy environment where the heavy waters eternally reflect in their depths vaporous and distant palaces." He was a poet who "must have felt the very soul of this queen of the Adriatic vibrate within him, mysterious, beautiful, and stinking beneath the jewels in which she dresses."[83] For Geffroy, Monet's lagoon city was a mournful, uninhabited place,

> *where the decor of ten centuries takes on a melancholy and mysterious aspect under the luminous veils that envelop it. The lapping water ebbs and flows, passing back and forth around the palazzi, as if to dissolve these wrecks of history... carrying away and drowning in its reflections all the dead splendors and all the abolished vanity. The serene magnificence of nature reigns alone in those parts of the landscape where the bustling city of pleasure is seen from far enough away that one believes in the enchantment of a dead city under the sun, where nothing is alive except the swift wake of the gondolas, skimming the water like black swallows.*[84]

The painter Walter Sickert also found the emptiness and stillness of Monet's Venice compelling: "It is very modern. The ghost of one gondola hurrying to the traghetto, but the rest, with the marionettes and the bautti [masks] have been put away in their boxes. The modern painter offers us the austere consolation

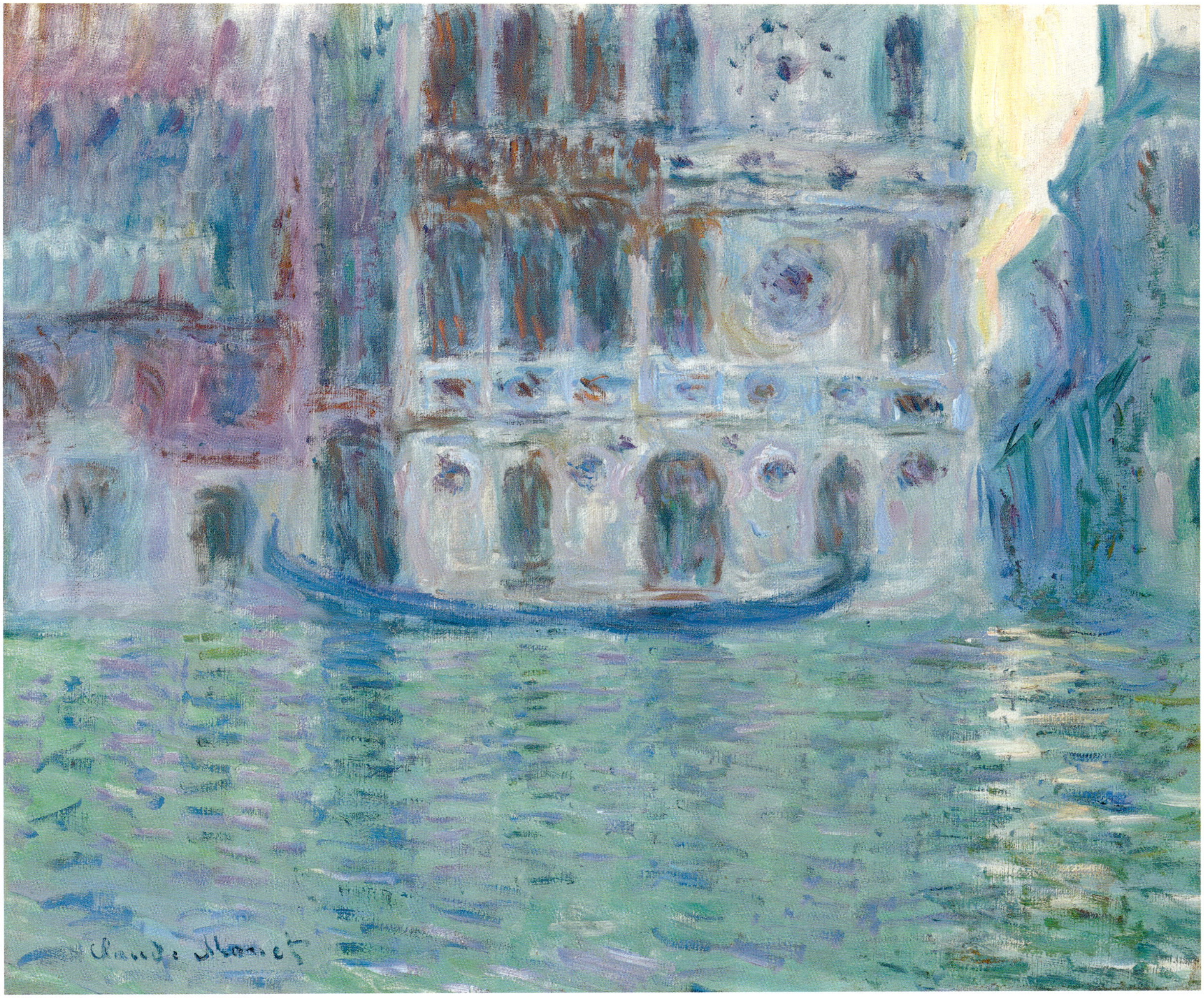

plate 22—Claude Monet, *The Palazzo Dario*, 1908, oil on canvas, 22×25⅔ in., private collection

plate 25—Claude Monet, *The Rio della Salute*, 1908, oil on canvas, 31⁹⁄₁₀ × 25⅔ in., Hasso Plattner Collection

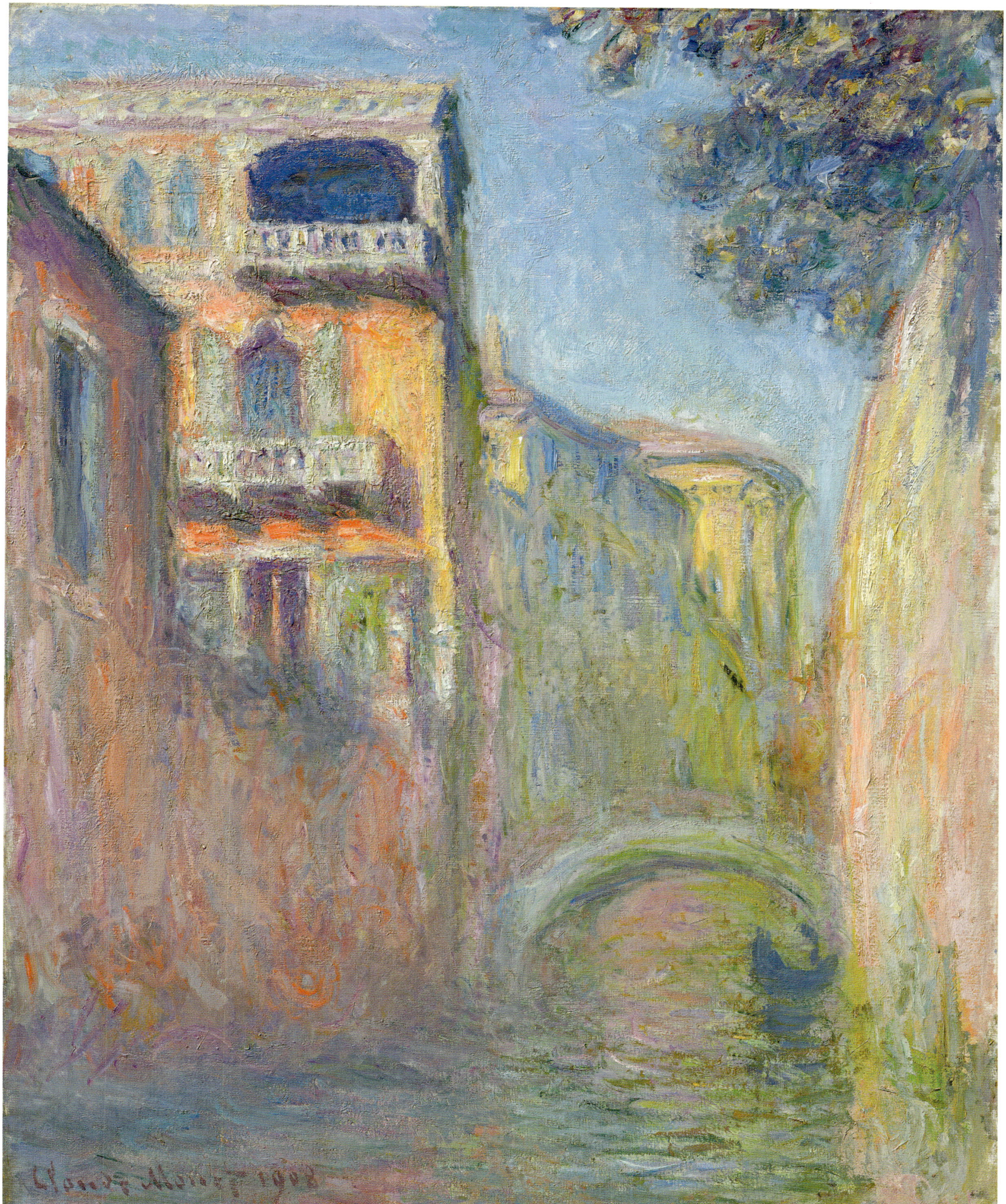

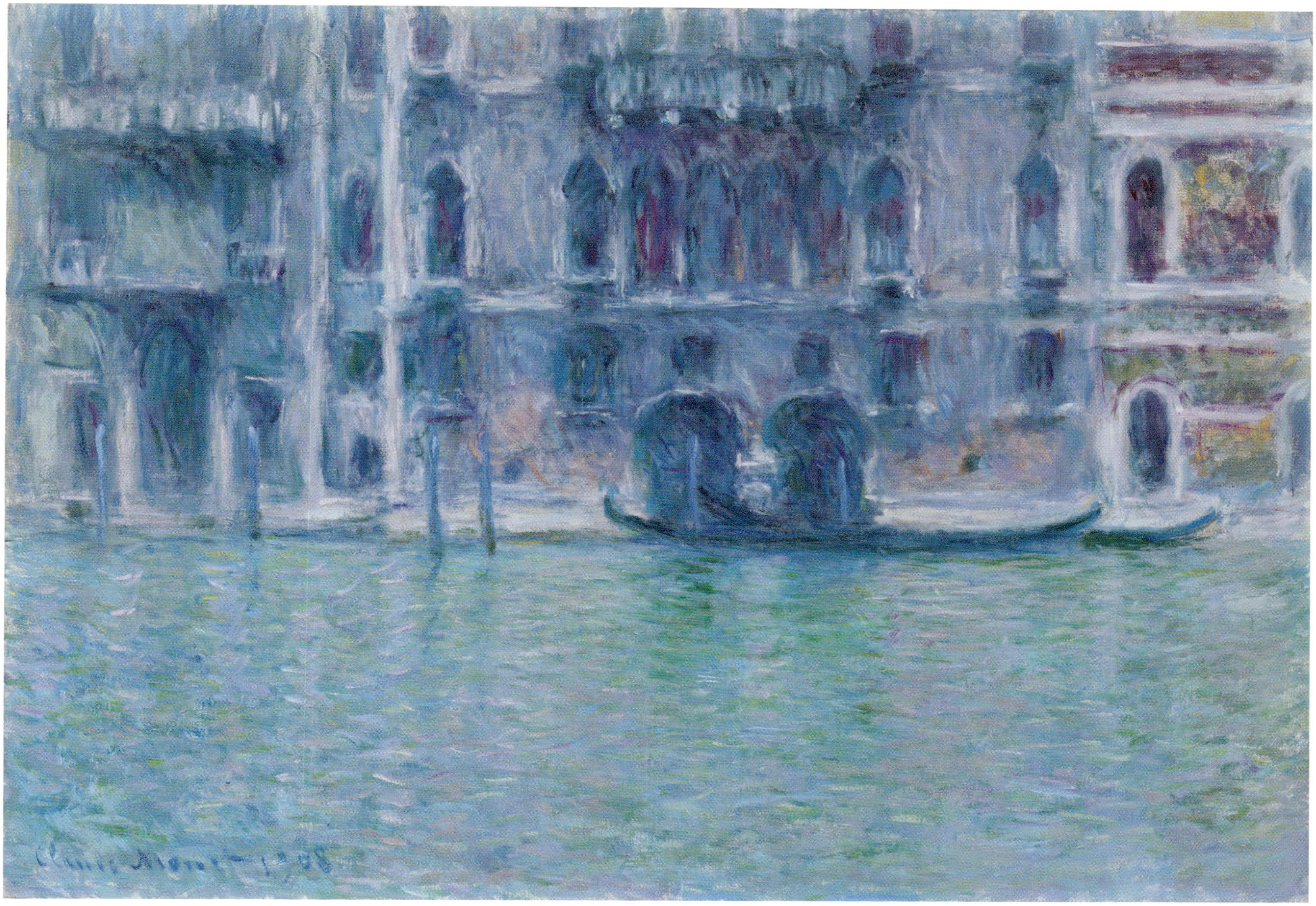

plate 28—Claude Monet, *The Palazzo da Mula*, 1908, oil on canvas, 26⅛ × 36¾ in., private collection

most elementary rules of painting, if there are any. In short, I let a good many mistakes show through when fixing my sensations. It will always be the same and this is what makes me despair. Thank you for your great and loyal friendship and trust in the no less loyal friendship of your old Claude Monet.[114]

But a month later, Monet insisted to Geffroy, "I was right, despite my good friends: these Venices are pitiful and I would have done better to keep them as a precious souvenir."[115] He did keep at least one—a Palazzo Dario canvas that he requested from the Bernheim-Jeune brothers and which can be seen in photographs at Giverny in 1913 and 1920 (figs. 82 and 106).[116]

Was Monet's assessment of his paintings correct? Should it inform how they are considered today? He offered no specifics and did not criticize any of them individually or compare them unfavorably to other of his works. For him, the Venice paintings represented his tremendous loss and dashed hopes for what might have been if Alice had lived, and they had been able to return together to that enchanted city to revisit the sensations that had so captivated him. One of the many critics who admired the Venetian works acknowledged that Monet "visibly executed these paintings in a state of anxiety."[117] What must be taken into account is not just Monet's opinion of them as paintings, but that he would only ever see them through the *envelope* of his tears.

—

I'm very sad that I'll soon have to leave this unique light.
It is so very beautiful, but we must resign ourselves
to the inevitable.... I comfort myself with the thought that
I'll come back next year... But what a shame I didn't come
here when I was a younger man, when I was full
of daring!... Still... I have spent some delightful hours here,
almost forgetting that I am now an old man.
{ Claude Monet to Gustave Geffroy, December 7, 1908 }

Monet's Venetian sojourn interrupted and replenished the increasingly immersive vision of his *Water Lilies* paintings. But what did he mean when he said that his trip had made him see those canvases "with a better eye"? Along with expanses of scintillating, reflective water, he encountered something else in Venice that may have affected his thinking. The concept of displaying his water lily paintings in a room as a single, encompassing panorama seems to have emerged around 1897 and then become stronger in 1909. He was likely aware of large-scale popular entertainment panorama installations and would have been familiar with the decorated public spaces of Paris.[118] But the encompassing, densely painted architectural settings he encountered in Venice—although entirely different in form and content from his own work—cannot help but have fed his imagination. When the couple first arrived in Venice, they "admired some superb Tintorettos." Alice did not say which ones, but most likely they saw the immense, multipart painting cycles at the Scuola Grande di San Rocco and in the Palazzo Ducale (figs. 81, 89, and 90).[119] In 1924, Marc Elder wrote that Monet recalled seeing in

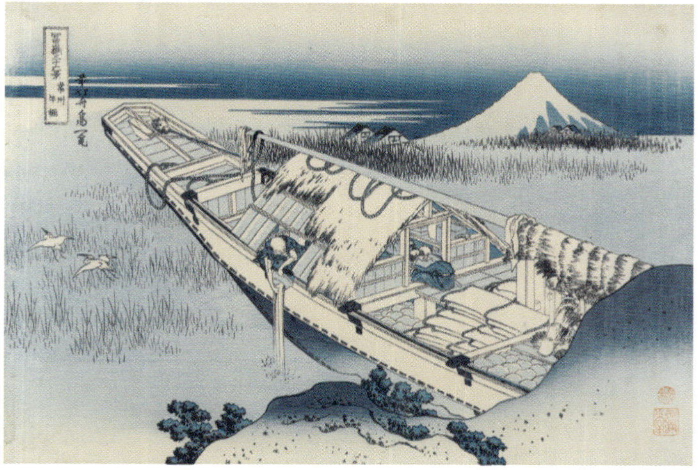

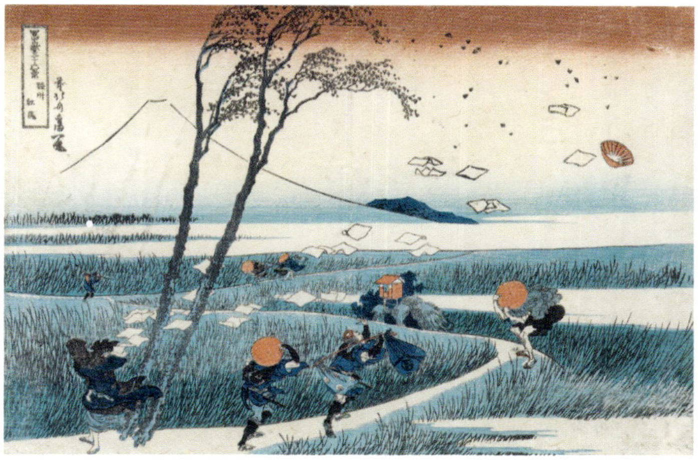

fig. 79—Katsushika Hokusai, *View of Mount Fuji from a Boat at Ushibori* from the series *Thirty-Six Views of Mount Fuji*, 1834, color woodblock print on paper, 10⅜ × 15¼ in., Brooklyn Museum

fig. 80—Katsushika Hokusai, *Ejiri in Suruga Province*, from the series *Thirty-Six Views of Mount Fuji*, c. 1830–31, color woodblock print on paper, 9 9/16 × 14 5/16 in., Brooklyn Museum

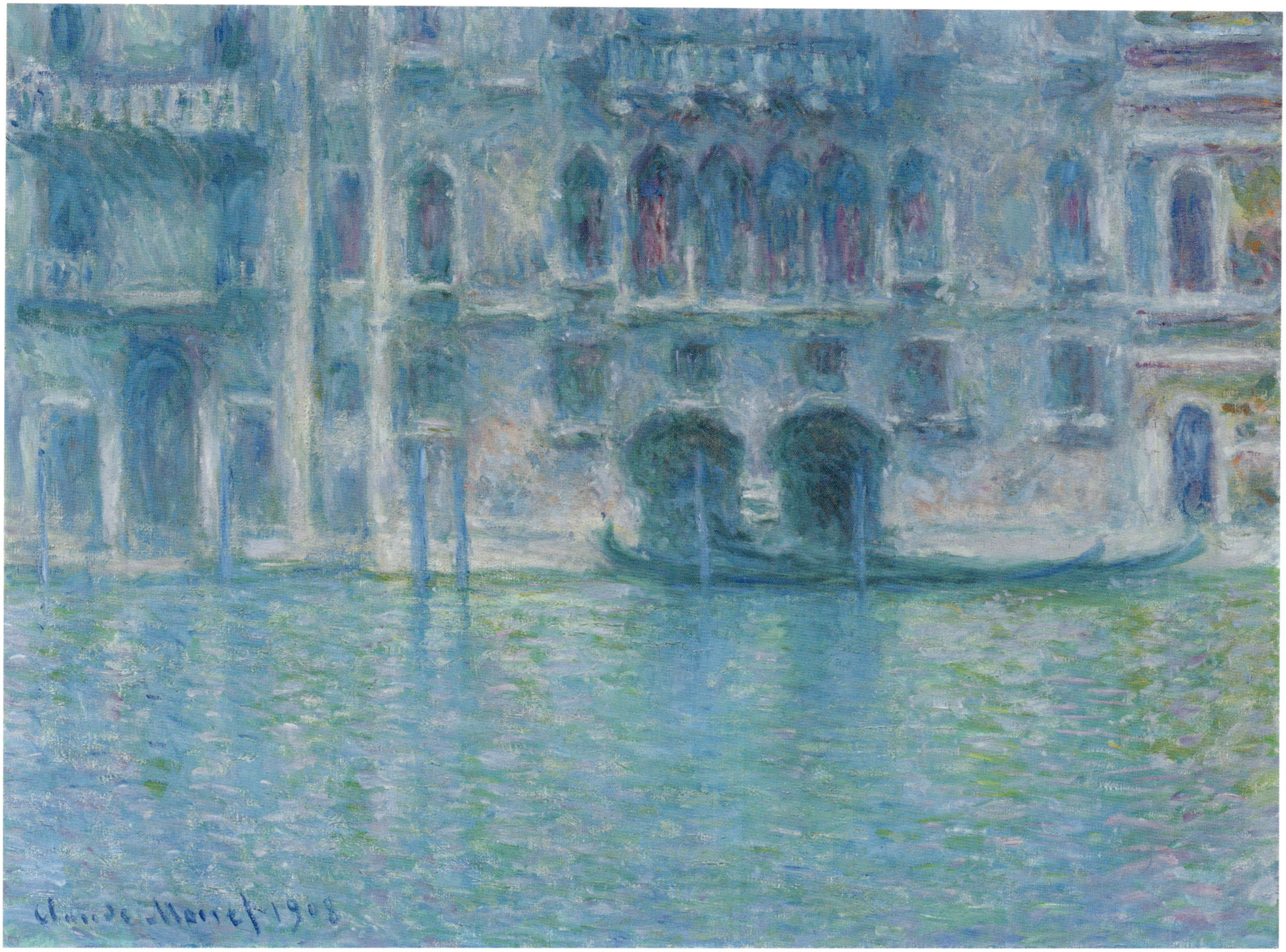

plate 29—Claude Monet, *The Palazzo da Mula, Venice*, 1908, oil on canvas, 24 3/16 × 31 11/16 in., National Gallery of Art

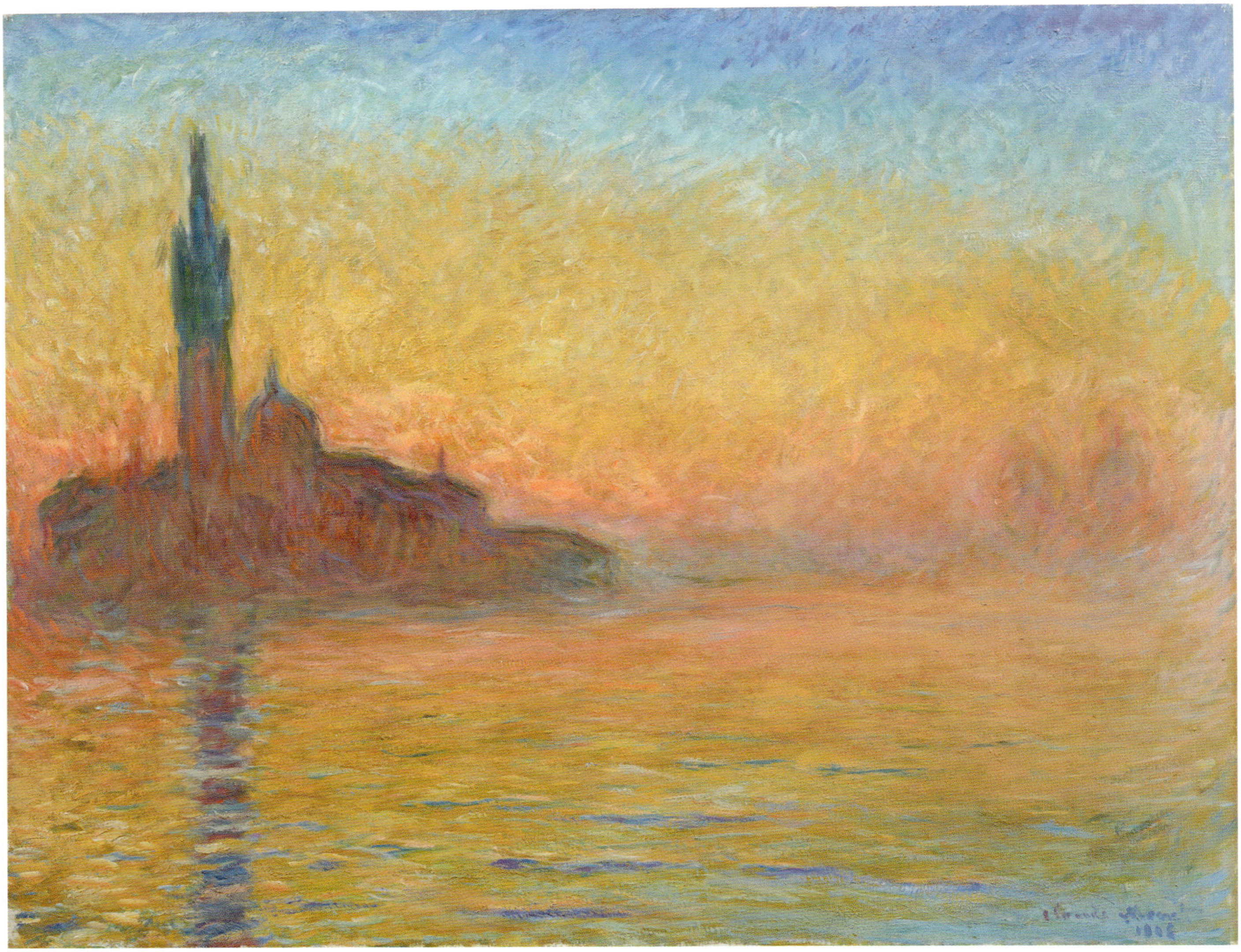

plate 32—Claude Monet, *Twilight, Venice*, c. 1908, oil on canvas, 28 ¾ × 36⅖ in., Artizon Museum

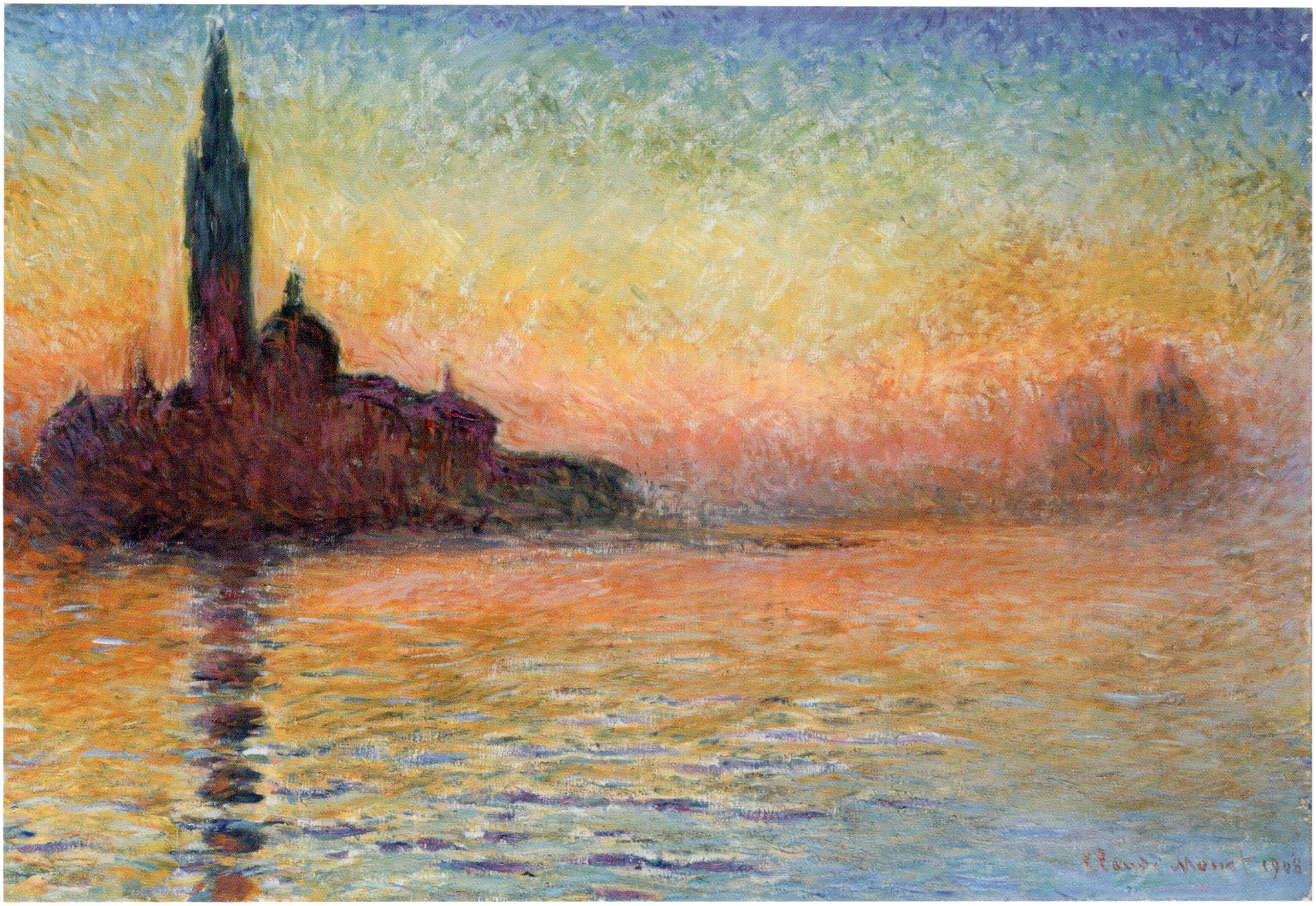

plate 33—Claude Monet, *San Giorgio Maggiore, Twilight*, 1908, oil on canvas, 25×36 in., Amgueddfa Cymru

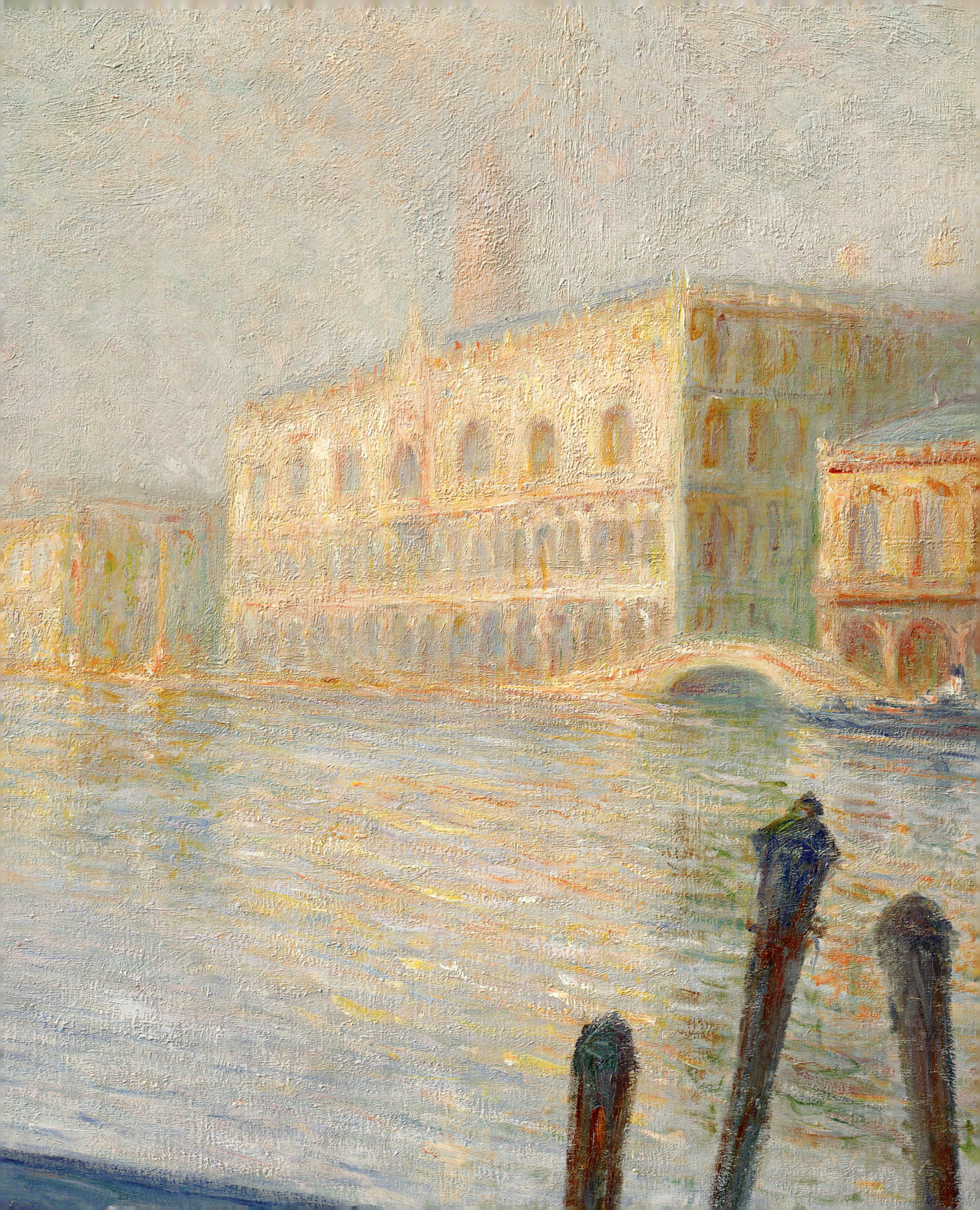

VENICE IN THE ERA OF MONET

Elena Marchetti

VENICE WAS "MILD AND BRIGHT" IN THE FALL of 1908, when Claude Monet arrived.[1] The autumn season, though not frequently documented in painting, had long stirred the imagination of poets. In his poem "Late Autumn in Venice," Rainer Maria Rilke remarked on the "radiant and deadly" wind of Venice.[2] At the first Venice Biennale, in 1895, Gabriele D'Annunzio offered his "Allegory of Autumn" as a tribute to the city,[3] and Henri de Régnier called autumnal Venice "the Venice I prefer, the Venice of cool and brightly lit days."[4]

Alice Monet's letters from the period make frequent mention of the weather, and as a landscape painter Claude Monet would have been acutely aware of meteorological conditions. When it rained, or the wind gusted, or it was too cold to work outdoors, Claude considered leaving, she wrote, but then each time the sun shone again, he changed his mind. The observations in Alice's letters are supported by the weather reports that appeared in newspapers at the time. Such reports detail high and low temperatures, atmospheric pressure, the speed and direction of the wind, rainfall, and even how much of the sky was covered in clouds each day, measured in one-tenths.[5] On October 1, 1908, the day the couple arrived in Venice, temperatures were mild, with a low of 14.8°C (58.6°F) and a high of 20°C (68°F). Sunset was at 5:48 p.m., but the temperature remained relatively warm even afterward (17.4°C/63.3°F at 9 p.m.), indeed so warm that the couple embarked upon a gondola ride to Piazza San Marco the evening they arrived from Milan, presumably on the 6:45 p.m. train on the day's schedule.[6] On October 4 the temperature reached 24.2°C (75.6°F) with relative humidity of 49 to 91 percent. This was too warm for Alice's taste. She asked the gondolier to set up the cabin roof "to avoid being made ill by the sun."[7] There were only four days of genuinely bad weather during the sixty-eight

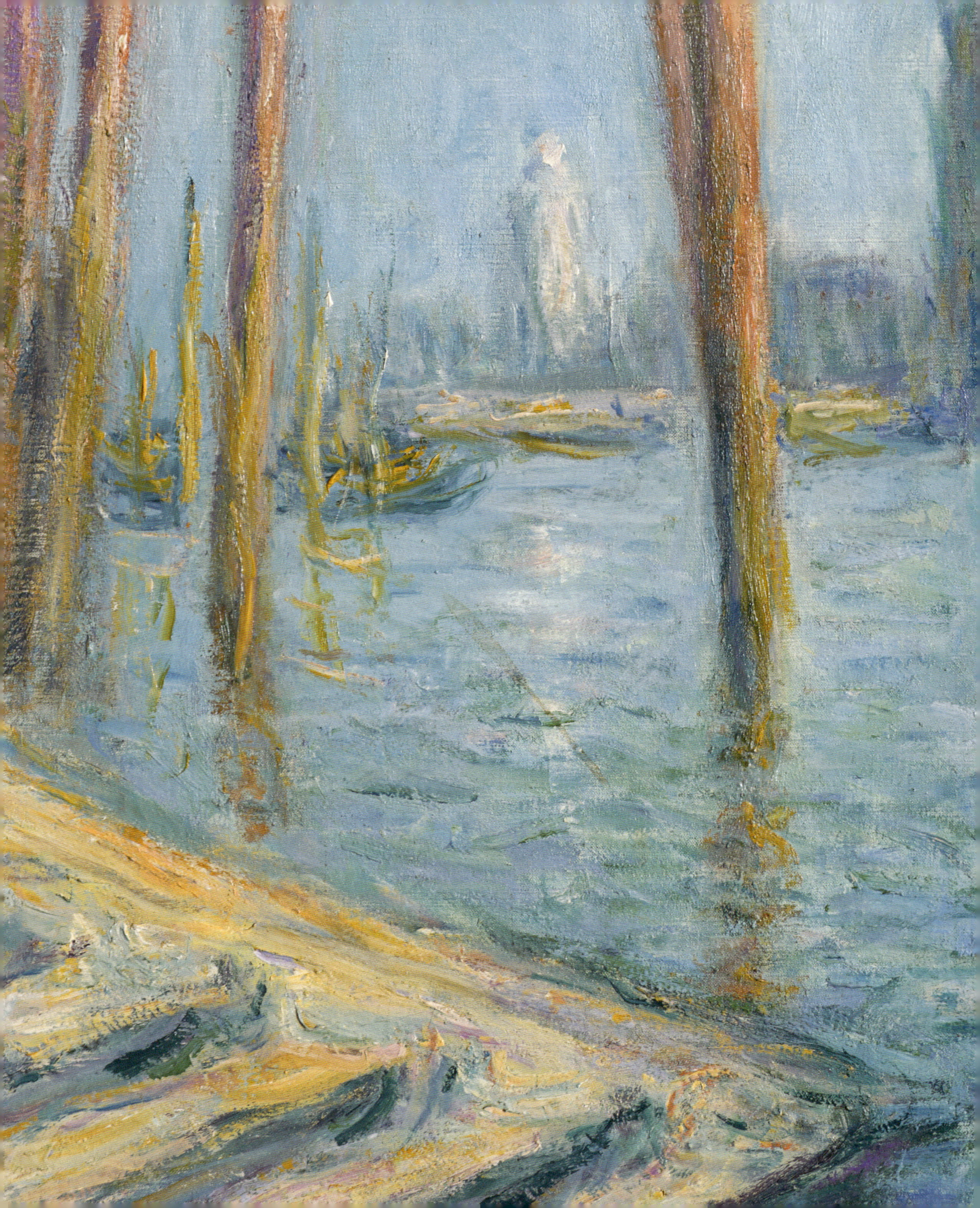

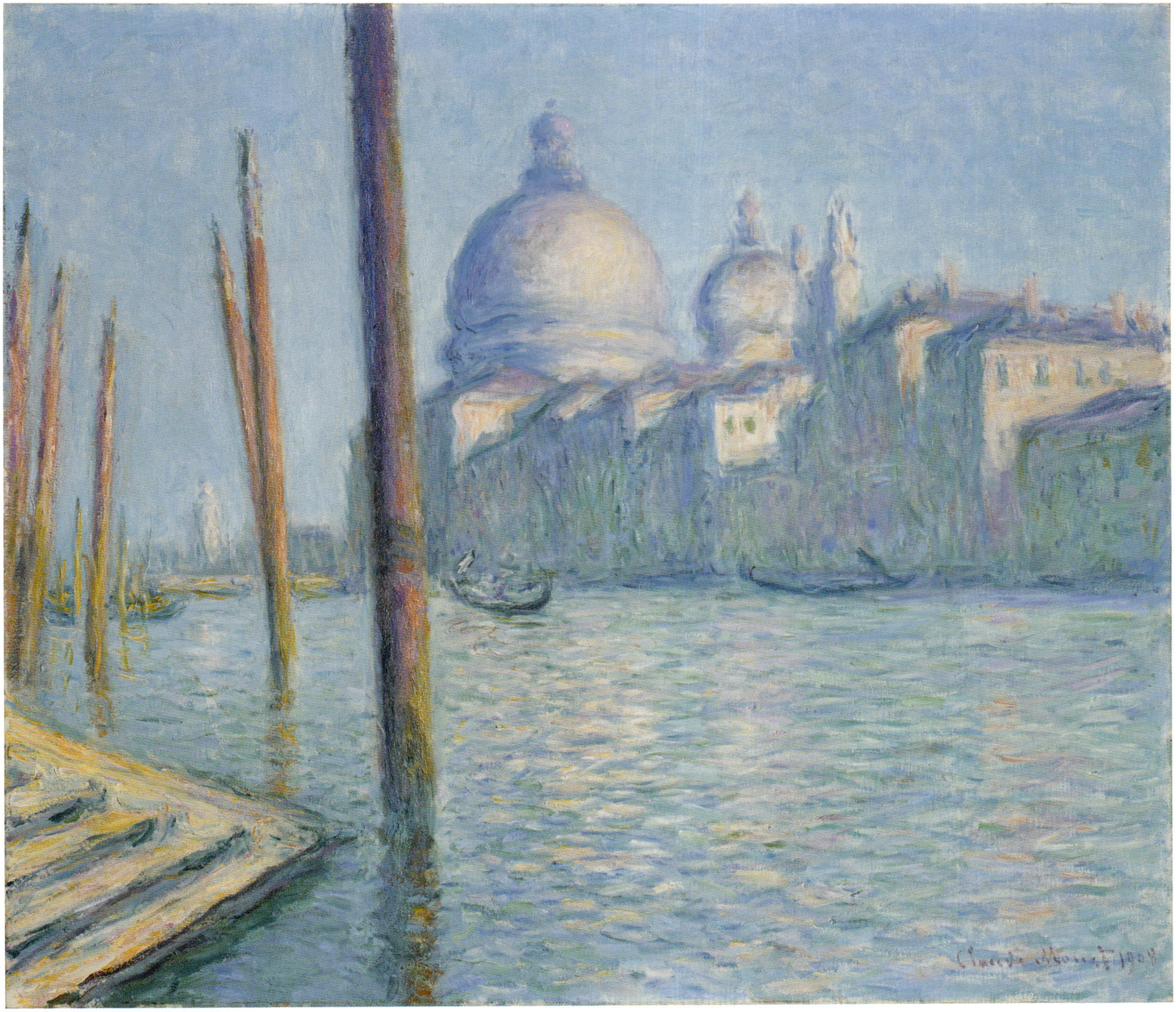

plate 4—Claude Monet, *The Grand Canal*, 1908, oil on canvas, 32⅛ × 36⁷⁄₁₆ in., private collection

it was, where it was," and the work lasted until April 25, 1912. Great strides were made during Monet's visit, as can be seen by comparing two photographs from April (fig. 86) and October 1908 (fig. 87). By the time Monet arrived in Venice, the reconstructed tower had reached 48.17 meters (158 feet) in height.[26]

The bell tower's collapse shined a spotlight on the urgent need to preserve the city's landmarks. A law passed on April 10, 1904, allocated state funds of 300,000 lire (approximately 1.75 million U.S. dollars today), and the city supplemented that contribution. An unprecedented campaign of reinforcement and restoration of buildings got underway.[27] By December 1908, work had been done on the Basilica di San Marco and the churches of Frari, Santi Giovanni e Paolo, San Francesco della Vigna, San Giacomo dall'Orio, Santa Maria della Salute, San Nicolò dei Mendicoli, San Giacomo di Rialto, and San Giorgio in Isola.[28] When Monet went for walks with his wife to visit "plusieurs églises," he must have seen this nearly completed work.[29]

A VAST MUSEUM

Venice was already a tourist destination in Monet's time, though travel was still an elite pursuit. The city's offerings were wide and varied. As early as 1882, Henry James noted, "The Venice of to-day is a vast museum where the little wicket that admits you is perpetually turning and creaking, and you march through the institution with a herd of fellow-gazers."[30] Famous international figures regularly toured the city.[31] More and more guidebooks were published in various languages and for different audiences.[32] Even the pigeons in Piazza San Marco (fig. 25) became famous: in December 1908 a resident of Venice, California—established in 1905 and modeled after its namesake city—imported some of the birds.[33] A ride in a gondola, which Monet took often, cost one franc per hour, though ten hours in a gondola was discounted to six francs.[34]

On October 1, 1908, when Monet arrived in the city, the ticket price to visit the Palazzo Ducale was raised to 1.5 lire, though entry was free on Sundays.[35] The funds collected went to maintain Venice's signature buildings.[36] A visitor at the time was admitted to the institutional rooms and the prisons, as is still the case today. But back then, visitors also were admitted to the Museo Archeologico in the Doge's Apartment (fig. 88). The Sala del Maggior Consiglio still contains the cabinets from the Biblioteca Marciana that John Singer Sargent (fig. 89) saw on his visit, but later work revealed the magnificent fourteenth-century fresco by Guariento di Arpo, *The Coronation of the Virgin*, on the back wall.[37] Damaged by fire in 1577, the fresco had been covered fifteen years later by a huge canvas, the famed *Paradiso* by Jacopo Tintoretto and his workshop. When cracks were discovered in the wall, the Tintoretto was temporarily relocated to the center of the room, where it was protected by a grate. (fig. 90) Monet was therefore able to observe it up close in a way that few ever had.[38] To allow repairs to be made, the Guariento fresco was detached from the wall and placed in the Sala dell'Armamento, where it remains today. When Monet was in Venice, that room, then the library director's office, also boasted a Paolo Veronese ceiling (fig. 91) from the church of San Nicolò della Lattuga ai Frari.[39]

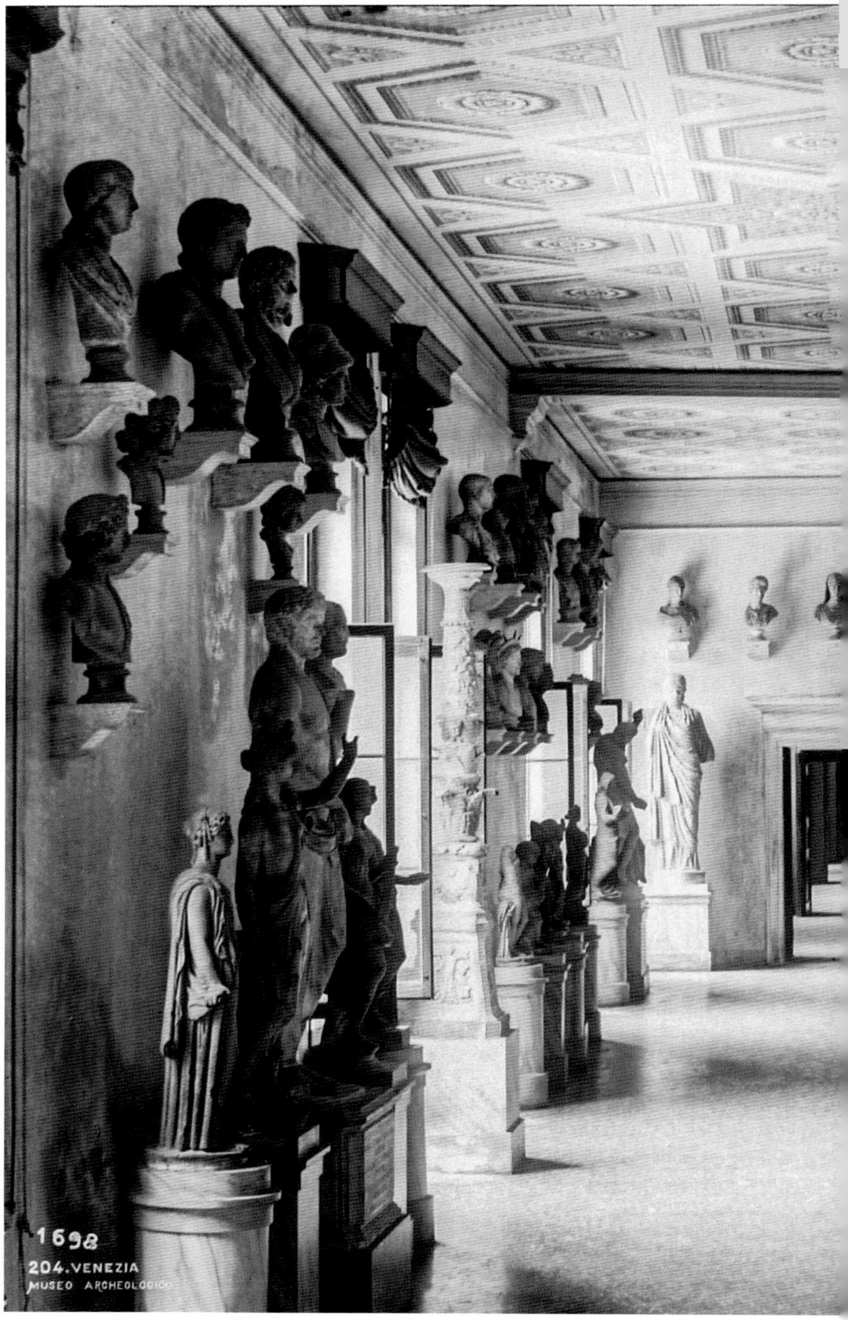

fig. 88—Carlo Naya photograph of the Museo Archeologico in the Doge's Apartment in the Palazzo Ducale, late 19th c., Palazzo Ducale

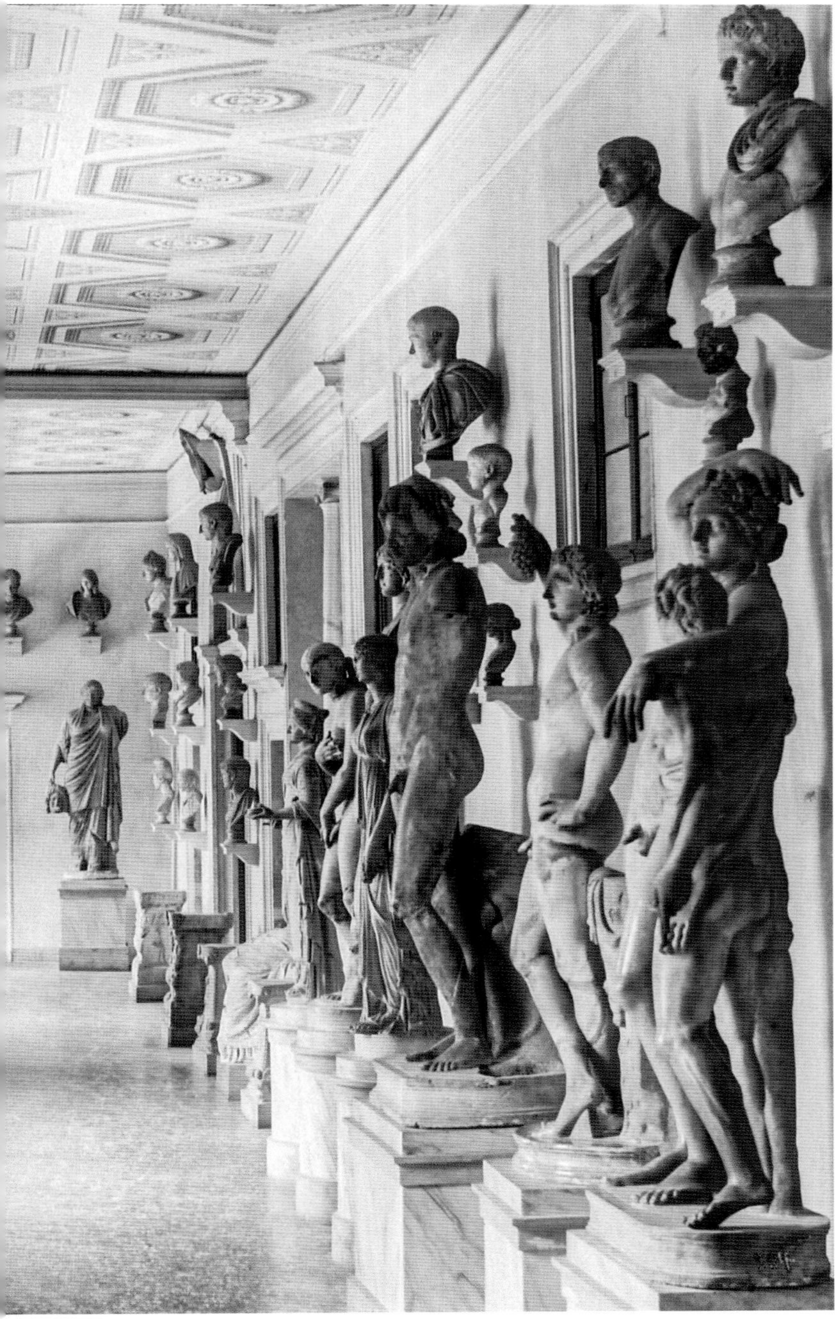

On one of their first tours around the city, the Monets "admired some superb Tintorettos"—very likely those in the Scuola Grande di San Rocco. (fig. 81)[40] Guidebooks of the era suggested visiting San Rocco only when natural light was cooperating. Indeed, in his 1909 travelogue, *Italian Hours*, Henry James cautioned, "Incurable blackness is settling fast upon all of [the pictures], and they frown at you across the sombre splendour of their great chambers like gaunt twilight phantoms of pictures."[41] October 5, 1908, was a sunny day.[42] This was fortunate, because an electric lighting system would not be installed at the Scuola Grande until 1937, based on a design by Mariano Fortuny.[43] The Monets also had a chance to appreciate Tintoretto masterpieces in the Sala Superiore: *The Miracle of the Loaves and Fishes*, *The Adoration of the Shepherds*, and *The Last Supper*, which the painter Giovanni Zennaro had just finished restoring in 1907 and 1908.

Some of the museums that could be visited in Monet's time are no longer accessible today: Palazzo Vendramin Calergi, Palazzo Labia, Collezione Giovanelli, and Museo Donà delle Rose. The Museo Correr was then located in the Fontego dei Turchi, as can be seen in the photos that document Prince August Wilhelm of Prussia touring the city (fig. 93). The prince, who had a deep interest in archaeology, visited during his honeymoon in Venice from October 27 to November 2, 1908.[44] The Giandomenico Tiepolo frescoes from Villa Zianigo were moved to the museum in August of that year. Today they are housed at Ca' Rezzonico.[45]

It is valid to wonder what materials Monet used in Venice. Alice noted that he had ordered canvases from Paris, but they were late in arriving, which stopped him from beginning to paint on October 7.[46] A notebook bears an elegant Liberty-style label from Emilio Aickelin's store (fig. 62) near Hotel Britannia at 2378-2038 Calle Larga XXII Marzo. There are also Emilio Aickelin labels on *San Giorgio Maggiore, Twilight* (pl. 33) and the original canvas for *Venice, Palazzo Dario* (pl. 21).[47] Emilio Aickelin's store sold a variety of supplies.[48] Emilio and his wife, Berta, both German, started the business, which was followed by Ars—owned by Emilio and Frieda Aickelin and operational from 1955 to 1971—where Giorgio de Chirico bought supplies.[49]

MUSIC, LITERATURE, AND ART: VENICE AS INTERNATIONAL CULTURAL HUB

Claude Monet and his wife traveled to Venice at the invitation of Mary Hunter. The artist and Hunter had met when Monet was in London in 1900; their mutual friend John Singer Sargent introduced them.[50] Sargent's portrait of Hunter was exhibited at the Biennale of 1907.[51] Sargent was a key player in the network of high-profile figures who transformed Venice into an international cultural hub in those years.[52] He was close with Ariana and Daniel Curtis, who were Bostonians and owners of Palazzo Barbaro (fig. 12). Though Sargent was said to be a distant cousin of the Curtis family, it was their shared cultural interests that drew them to each other beginning in the 1880s. In Paris, Sargent met Ralph Curtis, the Curtises' son and a painter himself. Sargent was a frequent guest at the lively literary and artistic salons hosted at Palazzo Barbaro, alongside such guests as Henry James, Robert

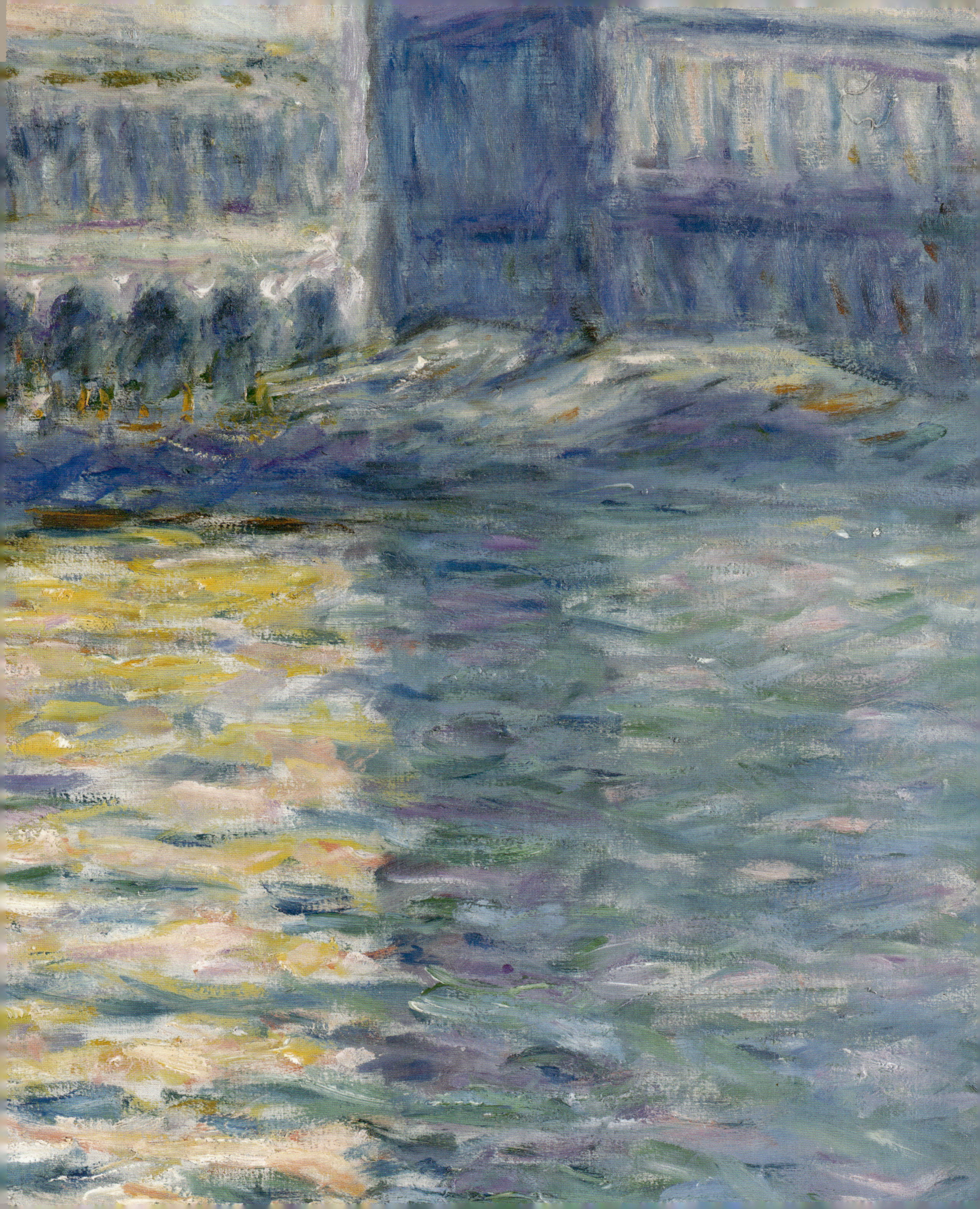

fig. 91—*L'Adorazione dei Magi* by Paolo Veronese in the Palazzo Ducale, photographed early 20th c., Museo Correr

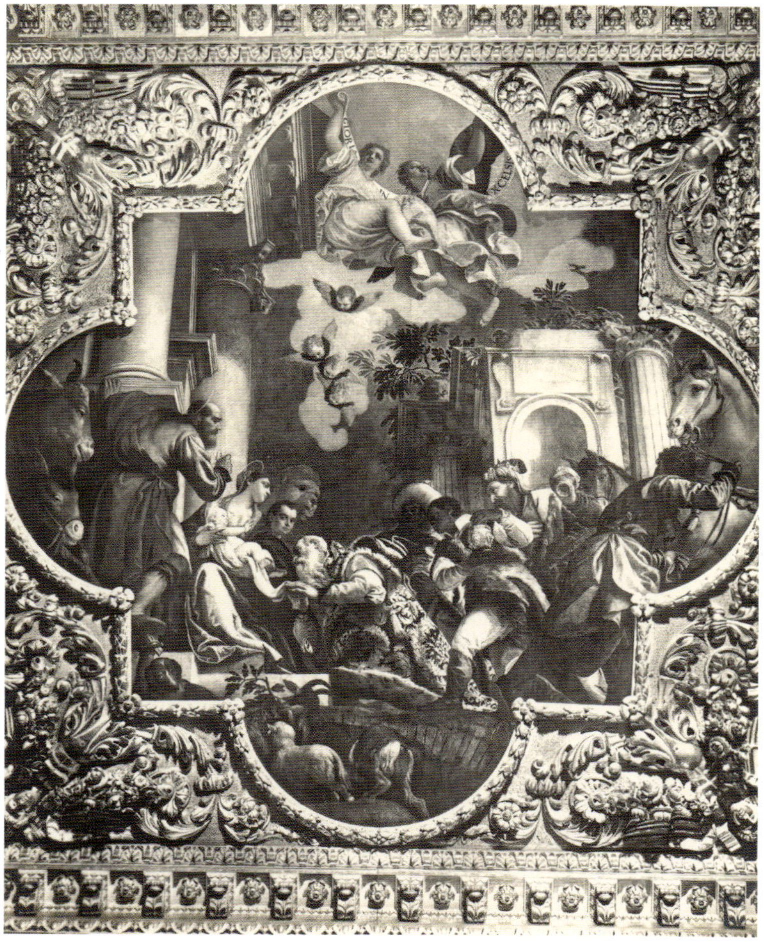

colored glass in Venice's streetlights is famous, few know the origin of this hue.[76] The turn of the century saw the introduction of the Auer incandescent gas mantle, which made electric light brighter without increasing consumption. This advancement was regarded warily at first. In 1907, the mayor of Venice protested in the pages of *Il Gazzettino* that "the artificial and blinding Auer light destroys the effects of the moonlight and wipes away the charm of Venetian nights."[77] In order to defend the beauty of Venice, the overly white and intense light cast would need to be softened. Various chemical experiments were conducted: when the mantle was soaked in sodium salts, the light was more yellow; potassium salts made it violet; lithium turned it reddish; and copper resulted in green.[78] In April 1908, the Società Civile per l'Illuminazione a Gaz announced that "the candelabra on the Caffè Florian side of Piazza San Marco" had been replaced with new gold-tinted mantles.[79] This was the light that Monet admired on his evening walks. The mantles would be replaced in September 1909 with manganese salt–soaked versions.[80] When electric lighting was installed, the glassmakers of Murano were instructed to maintain the previous color by creating the pink glass that still graces the outdoor lights in Venice today.[81]

Monet experienced a Venice that was undergoing many changes. Rife with contradiction, it was hurtling into a new century. Venice was both modern and eternal, and that is the vision of the city Monet represented in his paintings.

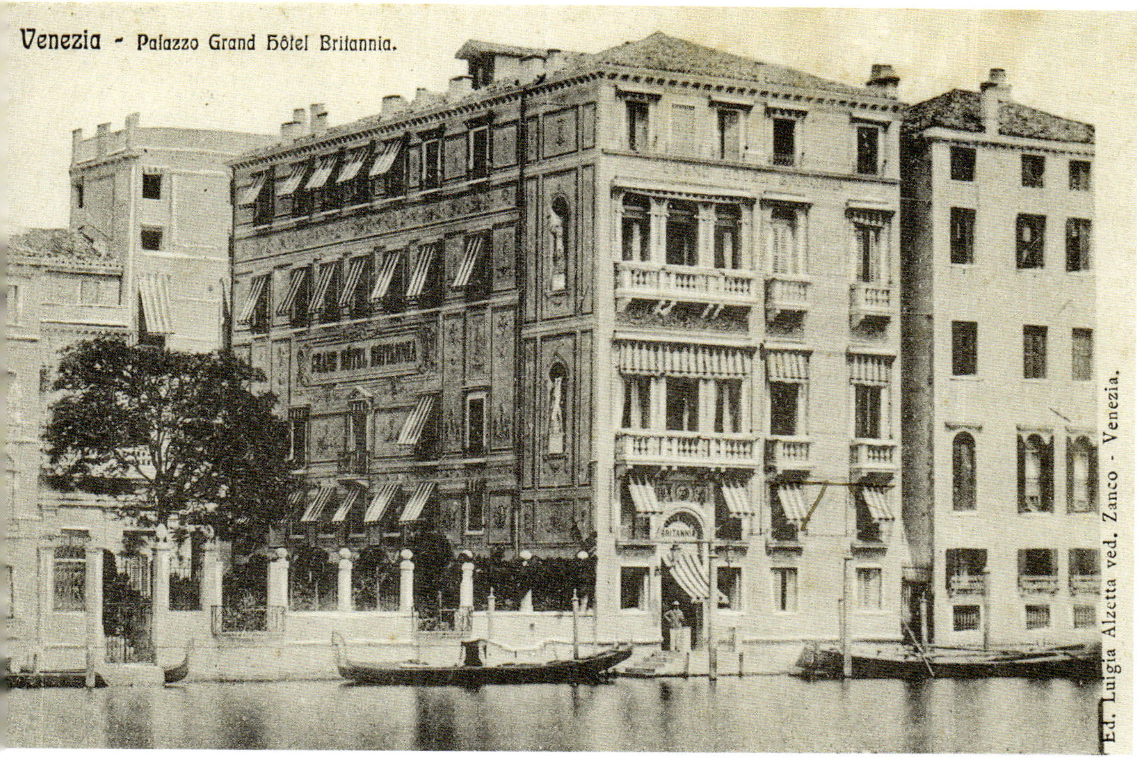

fig. 92—Postcard showing Grand Hotel Britannia sent by Alice Monet to her granddaughter Alice Butler, November 25, 1908, Collection Philippe Piguet

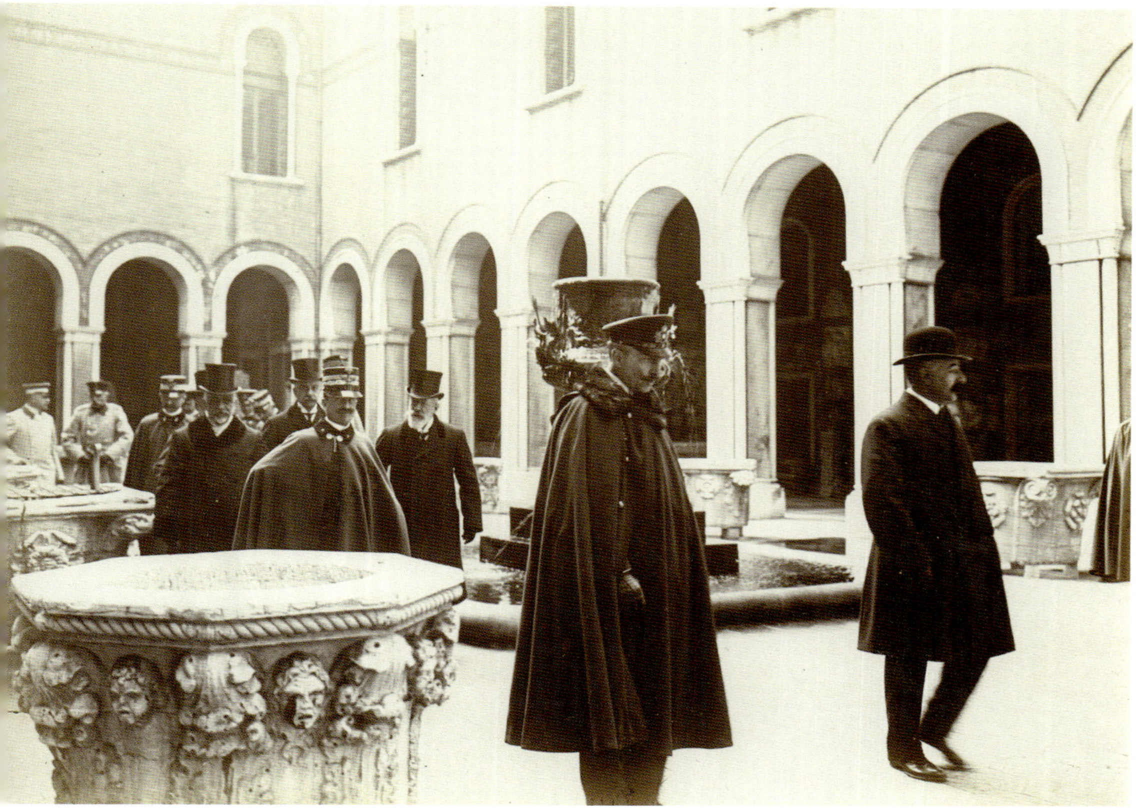

fig. 93—Wilhelm II at the Fondaco dei Turchi in 1908, Museo Fortuny

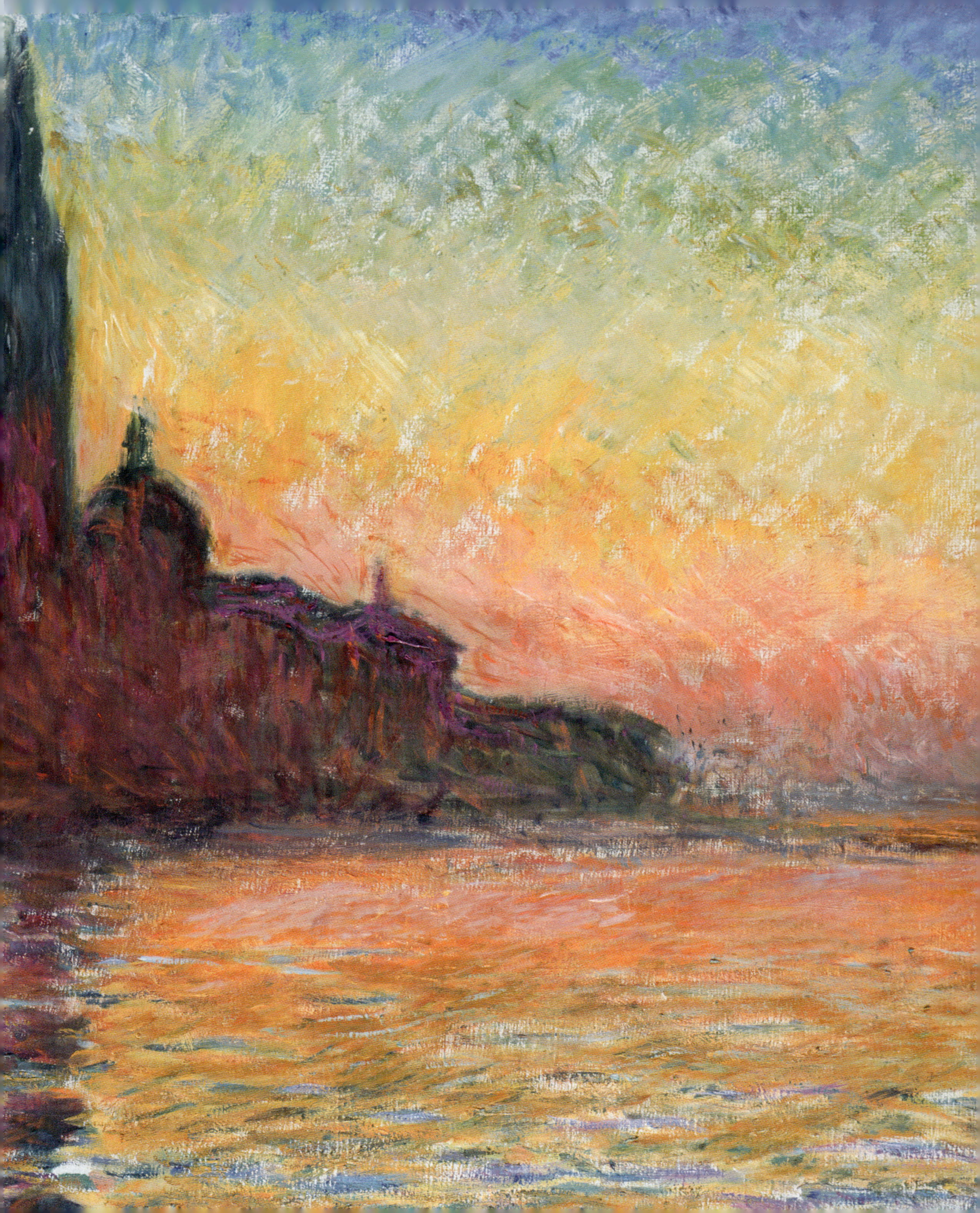

MONET'S VENETIAN HOURS

André Dombrowski

WHEN CLAUDE MONET PAINTED VENICE, critics felt in the late spring of 1912 as the canvases were on display at the Bernheim-Jeune gallery, he made the city disappear. Venice vanished in front of their eyes — *se volatiliser*, to evaporate or to turn vaporous, was one of their favorite and oft-repeated verbs — a city almost entirely unmoored from the usual parameters of the real and any concrete conditions of weather, light, and space.[1] Venice's churches and palaces dissipated within a colorful haze, hovering above their watery reflections as if they were mere projections and evanescent dreams, not actual buildings made of brick and stone. In the twenty-nine works on display, time seemed suspended as well, and the famed Impressionist "instant" was difficult to register and localize with precision. True, the paintings banked as much as any Monet on lending each image a different atmospheric look, but somehow, critics sensed, time was made more transcendent than present and particular.

In this temporal vacuum, Monet created his own metric of chronological and chronometric regularity. It is well known that, though less well understood why, Monet generated one of the most stringent and unforgiving painting schedules he ever employed while in Venice between early October and early December 1908, dividing his day into two-hour intervals of painting the same motif, then moving on. He and Alice got up at 6 a.m., and he was at work starting at 8, every day. This schedule overrode all other markers of time. It was followed more or less on each day of serious work (after an initial phase of touring and settling in) during his two-month stay, and, like any modern schedule, including those of train systems and workspaces, it knew nothing but the clocking of time itself. But why would a painter-tourist like Monet have a need for such orderliness and such a pedantic way of structuring his day, so

lunch, Monet works on the steps of Palazzo Barbaro—then at 3 o'clock on gondolas; we make a tour to admire the setting of the sun and return at 7 p.m."[11] A few days later, on October 17, with the couple now installed at the Grand Hotel Britannia, the schedule had shifted somewhat. As Alice noted in another letter: "At 8 a.m., every day, we find ourselves installed at the first motif until 10 o'clock: we therefore have to get up at 6 a.m.; then another motif from 10 a.m. to noon. From 2 to 4 p.m. in the canal, and from 4 to 6 from our window—you see how our hours are filled and, honestly, I don't know how he does it at his age without tiring."[12] In the few intervening days between palazzo and hotel, the agenda seems only to have hardened, and the two-hour interval became more binding and mandatory. Actual sunrise was irrelevant to this temporal scheme and was replaced with a uniform 6 a.m. start to the day, no matter if that time corresponded to the actual diurnal rhythm and first light. A distinct weather effect did not particularly matter to this schedule either, as long as it occurred within Monet's specific time intervals. When things needed to be packed up as the couple moved on to the next site at, say, 10 a.m. or 4 p.m., the specific effect was interrupted, too, no matter whether it had concluded. By Alice's accounting, natural times were no real match for cultural ones, and certainly no match for the industrial-age scheduling used here that dictated its exacting procedures at the expense of the untrammeled flow of nature and weather.

Pissarro says rightly that Monet had "a fixed appointment with his motifs at the same time each day."[13] At 8 a.m., when Monet started painting, he and Alice found themselves on the platform of the island of San Giorgio Maggiore, visible in the foreground of the paintings, looking over at the Palazzo Ducale, with the campanile the leftmost element in each iteration (pl. 14, 16-18). In a related version, he took a few steps farther to the left and centered the palace a little better within his visual field (pl. 15); in another, he walked down the platform farther to the right, so that the opposite shore appeared at a more diagonal angle (pl. 20). At some point during the later mornings, likely as part of his trip back in the direction of San Marco, Monet painted his three close-up views of the Palazzo Ducale from the perspective of a gondola, the unstable position that vexed him most, given how difficult it was to identify precisely the same viewing spot on the water day after day (pl. 6–8).

From noon until 2 p.m., the Monets took their lunch, and therefore no Venetian scene shows any true midday effect. The precise afternoon schedule is a little more difficult to reconstruct, since it includes a greater variety of motifs. In the earlier afternoons, it appears as if Monet spent some hours making views from Palazzo Barbaro and other positions along the Grand Canal. From here and other vantage points along the canal, he painted the six views of Santa Maria della Salute seen across the canal (pl. 1–5) and created his various views of Venetian palaces (such as Palazzo Contarini Polignac, Palazzo Dario, and Palazzo da Mula; (pl. 21–24, 28–29, and 30–31, respectively). After mid-October, he also painted from, or close to, the Grand Hotel Britannia, probably during the last two-hour shift of his day. Monet was now looking out from his accommodation or walking the short distance toward the Piazzetta San Marco or the platform of the Schiavoni in front of the Palazzo Ducale, looking back to where the day had started, to the island of San Giorgio Maggiore; he made six very similar versions of this view (pl. 9–13). In the initial schedule, it appears, these canvases were started in the late morning, from 10 a.m. to noon, but this likely shifted in the later schedule, as the final paintings seem to register an afternoon light effect, as Daniel Wildenstein has suggested.[14] Given some adaptation, however, this afternoon schedule fits, roughly, with Alice's second description: "From 2 to 4 p.m. in the canal, and from 4 to 6 from our window." Overall, as Pissarro has emphasized, "Monet moved from the point of observation to the point observed" (between San Giorgio Maggiore and San Marco) at least at some point during his long working day.[15] Finally, at the end of some days, Monet walked farther east, roughly to the entrance of Via Garibaldi, in order to paint his two sunset views of San Giorgio Maggiore (pl. 32 and 33). Given that sunset fell outside his usual working hours that ended at 6 p.m., Monet must have decided occasionally to labor in overtime, or perhaps these two paintings were started early during the stay when observing the sunset was still an explicit part of his daily schedule. Of course, we cannot be certain how strictly Monet followed this regimen, and surely it was adapted to the immediate needs of each day, but its existence as a rhetorical and practical tool remains crucial.

The resulting paintings, taken together, evince a curious admixture of temporalities. In general, because of Monet's strict schedule, time seems duplicated from one day to the next, and thus frozen and stilled. Each group has its specific light condition that, no matter the particularity or the haziness of the scene, stands repeated in each. Most often, light streams into the scenes from the right. In each version of Santa Maria della Salute, for instance, the buildings to the church's right are hit by steady afternoon light from the right, especially the side wall of Palazzo Dario (pl. 1–5). The light in every version of the Palazzo Ducale facade, no matter if seen from afar or in close-up, bathes the palace in roughly the same angle of morning light (pl. 6–8 and 14–20). As Pissarro has emphasized, the lighting in each version of the same motif is remarkably stable and repetitive, more like a light switch Monet turned on when he arrived at the preselected hour. But this does not mean time entirely disappears from view. It implies, rather, that time is present as an appointment with a monument, which is not a time outside of time but a modern, touristic version of time, naturalized *as* timeless. Monet scholar Paul Hayes Tucker argued similarly that in Venice, "At one moment [time] could be abandoned or falsified, at another, recovered and affirmed."[16]

Such appointments with monuments, otherwise known as opening hours, were the daily bread of any tourist in Venice and elsewhere. Indeed, in the guidebook to Italy that Monet bought in advance of his trip, the famed *Guide Joanne* for Italy, by Paul Joanne, opening hours are often the first thing one reads about. What is more, this then-newest of guidebooks included a novel kind of section called "emploi du temps," or "best use of time," which gave visitors tips about how to make the most of their precious few days in Venice, creating an early form of a practical, but also profoundly curated, daily itinerary. For a brief

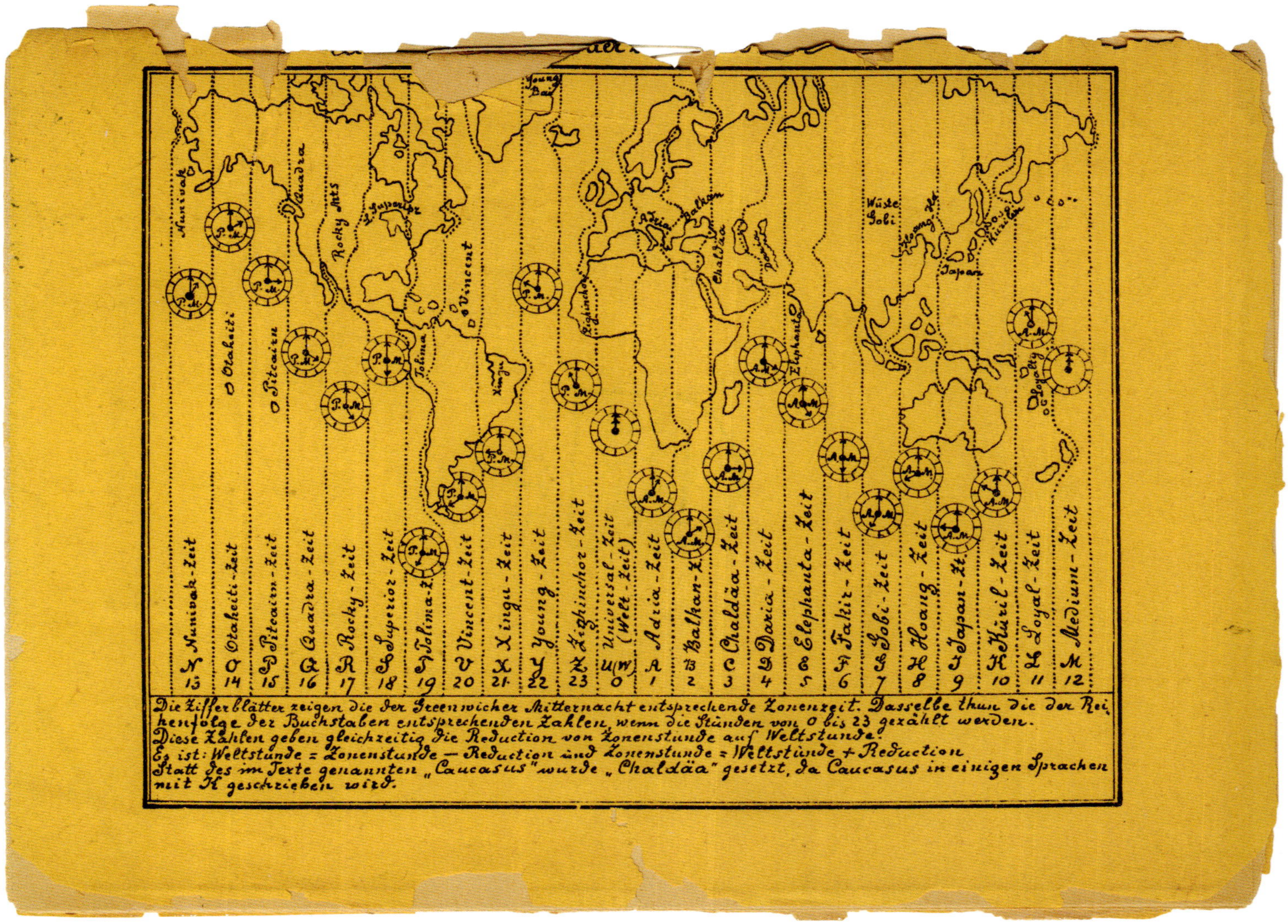

fig. 96—Time Zone Map, including *Adria-Zeit* (Adriatic Time), published on the back cover of Robert Schram, *Adria-Zeit*, excerpt from *Neue Freie Presse*, 1889

trip to Venice, Joanne recommended the following for the first day's sightseeing: "1st day.—morning: *piazza San Marco*...; *piazzetta*...; *basilica San Marco*...; afternoon, *Palazzo Ducale*...and excursion by gondola on the *Grand Canal*."[17] Joanne then divided the subsequent days according to an equally manageable itinerary that included a group of monuments in rough proximity, structuring the tourist day clearly and easily, so one could see three to four major sites per day; which means, given some period for lunch, that he budgeted about two hours per visit, or about the same time Monet spent painting one view. Monet's two-hour appointments per motif expressly mirrored a tourist's time frame and temporal economy. In the second guidebook Monet bought, Pierre Gusman's 1907 *Venise*, he would have found similar advice, including that Santa Maria della Salute should be admired with "its pale domes bulging at sunrise and in the harmony of evening" (pl. 21).[18]

None of the above, however, is to say that the instantaneity of Impressionism fully disappeared in Venice. It was, rather, profoundly domesticated, referenced briefly here and

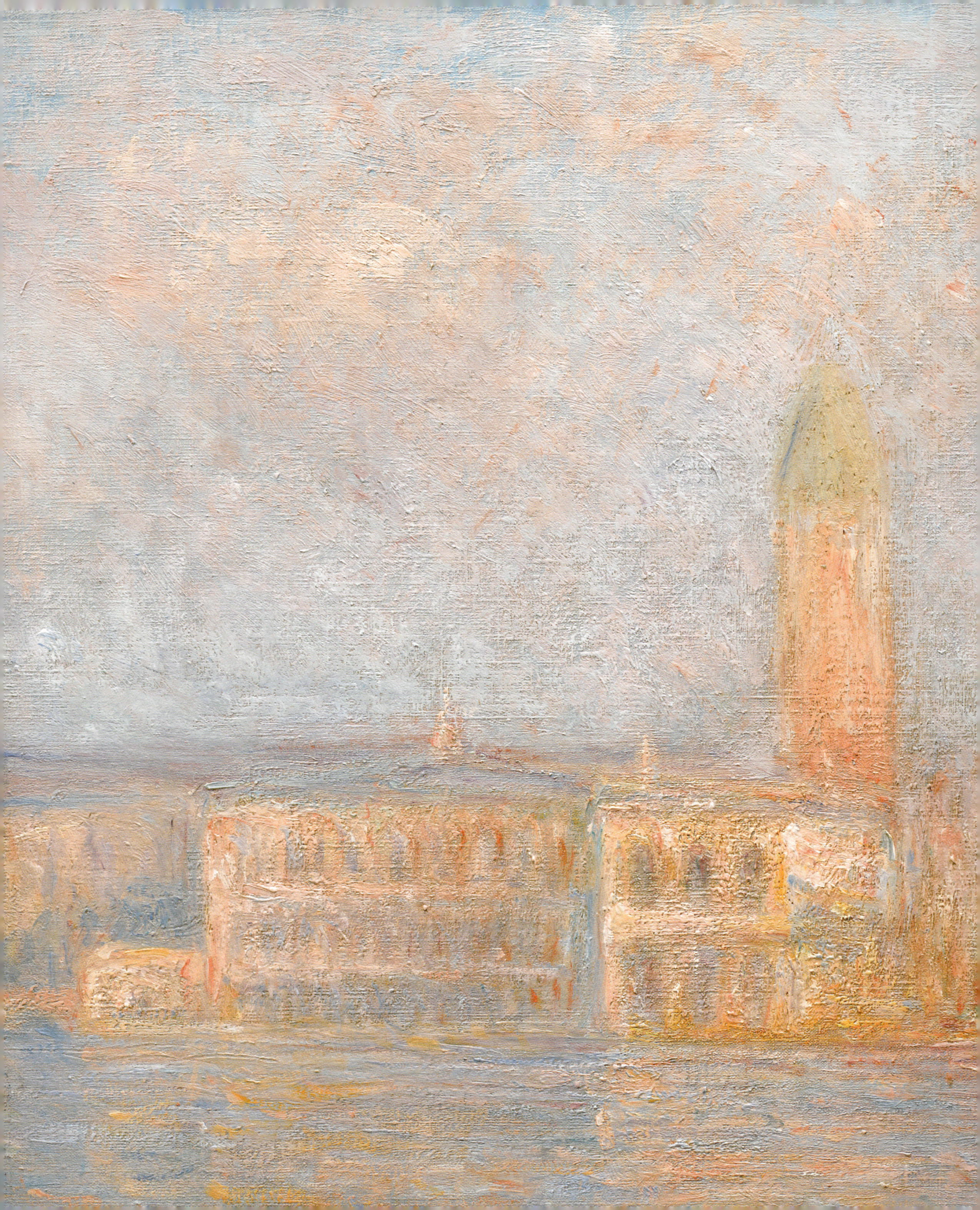

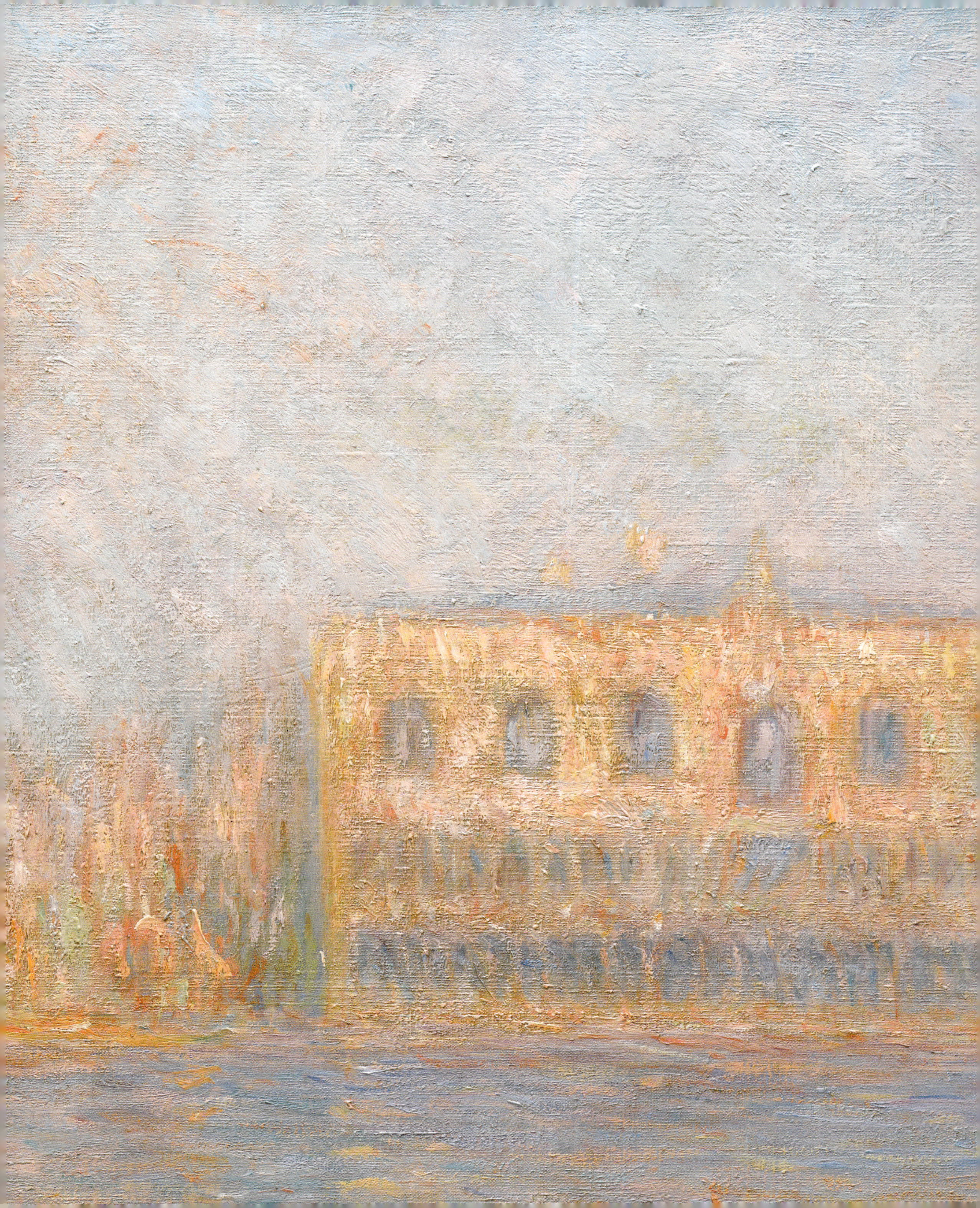

deeply contested entity of time, one known to have changed over the course of history and only recently taking its contemporary shape. When Monet painted Venice in regular two-hour intervals, he registered not just Venice's peculiar timelessness but the flattening and regularization of the modern hour as well. What he demonstrated in Venice was both the regularity of his schedule and that of an hour as a unit of time framing that schedule, features whose uniformity echoed — but only echoed — a city in which time had effectively stopped. To paint with regularity was precisely the means toward an image of timelessness, because uniform time now looked like *all* the time there was, or the only time there is.

Monet's paintings bear out such a reading. It has often been remarked, as Pissarro expressed it, that "this is unquestionably one of Monet's most systematic series. The six canvases [of the Grand Canal] are almost exactly the same dimensions (73 × 92 cm); the layout of the motif is virtually identical in all, and each of the canvases was painted at the same time of day" (pl. 1–5).[28] Let me add to that the striking visual fact that all the Venice pictures, in their overall compositions, focus on the watery surface in the bottom half and on the buildings in the upper half, as if the world were nearly perfectly divided between the real and its reflection, a distinction Monet then tended to diminish by making the structures appear ethereal and enveloped in haze as if mere apparitions. Overall, the Venetian group is a study in regularity, in terms of set up, format, composition, paint handling, and also time frame; it is an utterly "controlled environment," as Pissarro has rightly put it.[29] But this formal uniformity, which looks so timeless, is in fact lodged deeply inside the works, registering the regular schedule by which they were created. Such is the modern temporal condition itself: its regularity becomes visible only through the emotional charge of timelessness.

Looking backward and forward from the Venice paintings briefly will aid in making this point. The other times when Monet had painted architecture with as much verve as he did in Italy were in his Rouen Cathedral series between 1893 and 1895 and the group of paintings showing London's Houses of Parliament in the very first years of the twentieth century. In both, the instant seems to reign much more supreme than a few years later in Venice, and each of the two important structures of Rouen and London was painted at different times of day and under different weather and light conditions (figs. 58, 97, and 102). Even though the viewpoints are often similar, the painted effects vary dramatically, prompting Georges Clemenceau to write famously of the Rouen paintings that they constituted "not just more than twenty, but more than a hundred, a thousand, a billion states of the eternal cathedral in the immeasurable cycles of the sun."[30] A few years later, no critic of the Venice paintings would make such a hyperbolic statement about their internal differences; the critics instead focused on the paintings' strange timelessness. Finally, in the 1920s, during the last years of his long life, when Monet painted several versions of the facade of his Giverny estate seen at a dramatic angle, the house nearly disappears from view entirely (fig. 98). Barely there in a flurry of brush marks and colorful dabs of paint, the instant had fully disappeared and

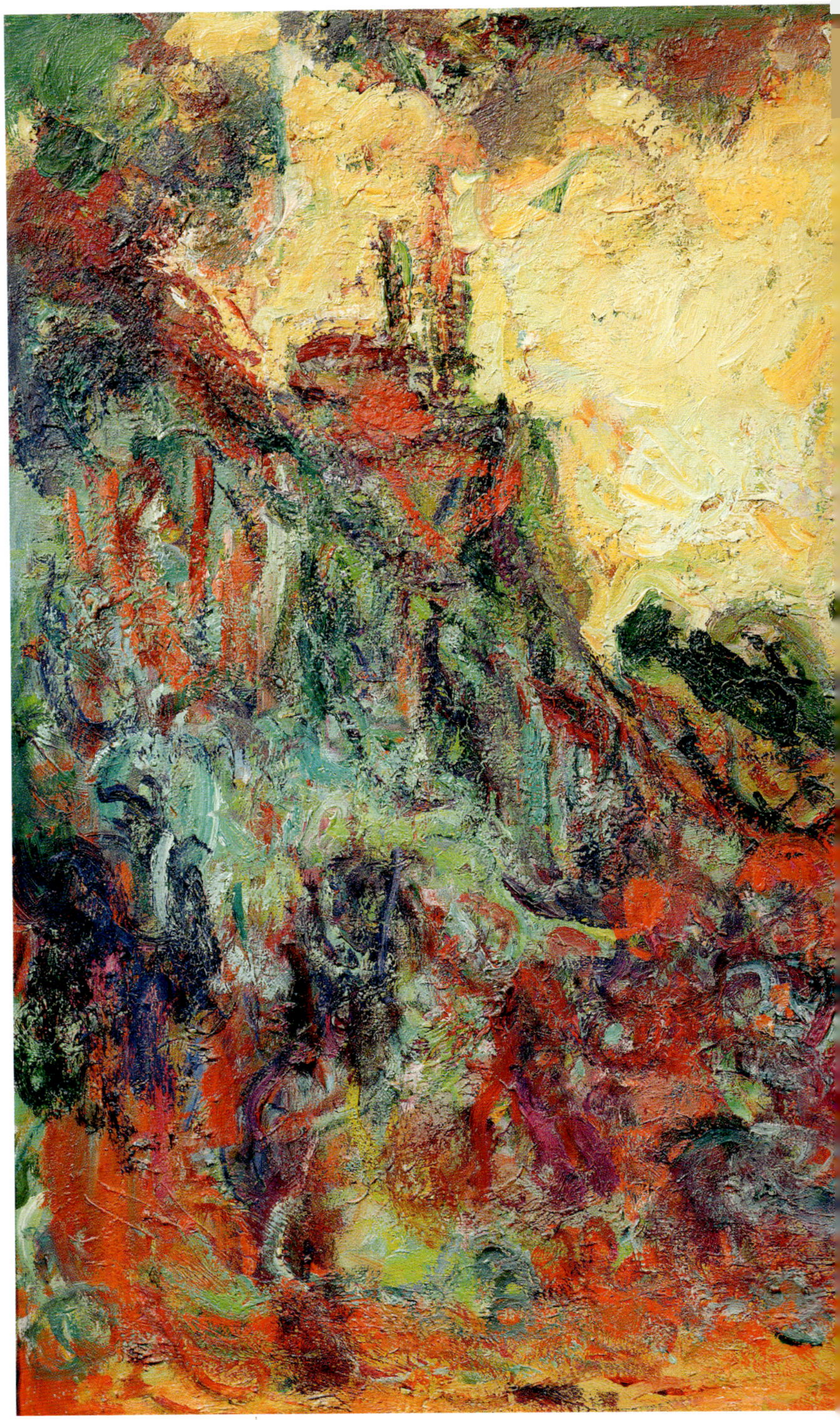

was no longer a viable category for painting. Nothing indicates these late works' parameters of time, space, light, or weather, all having been rendered as nothing but an artificial network of vibrant coloration and performative paint handling. Venice sits roughly between these two approaches to pictorial time, one hypersensitive to the instant, the other dismissive of it. In Venice, instant, hour, and timelessness still walked hand in hand across Monet's canvases, perhaps for the last time in his career. Time was there, but it was dissolving and becoming more and more unrecognizable and useless for Monet's art. In his *grandes décorations* and his *Water Lilies*, his major preoccupations in the final three decades of his life, he no longer worried much about time at all. The plants themselves did this for Monet, so he did not have to: "The master took his watch: It is 10:30, [Monet] said, let's go see them. [The water lilies] are open," recalled the critic Marc Elder when visiting the aging Monet in the mid-1920s.[31] Time was simply *there*, a given, and the paintings, now perfectly timeless, embody a particular state of modern art toward which Monet's Venice sojourn helped pave the way.

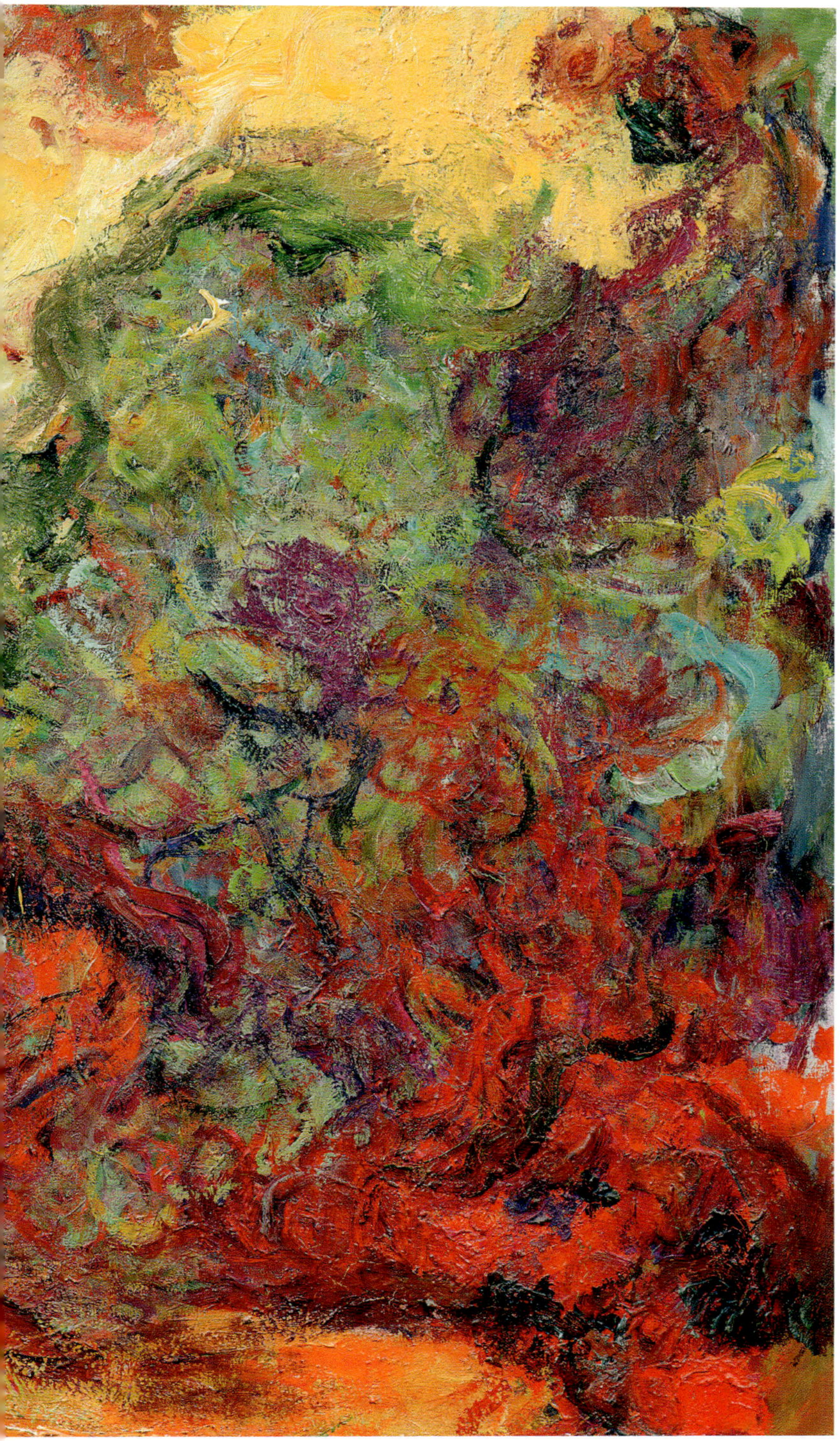

fig. 98—Claude Monet, *The Artist's House from the Rose Garden*, 1922–24, oil on canvas, 31 9/10 × 36 2/3 in., Musée Marmottan Monet

The specific time of representation is rarely evident in an Impressionist painting, and the time of day is difficult to read. Still, the basic desire to capture a specific time was always there when Monet and his colleagues painted. In Venice, this desire for the specificity of the instant was overshadowed by an overwhelming sense of historical time, more invested in making Venice appear timeless than specifically temporal. In his versions of the city's atmosphere, Monet brought out the full contradictions in these divergent yet linked temporal pursuits and made paintings that allowed the modern codification of timelessness to appear in painting. We thus witness the beautiful disappearance of time—perhaps the most modern of anti-modern desires—as emerging precisely from the perspective of instantaneity. When instant and hour were as conflated as they were here, however, it became difficult to disentangle them or to see them for what they really were. What Monet showed, truly, was the modern hour's deep investment in making Venice look timeless. He demonstrated that timelessness was hard-won from the regularity of modern time. When Monet was back in Giverny by mid-December, the very first letter he sent (as far as has come down to us) was a brief missive to Geffroy, dating to the twentieth of the month: "I ask you to please send me word immediately to the [Hotel] Terminus telling me which day, Tuesday or Wednesday, I can stop by around 9 in the morning to pick you up to have lunch with my wife and myself. In haste and friendship, Claude Monet."[32] When Monet wrote in haste and wanted clarity on the appointment ahead, as we all do on occasion, Venice seems already to have retreated far into distant memory. What is less clear is whether Monet had brought this temporal pressure to Venice and sublimated it there into his painting schedule, or whether he had brought it back from Venice to Giverny, now a fundamental aspect of his late Impressionism. Most likely, it was both.

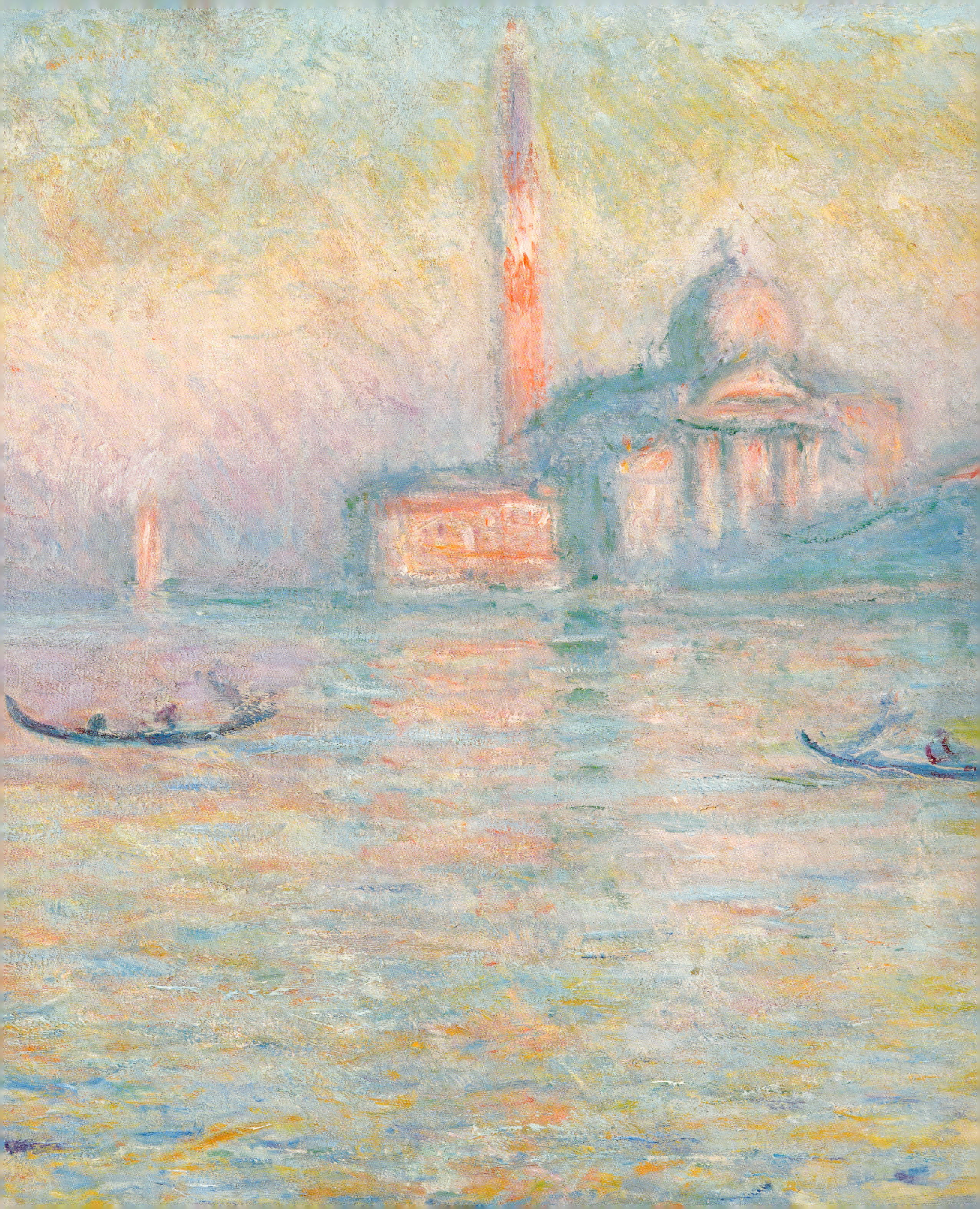

Jonathan P. Ribner

"A ROSE VEIL": AIR QUALITY AND COUNTER-TOURISM IN MONET'S VENETIAN PAINTINGS

IT WAS HARDLY THE FIRST TIME Claude Monet sought out sulfurous haze. Thrice, polluted fog had drawn him to London (September–October 1899, February–April 1900, and January–April 1901).[1] His sojourn in Venice (October–December 1908) coincided with the region's annual foggy season, and the city was surprisingly industrialized in the early twentieth century.[2] Having visited the exhibition of the Venetian paintings at the Paris gallery of Gaston and Joseph Bernheim-Jeune (May–June 1912), Pablo Picasso's friend Guillaume Apollinaire anticipated that viewers subscribing to the conventional notion of Venice as multicolored and accustomed to Monet's rich palette might be taken aback that "he painted the hazy aspects of the city of canals."[3] Infused with moisture and sulfur dioxide, Venetian air admirably suited an aspiration the artist first mentioned in 1888 and became preoccupied with around 1890: a desire to capture the *enveloppe* — a site's particular light and atmosphere.[4] And Monet was willing to leave his Giverny flowers for odoriferous sites offering such quarry.

Consideration of the impact of air quality on paintings of the outdoors is timely. Atmosphere scientists Anna Lea Albright and Peter Huybers recently marshaled historical sulfur dioxide emissions data and quantitative analysis of contrast and of light intensity in thirty-eight paintings by Monet and sixty by J. M. W. Turner to persuasively argue for correlation between visual features of the canvases and contemporaneous levels of air pollution in London and Paris.[5] Providing evidence of the artists' responsiveness to the specific environmental conditions in which they worked, the investigators aptly view pollution-impacted conditions of visibility not as the exclusive factor determining the paintings' appearance, but rather as a spur to creativity. Turner's richly imaginative Romantic painting is distant from that of the

Impressionist Monet—born more than three generations later, uncompromisingly committed to contemporaneity for much of his career, and uninterested in grandiose theatrics. Yet the effects of air pollution on what they could see are germane to the work of both artists, each of whom was a keen observer of weather and light willing to assimilate modern industry and technology within his repertoire.

Dovetailing with my art historical research on the "poetics of pollution," this scientific evidence of environmental history's relevance to painting opens an avenue to address a central aspect of Monet's art.[6] At issue is the fruitful tension between, on the one hand, Monet's dogged commitment to recording what he observed and, on the other, the fictitiousness of his claim to see with an innocent eye.[7] Intrepidly working in the open air, Monet—raised in Le Havre on the Norman coast—had "a fisherman's sensitivity to the weather," as William C. Seitz put it.[8] However, throughout his career, this master manipulator of composition and color usually completed his paintings indoors.

That was the case with the paintings begun in Venice and finished at Giverny prior to the 1912 exhibition. As the artist told his close friend and ardent admirer Gustave Geffroy, the canvases brought home from Venice were embryonic: "I've only made some studies, some beginnings."[9] Relying on visual evidence, the city's seasonal conditions of visibility, and the historical record of local industrialization, I contend that the completed works retained and creatively transformed traces of the atmospheric and environmental conditions prevailing when the studies and beginnings were brushed on canvas.

As Monet worked in Venice, a large industrial plant incorporating a steam-powered flour mill and a pasta factory was spewing dark smoke above the western end of Giudecca, the cluster of islets south of the urban center. Property of the Swiss-Venetian industrialist Giovanni Stucky, the Molino Stucky (begun 1896, expanded 1907 to 1925) was designed by the German architect Ernst Wullekopf in a northern, neo-Gothic style alien to the city (fig. 99).[10] A world-class flour producer with 194 employees in 1901, the Molino Stucky was shuttered in 1954. Permitted for redevelopment in 1995, it was reborn in 2007 as the five-star Hilton Molino Stucky Venice.

A monument to industry's demise and tourism's triumph, the Molino Stucky hardly introduced steam technology and air pollution to Venice.[11] A lighting gas factory, opened by a French firm in the early 1840s on the city's outskirts, is a prominent pioneering example. At the end of the 1860s, it annually consumed approximately 10,000 tons of English hard coal and 2,400 tons of Istrian coke. In the 1880s, Venetian industrialization accelerated and sulfur dioxide emissions increased, abetted by regulatory relaxation. Concentrated at the city's periphery—Giudecca was a prime site—industry within Venice's historic boundaries began to evaporate following World War I and the establishment in 1917 of the new industrial port of Marghera on the mainland.[12]

By the time of Monet's arrival, smoky modernization had long been symbolized by locomotives puffing along the railway bridge (opened 1846) spanning the Venetian lagoon. Sojourning

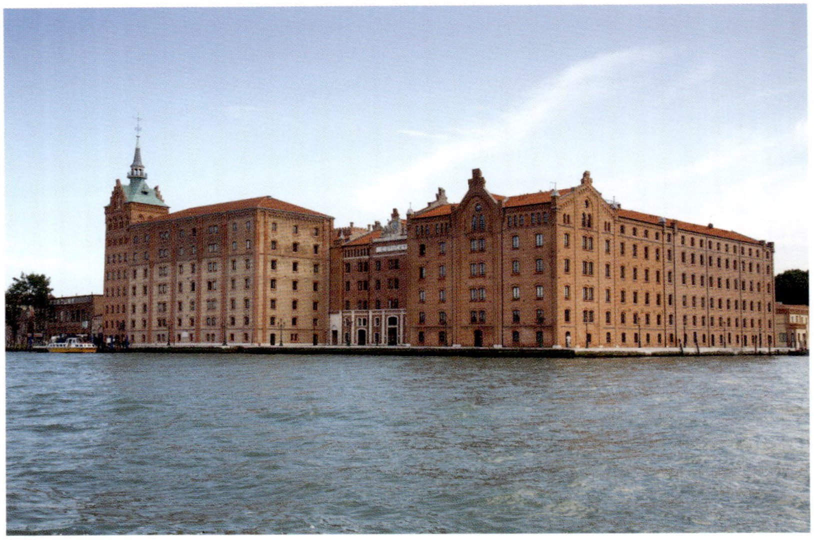

fig. 99—Exterior of the Hilton Molino Stucky Venice hotel in Giudecca

in Venice in 1845 and again the following year, John Ruskin was dismayed by the bridge and witnessed a troubling sight: "a sullen cloud of black smog" issuing from the bell tower of the former church of San Girolamo.[13] Housing what was then Italy's most technologically advanced steam-powered flour mill, the odd, hybrid edifice, with engine fired up, was drawn in 1847 by Giovanni Pividor (fig. 100). Ruskin's nemesis, James McNeill Whistler, inadvertently reversed that conversion of campanile to chimney in the *Ten O'Clock* lecture (1885). Receptive to visual subtlety within hardscrabble urban scenery, the aesthete delighted in the beautifying crepuscular moment "when the evening mist clothes the riverside with poetry, as with a veil, and the poor buildings lose themselves in the dim sky, and the tall chimneys become campanili."[14] Whistler performed that alchemy in the *Nocturnes* of the 1870s and 1880s, in which the contours of river- and canal-side structures are subsumed within nuanced tones of sepia, gray, blue, or green, sometimes shading to black. In their dense, unifying atmosphere, the nearly monochrome *Nocturne* Thames paintings and their etched Venetian counterparts (e.g., *Nocturne*, figs. 154, 156, and 157) prefigure Monet's richly hued views of Venice.

As Albright and Huybers pointed out, aerosolized sulfur dioxide scatters light. This increases light intensity — which has a whitening effect — and diminishes contrast, reducing the sharpness of edges.[15] Typical of the Venice paintings, these characteristics appear, for example, in a view of the church of San Giorgio Maggiore (pl. 12). Here, white was added to a gamut of hues reflected from buildings, water, and sky. Value (i.e., degree of lightness or darkness) is lightened and restricted to a narrow range, making edges indistinct. The yellow-green-tinged sky, dulled color, and low contrast of *San Giorgio Maggiore* suggest that the haze through which Monet viewed the church — located off the eastern end of Giudecca — contained smoke. The same could be said of Monet's paintings of the Palazzo Ducale on the other side of the Grand Canal (pl. 14–20).

Accordingly, Geffroy observed that in some of the paintings of San Giorgio Maggiore, "nacreous and sulfurous vapors half veil the delicate church."[16] Those effects are amplified in a foggier, seemingly more effluent-rich, version of that motif (pl. 9). Here, campanile and dome nearly vanish and the horizon is obliterated. Pervading the sky, murky yellow-green is reflected by the water below. Transitions between hues as distant as yellow and violet are fluid, such that the overall effect, as in the Indianapolis canvas, approaches monochrome.

Those traits gain relief through comparison to a canvas painted under dissimilar conditions of visibility. Working in the strong light of the French Riviera (mid-January to early May 1888), Monet set the Fort Carré and the Château Grimaldi at Antibes in transparent atmosphere in *Antibes* (*Afternoon Effect*) (fig. 101). Contrast is orchestrated rather than muted, with the sunstruck buildings and shore boldly set against the variegated blue-green Mediterranean, tinted Maritime Alps, and pale sky. Whereas Monet might have inhaled sulfur dioxide as he painted San Giorgio Maggiore, viewing *Antibes* (*Afternoon Effect*), we can almost smell bracing sea air.

Soft edges, muted value contrast, and coloristic consonance cannot be attributed solely to empirical observation of Venice's tainted air and seasonal fog. Dependent on the painter's craft, persuasive mimicry of Venetian atmosphere advanced Monet's artistic goals. By imparting tonal unity, Monet enforced perception of the image as a cohesive whole, rather than as a sum of its parts. This aspect of the Venice paintings points to enduring respect for the late work of Jean-Baptiste-Camille Corot, whom Monet had especially esteemed in the late 1890s, as evidenced by his paintings of *Morning on the Seine, near Giverny* (1897; examples in the Museum of Fine Arts, Boston, and the Metropolitan Museum of Art, New York). For example, Corot's silvery-misted *Memory of Mortefontaine*, exhibited in the Salon of 1864, has an evenness of value so ingrained in that painter's sensibility as to be prophesied by his earlier sunlit views of Venice (e.g., figs. 147 and 148).

In the Indianapolis and Cardiff canvases, composition serves to reinforce the homogenizing effect of diminished visibility. The church is relegated to the upper half of a bisected field, such that its campanile nearly reaches the frame's top edge and water occupies the lower half. Reinforcing continuity between water and sky, this flattening is tenuously tempered by a gondola and another slender boat that provide way stations between viewer and buildings.

In *The Grand Canal* (pl. 1–5), counterpoint upstages cohesion, as the vaporous form of Santa Maria della Salute is juxtaposed with gondola mooring posts assertively funneling into depth. Cropped by the top edge of the canvas, the foremost post locates the position of the painter while providing a bold chromatic accent. That post's relatively sharp silhouette, darker value, and richly variegated color — an unrealistically intense stripe of cool blue, green, and violet shadow is paired with warm, sunlit reddish brown and magenta — provide a foil to the nuanced coloration and soft contours of the church.

Creative response to translucent atmosphere had long been a feature of Monet's art. It is key to his London paintings. Europe's largest and smokiest city, the British capital offered displays of scattered light more extreme than those the painter could have witnessed in Italy. At the turn of the century, blanketing London fogs of the sort that first appeared in the 1840s were known as "pea-soupers" due to their color — usually yellow, though other hues appeared. That the frequency of fog in London began to increase gradually about 1750, peaked in the 1890s, and subsided around 1904, constituted a long-term meteorological pattern. Yet the composition of what, in *Bleak House* (1852), Charles Dickens called "London particular" was due to human input. The effluent-charged fog was rich in sulfur dioxide emitted from combusted coal, of which, by the end of the nineteenth century, Londoners annually burned approximately eighteen million tons. Louis C. Parkes, a health official for Chelsea, put the daily portion of fine soot going into the London atmosphere in 1892 at more than two hundred tons.[17] Londoners inhaled smog in the sense of the term as coined in 1905, smoke plus fog.

Sufficiently dense to muffle sunlight and unify contrasting hues, London's fog provided matchless opportunities to apprehend the *enveloppe*. Monet told the dealer René Gimpel, "I adore London... But what I love more than anything is the fog."[18] And this infatuation was consonant with the Parisian notion that London was almost always foggy. According to Max O'Rell (pseudonym for Léon Paul Blouet)—a French humorist specializing in things English and American—on the rare occasions that the sun appears in London, it is photographed "in order not to forget it."[19]

In the most negative review of the Venice paintings—for more positive responses, see the essay by Félicie Faizand de Maupeou in the present volume—Camille Mauclair indicated their kinship with those representing London. The artist, he wrote, depicted San Giorgio Maggiore "with various effects of greenish or inflamed skies, which hardly differ from the beautiful skies he painted in his Thames series."[20] Yet examination of a Thames-side view brings home the distinction in visibility separating the two cities. Consider, for example, *Houses of Parliament, Sunlight Effect* (fig. 58) and *The Thames at Charing Cross* (fig. 102). Asphyxiating fog reduces the Palace of Westminster to a milky, lavender silhouette and blunts its Gothic Revival skyline. Melded with the shaded reach of the Thames at its base, the pinnacled building is set against the sky's pale murk. Reflections of the enshrouded sun glint on the river, providing a pronounced, asymmetrical contrast that enlivens the nearly monochrome view. Such nuanced hue and controlled luminosity required revision in the studio. Like the canvases later brought home from Venice, those from London were begun in situ and completed at Giverny.

Notwithstanding their unconventional style, the London paintings sold well. When exhibited at Paul Durand-Ruel's Paris gallery (in May and June 1904), they readily found buyers. According to Robert L. Herbert, Monet was "obsessively and often ruthlessly devoted to making money." [21] Since the 1880s, the artist's pursuit of affluence had been rewarded. In 1890, he purchased the gardened house at Giverny, rented since 1883. To provide watery settings, the painter acquired an adjacent lot on the opposite side of a railway line in 1893. Between 1891 and 1904, his income from painting nearly tripled.[22] Sales were guaranteed by the artist's name; the Bernheim-Jeune brothers purchased the yet-to-be-finished Venice canvases for 12,000 francs each when Monet returned to Giverny.[23] Keen to support a lifestyle that included maintenance of the Giverny property and ownership of a chauffeured automobile, Monet had an eye for business as well as color. With that acumen, he had shown eight views of the Gare Saint-Lazare in the third Impressionist exhibition (1877), initiating his commercially advantageous practice of exhibiting together works sharing a common subject. Fortunately for his collectors, Monet's sly entrepreneurship did not conflict with the consistently high quality of his prolific output.

Monet also exploited tourist appeal to increase marketability.[24] The London canvases, for example, provided his clientele with startling views of a common destination for French travelers in search of novelty or thrillingly forbidding sights. While Gallic Anglophobes relished opportunities to decry London's fog as a crime-concealing menace and to attribute suicides to the city's premature darkness, some of their compatriots crossed the

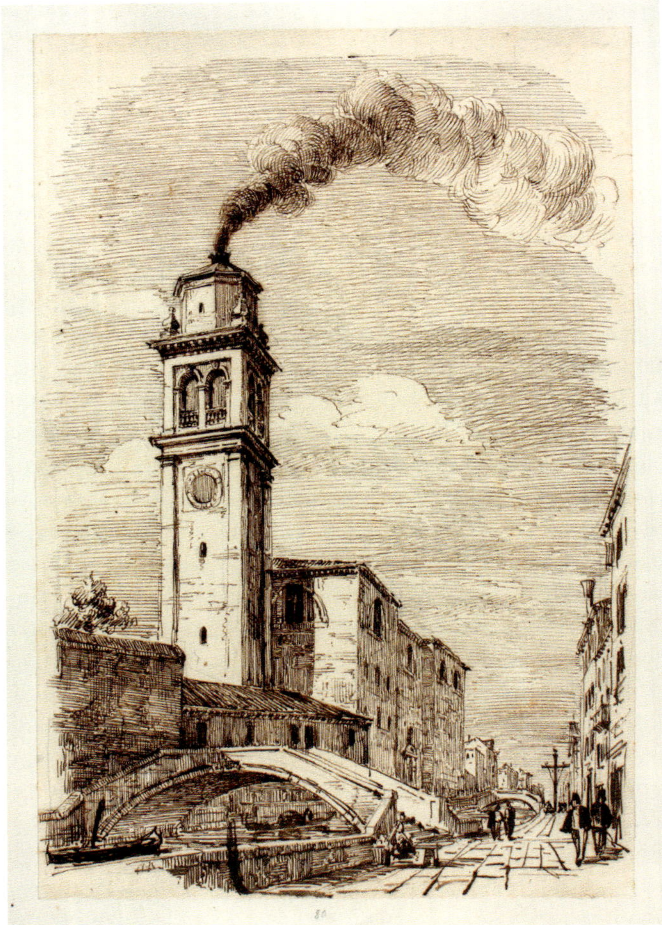

fig. 100—Giovanni Pividor, *San Girolamo, Venice*, 1847, paper, pen, and India ink, 11⅛ × 7⅖ in., Museo Correr

Channel expressly to experience the light-blocking fog.[25] In the 1890s, a splendid view of the Thames in fog was advertised as one of the advantages of the Savoy Hotel, where Monet lodged.[26] Determined to record that commercially valuable spectacle, the painter wrote from London to his wife, Alice, of his panic on seeing clear sky when he arose to work.[27]

Given that Venice's tourist appeal outstripped that of London, and in light of Monet's acquisitiveness, it is striking that the profit-seeking painter did little to capitalize on the city's mystique. Demonstrating scant interest in the specifics of celebrated monuments, the Venice paintings either understate or expunge architectural detail. With displeasure, Mauclair criticized Monet's reduction of the dome of Santa Maria della Salute to "a bluish bulb, whose characteristic traits are suppressed."[28] "The monuments of Venice don't interest him," quipped André Michel. "He presents them as rickety and keeled over, such that one would say their rotten foundation posts totter and will

fig. 101—Claude Monet, *Antibes (Afternoon Effect)*, 1888, oil on canvas, 32 ½ × 26 in., Museum of Fine Arts, Boston

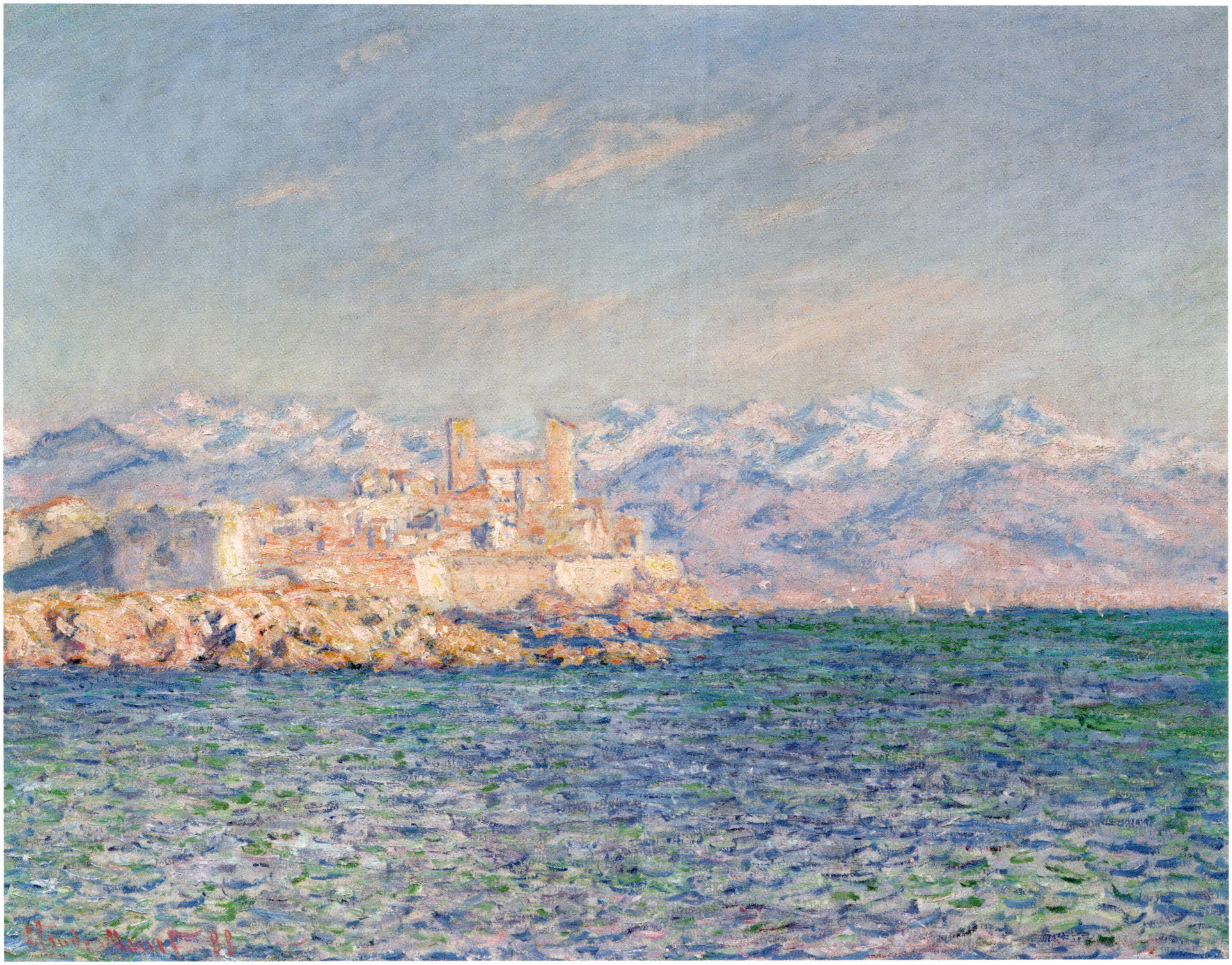

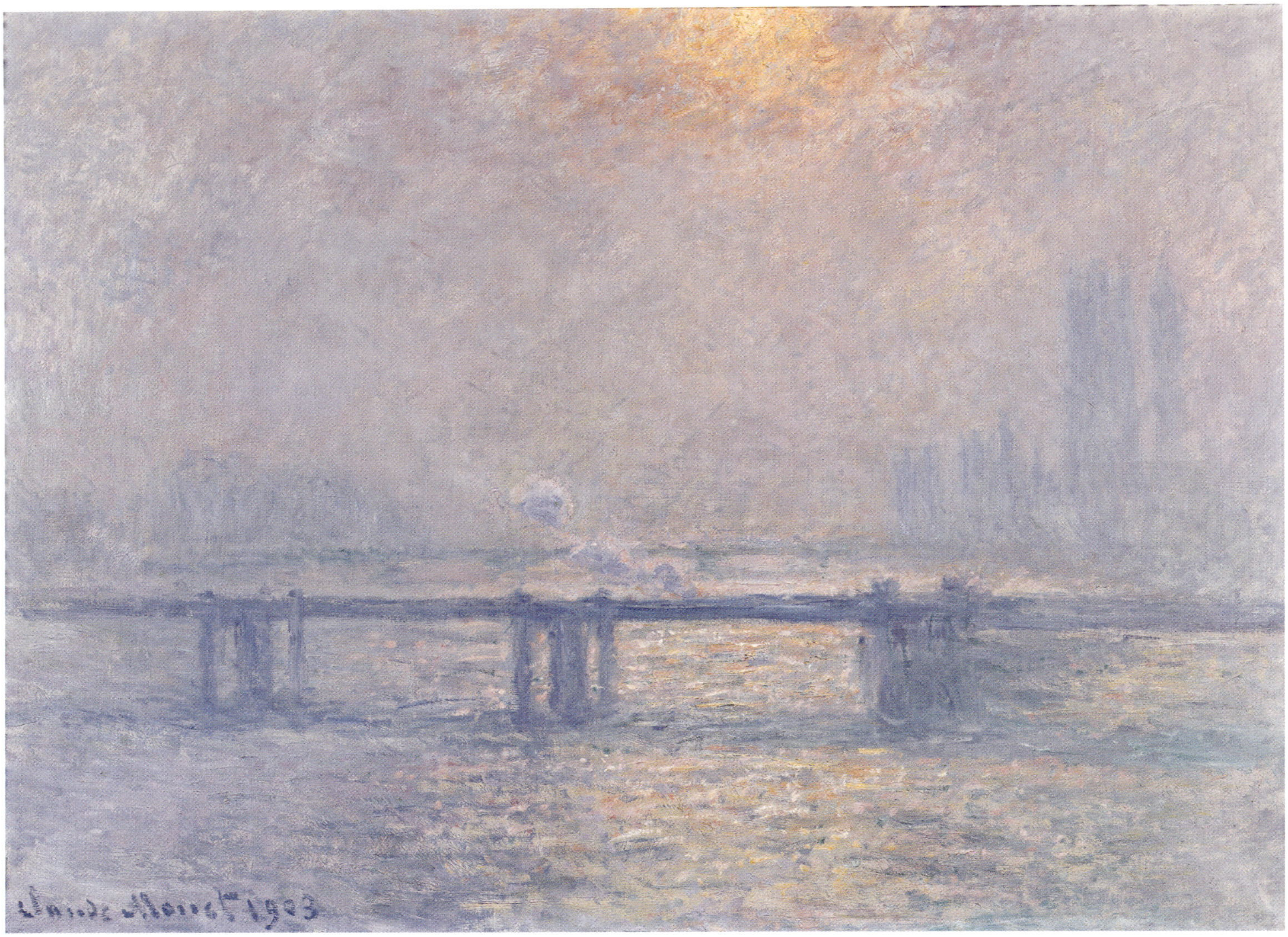

collapse for good."[29] I hold that Monet's reticence regarding familiar Venetian tourist sites was a function of his avid quest for the *enveloppe*. And the poetic dimension of his audacious approach was admired within the artist's inner circle. What bothered Mauclair and Michel, Geffroy prized. Monet's Venice, he noted, is not "in the foreground, constructed, sculpted, inventoried, it is suspended in the haze and in a distant space that evokes temporal remoteness."[30]

Geffroy's delight in the distancing atmosphere Monet rendered runs counter to an appetite for the picturesque that, over the centuries, has brought to Venice untold numbers of visitors, from eighteenth-century British Grand Tourists nurtured by Canaletto's views (e.g., figs. 32 and 149) to twenty-first-century purchasers of prime vacation real estate. Here, for example, is the Piazza San Marco, packed with humanity during a festival (fig. 103). Despite his affection for Venice, John Singer Sargent did not return after 1913, when he found it spoiled by "swarms of smart Londoners."[31] Previously, Henry James lamented, "You are reminded from the moment of your arrival that Venice scarcely exists any more as a city at all; that she exists only as a battered

fig. 102—Claude Monet, *The Thames at Charing Cross*, 1903, oil on canvas, 39½ × 29 in., Musée des Beaux-Arts de Lyon

fig. 103—(opposite) Crowd at a festival in Piazza San Marco, Venice

peep-show and bazaar."[32] In an eloquent jeremiad decrying the destruction of all that makes the city unique and vital, *If Venice Dies* (2014), Salvatore Settis adduced startling figures regarding population decline and the explosion of tourism in Venice's historic center. As of 2014, tourists outnumbered residents by 140 to 1. "Venice," Settis warned, "runs the risk of soon becoming devoid of Venetians."[33] That grave prediction would hardly have troubled Monet, absorbed by the city's illuminated atmosphere. Minimally present in the Venice paintings, human figures, whether inhabitants or visitors, seem to have held little interest for the painter as he worked there.

The grievances of Sargent, James, and Settis resonate with Octave Mirbeau's preface to the catalogue of the 1912 exhibition of Monet's Venice paintings. There, the artist's friend and fellow garden enthusiast reported that Monet resisted travel to that clichéd location, declaring "Venice... no... I will not go to Venice."[34] No longer a real city, Mirbeau sneered, Venice was but "a colored postcard."[35] Whereas, the critic asserted, we are moved by the atmosphere of cities, in Venice "there is no atmosphere, since a rose veil hangs over Venice, like a scarf around a dancer."[36] Evoking physical atmosphere as well as cultural ambience, Mirbeau's intriguing simile suggests awareness of the quality of Venetian air.[37] Blinkered to the factitiousness of the Venice paintings, Mirbeau acerbically insisted on their fidelity: "The stupidity of writers and painters uprooted Venice from nature. Claude Monet went to Venice and returned it to nature."[38] Just as Monet bristled at mention of his studio, so, too, had Mirbeau long endorsed the myth of his friend's innocent eye. Paris does not suit Monet, the writer asserted in 1889: "He lives in the countryside in a superb landscape, in constant contact with his models, and the open air is his sole studio."[39]

That such was hardly the case is evidenced with particular force by the spectacular coloration of San Giorgio Maggiore at dusk (pl. 32 and 33).[40] This chromatic fantasy sprang from a kernel of environmental truth: smoke pollution can heighten orange and red in sunsets. At Giverny, Monet exuberantly expanded the range of hue, spanning the spectrum from tinted red to shaded violet. Such willingness to depart from sensitively studied visual fact was previously evident in Monet's sometimes extravagantly colored, serial representations of grainstacks, poplars, and the Rouen Cathedral of the 1890s (fig. 97), as well as in his London paintings, commenced at the decade's close. Liberty from faithful imitation was integral to Monet's art from the outset, having permitted the physiognomic and anatomical distortions of his youthful caricatures of Le Havre locals.[41] In the Venice paintings—as throughout his career—Monet applied his skill as caricaturist, amplifying salient features, suppressing others, and demonstrating astonishing agility as an inventor of pictorial equivalents of fleeting observations.[42]

Mimetic and mediated, the Venice paintings are informed by Monet's scorn for the influence of preconception on sight. The artist's posture that he wished to have been born blind and later gained vision squares with Mirbeau's report of his friend's initial unwillingness to visit Venice—a city that attracted tourists with preconceived notions of what was on view.[43] As James observed, "Venice has been painted and described many thousands of times, and of all the cities of the world is the easiest to visit without going there."[44] Declining to produce predictable souvenirs, Monet captured in Venice visual effects that outshone monetary potential. It is indicative of the artist's virtuosity and brand recognition that, like the London paintings, those from Venice were a financial success.

Awareness of the environmental conditions in which Monet worked can only tighten our grasp on an elusive—albeit seemingly direct—art, both ingeniously wrought and resolutely of its time and place. His determination to seize the Venetian *enveloppe*, even at the expense of the paintings' tourist appeal, aligns with an opinion expressed by James a decade before souring on the city's commercialization and tourism: "The mere use of one's eyes in Venice is happiness enough, and generous observers find it hard to keep an account of their profits in this line. Everything the attention touches holds it, keeps playing with it—thanks to some inscrutable flattery of the atmosphere."[45]

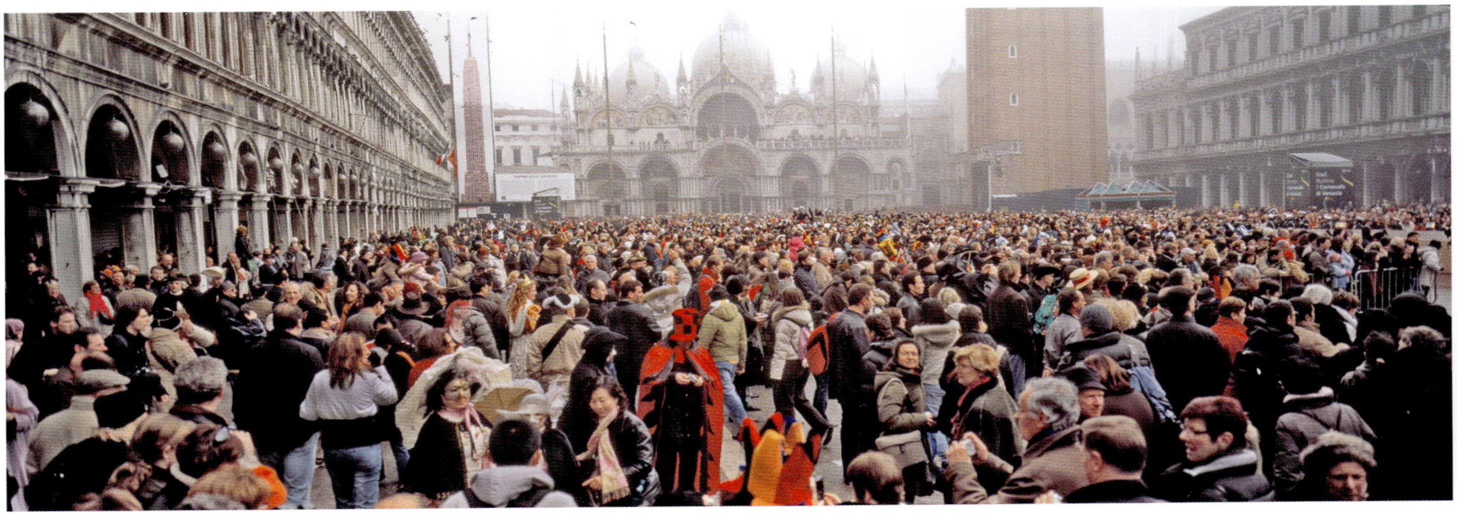

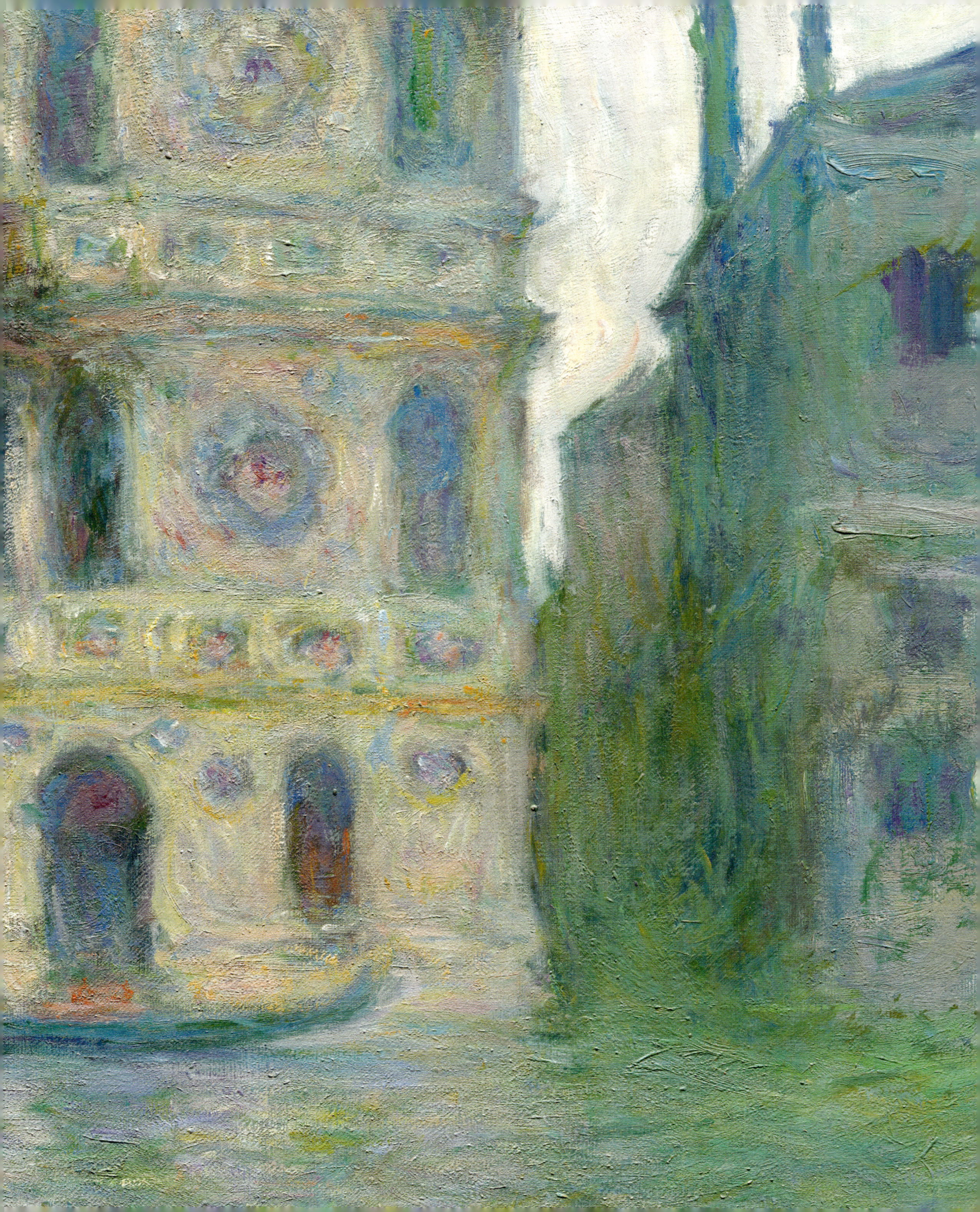

BEHIND ONE DEALER LIES ANOTHER, AND A SHOW: EXHIBITING THE VENICE PAINTINGS

Félicie Faizand de Maupeou

ON OCTOBER 1, 1908, CLAUDE MONET arrived in Venice accompanied by his wife, Alice. Venice, a beloved place for painters, was a place Monet had refused to visit until then, as he had confided to his friend Octave Mirbeau: "Venice . . . no . . . I will not go to Venice."[1] But an invitation from Mary Hunter, an English friend of the couple's, finally seems to have persuaded him to leave the water garden that had become his primary source of inspiration since his move to Giverny in 1883. It was a fortuitous decision: after several days spent appraising the architecture and the quality of light in his new environment, a dazzled Monet took up the brush. In Venice, he "returned to a subject he hadn't tackled in more than five years — the meeting of solid and liquid, and their intermingling in light."[2] Monet selected a limited number of views, which he depicted multiple times. He ultimately brought back thirty-seven canvases from his time in Venice — or, rather, thirty-seven sketches, all but two of which would be substantially reworked in his studio.

These paintings would become the object of a fierce competition between Paul Durand-Ruel, the Impressionists' longtime dealer, and the brothers of the Bernheim-Jeune gallery (fig. 105). Both galleries vied to obtain the exclusive rights to represent these canvases and to organize their public unveiling. A study of this inaugural exhibition, based largely on correspondence between the painter and his dealers and on the fortunes of the works shown in it, illuminates not only Monet's stature at the dawn of the twentieth century vis-à-vis his dealers and collectors, but also the mechanics of the art market — a mix of rivalry and collaboration — on a national and international scale.[3]

TWO RIVAL DEALERS

The moment Durand-Ruel and the Bernheim-Jeune brothers learned of Monet's trip to Venice, they started jockeying to obtain exclusive rights to that group of paintings. But to both, Monet gave the same answer. To Gaston Bernheim-Jeune, he wrote, "M. Durand-Ruel has already made the same request of me. It is with sincere regret, therefore, that I cannot accede to yours. But please rest assured: while I've become quite enamored of Venice and have started several paintings here, I fear I'll bring back only a few initial sketches, which will mainly serve me as reminders."[4] Several days later, to an insistent Durand-Ruel, he replied in more or less the same terms: "Your last letter again urges me to reserve for you anything I might produce here; I'm very flattered, but I must tell you that the Bernheims have made the same request, and besides, as I've already said, I have no idea what I might bring back with me, maybe just a few attempts or sketches, so what would be the point of committing myself, to you or anyone else?" He added: "No, I don't want to do that anymore. I wish to remain absolutely free, and besides, these commitments never turn out well, since every series [of paintings] only leads us into an endless debate."[5]

Monet was most likely referring to the exhibition of his *Water Lilies* series, which had been in the works since 1905 and which the painter had repeatedly delayed. It is true that the older Monet got, the less satisfied he became with his work and the more he labored over his canvases, unable to let them go. The *Water Lilies* exhibition, which strained relations between Monet and Durand-Ruel, provides an important contextual key to understanding the artist's decisions regarding his Venice paintings. In fact, having returned to Giverny on December 16, Monet wrote to Durand-Ruel on December 29 to let him know he had been beaten out by Bernheim-Jeune. It seems the brothers had seized upon the pretext of a trip to force an invitation to Giverny, and there "they did such a skillful job of presenting such excellent arguments that [Monet] had to give in." The painter justified his decision by claiming, "For you as much as for me, it's a good and useful thing for you not to be the sole handler of my works."[6]

This sort of dispute between Monet and his dealer was nothing new. While Durand-Ruel based his business strategy partly on obtaining exclusive representation of his artists, Monet resisted this desire for monopoly. In 1886, when he decided to show for the second time at the *International Exhibition* mounted by Georges Petit, an important rival of Durand-Ruel's, Monet wrote to Durand-Ruel to explain his decision: "It is indisputable that the last exhibition did me (and also you) a world of good, and this will be borne out by the show later this year. Moreover, had I refused, I would have appeared to be openly siding with you against him and that would have been imprudent . . . Besides, I don't think it would be a bad thing if in the eyes of the public and the collectors we didn't appear to be wholly under your tutelage and in your hands."[7] Time seems to have proved Monet right. In any case, that is the coloration he gave to this strategy after the fact, as he told François Thiébault-Sisson in 1900: "Came the day when [Durand-Ruel] had to cut back, acquire more sparingly. We thought we were heading for ruin, but instead

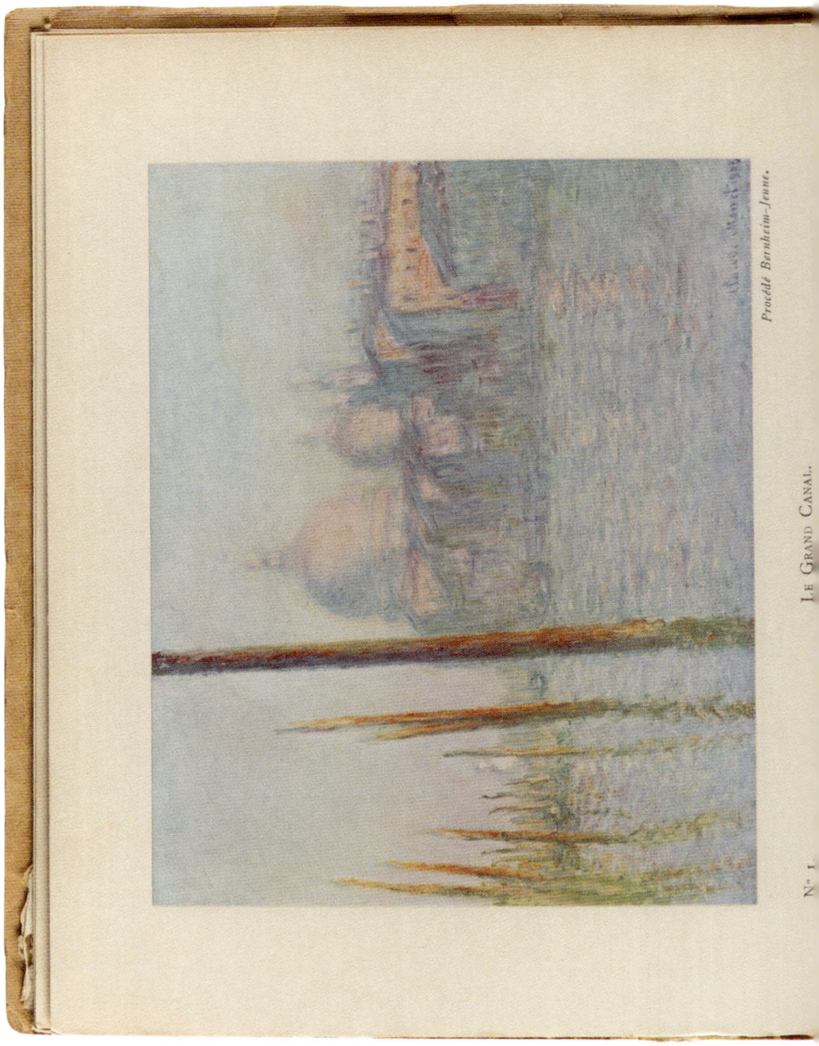

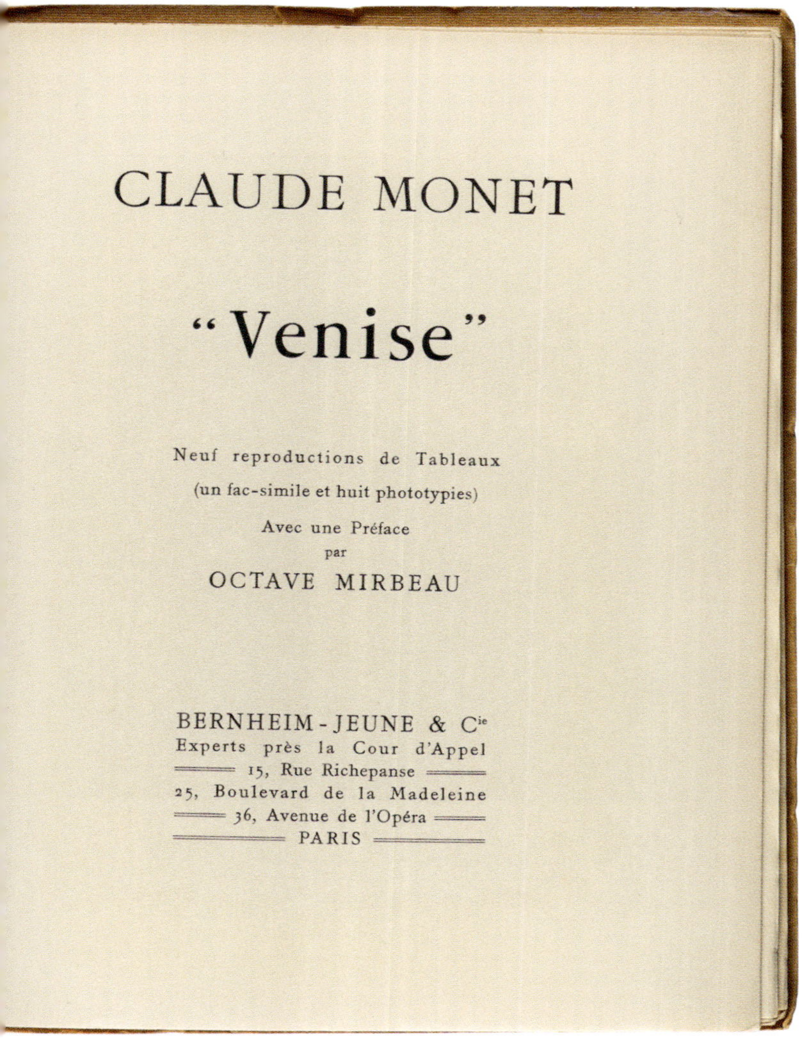

CLAUDE MONET

“Venise”

Neuf reproductions de Tableaux
(un fac-simile et huit phototypies)
Avec une Préface
par
OCTAVE MIRBEAU

BERNHEIM-JEUNE & Cie
Experts près la Cour d'Appel
15, Rue Richepanse
25, Boulevard de la Madeleine
36, Avenue de l'Opéra
PARIS

fig. 104—Catalogue for the 1912 *Venise* exhibition, Galerie Bernheim-Jeune, Collection of Paul Hayes Tucker lent in honor of Robert L. Herbert

we met with success. When our works were placed with the Petits and the Boussods [the Boussod-Valdon and Co. gallery], they found buyers. Suddenly they weren't considered to be so awful. At Durand-Ruel's, no one wanted them; when they were represented by others, people became more enthusiastic. They bought, things started moving.”[8] While Georges Petit mainly promoted artists endorsed by the official art system—safe values—Durand-Ruel was known for his support of modern and more controversial artists. By 1908, then, Monet was already working with different dealers and was utterly convinced that this diversification was beneficial.

Work continued with Bernheim-Jeune. In a letter of December 30, 1908, Monet invoked, in order to have it amended, his contract with the dealers regarding the Venice paintings—which tells us that the painter had ultimately gone back on his refusal to make commitments on unproduced works.[9] Had he truly altered his stance, or did the fact that he was not dealing with Durand-Ruel cause him to change his mind? While Monet's longtime dealer contended with a number of setbacks, Durand-Ruel would ultimately benefit indirectly from the trip to Venice. Most likely thanks to the perspective afforded by the trip, Monet looked upon his work with new eyes and, perhaps embarrassed at having favored the Bernheim-Jeune brothers, after the long-standing relationship and the support Durand-Ruel had given the artist throughout his career, he finally completed his *Water Lilies* canvases and committed to exhibiting them as of early May 1909.

Because of this, the Venice paintings were set aside for several months, after which Monet was beset by various difficulties. The intense winter rains had caused major flooding. Giverny was cut off from the rest of the world, and the painter was frantic about his garden. Worst of all, Alice had fallen ill on their return from Venice. Though she had slowly been recovering, she suffered a relapse in March 1910, leading to long months of illness; during this time, Monet hardly left her bedside and was entirely preoccupied with her care. When Alice passed away on May 19, 1911, Monet was devastated by the loss, and it was some time before he began painting again. As he announced to Joseph Bernheim-Jeune in late January or early February 1912: “As there is no remedy for what is irreparable, I have bravely gone back to work, which I had once again entirely abandoned, and I believe I'll soon have completed my Venice canvases, that is, the ones worth completing, and so we could do an exhibition.” Nevertheless, acutely aware of the time elapsed since his trip and his agreement with the Bernheims, he offered them the option of canceling their contract should they wish.[10]

AN EXHIBITION AT LAST

On March 29, a letter addressed to the Bernheim brothers confirmed Monet's good progress, as fifteen paintings had already left his studio for the Galerie Bernheim-Jeune on Rue Richepanse. In the weeks following, preparations continued and various matters were settled: the price of each canvas, the selection of works for the exhibition,[11] the catalogue and its preface, for which they commissioned Mirbeau.[12] But the more time that went by, the more Monet became prey to doubts. Dissatisfaction, which habitually seized the painter at the idea of letting go of his canvases, took hold: "I simply cannot give you any more Venice paintings. Try as I might to convince myself otherwise, the remaining ones are too poor to be shown. Please don't insist, this is nonnegotiable. I have sense enough to know whether what I do is good or bad, and this is absolutely bad, and I cannot believe that people of taste, if they know anything at all, will find what I've done any good."[13] Although he was totally familiar with this psychological mechanism—"As always, alas, just as I'm about to deliver [my paintings], I again find myself dissatisfied, working up to the last moment and not ending up with anything good. It will be a huge relief when they've all been packed up and I can't see or retouch them anymore"[14]—Monet was waging a veritable battle against himself. For several weeks, he vacillated between deep despair, which led him to question his entire career ("I realized how fake is the undeserved success I've gained"[15]), and slight respites that allowed him to resume work: "I can't say that I've recovered from my discouragement, but at least I want to do the impossible and struggle to the finish out of consideration for you and so as not to put you in a difficult spot."[16]

Durand-Ruel joined the Bernheim-Jeune brothers in their efforts to persuade Monet to deliver fourteen new canvases on May 15.[17] Durand-Ruel had a commercial interest in this, but he was also a true supporter of Monet and had always encouraged him in his moments of doubt in the name of art and their friendship. The exhibition opened on May 28 and comprised twenty-nine paintings (fig. 104). They were listed in the catalogue under simple descriptive titles, grouped by subject: six views of the Grand Canal, two of the Palazzo Ducale, five of San Giorgio Maggiore seen from across the lagoon, five of the Palazzo Ducale seen from San Giorgio Maggiore, three of the Rio della Salute, one of San Giorgio Maggiore at dusk, and seven frontal views of the palaces along the Grand Canal: three of Palazzo Dario, two of Palazzo da Mula, and two of Palazzo Contarini. The works' dimensions were also given, and eight reproductions accompanied Mirbeau's introductory essay.

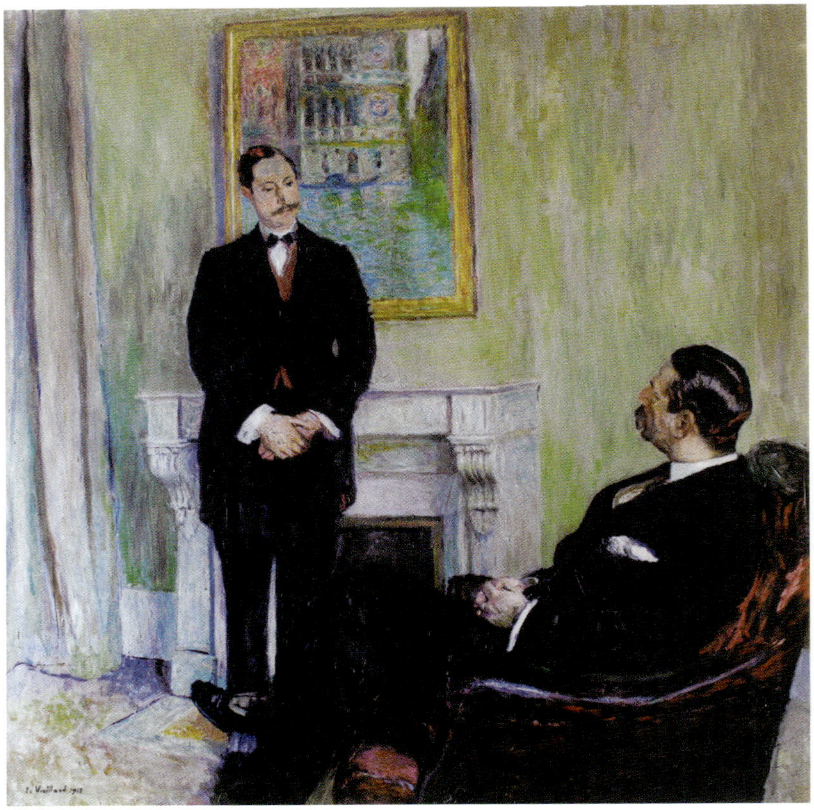

fig. 105—Édouard Vuillard, *Portrait of Josse and Gaston Bernheim-Jeune*, 1912, oil on canvas, 61 ¾ × 62 ¼ in., private collection, Courtesy Bernheim-Jeune

THE CRITICAL RESPONSE TO THE EXHIBITION

The exhibition was generally very well received by both the public and the critics. No fewer than twenty-three articles appeared in the national press. Several, such as Adolphe Tabarant's in *Paris Midi*[18] and Georges Lecomte's in *Le Matin*,[19] took the opportunity to review the phases of Monet's career, from his difficult beginnings to his eventual acclaim, before briefly discussing the Venice works. Most of the reviewers noted the repetition of a limited number of subjects; it led some of them to speak of a series,[20] whereas the term was never used in the catalogue and Monet insisted, "There are no series in these views of Venice, only different subjects repeated one, two, or three times."[21] In addition to their recurrence, the choice of subjects was itself called into question, in highly contrasting ways. Camille Mauclair, who published in *La Semaine Littéraire* the most critical article of the lot, regretted that Monet had confined himself to extremely well-known motifs, familiar to all.[22] On the other hand, most critics, such as "Parisiana" in *L'Art et la Mode*, André

Michel in *Le Journal des Débats Politiques*, and Max Goth in *Les Hommes du Jour*, insisted that the choice of subject was unimportant, even that "the monuments of Venice are of no interest to [Monet]."[23] The important thing was "not the exaggerated Venice, as sung and familiar as the refrain of a popular tune, nor the Venice glimpsed by newlyweds yearning for poetry and sentimentality,"[24] but rather that "the vision that Claude Monet provides of Venice forever delivers us from the outdated charms of flower-laden gondolas, serenades, and guitars."[25] Even more than the subjects, what the critics questioned was Monet's decision to take on Venice and the whole painterly tradition that the city carried with it. Both the ancients — such as Canaletto,[26] Guardi,[27] Leonardo da Vinci, Tiepolo, Titian, and Carpaccio[28] — and the moderns — Turner,[29] Félix Ziem,[30] Henri Le Sidaner, Whistler[31] — were cited either as deterrents or, conversely, as exemplars. And the comparisons were not limited to painting. Music and poetry were also invoked in an attempt to describe the emotions inspired by Monet's canvases, in which "space imbues his work [and] his brushstrokes are rhythms,"[32] and which were "magnificent poetry in pigment."[33] Gustave Geffroy, whom Monet had also considered for the catalogue's preface,[34] was another who compared the Venice canvases to the pages of a poem.[35] While Monet thanked his friend for his laudatory articles, he refuted the comparison, denying that he was a "great poet" or even a "great painter."[36]

ONE DEALER? ONE SHOW?

Bernheim-Jeune was cited in the catalogue, both on the title page and in the colophon, with this specification: "The paintings in this album were exhibited at the Bernheim-Jeune gallery, 15 Rue Richepanse, Paris, from May 28 to June 8, 1912." Mentioning only the Bernheim-Jeune gallery seems logical, since the brothers had exclusive rights to the Venice paintings, to Durand-Ruel's detriment. Nonetheless, in his catalogue raisonné, Daniel Wildenstein mentions both dealers as owning the works in the exhibition. This information is confirmed by the Durand-Ruel archives, which indicate that the paintings were purchased jointly with Bernheim-Jeune: twelve in March 1912 and the others in May of the same year, at prices ranging from 10,000 to 15,000 francs.[37] The Bernheim brothers' supposed exclusivity in fact masked a collaboration between the dealers. Although they did their utmost to obtain priority for the paintings in Venice, it was important above all from the point of view of the exhibition, which, thanks to Monet's name, ensured the gallery's reputation. From an economic point of view, however, the alliance with Durand-Ruel reduced purchasing costs and broadened the market. Since the prices for Monet's canvases had risen quite high, this system of joint purchasing allowed them to acquire an entire group of paintings and thereby maintain their exclusivity over series even if shared. This was not the first time the two galleries had banded together to buy a grouping of Monets. When the first *Water Lilies* were shown in 1900, Durand-Ruel acquired several paintings with Bernheim-Jeune and dealer Isidore Montaignac. And in 1909, at the time of the second *Water Lilies* exhibition, a joint acquisition occasioned lengthy negotiations between Monet and Durand-Ruel, as the painter was insistent that the two galleries agree on the selection of works before the show opened.[38] There is no such trace of similar discussions in Monet's correspondence at the time of the Venice exhibition, which suggests that the dealers settled matters between themselves without bringing in Monet,[39] who for his part considered his contract to be with Bernheim-Jeune.

While the joint purchase facilitated buying the works from the painter, it was equally beneficial for their sale, as it allowed the dealers to expand their market; while Bernheim-Jeune operated solely in France, Durand-Ruel had a significant presence in the United States. He was one of the main architects of the dissemination of Impressionism in America, organizing in New York, in 1886, a major exhibition of his holdings, mostly works by the Impressionists. In addition to New York, where Durand-Ruel opened a branch office in 1888, other cities played an important role in the reception of Impressionism in America. Before the New York exhibition, there had been the *American Exhibition of Foreign Products, Arts, and Manufactures* in Boston in 1883, to which Durand-Ruel had lent paintings by Manet, Renoir, Monet, and Pissarro. The latter mentioned this loan in a letter to Monet of June 12, 1883: "Several of our canvases went traveling to the Boston show; according to some Americans, I learned that it was a mediocre exhibition that had no impact. I mentioned this to Durand, who called it a trial run, saying he'd taken advantage of the opportunity to exhibit us, especially since it was exempt from any customs duties."[40] Regardless, from very early on, Boston was establishing connections with Impressionism and Monet.[41] During the painter's lifetime, his works would be shown thirty-four times in Boston; seventeen of those exhibitions were instigated by Durand-Ruel.

It was therefore through Durand-Ruel that, after the exhibition in Paris, several of the Venice canvases were sent to the United States to be shown at the Brooks Reed Gallery in Boston. This information is given by Wildenstein in the "List of Exhibitions" appendix in his catalogue raisonné. Despite our best efforts, we have found out very little about this gallery, which nonetheless exhibited works by Monet no fewer than fourteen times.[42] The Venice show was the only monographic exhibition; all the others were group shows, featuring works from Durand-Ruel's inventory or collection. Given that the dealer organized a number of shows in Boston, despite not having a gallery there, it is likely that the Brooks Reed Gallery, located at 19 Arlington Street, was an exhibition space that could be rented out. Not only do we have precious little information about this space, but we also know little about that particular exhibition. We must therefore rely on the data provided by Wildenstein, who indicates that the show, titled *Monet, Venice: Tableaux Durand-Ruel*, was held in late October 1912 (with no further details) and that seven canvases were displayed.[43] All the works presented in Boston had already been included in the Paris exhibition, indicating that no exclusivity applied to the United States. The seven paintings all depicted different views, giving a wide overview of the range of subjects Monet brought back from Venice. And while these works were initially bought jointly by Durand-Ruel and Bernheim-Jeune, they appear to have been repurchased by

Durand-Ruel's New York annex, which then showed them at the Brooks Reed Gallery before selling them on the American market.

THE SALE OF THE PAINTINGS

Of the twenty-nine canvases shown in Paris, four were sold during the run of the exhibition or immediately afterward, nine over the rest of 1912, and seven in 1913. Among these, the seven paintings shown in Boston were all sold during or soon after the exhibition. Twenty paintings out of twenty-nine were therefore sold in the wake of the Paris and Boston exhibitions, proof positive that showing the works in public played a preponderant role in encouraging sales. While Monet's renown was by then well established, it was still important to create a sense of occasion with a well-curated exhibition, which showcased works and inspired collectors to acquire them. Monet was quite savvy about such matters, and throughout his career he used exhibitions, first in group shows with his Impressionist colleagues, then alone in monographic shows, to promote his work and career.[44] In 1912, after some hesitation, Monet did not go to Paris to install his paintings,[45] which suggests that he was more willing to leave control of this exhibition to his dealers. They were the ones who acted as their artist's promoters, inviting all "the major collectors, directors of European museums, and art lovers" to the opening.[46]

Following the path taken by these works after the two exhibitions is also highly instructive. Notably, it confirms the international dimension of the Venice canvases, since out of the twenty sold in 1912 and 1913, thirteen were bought by American collectors.[47] Three of them were women, each of whom bought a painting after the Boston exhibition. Miss Grace M. Edwards acquired a *Palazzo Ducale Seen from San Giorgio Maggiore* (pl. 14), which would not remain in her collection very long, as she exchanged it at Durand-Ruel in March 1916; it was therefore not among the works that she, along with her brother and sister, would donate to the Museum of Fine Arts, Boston, in memory of their mother. Mrs. Breckinridge Long, for her part, acquired a view of San Giorgio Maggiore (pl. 12). Born Christine Alexander Graham, she was the wife of Samuel Miller Breckinridge Long, himself a collector who later held positions in the U.S. State Department. The painting was shown as early as 1913 at the Saint Louis Art Museum in an exhibition of works lent by collectors. The last of the three women, Ellen Hunt Henderson, bought a Rio della Salute (pl. 26). Henderson was the daughter of a sugar magnate and the sister of Hunt Henderson, a major collector of works by the Impressionists and Whistler. Her brother also bought a Venice painting, a view of the Grand Canal, acquired in 1913 from Durand-Ruel, of whom he had been a steady client since 1908 (pl. 3). Among the other buyers of works shown in Boston, Arthur B. Emmons was the owner of four Venice canvases. He bought the first one right after the Boston show, then the three others over the course of 1913 (pl. 6, 17, 21, 29). All were sold, along with fifteen other paintings by Monet and five by Renoir, in a sale orchestrated by Durand-Ruel and Knoedler in January 1920.[48] Along with the Venice works, Emmons owned five paintings from London, which are aesthetically fairly close to the Venice paintings in their interplay of water, architecture, and light. Alexander

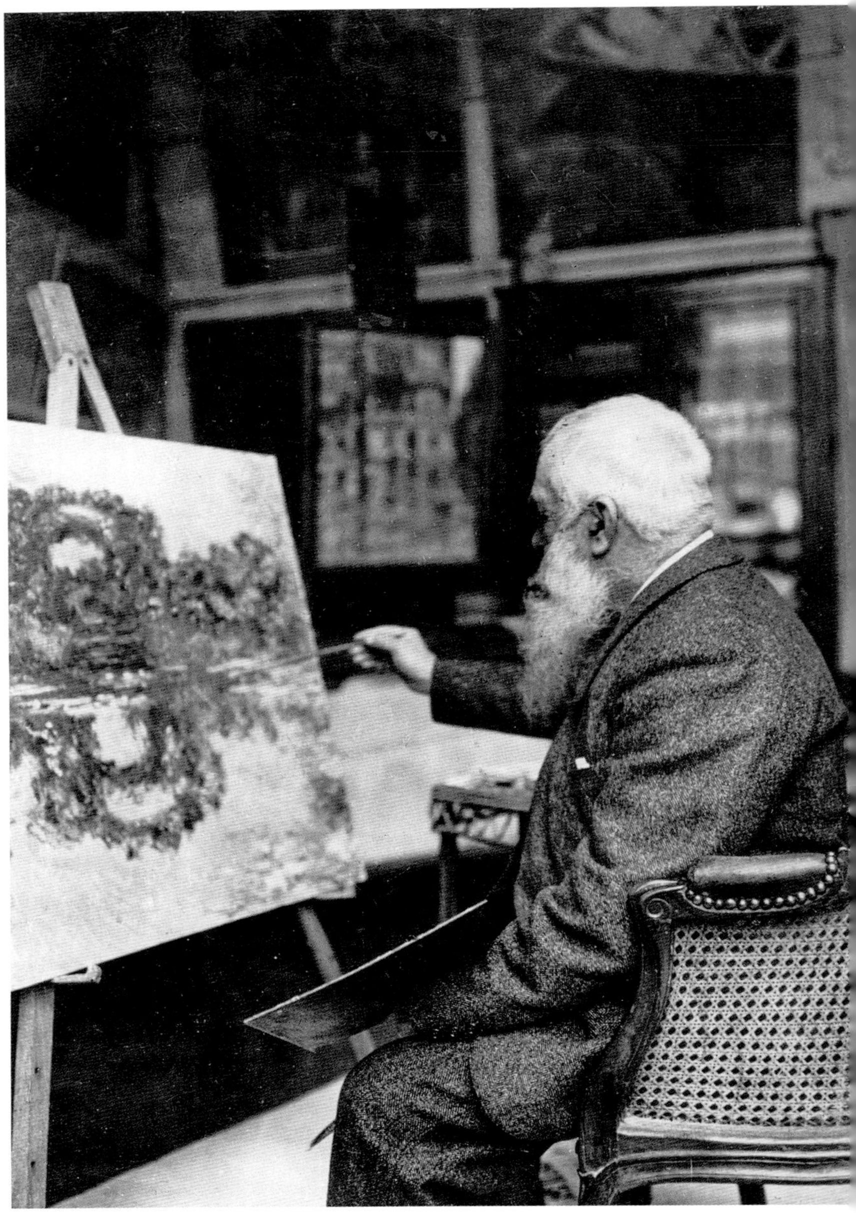

fig. 106—Monet in his Giverny studio, circa 1913, with a painting of Palazzo Dario visible in the background

Cochrane, a Boston collector, bought a painting of San Giorgio Maggiore in July 1912, therefore even before the works were shown at Brooks Reed (pl. 10). The exhibition, however, seems to have persuaded him to buy another, as he acquired a view of the Grand Canal in November 1912. A member of the board of trustees of the Museum of Fine Arts, Cochrane would bequeath part of his collection, including the Grand Canal view, to that institution (pl. 2).

Of the six paintings not bought by Americans, only two were acquired by Frenchmen; one of them was Monet himself, to whom a *Palazzo Dario* was retroceded in June 1912 (fig. 106 and pl. 23).[49] The painting would remain in Giverny in the collection of his younger son, Michel, before being auctioned in the 1960s. The couturier Jacques Doucet was the purchaser, from Bernheim-Jeune during the exhibition, of the second item in the catalogue, a view of the Grand Canal. The last four canvases went to Wales, bought by the sisters Margaret and Gwendoline Davies, whose vast acquisitions form the basis of the modern art holdings of Amgueddfa Cymru–Museum Wales, which are displayed in the National Museum Cardiff. They visited the Venice exhibition at Bernheim-Jeune in 1912, buying a first painting there, then two others a few months later, also from Bernheim-Jeune. Margaret completed this small grouping with a *Palazzo Dario*, which she acquired nearly a year after that, this time from Durand-Ruel. This change of intermediary vis-à-vis the Welsh sisters confirms that Bernheim-Jeune was limited to the French market, whereas Durand-Ruel had international reach. Three of the four works the Davies sisters bought in 1912 and 1913 remained in their collection and are now at the Cardiff museum; the fourth was sold to the collector Osgood Hooker, who in 1960 gave it to the Fine Arts Museums of San Francisco.

Of the eight paintings that were not shown, two were given as gifts by Monet: a view of San Giorgio Maggiore went to Mary Hunter in gratitude for her hospitality during Monet and his wife's stay in Venice, and *Gondola in Venice* was given to Georges Clemenceau. One remained in Giverny, and the other five entered the market at a much later date. This confirms yet again the importance of exhibitions to the sale of works. While works of art are, of course, sold outside of exhibitions, the latter play an especially crucial role, something that Monet understood perfectly and that he used to his advantage throughout his career. As someone whose works were shown in no fewer than six hundred exhibitions during his lifetime, including about fifty monographic ones, he truly built his career on public displays. He used them to forge his reputation, sell his paintings, and publicize his visual experiments. Monet would never again travel after Venice, instead concentrating exclusively on his water garden, which he depicted tirelessly. He embarked on a vast mural project, what he called his *grandes décorations*, with the idea of plunging the viewer into the center of his water lily pond. For the armistice of World War I, he gave these canvases to the French state and designed their installation in the Musée de l'Orangerie. With this gesture, Monet severed his career-long connection between exhibition and sale, removing his final paintings from that marketing strategy in an exhibition that, this time, was not temporary and organized by a dealer, but permanent and in a museum.

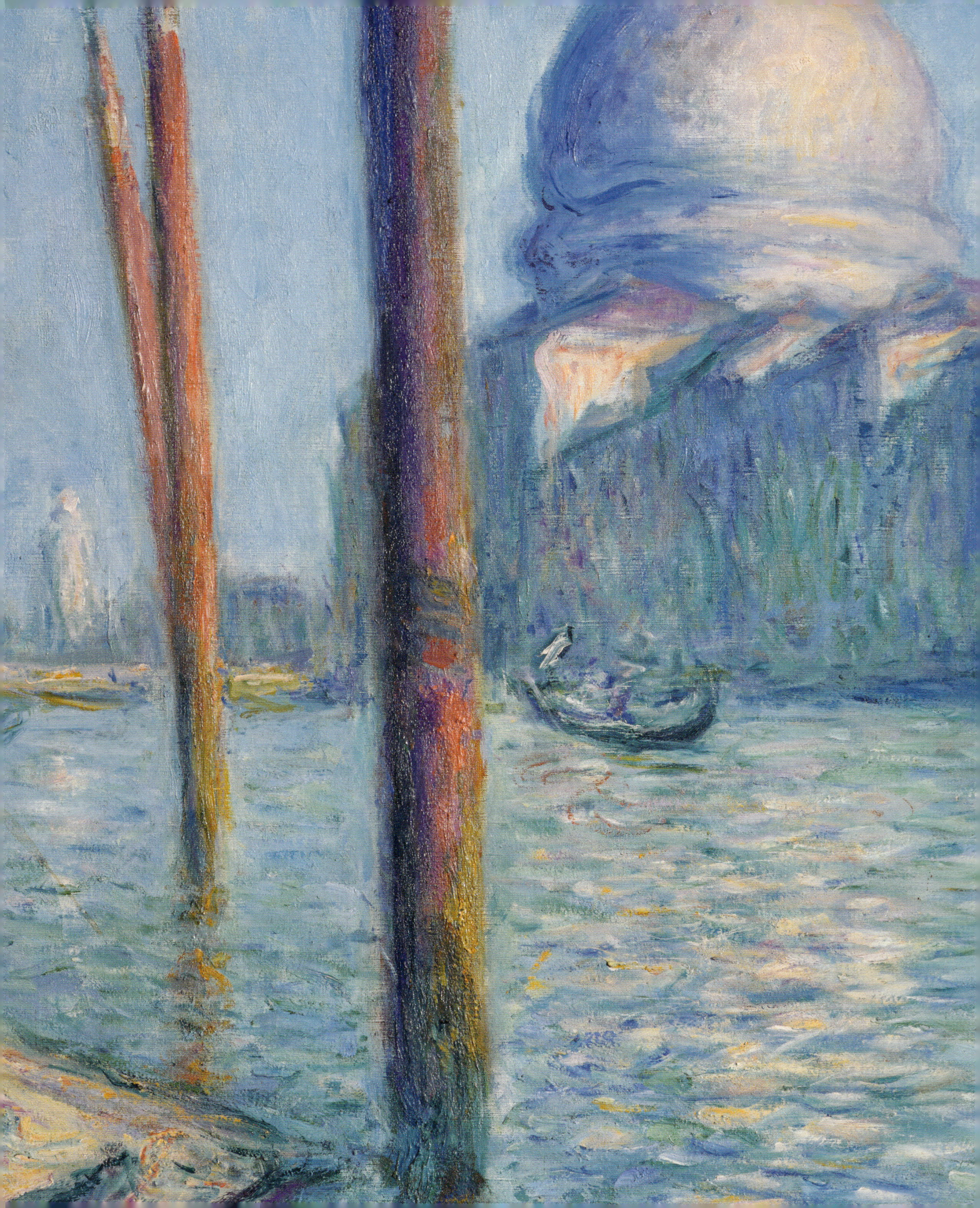

PART FOUR

VISIONS AND VARI-ATIONS

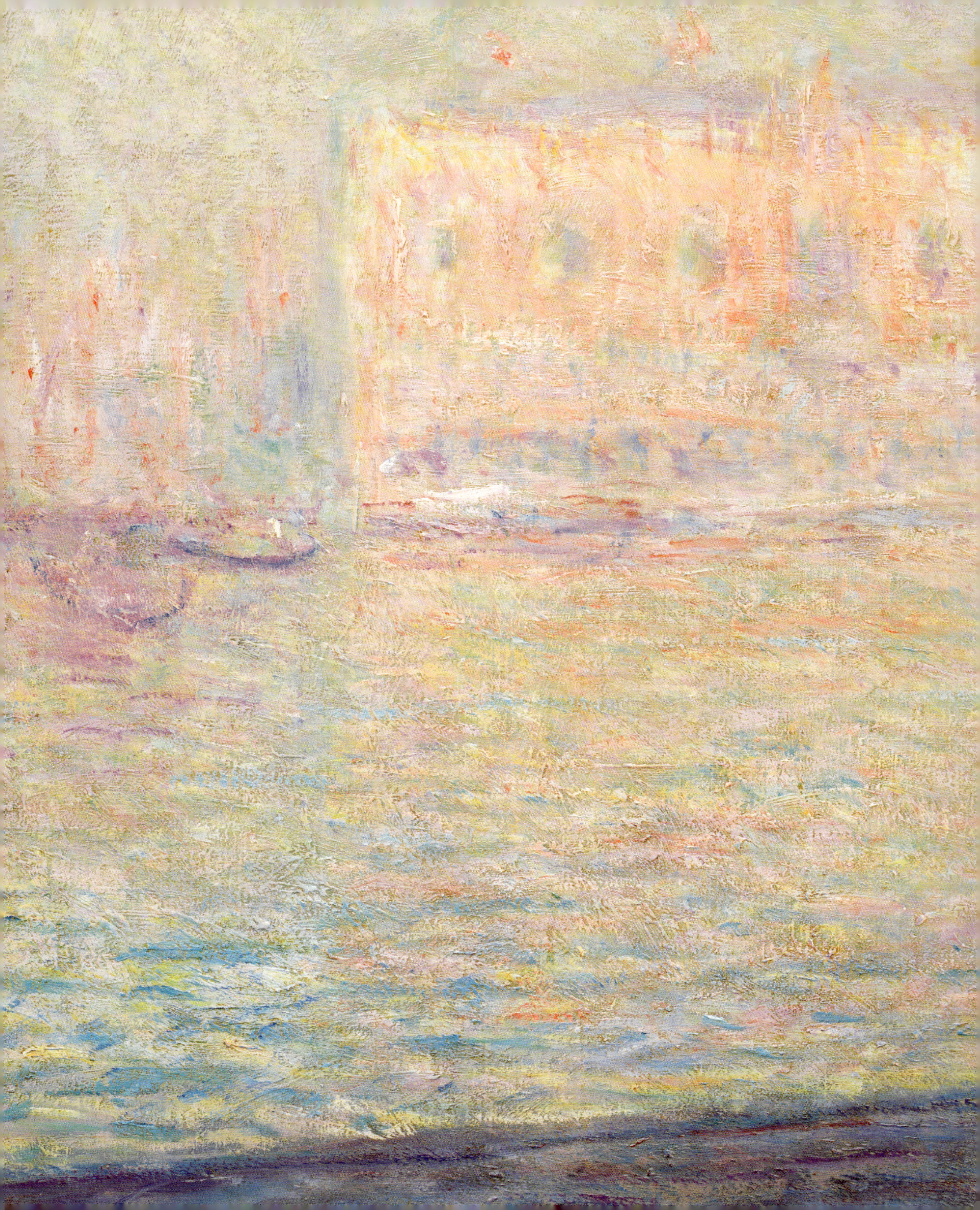

VISIONS OF VENICE: BETWEEN PARIS AND LONDON

Donato Esposito

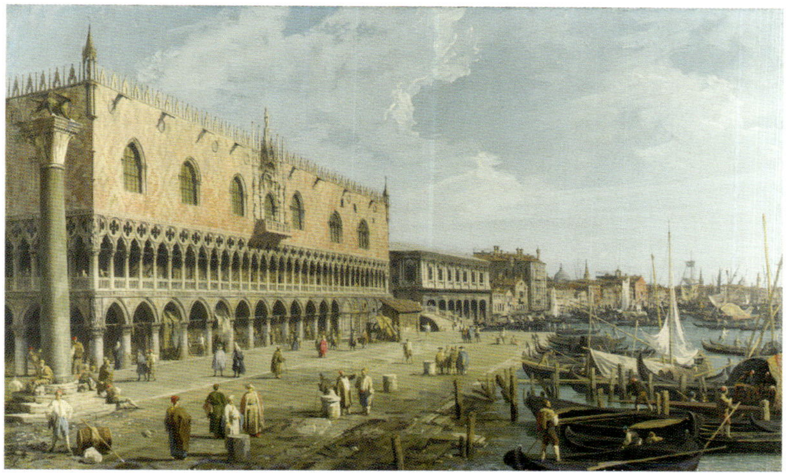

fig. 107—Canaletto, *Venice: The Doge's Palace and the Riva degli Schiavoni*, late 1730s, oil on canvas, $24\frac{1}{8} \times 39\frac{1}{4}$ in., The National Gallery

CLAUDE MONET VISITED VENICE for the only time in 1908. Decades before he ventured there, the city had visually impressed itself on him through a long tradition of its artistic representation. Depictions of Venice were found in great numbers in both London and Paris and informed and shaped his encounter. Monet's work is in many respects in the *vedute* tradition of Canaletto and Francesco Guardi, but also Jean-Baptiste-Camille Corot and Richard Parkes Bonington, and it shares a historical vision with that of J. M. W. Turner and James McNeill Whistler. In Paris, Monet had access to the French national collection of old masters at the Musée du Louvre and contemporary work at the Musée du Luxembourg (now absorbed into the Musée d'Orsay). He first went to London in 1870 to escape the Franco-Prussian War and returned there three times over the course of his long career. London had the most numerous and finest Canalettos in Europe, both at the National Gallery and later (after it opened in 1900) at the Wallace Collection. The latter even had a "Canaletto room" upon opening. In the national collection at Trafalgar Square, where both foreign and British works could be seen together, Monet would relish further Venetian scenes by Canaletto and Guardi, but also those of more recent production by Turner and others. In addition, the Turner bequest was on view there before the Tate Gallery (now Tate Britain) opened in 1897. In assembling works by Monet of Venice, his collectors, such as the Davies sisters in Newtown, Wales, hung his works in dialogue with other depictions of the same city by other artists. Thus, a canvas by Walter Sickert (bought in 1935) and one by Whistler (bought in 1912) hung in the same collection with *The Grand Canal, Venice* (pl. 1) and *The Palazzo Dario* (pl. 24) by Monet. His dialogue with art and Venice went both ways.

PARIS

The greatest painter of Venice, and the one most associated with that city up to the nineteenth century—perhaps even now—was Giovanni Antonio Canal, known as Canaletto, closely followed by Francesco Guardi. Paul Leroi identified the attraction of these two artists: "Canaletto shows us the real Venice, Venice as it exists materially; the other unfolds it for me as I dream it and my dream is dear to me. Long live Guardi! . . . The true historian of our Venice!"[1] The faded glory of the city was evidenced for Leroi in even the "smallest of the paintings" by Guardi.[2] For Monet, living in Paris, there was limited opportunity to study paintings by either Canaletto or Guardi at the Louvre.[3] The best ones were the superb *Entrance to the Grand Canal and the Salute Church in Venice*, which had been in the Louvre since 1818 and was thought to be a Canaletto until the late twentieth century but is now considered to be by Michele Marieschi, and Guardi's *Le Doge de Venise Suit la Procession du Corpus Domini sur la Place Saint-Marc*, which had arrived into the collection in 1797 (fig. 110).[4] The architecture of the city in the bold work by Marieschi, complete with the jutting quay outside Santa Maria della Salute, both frames and dominates the composition. Closer to Monet's time was the work of the British artist Bonington, which offered vivid and freshly captured views of Venice departing from earlier depictions marked by crystalline clarity. Bonington had made his trip to Italy in 1826, shortly before Corot was in Venice in 1828. Bonington's *The Ducal Palace Venice, from the Riva degli Schiavoni* (1827–28), was in the Louvre by 1883.[5] The view is close to one that Monet later adopted (fig. 112).

There was a burgeoning interest in Guardi during the nineteenth century. Leroi, writing in 1878, again signaled this appreciation, and his new contemporary appeal: "I saw the Guardis again [at the Louvre] and this devil of a man . . . bewitched me. That's because he's a musician and a poet, this painter; his palette modulates the finest harmonies."[6] This interpretation of Guardi's work broadly anticipates Monet's future work in Venice with its harmonious colorways.

Though there were relatively few publicly accessible pictures by either Canaletto or Guardi available to Monet in Paris, auction houses supplemented museums and art galleries. Frequent auctions in Paris provided opportunities to encounter Venetian subjects by historic and contemporary artists. These artworks were displayed for a few days, available to all, before they were put up for sale. One of the major sales of Venetian *vedute* pictures in the last quarter of the nineteenth century in Paris was that of Alexis Febvre.[7] The sale of the large collection took place in mid-1882 and garnered wide coverage in the art historical press. The journal *L'Art* took the opportunity to commission large full-page etchings after four major paintings by Guardi that all appeared in early 1882 ahead of the sale. The prints after Guardi accompanied a biographical note about Febvre, who had died the year before, and are "planches hors texte."[8] Guardi's quartet of paintings in the sale were identical in size and format and the artist may have intended them to form a group or series: *Piazza San Marco*, *La Piazzetta*, *San Giorgio Maggiore*, and *Santa Maria della Salute*.[9] In the auction *livret* they were described as offering a range of views of the city that "reproduce and summarize Venice in its most attractive aspects, at different times of the day." That remark reveals some awareness of the Impressionist project, and of Monet's seriality in particular. Monet may also have encountered the many Venetian subjects in Gustave Rothan's collection dispersed in 1890.[10]

In 1892, two large works by Canaletto were sold at the Galerie Sedelmeyer in Paris: *La Place Saint-Marc, Venise* and *Saint-Georges-Majeur, Venise*.[11] In 1895, Sedelmeyer also had a fine Bernardo Bellotto, then considered a Canaletto, that later ended up in the Louvre in 1961.[12] That same decade this gallery also handled late works by Turner, including the painting *Rockets and Blue Lights (Close at Hand) to Warn Steamboats of Shoal Water*, from 1840, now in the Clark Art Institute in Williamstown, Massachusetts.[13] The sale in 1904 of artworks from the collection formed of Mathilde Bonaparte—niece of Emperor Napoléon I—also drew interest. In it were four Venetian views, two each by Canaletto and Guardi. All four are now untraced.[14]

In the years immediately before Monet's trip to Venice in October 1908, many other Venetian scenes appeared at auction in Paris and may have had a chance to impress themselves on Monet. For example, a sale on May 16, 1904, included *La Piazzetta, à Venise* by Canaletto and *Le Grand Canal, à Venise* by Guardi.[15] In March 1908, the painting *La Place Saint-Marc de Venise* by Canaletto was sold.[16]

Beyond auctions and the old masters at the Louvre, in Paris Monet was surrounded by contemporary art on permanent or temporary display. The annual state-sponsored, though typically conservative-leaning, Paris Salon showcased contemporary art. Most years included something painted (or inspired) by Venice. Fellow Impressionist Pierre-Auguste Renoir visited Venice before Monet. Renoir exhibited two 1881 Venice images, *Grand Canal, Venice* and *Venice, the Doge's Palace*, at the 1882 Impressionist exhibition (fig. 185).[17] Renoir's depictions reinforce the *vedute* tradition. The French painter Corot also visited and painted in Venice, though none of his works were acquired for the French national collection until 1909. Undoubtedly the French artist most closely associated with Venice during Monet's lifetime was Félix Ziem. In 1887, a writer in London noted that the novelty of approaching Venice for the first time was marred by prior exposure to its many artistic depictions and lamented that they wished they had "never seen a Canaletto or a Ziem" beforehand.[18] Ziem's work was exhibited at the Paris Salon, won medals, and was in the Musée du Luxembourg.[19] In his works, widely known from publication as prints, Venice is conveyed as a working mercantile center, with its illustrious landmarks in second place. This contrasts markedly with the approach of Monet, who never depicted any commercial activity in Venice at all.[20]

Ziem's profile rose even further in 1900—and likely attracted Monet's attention—when one of his paintings set the highest sale record for a living artist in France. Amid great fanfare, Ziem's *Le Grand Canal à Venise* was sold in Paris from the collection of Étienne Moreau-Nélaton for 49,500 francs

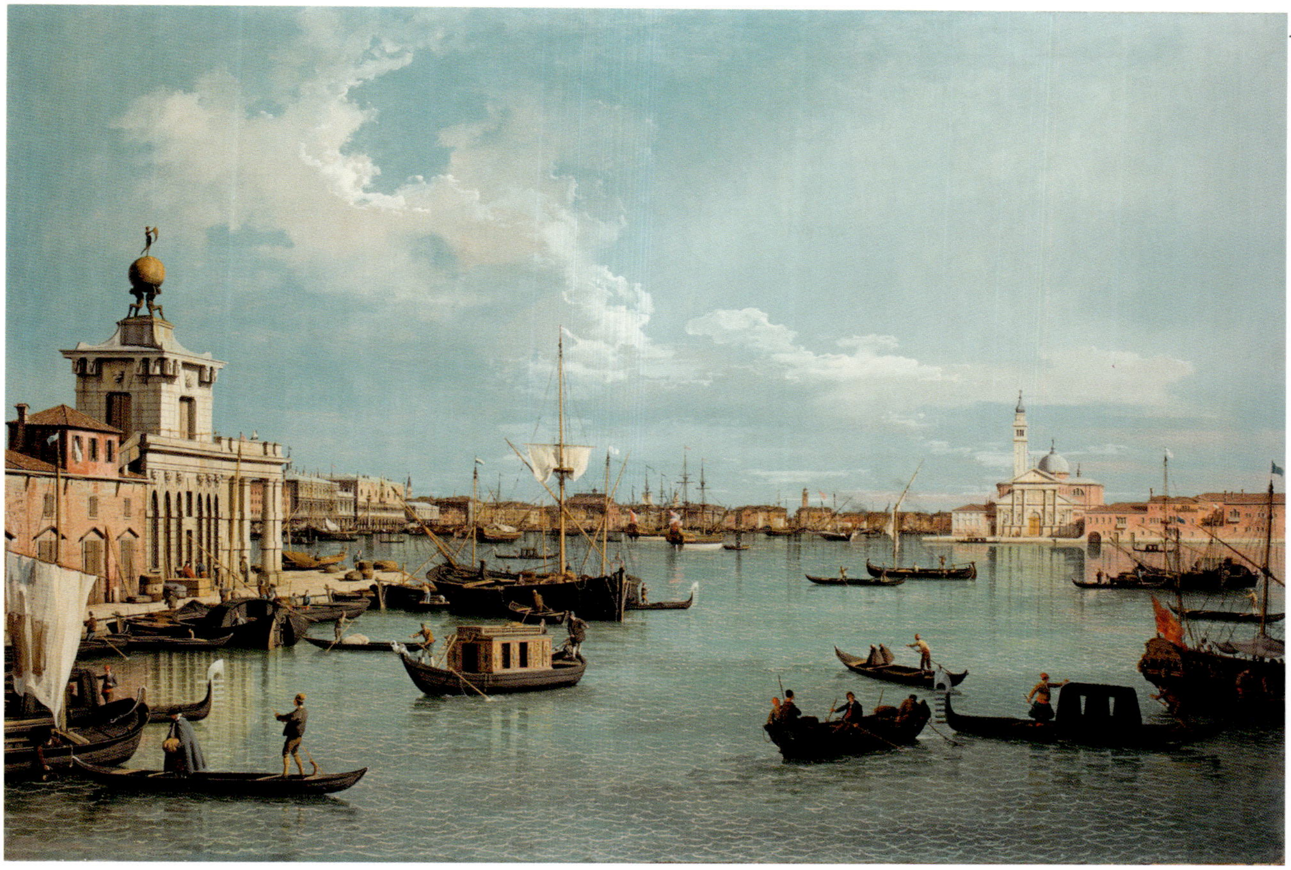

fig. 108—Canaletto, *Venice: The Bacino di San Marco from the Canale della Giudecca*, c. 1735–44, oil on canvas, 51¼×75 in., The Wallace Collection

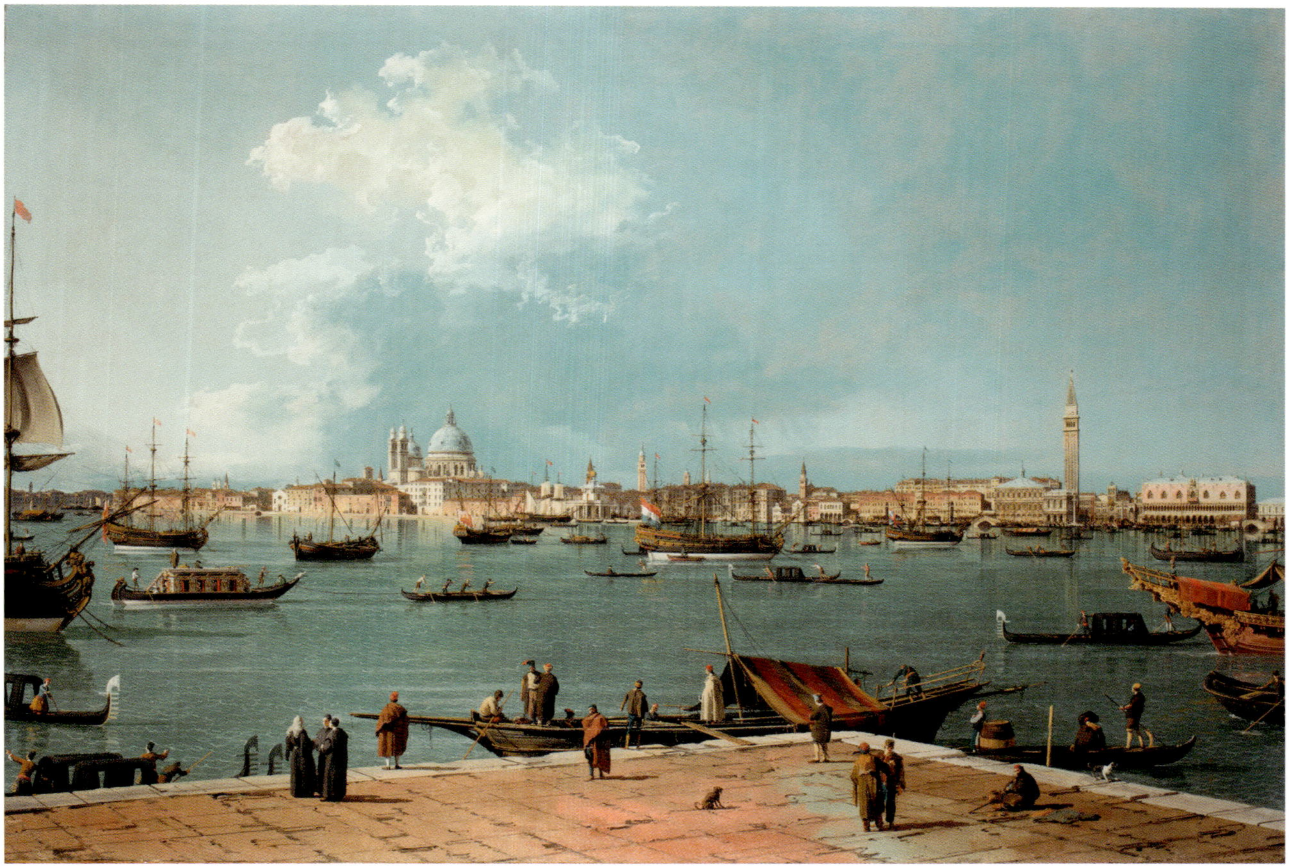

fig. 109—Canaletto, *Venice: The Bacino di San Marco from San Giorgio Maggiore*, c. 1735–44, oil on canvas, 50⁹⁄₁₀×74⅓ in., The Wallace Collection

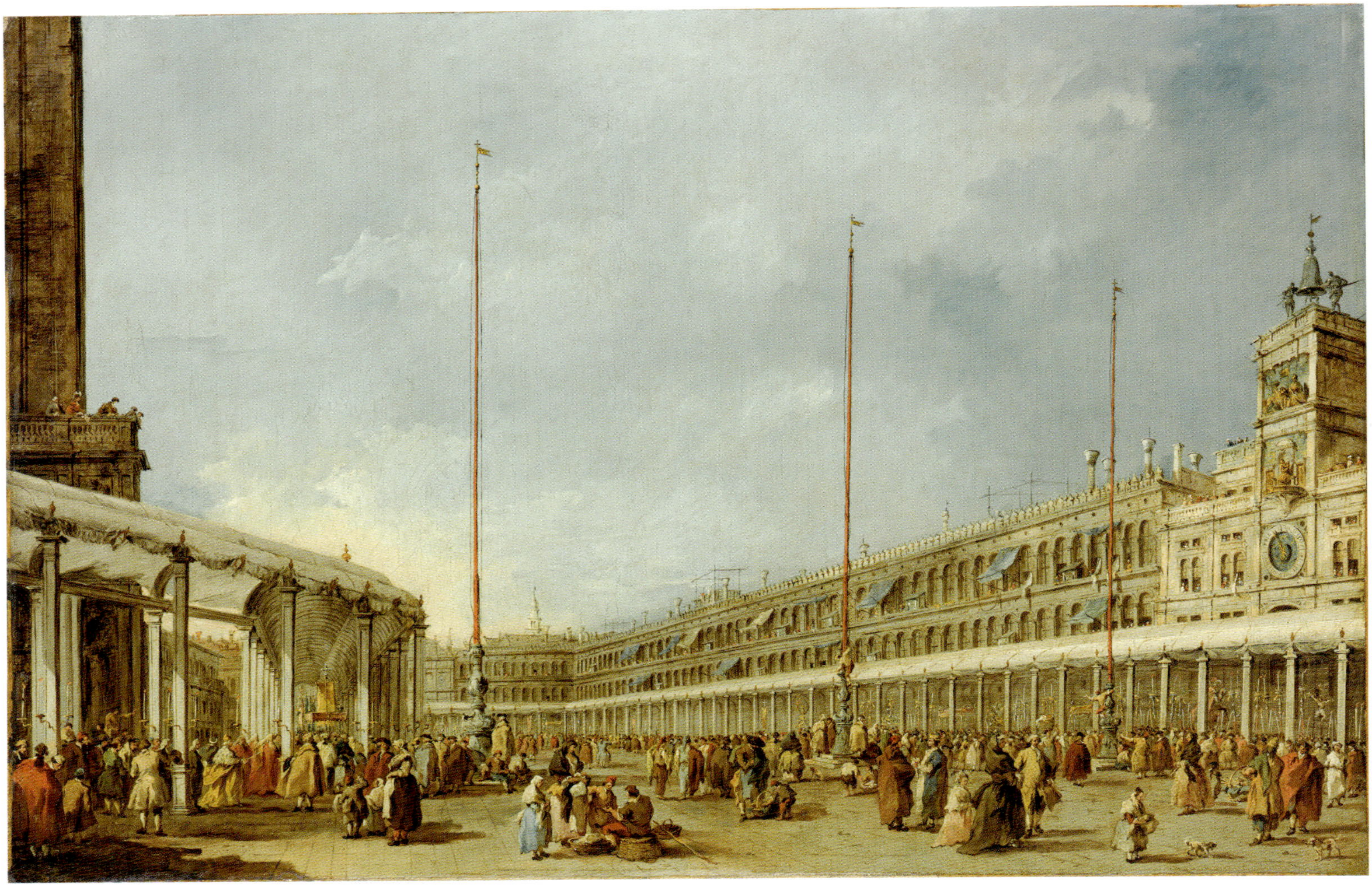

fig. 110—Francesco Guardi, *Le Doge de Venise Suit la Procession du Corpus Domini sur la Place Saint-Marc*, c. 1770–80, oil on canvas, 26×31¾ in., Musée du Louvre

(or 274,000 U.S. dollars in today's value).[21] In Britain, Ziem was dubbed the "French Turner" in 1906.[22] Even in London, Monet could not escape Ziem, as one of his large paintings, *Venice: The Bacino di San Marco with Fishing Boats*, was in the Wallace Collection.[23]

The examples by Ziem that most likely imprinted upon Monet in the years immediately before 1908 were the sketches donated by the artist to the city of Paris in 1905. Perhaps aware of the positive effect of the Turner bequest on that artist's reputation, Ziem donated several dozen oil sketches and works on paper to the Petit Palais museum (then recently opened following the Exposition Universelle in 1900).[24] In these sketches, Ziem is at his most daring, and in a few examples he approaches the subtlety and touch of Turner. The "salle Ziem" opened to the public in July 1905 and was officially inaugurated on December 13, 1905.[25] Crucially, on opening, the whole gift was shown in its entirety—including the type of preparatory or loosely finished work that was seldom exhibited to the public at the time.

Ziem's oil sketches bear aesthetic and compositional parallels with the work of Monet. The dreamy *Venise, le Grand Canal au Soleil Levant* (fig. 116) closely approaches Turner in the soft handling of the setting sun, vaporous, hazy clouds, and dissolving forms of the Palazzo Ducale on the left.[26]

LONDON

On Monet's working trips to London in 1899, 1900, and 1901, that city's public collections offered him a wider selection of Venetian artworks than his native Paris. Prized among these depictions were works by Canaletto and Turner. The latter granted Monet the greater Venetian pictorial legacy, and Monet's work is much indebted, in spirit and method, to the earlier British painter. London provided access to the full range of Turner's output, encompassing works on paper as well as paintings, whereas in nineteenth-century Paris few opportunities were to be had to see Turners (of any kind), and usually these were exclusively at dealers' galleries.[27] The Louvre did not acquire any Turners during Monet's lifetime and indeed did not receive its first painting until 1967.[28] The first public exhibition of any Turners in Paris came only in 1900, when several were included in the Exposition Universelle. These included *Depositing of John Bellini's Three Pictures in La Chiesa Redentore, Venice* (fig. 153), which anticipates the mood of Monet's future depictions of Venice.[29]

In London, the Turner bequest, finally settled in 1856, had made Turner's work accessible. The artist's bequest to the British state included hundreds of paintings (some complete, others not) and thousands of drawings and watercolors in various stages of completion. These were initially housed and put on display at the National Gallery in Trafalgar Square, where they were joined by other work by Turner from other sources. When Monet visited the institution at the turn of the century, he would have seen the newly configured "Turner room" for framed works on paper that had opened in 1890.

The critic Frederick Wedmore was delighted by the new offerings in the Turner room in the National Gallery, where

fig. 111—Richard Parkes Bonington, *Venice: The Piazza San Marco*, 1828, oil on canvas, 39 3/25 × 31 3/50 in., The Wallace Collection

fig. 112—Richard Parkes Bonington, *View of Venice, the Riva degli Schiavoni, and the Palazzo Ducale*, 1826, oil on canvas, 16 3/20 × 21 1/4 in., Musée du Louvre

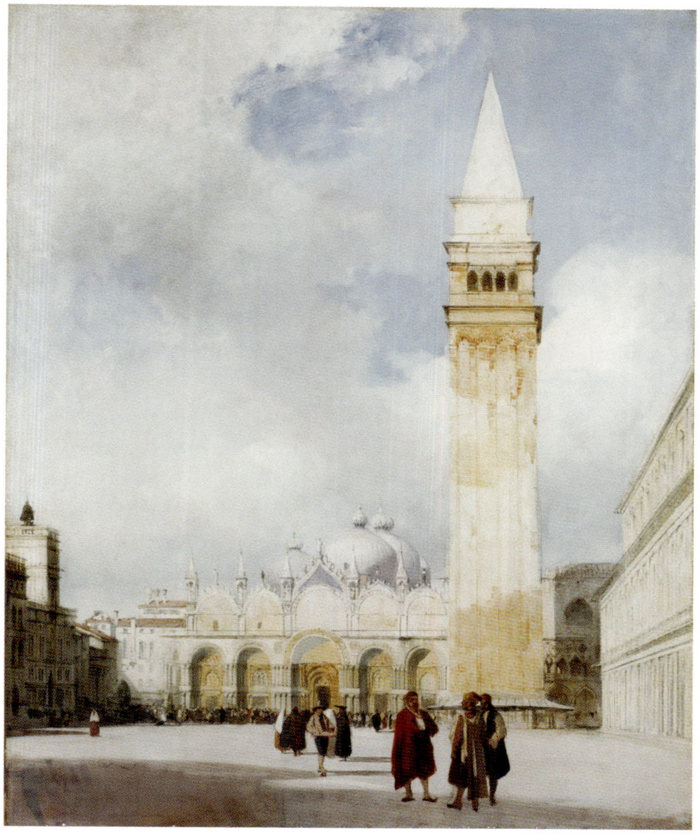

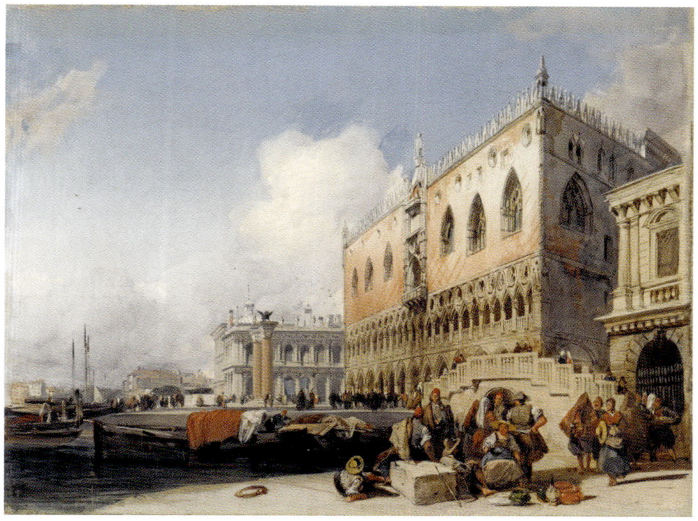

"something like a hundred drawings, which have never before been exhibited, have suddenly become visible in a room newly devoted to the work of Turner." Many of them, he added, appeared "rapid and impetuous."[30] The coverage of the new display extended nationally, and the critic of the *Liverpool Mercury* declared that 104 works by Turner "never before exhibited, are now to be seen in one of the rooms of the basement of the National Gallery."[31] The *Magazine of Art* enthused over the "important addition made to the number of the [late] Turner drawings on view" in which he "exquisitely idealised and refined" nature. It demonstrated "how masterly an 'Impressionist,' in the best of all senses, Turner became in his later life."[32]

The Turners on view would have offered fertile inspirational ground for Monet. For example, Monet may have noticed *Venice—Noon* (fig. 115).[33] It was first exhibited at the Royal Academy of Arts in 1845 and was on display (on rotation) at the National Gallery until it was transferred to the Tate Gallery in 1929. Inventoried in 1856, it was one of 106 "finished pictures" (to use Turner's own description in his later codicils of 1848 and 1849) that were immediately available on view.[34] In 1901 and 1905, additional oil paintings were inventoried and added to the public presentation.[35] In 1897 the opening of the Tate Gallery precipitated the gradual transfer of most Turners from Trafalgar Square to Millbank.

In *Venice—Noon*, Turner avoided the many obvious landmarks of the city, so that only the campanile—and perhaps the gondolas in the foreground—marks the canvas as being situated in Venice at all. Water and sky seem to merge and their similar treatment in brushwork dissolves the cityscape altogether. This late treatment by Turner contrasts with work from the decade before, and freely on view at the National Gallery, like *Bridge of Sighs, Ducal Palace and Custom-House, Venice: Canaletti Painting* (1833; Tate),[36] and *Venice, the Bridge of Sighs* (1840; Tate), in which the architecture is central. The former was among the first Venetian works Turner exhibited at the Royal Academy in 1833. In 1847 Robert Vernon donated the painting to the National Gallery; it remained on view there until 1912, when it was transferred to the Tate.[37]

The other great Turner of Venice on view during one of Monet's visits was the stunning *Venice from the Giudecca* (fig. 113). First shown at the Royal Academy in 1840, it was donated to the Victoria and Albert Museum in 1857 by John Sheepshanks, with the intention of founding a British national gallery there. Ultimately, this was usurped by the founding of the Tate Gallery in 1897.[38] Here the majestic white form of the church of Santa Maria della Salute rises above the bustling mercantile life of the city on the water. The white forms merge with the white cloudy sky to form a continuously modulated setting.

Some Turner watercolors had been on view long before 1890. Beginning in 1879, visitors to the National Gallery could see these, including many late works, which are often unresolved and loose. The move was a cause to congratulate the authorities of the National Gallery, because "hitherto the Turner sketches have been more difficult of access" but they were now freely available with the rest of the permanent collection, without special permission.[39] The new range on display included much late work from Turner's trip to Venice (and elsewhere) and of a type unavailable elsewhere: "coloured sketches of the artist's later period—brief but pregnant records of a crowd of impressions received by Turner in Venice, on the Alps, and on the lakes of Switzerland."[40]

In London Monet could see more Venetian work by Bonington than in Paris. In the National Gallery, together with the many Turners, was *The Piazzetta, Venice* (1827; Tate).[41] In the Wallace Collection was another unusual viewpoint by Bonington, *Venice: The Piazza San Marco* from 1828 (fig. 111). The bold thrusting form of the campanile, depicted close-up, dominates the work and looms over the adjoining piazza. The Wallace Collection and the National Gallery offered Monet a combined equivalent of the Louvre and the Luxembourg, with contemporary works under the same roof as historic works, foremost among them the many paintings by Canaletto and Guardi. In the aggregate, these must have impressed upon Monet the pictorial possibilities of Venice.[42]

The Wallace Collection's superb Canalettos included *Venice: The Bacino di San Marco from San Giorgio Maggiore* and *Venice: The Bacino di San Marco from the Canale della Giudecca* (figs. 108 and 109). The overall blue tonality is dominated by the sky and water, casting the city in both paintings into a narrow strip on the horizon. This resonates with Monet's painting *The Palazzo Ducale Seen from San Giorgio Maggiore*[43] with its jutting quayside that breaks into the picture plane in a similar way. The major *Venice: The Doge's Palace and the Riva degli Schiavoni* by Canaletto in the National Gallery may also have offered a pictorial solution to depicting the palace up close while retaining the picture's broader visual appeal (fig. 107).

In his 1899 book, *Venise, Reine de la Couleur*, Léon Rosenthal extolled the mesmeric attraction of the city and the way that "the name of Venice evokes in everyone's mind brilliant and radiant images."[44] He continued: "For the popular imagination, for painters and for poets, for those who have seen it and for those who have dreamed of it, Venice is a symbol—a symbol of warm richness, light, and color."[45]

These words could have resonated with Monet and Whistler before him. In London, Monet could have seen many works by Whistler, but (excluding pastels and prints) it is difficult to pinpoint with certainty any of Venice specifically. Whistler's *Nocturne: Blue and Gold—St. Mark's, Venice* (1880), completely dissolves the architecture into inky blackness, with just a few streetlamps to anchor the scene.[46] It was exhibited in London at the Royal Society of British Artists in 1886 and 1887 and in Paris in both 1891 and 1892, when Monet may have seen it close to home. One other work by Whistler of Venice was sold in Paris in 1903 and was in a French collection before that.[47] The buyer of the former work, Gwendoline Davies, was a direct purchaser from the Galerie Bernheim-Jeune Venice show in 1912, and had many works of Venice in her collection, including works by Sickert (fig. 114), as well as Whistler and Monet. Monet's visit to London in 1899 provided many opportunities to see Turner's work outside of public collections.[48] In particular, auction houses

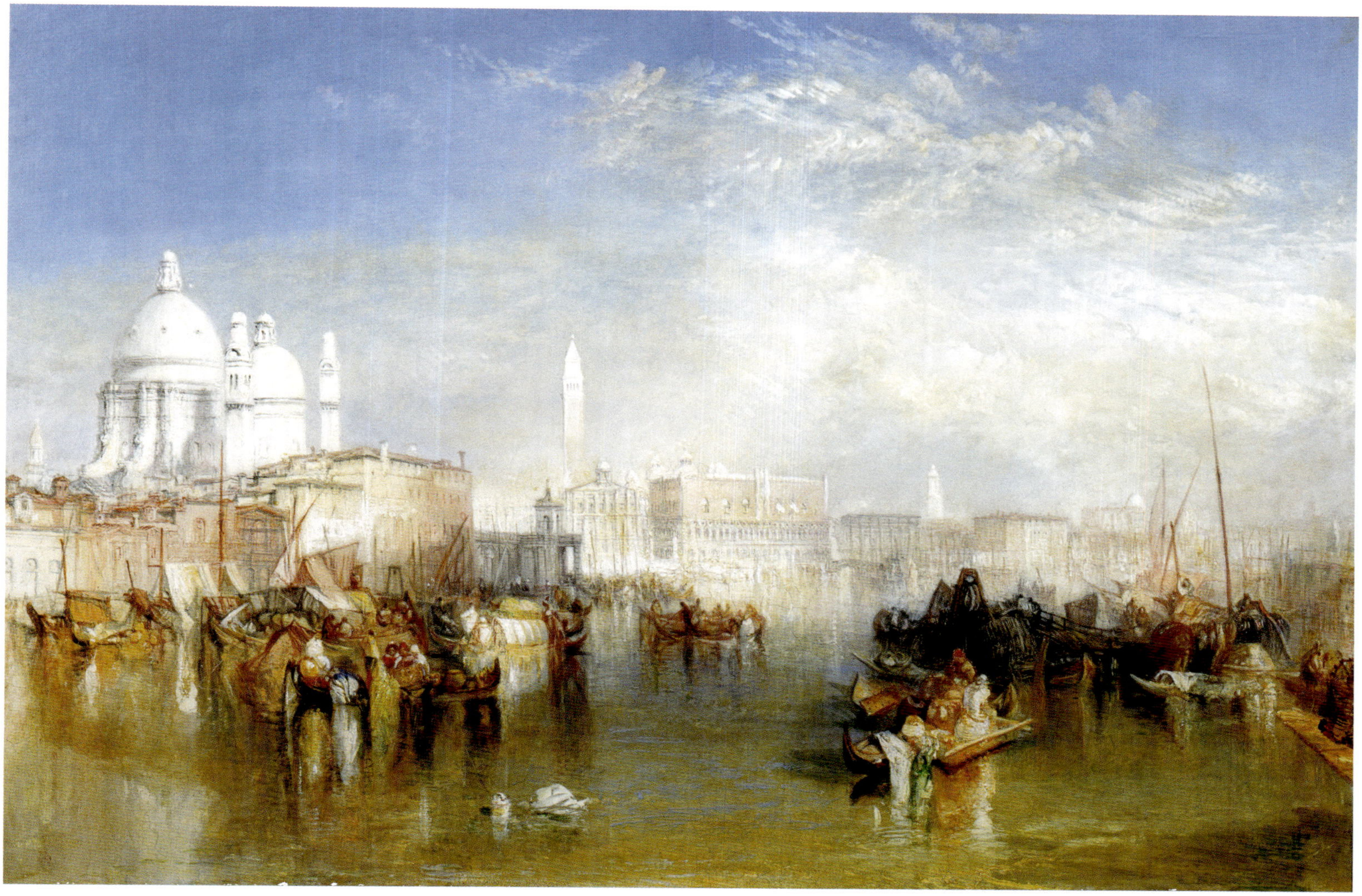

fig. 113—J. M. W. Turner, *Venice from the Giudecca*, 1840, oil on canvas, 24 × 36 in., Victoria and Albert Museum

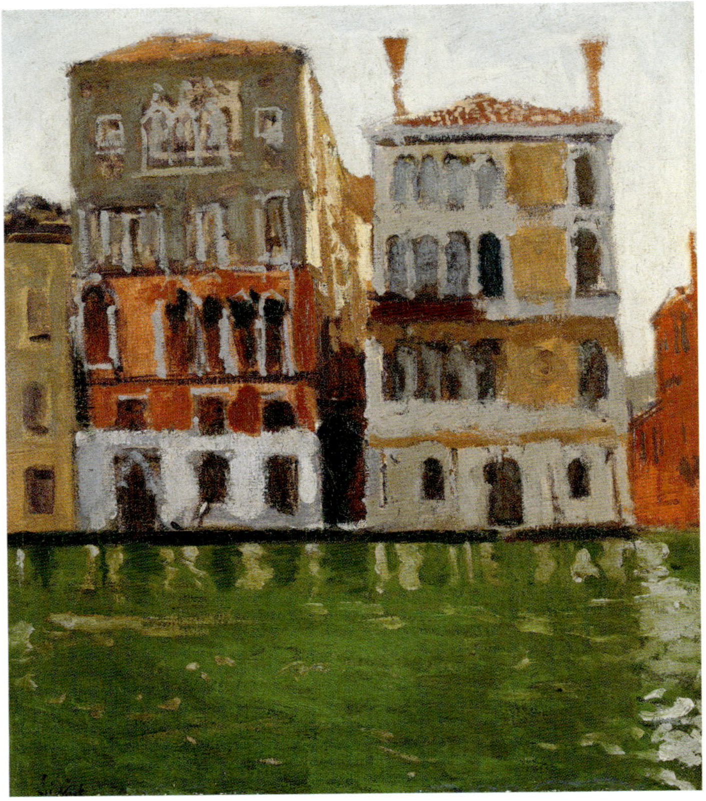

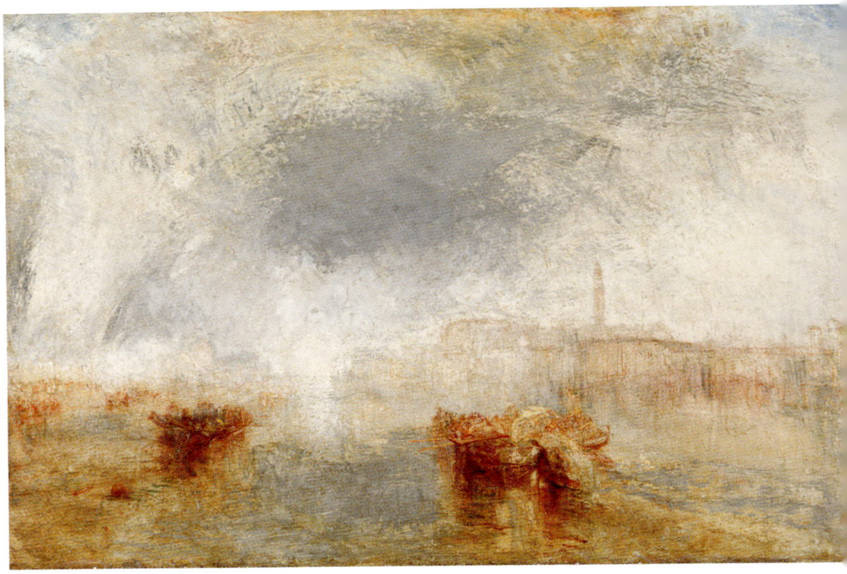

and galleries offered other chances to see Turners of Venice. On May 6, 1899, the collection formed by John Fowler came to auction, and it included the luminous *The Dogana and Santa Maria della Salute, Venice* (1843).[49] The work made the news, as it set a new auction record for the British artist at 8,200 guineas (or 1.85 million U.S. dollars in today's value).[50]

Monet again was not in London at the time. But later that year there was a chance for him to see the work on the Old Bond Street premises of Thomas Agnew & Sons. Included as part of the loan show *Twenty Masterpieces of the English School* held there in November and December 1899 (when Monet was in London), it made a marked impression on the art press. The critic of the *Pall Mall Gazette* found rapture before the "quivering glory of Turner's *Venice*, and linger so long in thrall before its invisible orchestra that painting becomes a worship and a religion."[51]

The tondo *Venice: Moonlight*[52] together with *The Grand Canal, Venice* and *The Colleoni Statue, Venice* by James Holland, were displayed in the *Winter Exhibition* held at the Royal Academy of Arts from January 7 to March 16, 1901.[53] The middle work depicts a view up the Grand Canal with the church of Santa Maria della Salute on the left and the Piazzetta di San Marco on the right. The first was a view of an anonymous canal, away from the famous sights. Monet, in London in February that year, may have visited the prominent exhibition. Avid Turner collector Donald Currie lent *Venice* (1841) to the same exhibition, where it was displayed among other Turners, all "very well known."[54] The painting is now known as *Giudecca, La Donna della Salute and San Giorgio*, one of Turner's most beautiful pictures of Venice.[55]

Finally, on his last visit to London (and before heading to Venice in 1908) Monet may have noticed a large painting by Edward William Cooke, then recently acquired for the national collection, *Canal of the Giudecca, Venice* (1867, Tate).[56] The notable landmarks of Venice are diminutive, and the work is dominated by a dappled blue sky streaked with pink-tinged clouds.

While we can't always know for certain which specific Venice-themed works Monet encountered, there is no doubt that the artist's engagement with the city of Venice was embedded in a firmly established tradition of its depiction over the previous centuries. He saw Venice in 1908 conditioned by such artworks. In London and Paris, the artist encountered many such views (both historic and contemporary), and these varied cityscapes impressed on him the different—and competing—possibilities for capturing in paint the many facets of Venice. From Canaletto through Turner, the modes of representation and the temporal span were wide, and Monet sought to add his own engaging contribution to this imagery, and render in other and different ways the particular attraction of this luminous city. By doing so Monet reimagined Venice.

fig. 114—Walter Sickert, *Palazzo Eleonora Duse, Venice*, c. 1901, oil on canvas, 21×18 in., Amgueddfa Cymru–Museum Wales

fig. 115—J. M. W. Turner, *Venice—Noon*, exhibited 1845, oil on canvas, 36⅛×24 in., Tate

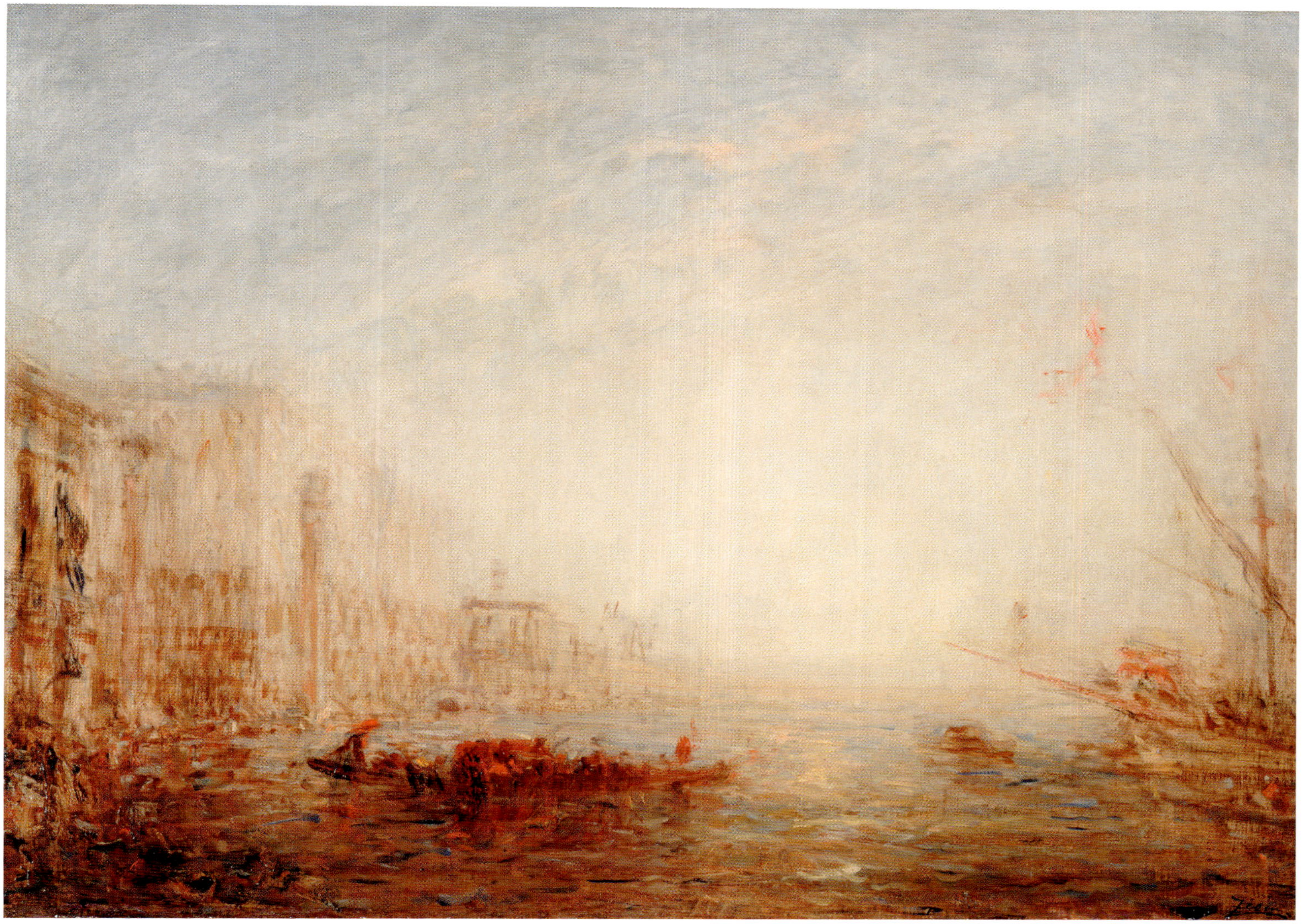

fig. 116—Félix Ziem, *Venise, le Grand Canal au Soleil Levant*, c. 1880–90, oil on canvas, 29 × 39 ¾ in., Petit Palais, Musée des Beaux-Arts de la Ville de Paris

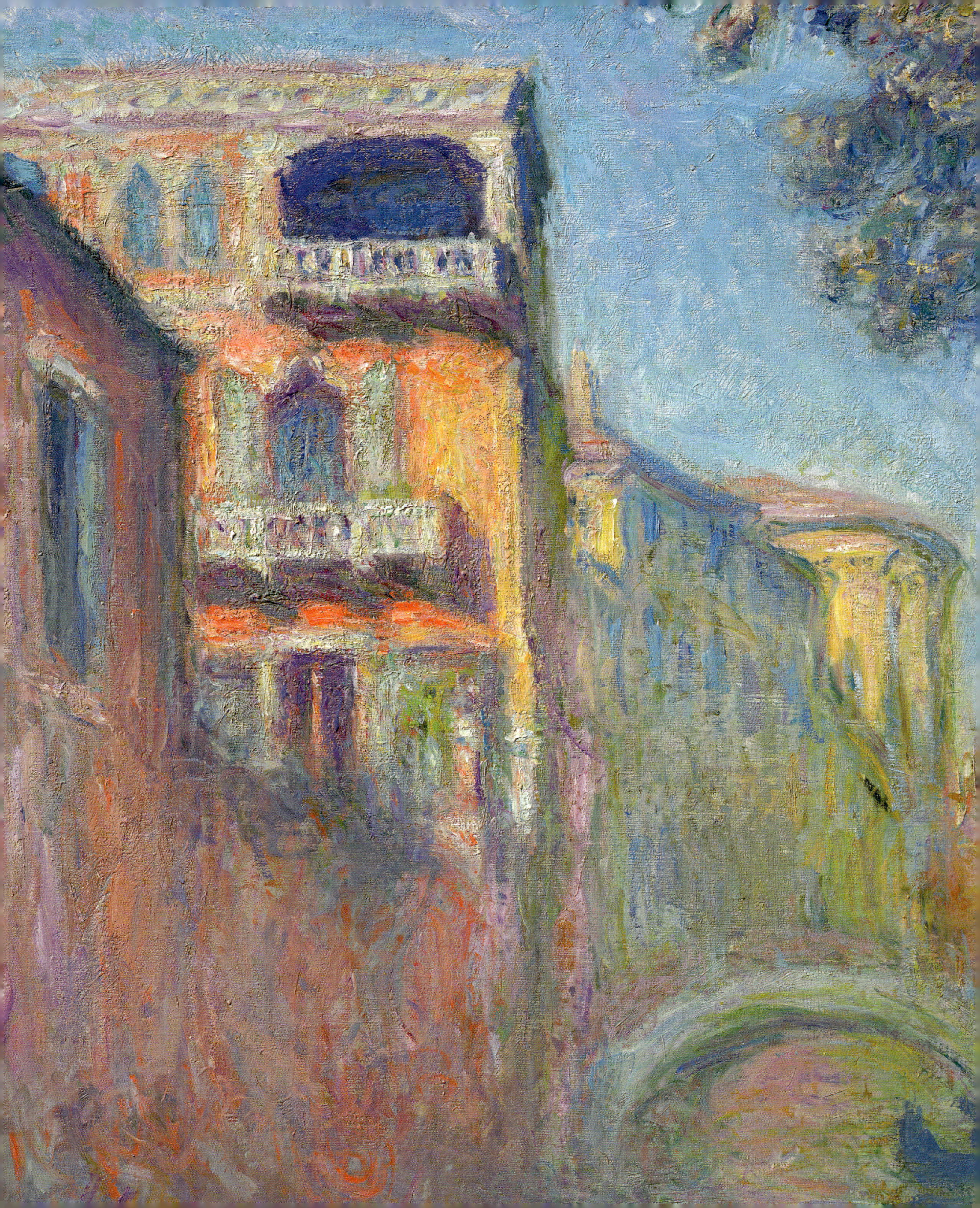

Richard Thomson

VARIATIONS ON VENICE: THE CULTURED, THE CAPTIVATED, AND THE CONTRARY, c. 1880–1910

SURVEYING RESPONSES TO VENICE among Claude Monet's fellow artists in the decades immediately before his campaign there in 1908 throws into relief strong contrasts that sharpen our understanding of Monet's work in the city. Monet shared the enthusiasm of many of his predecessors and contemporaries for the celebrated sites and vistas of Venice. He was, after all, planning a future exhibition of his Venice work following the success of shows of his Rouen and London series in 1895 and 1904, respectively, and was well aware of the expectations of prospective purchasers. Like many visiting artists, Monet mainly chose to paint identifiable buildings such as the Palazzo Ducale, the basilica of Santa Maria della Salute, and the church of San Giorgio Maggiore. These he pitched between luminous sky and reflective water, motifs that challenged his remarkably personal eye for ambient light and evocative color. In so doing, he evoked a Venice distinct from both the frank descriptiveness of Emmanuel Lansyer and Frits Thaulow and the orchestrated suggestiveness of Henri Le Sidaner and Lucien Lévy-Dhurmer. The play of light in Monet's canvases is vivid and varied, but he did not seek to suggest mood as consciously as some others did. When the exhibition of Monet's Venice canvases finally took place in 1912, it registered a great painter's celebratory response to the city, but it also followed a busy sequence of other shows and displays with the same focus, by painters as different as Eugène Boudin, Henri Martin, Alfred Smith, and Paul Signac. The contexts in which Monet's Venice paintings were made place his work in the complex cultural, creative, and commercial history of his time, but they do not detract from the magnificence of his own response to the Queen of the Sea.

The fabled city drew a range of reactions as the nineteenth century ended and the twentieth began. These were based on the individual visitor's experience and interests. Many responses were defined by difference. Venice is such an unusual place, with canals rather than streets, buildings a combination of the European and the Islamic, the absence not only of trees but also of the evident modernity of buses, department stores, and telegraph wires. In the mid-nineteenth century, Italy had been slow to develop a railway system. It was not until 1846 that Venice could be approached by rail from Padua or Vicenza; that year the ruling Austrians built a bridge crossing the lagoon between San Giuliano, on the mainland, and Santa Lucia, in Venice.[1] As the century came to a close, increasing ease of travel made the city a growing attraction, and the cultivated French—painters, writers, but also the well-educated and more broadly curious—joined other nationalities in visiting.

Of course, Venice had been long admired for its artistic heritage, from Carpaccio and the Bellinis, through Giorgione, Titian, Tintoretto, and Veronese, to the eighteenth-century topographical painters, such as Canaletto and Guardi, whose work was collected by contemporary travelers (especially the British). This in turn enhanced the city's reputation as a venue for the tasteful Grand Tourist. There seems to have been a gradual shift in the responses of French artists in particular to Venice during the second half of the nineteenth century. The generation born in the 1820s and 1830s considered the city a place to study the ideals of Italian Renaissance art, to add other dimensions—the coloristic and painterly—to the idealized and linear models, such as those of Michelangelo and Raphael, that the academic system encouraged them to study in Rome and Florence. In late 1860, Jean-Jacques Henner made eight copies of old master pictures in the Gallerie dell'Accademia and elsewhere, and a single view of a back canal.[2] Two years earlier, Gustave Moreau had copied Carpaccio. (Both would be invited in 1895 to serve as patrons of the first Venice Biennale.)[3]

Of course, not all academically trained artists went to Venice. Edgar Degas never did, though from Florence in 1858 he wrote to Moreau in Venice asking to be briefed about the artists his friend was seeing there.[4] Édouard Manet visited Venice as a student in September 1853 and again in 1857. James Tissot visited in the summer of 1862 and used the experience to create Carpaccio-esque paintings such as *Departure of the Prodigal Son* (1863). Manet and Tissot returned to the city together in 1875. Manet painted two canvases of gondolas on the Grand Canal, both featuring striped *pali* (mooring posts) in the foreground rather than the typical architectural detail, and depicted the play of light on the water in a way that reminds us that the previous summer he had painted alongside Monet at Argenteuil (fig. 184).[5] But Manet's water-level and close-up interest in the gondolas was not something Monet would pursue on his much later visit. Another painter from the Impressionist circle, Monet's good friend Pierre-Auguste Renoir, visited Venice in late October and early November 1881. He painted the typical sites with a loose handling and attentive observation of both weather effects and reflected light; witness his canvas of the Palazzo Ducale seen from San Giorgio Maggiore (fig. 185). Renoir was taken not only by the light clouds scudding across the breezy sky, the famous

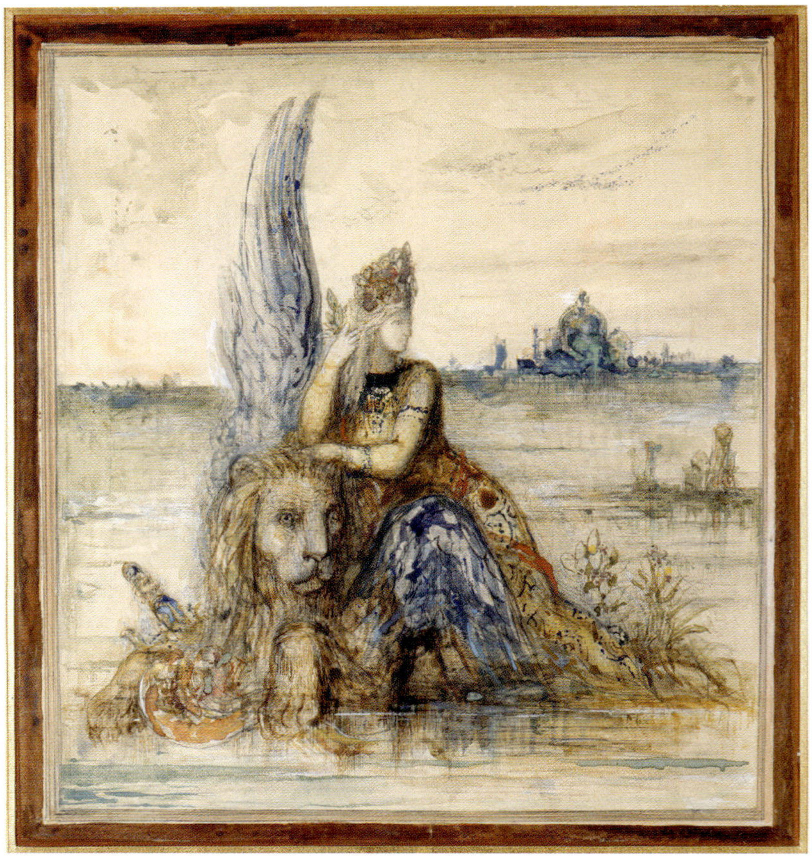

fig. 117—Gustave Moreau, *Venice*, c. 1885, watercolor on paper, 10 × 9 ¼ in., Musée Gustave Moreau

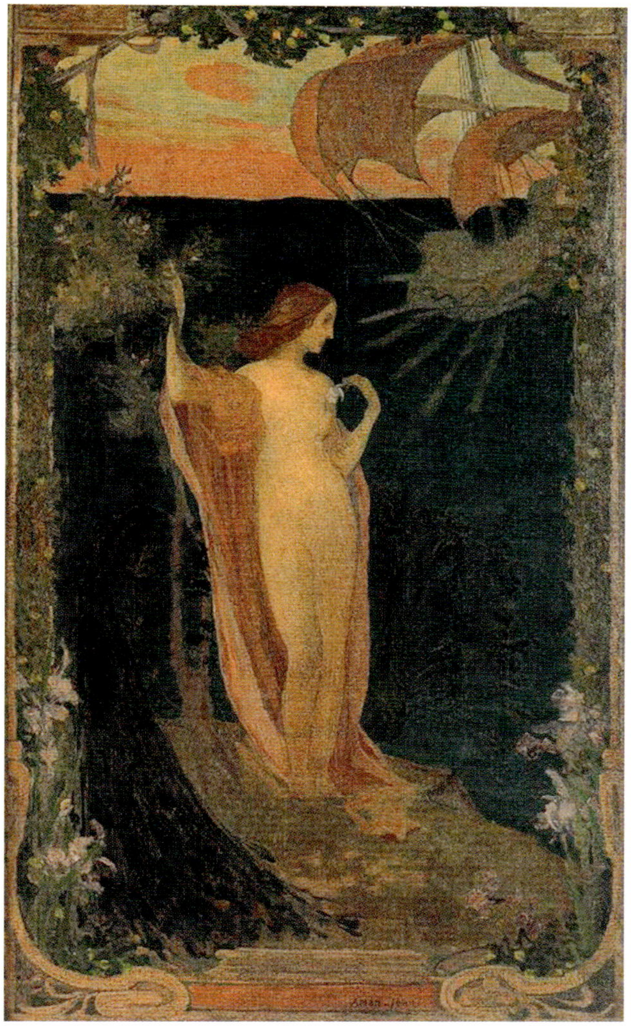

fig. 118—Edmond Aman-Jean, *Venice*, 1892, oil on canvas, 41×24¾ in., private collection

buildings and towering campanile, but also by the bustle of the busy city. The middle-ground is hectic with passing gondolas, full sails, and the suggestion of crowds on the *molo*. This was the Impressionism of its day; almost three decades later, Monet would see the city differently.

The experience of Venice could have a lasting impact. After Carolus-Duran, who had first been to Venice in 1863 as a student, was given a commission for an important ceiling painting for Paris, he returned in 1877 with student assistants for the express purpose of examining Veronese's decorations to aid him with the project.[6] The sculptor Auguste Rodin's visit to Venice in March 1876 was brief.[7] But three and a half decades later that experience remained with him, and when asked by the National Art Collections Fund how his *Burghers of Calais* group should be displayed outside the Houses of Parliament in London, he suggested that it should be on a plinth like Verrocchio's sculpture of Bartolomeo Colleoni in the Campo Santi Giovanni e Paolo.[8] These were two artists Monet knew personally and whose objectives in visiting the city were entirely different from his, and while their initial responses to the city had resonance in their later careers, Monet's 1908 sojourn in Venice culminated and closed with the 1912 exhibition of that body of work.

Venice resonated with Gustave Moreau, too. Almost thirty years after he had visited he painted an allegory in watercolor that represents the female embodiment of the city resting upon the back of the winged lion of Saint Mark as they float in the lagoon, with a dome and towers on the distant horizon (fig. 117). The work was purchased by the wealthy Parisian collector Charles Hayem, who had once owned and soon sold an Impressionist canvas by Monet.[9] In 1893, the critic Jean Lorrain saw the Moreau in Hayem's collection and greatly admired "this beautiful, pensive figure of a woman reclining in her nudity as princess of the sea," happy to praise an allegory that with the "dull blue of a melancholy gulf" evokes "a Venice still regal and yet fallen, dreaming of her splendor, of times gone by, alone with her regrets upon the Adriatic."[10]

By the 1880s a younger generation of academically trained artists, born in the 1860s, adopted a different attitude from that of their predecessors. Not long out of the École des Beaux-Arts, Edmond Aman-Jean and Ernest Laurent had won travel grants for their submissions to the Paris Salon of 1885 and they traveled together to study art in Italy. In Florence they met their contemporary Henri Martin, and together the three traveled on to Venice.[11] Once again, the experience lingered in the artistic memory, and while Martin went on to visit the city regularly to paint views, Aman-Jean responded with decorative allegories shown at the Salon de la Société Nationale des Beaux-Arts in 1893. One was a vertical panel, with the nude figure of Venice set against the deep blue Adriatic with a galleon in the background, and the other a profile head, once more against the sea with a vessel, inscribed *Venezia Regina del Mare* (figs. 118 and 119). Reviewing the exhibition, Lorrain did not like Aman-Jean's decorative panel, with its consciously antiquated lettering and "sense of facility and pastiche" of the Italian Quattrocento. Indeed, it prompted him to remember his recent, more satisfying, experience of the Moreau.[12]

Such allegorical encapsulations underline the resonance of Venice as a cultural totem, but they are far distant from the immediate individual response of a painter such as Monet.

As one century ended and the next began, as tourism burgeoned and academic prescription weakened, what artists desired and drew from their experience of Venice gradually changed. One of the fascinations of Venice for French and other foreign travelers during the so-called Belle Époque was that it offered a counterpoint to the modernity that was such an emphatic presence in other European and, of course, American cities. London was known as the imperial capital, with an underground railway system that had opened in 1863, a telephone network in 1878, and a port that in 1910 handled 18.6 million tons of cargo. Paris had celebrated the Exposition Universelle in 1889 with the Eiffel Tower, a prefabricated iron structure then the tallest building in the world. The subsequent Exposition Universelle in 1900 saw the opening of the Paris Métro and *trottoirs roulants* (people movers), as well as the second Summer Olympics.

The enthusiasm for Bruges at this period, in Georges Rodenbach's novel *Bruges-la-Morte* (1892) or the paintings of artists such as Fernand Khnopff, echoed that for Venice. These were two cities with deep histories not Classical but stretching back to the Middle Ages, graced by noble buildings and traversed by canals, an ancient and unhurried transport system. Of course the paradox was that, for the tourist to reach Venice, it was convenient to travel by a modern railway system, which served a relatively untouched historic environment. If the attraction of Venice for the developing tourist trade in this period was based on (momentary) repudiation of modernity in favor of palazzo-lined canals, then the case is emphatically proved by Monet. Prior to his visit to Venice in 1908, Monet's last campaign of work painting in a city had been the sequence of images made in London between 1899 and 1901. These were distinctly modern in subject: the road and rail traffic across Waterloo and Charing Cross Bridges, the factories and chimneys on the south bank of the Thames, and even the most grand, palatial buildings—the Houses of Parliament and Big Ben—completed scarcely half a century before (figs. 58, 102, and 152). In addition, the atmosphere that surrounded those structures, the smog and pollution of the industrial city that so enraptured Monet and tested his nuanced ability to paint light on shifting wafts of smoke and haze, were created by the boilers, furnaces, and mechanisms of modern industrial production.[13] (For more on pollution in Venice, see Jonathan P. Ribner's essay in this volume.)

But while Venice's history, buildings, and reputation brought in tourists and artists alike, their responses were neither consistent nor uniformly laudatory. In *The Innocents Abroad* of 1869, Mark Twain swerved from eulogy—"very soft and dreamy and beautiful"—to critique—"vast, gloomy marble palaces, black with the corroding damp of centuries."[14] A decade later he voiced similar mixed feelings in *A Tramp Abroad* about the Basilica di San Marco, inevitably a subject of "strong fascination" but "propped on its long row of low thick-legged columns, its back knobbed with domes, it seemed like a vast warty bug taking a meditative

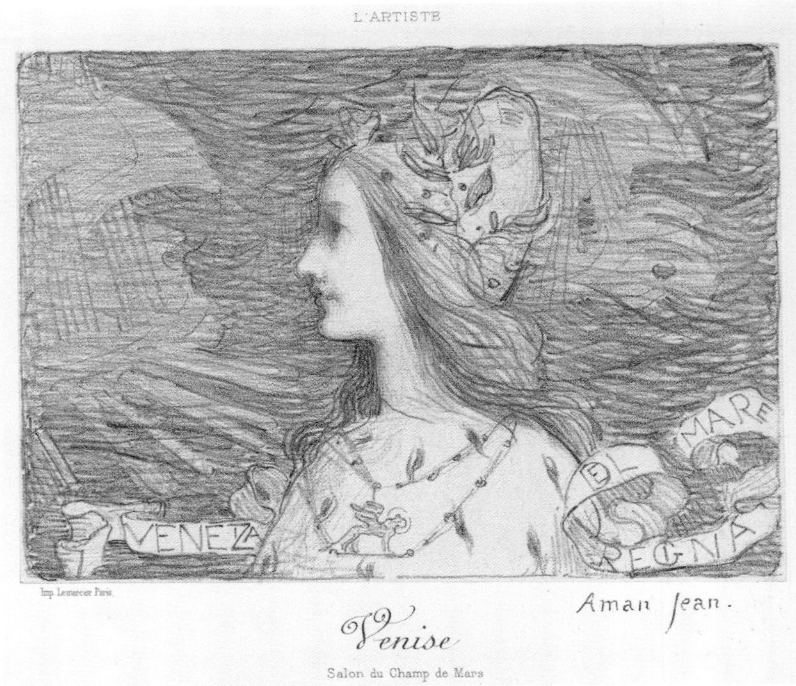

fig. 119—Edmond Aman-Jean, *Venice*, 1892, lithograph on chine-collé, Cleveland Museum of Art

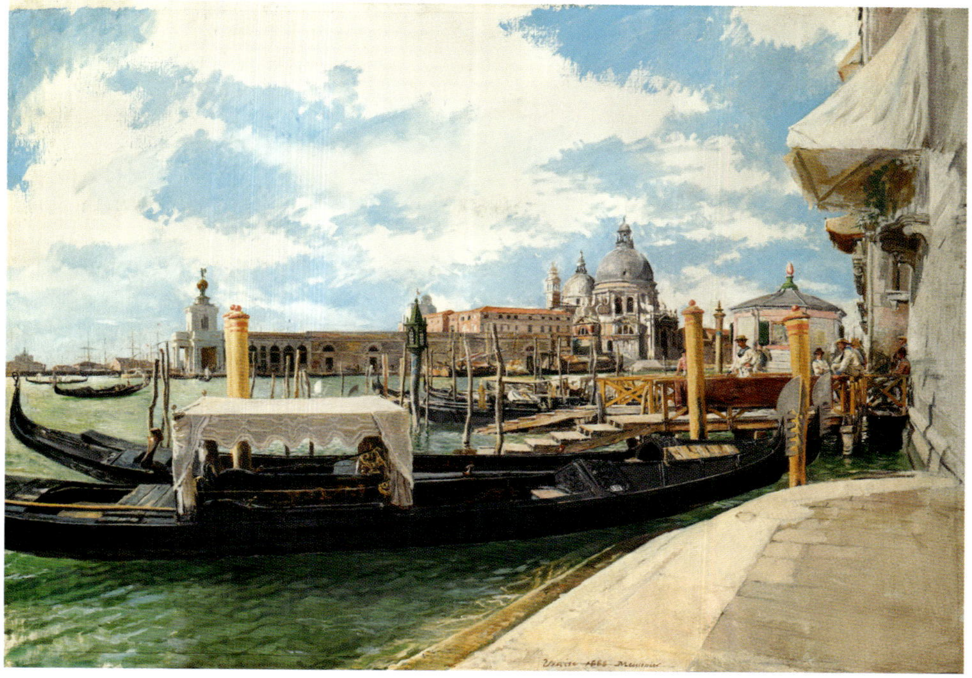

fig. 120—Ernest Meissonier, *Venice: The Grand Canal*, 1888, oil on canvas, 3×42 ½ ft., Musée d'Orsay

walk."[15] In 1885, another writer, Guy de Maupassant, shared that ambivalence, reporting on a recent trip he had made to the city in the company of the painter Henri Gervex. He told the readers of *Gil Blas* that Venice was exceptional as a name that "instantly calls to mind a striking parade of magnificent memories and a whole sweep of enchanting dreams." But he could not help pointing out the unhygienic filthiness of the canals that forced the inhabitants "to navigate along their sewers."[16] This ambivalence was countered by others. A subtler view was voiced by Henry Havard in his book *Amsterdam et Venise*, a comparison of the two canal-crossed cities published in 1876. As it happens, Havard and Monet had met while both were in the Netherlands in the summer of 1871, though Havard's book was not in Monet's library. Havard wrote appreciatively of what he sensed were the two essential, if apparently contradictory, aspects of Venice: "the melancholy of its past grandeur, and the joyous madness of its eternal light."[17]

Toward the end of the nineteenth century, many artists traveled to paint the city's celebrated architecture and picturesque canals rather than to study Venetian art. In this they were following the *vedute* tradition of the eighteenth-century topographical painters and, like them, they both satisfied their inclinations to record the cityscape and worked for a tourist clientele keen to buy painted souvenirs. The proliferation of such subjects in the repertoire of French artists at the end of the nineteenth and beginning of the twentieth century is notable. Many of these works were simply descriptive records of the actuality of Venice's highly individual cityscape. Ernest Meissonier, famous and wealthy thanks to his precisely painted military and costume pieces, had first traveled to Venice in 1860. But some two decades later he began to visit the city regularly, eventually buying a property, the Casa Fumagalli. This gave him a view southward across the Grand Canal to the Dogana and Santa Maria della Salute, which he rendered first

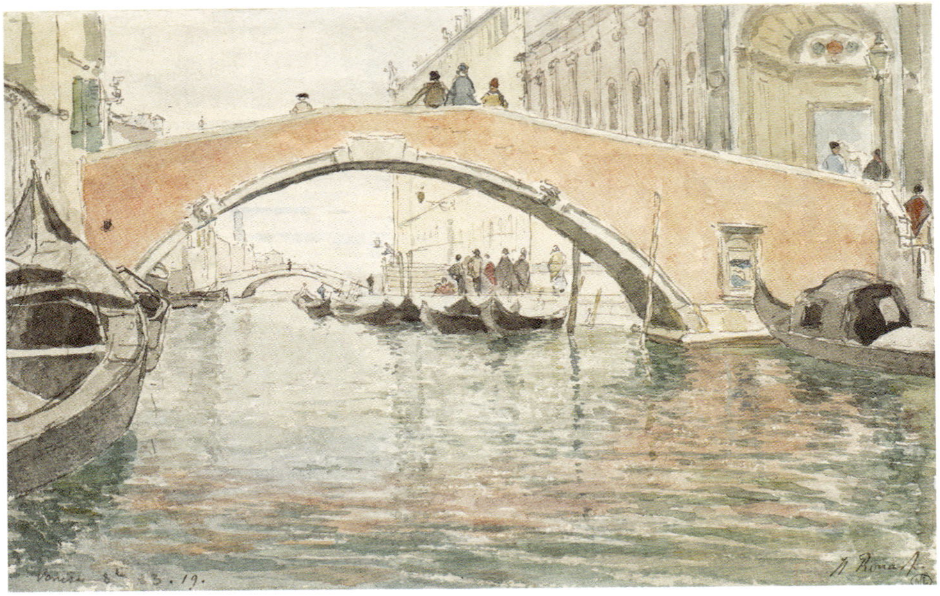

fig. 121—Henri Rouart, *Canal in Venice*, 1883, gray ink and watercolor, 6⅓ × 10 in., Musée d'Orsay

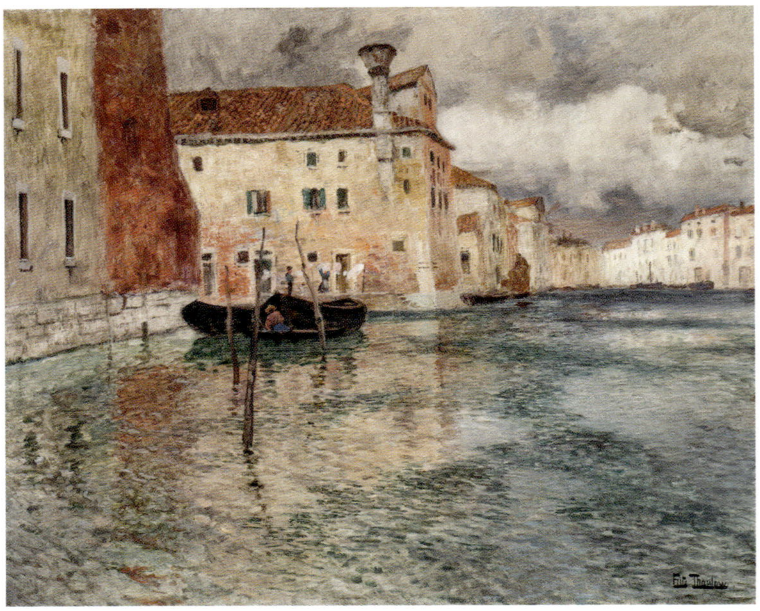

fig. 122—Frits Thaulow, *Venice*, c. 1899, oil on canvas, 25½ × 32 in., private collection

in a watercolor of 1886 and then in an oil painting two years later (fig. 120).[18] Jules Bastien-Lepage, famous for peasant subjects from his native northeast France, traveled to Venice in autumn 1881, and at the retrospective exhibition held in 1885, the year after his death, five views of Venice, four of them now untraced, were on view.[19] In short, celebrated naturalist artists were seeking out Venice at a time when Monet was discovering the coastline of northwestern Italy at Bordighera, where he worked in early 1884.

Degas's friend Henri Rouart, an industrialist, collector, and amateur artist, went to Venice in 1883, and at the eighth and final Impressionist exhibition in 1886 he exhibited a group of watercolors that included two of these, in all likelihood *Pont Saint-Zanni et Paolo* and *À Murano*.[20] How apt that one critic who drew attention to them in his review of the exhibition was none other than Henry Havard, author of the volume on Venice and Amsterdam published a decade previously.[21] Like Bastien-Lepage, Rouart did not feature grand and famous buildings but favored more modest, but nevertheless distinctly Venetian, motifs of back canals and churches not in the city center (fig. 121). That choice was consistent with the naturalist aesthetic then dominant in French art and literature, which stressed the accurate description of actuality in all its bland and factual character, precisely because that was objective and could be experienced by all. Monet, too, was later to paint a few motifs off the main canals, such as the Rio della Salute and the Fondamenta Bragadin (fig. 6), though by 1908 his strong personal aesthetic was distinctly more individualistic than the naturalism that dominated so much late-nineteenth-century painting.[22]

One painter who consistently sought out the ordinary in Venice was the Norwegian Frits Thaulow, who had worked a good deal in France during the 1870s and in the spring of 1885 made his first visit to Venice. On this and subsequent trips Thaulow was drawn to the back canals. This corresponded to his naturalist aesthetic, with its commitment to the actual and the ordinary. A canvas made at the turn of the century typifies this approach.

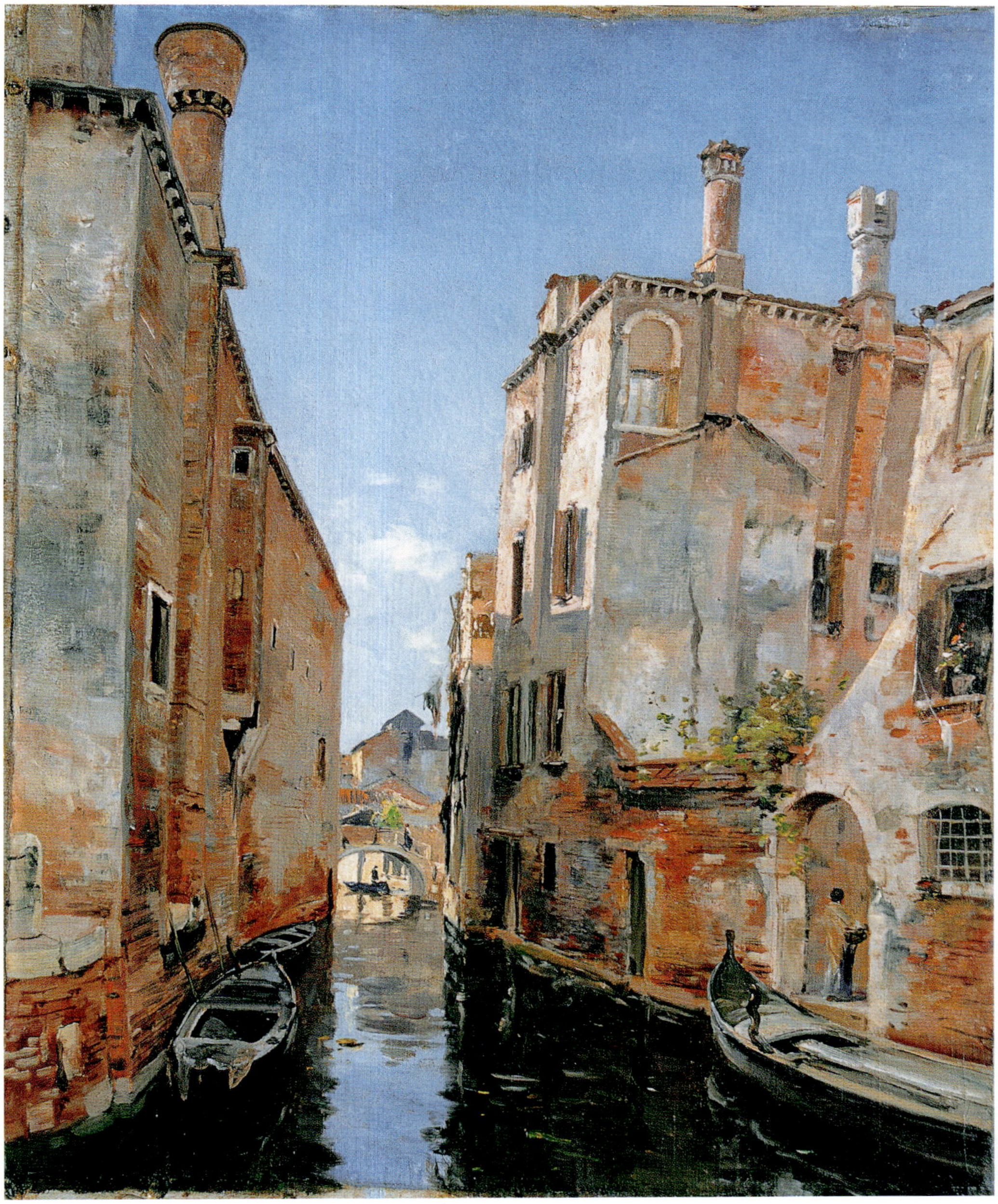

fig. 123—Emmanuel Lansyer, *San Sebastian Church, Venice*, 1892, oil on canvas, 12¾ × 15⁹⁄₁₀ in, Musée Lansyer

While Thaulow was fascinated by the play of the mounting rain clouds on the surface of the broad canal and the light on the far facades, he chose a motif of unexceptional buildings with small local figures going about their business on the quayside, the type of quotidian detail Monet ignored (fig. 122).

A painter with a similar approach to that of Thaulow was Emmanuel Lansyer. He had traveled widely in France, painting in Normandy, Brittany, and Touraine and on the Provençal coast. He spent much of September and October 1892 in Venice, where he produced six canvases, one of which was shown at the Salon of 1893.[23] While that painting, *View from the Church of Madonna della Salute*, was of a famous, eye-catching building, Lansyer also painted narrow back canals and their modest housing with the characteristic tall chimneys, and so was drawn to a similar variety of motifs as Monet was later (fig. 123). The conservative critic

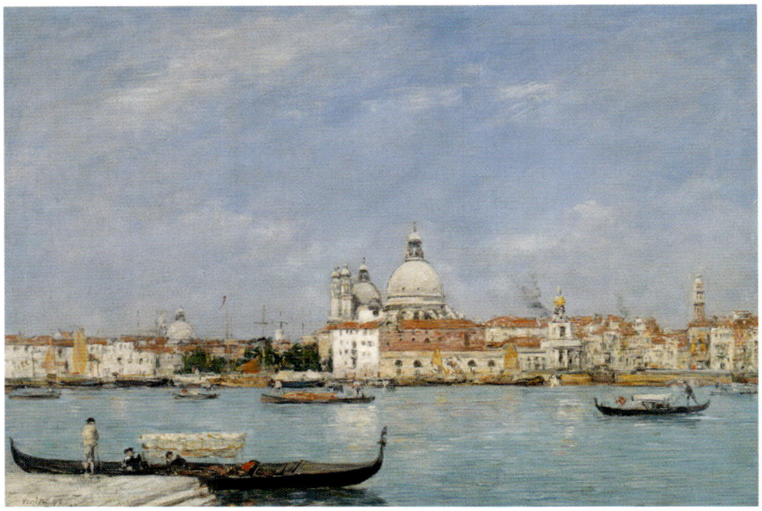

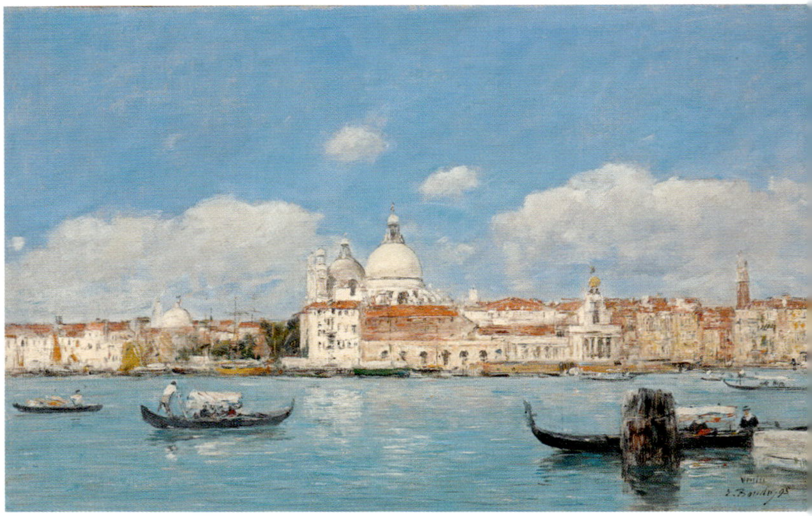

Georges Lafenestre appreciated Lansyer's handling of light in the Salute painting and his avoidance of the "horror of exactitude" that in Lafenestre's view increasingly afflicted French landscape painters.[24] Topographical naturalism, of both celebrated and mundane sites, was very much the order of the day. The contrast with Monet's work a few years later could hardly be better made.

Eugène Boudin, native of Honfleur on the English Channel coast and Monet's mentor in the early 1860s, discovered the Mediterranean in 1890, a year after his wife died, when he went to Villefranche in search of a change of scene. In 1895 he visited Venice.[25] At the Salon de la Société Nationale des Beaux-Arts two years later he showed eight studies made in the city in the same frame: evidence of his intense focus on work *sur le motif*.[26] Some of the smaller works on panel, made rapidly *sur le motif*, perhaps as Boudin accustomed himself to his new surroundings, represent ships in the harbor under expansive skies, with only a gondola differentiating the scene from his typical motifs on the coast of the English Channel. An interesting aspect of Boudin's Venice work is that he painted the same scene more than once, perhaps with a minimal variation in the point of view—just as Monet would do later. An instance of this is a panoramic view from the island of San Giorgio Maggiore looking across the Bacino toward the Punta della Dogana and with the church of Santa Maria della Salute seen from the side (figs. 124 and 125). This gave the artist the challenge of painting the same motif—a foreground panorama of water and central mass of identifiable buildings and the upper expanse of sky—under different light and atmospheric effects, as his friend Monet was doing with his series paintings and would develop further when he in turn visited Venice more than a decade later. One of Boudin's variants was bought by an S. Reichard, who then sold it to the dealer Durand-Ruel's New York branch on June 2, 1899. Here, it seems, was the painted motif demonstrating its cosmopolitan commerciality: the motif of Venice painted by a visiting artist, sold probably to somebody with a tourist's experience of the city, and then available for purchase on another continent to a new buyer who might well have visited that same site.[27] Monet and his dealers the Bernheim-Jeune brothers would

fig. 124—Eugène Boudin, *Venice, Santa Maria della Salute from San Giorgio*, 1895, oil on canvas, 18¼ × 25¾ in., Museum of Fine Arts, Boston

fig. 125—Eugène Boudin, *Venice, the Salute, the Customs House and the Beginning of the Grand Canal*, 1895, oil on canvas, 14⅓ × 23 in., private collection

fig. 126—Henri-Jean Guillaume Martin, *San Giorgio Island in Venice*, 19th c., oil on board, 19 × 26 ¾ in., Palais des Beaux-Arts de Lille

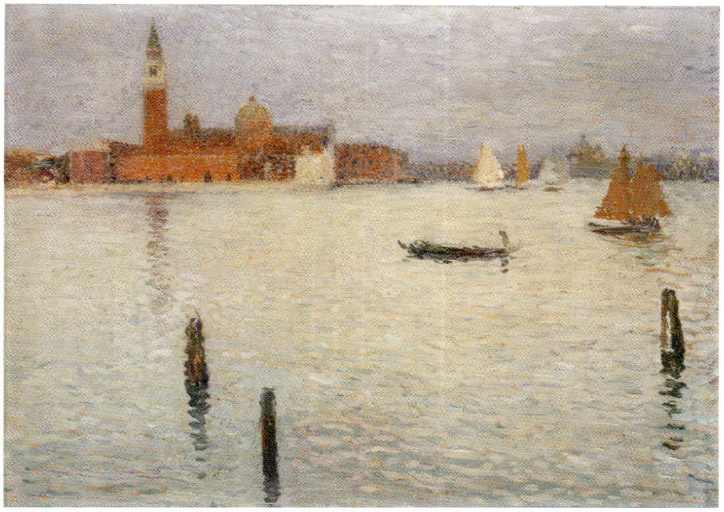

have expected similar patterns on the art market when his work was exhibited and sold in 1912.

By the 1890s Venice had become a regular destination for certain French painters. The Toulousain Henri Martin, who had first visited with Aman-Jean and Laurent in 1885, returned frequently, and in 1910 at the Galerie Georges Petit in Paris held an exhibition that was almost exclusively given over to views of Venice (fig 126).[28] Alfred Smith, whose father was British but who grew up in Bordeaux, stayed in Venice over the winter of 1896 to 1897 and painted a number of canvases. At the 1897 Salon de la Société Nationale des Beaux-Arts in Paris, Smith exhibited nine paintings of Venetian motifs, and the following year another thirteen.[29] In 1898 he also showed twenty-one Venice subjects at the Salon de la Société des Amis des Arts at Bordeaux. This consistent use of the city as a subject continued in Smith's output until the outbreak of World War I, with the French state buying one of his Venice motifs in 1905 and another in 1914 (fig. 127).[30]

Such concentrated output of Venetian subjects in the 1890s and 1900s demonstrates more than individual artists' fascination with the jewel of the Adriatic. Painters knew that their enthusiasm for Venice was shared with a variety of fellow visitors, tourists from a wide range of classes—from the wealthy who arrived in yachts and rented palazzi to those booked on the train by Thomas Cook—and that those tourists formed a large pool of potential purchasers for characteristic views of the city. Indeed, the current fascination with Venice was used to promote Italy, whose large national pavilion at the 1900 Exposition Universelle in Paris, designed by Carlo Ceppi and Giacomo Salvadori, had copies of the portal of the Palazzo Ducale on all four facades and gondolas

fig. 127—Alfred Smith, *La Gondole*, 1905, oil on canvas, 22⅛ × 30⅓ in., Musée des Beaux-Arts de Bordeaux

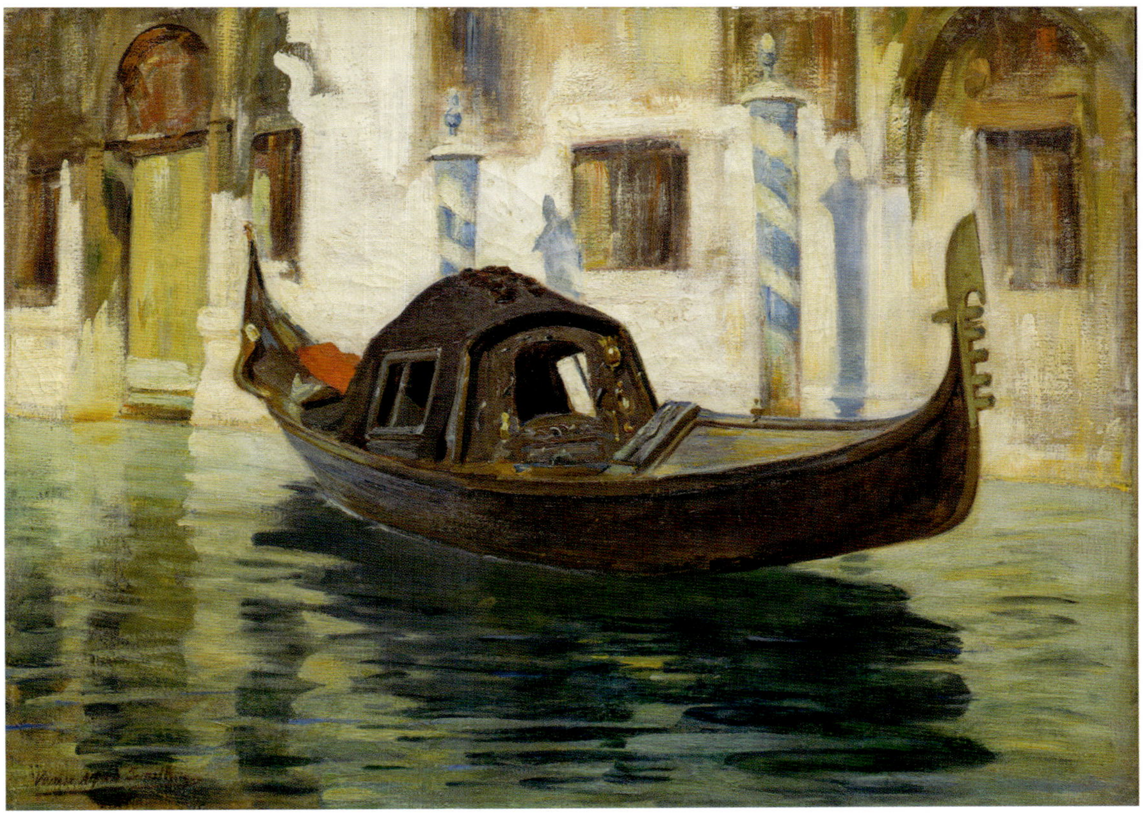

to take visitors on the river Seine in front (fig. 128). There was also a question of how artists represented Venice, an issue particularly in focus beginning in the 1890s, as styles and aesthetics veering away from the broadly shared naturalism of Lansyer, Boudin, and Thaulow became increasingly notable. How an artist could rise to the challenge of painting Venice's Mediterranean light, extensive planes of water reflecting sky and city, and famous buildings demanding specificity and grandeur was at issue. Henri Martin was not entirely successful, according to the critic Achille Segard; he failed to catch the "something Oriental under an Italian sky . . . the psychology of that sky," but painted Venetian motifs as if still in Quercy, which he frequently depicted.[31] The same charge might be laid on Eugène Carrière, whose views of Venice were washed in the thin brown mist that typified his paintings of family, intellectual friends, and Parisian scenes (fig. 129). Walter Sickert, a British painter who had spent much time in France, first visited Venice in May 1895, then returned for several months in 1901 and for a longer period in 1903 to 1904. His architectural compositions are strikingly individual. *The Lion of St. Mark* (fig. 130) from his first trip, by centering on the columns and sculptures seen across the Grand Canal, views the Palazzo Ducale from an odd angle, its waterside face catching the light and the facade facing the Piazza San Marco receding repetitively across the center space with its angled arches and carved columns. Only the blues of the nearby water and patch of sky bring cool elements to a canvas chiefly brushed in warm tones, be they mid-brown stonework, terracotta brick patterning, or blanched pillars. The complications of the composition and the predominant warmth of the chromatics mark the divergence between Sickert's maturity and the cool, reductive approach of his master, James McNeill Whistler.

The generation of both writers and artists born in the 1860s, who developed in the 1890s in an aesthetic climate that increasingly preferred the suggestive and emotive to the frankly descriptive, found Venice richly evocative. In 1889, the emerging novelist Maurice Barrès wrote of how "the almost colorless sky becomes accented toward dusk with the vast redness of the declining sun," while the young Pierre Louÿs wrote to his friend André Gide that he was struck by "the evening flaming in the sea": both were responding to the visual experience of the light and not just the historical resonance of the city.[32] Lucien Lévy-Dhurmer worked at a faïence factory in Golfe-Juan in the early 1890s and made trips to Italy. A number of pastels of Venetian subjects stemmed from these trips, and in 1898 the periodical *Art et Décoration* reported that many of these "noble visions" with "the transparency of these turquoise nights, clear as dawns" were done from memory and imagination rather than observation, thus corresponding with the Symbolist aesthetic (fig. 131).[33] Henri Le Sidaner, who first visited Venice in 1892, returned in 1905 and the two following years.[34] He painted the Ponte dei Sospiri in 1906, contrasting the open space of the foreground with the elegant but sinister span like a great devouring mouth beyond, the cramped channel of the Rio di Palazzo beneath (fig. 132). A small oil sketch of the Palazzo Ducale shows him exploring the layers of arches on the facade that had also fascinated Sickert (fig. 134). By contrast, Monet's views of the facade of the Palazzo

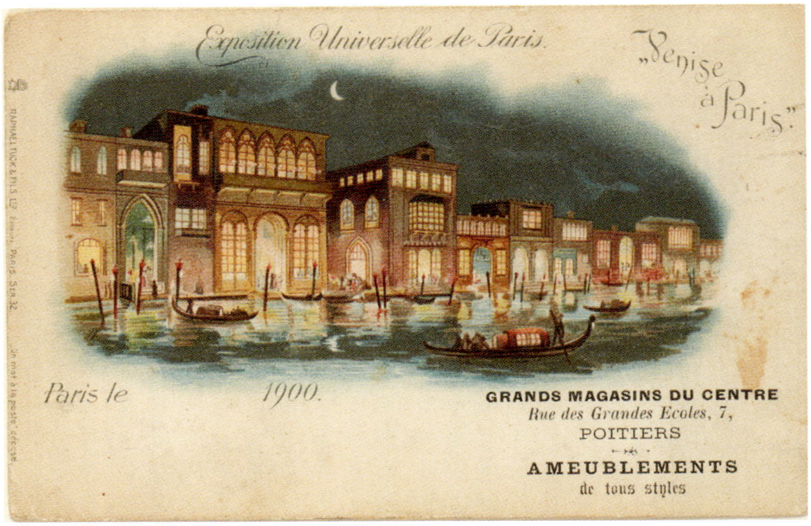

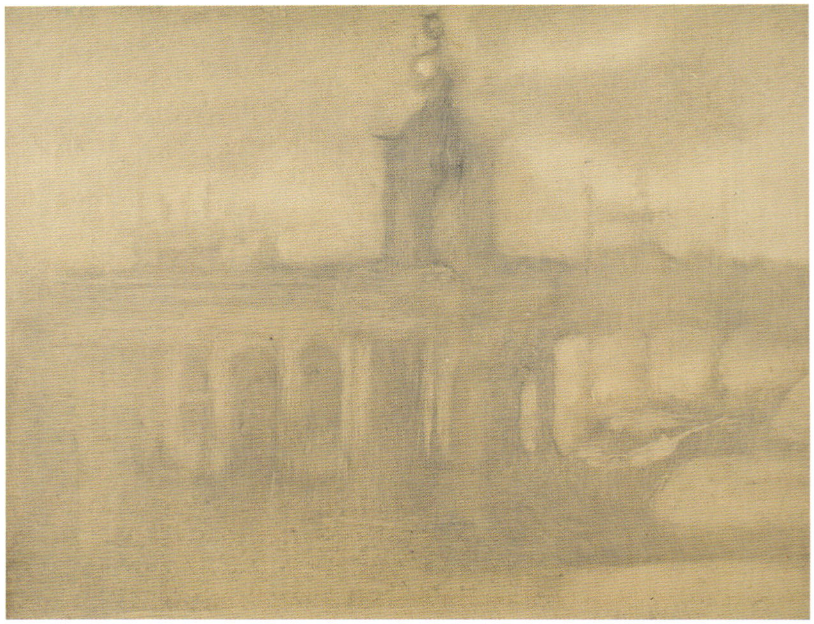

fig. 128—Postcard from the Exposition Universelle, 1900, Musée Carnavalet

fig. 129—Eugène Carrière, *Venise, la Dogana*, c. 1897–99, oil on canvas, 11 × 13¾ in., Musée Lambinet

fig. 130—Walter Sickert, *The Lion of St. Mark*, c. 1895–96, oil on canvas, 35½ × 35½ in., The Fitzwilliam Museum

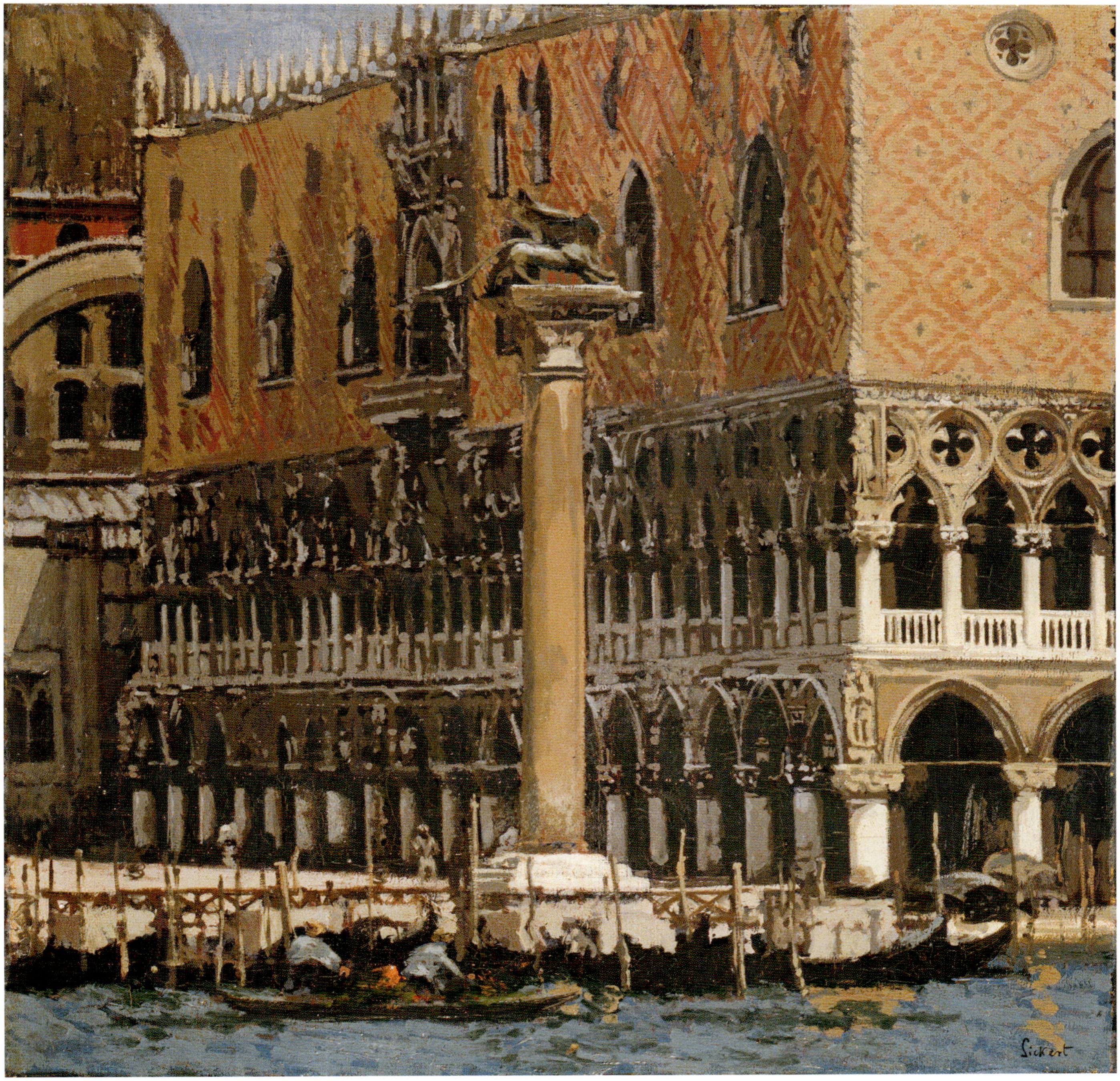

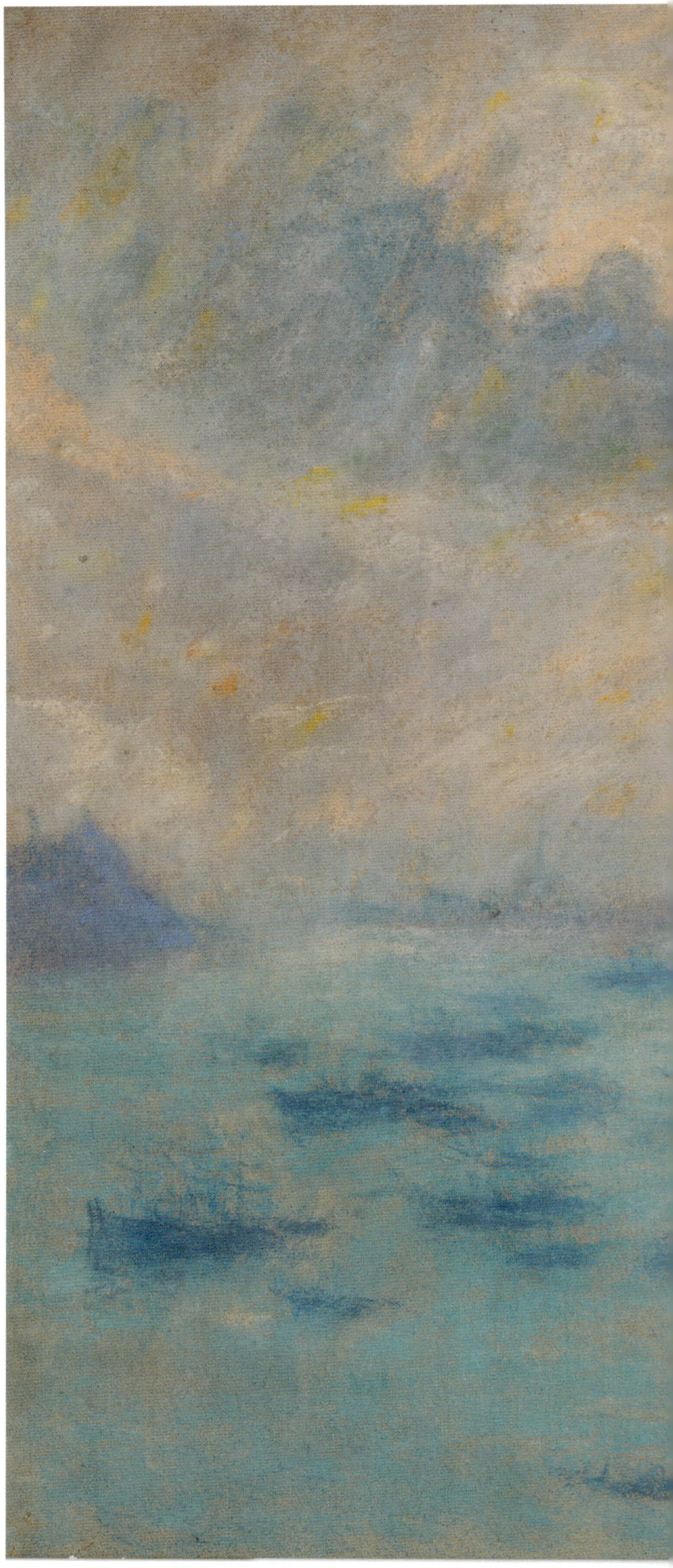

fig. 131—Lucien Lévy-Dhurmer, *Venice: The Grand Canal at Night*, c. 1895, pastel on paper, 23×32 in., Collection of Celia Morrissette/Keith Johnson

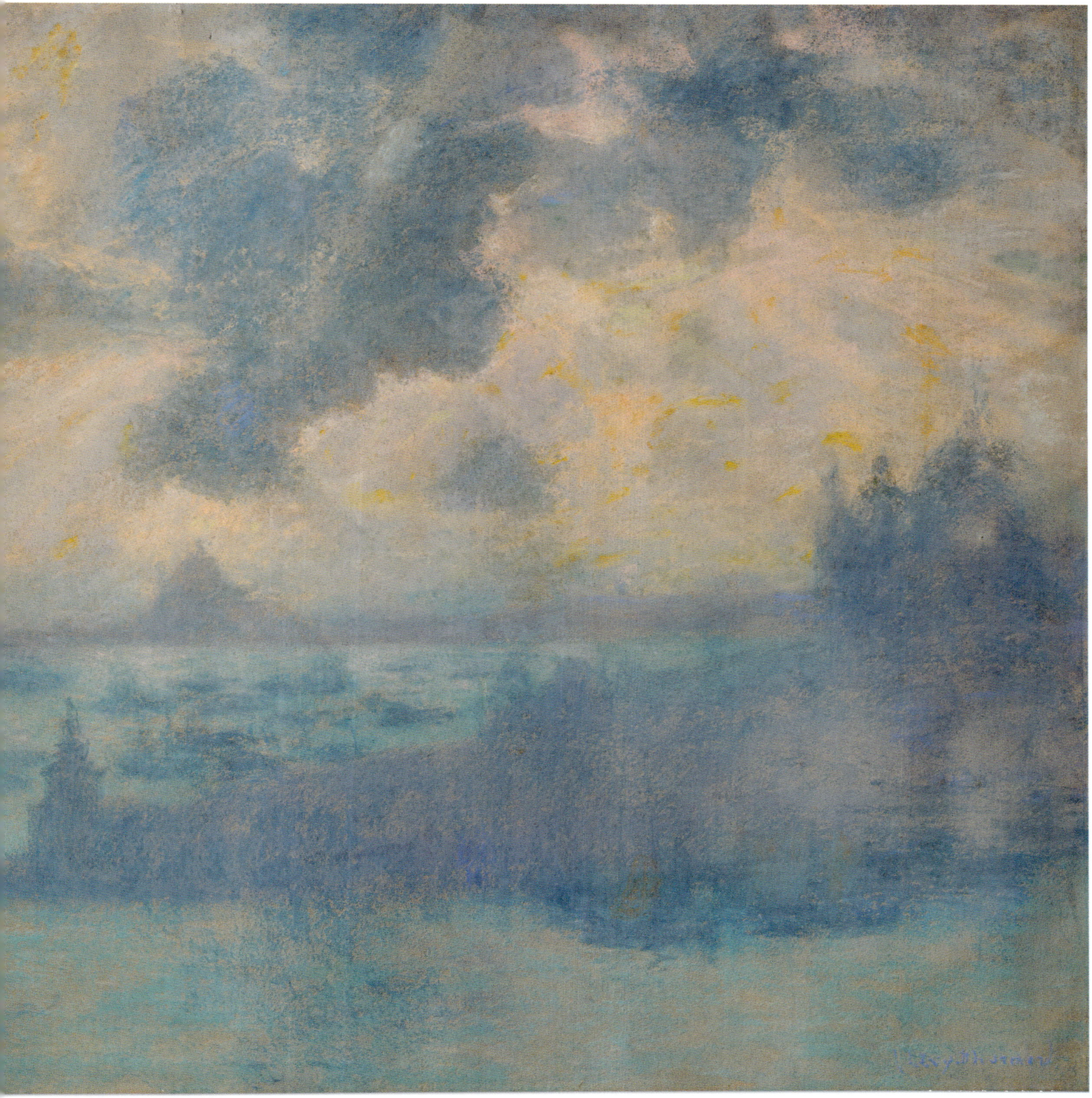

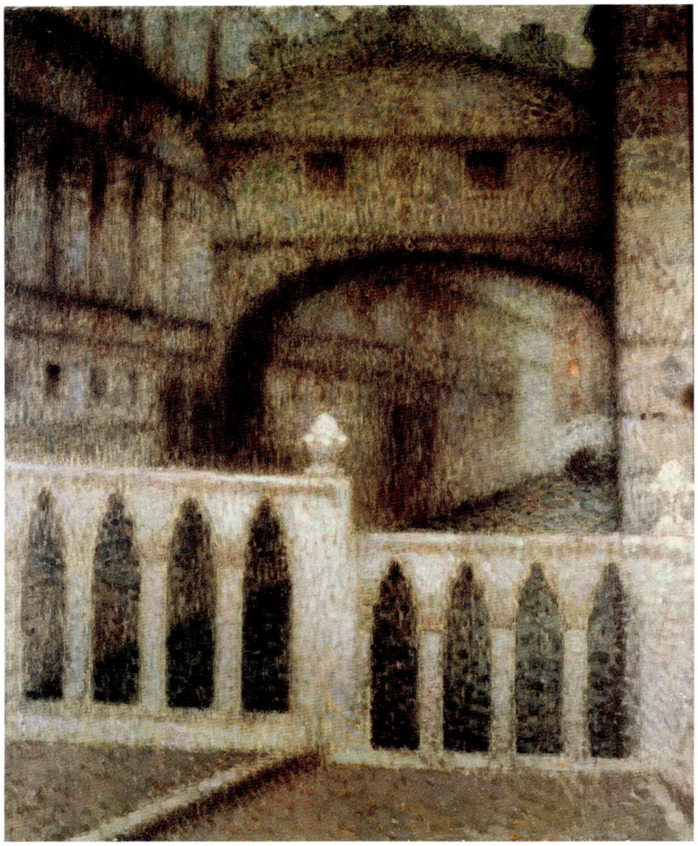

Ducale, probably painted from a boat, spread the building across his canvas, the better to use the facade as a screen on which play the reflections from the water below, an alternative—but also subtly suggestive—approach (pl. 6–8).

Utterly different approaches to the city were also spawned in the new century. Odilon Redon, a leading figure among the Symbolists, visited Venice two years later and, perhaps typically, avoided obvious city motifs, painting from memory imprecise but vivid images of the expanse of sky and water (fig. 135). Divergent again was Maurice Denis, who had first seen the city in 1895. A subsequent visit in 1907 inspired him to use a Venetian vista, with the Salute in the distance, and his experience of bathers at the Lido, for a painting illustrating the opening chapter of his friend Gide's *Le Voyage d'Urien* (1892), in which enslaved people are unloaded at a quayside (fig. 133).[35] Such paintings are quite distinct from Monet's Venetian paintings in subject and style, but the yearning for the evocative and suggestive that the Symbolist aesthetic engendered did resonate when his canvases were exhibited in 1912. Gustave Kahn, a poet and leading figure in the emergent movement in the late 1880s, wrote a review for the *Mercure de France* saying that while some might have preferred Monet to make the buildings more solid and volumetric—in other words, more simply naturalistic—he much admired "the fairy presence of the light" in these "luminous poems executed with care to render all the beauties, all the fantasies, all the finesse, all the exuberances of the light": an archetypal Symbolist response.[36]

But for all that expectation of being seduced by the extravagant eccentricities of the city, it was possible to be disappointed. Marcel Proust, who so admired John Ruskin's intense writing that he undertook the difficult task of translating it into French, was so imaginatively excited by the prospect of seeing the city that he read *The Stones of Venice* aloud to his mother as their train crossed the plains of Lombardy. They stayed at the Hotel Danieli on the Riva degli Schiavoni, where the English aesthete had

fig. 132—Henri Le Sidaner, *The Bridge of Sighs*, 1906, oil on canvas, 35×29½ in., Petit Palais, Musée des Beaux-Arts de la Ville de Paris

fig. 133—Maurice Denis, *Les Captifs*, 1907, oil on canvas, 31½×47½ in., Musée des Beaux-Arts de Reims

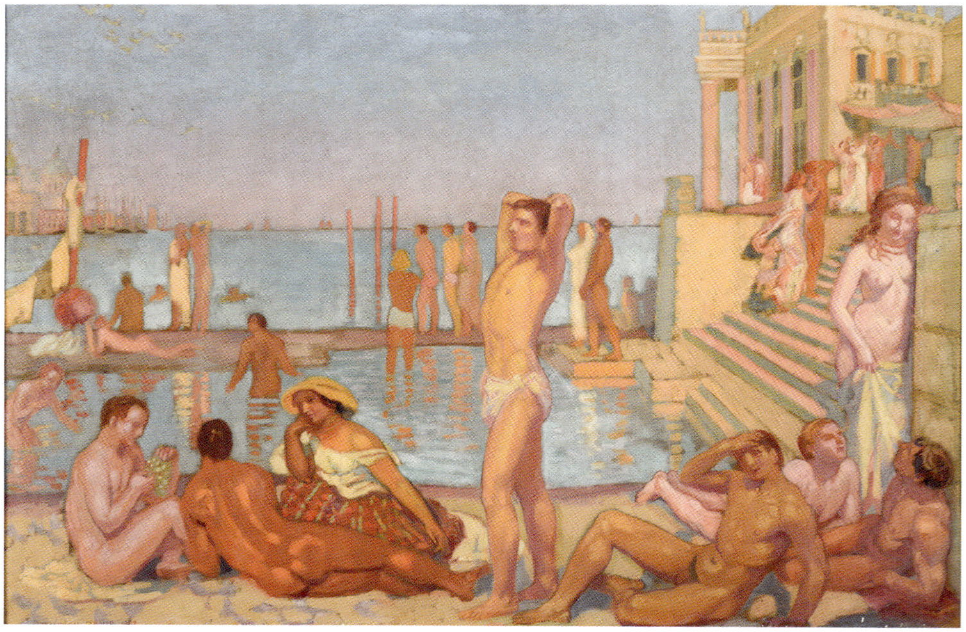

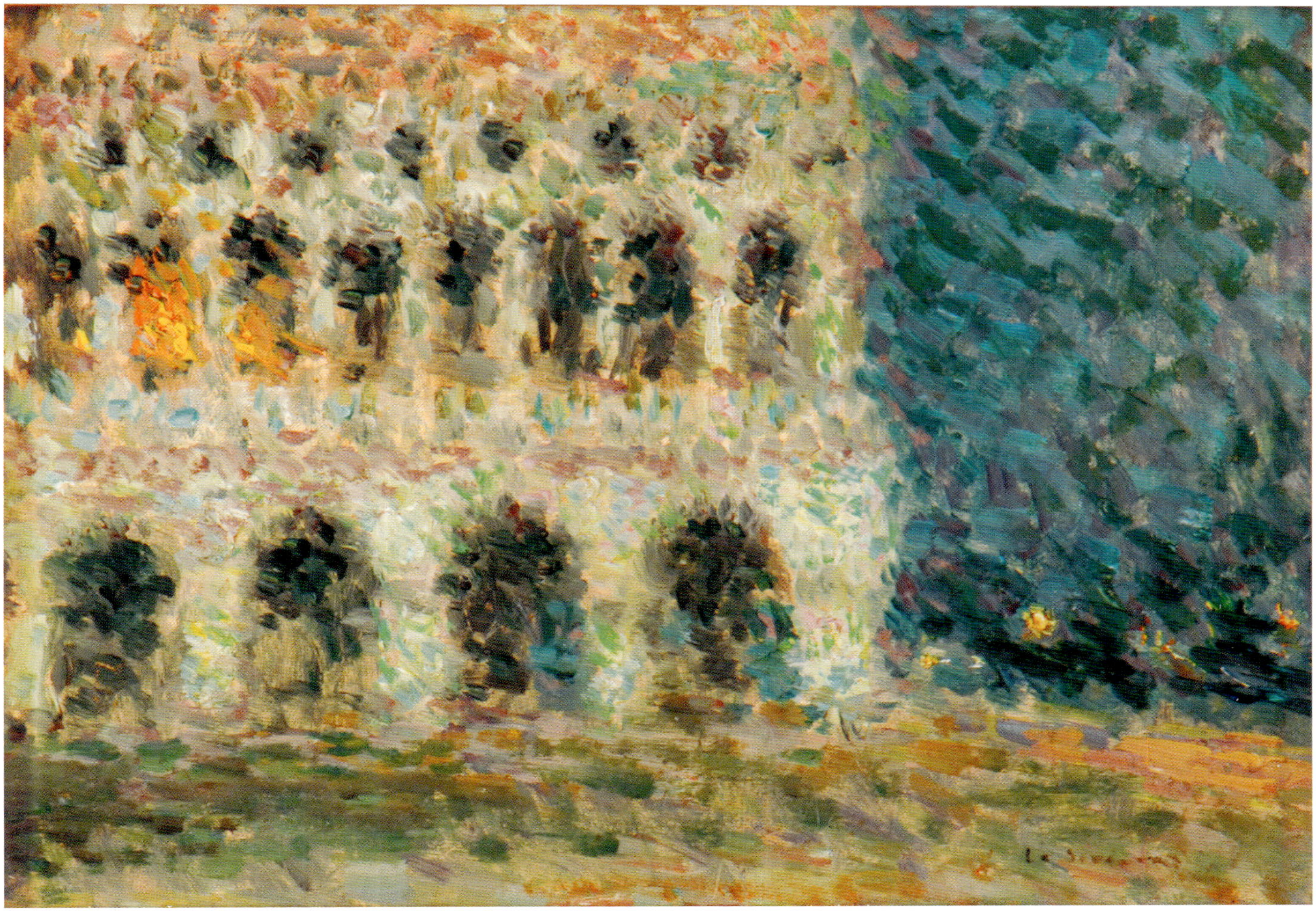

fig. 134—Henri Le Sidaner, *The Palazzo Ducalew, Venice*, c. 1906, oil on panel, 5⅝ × 7⅞ in., La Salle University Art Museum

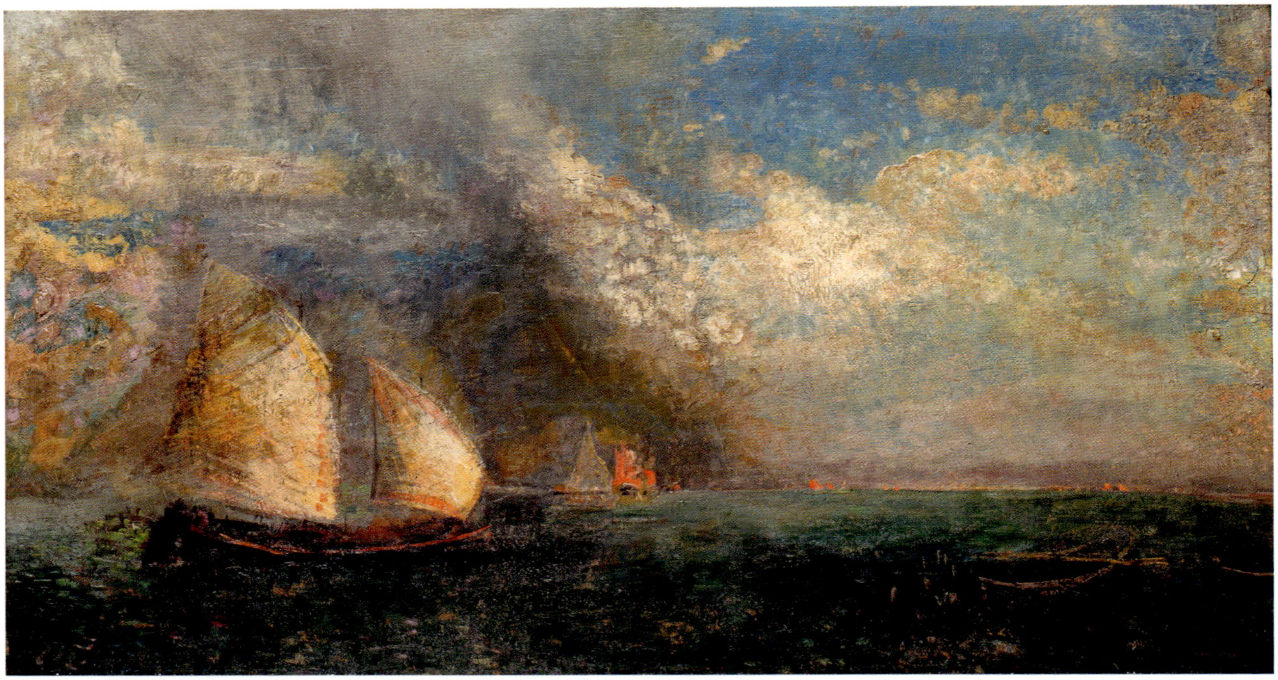

lodged. But when Proust saw the facade of San Marco he was saddened to discover Ruskin's description of it in terms of pearls and rubies too extravagant.[37]

Yet naturalistic representations continued after 1900. In 1912—the very year Monet's Venice show was staged in Paris—René Ménard, who had made his reputation painting the ruins of Greek civilization, executed a view of the Piazzetta (fig. 136), a conventional enough site rendered interesting by marginalizing the Palazzo Ducale and playing off the twin columns of the Lion of Saint Mark and Saint Theodore against the *campanile* of San Giorgio Maggiore across the Bacino di San Marco. This was the kind of precise topographical motif—almost requiring a Baedeker in hand—that Monet's paintings had eschewed. In his painting Ménard discreetly omitted the tourist crowds, whereas Jean-François Raffaëlli, an artist who had shown images of the poor of suburban Paris at the 1880 and 1881 Impressionist exhibitions (at neither of which Monet showed) before switching to more genial cityscapes, represented the Riva degli Schiavoni and the waterfront busy with the daily bustle of ordinary Venetian life (fig. 137). Ambivalent reactions continued, too. The rakish aristocrat Boni de Castellane and his plutocratic wife, Anna Gould, arrived in their yacht in 1903. His disgust and delight were similar to that of Maupassant almost twenty years before. Castellane found the city "absurd" and resented the proliferation of cabbage stalks, dead cats, and mosquitoes, yet thrilled that "the city seems to be made in a pinkish gold and one always seems to see it through a sapphire light."[38]

Avant-garde painters also discovered the city. Henri-Edmond Cross arrived in July 1903 and stayed five weeks. On-site he painted watercolors and developed paintings to be completed on his return. His *Regatta in Venice* (fig. 138) takes on Venice's particular light with a Neo-Impressionist touch and chromatics,

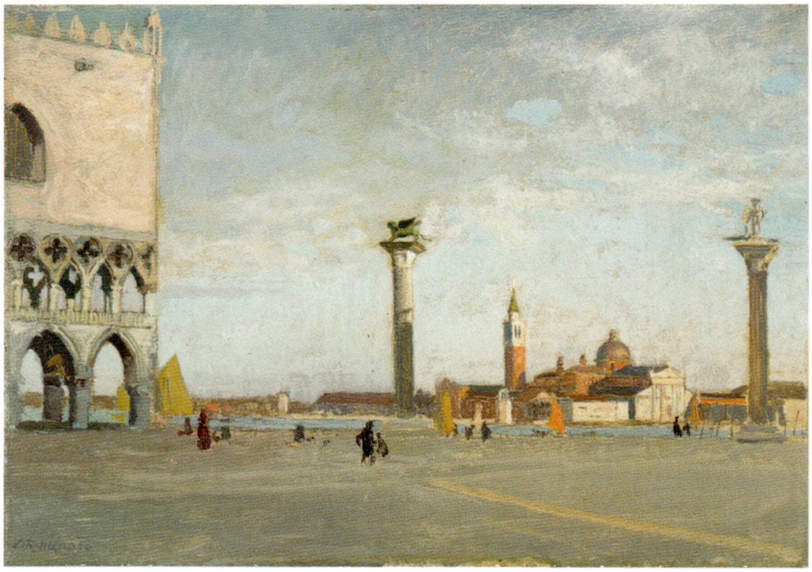

fig. 135—Odilon Redon, *Fishing Boats, Memory of Venice*, c. 1908, oil on wood, 15 ¾ × 29 in., Museum Langmatt

fig. 136—Émile René Ménard, *La Piazzetta*, 1912, oil on canvas, 10½ × 14½ in., Musée d'Orsay

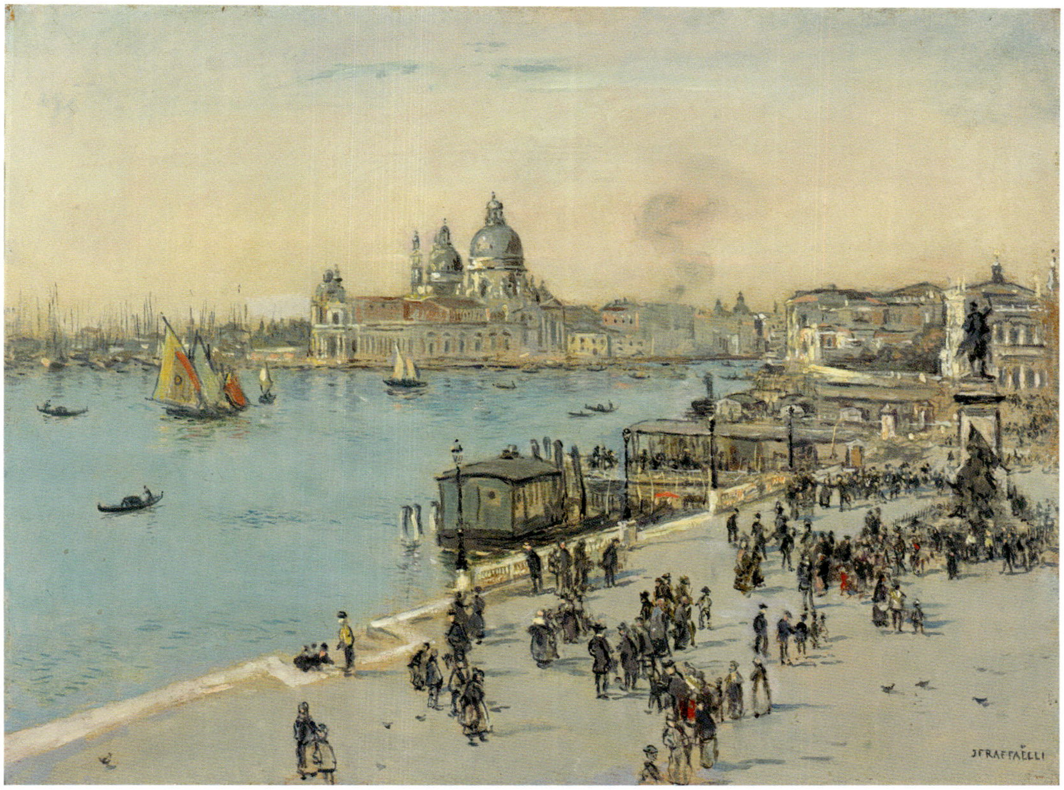

fig. 137—Jean-François Raffaëlli, *Le Quai des Esclavons (Venetië)*, c. 1913, oil on canvas, 22×17⅞ in., Museum Boijmans Van Beuningen

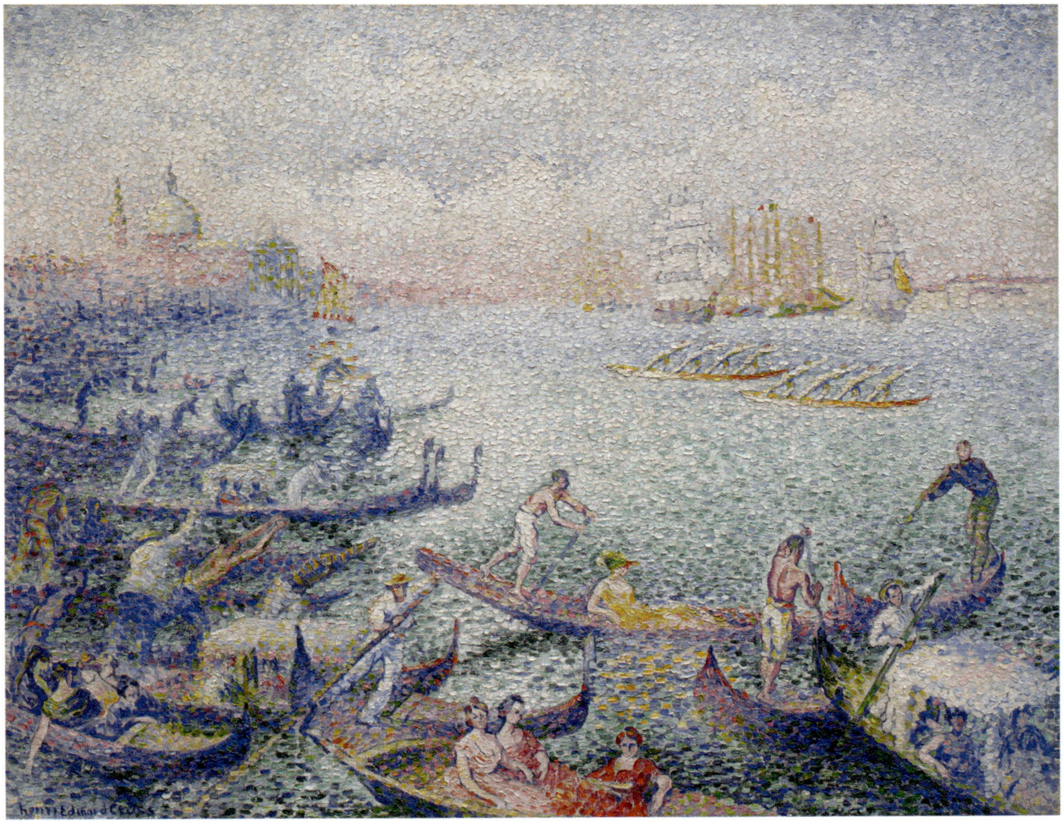

fig. 138—Henri-Edmond Cross, *Regatta in Venice*, 1903–04, oil on canvas, 29 × 36½ in., Museum of Fine Arts, Houston

and by representing not only tourists but also gondoliers and the working port in the background, he rendered a more egalitarian view of Venice consistent with his anarchist ideology. The notes Cross made record his responses to Carpaccio, Veronese, and Tiepolo, observations of ordinary Venetians, and regret that the July sky was persistently azure.[39] His fellow Neo-Impressionist and anarchist Paul Signac followed him in 1904. Signac's *The Green Sail* uses the muted profiles of San Giorgio Maggiore and, farther back, the Salute to set the Venetian scene, but around the decoratively rigged foreground boat are fishing nets and the silhouettes of passing gondoliers. Signac's *The Lagoon of Saint Mark, Venice* (fig. 186), completed the following year, presents a pageant-like quality with decorative sails but focuses attention on the boatsmen in the foreground, while the celebrated buildings slip softly into the ambient distance. Of the fifteen paintings resulting from this campaign, two of which were shown at the Salon des Indépendants in 1905 and three the following year, five—including the largest, the *Lagoon of Saint Mark, Venice*—were purchased by the wealthy Béziers vineyard owner Gustave Fayet and others by German collectors such as Count Harry Kessler, Victor von Mutzenbecher, and Alfred Wolff.[40] Monet himself admired Signac's Venice work, and in May 1909 he purchased from the Bernheim-Jeune gallery a watercolor the younger artist had made the previous year. (fig. 187)[41] Here was evidence not only of Neo-Impressionism's status among progressive amateurs but also the cosmopolitan appreciation of Venice as a tourist destination for the cultivated and curious, precisely the élite audience at which Monet's 1912 exhibition was aimed. Indeed, Fayet himself had spent his honeymoon in Venice in 1893. Although an agriculturalist, businessman, and collector, Fayet was also an amateur artist, and—as it happens—this aspect of his life spans the range of responses to the great Adriatic city. Much of the work that Fayet made in 1893 is reliably naturalistic (fig. 139), like that of Thaulow, Lansyer, and, among fellow amateurs, Rouart. But a view of the Dogana and Salute silhouetted against the evening glow responds to the magical light admired by Havard, Louÿs, and so many others and looks forward to Fayet's later collecting of the work of artists such as Paul Gauguin, which was reductive in form and suggestive in color.

This survey sites Monet in the cultural and artistic context of his day. In so doing it makes clear how remarkably individual his paintings of Venice are. We have seen his contemporaries use the Queen of the Sea in allegories, represent the city as a locus of busy activity, veil it in subtle light, and depict its buildings with exactitude but also suggestive nuance. We have heard their ambivalence about its architectural glory and grubby conditions. But when we look at Monet's canvases in comparison to the pictures of his fellow artists, we are struck by how deeply personal they are, how his exquisitely refined eye could realize on canvas the nuances of shifting Adriatic light, the movement of the reflecting surfaces of the water, and the historic identity of the buildings even as they bask in the extraordinary illumination that characterizes the magical city of Venice.

fig. 139—Gustave Fayet, *View of Punta della Dogana Venice*, 1893, painting on cardboard, 8¼ × 6⅓ in., Musée d'Art Gustave Fayet à Fontfroide

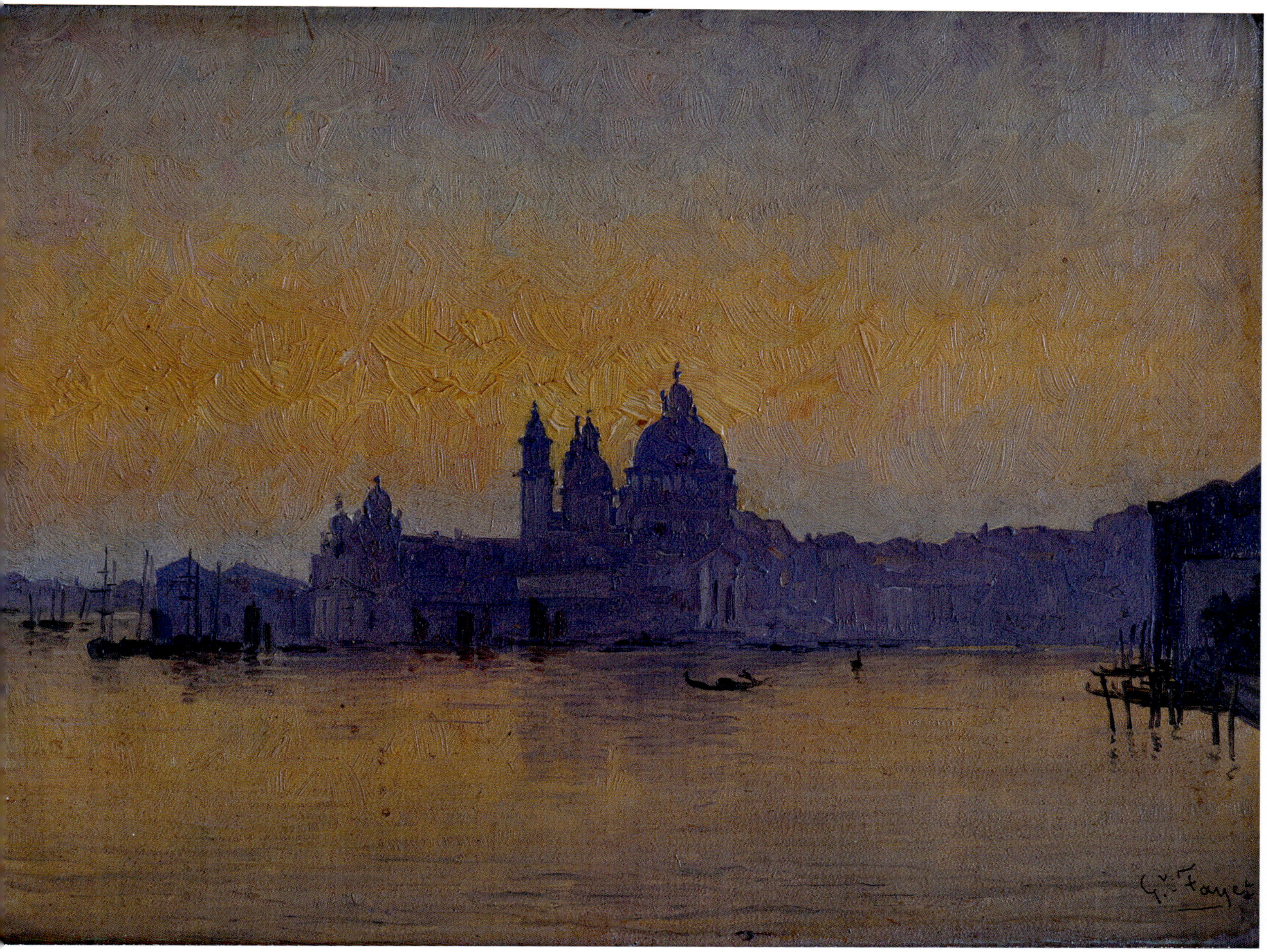

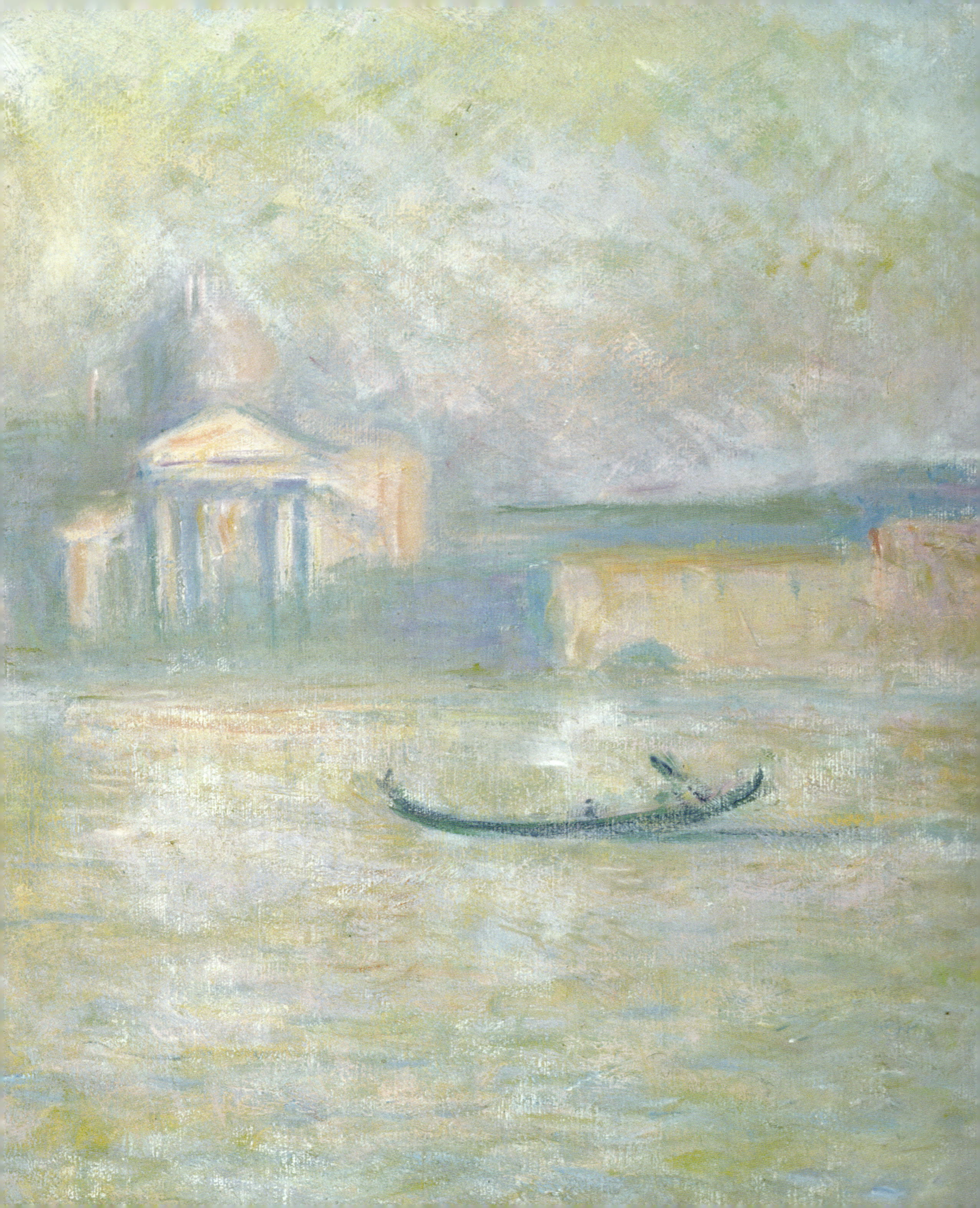

Lisa Small

"NO ONE HAS EVER GIVEN THE IDEA OF VENICE": MONET'S PREDECESSORS AND CONTEMPORARIES

PORTRAYED BY ARTISTS FOR CENTURIES, the spectacular city of Venice has long maintained an indelible visual presence in the European cultural imagination. But when Claude Monet visited the city in 1908, he nonetheless found it "unrealizable" and insisted that "no one has ever given the idea of Venice."[1] It is not clear how much Claude Monet engaged—or not—with works depicting the city by other artists, past or contemporaneous. He did not frequently share his thoughts about historical art in general. One of the most famous anecdotes about him recounts that when as a young man he went with fellow artists to copy in the Musée du Louvre, he turned his back on the old masters and looked out a window to paint Paris. Yet when he visited the Museo del Prado in Madrid in 1904, he was apparently quite moved: "When I found myself in these rooms, in the middle of the Titians, the Rubenses, the Velázquezes, the Tintorettos that seem to be made yesterday, which burst with strength, light, color, the emotion seized me in the heart, the throat, and I cried, cried without being able to contain myself."[2] Also, like many of his European and American contemporaries, Monet had a deep admiration for Japanese woodblock prints of the eighteenth and nineteenth centuries. Not only was he inspired by their bold colors and innovative compositions; his choice to capture the essence of a place like London or Venice through multiple characteristic views, or in different seasons and at different times of day, reflects his appreciation of sets like Hokusai's *Thirty-Six Views of Mount Fuji* (figs. 79 and 80) and Hiroshige's *100 Famous Views of Edo*, individual prints from which he owned.[3]

Monet's regard for key figures of the previous generation—Eugène Delacroix's fluid brushwork and color and the Barbizon landscapists' practice *en plein air*, for example—is well-known, although the competitive Monet rarely compared

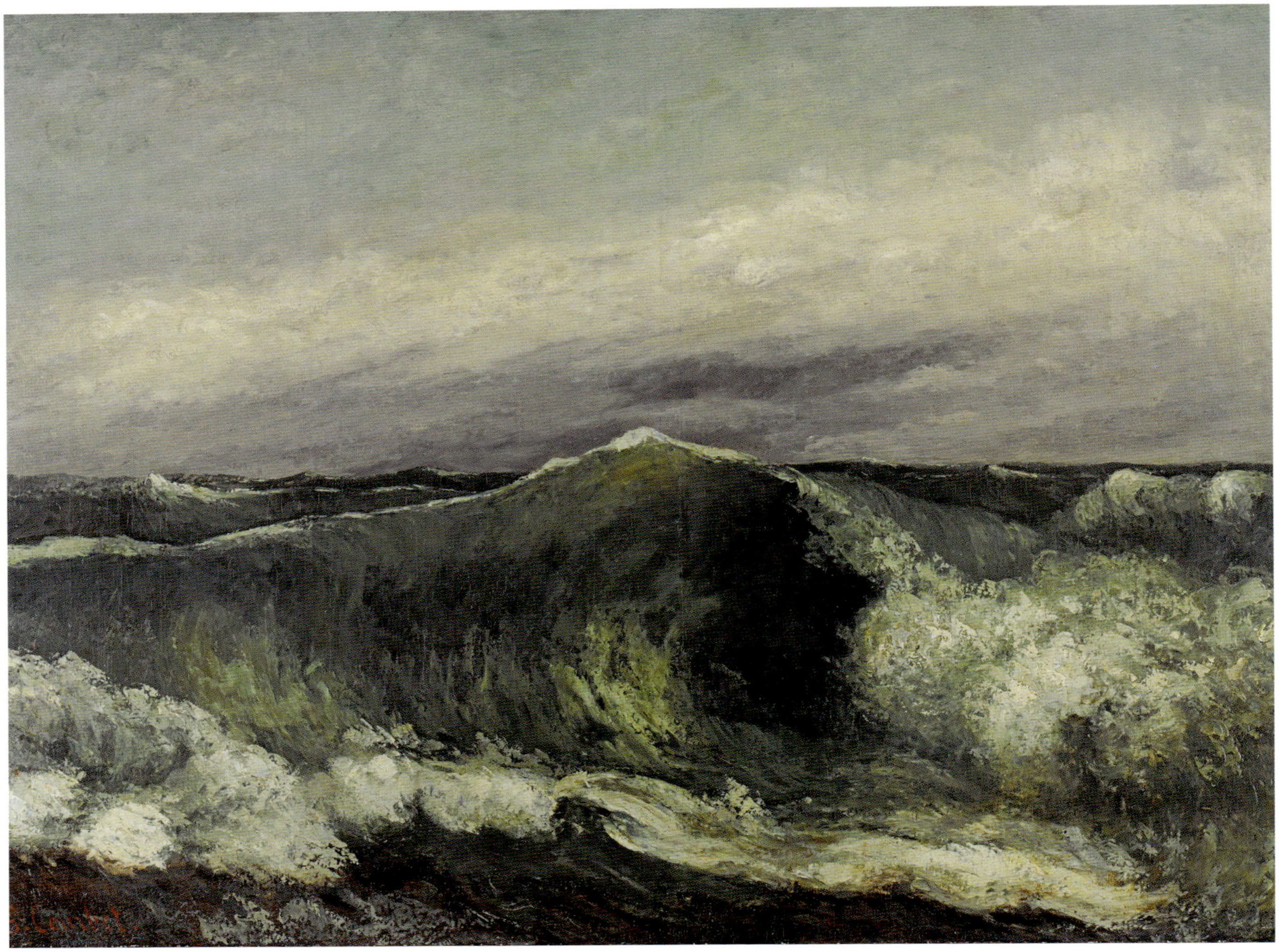

fig. 140—Gustave Courbet, *The Wave*, c. 1869, oil on canvas, 25¾ × 34¹⁵⁄₁₆ in., Brooklyn Museum

himself directly to anyone. He came close to doing so—while still emphasizing reliance on his own vision—when he wrote to his wife, Alice, from Normandy in 1883: "I am planning to do a large canvas of the cliff at Étretat, even though it is terribly bold of me to do so after Courbet did it so wonderfully, but, I will try to do it in a different way."[4] The influence of what Gustave Courbet called his "sea landscapes" is indeed evident in Monet's Normandy coast paintings, such as *Waves Breaking* (figs. 140 and 141).

As an artist attuned to the present moment, Monet was more forthcoming about his own mentors and contemporaries. He admired the naturalism and painterly touch of landscapist Charles-François Daubigny, who was an important supporter of Impressionism and introduced Monet to Paul Durand-Ruel in London. Daubigny's river scenes were initiated with great immediacy from his purpose-built "studio boat," a structure and strategy that Monet emulated throughout his career, including in Venice (figs. 142, 143, and 144). Monet also acknowledged the influence of Johan Barthold Jongkind, with whom he worked on the Normandy coast in the 1860s. Monet absorbed the Dutch artist's manner of structuring compositions with pronounced

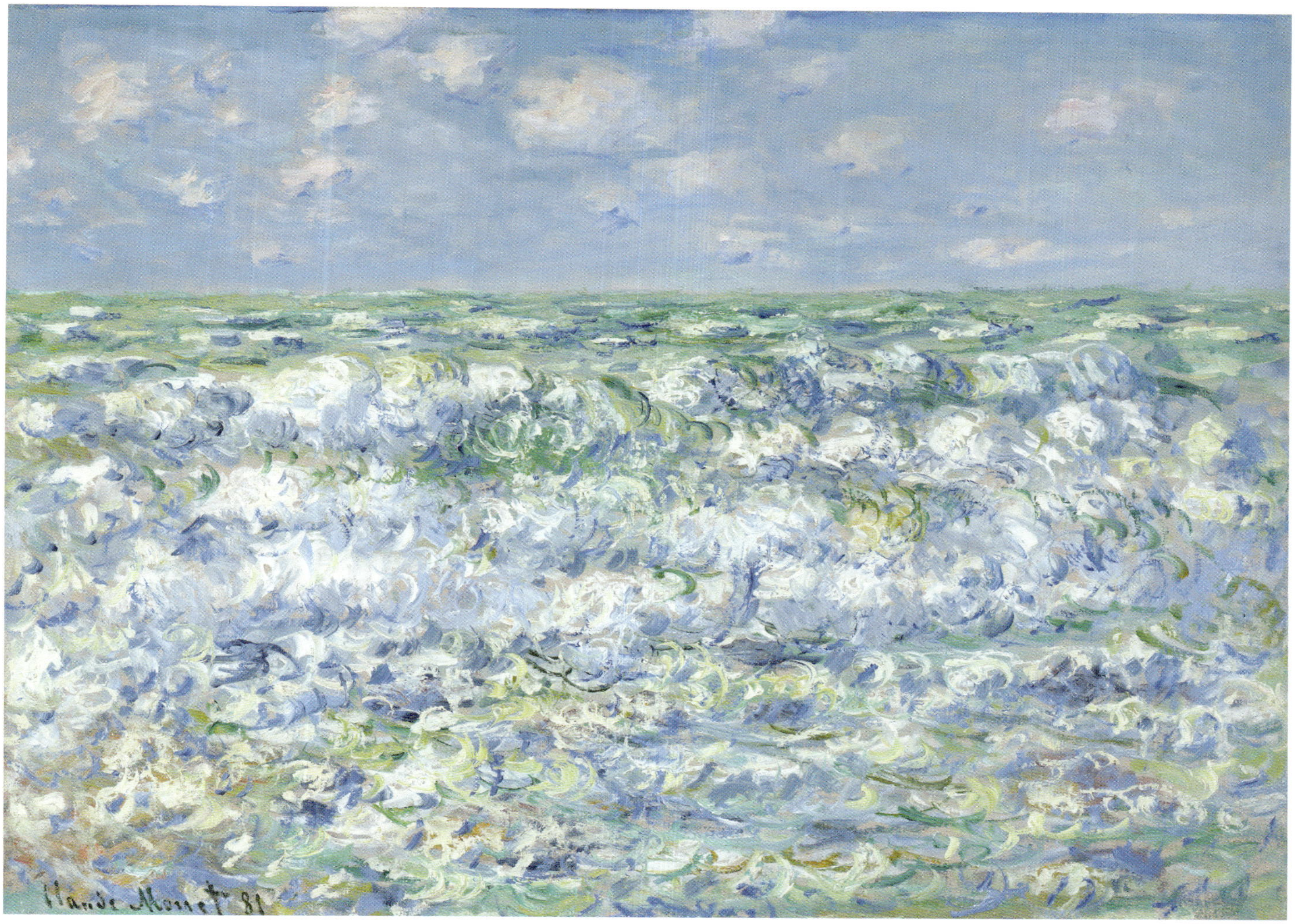

fig. 141—Claude Monet, *Waves Breaking*, 1881, oil on canvas, 23½ × 32 in., Fine Arts Museums of San Francisco

diagonals and expanses of sky (fig. 145). Monet claimed that he owed to Jongkind "the definitive education of my eye."[5]

Some of the artists important to Monet's early development had also spent time painting in Venice. Jean-Baptiste-Camille Corot's serene, silvery landscape paintings and dazzling *plein air* oil sketches, particularly his Italian scenes, were generally known and admired by Monet and his cohorts. (fig. 148)[6] For Monet, he was a touchstone, the greatest landscape painter of all: "There is only one master here—Corot. We are nothing compared to him, nothing."[7] Monet may not have had firsthand knowledge of Corot's oil sketches of Venice, but he would have appreciated their spontaneous handling, bright colors, and brilliant light. The immediacy of the older artist's visual impression is underscored in an 1828 sketch by his notation, *Venise, 12 Juillet*, inscribed in the wet paint with the brush handle (fig. 147).

And Monet acknowledged his formative relationship with Eugène Boudin, who used lively touches of paint to capture the transient effects of light in cloud-filled skies and on the water's undulating surfaces (fig. 146). When the two were on campaigns together on the Normandy coast in the late 1850s, Boudin opened

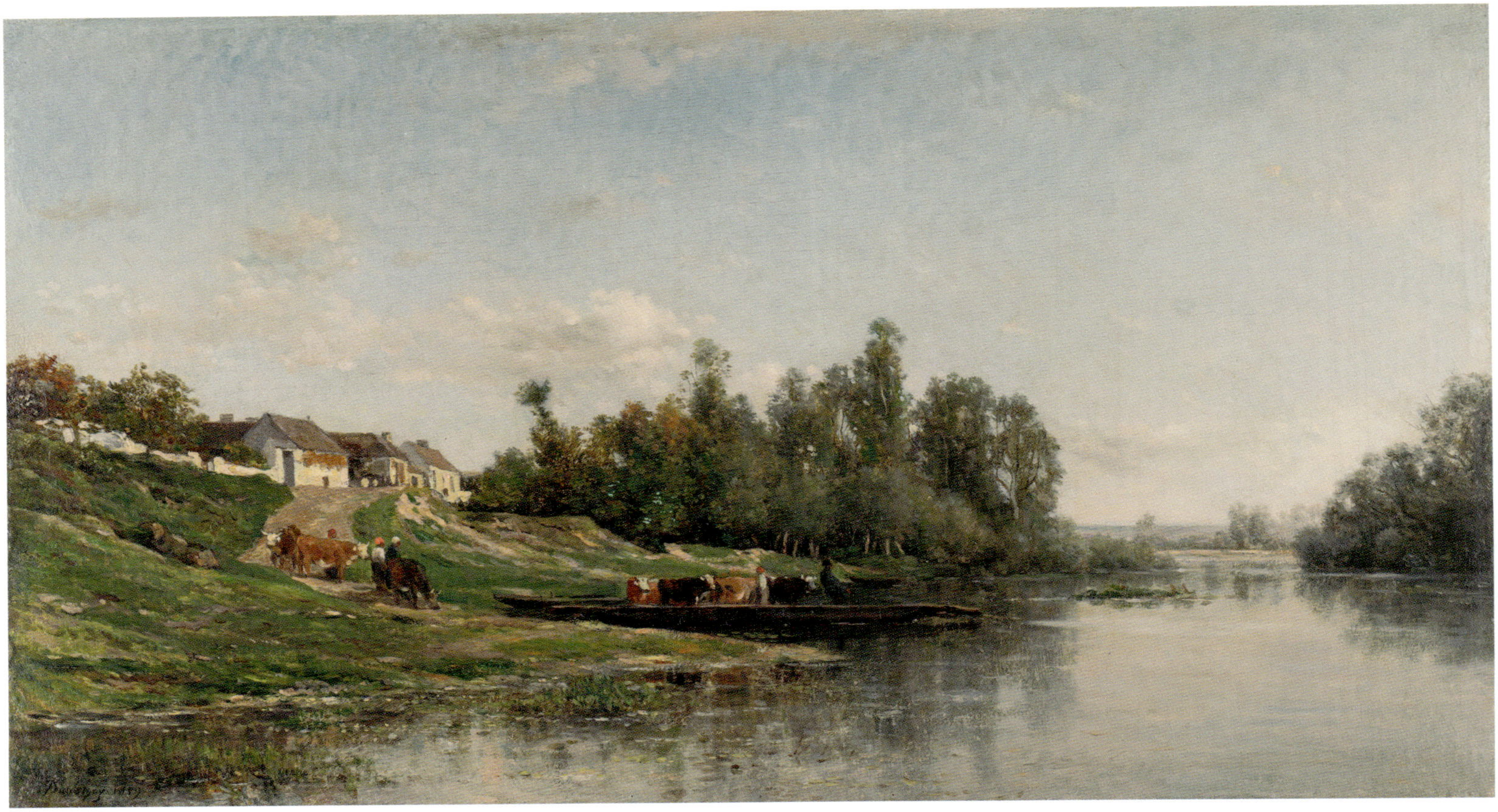

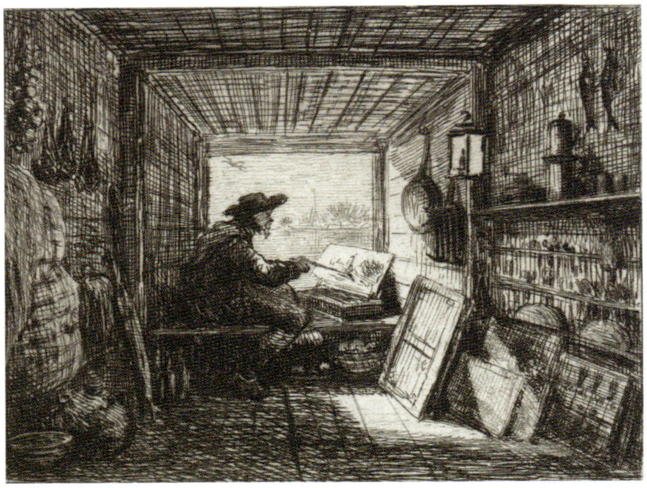

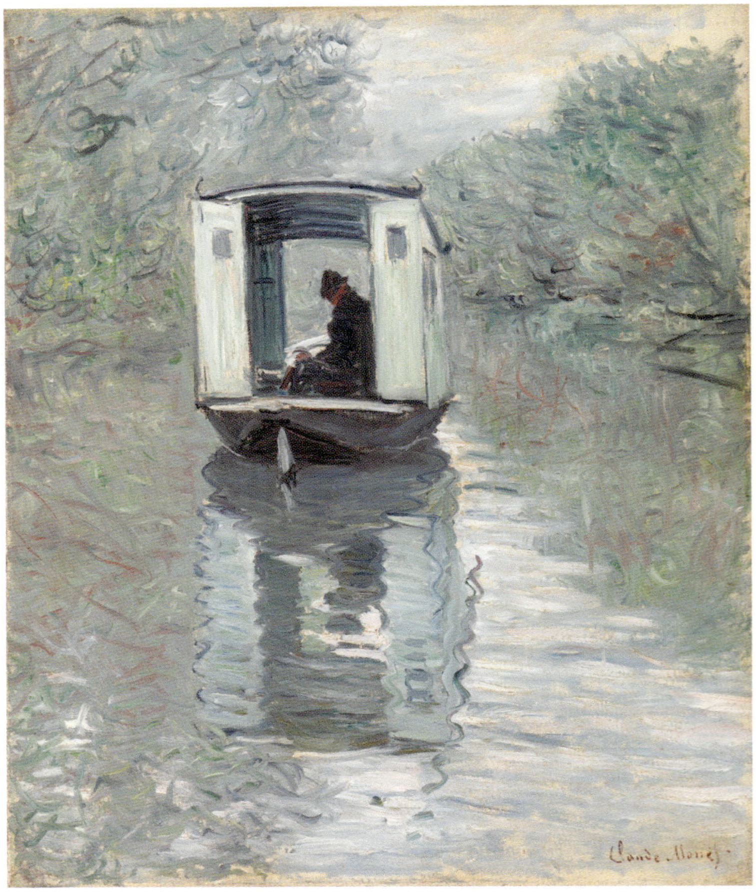

fig. 142—Charles-François Daubigny, *River Scene*, 1859, oil on panel, $14\frac{1}{4} \times 25\frac{3}{4}$ in., Brooklyn Museum

fig. 143—Charles-François Daubigny, *Le Bateau-Atelier* from the album *Voyage en Bateau*, 1861, etching, $5\frac{1}{16} \times 7$ in., Fine Arts Museums of San Francisco

fig. 144—Claude Monet, *The Studio Boat (Le Bateau-atelier)*, 1876, oil on canvas, $28\frac{5}{8} \times 23\frac{5}{8}$ in., The Barnes Foundation

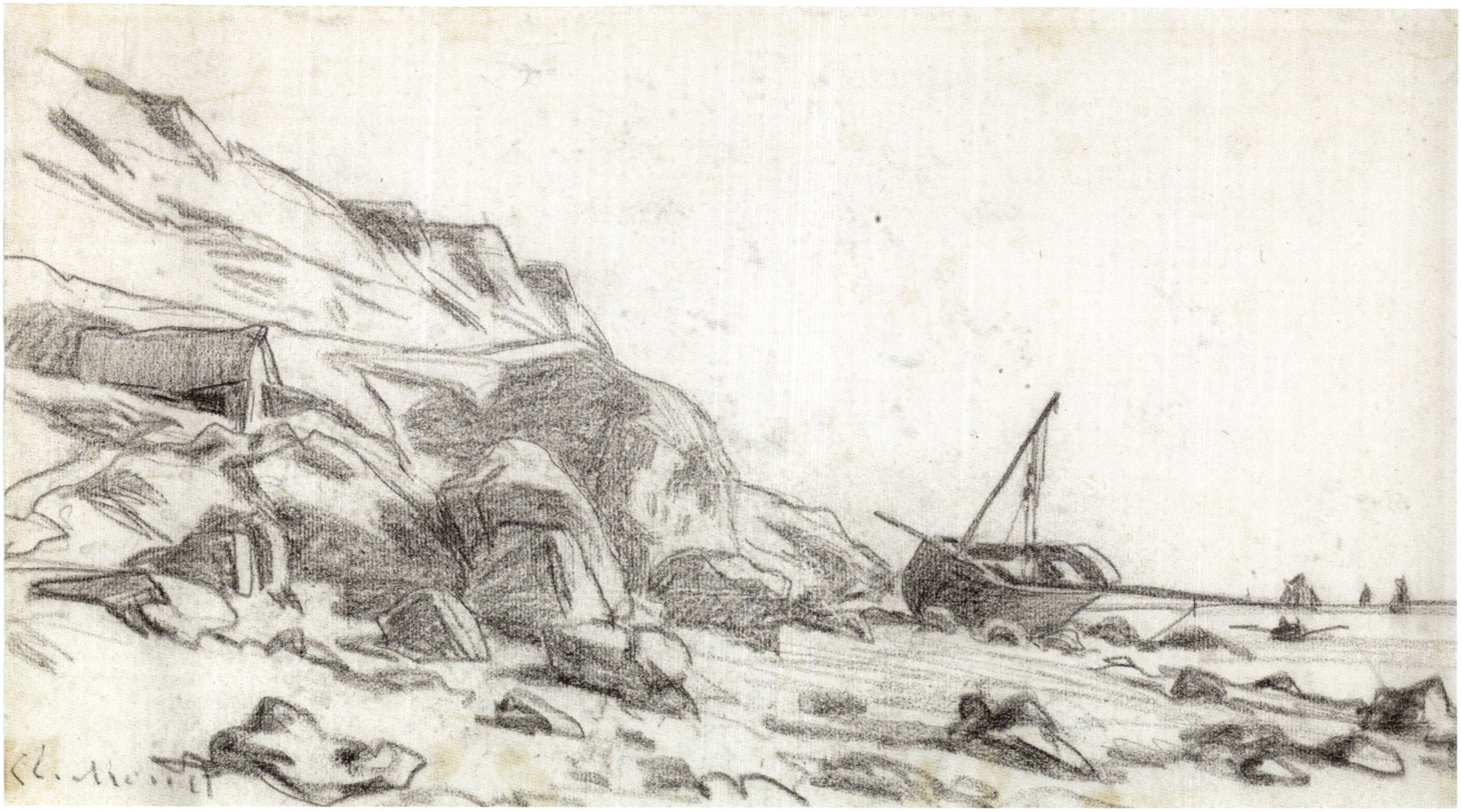

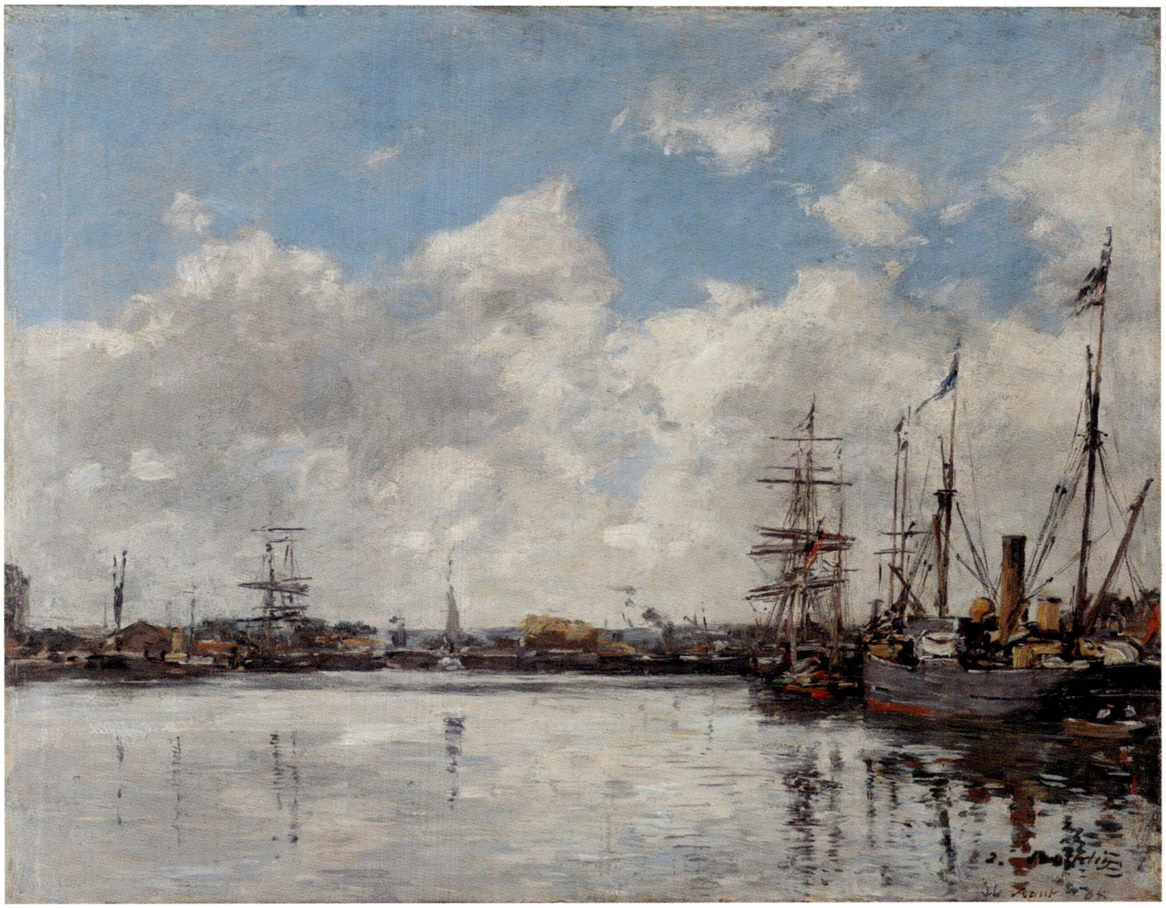

fig. 145—Claude Monet, *The Coast of Normandy Viewed from Sainte-Adresse*, c. 1864, black chalk on cream laid paper, 7⅟₁₆ × 12⅛ in., Fine Arts Museums of San Francisco

fig. 146—Eugène Boudin, *Le Havre, The Port*, 1884, oil on panel, 12¾ × 16³⁄₁₆ in., Brooklyn Museum

Monet's eyes to atmospheric nuances and to *plein air* painting: "It was as if all of a sudden a veil had fallen from my eyes: I had understood. I knew what painting could be."[8] Like Monet, Boudin painted in Normandy throughout his career and was in his late sixties when he first traveled to Venice. Over several trips to Venice, Boudin made numerous paintings of the lagoon that echo the format and sketchy handling of his Normandy port images (figs. 124 and 125). (For more on Boudin's Venice work, see Richard Thomson's essay in this volume.) Indeed, Boudin was surprised to discover that instead of being bright and hot, "Venice, like all luminous cities, has a grey hue, the atmosphere is mild and misty and the sky arrays itself with clouds, just like the sky of our Norman and Dutch regions."[9]

Monet was undoubtedly aware of the centuries-long tradition of painting Venice through his visits to museums, as well as reproductions he would likely have encountered in books and art journals. But there is no clear evidence of what he thought even of that genre's most famous eighteenth-century practitioners, Canaletto (figs. 32, 107, 108, 109, and 149) and Francesco Guardi (figs. 110 and 150), although he would have had access to their works in both London and Paris and he painted some of the same

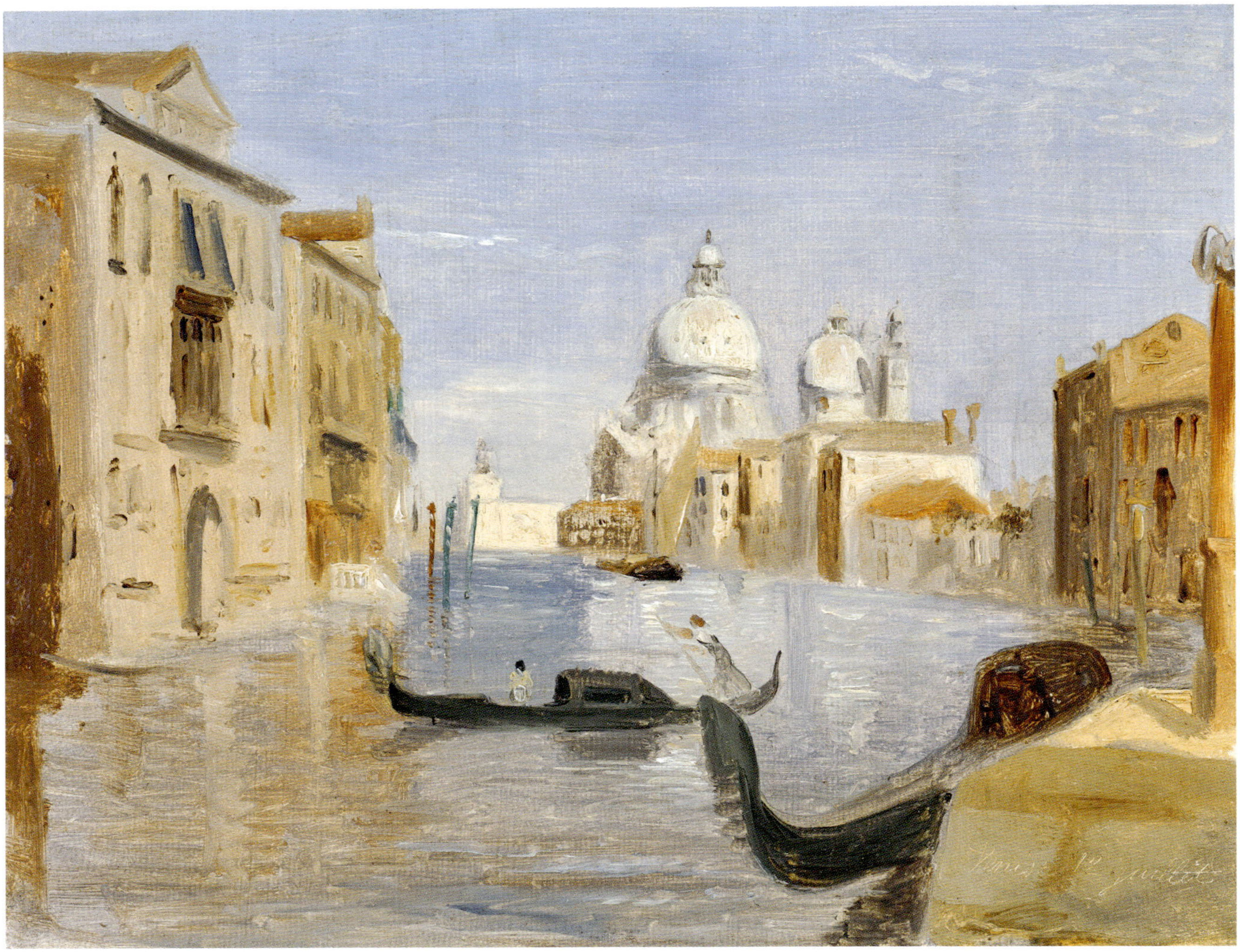

fig. 147—Jean-Baptiste-Camille Corot, *View of Venice (Santa Maria della Salute from Campo della Carita)*, 1828, oil on paper laid down on canvas, 9⅜ × 12⅝ in., Gallery 19C

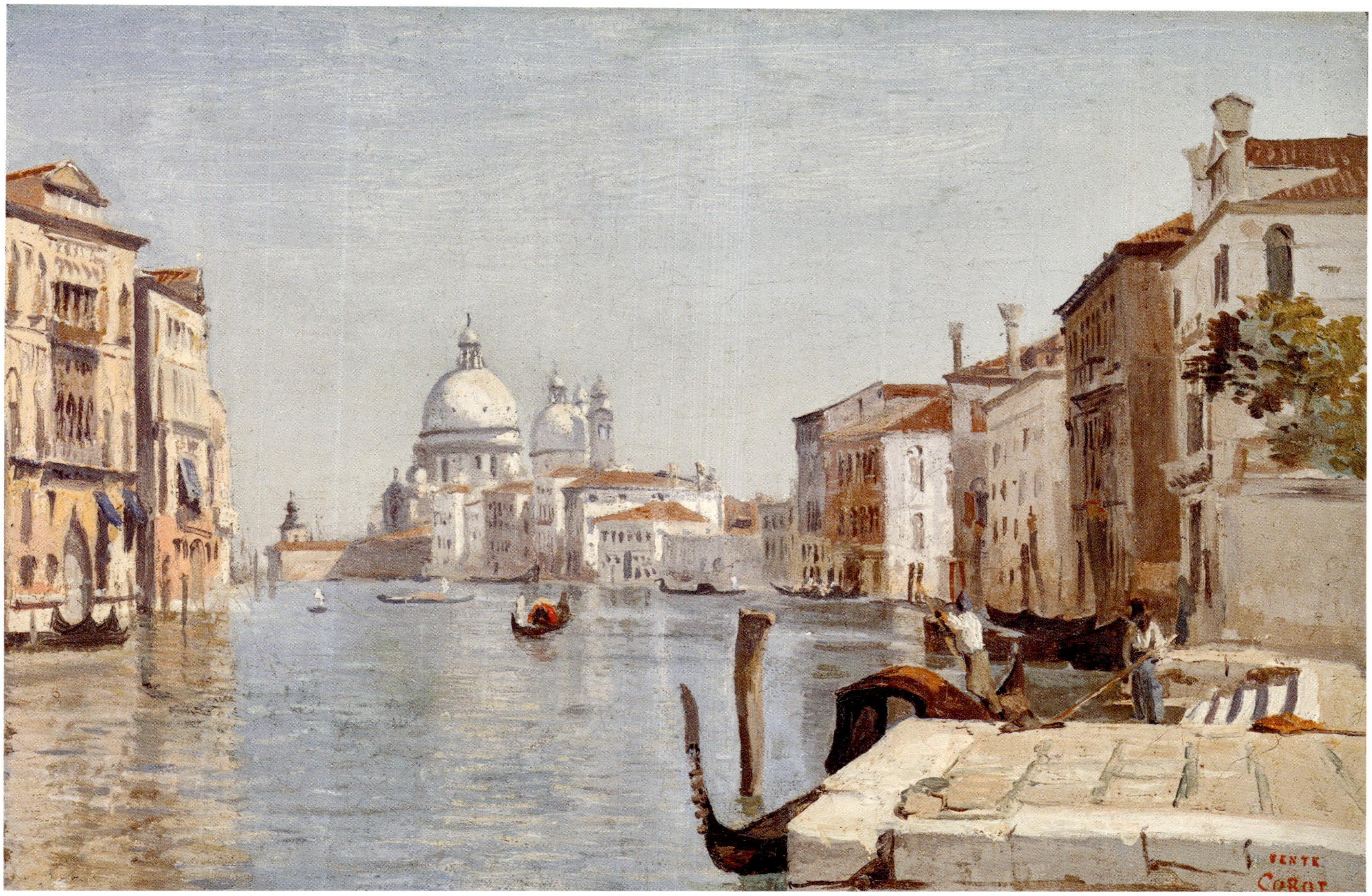

fig. 148—Jean-Baptiste-Camille Corot, *Venise—View of Campo della Carità Looking Toward the Dome of la Salute*, 1834, oil on paper laid down on canvas, 10½ × 15 in., Gallery 19C

vistas they did.[10] (See Donato Esposito's essay in this volume.) Indeed, Monet's focus on some of the city's primary viewpoints parallels the approach of the Venice view painting sets commissioned from Canaletto by wealthy collectors, or more affordable print portfolio versions (figs. 34–54). From a stylistic perspective, Monet would have been drawn more to Guardi: freer, feathery brushwork and delicate colors that were more consonant with his own. In his 1907 book, *Venice in the Eighteenth Century*, the historian Philippe Monnier recognized Guardi's modern appeal: "Look at the fine quality of the silvered greys of his skies, and, through all these translucent tints, the little dash of sobriety and grace he throws in with his supple and sure touch; the light parts washed in, a tiny point of light, an accentuated colour, the bright red of a cloak, or the yellow sheen of a boatman's tunic. It is the utmost pitch of skill, and as modern as today. Francesco Guardi began a new era."[11] Guardi himself described his own style as "tocco forte," a thick and often rough application of paint; on the back of one of his drawings, he wrote that he sought buyers who appreciated deliberately rough, rather than fine, brushwork.[12]

The assumption that Monet would not have been particularly inspired by Canaletto's architectural clarity might be inferred from a 1909 article by Roger Marx about the *Water Lilies*. Writing in Monet's voice, Marx asserted the artist's affinity for "our own eighteenth-century painters, with whom I recognize a close kinship of sensitivity and technique." While this likely referred to

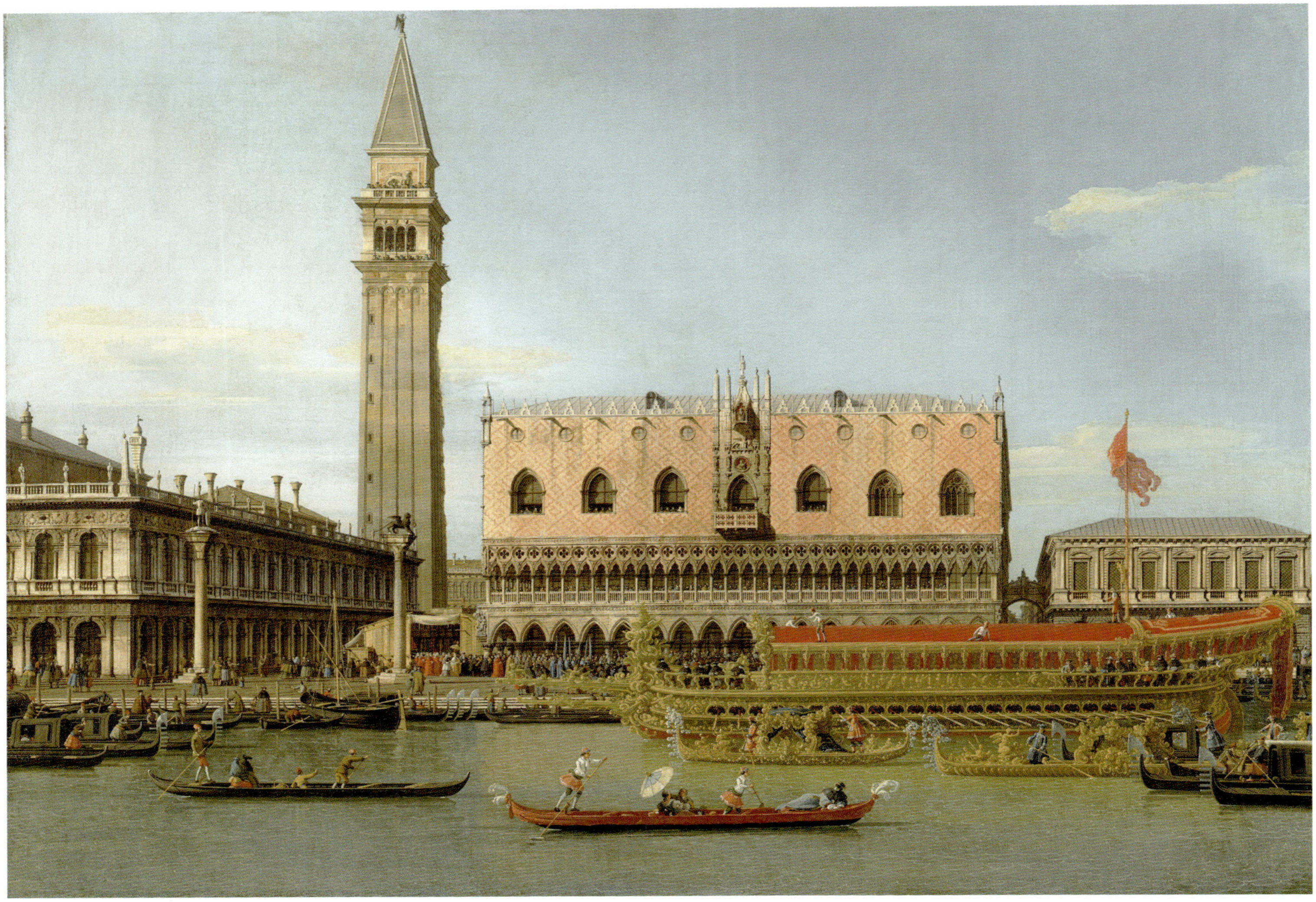

a French artist such as Antoine Watteau, the Italian Rococo artist Guardi, with his flickering brushwork and subtle light effects, is another plausible eighteenth-century candidate for Monet's kinship.[13] Louis Gillet also channeled Monet's voice in a 1909 article in which he asserted the artist's emphasis on sensation rather than description: "You demand from my painting the information of an engineer; you have come to the wrong address."[14] This passage could equally rebut any insistence that instead of hazy dissolution, Monet should offer the kind of topographical accuracy Canaletto's paintings were thought to exemplify. Several reviews of Monet's 1912 *Venise* exhibition noted his transfiguration of the eighteenth-century *vedute* tradition epitomized by Canaletto, "where the architecture is written with a marvelous concern for precision."[15] Monet instead looked "in a new way" at the city; it was no longer "the Venice in picturesque decadence of the painters of the eighteenth century.... Venice is there, very present and recognizable, but it is not in the foreground, built, sculpted, inventoried; it is suspended in the mist and in a distance of space."[16]

In the nineteenth century, Venice's growing reputation as a dreamlike place of melancholy and bedazzlement attracted

fig. 149—Canaletto, *The Bucintoro at the Molo on Ascension Day*, c. 1745, oil on canvas, 45¼ × 64 in., Philadelphia Museum of Art

new generations of European and American artists. They used a variety of pictorial strategies—from vistas to vignettes—to match their talents against the city's natural and architectural beauty. J. M. W. Turner, who combined the breadth of Canaletto's influential panoramas with lush color and gestural effects, was synonymous with Venetian imagery in the early nineteenth century, and he was Monet's most consequential artistic predecessor there. The English painter's expressive, abstracted style had been cited by critics in relation to Monet's work since the 1870s. When paintings by both artists appeared in the 1900 Exposition Universelle in Paris, Roger Marx wrote of Monet, "Apart from Turner and Corot, modern landscape cannot count a master of more noble ability."[17] The two artists were also linked during Monet's 1904 exhibition of his London paintings at Durand-Ruel's gallery in Paris (fig. 152). One writer referred to Monet as "our French Turner" and another wrote that placing certain Monets beside certain Turners would reveal two branches of Impressionism and "integrate two moments in the history of visual sensitivity."[18] Even Henri Matisse recognized a formal affinity: "It seemed to me that Turner must have been the link between the academic tradition and impressionism. I have, in fact, observed a close relationship in the construction of works using colour between Turner's watercolours and the paintings of Claude Monet."[19]

fig. 150—Francesco Guardi, *View of the Grand Canal with the Dogana*, c. 1780, oil on canvas, 16¾ × 26⅜ in., Columbia Museum of Art

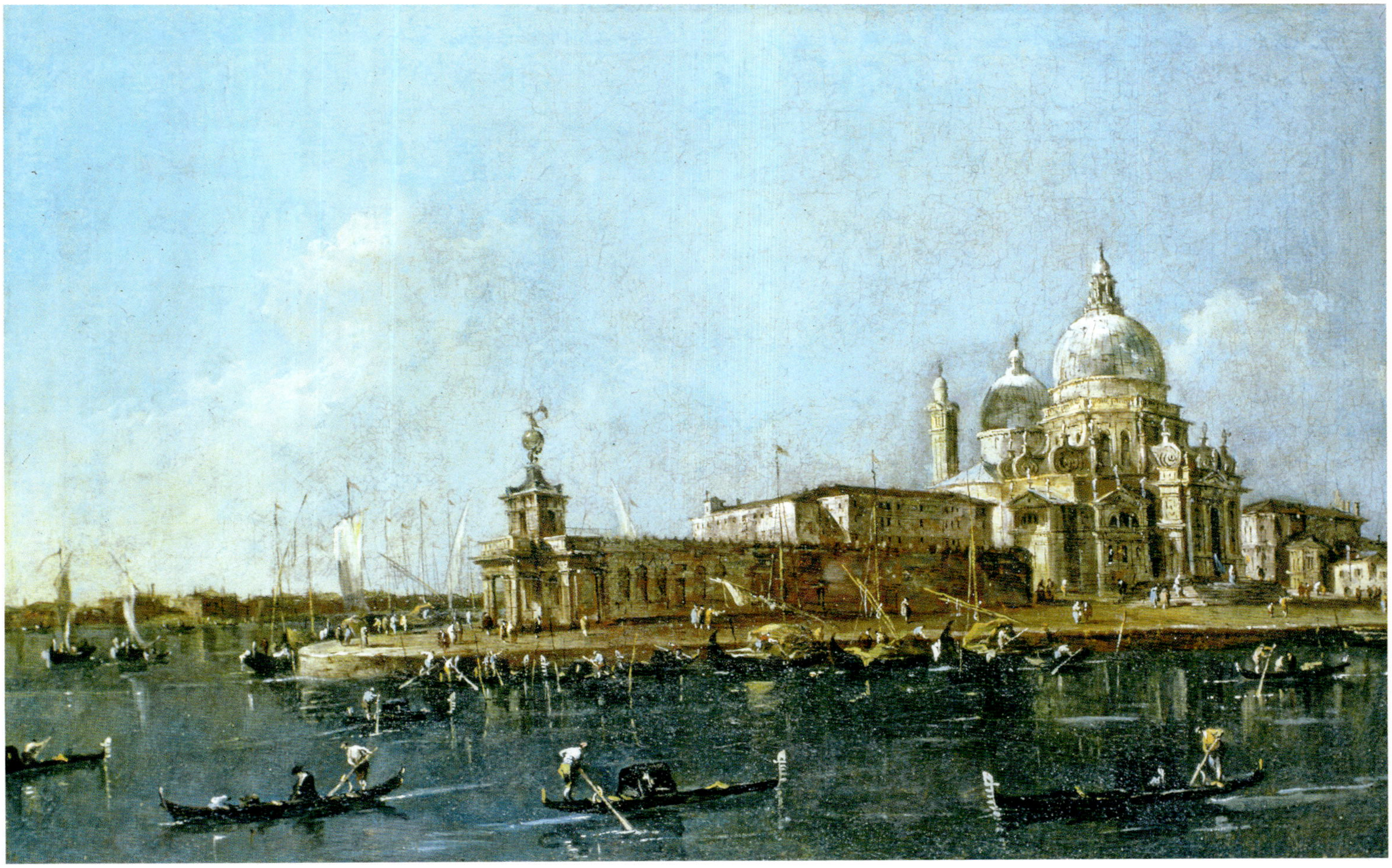

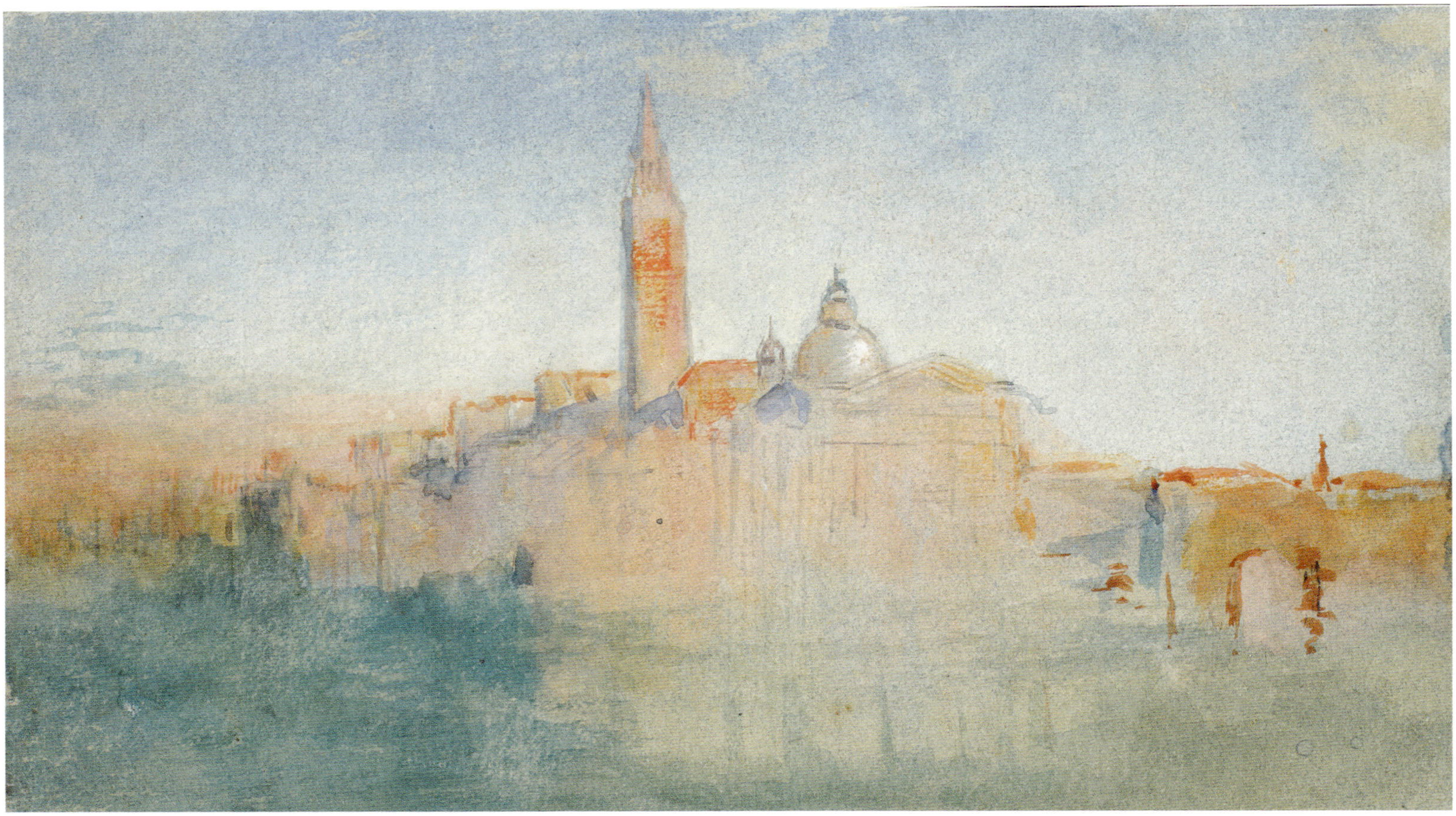

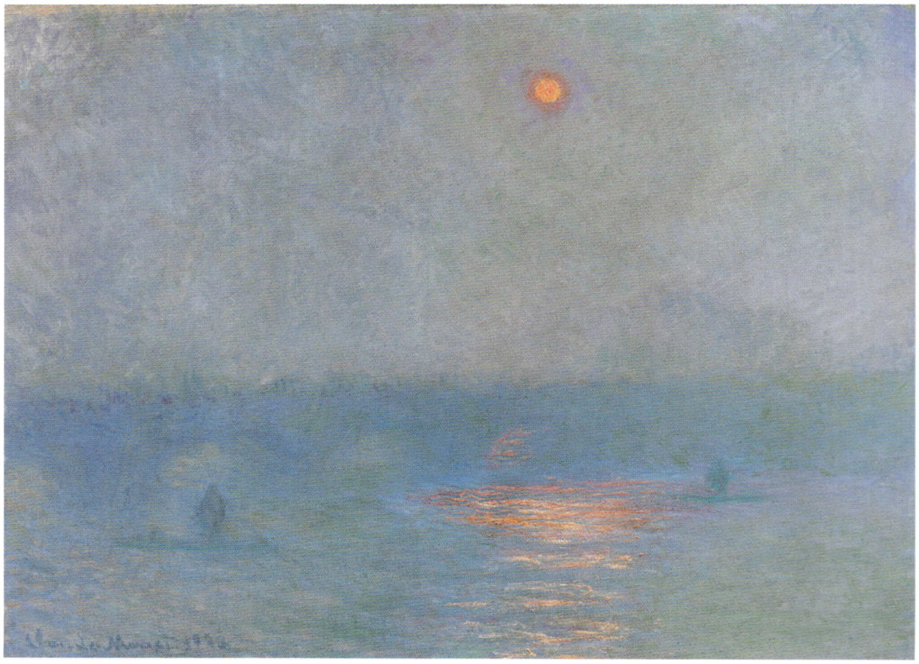

fig. 151—J. M. W. Turner, *San Giorgio Maggiore*, c. 1835, gouache on gray paper, 5 × 8⅔ in., Victoria and Albert Museum

fig. 152—Claude Monet, *Waterloo Bridge: Effect of Sunlight in the Fog*, 1903, oil on canvas, 29 × 39½ in., National Gallery of Canada

Monet's own attitude toward Turner, however, appears to have been complicated. He probably first encountered Turner's paintings at the National Gallery in London, the city where he and his family took refuge from the Franco-Prussian War in 1870. (See Donato Esposito's essay in this volume.) Although Monet would later downplay his admiration for the English artist, in the 1890s he spoke highly of atmospheric Turner paintings such as *Rain, Steam, and Speed* and his watercolor studies. White clouds scudding across blue skies and the diffusion of hazy light across architecture and water, as seen in a painting like *Depositing of John Bellini's Three Pictures in La Chiesa Redentore, Venice* (fig. 153), and the vaporous, crepuscular mist out of which the church emerges in the gouache *San Giorgio Maggiore* (fig. 151) were the types of atmospheric Turnerian effects that surely would have come to Monet's mind in Venice.[20] Monet shared some of Turner's chosen viewpoints, but he was not at all interested in the romanticized historical references that appear in some of the other artist's Venetian imagery, like the imagined procession of Bellini paintings in the aforementioned canvas, a motif that suggests Turner paying an explicit homage to an earlier Venetian colorist.[21]

James McNeill Whistler, a younger contemporary whom Monet had known at least since the mid-1880s, would have loomed large in his mind when he was painting in London, and quite likely again a few years later when he went to Venice. Monet

fig. 153—J. M. W. Turner, *Depositing of John Bellini's Three Pictures in La Chiesa Redentore, Venice*, 1841, oil on canvas, 29×45½ in., private collection

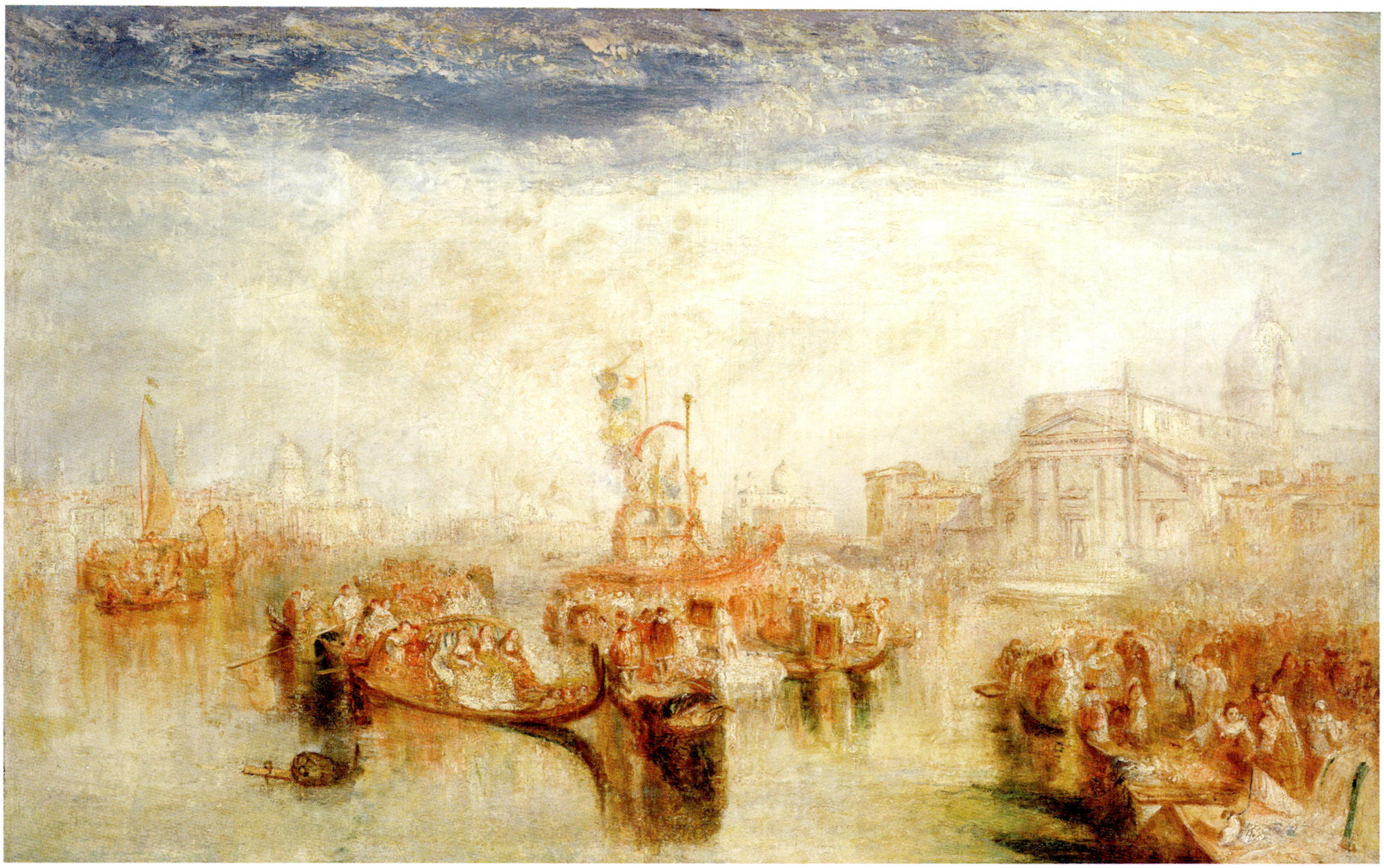

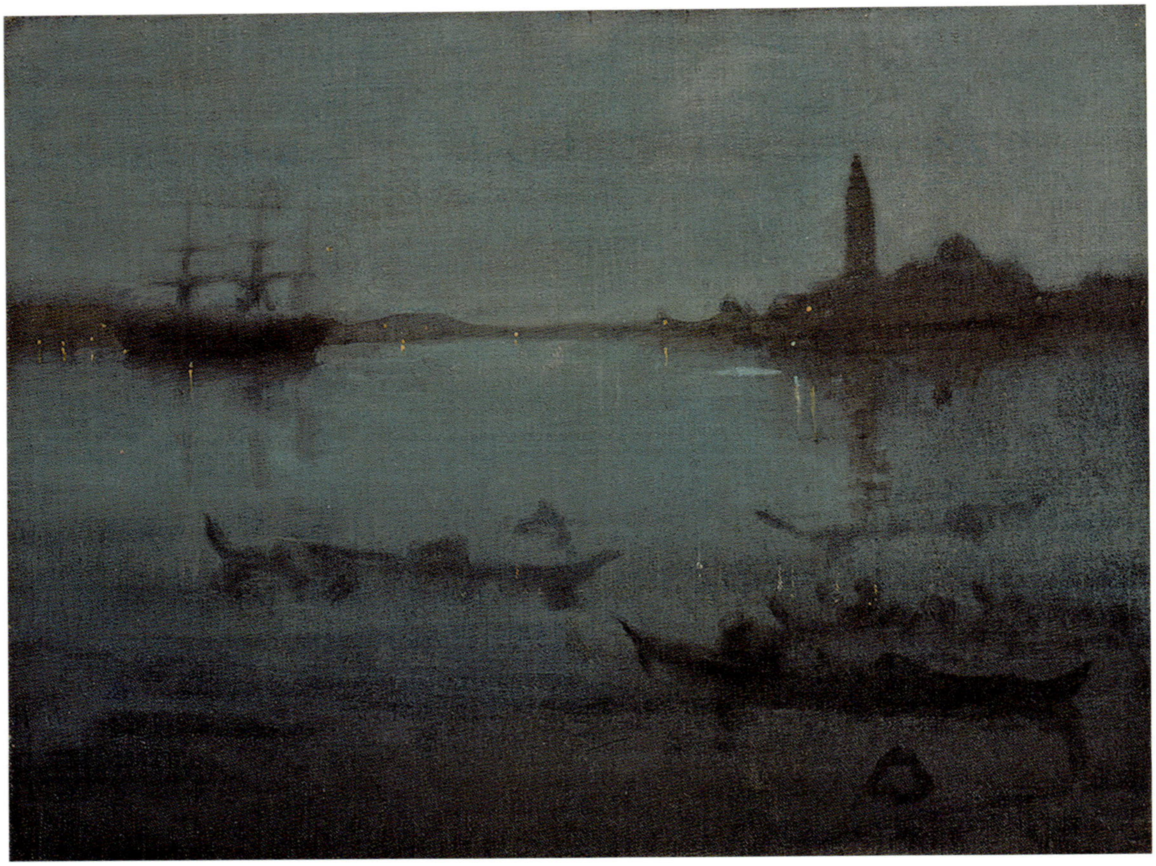

admired his American friend's emphasis on sensation and subjectivity and his glowing, tonal paintings of impalpable, twilit forms (fig. 154).[22] Recognizing their mutual creative interests, he introduced Whistler to a friend, the writer and early champion of Impressionism Stéphane Mallarmé, who translated Whistler's 1885 aesthetic manifesto, *Ten O'Clock,* into French. As Jonathan P. Ribner points out in his essay in this volume, Monet would have been familiar with the passage in which Whistler exhorts artists to contemplate and transform ephemeral moments into visions at once real and imaginative, such as "when the evening mist clothes the riverside with poetry, as with a veil."[23]

After Whistler was bankrupted by his Pyrrhic libel suit against the art critic John Ruskin for an insult directed at a painting by the artist—he won the case but was awarded almost nothing—he accepted a much-needed commission from the Fine Art Society in London to make twelve etchings of Venice. Whistler lived there from September 1879 through November 1880 (encompassing two autumns, the same season Monet would spend there in 1908). He ultimately made around fifty prints of the city, thirty-eight of which were included in two sets he published in 1880 and 1886.[24] Together, these etchings (figs. 155, 158, 159, and 163) challenge the pervasive visual stereotypes of Venice, offering intimate and often fragmentary visions of the lagoon city's canals and architectural details (especially its surface textures) rendered in delicate, economic lines. And by using more or less ink and different plate-wiping techniques in

fig. 154—James McNeill Whistler, ***Nocturne in Blue and Silver: The Lagoon, Venice***, 1879–80, oil on canvas, 19¾ x 25¾ in., Museum of Fine Arts, Boston

fig. 155—James McNeill Whistler, *Long Lagoon*, c. 1879–80, etching printed in brown ink, 6⅛ × 9 in., Fine Arts Museums of San Francisco

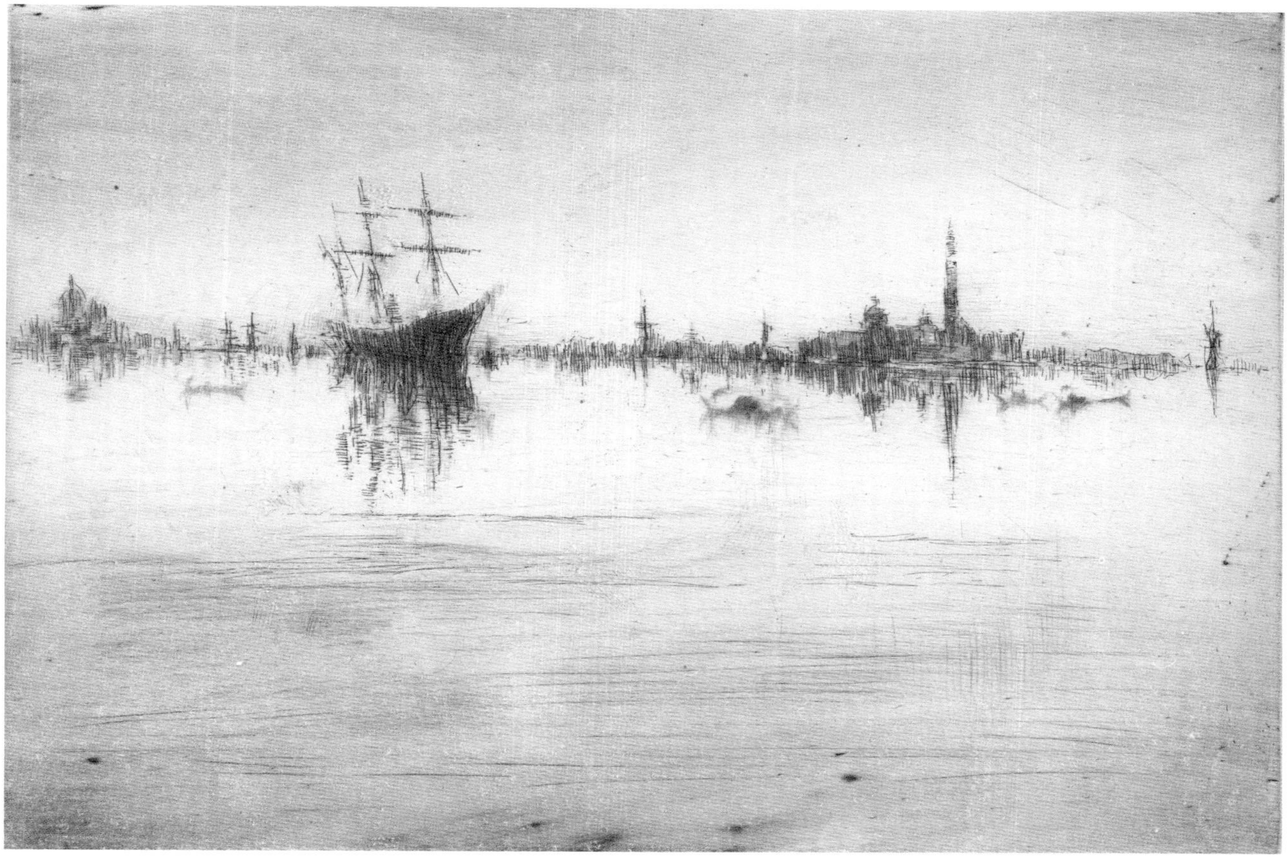

fig. 156—James McNeill Whistler, *Nocturne*, 1879–80, etching, $7\frac{15}{16} \times 11\frac{9}{16}$ in., Fine Arts Museums of San Francisco

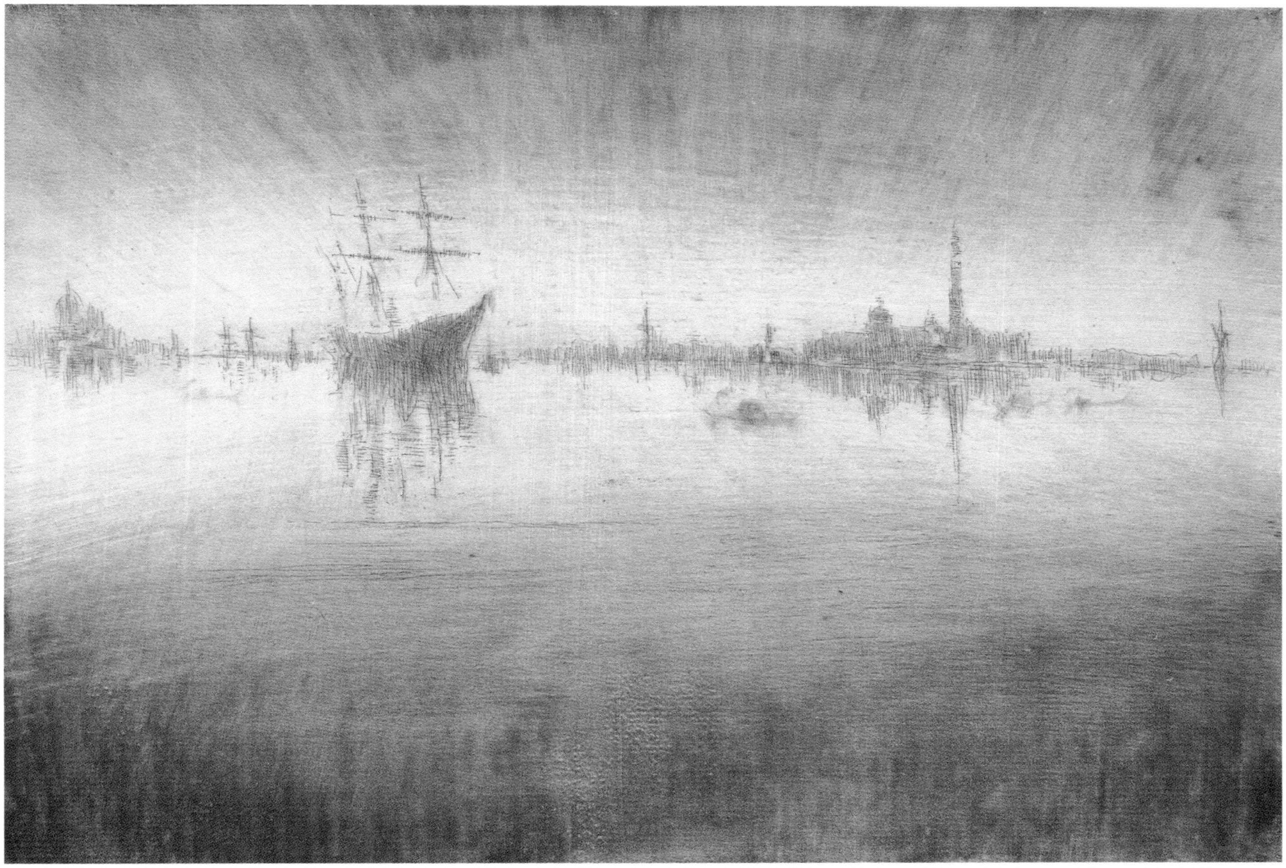

fig. 157—James McNeill Whistler, *Nocturne*, 1879–80, etching, $7\frac{15}{16} \times 11\frac{9}{16}$ in., Fine Arts Museums of San Francisco

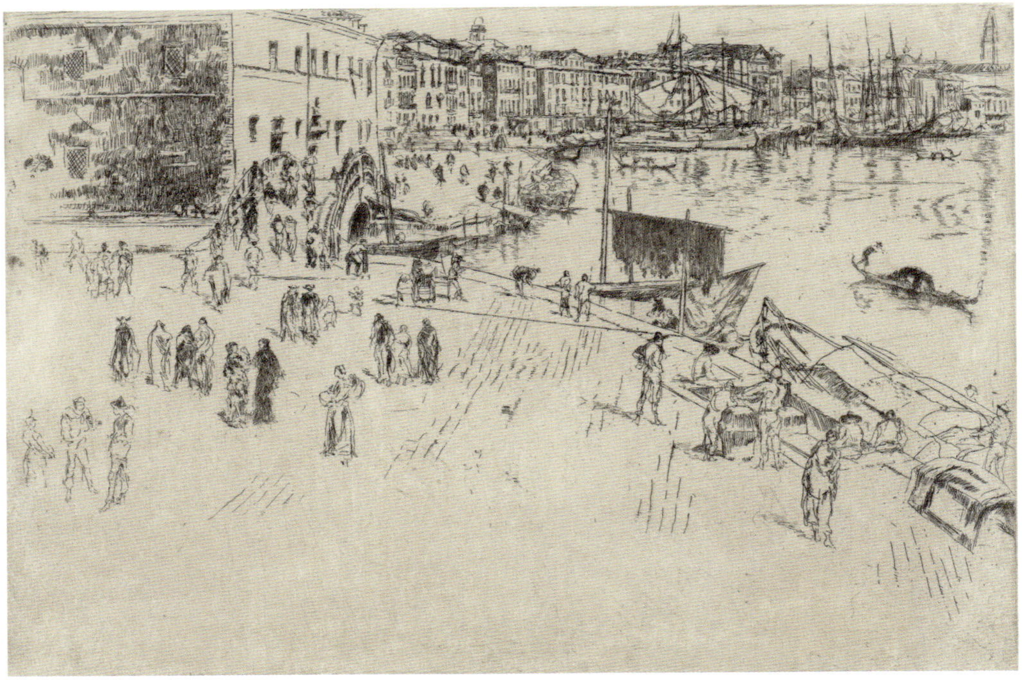

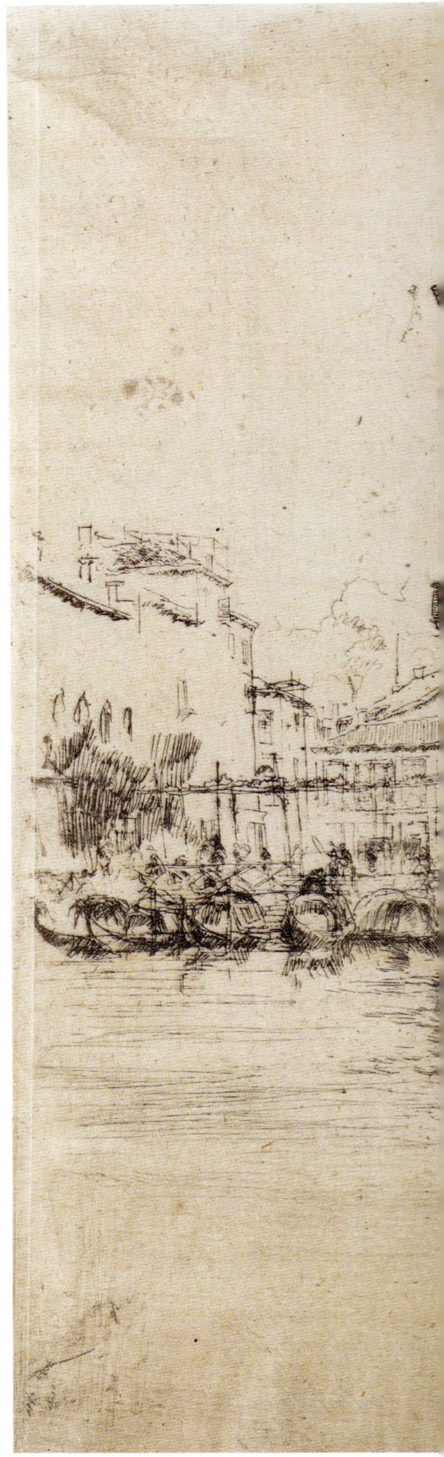

fig. 158—James McNeill Whistler, *The Riva, No. 1*, 1879–80, etching and drypoint, 7¹⁵⁄₁₆ × 11¾ in., Fine Arts Museums of San Francisco

fig. 159—James McNeill Whistler, *The Palaces*, c. 1880, etching and drypoint on paper, 10¹⁄₁₆ × 14 in., Brooklyn Museum

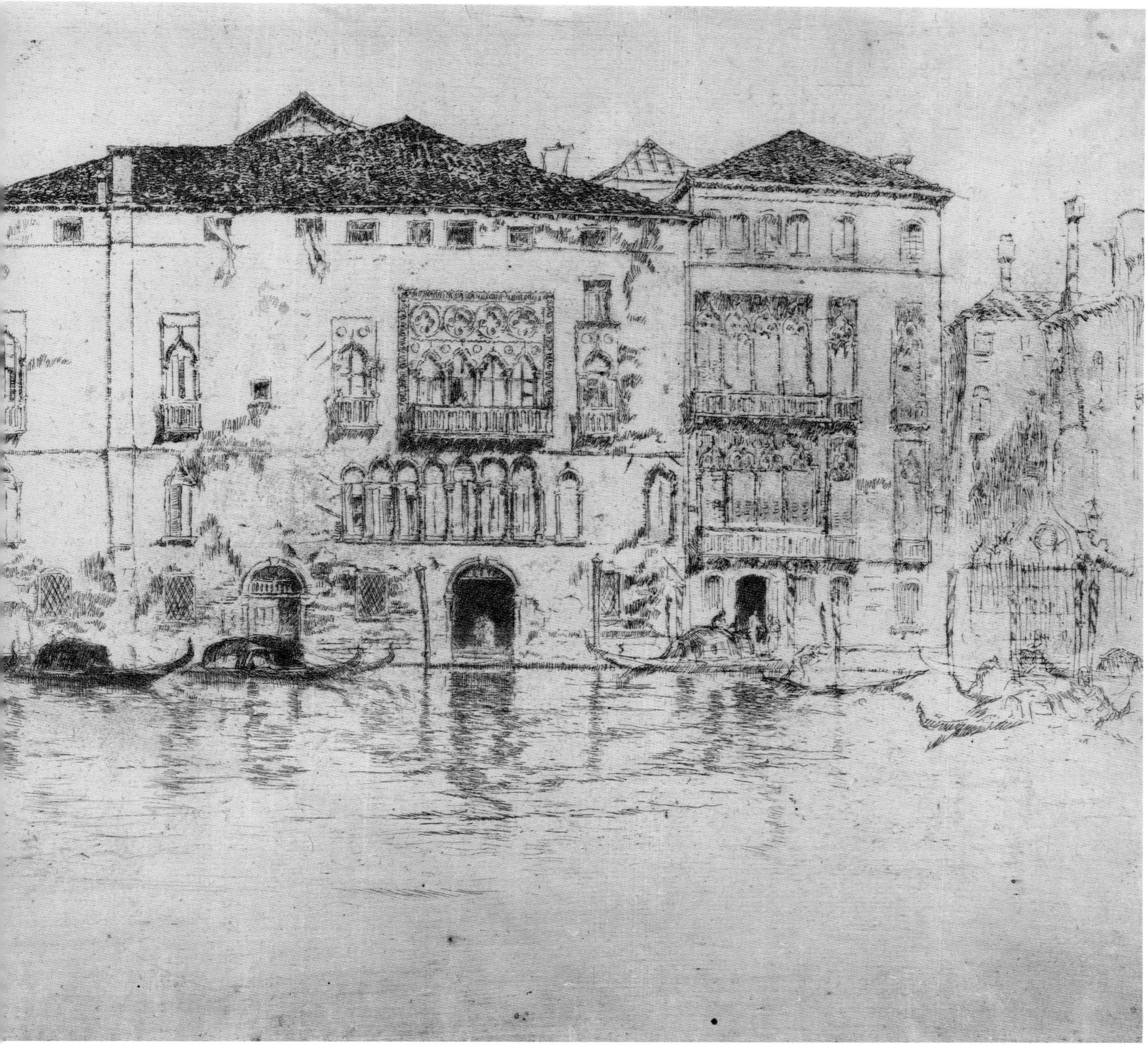

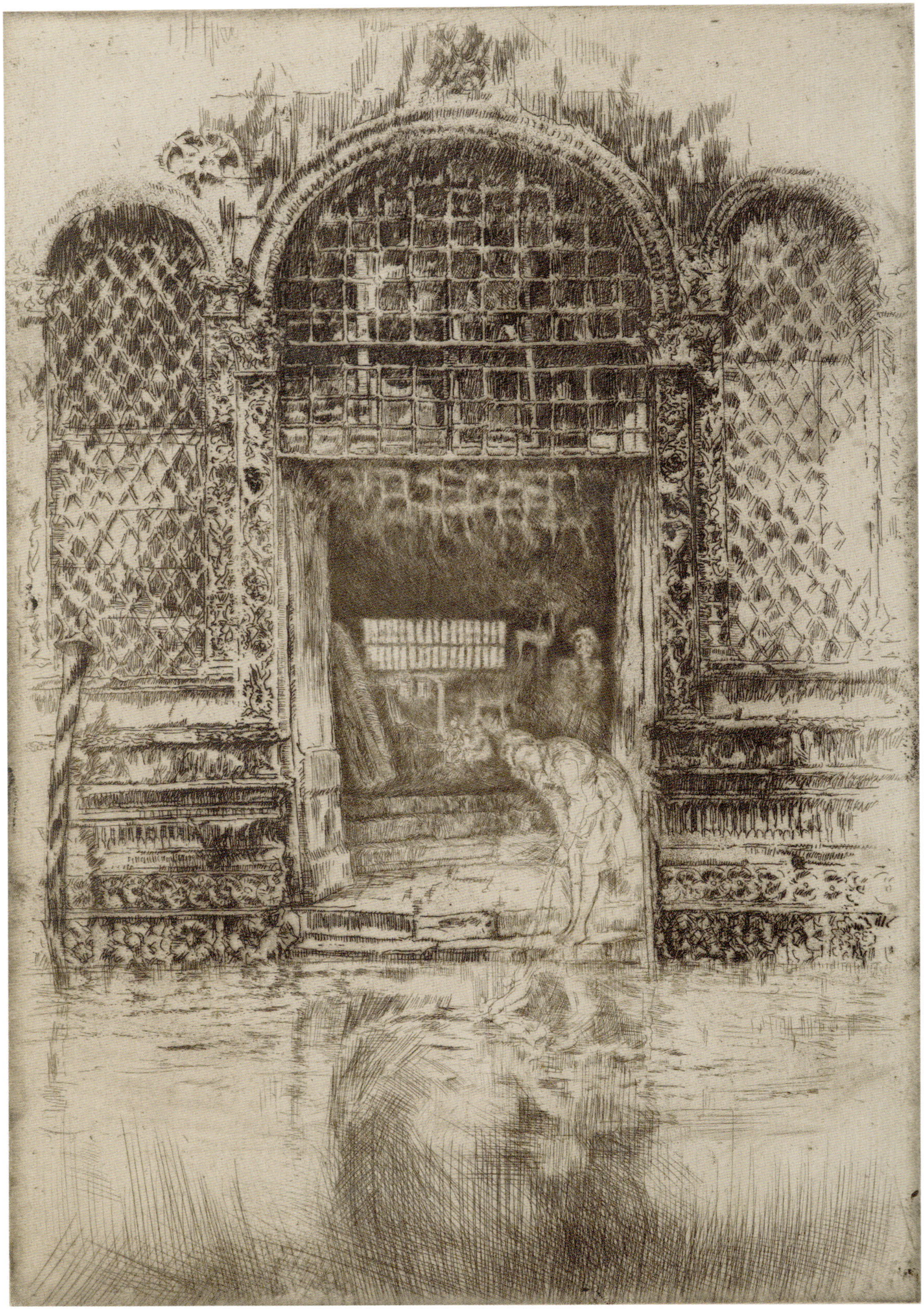

fig. 160—James McNeill Whistler, *The Doorway*, 1880, etching and drypoint on paper, $11\frac{9}{16} \times 7\frac{15}{16}$ in., Brooklyn Museum

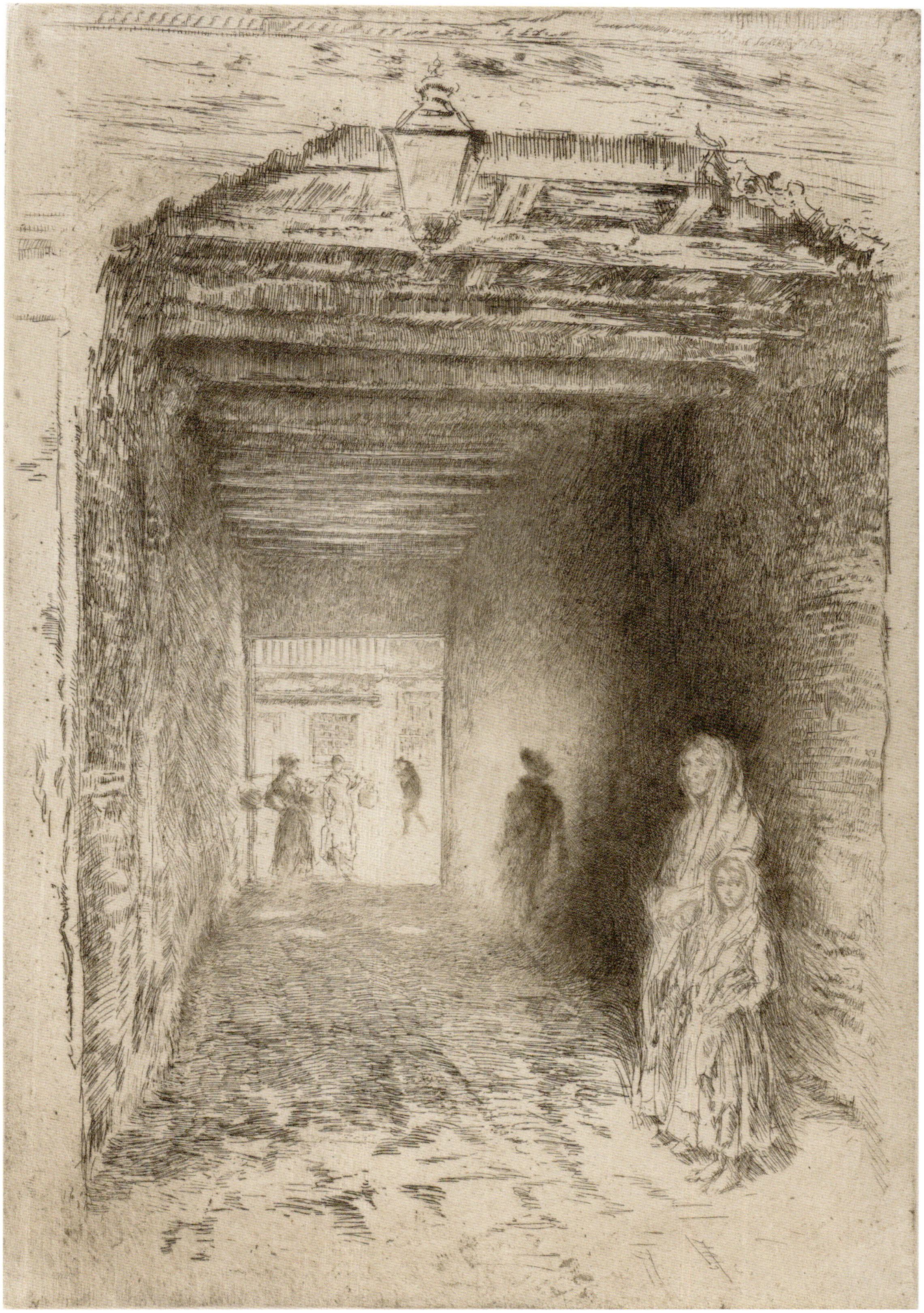

fig. 161 — James McNeill Whistler, *The Beggars*, 1880, etching on paper, 12⅛ × 8¼ in., Brooklyn Museum

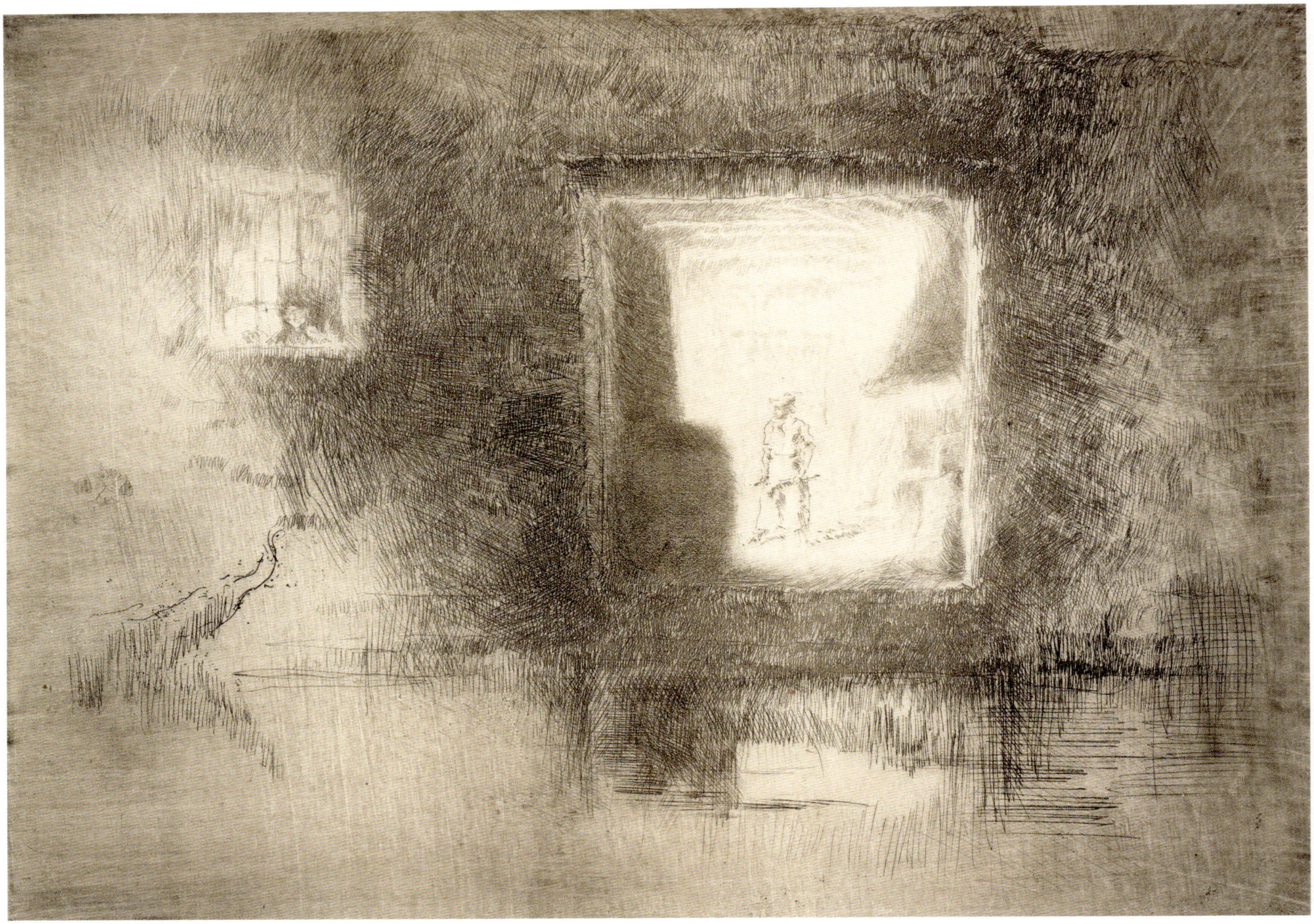

fig. 162—James McNeill Whistler, *Nocturne: Furnace*, 1878–80, etching, 6⁹⁄₁₆ × 9⁹⁄₁₆ in., Fine Arts Museums of San Francisco

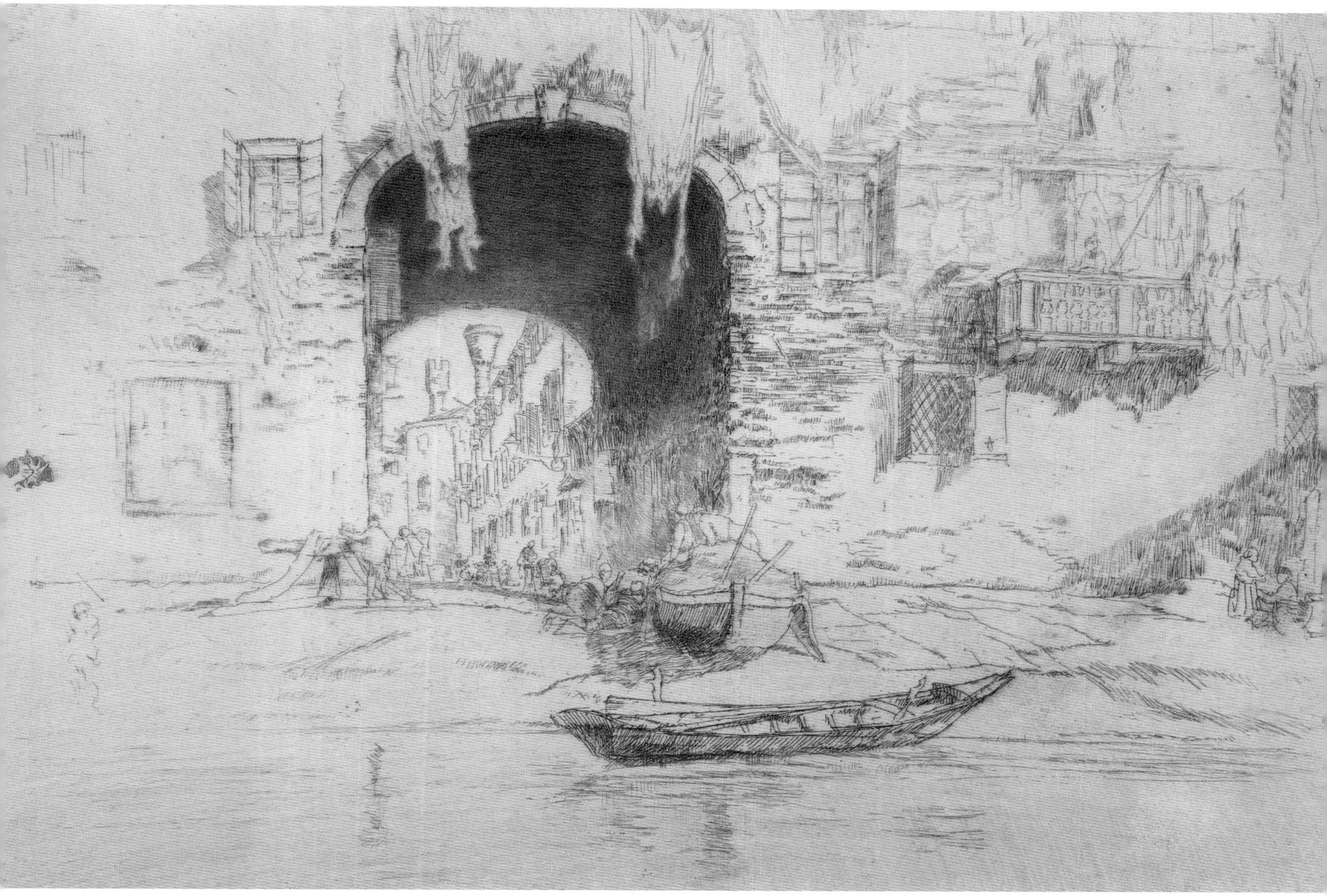

fig. 163—James McNeill Whistler, *San Biagio*, 1879–80, etching and drypoint printed in brown-black, 8$\frac{3}{16}$ × 11$\frac{13}{16}$ in., Fine Arts Museums of San Francisco

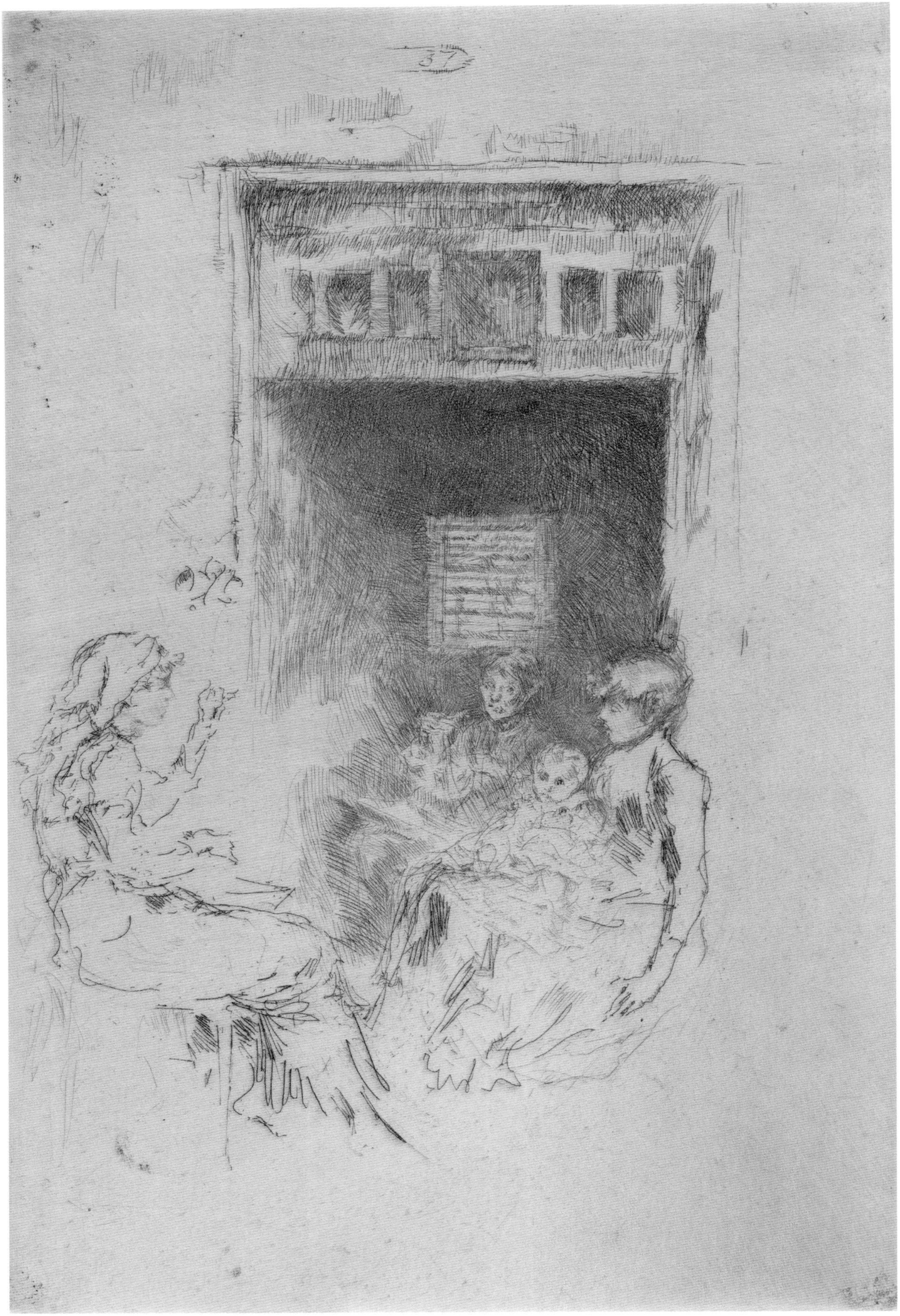

fig. 164—James McNeill Whistler, *Bead Stringers*, 1886, etching, 8$\frac{15}{16}$ × 6 in., Brooklyn Museum

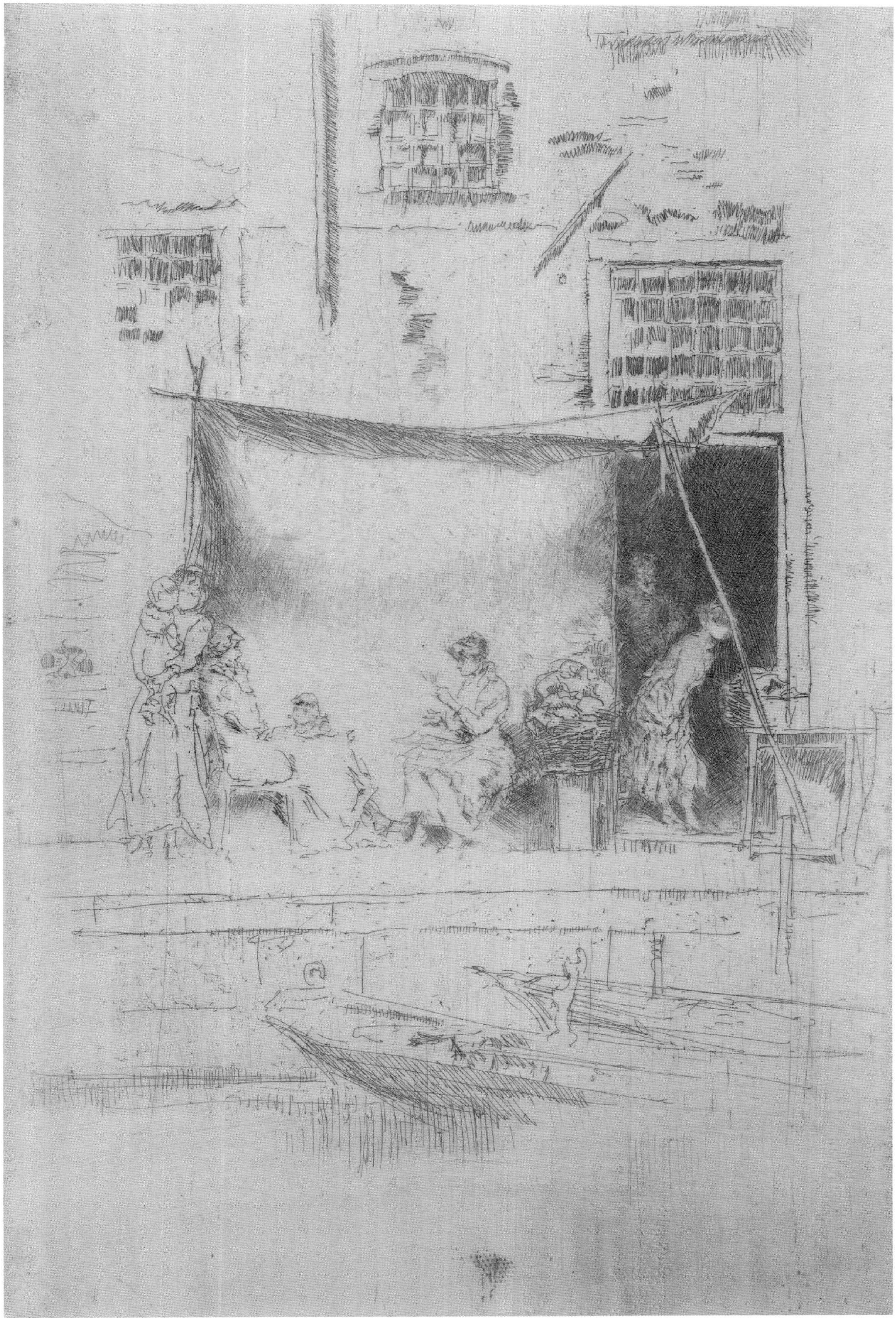

fig. 165—James McNeill Whistler, *Fruit Stall*, 1886, etching, 8⅞×5⅞ in., Brooklyn Museum

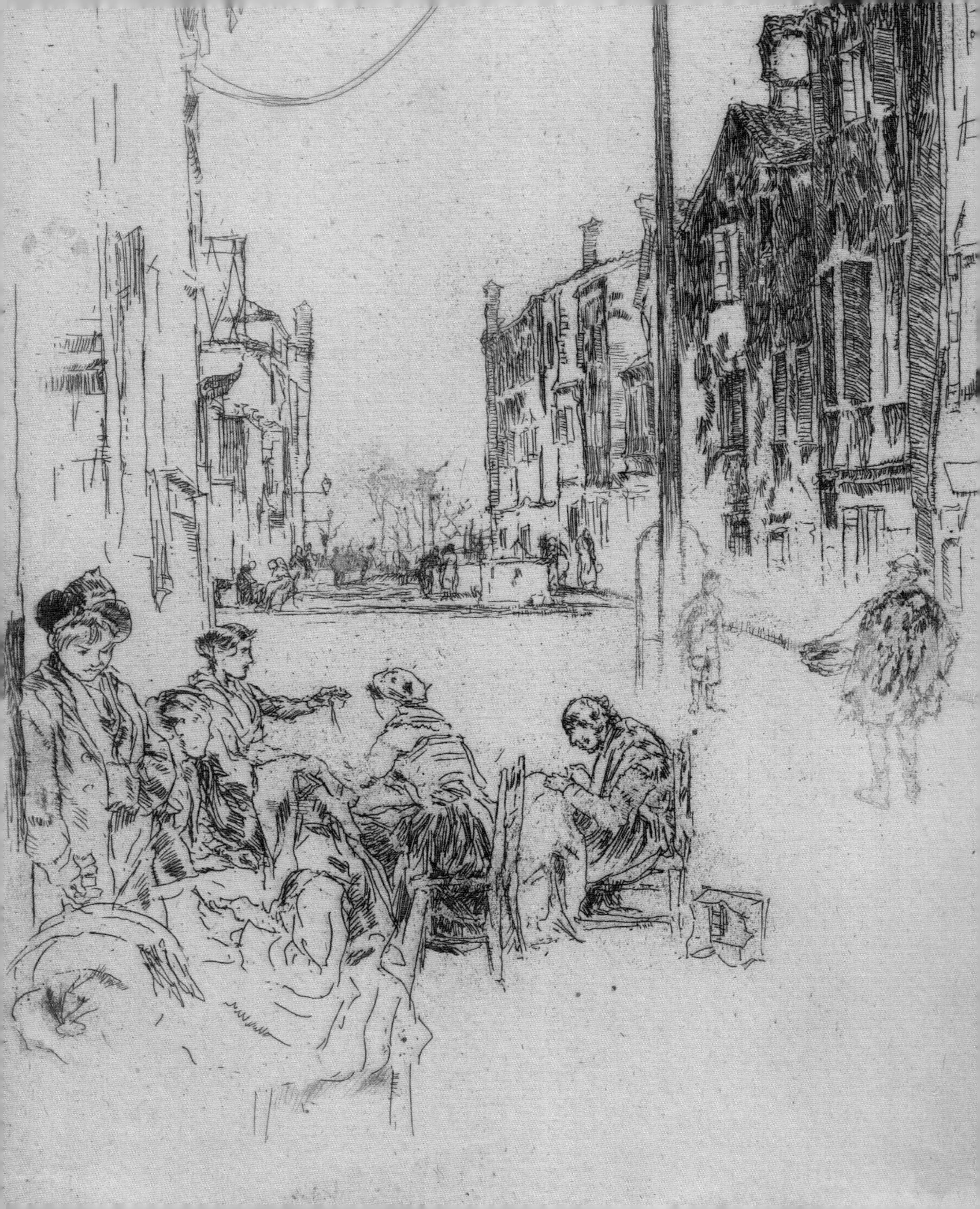

fig. 166—James McNeill Whistler, *The Mast*, 1880, etching on paper, 13½ × 6⁷⁄₁₆ in., Brooklyn Museum

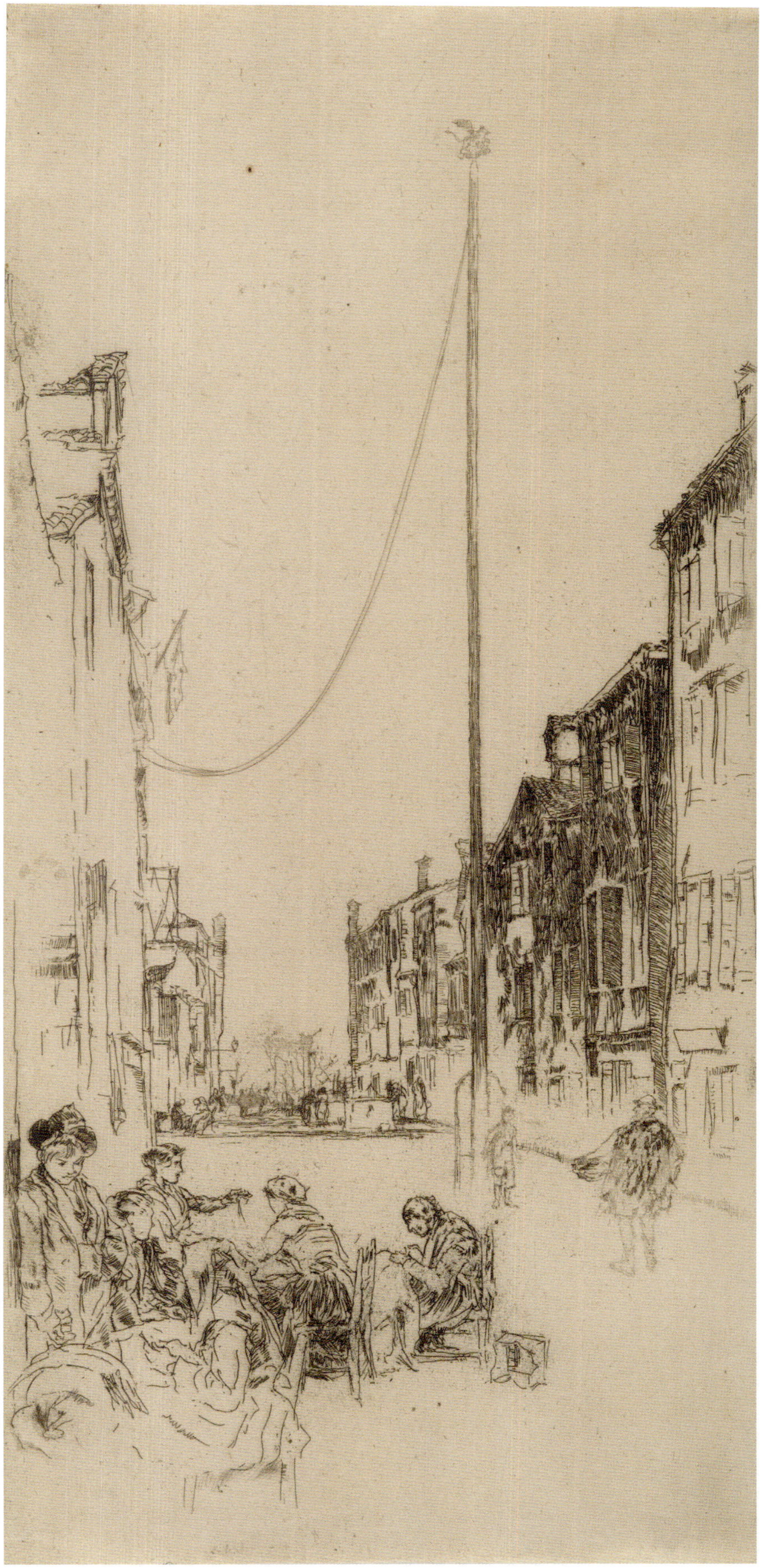

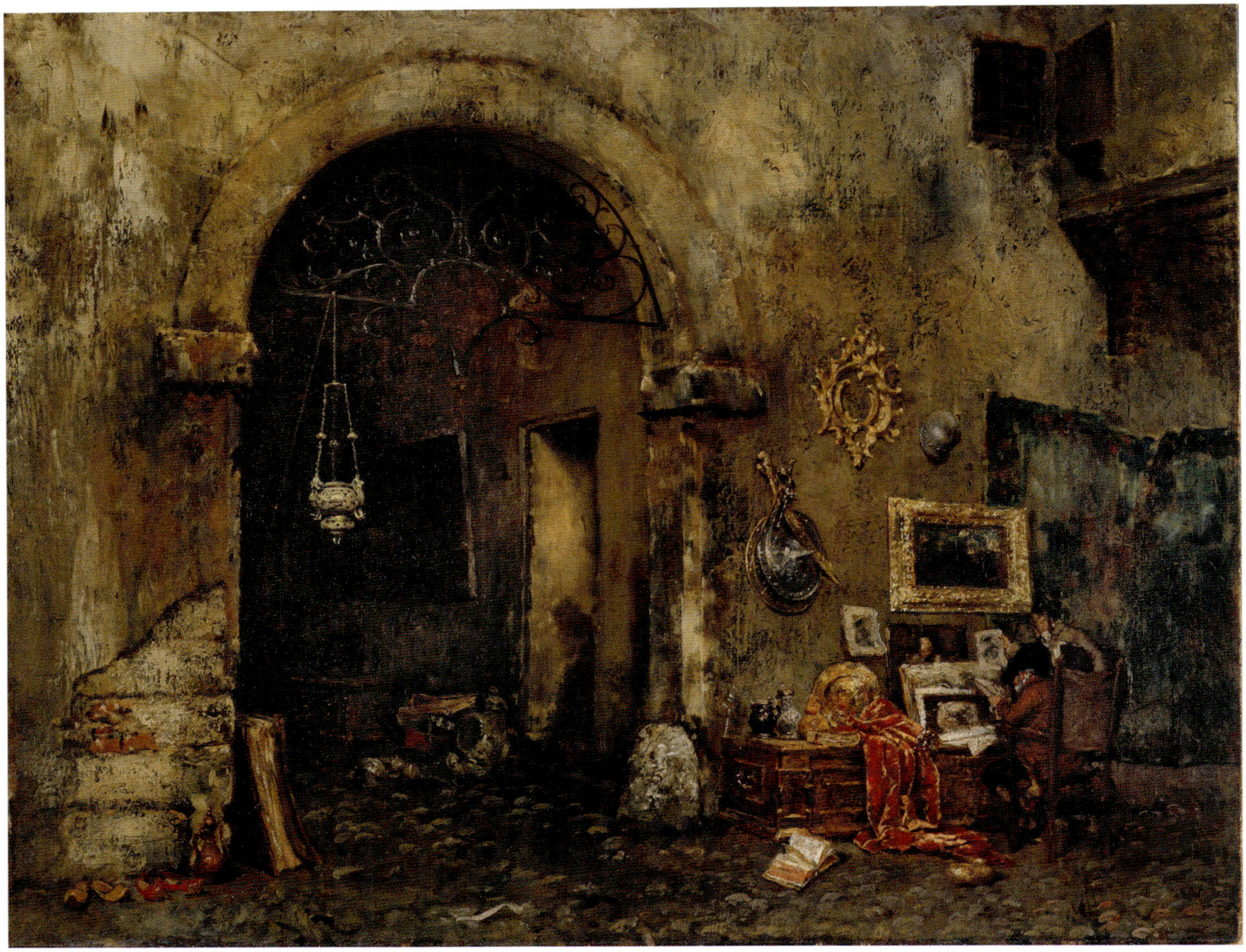

fig. 167—William Merritt Chase, *The Antiquary Shop*, 1879, oil on canvas, 26½ × 33¹⁵⁄₁₆ in., Brooklyn Museum

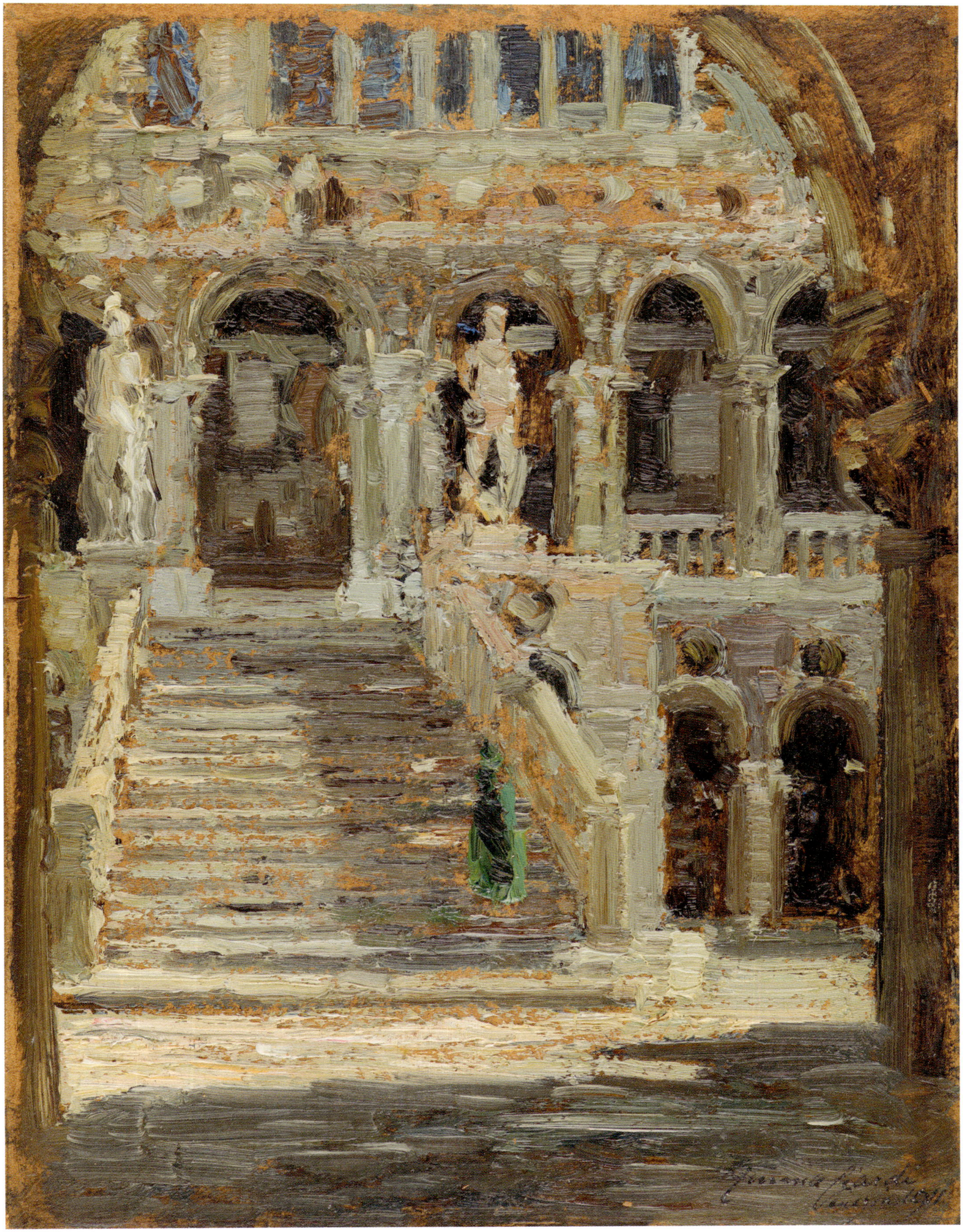

fig. 168—Emma Ciardi, *La Scala dei Giganti*, 1911, oil on beaverboard, 14 × 11½ in., Brooklyn Museum

fig. 169—John Singer Sargent, *The Church of San Stae, Venice*, c. 1907, oil on canvas, 22 × 28 in., private collection

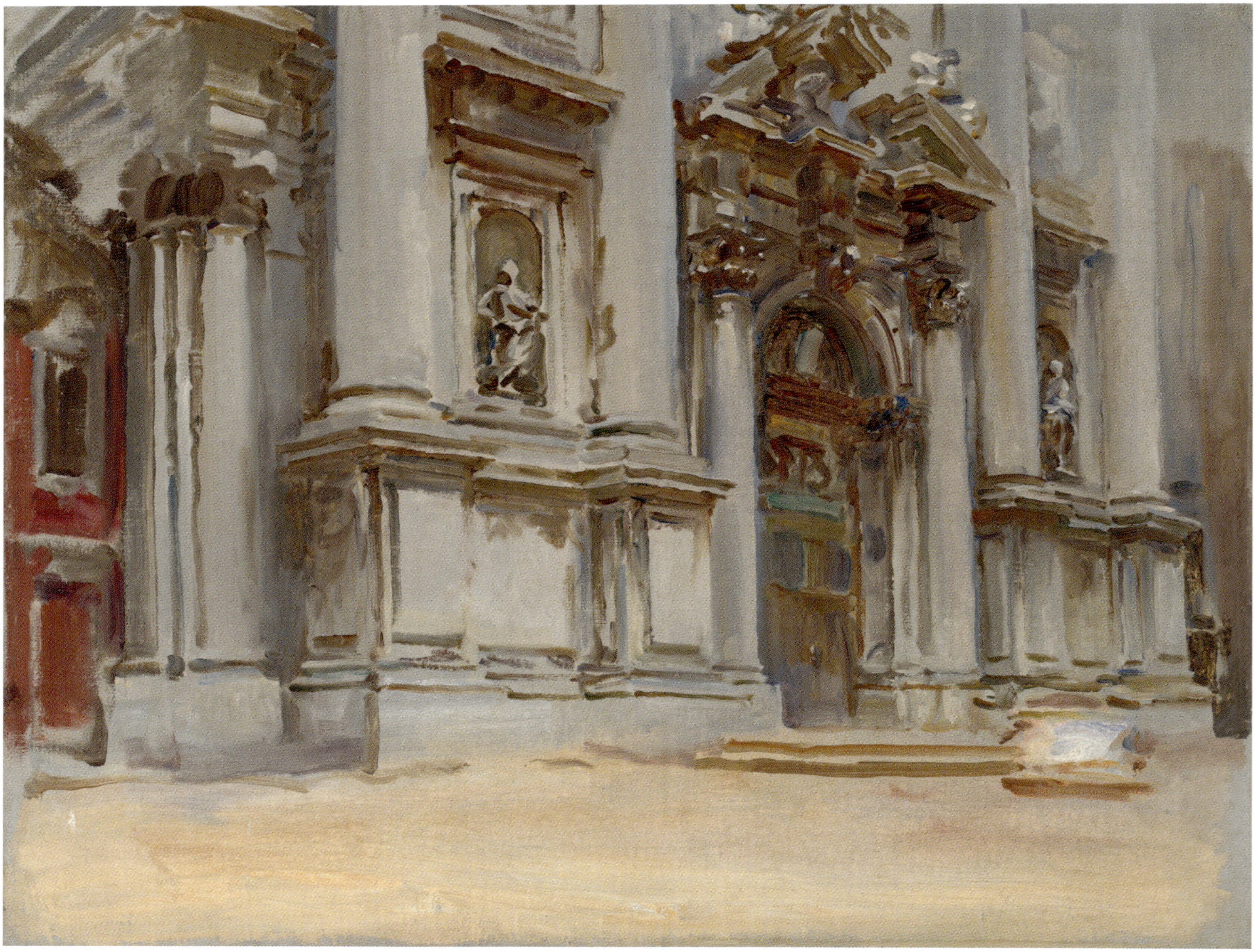

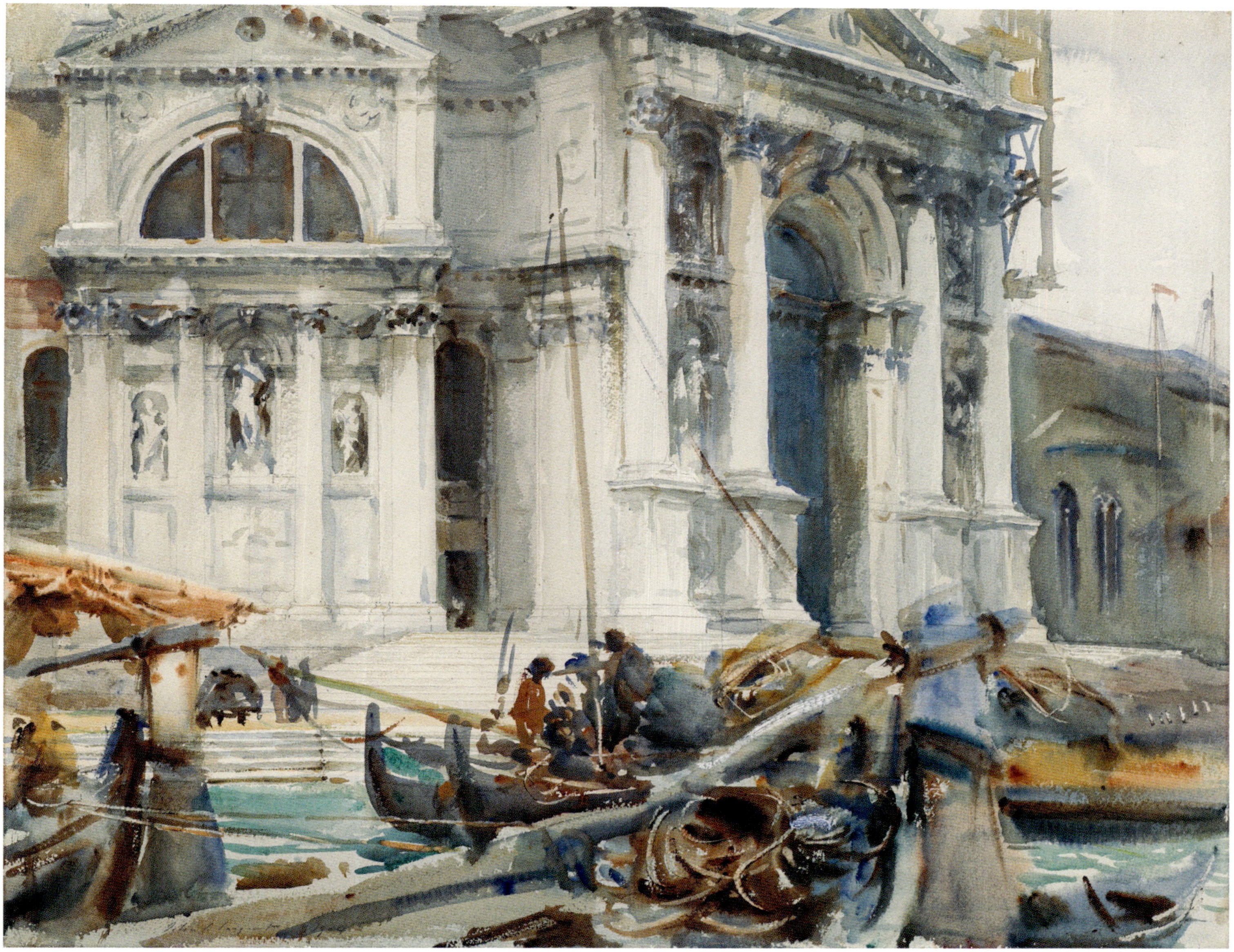

fig. 170—John Singer Sargent, *Santa Maria della Salute*, 1904, translucent and opaque watercolor and graphite, with graphite underdrawing, $18\frac{3}{16} \times 22\frac{15}{16}$ in., Brooklyn Museum

different impressions of *Nocturne*, for example, he was able to convey a range of tonal intensities that suggest changing atmospheres (figs. 156 and 157). He often included local figures in his glimpses of quays, alleys, shops, and doorways (figs. 162, 164, 165, and 166)—workaday subjects that also appealed to fellow American William Merritt Chase (fig. 167).

The Florence-born American artist John Singer Sargent was another significant figure in Monet's orbit who had a sustained and distinctive artistic relationship with Venice. He first visited as a young man in the 1870s, again in the early 1880s, and then nearly every year between 1898 and 1913, producing almost two hundred paintings and watercolors of the city. After Sargent and Monet met at Durand-Ruel's Paris gallery in 1876, they remained lifelong friends, and Sargent was a key promoter of Monet's work in the United States.[25] He revered Monet, painted alongside him in Giverny (fig. 171), emulated his broken brushwork and interest in the transitory effects of natural light (particularly in the late 1880s), sought professional advice from him, and added several of the French artist's paintings to his personal collection.[26]

On Monet's visits to London, Sargent was especially solicitous, arranging for him to visit art collections such as Sir Richard Wallace's (where he would have seen Canalettos and Guardis), and introducing him to his future hostess in Venice, Mary Hunter. She helped him secure access to a terraced room at Saint Thomas' Hospital from which he could paint the Houses of Parliament at sunset across the Thames.[27] Even before Monet embarked on his London series, Sargent must have been aware of his friend's desire to paint city views under varying atmospheric conditions. He wrote to tell Monet of the city's "settled fog" and "absinthe colored weather," and he wondered, "Is that not enough to lure you here?"[28] Given Sargent's extensive knowledge of and experience in Venice, it is fair to assume that the subject of painting that city's architecture, enveloped in its distinguishing light, also may have come up between them. Sargent had an opportunity to see Monet's as-yet-uncompleted Venice paintings on a social visit to Giverny in April 1909, as Alice recounted: "Our party was a success.... Sargent was pleased to be here again; he was so enthusiastic about the Venice and Waterlilies paintings."[29]

Sargent's own extraordinary body of Venetian work encompasses cropped architectural views (fig. 169), images of young people working in partially illuminated rooms, enigmatic scenes of couples in narrow passageways (fig. 172), and spaces closer to his own life, like the group portrait of his purportedly distant relatives Daniel and Ariana Curtis and their son and daughter-in-law in the grand salon of Palazzo Barbaro, a room Monet would also come to know well (fig. 5). Sargent did not paint the wall of windows on the right that face the canal, but he captured the light streaming through them and bouncing off gilded furnishings and fabrics.[30] His sister Emily also painted with him in Venice, as did his friend, frequent traveling companion, and sometime model the artist Jane de Glehn (figs. 175, 176, and 177). Perhaps the most dazzling of Sargent's Venetian works are his bravura watercolors, vignettes of reflective canals filled with boats and gondolas, surrounded by light-struck architecture, that are often cropped in ways that replicate the experience of a scene quickly

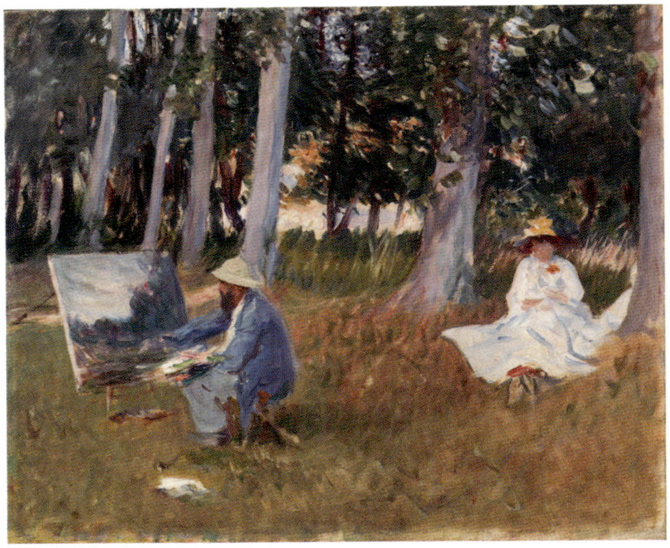

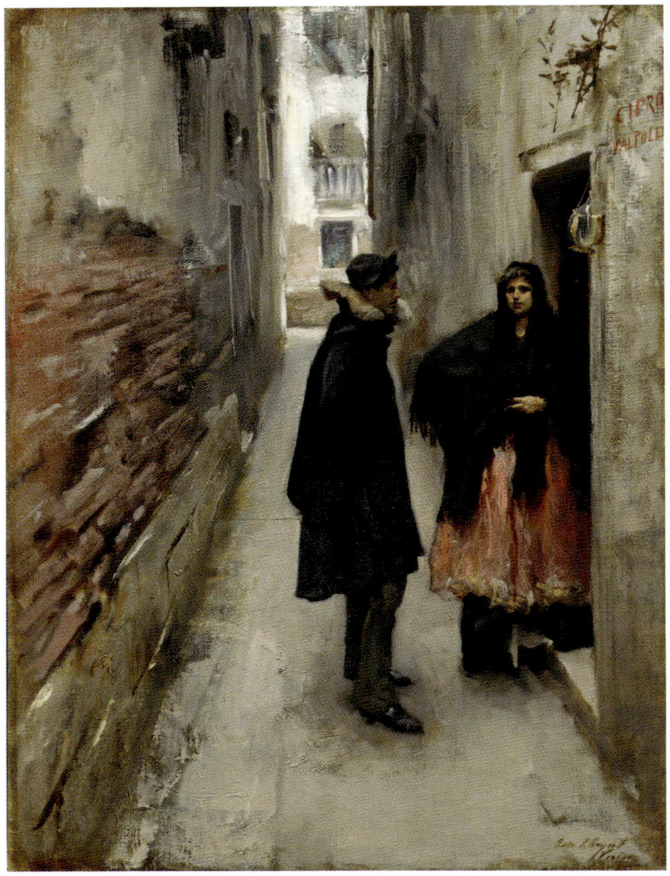

fig. 171—John Singer Sargent, *Claude Monet Painting by the Edge of a Wood*, c. 1885, oil on canvas, 21¼ × 25½ in., Tate

fig. 172—John Singer Sargent, *A Street in Venice*, c. 1880–82, oil on canvas, $29\frac{9}{16} \times 20\frac{5}{8}$ in., Clark Art Institute

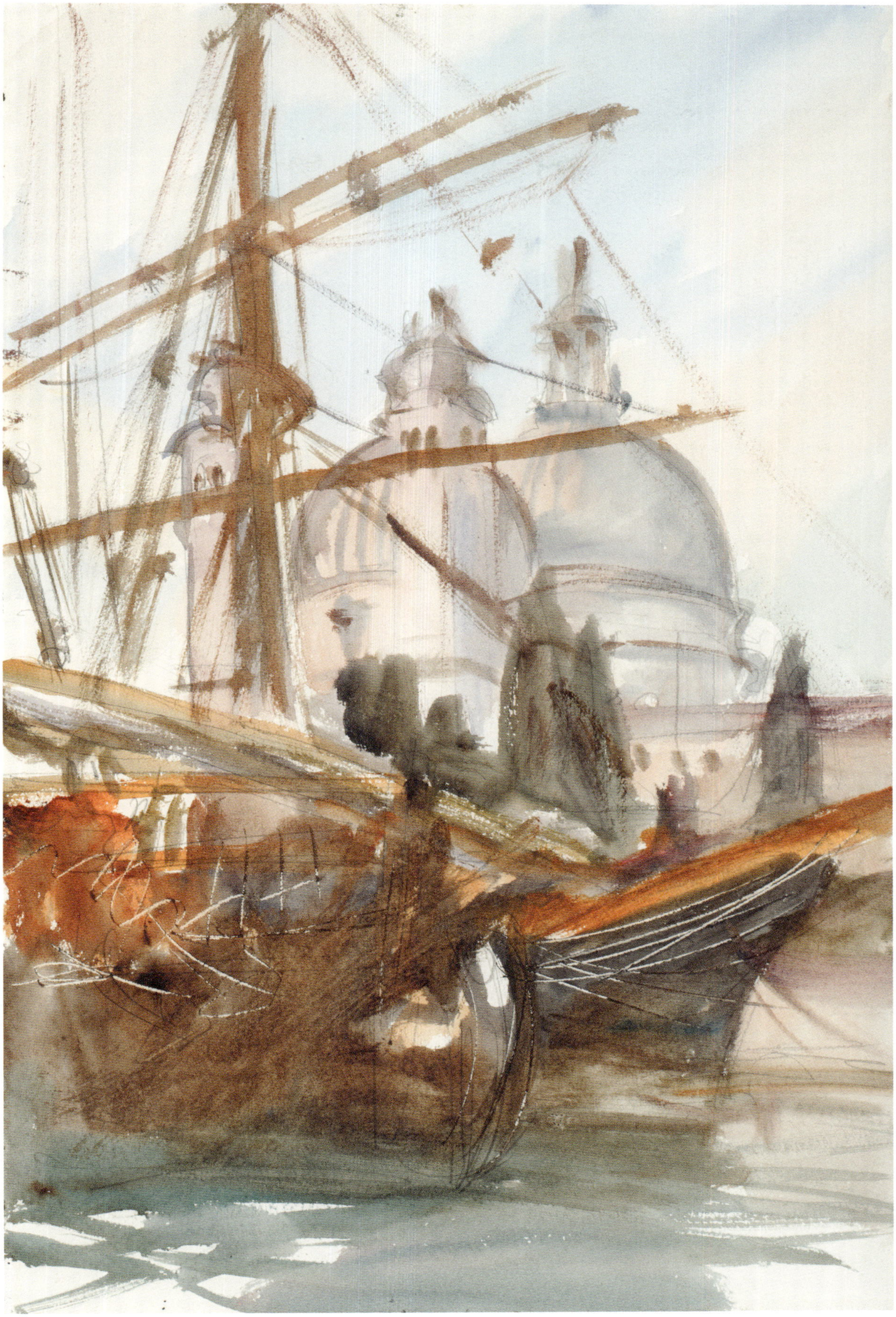

fig. 173—John Singer Sargent, *Santa Maria Della Salute, Venice*, c. 1904–09, watercolor on paper, 18×12 in., Victoria and Albert Museum

fig. 174—John Singer Sargent, *Venetian Boats*, c. 1903–08, watercolor on paper, 9 15/16 × 13 13/16 in., Brooklyn Museum

fig. 175—John Singer Sargent, *Jane de Glehn in a Gondola*, 1904, watercolor on paper, 17 ½ × 12 ½ in., private collection

fig. 176—Emily Sargent, *Interior of the Frari*, 1885, pencil and watercolor, 12 × 9⅜ in., Brooklyn Museum

fig. 177—Jane Emmet de Glehn, *Canal View, Venice*, early 20th c., oil on canvas, 16 × 19 in., Collection of Mary McClean

or partially glimpsed. (figs. 170, 173, 174, 178, 179, 180, 181, and 182)[31] As Monet had done throughout his career, Sargent painted from a position on the water—in a gondola—and in many of his compositions, he explicitly invites the viewer to imagine themselves in his position by including the prow of his boat (figs. 170 and 179).

There are three other noteworthy contemporaries whose paintings in Venice bear mention in connection with Monet's. In 1874, Édouard Manet spent the summer working with Monet near Argenteuil, often painting similar motifs *en plein air* (fig. 183). Just after this, when Manet was most affected by the Impressionist interest in the visual effects of light and atmosphere, he went to Venice, where sparkling canals offered him the perfect opportunity to prove himself equal to Monet, whom he called the "Raphael of the water."[32] Manet's *The Grand Canal (View of Venice)* (fig. 184), one of only two known paintings that resulted from his trip, features his signature bold brushwork and saturated color, including his extraordinary handling of deep blacks and

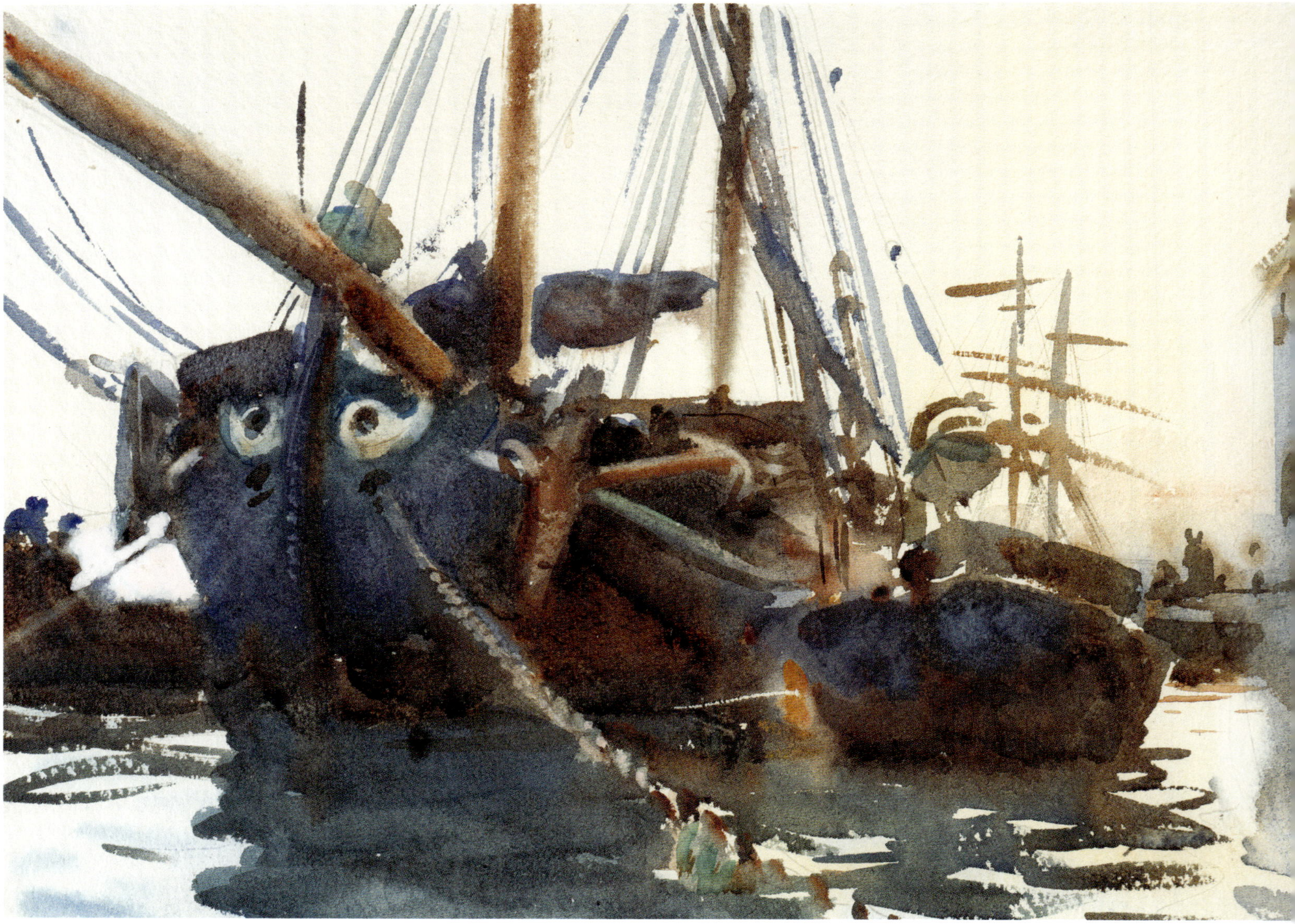

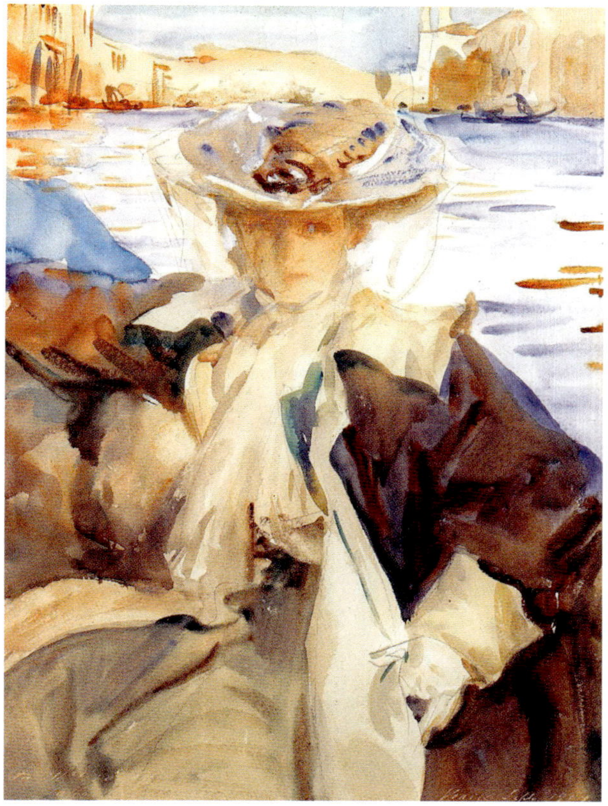

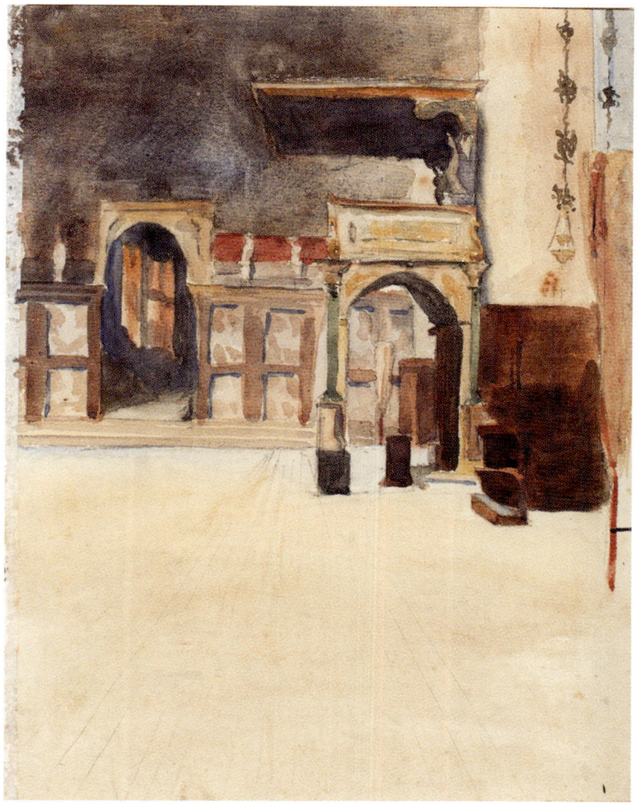

bright whites. As Monet would do years later, he likely worked from a gondola moored near the steps of Palazzo Barbaro. Unlike his friend, whose Venice included no trace of the human form, Manet featured an upright gondolier while just barely including the famous view of Santa Maria della Salute, rhyming its cupolas with the tops of the *pali*, or mooring posts. Charles Toché, an artist who befriended Manet in Venice, recalled his delight in what the city had to offer, and this painting: "I shall not forget Manet's enthusiasm for the motif . . . the white marble staircase against the faded pink bricks of the façade, and the cadmium and greens of the basements. Oscillations of light and shade made by the passing barges in the rough water that drew from him the exclamation, 'Champagne-bottle ends floating!' Through the row of gigantic twisted posts, blue and white, one saw the domes of the incomparable Salute, dear to Guardi. 'I shall put in a gondola,' cried Manet, 'steered by a boatman in a pink shirt, with an orange scarf.'"[33] Exhibited in Paris in 1906, Manet's composition was surely known to Monet.

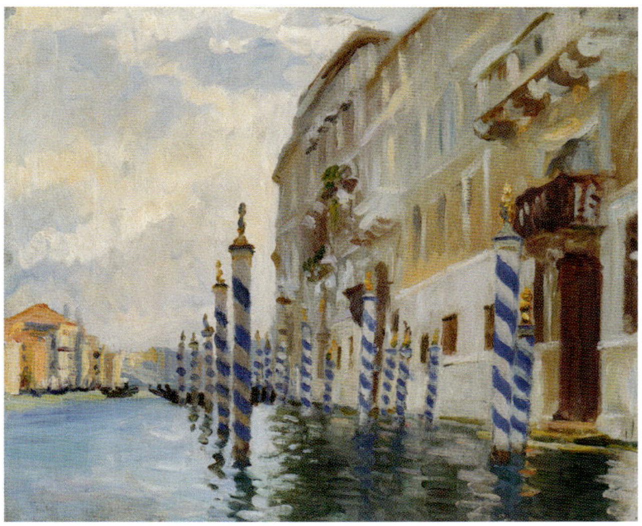

Pierre-Auguste Renoir accompanied Monet on his first trip to Italy in 1883. Venice was not on their itinerary, but Renoir had already been there a few years earlier. He produced several lively Venetian subjects, including *Venice, The Doge's Palace* (1881), which, despite its creamy dabs of bright pigment, presents a relatively clear view of the building's architectural elements (fig. 185). As Monet would do twenty-seven years later, Renoir painted some of the city's most famous vistas and he understood that he was not the only artist to do so, jokingly writing: "I have painted

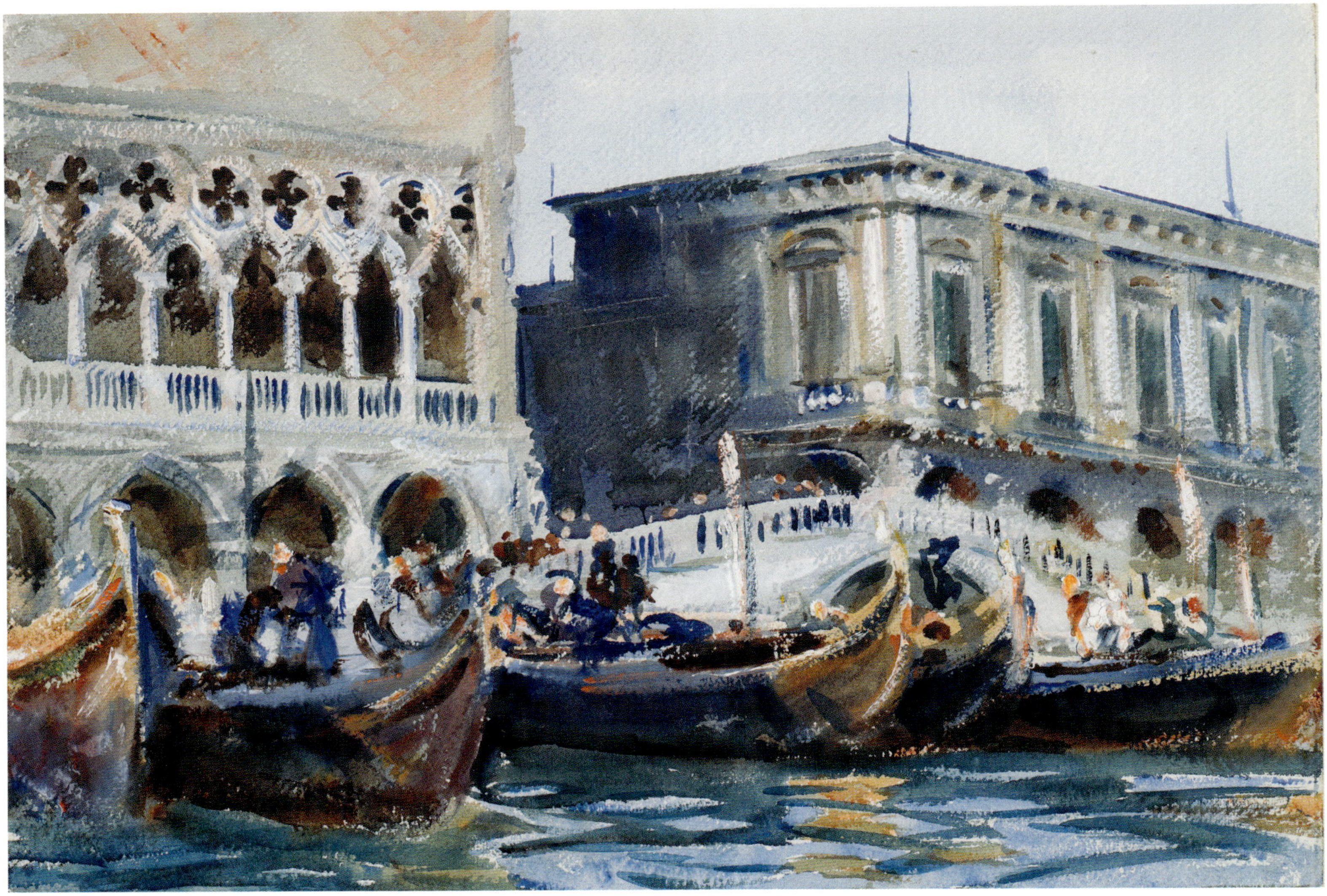

fig. 178—John Singer Sargent, *La Riva*, c. 1903–04, opaque and translucent watercolor with graphite underdrawing, 14 × 20¹⁄₁₆ in., Brooklyn Museum

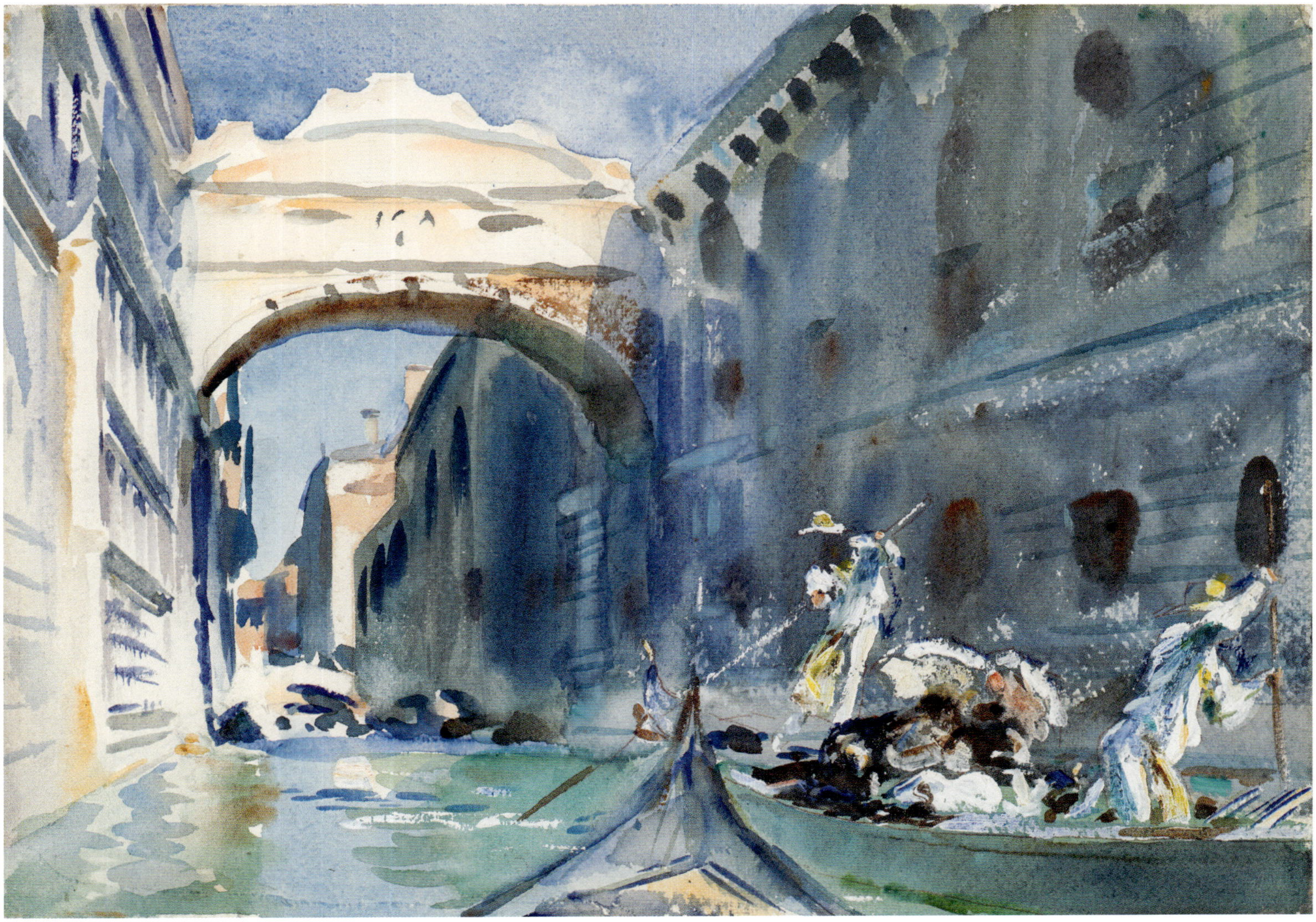

fig. 179—John Singer Sargent, *The Bridge of Sighs*, c. 1903–04, translucent and opaque watercolor with graphite and red-pigmented underdrawing, 10×14 in., Brooklyn Museum

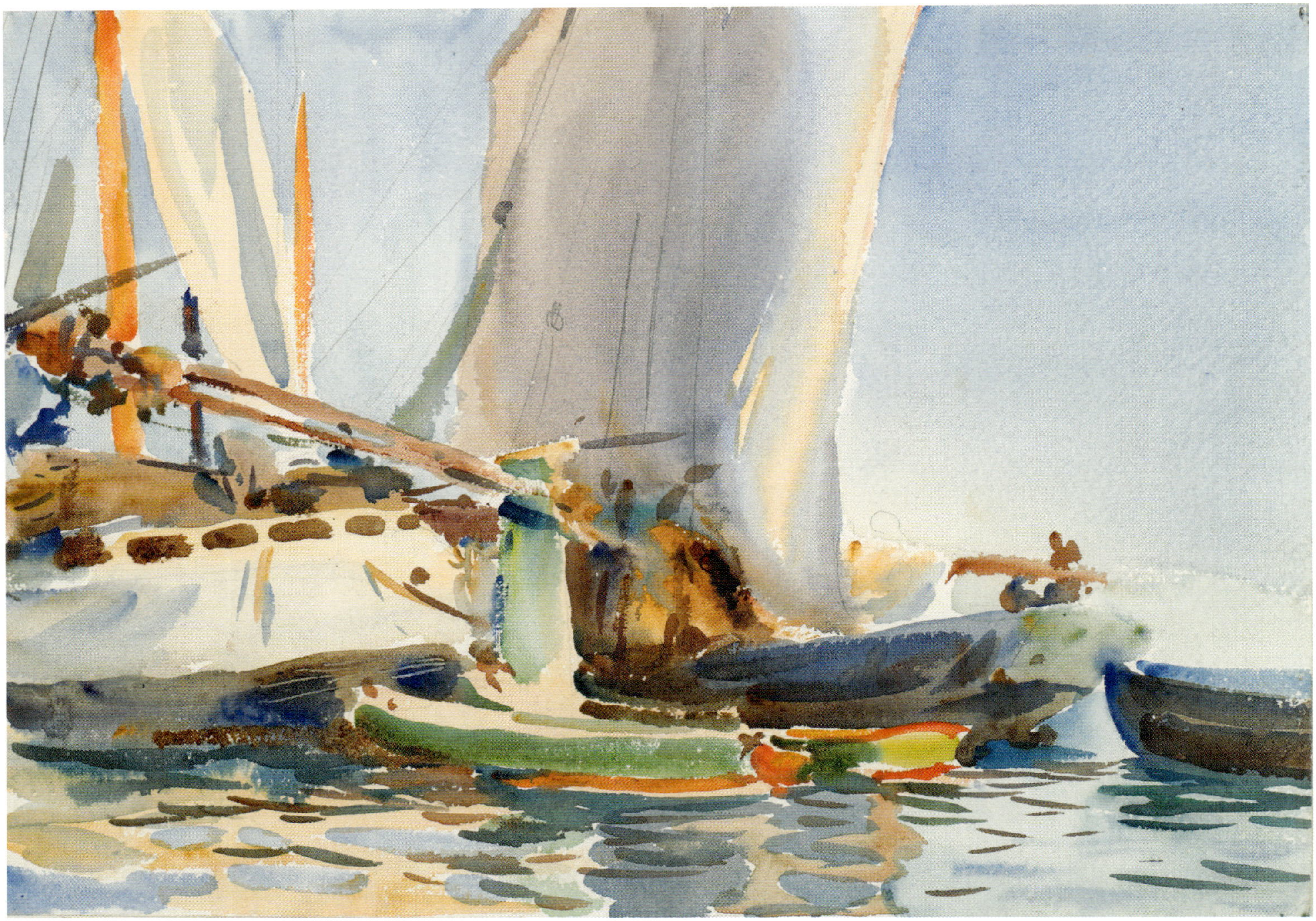

fig. 180—John Singer Sargent, *The Giudecca*, c. 1904, translucent watercolor and touches of opaque watercolor and graphite, with graphite underdrawing, 10 × 14 in., Brooklyn Museum

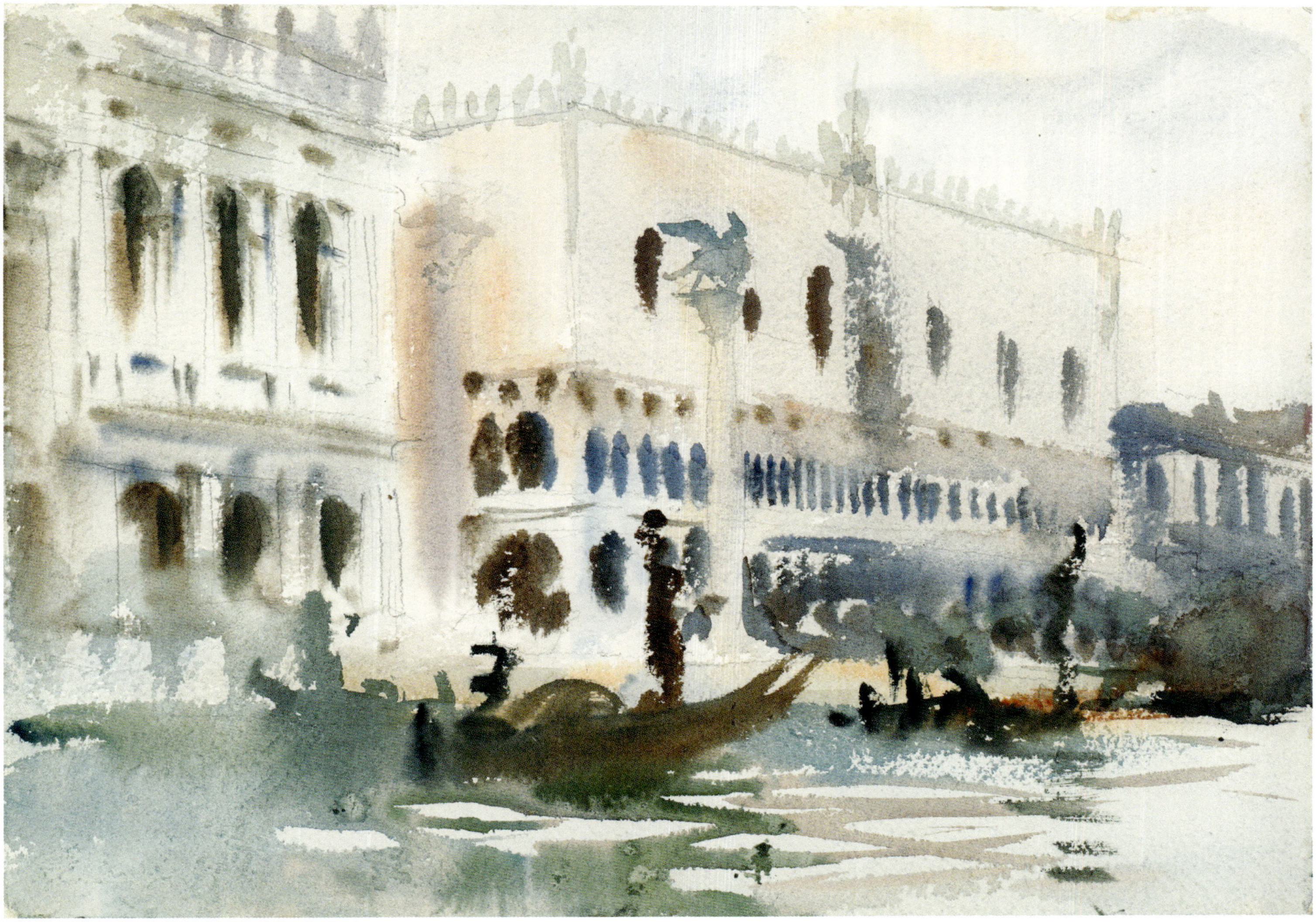

fig. 181—John Singer Sargent, *From the Gondola*, c. 1903–04, translucent watercolor and touches of opaque watercolor and graphite, with graphite underdrawing, 10×14 in., Brooklyn Museum

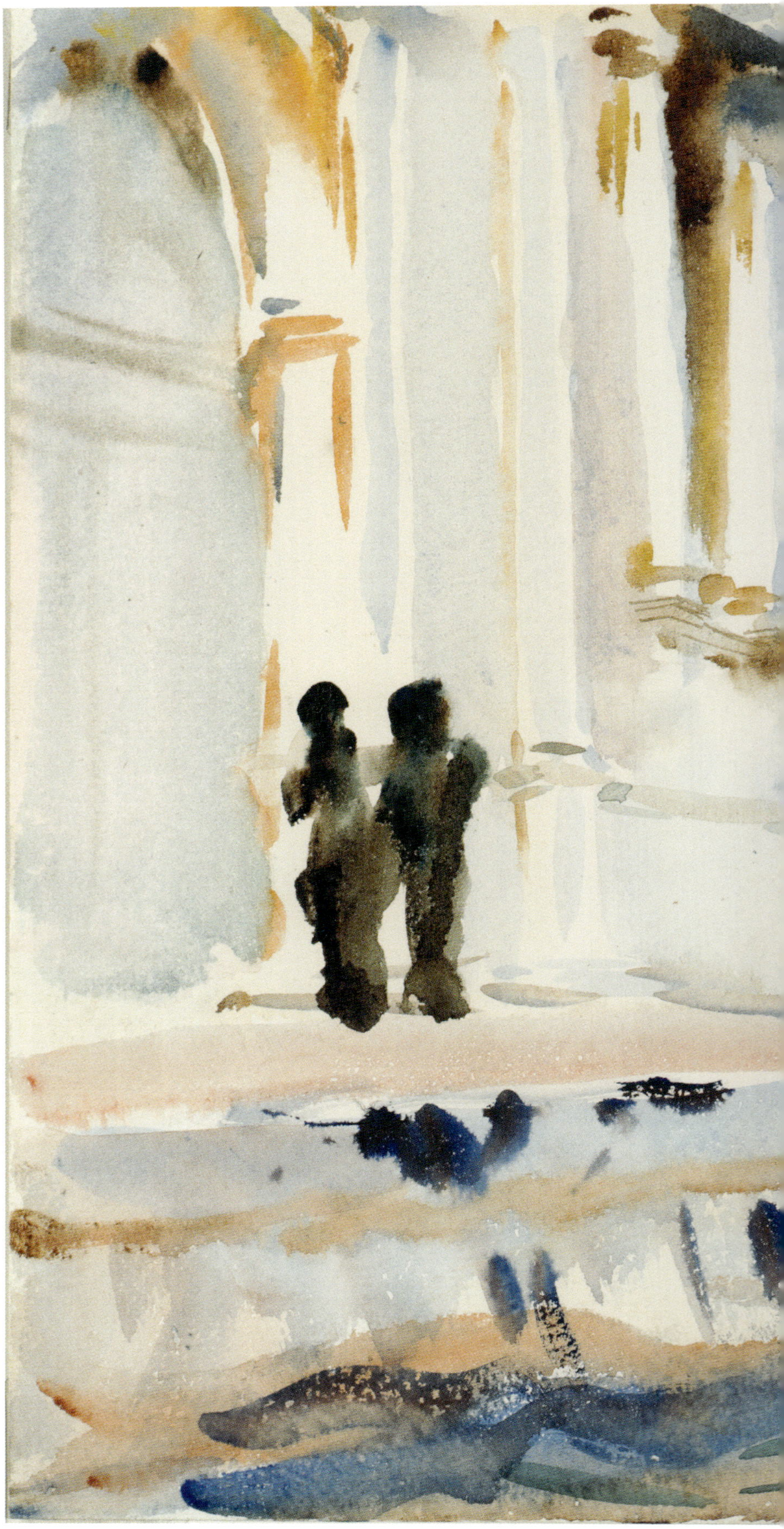

fig. 182—John Singer Sargent, *All' Ave Maria*, c. 1902–04, translucent watercolor and touches of opaque watercolor, 10 × 14 1/16 in., Brooklyn Museum

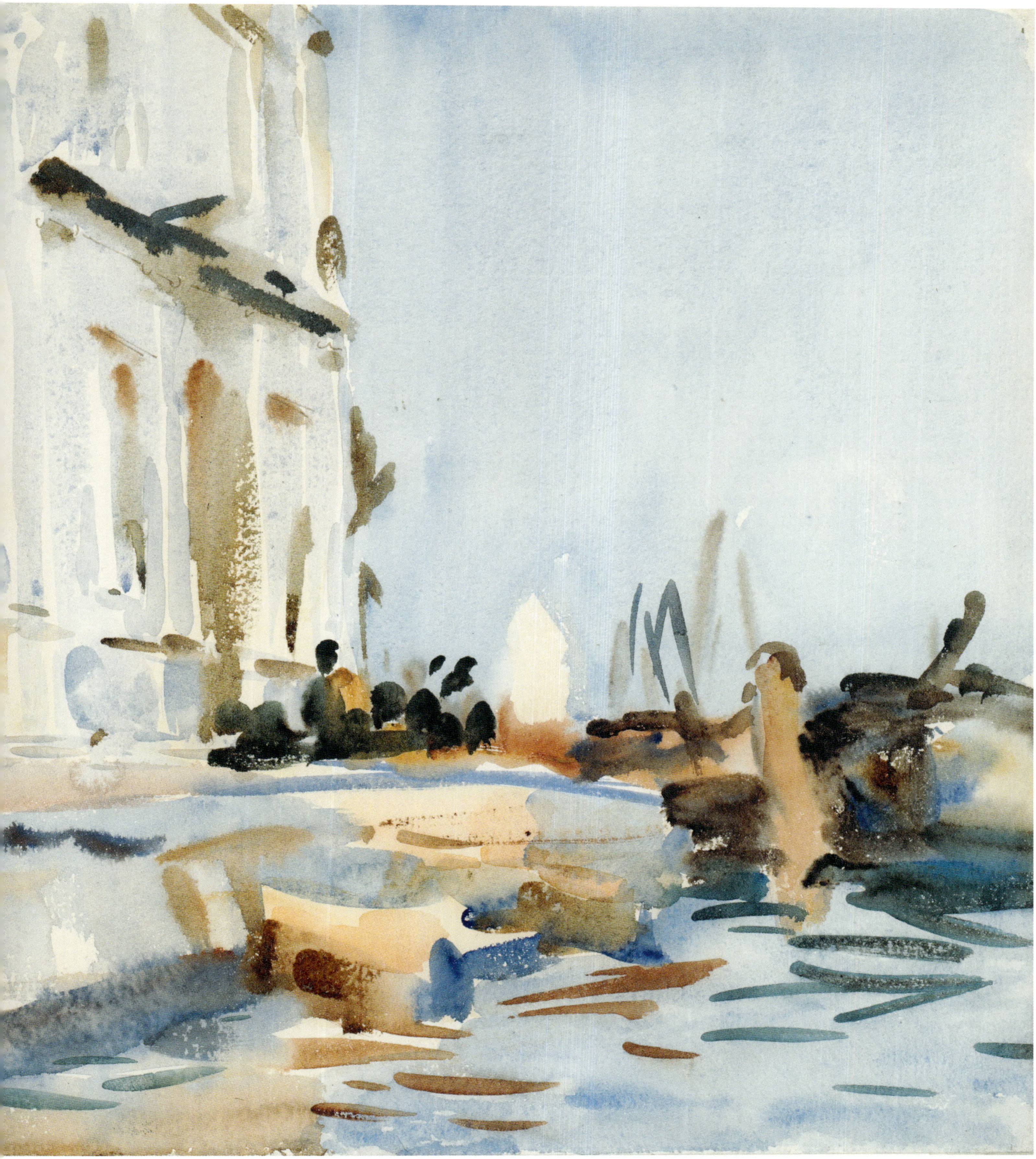

the Doge's Palace seen from San Giorgio; that has never been done before, I think. There were at least six of us queuing up to paint it."[34] This painting was likely one of two Venetian views that Durand-Ruel loaned to the *Seventh Impressionist Exhibition* in 1882, where Monet would have seen it. He might also have been aware of the mostly negative critical response to Renoir's Venice paintings. One writer described them as "the most outrageous series of ferocious daubs that a calumniator of Venice could possibly imagine."[35]

Venice's natural luminosity and distinctive decorative forms were well-suited to the shimmering mosaic paint touches that characterized Paul Signac's later Neo-Impressionist style. On a trip to Venice in 1904, Signac made hundreds of watercolor sketches that provided the basis for large studio paintings such as *The Lagoon of Saint Mark, Venice* (fig. 186). This was among several of Signac's Venetian subjects included in his exhibition at Galerie Bernheim-Jeune in 1907, the year before Monet's trip and five years before his own Venice exhibition at the gallery.[36] A sweeping view of the lagoon that comprises the Palazzo Ducale, Santa Maria della Salute, and San Giorgio Maggiore, it probably reflects a composite of the artist's studies from different vantage points on the opposite quay. Under the influence of Turner's grand harbor scenes, Signac portrays a lagoon bustling with life and movement: bragozzi with their colorful sails and gondolas carrying tourists wielding parasols, precisely the kind of teeming prospect Monet would take pains to avoid.

Signac was a lifelong admirer of Monet and wrote in a letter to him in the early 1880s that the older artist's paintings were his only models. After seeing Monet's *Venise* exhibition in 1912, Signac wrote again to praise his "superb interpretation of those motifs I know so well."[37] The only known artwork depicting Venice other than his own to which Monet can be definitively connected is a 1908 watercolor of the Salute and gondolas by Signac (fig. 187) that he acquired in May 1909 from the Bernheim-Jeune gallery. Along with one of his own paintings of Palazzo Dario, this serene Signac watercolor hung in his Giverny home (possibly along with one of the charming pigeon-filled photographs taken in Piazza San Marco), reminders of his time in that splendid city with his beloved Alice.[38]

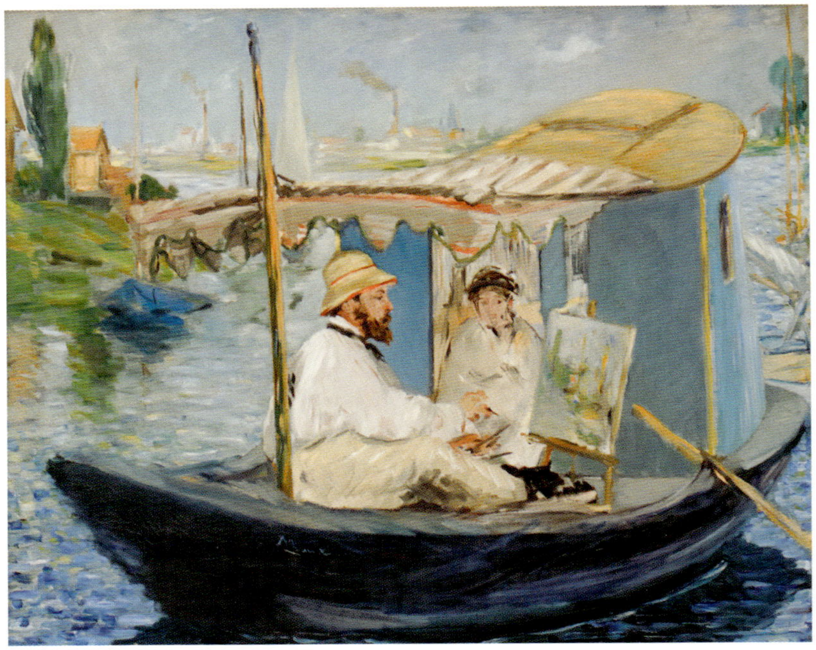

fig. 183—Édouard Manet, ***Claude Monet Painting in his Studio Boat***, 1874, oil on canvas, 31⅖ in × 38½ in., Neue Pinakothek

fig. 184—Édouard Manet, *View of the Great Canal in Venice*, 1875, oil on canvas, 22⅝ × 18⅞ in., private collection

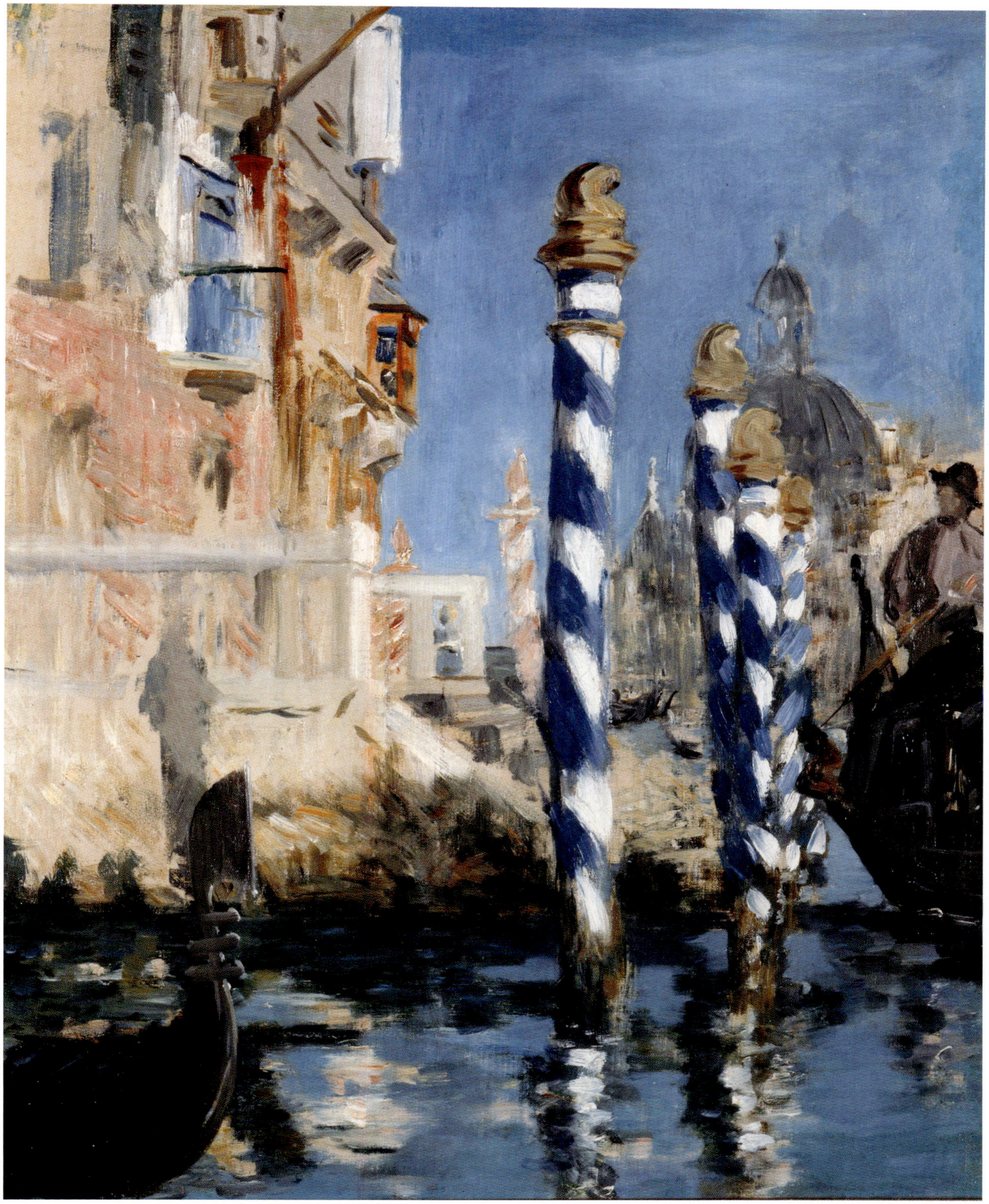

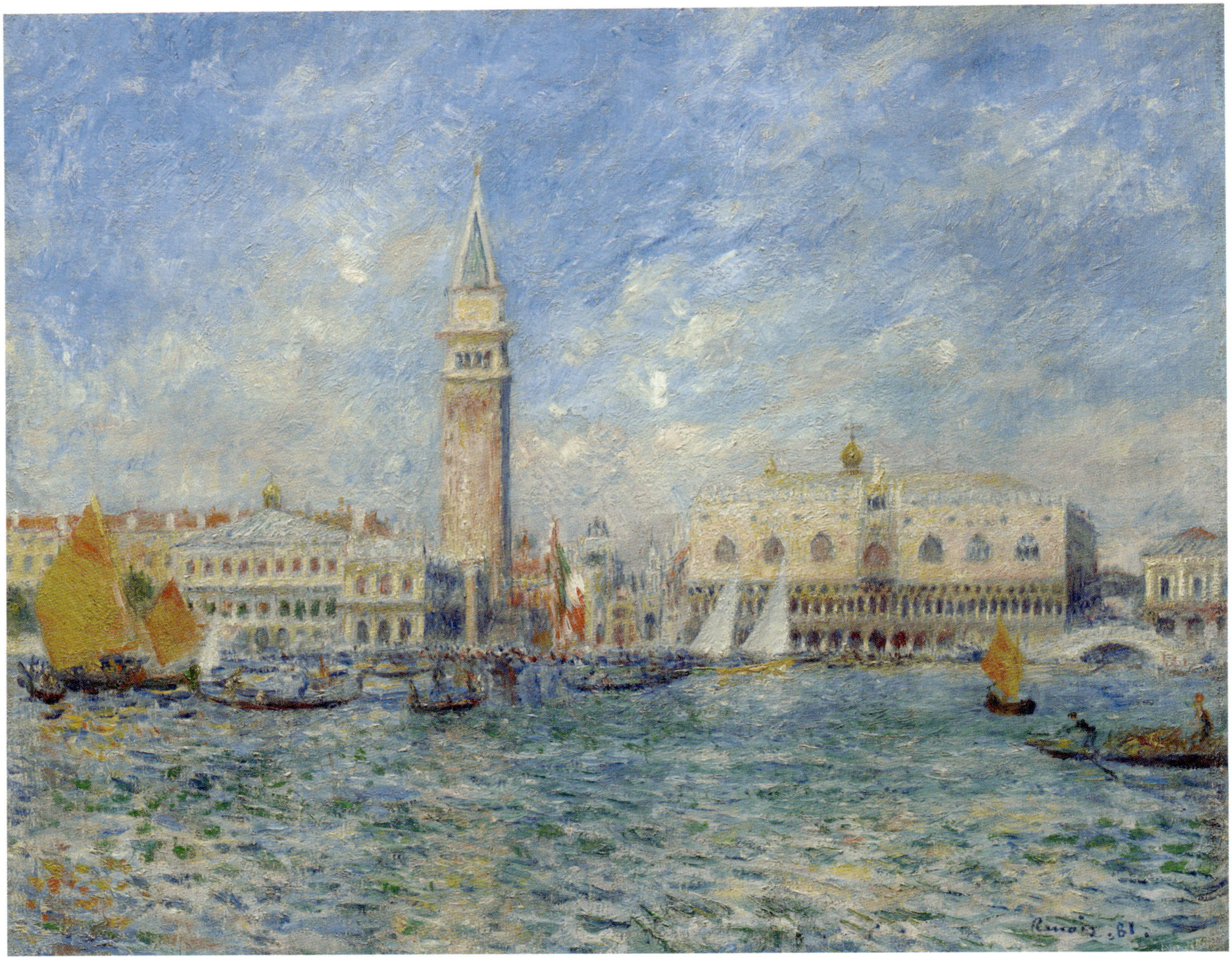

fig. 185—Pierre-Auguste Renoir, *Venice, the Doge's Palace*, 1881, oil on canvas, 21 7/16 × 25 7/8 in., Clark Art Institute

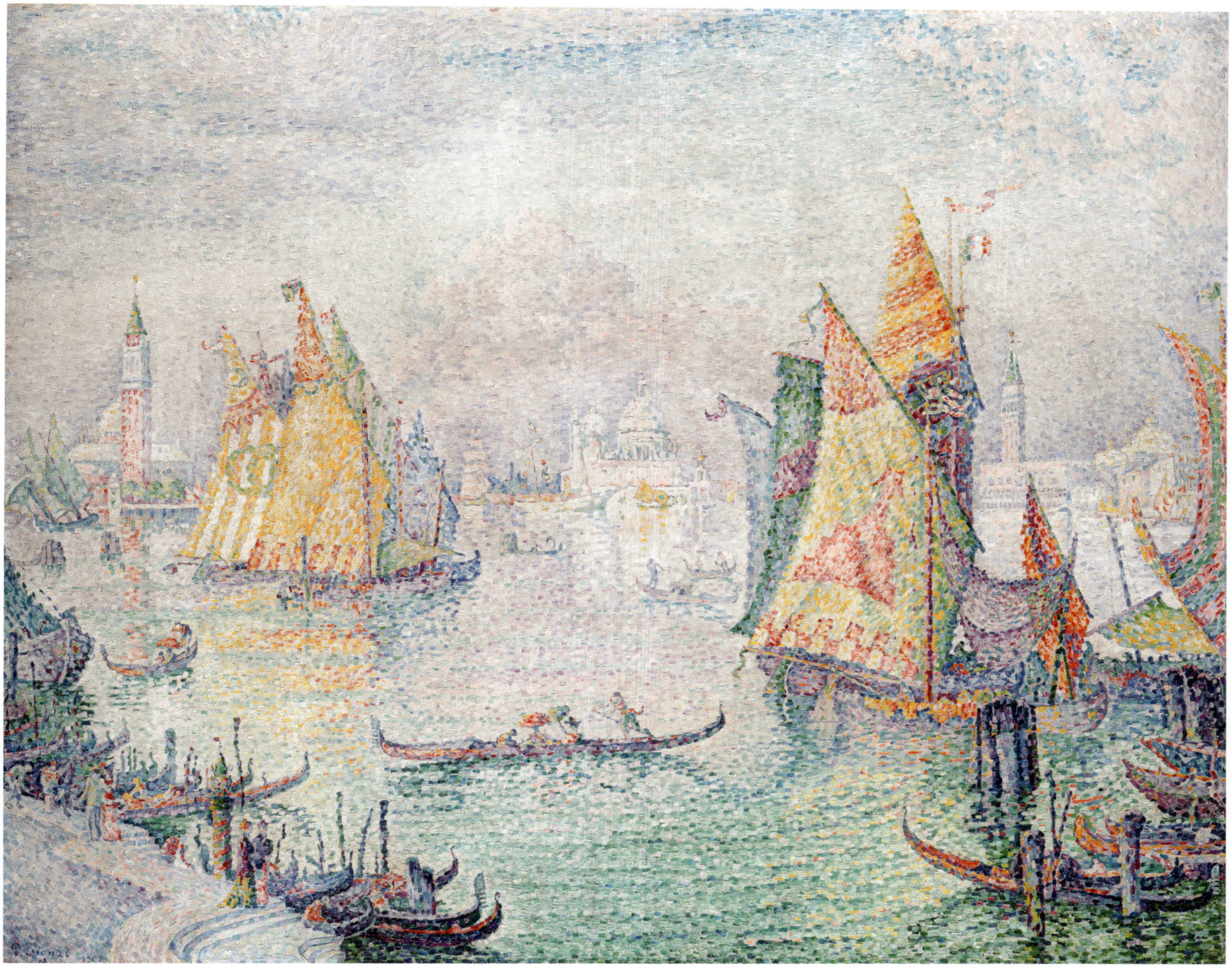

fig. 186—Paul Signac, *The Lagoon of Saint Mark, Venice*, 1905, oil on canvas, 51×64 in., Chrysler Museum of Art

fig. 187—Paul Signac, *Venice or, The Gondolas*, 1908, black chalk and watercolor on paper, 7 ½ × 9 ⅘ in., Musée Marmottan Monet

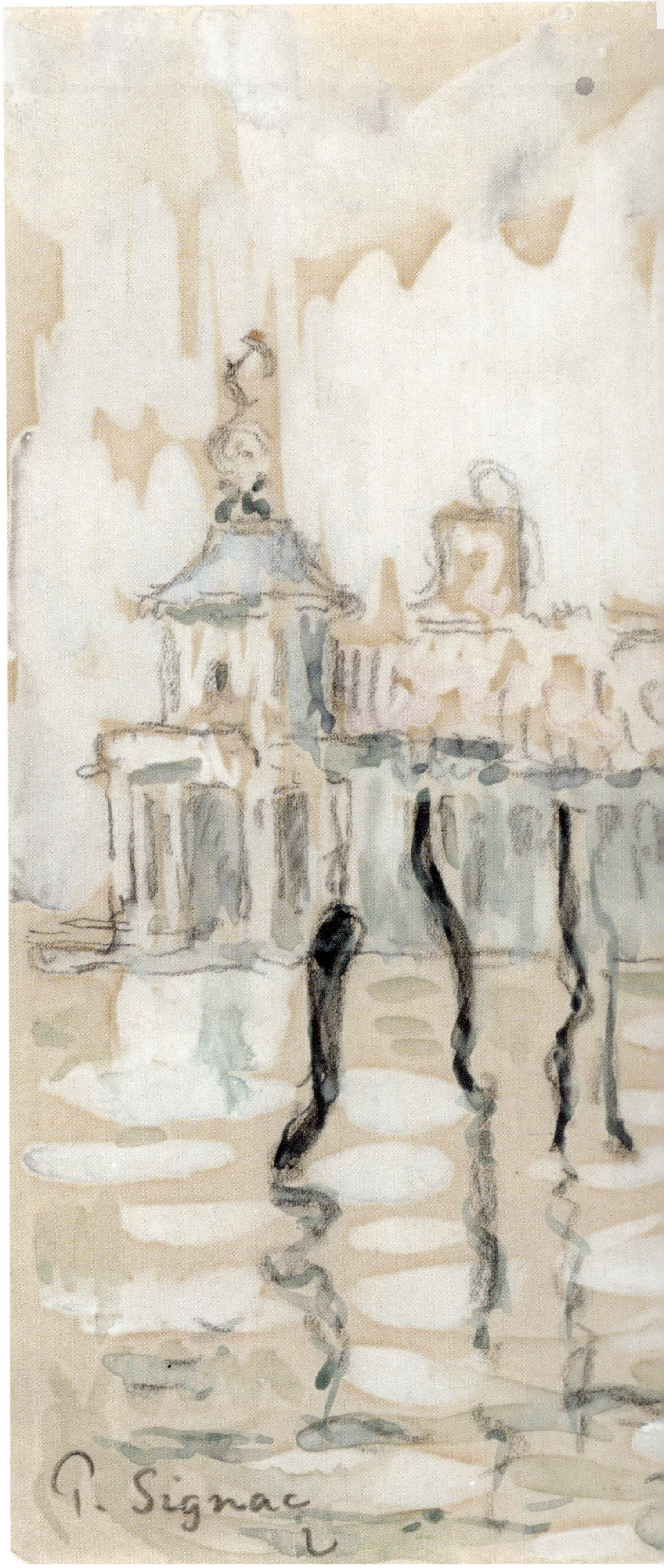

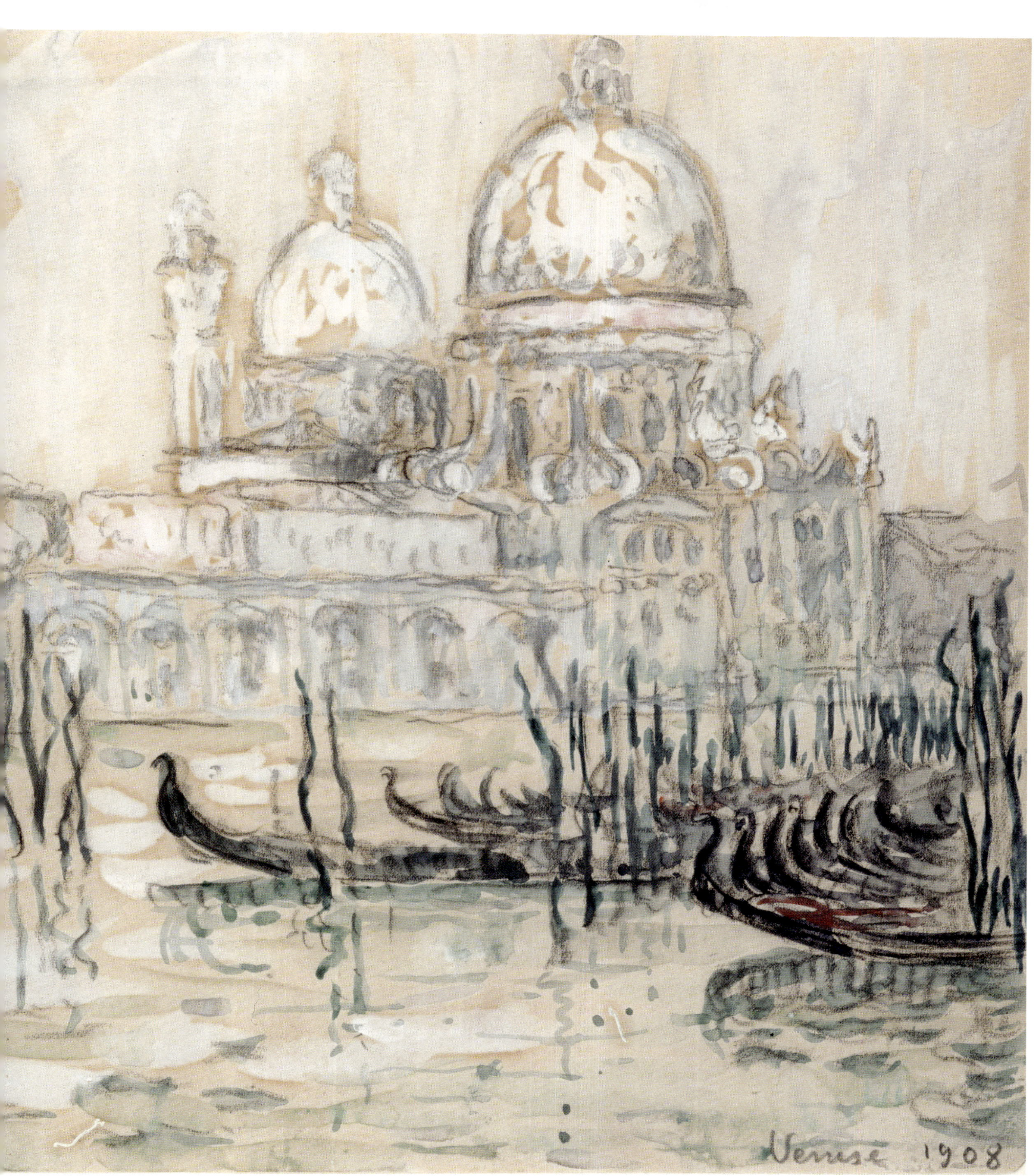
Venise 1908

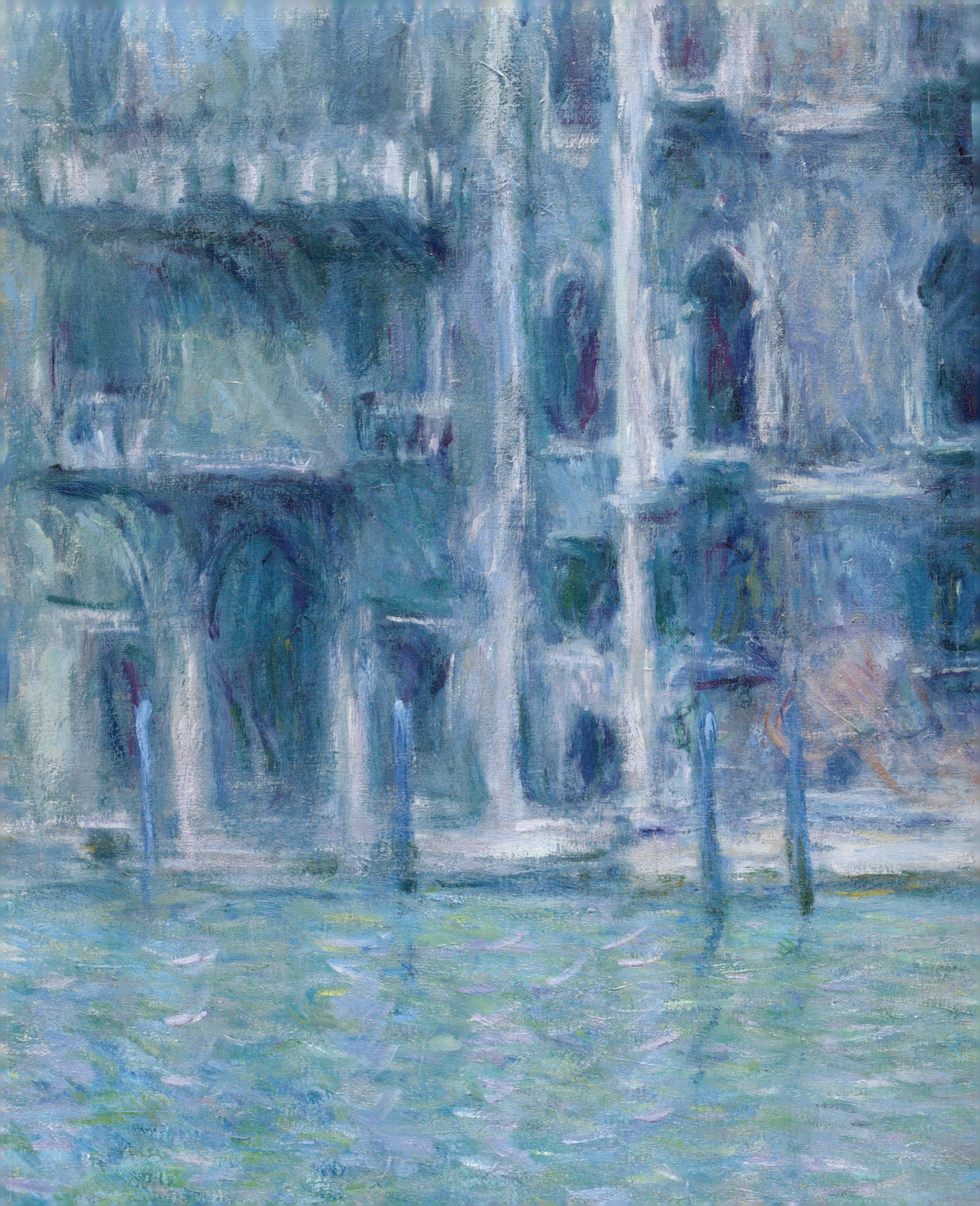

BETWEEN OBSERVER AND OBSERVED: MONET, VENICE, AND THE MUSICAL GAZE

Niles Luther

CLAUDE MONET'S VENICE PAINTINGS, with their masterful interplay of color, light, and atmosphere, emerged from the unlikeliest of sources: a vacation he had initially resisted. I am struck by the thought that had his wife, Alice, not insisted on the trip, these masterpieces might never have come to be. The paintings themselves, in their forthright beauty, whisper of melancholy when we learn they were completed only after Monet's return from Venice—and following the death of his beloved Alice more than two years later. Viewed through Monet's own description, the French word *souvenirs*, their meaning deepens, transcending mere landscape studies to become profoundly personal: the imprint of a man's life on canvas, memories of a foreign land imbued with the presence of a familiar love.

This recasting of lived experience into art invites fundamental questions about the nature of representation. One might ask, could the French Academic style, with its photographic rendering of reality, not provide a more potent mimetic capture? It is apparent, however, that Monet's vision of the world, and his consequent relationship to the architecture of Venice, the painters who came before him, his Alice, and the very light itself, manifested in the diffuse style we now know of him. It is as if the *enveloppe* that he created, and the atmosphere with which he subsumes the viewer, unveils an emotion unto itself rather than oil on canvas. This impulse—the need to translate experience into something beyond representation—lingers in the air, waiting to be heard as well as seen.

The genius of Monet's oeuvre did not go unnoticed; the critic Théodore Duret recognized something revolutionary in these late works. "Impressionism found the extreme reach of its attainment," he wrote of Monet's Venice pictures, observing that "painting which has arrived at this degree of fluidity in some measure approaches music, executing variations upon a theme of colour analogous to those of sound."[1] To further Duret's astute observation, fluidity is embedded within the very nature of music: morphing sets of motifs, continuously surging and receding as they develop from a singular point in time before expanding outward. As such, the ascription of fluidity to Monet's Venice paintings, and the musical qualities they evoke, is precisely what gives these works their unparalleled significance. It is in the brushwork—refusing conformity, shaking definition, and grappling with light—that the Venice paintings reach beyond the canvas, entering the intangible domain of the ephemeral. The music composed for these paintings must embrace this fluidity, lifting the image from its frame and into the air as song: flowing, undulating, and infinitely enveloping.

Monet's embrace of loose, visible brushwork over the sharp, detailed technique of the Academy as his primary means of expression was not a calculated decision. Similarly, my compositions in response to his paintings did not arise from a conscious intention to subvert traditional musical form. These expressions are rooted not in logos but in pathos: a fundamental desire to convey that which is seen, heard, felt, and experienced. What we now call Impressionism became the tool through which Monet captured the world as he felt it. For my compositions, meaning lies in thrusting the score beyond itself—evolving it past ink on a staff, live performance, or traditional recording, to sculpt the sounds as if they were physical objects in their own right, occupying not only the dimension of time, as music does inherently, but also the dimension of space. It is not a decision but a necessary prerequisite to communicate the vision witnessed by both Monet and me, a movement forward as natural as light.

Such movement—as with the relationship between art and music—unfolds in nonlinear currents, resisting a simple, direct progression. This becomes exemplified in the act of composing a musical response to Monet's work. The creative terminus lies not in the act itself but in the dialogue that emerges between these mediums, a meta-conversation of forms. At large, the choreography of disciplines has been a human pursuit since antiquity, spanning centuries from its theatrical origins in ancient Greece to the hybridity aesthetics lauded in the modern era. The ancient Greeks, in their exploration of this dialogue, gave it a name that endures: *ekphrasis*. This was—

> *a type of speech or writing* (logos) *that appealed to the audience's visual imagination and made its members feel as if they could see the subject matter in their mind's eye.... In modern criticism, [ekphrasis] has come to be defined as the "description of a work of art...." [Ekphrasis] in this new guise is often used as the title of a genre or even as a distinct poetic mode or principle in which the relation of the verbal and the visual is explored.... The ancient definition of [ekphrasis] as a "speech that brings the thing shown vividly before the eyes" naturally included graphic descriptions of paintings, sculptures, and other artifacts.*[2]

Like the poets of antiquity, I, too, seek to render the visual into the tangible—but through sound. This power of ekphrasis—to conjure the spirit of a visual with stunning clarity—raises an essential question: Why must this practice be bound to words alone? In other words, why can't music, too, serve as a language that brings "the thing shown vividly before the eyes"?

In my practice, I approach this question through what I call Art Music:[3] a process of transmutation in which both medium and meaning shift, distilling the spirit of a visual work and reconstituting it in the language of music. This approach departs from written ekphrasis; where words must describe, music can simply evoke. Like a painting, music resists a single, fixed meaning—its essence is absorbed uniquely by each listener. In transmuting the spirit of a visual work into sound, Art Music therefore invites an intimate relationship, creating a space where every individual encounters and interprets its presence in a personal way.

Yet in crossing the threshold between visual art and music, we confront deeper questions: How do we experience these forms? What does it mean to see? To hear? To feel? Though both art and music invite interpretation, their phenomenological nature sets them apart. Art is fixed, suspended in time, its presence etched into material, while music is fleeting—vanishing as it is heard, existing only in the act of becoming. This chasm is at once a limitation and a possibility. Can music's fleeting beauty lend movement to a work of art? And in return, can art's permanence concretize our fading music?

Beyond form and perception, there is something deeper still: narrative. Art Music—musical ekphrasis—is no sterile exercise in technique. As a composer, my aim is not to map a brushstroke in counterpoint, nor to reduce music to calculated gesture. My approach is to uncover the essence of a visual work—to grasp its nature, its core, and the truth it seeks to express. What does it *say*? The technique conveys the message, but it is not the message itself. Thus, my practice in Art Music, through a different language and by different means, seeks to express the same truth.

If Monet's paintings invite musical interpretation, it is my charge to give them voice. What the critics sensed intuitively, I render explicit: translating Monet's serial visions of Venice into music, not as allegory but as experience. What lingers in these works beyond what the eye can see? More specifically, how does Monet's shifting vision of Venice echo my own unfolding perception of these spaces? The key lies in his sequential works—we must look closer, listen deeper.

At first glance, these works seem to chart the shifting moods of Venice—its changing light, its weather, its air: each shaping Monet's perception of atmosphere. Just as vital, however, was the space between artist and subject—the air itself, mediating perception. Yet my inquiry diverges from Monet's, not in the subject, nor in the air between man and motif. What captures my attention is the through line of Monet's work, necessitating both a point of origin and a destination. Monet exists and he observes. The distance he painted, the atmosphere he sought to capture, is the space between these two points: the observer and the observed. Seen from this perspective, the act of observation itself alters the object being observed. Thus, Monet himself—his mood, his emotions, his reasons for being in Venice, his very humanity—is embedded in the canvas.

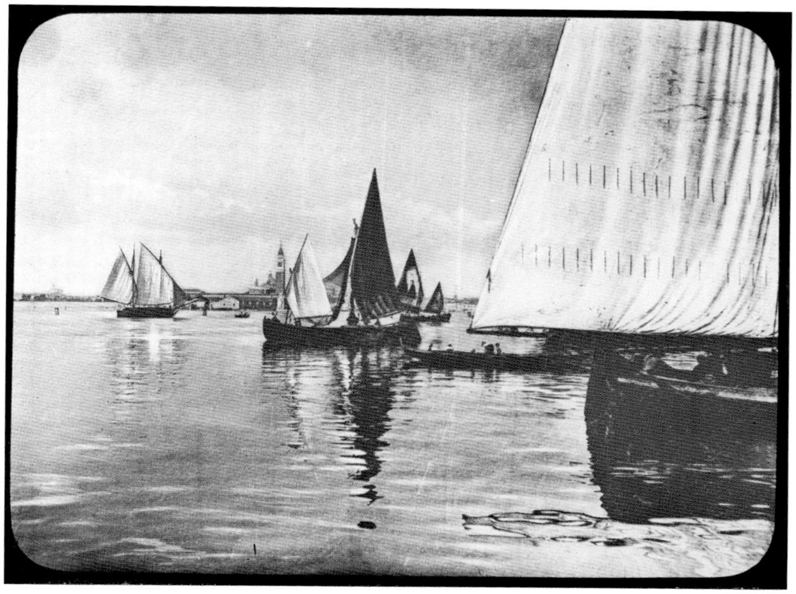

fig. 188—*Venice Bay with Fishermen's Boats*, lantern slide, F.C. Lockwood, Brooklyn, N.Y., Brooklyn Museum Libraries and Archives

This interplay reveals multiple layers, each demanding closer examination. There is the physical reality of Venice: its canals, palazzi, and churches. There is the space between Monet and his motif—the air that separates and connects them. And finally, there is Monet himself. Together, these three elements—the city, the space, and the man—interweave to shape the subtle variations that define each motif. Thus, from a musical perspective, my inquiry extends beyond "What does Venetian architecture sound like?" or "What do Monet's paintings of Venetian architecture sound like?" Instead, I ask, "Who is this man—this human presence—within the shifting atmosphere of the city he painted?" The sequential motif is not merely the physical object, nor just the space between observer and observed; it is both, and it is also the observer himself. This triadic relationship is what must be rendered into music.

Beyond this, we must also consider the interplay of cultural and historical layers—an ancient Italian city, an early-twentieth-century French painter, and a contemporary American composer. How do these seemingly disparate elements converge within the sequential motif? I cannot claim lineage within these histories, nor do I stand within their inherited traditions. My tether to the French Impressionists—and further still, to Venice itself—is not one of heritage but of intent: a profound desire to give voice to something witnessed.

In many ways, my journey to Venice was less about Monet's paintings and more about immersing myself in the environment that gave rise to them. This distinction is crucial. It sets these works apart from his *Water Lilies*, an environment he shaped and controlled entirely, whereas in Venice, he was directly confronted with the city's vast, inescapable presence. Forced to reckon with the city itself—its storied history, its aging magnificence, and the artists who had glorified it before him—I, too, had to journey there, to stand within its presence, to contend with the very elements that shaped Monet's vision.

These layers of cultural translation—one of the great Italian cities was captured by a French Impressionist, and now the works of that French Impressionist will be transliterated by an American composer—compel a response, not merely as artistic choice, but as necessary homage. I turn to the Italian composer Ottorino Respighi's[4] *Ancient Airs & Dances, Suite III, P. 172*—a work that distills the essence of Italian musical expression—and to the viola da gamba, an instrument refined by Italian luthiers into a voice that resonates most purely in pieces such as Carl Friedrich Abel's[5] Suite in D Minor: I. Arpeggiata. These works embody the Venetian sonorities that form the first layer of this cultural translation. From Venice, we move to Monet's France, where his painterly vision finds its musical parallel in the French Impressionist composers—artists who reimagined functional harmony as pure color rather than merely as architectural support for tonal progression. In Claude Debussy's[6] moonlit reverie "Clair de Lune," L. 32, and the delicate impressions of "La Fille aux Cheveux de Lin," L. 33; in Frédéric Chopin's[7] 21 Nocturnes for Solo Piano, with their liquid arpeggios; and in Maurice Ravel's[8] elegiac "Pavane pour une Infante Défunte," M. 19, we hear color becoming sound, the synesthetic representation of hue, shade, and saturation.

Yet to compose a response to Monet's works solely within the French Impressionist idiom—with its shimmering textures and liberated harmony—would be to deny the very cultural fluidity that his Venice paintings embody. Such an approach would not only echo what these French masters have already accomplished but would also fail to acknowledge the final layer in this palimpsest of cultural translation: that these Venetian visions, filtered through French sensibilities, now resonate in the present moment through an American musical voice—more than a century after their creation. In this American layer, the orchestral works of Samuel Barber[9] emerge as vital references: the penetrating lyricism of his Violin Concerto, Op. 14: II. Andante; and the profound emotional depth of his Adagio for Strings, Op. 11, a work whose concentrated sorrow has few equals in the musical canon. Barber's compositional voice stands in stark contrast to those of his French predecessors: embracing rather than veiling explicit melodic statements, luxuriating in the full tonal palette of the orchestra, and working within traditional forms while subtly expanding their boundaries. His music projects an unmistakable American sensibility: direct, emotionally forthright, and unapologetically expressive.

These three currents converge in my approach: Venice's architectural grandeur demands the resonance of Italian instruments; Monet's luminous interpretation calls for the coloristic sensitivity of the French tradition; and my own perspective inevitably channels the expansive and cinematic sonorities of the American orchestral voice. None dominates; all three flow together. This prismatic view allows us to peer into Venice from multiple perspectives, each one revealing different facets of the city's essence and the cultural artifacts that have been created from it. What emerges from this confluence is something entirely new, neither purely Venetian, French, nor American, but a living synthesis that exists only in our present moment. In this way, Monet's paintings, like the musical works that inspire me, are not merely historical artifacts but perpetually contemporary experiences. Their true essence is not locked in the past but continuously reborn in each encounter, as viewers and listeners engage with them through the lens of their own time and consciousness.

Ultimately, Monet and I pursue the same elusive vision: to translate the profound sensation of being subsumed. For him, it was light; for me, it is sound. Monet's primary thesis asserts that the viewer is not merely observing the painted subject, but is observing the ether in between himself and the motif, placing us within an interstitial space that is neither opaque nor transparent. It exists between two points, and invariably it becomes the point, or nexus, unto itself. Similarly, I aim to deconstruct the traditional form of orchestra versus audience, a clearly defined format that separates the music from the creator and the receiver. What Monet visually articulated, and what I am musically articulating, is that there exists a method of dissolving the rigid boundaries between observer and observed, allowing perception itself to flow unimpeded between traditionally separated elements. What does it sound like if an individual is actually the focal point for the orchestra? The sound does not merely travel toward you from a distance, but rather flows around and through you, constellating as a fluid architecture of tone with you at its center, wholly enveloped within its sonic current. To return to my earlier exploration of the fluid relationship between observer and observed, here we witness this boundary dissolving once more, but now flowing across mediums themselves. Just as a conductor stands at the podium, shaping waves of sound from the orchestra, the listener now becomes the center of the sonic field, the still point around which the music naturally gathers. In this way, they serve two roles, the guide and the guided, for without them as a point of gravitational force, there is nothing for the sound to constellate around. This is the essence of the *enveloppe*, both musically and visually: its very nature resides in its capacity to enfold. We, the observer, are enfolded and enveloped. Pursued to its fullest potential, the *enveloppe* demarcates a fundamental change in the very nature of what music is, for unlike the written score, live performance, or traditional recording, the musical realization of the *enveloppe* is the sculptural, spatial, and, most importantly, invisible manifestation of lived experience.

EXPERIENCE THE MUSIC

To extend this conversation beyond words and into sound, I invite you to engage directly with the music itself. Type the link below into your browser of choice to hear my original symphonic compositions inspired by these works. This immersive audio experience is designed to be enjoyed while viewing the paintings in this catalogue, creating a multisensory dialogue between visual and aural impressions. I encourage you to listen actively while looking—to experience how music can reveal new dimensions within Monet's brushwork, light, and atmosphere.

MONETANDVENICESYMPHONY.ETH.LIMO

ENDNOTES

(Unless otherwise indicated, all translations are by each author.)

MELISSA BURON, pp 17–29

1 Mark Evans, "The Davies Sisters of Llandinam and Impressionism for Wales, 1908–1923," *Journal of the History of Collections* 16, no. 2 (2004): 219–53. Their extraordinary Impressionist collection was bequeathed to Amgueddfa Cymru–Museum Wales and are now displayed in the National Museum in Cardiff. See also Mark Evans, *Impressions of Venice from Turner to Monet* (National Museum of Wales, 1992), 22–26.

2 Evans, "The Davies Sisters," 242.

3 The sole painting in an American public collection not included is the National Gallery of Art's *Palazzo da Mula* (pl.29) from the Chester Dale Collection, which can never be lent due to the terms of the donor's gift.

4 See Karen Serres, ed., *Monet and London: Views of the Thames* (Paul Holberton Publishing, 2024), 49.

5 *Monet and London*, 21.

6 Boudin visited in 1892, 1894, and 1895; Manet in 1853 and from 1874 to 1875; Renoir in 1881; Sargent nearly every year between 1902 and 1913; Signac in 1903, 1904, and 1908; and Whistler from 1879 to 1880.

7 Alice Monet to Germaine Salerou, October 2, 1908, in Philippe Piguet, *Monet et Venise* (Editions Herscher, 1986). All subsequent references to Alice Monet's letters come from this source unless otherwise cited, and all of Alice Monet's letters are written to Germaine Salerou unless otherwise cited.

8 This was not the first instance when Monet canceled an exhibition in frustration. He had ended plans for a 1903 exhibition of London paintings, which he eventually presented the following year in Paris. *Monet and London*, 40

9 Quoted in Ross King, *Mad Enchantment: Claude Monet and the Painting of the Water Lilies* (Bloomsbury, 2016), 40.

10 The sensational, headline-making June 1908 murder of Alice's brother-in-law Auguste Rémy may have prompted a desire to seek a low profile outside France.

11 Sargent's portrait of Hunter (fig. 4) was shown at the Venice Biennale in 1907 (English Pavilion, 27). It was later gifted by her through the National Art Collections Fund in 1929 "in memory of a great artist and a great friend" and is today in Tate Britain's collection. Sargent also arranged for Monet to watch Queen Victoria's 1901 funeral with the author Henry James as his translator. These connections may have bolstered Monet's interest in visiting Palazzo Barbaro, where both Sargent and James had stayed in Venice.

12 Daniel Curtis died on July 2, 1908, which accounts for the Curtis family's absence from Palazzo Barbaro in the autumn of 1908, when Hunter invited the Monets to visit.

13 Ariana rejected the painting, reputedly claiming that her son's pose was too casual. Sargent presented the family portrait to the Royal Academy as his diploma painting in 1900.

14 Isabella Stewart Gardner visited Monet in Giverny in 1906, two years before the Monets went to Venice. She tried to buy works directly from him, but the artist refused, telling her that he was not ready. It is interesting to speculate whether her time in Venice at Palazzo Barbaro was ever discussed. See Elizabeth Anne McCauley et al., eds., *Gondola Days: Isabella Stewart Gardner and the Palazzo Barbaro Circle* (Isabella Stewart Gardner Museum, 2004), 244, note 24.

15 See *Gondola Days*. Gardner would later, through Sargent's intervention, acquire works from Hunter's art collection for her museum in Boston, which was inspired by Palazzo Barbaro and features a transplanted Venetian palazzo as its interior courtyard.

16 Quoted in Octave Mirbeau, *Claude Monet: Venise* (Galerie Bernheim-Jeune, 1912), n.p.

17 October 8, 1908.

18 A musical child prodigy, in adulthood Smyth was a suffragette and the first female composer to be made a dame in 1922. She had friendships and romantic relationships with notable figures of her time, including Oscar Wilde's brother, Willie, to whom she was briefly engaged, writer Virginia Woolf, and fellow suffragette Emmeline Pankhurst.

19 October 9, 1908.

20 Hunter hosted a lunch where Monet was introduced to Italian critic Carlo Placci, who arranged access for the artist. *Gondola Days*, 240 and 244, note 11. Hunter helped Monet with similarly exclusive access in London, where she facilitated his gaining permission to paint the Houses of Parliament from a covered terrace at Saint Thomas' Hospital across the Thames. *Monet and London*, 31.

21 *Gondola Days*, 240. A large ship ultimately blocked his view and prevented this vantage point from working well.

22 October 16, 1908.

23 Attesting to her friendship with Hunter, Alice Monet wrote to Salerou on October 19, 1908, asking her to source, as a gift for their host, an edition of the eighteenth-century novel [*La Vie de*] *Marianne* by Pierre de Marivaux, which Alice was concerned could be difficult to find.

24 Ségolène Le Men et al., *La Bibliothèque de Monet* (Citadelles & Mazenod, 2013), 50 and 251. The version documented in Monet's library is John Ruskin and K. Johnston (trans.), *Le Repos de Saint-Marc: Histoire de Venise Pour Les Rares Voyageurs Qui Se Soucient Encore de Ses Monuments* (Hachette & Cie, 1908).

25 John Ruskin / Abitò questo casa (1877) / Sacerdote dell arte / Nelle nostre pietre nel nostro S Marco / Quasi in ogni monumento d'Italia / Cerco insieme / L'anima dell'artefice e l'anima del popolo / Ogni marmo ogni bronzo ogni tela / Ogni cosa gli gridò / Che bellezza è religione / Se virtù d'uomo la susciti / E riverenza di popolo l'accolga / Il comune di Venezia riconoscente / P[osuit] XXVI Gennaio MDCCCC. I am grateful to Elena Marchetti and Natalie Danford for their careful translation of this memorial text.

26 John Ruskin, *The Complete Works of John Ruskin, Modern Painters*, vol. 3 (National Library Association, n.d.), 63.

27 John Ruskin, *The Stones of Venice*, vol. 3 (National Library Association, n.d.), 307–8.

28 October 6, 1908.

29 Joachim Pissarro, *Monet and the Mediterranean* (Rizzoli, 1997), 181, note 1.

30 Claude Monet to Paul Durand-Ruel, October 19, 1908, in Daniel Wildenstein, *Monet: Biographie et Catalogue Raisonné*, vols. 1–5 (Wildenstein Institute and La Bibliothèque des Arts, 1974–1991). All subsequent references to Claude Monet's letters come from this source unless otherwise cited.

31 December 7, 1908, quoted in Katharine Lochnan et al., *Turner Whistler Monet: Impressionist Visions* (Art Gallery of Ontario/Tate, 2004), 205 and 243, note 21.

32 For more on his practice of working from photographs, see *Monet and London*, 54 and 151. Mary Hunter helped Monet source a photograph as an aide-mémoire as he finished a painting of the Houses of Parliament when he was back in Giverny.

33 It would later enter the collection of the Musée Marmottan Monet, when the artist's childless son Michel transferred the family's remaining collection after his death in 1966. A facsimile can be seen today on the walls of the artist's home in Giverny, France. For more, see Marianne Mathieu and Dominique Lobstein, *Monet the Collector* (Yale University Press, 2018), 278–79.

34 Gustave Geffroy Notre Époque:, "La Venise de Claude Monet," *La Dépêche* 43, May 30, 1912.

35 Wildenstein, *Monet*, 824. It is possible that Monet knew the rumors about Palazzo Dario and the tragic fates of those who spent prolonged time there, which persist today, as relayed to the author in October 2024 by Venetian residents.

36 December 7, 1908.

37 Georges Clemenceau, *Claude Monet: Les Nymphéas* (Plon, 1928).

38 July 11, 1911.

39 Jackie Wullschläger, *Monet: The Restless Vision* (Penguin, 2023), 390.

40 January 28, 1909.

41 See Steven Z. Levine, *Monet and His Critics* (Garland, 1976), 297–334.

42 Roger Marx, "Les Nymphéas' de M. Claude Monet," *Gazette des Beaux-Arts* 4, no. 1 (June 1909): 523–32.

43 Quoted in Paul Hayes Tucker, *Claude Monet: Life and Art* (Yale University Press, 1995), 196.

44 Paul Hayes Tucker, *Monet in the 20th Century* (Yale University Press, 1998), 49.

45 Later that year, seven of Monet's Venice paintings were shown in Boston at Brooks Reed Gallery, and Durand-Ruel's gallery in New York would showcase them in 1913.

46 Paul Signac to Claude Monet, May 31, 1912, quoted in Lochnan et al., *Turner Whistler Monet*, 207.

47 W. R. Sickert, "From 'Nineteenth-Century Pictures at Messrs. Knoedler's'" (originally published in *The Burlington Magazine* in July 1923) in *A Free House! or The Artist as Craftsman*, ed. Osbert Sitwell (Arcade Publishing, 1947), 156.

48 Jonathan Keates, *La Serenissima* (Apollo, 2022), 360.

49 Wullschläger, *Restless Vision*, 392.

50 Pissarro, *Monet and the Mediterranean*, 65.

51 January 28, 1909.

LISA SMALL, pp 31–69

1 Simon Kelly, "How Monet Became a Millionaire: The Importance of the Artist's Account Books," *Journal of Cultural Economics* 47 (September 2023): 443, note 12.

2 On the *enveloppe*, see John House, *Monet: Nature into Art* (Yale University Press, 1988), 220–25. See Paul Hayes Tucker, *Monet in the '90s: The Series Paintings (Museum of Fine Arts, Boston/ Yale University Press, 1989)* on how Monet's choice of motifs resonated beyond just the capturing of light effects and reflected his engagement with a range of contemporaneous cultural and political concerns.

3 From an 1895 interview with Herman Bang published in Norway, quoted in Jean-Pierre Hoschedé, *Claude Monet, Ce Mal Connu: Intimité Familiale d'un Demi-siècle à Giverny de 1883 à 1926* (Pierre Cailler Éditeur, 1960), in turn quoted in House, *Monet: Nature into Art*, 29.

4 See Tony Tanner, *Venice Desired* (Harvard University Press, 1992); *Venice and the Cultural Imagination: 'This Strange Dream Upon the Water,'* ed. Michael O'Neill et al. (Routledge, 2016).

5 July 17, 1893, letter from Monet to the Prefect of the Eure petitioning for permission to divert water from the Epte to cultivate his aquatic plants in his pond at Giverny, in Richard Kendall, *Monet by Himself* (Little, Brown, 1989), 170–80.

6 Marcel Proust, "Les Éblouissements," *Le Figaro*, June 15, 1907, quoted in *Monet's Garden: Masterpieces from Musée Marmottan Monet* (Sakip Sabanci Museum, 2012), 169.

7 Claude Monet to Gustave Geffroy, August 11, 1908, in Daniel Wildenstein, *Monet: Biographie et Catalogue Raisonné*, vols. 1–5 (Wildenstein Institute and La Bibliothèque des Arts, 1974–1991). All subsequent references to Claude Monet's letters come from this source unless otherwise cited.

8 Claude Monet to Durand-Ruel, January 28, 1909.

9 Gustave Kahn, "Une Exposition d'Impressionnistes," *Mercure de France*, July 1, 1912.

10 Katie Hornstein and Caty Telfair, review of *Claude Monet, 1840–1926*," *Nineteenth-Century Art Worldwide* 10, no. 1 (Spring 2011): 19thc-artworldwide.org/spring11/claude-monet-18401926. The authors comment on the five Venice paintings included in the major Monet retrospective at the Grand Palais from 2010 to 2011, "Isolation serves them well as it both underscores them as anomalies for Monet, and emphasizes their strangeness as images of Venice."

11 Selected Venice paintings have been featured in several monographic exhibitions. The most detailed accounts of the trip and the paintings are found in Philippe Piguet, *Monet et Venise* (Éditions Herscher, 1986); Joachim Pissarro, *Monet and the Mediterranean* (Rizzoli, 1997); Paul Hayes Tucker, *Monet in the 20th Century* (Yale University Press, 1998); and Richard Thomson, *Monet & Architecture* (National Gallery, 2018). Stephen F. Eisenman, "Death and Tourism: Claude Monet's Paintings of Venice," in *Value, Art, Politics*, ed. Jonathan Harris (Liverpool University Press, 2007) is also an important contribution. Some of Monet's Venice paintings have also been included in thematic exhibitions. For two notable examples, see the catalogue by Katharine Lochnan et al., *Turner Whistler Monet: Impressionist Visions* (Art Gallery of Ontario/Tate, 2004) and especially Gottfried Boehm's essay in Martin Schwander, ed., *Venice: From Canaletto and Turner to Monet* (Fondation Beyeler, 2008).

12 Until the mid-twentieth-century "rediscovery" of Monet (fueled by the efforts of Parisian dealer Katia Granoff, who purchased the studio collection from Monet's son Michel in 1956), his enormous late *Water Lilies*, like the Musée de l'Orangerie works, were not held in critical or popular high esteem. See *Monet: The Late Years* (Kimbell Art Museum, 2019). The Museum of Modern Art acquired its first Monet *Water Lilies* painting in 1955, around the same time that American art critics like Thomas Hess and Clement Greenberg connected Monet's *Water Lilies* to Abstract Expressionist artists such as Mark Rothko, Joan Mitchell, and Clyfford Still. See James H. Rubin, *Why Monet Matters: Meanings Among the Lily Pads* (Pennsylvania State University Press, 2021), 267–296. Several exhibitions have been devoted to the relationship of these late Monets to twentieth-century abstraction, the most recent of which was *Monet-Mitchell* at the Fondation Louis Vuitton in 2022.

13 Jennifer Scappettone, *Killing the Moonlight: Modernism in Venice* (Columbia University Press, 2014), 11.

14 F. T. Marinetti, Umberto Boccioni, Carlo Carra, and Luigi Russolo, "Against Passéist Venice," in *Futurism: An Anthology*, ed. Lawrence Rainey et al. (Yale University Press, 2009), 67.

15 To Gaston or Joseph Bernheim-Jeune, April 8, 1912. Théodore Duret, who would have been able to see the Venice paintings at Giverny not long after Monet's return, called each group of individual Venice motifs a series, as did Marc Elder in his 1924 book *À Giverny, Chez Claude Monet* (published by Bernheim-Jeune). The Bernheim-Jeune brothers referred to the Venice "series" in their correspondence with Monet. Today, one can see multiple examples of Rouen Cathedral, *Grainstacks*, London, and *Water Lilies* series paintings at the Musée d'Orsay, the Art Institute of Chicago, the National Gallery of Art, Washington, DC, and the Museum of Fine Arts, Boston. By contrast, the only public collections that contain more than one Venice painting are the Amgueddfa Cymru–Museum Wales and the Museum Barberini in Potsdam. For overviews of Monet's series paintings, see Charles Stuckey, "The Predications and Implications of Monet's Series," in *The Repeating Image* (Walters Art Museum, 2007); and Tucker, *Monet in the '90s*.

16 A selection of commentary provides a snapshot of the way in which the Venice paintings sometimes have been construed as primarily picturesque or accorded less general significance within Monet's career. John House referred to the paintings as "rather synthetic arrangements that threaten to make his Venice as unconvincing as that of Félix Ziem, creator of the orange-blue Venetian stereotype of the later nineteenth century." House, *Monet: Nature into Art,* 129. In his review of *Monet and the Mediterranean*, which featured many of the Venice paintings, George Shackelford asserts that "having completed the Water Lily paintings Monet made a distinct return to the picturesque in undertaking the Venetian views." George T. M. Shackelford, "Monet and the Mediterranean: Fort Worth and New York," *The Burlington Magazine* 139, no. 1135 (1997): 719. That sentiment was reiterated in Tucker, *Monet in the 20th Century*, 178. In *Claude Monet: Late Work* (Gagosian, 2010), Tucker stated, "Monet could not permit the latter [Venice] to be his last pictures, given their deeply romantic bent."

17 Arsène Alexandre, *Claude Monet* (Bernheim-Jeune, 1921), 110.

18 Henri Genet, "Les Venises de Claude Monet," *L'Opinion*, June 1, 1912, quoted in Gustave Geffroy, *Claude Monet: Sa Vie, Son Temps, Son Oeuvre* (G. Crès et Cie, 1922), 247.

19 Georg Simmel, *The Art of the City: Rome, Florence, Venice*, trans. and ed. Will Stone (Pushkin Press, 2018), 62; *Venedig* originally published in 1907.

20 Alexandre, *Claude Monet*, 110.

21 "Personal Intelligence: In Sunny Italy. M. Claude Monet in Venice," *The New York Herald Tribune*, October 11, 1908, quoted in Piguet, *Monet et Venise*, 124. See Melissa Buron's essay in this volume for more information on Hunter and the Curtises.

22 Alice Monet to Germaine Salerou, September 27, 1908, in Philippe Piguet, Monet et Venise, 1986. All subsequent references to Alice Monet's letters come from this source unless otherwise cited, and all of Alice Monet's letters are written to Germaine Salerou unless otherwise cited.

23 October 17, 1908; October 25, 1908; October 30, 1908.

24 November 16, 1908.

25 November 12, 1908.

26 October 3–4, October 12, October 15, October 19, October 27, October 29, October 31, November 3, November 5, November 14, November 28, November 30, and December 3, 1908.

27 To Paul Durand-Ruel, October 19, 1908; to Gustave Geffroy, December 7, 1908.

28 October 2, 1908.

29 October 4, 1908.

30 All three of these books were in Monet's library: see Ségolène Le Men et al., *La Bibliothèque de Monet* (Citadelles & Mazenod, 2013). André Dombrowski also discusses guidebooks in his essay in this volume. Pierre Gusman, *Venise* (Renouard, H. Laurens, 1907), 11.

31 Emilio Aickelin's artists' materials shop on Calle Larga XXII Marzo was patronized by Sargent as well. Aickelin's was one of two such shops listed in Venice in John Murray's *Handbook for Travellers in Northern Italy* in 1897. For more on Emilio Aickelin's shop, see Elena Marchetti's essay in this volume. For the ubiquity of photographs and postcards, see Liana Amanda Bellon. "Souvenirs of Venice: Reproduced Views, Tourism, and City Spaces" (PhD thesis, McGill University, 2016). The publication *Monet Paintings and Drawings at the Art Institute of Chicago* (2014) notes that the museum's Monet, *Venice, Palazzo Dario*, was painted on a canvas purchased in Venice. In her letters of October 21 and 30, 1908, respectively, Alice mentions Monet having ordered more canvases and their taking walks together to art supply and postcard sellers.

32 John Ruskin, *Notes by Mr. Ruskin on Samuel Prout and William Hunt* (The Fine Art Society, 1880), 67.

33 Pietro Casola, quoted in Robert C. Davis and Garry R. Marvin, *Venice, the Tourist Maze: A Cultural Critique of the World's Most Touristed City* (University of California Press, 2004), 15.

34 Lord Byron, *Childe Harold's Pilgrimage*, Canto IV. Lord Byron to Thomas Moore, *Letters and Journals of Lord Byron* (John Murray, 1830), 52.

35 Henry James, *Italian Hours* (Riverside Press, 1909), 3.

36 Octave Mirbeau, *Venise* (Bernheim-Jeune, 1912), n.p.

37 Mirbeau, *Venise*, n.p.

38 October 2, 1908, and October 8, 1908.

39 Arsène Alexandre, "La Vie Artistique: Claude Monet et Venise," *Le Figaro*, May 29, 1912.

40 Guillaume Apollinaire, "La Vie Artistique: Claude Monet," *L'Intransigeant*, May 31, 1912.

41 October 6, 1908.

42 October 7, 1908.

43 October 8, 1908, October 12, 1908, and October 27, 1908; Alice Monet to Geffroy, November 1908, quoted in Wildenstein, *Monet or the Triumph of Impressionism*, vol. 1 (Taschen, 1996), 387; November 1, 1908, and November 6, 1908. By October 19, 1908, Alice reported that a passionate Monet had twelve canvases underway; more than a month later, on November 26, she reported that he was able to work on nine canvases in a single day.

44 Monet's Venice schedule is described in Jacqueline Guillaud and Maurice Guillaud, *Claude Monet at the Time of Giverny* (Centre Culturel du Marais, 1983) and further outlined by Pierre Schneider in his essay in Piguet, *Monet et Venise*.

45 November 9, 1908.

46 October 22, 1908.

47 October 27, 1885.

48 Quoted in Karen Serres, "Monet's Views of the Thames, 1899–1904," in *Monet and London: Views of the Thames* (Paul Holberton Publishing, 2024), 32.

49 April 12, 1889.

50 Quoted in Ross King, *Mad Enchantment: Claude Monet and the Painting of the Water Lilies* (Bloomsbury, 2016), 38.

51 Monet's *Venise* exhibition included nine motifs: the Grand Canal; Palazzo Ducale close-up; Palazzo Ducale from a distance; San Giorgio Maggiore; San Giorgio Maggiore at sunset; Palazzo Dario; Palazzo Contarini; Palazzo da Mula; and Rio della Salute. His two other Venetian canvases, the red house and the gondola, which remained in the form of oil sketches, were not exhibited.

52 Monet wrote to Mary Hunter in 1903 from Giverny to ask for two photos of the silhouette of Parliament taken from the spot in Saint Thomas' Hospital where he had worked: one with calm water and reflections on the water, and the other with ripples on the water, both at high tide and preferably in the afternoon. See Serres, "Exhibiting the Thames Series in Paris and London, 1904–05," in *Monet and London*, 54.

53 See Robert L. Herbert, *Monet on the Normandy Coast: Tourism and Painting, 1867–1886* (Yale University Press, 1994).

54 In 1912 Bernheim-Jeune paid Monet the very large sum of 339,000 francs for the twenty-nine paintings they would exhibit. That year, Monet's income was the equivalent of between over 2 million and 12.4 million U.S. dollars, depending how the relative values are calculated. For a study of Monet's commercial acumen and his resulting financial success, see Kelly, "How Monet Became a Millionaire," 437–60.

55 André Michel, "Promenades aux Salons," *Journal des Débats Politiques et Littéraires*, June 5, 1912; "Les Arts: Claude Monet," *Paris Journal*, June 12, 1912; Parisiana, "Art et Chiffon," *L'Art et la Mode*, June 15, 1912; "Vision d'Art: Venise par Claude Monet," *Le Gaulois*, June 14, 1912.

56 "Expositions Impressionistes," *La Chronique des Arts et de la Curiosité*, June 15, 1912.

57 November 6, 1908.

58 Camille Mauclair, "Les 'Venise' de Claude Monet," *La Semaine Littéraire*, June 15, 1912, 282. Paul Hayes Tucker compares this compositional strategy with the geometric forms Georges Seurat incorporated into his coastal views of the late 1880s and early 1890s. Tucker, *Monet in the 20th Century*, 56.

59 Rainer Maria Rilke, "Venetian Morning," in Birgit Haustedt, *Rilke's Venice* (Haus Publishing, 2019), Everand.

60 October 16, 1908.

61 October 31, 1908.

62 Monet saw Fauvist paintings at the 1906 Salon d'Automne in Paris. "Claude Monet, *The Palazzo Ducale, Seen from San Giorgio Maggiore*," Guggenheim, guggenheim.org/artwork/3054. See Tucker, *Monet in the 20th Century*, 56. For more on Derain, see Serres, "Exhibiting the Thames," 57.

63 Alexandre, "La Vie Artistique: Claude Monet et Venise."

64 November 14, 1908.

65 Elisabeth Anne McCauley et al., eds., *Gondola Days: Isabella Stewart Gardner and the Palazzo Barbaro Circle* (Isabella Stewart Gardner Museum, 2004), 241–42.

66 Although Monet was a talented draftsman and maintained sketchbooks throughout his career, drawing did not play a prominent role in his mature artistic or commercial practice. See House, *Monet: Nature into Art*, 227–30, and Marianne Matthieu, "Monet as a Draftsman: From Drawings to Inner Images," in *Claude Monet: The Truth of Nature*, ed. Ortrud Westheider et al. (Prestel, 2019), 34–41.
67 Gustave Geffroy, "La Venise de Claude Monet," *La Dépêche*, May 30, 1912.
68 November 25, 1908.
69 See McCauley et al., *Gondola Days*, 242. On October 5, Alice noted, "We had to put the canopy on the gondola to avoid being made ill by the sun." Again on October 25, she wrote, "So that Monet could paint outside, we had to take the covered gondola with its black cabin."
70 Both of these images appeared as photogravures in *Camera Work*—Coburn's in 1908 and Stieglitz's in 1913.
71 For information on the circumstances surrounding this early footage, see Alexandre Promio, "A Travelogue," trans. Gerard-Jan Claes, *Sabzian*, May 27, 2020, sabzian.be/text/a-travelogue. The pigeons and tourists in Piazza San Marco were also featured in this footage.
72 November 17, 1908.
73 December 3, 1908. Refer to the appendix in this catalogue for a full illustrated list of the thirty-seven works. Monet gave the gondola sketch to his friend Georges Clemenceau.
74 November 28, 1908.
75 Alice to her son Jean-Pierre Hoschedé, October 29, 1908.
76 November 20, 1908.
77 Monet to Carlo Placci, October 20, 1908.
78 October 29, 1908.
79 John Ruskin, *St. Mark's Rest* (John Wiley & Sons, 1877), 4.
80 Lord Byron, *Childe Harold's Pilgrimage*, Canto IV.
81 John Ruskin, *The Stones of Venice*, vol. 1 (George Allen, 1888), 2; originally published in 1851.
82 Thomas Mann, *Death in Venice* 1912; (Vintage Books, 1958), 21.
83 Intérim, "La 'Venise' de Claude Monet," *La Chronique des Arts et de la Curiosité*, June 15, 1912; "Les Arts: Claude Monet," *Paris Journal*, June 12, 1912; Adolphe Tabarant, "Venise: L'Exposition de Claude Monet," *Paris Midi*, May 29, 1912.
84 Geffroy, "La Venise de Claude Monet."
85 Walter Sickert, "French Pictures at Knoedler's Gallery," *The Burlington Magazine* 43, no. 244 (July 1923): 39–40.
86 Mirbeau, *Venise*, n.p. Gustave Geffroy, *Claude Monet: Sa Vie, Son Temps, Son Oeuvre*, 320.
87 Arthur Symons, "Venice," All Poetry, allpoetry.com/poem/8529017-Venice-by-Arthur-Symons.
88 Théodore Duret, *Les Peintres Impressionnistes* (Harvard University Press, 1878), 19; Louis Gillet, essay first published in 1924, in *Trois Variations sur Claude Monet* (Plon, 1927), 71.
89 Gillet, *Trois Variations*, 71.
90 Claude Monet to Alice Monet, October 30, 1886.
91 Georges Lecomte, "Un Radieux Poème à la Gloire de Venise," *Le Matin*, June 3, 1912.
92 Piguet, *Monet et Venise*, 61.
93 "Monet, the Artist," *The Lewiston Daily Sun*, January 24, 1905, quoted in Jennifer A. Thompson, "Unveiling the Fogs of London: The Year-long Debut of the Thames Series," in *Monet and London*, 78.
94 For Monet's inner vision see Mathieu, "Monet as a Draftsman," and Angelica Daneo, "'These Palm Trees Are Driving Me Crazy': Monet, the South, and the Intentional Motif," in *Claude Monet: The Truth of Nature*, 34–41 and 42–49.
95 Gustave Geffroy, "Salon de 1887. VI. Hors du Salon: Claude Monet," *La Justice*, June 2, 1887, quoted in Steven Z. Levine, *Monet, Narcissus, and Self-Reflection* (University of Chicago Press, 1994), 72.
96 Marcel Proust, *In Search of Lost Time*, vol. 5, ed. D. J. Enright (Random House, 2010), 852.
97 Geffroy, *Claude Monet: Sa Vie, Son Temps, Son Oeuvre*, 320.
98 Claude Monet in conversation with Herman Bang, *Bergens Tidende*, April 6, 1895, quoted in Wildenstein, *Monet: Biographie et Catalogue Raisonné*, 304.
99 October 18, 1908.
100 Claude Monet to Paul Durand-Ruel, October 19, 1908, and November 4, 1908. Claude Monet to Gaston Bernheim-Jeune, October 25, 1908. Alice Monet to Germaine Salerou, October 14, 1908, October 18, 1908, and October 23, 1908.
101 At this point, Monet thought he'd be going back to Venice for another round of work. For more on Durand-Ruel's involvement as a financial partner—seemingly unbeknownst to the artist—see the essay by Félicie Faizand de Maupeou in this volume.
102 December 7, 1909.
103 Alice Monet to Germaine Salerou, February 2 and February 3, 1910, quoted in Guillaud and Guillaud, *Claude Monet at the Time of Giverny*, 275–76.
104 October 6, 1908.
105 November 11, 1910.
106 Maurice Guillemot, "De Venise à Giverny," *Le Siècle*, May 27, 1912. It was not until much later in his career that the fact that Monet regularly worked on and finished paintings in his studio became more widely known. See House, *Monet: Nature into Art*, 147–56.
107 Claude Monet to Alice Monet, November 8, 1886.
108 To Paul Durand-Ruel, October 10, 1911; to Gaston Bernheim-Jeune, October 17, 1911.
109 To Blanche Hoschedé, December 4, 1911.
110 To Joseph Bernheim-Jeune, February 1, 1912.
111 To Germaine Salerou, April 26, 1912. It should be stressed that in letters to close friends and family throughout his career Monet expressed doubt and even hatred toward his works in progress, even to the point of destroying some of them.
112 May 10, 1912.
113 See the appendix in this volume, which offers an illustrated list of all thirty-seven of Monet's Venice paintings and indicates the twenty-nine included in the Bernheim-Jeune exhibition. One of the eight paintings not exhibited in that show was sold by Monet the following year to Bernheim-Jeune. Of the remaining seven, one was given by Monet to Mary Hunter, one to his friend Georges Clemenceau, one he sold to a Japanese collector, and the remaining four were sold after Monet's death. For more, see Félicie Faizand de Maupeou's essay.
114 June 7, 1912. (The articles referenced are Geffroy, "La Venise de Claude Monet" and Gustave Geffroy, "Claude Monet," *La Vie*, June 1, 1912.)
115 To Gustave Geffroy, July 6, 1912. In her book about Monet, Marthe de Fels recounts Monet's feelings about his Venice paintings—quoting him as calling them "detestable," although it is not clear how reliable these quotes are, given that in teh book Fels has Monet erroneously stating that he went to Venice twice. Marthe de Fels, *La Vie de Claude Monet* (Librairie Gallimard, 1929), 190.
116 To Gaston and Joseph Bernheim-Jeune, April 1, 1912.
117 Alexandre, "La Vie Artistique: Claude Monet et Venise."
118 See *Monet: The Late Years*; Anthony Portulese, "A Phenomenology of Display: Monet's L'Orangerie, the Panorama Rotunda, and the History of Proto-Installation Art," *Rutgers Art Review* 37 (2021); and Félicie Faizand de Maupeou, "An Unprecedented Artistic Gesture: The Exhibition of Monet's Water Lilies at the Orangerie des Tuileries," *exposure* 3, no. 17 (2017).
119 October 6, 1908.
120 Quoted in Marc Elder, *À Giverny, Chez Claude Monet* (Bernheim-Jeune, 1924), 53.
121 Louis Gillet, *Trois Variations*, 81–82.
122 Alexandre, *Claude Monet*, 110.
123 Tucker, *Monet in the 20th Century*, 49.
124 Alexandre, *Claude Monet*, 110.

ELENA MARCHETTI, pp 125–35
(translated by Natalie Danford)

1 Gustave Geffroy, *Claude Monet: Sa Vie, Son Oeuvre. Neuf Reproductions hors Texte*. (G. Crès et Cie, 1924), 156.
2 Rainer Maria Rilke, "Late Autumn in Venice," in *The New Poems: The Other Part*, trans. Len Krisak (Boydell & Brewer, 2015), 295.
3 Gabriele D'Annunzio, *L'Allegoria dell'Autunno: Omaggio Offerto a Venezia* (Roberto Paggi, 1895), n.p.
4 Henri de Régnier, *L'Altana, ou la Vie Vénitienne* (1899–1924) (Mercure de France, 1928), 184.
5 Reported in various editions of the newspapers *La Gazzetta, L'Adriatico, and La Difesa* of September 29 to December 7, 1908.
6 Railway schedule, *La Gazzetta di Venezia*, October 1, 1908.
7 Alice Monet to Germaine Salerou, October 5, 1908, in Philippe Piguet, *Monet et Venise* (Éditions Herscher, 1986). All subsequent references to Alice Monet's letters come from this source unless otherwise cited, and all of Alice Monet's letters are written to Germaine Salerou unless otherwise cited.
8 Régnier, *L'Altana*, 183, 196, 206.
9 October 26, 1908. "Pioggia e Pioggia," *L'Adriatico*, October 26, 1908. The article noted, "The tide is very high, but only the lowest points in the city have flooded."
10 October 31, 1908.
11 November 30, 1908.
12 November 18, 1908.
13 I consulted a wide range of publications from the time period in question. Newspapers: *La Difesa*, July 10–December 26, 1908; *La Gazzetta*, September 29–December 25, 1908; *Il Gazzettino*, July 1–December 27, 1908; *L'Adriatico*, July 1–December 25, 1908. Periodicals: *Il Leone di San Marco*, October–December 1908; *Sior Tonin Bonagrazia*, October–December 1908; and *Secolo Novo*, October–December 1908. Grateful acknowledgment to Juliette Ardissone and Gabriel Barnagaud for their assistance.
14 See Gianfranco Pertot, *Venice: Extraordinary Maintenance* (Paul Holberton Publishing, 2004), 82–85; Margaret Plant, *Venice, Fragile City: 1797–1997* (Yale University Press, 2002), 256–58; "L'Inchiesta sulle Abitazioni," *Il Gazzettino*, November 13, 1908. These conditions were lamented in various reports over the years (1891, 1900, 1910). Implementation of the regulatory plan began in 1891 and was expected to take forty-two years. When Monet was in Venice, municipal police were performing house-to-house inspections in the San Marco neighborhood to investigate living conditions.
15 See *Venezia, Città Industriale: Gli Insediamenti Produttivi del 19o Secolo* (Assessorato alla Cultura e alle Belle Arti, 1980). See also the essay by Jonathan P. Ribner in this volume. According to Elsa Gregori, "Traditionally accustomed only to real estate investments, Venetian inhabitants were not able to explore other possibilities, while French, German and Austrian entrepreneurs did not waste the opportunity to take part in the industrial activities." Elsa Gregori, *Palace of Wonders Venice: History of the Palaces, Families and Events That Shaped the Insula of St. Moisè* (Supernova, 2020).
16 See Giandomenico Romanelli, *Venezia Ottocento: L'Architettura e l'Urbanistica* (Albrizzi, 1988); Giuseppe Pavanello and Giandomenico Romanelli, eds., *Venezia nell'Ottocento* (Electa, 1983); Giandomenico Romanelli, "Venezia nell'Unità d'Italia," in Giorgio Bellavitis and Giandomenico Romanelli, *Venezia* (Laterza, 1985), 196–255; Giandomenico Romanelli, "Dalla Storia alla Modernità: Materiali per un Secolo di Architettura Veneziana: l'Ottocento," *Bollettino dei Civici Musei Veneziani di Arte e Storia* 31 (1987): 1–4, 5–83. See also Pertot, *Venice*, 82–111; and Plant, *Venice, Fragile City*, 159–230. For useful documentary photographs, see Alvise Zorzi, Venezia ritrovata 1895-1939 (Arnoldo Mondadori Editore, Milano 1995).
17 Romanelli, "Dalla Storia," 15, 40.
18 Romanelli, "Dalla Storia," 16–17, 43–46; Gregori, *Palace of Wonders Venice*, 82–83.
19 Romanelli, "Dalla Storia," 18–19; "Le Luci di Venezia," *Arredo & Città* 33, no. 2 (2022): 136–55.
20 Clemens F. Kusch, ed., Eugenio Miozzi, Venezia tra Innovazione e Tradizione 1931-1969 (La Toletta, 2023). Both bridges were designed by Eugenio Miozzi.
21 Also in 1908, the Rialto fish market designed by Domenico Rupolo and Cesare Laurenti opened. Important architects in the years from 1890 to 1915

included Giuseppe Torres and Giovanni Sardi.

22 *La Gazzetta*, August 23, 1908, September 8, 1908, October 1, 3, 4, and 5, 1908; *Il Gazzettino*, September 16, 1908, October 2, 3, 4, and 5, 1908; *L'Adriatico*, July 19 and 27, 1908, August 15 and 23, 1908, September 29, 1908, October 1, 4, and 6, 1908; *La Difesa*, July 14, 15, and 18, 1908, October 3, 1908; *Sior Tonin Bonagrazia*, July 25, 1908.

23 *La Gazzetta*, July 11 and 17, 1908, October 3, 7, and 13, 1908, November 25, 1908; *Il Gazzettino*, July 24 and 27, 1908, August 6, 19, and 25, 1908, September 2, 5, and 6, 1908, October 3, 1908, November 25, 1908; *L'Adriatico*, July 17, 24, and 26, 1908, August 19, 1908, September 5 and 6, 1908, October 3 and 7, 1908, November 29, 1908; *La Difesa*, July 25, 1908, August 18, 1908, September 7 and 29, 1908, October 3, 1908. *Esposizione Permanente di Arti e Industrie Veneziane*, September 6–November 30, 1908, open every day from 9 a.m. to 4 p.m. at Ca' Pesaro, free of charge. Just one example of an exhibition review among many is "L'Esposizione di Palazzo Pesaro," *L'Adriatico*, July 17, 1908: "Though that may be accompanied by immoderation or flaws, the fresh mode of thought, the emotional fervor, the desire for novelty, and the quick reaction to any emotional stimulation that are typical of youth are its most potently attractive and richly expressive qualities." See also Luca Massimo Barbero, ed., *Cent'Anni di Collettive* (Cicero, 1999); and Luca Massimo Barbero, ed., *Emblemi d'Arte da Boccioni a Tancredi: Cent'Anni della Fondazione Bevilacqua La Masa 1899–1999* (Electa, 1999).

24 Monet had participated in the three previous iterations of the Biennale (1897, 1903, and 1905), contributing two paintings to each. Per the exhibition catalogues, in 1897 he exhibited *View of Ventimiglia* and *Spring Landscape*. in 1903 he showed *The Pyramids of Port-Coton* and *On the Cliff near Dieppe*; and in 1905 he showed *Sentiero Profondo* and *Au Cap Martin*.

25 Régnier, *L'Altana*, 109.

26 "Il Campanile di San Marco," *L'Adriatico*, September 29, 1908; "Nel Cantiere del Campanile," *La Difesa*, September 29, 1908.

27 "Il Campanile di S. Marco," *L'Adriatico*, August 27, 1908. In an interview, Moretti, an architect and director of the Office for the Conservation of Monuments of Lombardy and the Veneto and chair of the commission for the reconstruction of the Piazza San Marco bell tower: "Venice was actually very fortunate that the Piazza San Marco bell tower collapsed. Without that blaring *sui generis* alarm, much more damage in more serious and irreparable form might have tragically occurred! Upon arriving in Venice, I visited the major monuments and I was amazed and shocked that by some miracle of balance they were still standing." See also Pertot, *Venice*, 103–11.

28 "Per i Monumenti Veneziani. Un Fondo di 500 Mila Lire per i Restauri," *L'Adriatico*, December 12, 1908.

29 "Several churches." October 8, 1908.

30 Henry James, *Italian Hours* (Ecco Press, 1909), 5.

31 While Monet was in Venice, newspapers reported the arrival of the Duke of Connaught, Prince August Wilhelm of Prussia, and Princess Sophie of Greece, among others.

32 Andrea Zannini, *La Costruzione della Città Turistica* (Enciclopedia Treccani, 2002).

33 "Dieci Piccioni di San Marco da Venezia alla California," *L'Adriatico*, December 10, 1908.

34 The currency of the Kingdom of Italy was the lira. The Latin Monetary Union currency also circulated. That was a kind of precursor to the euro used in the member states (France, Italy, Belgium, Switzerland, Greece, Spain, and Austria). Cristina Crisafulli, "Dalla Nascita della Monetazione Moderna alle Soglie della Prima Guerra Mondiale," in *Alle Radici dell'Euro: Quando la Moneta Fa la Storia* (Canova, 2001), 167–69. In Venice, the lira, the franc, the mark, the florin, and the ducat were used interchangeably.

35 "L'Ingresso a Palazzo Ducale," *Il Gazzettino*, September 30, 1908; "La Tassa d'Ingresso nel Palazzo Ducale," *La Gazzetta*, October 2, 1908; "Visite al Palazzo Ducale," *L'Adriatico*, September 30, 1908; "Nel Cantiere del Campanile," *La Difesa*, September 29, 1908. Broken down as follows: one lira to visit the first and second floors, fifty cents for the prisons. Children under the age of nine paid half price. Ferdinand Baccovich, *Souvenir de Venise: Guide Historique Illustré* (Tipo-Litografia Veneziana, 1903), 30; Camillo Tonini, "The Light in the Venice Ducal Palace," in *From Darkness to Light*, 82. In 1902 a ticket cost 1.20 francs (or lire). Entry to the Palazzo Ducale required a ticket beginning in 1873.

36 "I Monumenti di Torcello," *L'Adriatico*, November 30, 1908.

37 "Dipinto del Guariento nella Sala del Maggior Consiglio," Archivio Storico della Soprintendenza Archeologia, Belle Arti e Paesaggio per il Comune di Venezia e Laguna, No. 13 A 5–6.

38 "Dipinto del Guariento nella Sala del Maggior Consiglio," Archivio Storico della Soprintendenza Archeologia, Belle Arti e Paesaggio per il Comune di Venezia e Laguna, No. 9 A 5–6. The Tintoretto painting was hung on the wall again on May 22, 1909.

39 Paolo Caliari, known as Paolo Veronese, *Adorazione dei Magi* (1582), oil on canvas, Gallerie dell'Accademia, Venice (inv. no. 955). Francesco Zanotto, *Il Palazzo Ducale di Venezia*, vol. 3 (Antonelli, 1858), 1–7; Sandra Moschini Marconi, *Gallerie dell'Accademia di Venezia: Opere d'Arte del Secolo XVI*, vol. 3 (Istituto Poligrafico dello Stato, 1962), 87–89. The work, originally located in the oratory of the church of San Nicolò della Lattuga ai Frari, was removed after suppression of the church by Napoleonic decree. In 1826, it was moved to the Palazzo Ducale, and it was transferred to the Gallerie dell'Accademia on April 9, 1909.

40 October 6, 1908.

41 Henry James, "Venice, an Early Impression," in *Italian Hours*, 53. James wrote these lines in 1872.

42 Baccovich, *Souvenir*, 43.

43 Demetrio Sonaglioni, "Light in the Scuola Grande di San Rocco," in Mamoli Zorzi and Manthorne, *From Darkness to Light*, 71–78.

44 *L'Adriatico*, October 28 and 31, 1908, November 2 and 3, 1908.

45 Archivio Storico del Museo Correr, 1908, 11.

46 October 5, 1908 and October 6, 1908.

47 Jill Shaw posits that the fact that Monet bought new materials on-site means that "presumably . . . he was painting more than he had originally intended." Jill Shaw, "Entry for Cat. 45. *Venice, Palazzo Dario*, 1908," in Gloria Groom and Jill Shaw, *Monet Paintings and Drawings at the Art Institute of Chicago*, publications .artic.edu/node/135622. The store was only two hundred meters from the Grand Hotel Britannia, on the main street that connects Piazza San Marco to Campo Santo Stefano, which in turn leads to Palazzo Barbaro.

48 The store advertised in the catalogue for the third Venice Biennale in 1899 and was listed in the *Guida del Commercio e dell'Industria di Venezia* of 1902.

49 *Il Catalogo Generale di Giorgio de Chirico: Perché Dà Fastidio a Paolo Baldacci?*, Fondazione Giorgio e Isa de Chirico, 8–10, fondazionedechirico.org/il-catalogo-generale-perche-da-fastidio-a-paolo-baldacci-una-verita-semplice/.

50 Daniel Wildenstein, *Claude Monet: Biographie et Catalogue Raisonné*, vols. 1–5 (Wildenstein Institute and La Bibliothèque des Arts, 1974–1991). Monet gave Mary Hunter a painting he had done in Venice, *San Giorgio Maggiore*. Daniel Wildenstein, *Monet or the Triumph of Impressionism*, vol. 4 (Taschen, 1996), 818.

51 Sargent's *Mrs. Charles Hunter* portrait was shown at the 1907 Biennale, along with his celebrated portrait of Lord Ribblesdale (1902, National Gallery, London). *VII Esposizione Internazionale d'Arte della Città di Venezia, 1907* (C. Ferrari, 1907), 12–13.

52 See John Pemble, *Venice Rediscovered* (Clarendon Press, 1995).

53 Elisabeth Anne McCauley et al., eds., *Gondola Days: Isabella Stewart Gardner and the Palazzo Barbaro Circle* (Isabella Stewart Gardner Museum, 2004), 53–86.

54 McCauley et al., *Gondola Days*, 3–52, 177–90; Nathaniel Silver and Diana Greenwald, *Isabella Stewart Gardner: A Life* (Princeton University Press, 2022), 59–62.

55 Ethel Smyth, *Streaks of Life* (Longmans, Green, and Co., 1921). Smyth's most notable compositions are *Der Wald* (1902) and *The Wreckers* (1906) and the symphony *The Prison* (1931). Smyth had been to Venice at least two previous times; she stayed at Palazzo Contarini Polignac in 1903 and at Ca' Dario in 1904.

56 On Winnaretta Singer in general, see Michael de Cossart, *The Food of Love: Princesse Edmond de Polignac (1865–1943) and Her Salon* (Hamish Hamilton, 1978); Sylvia Kahan, *Music's Modern Muse: A Life of Winnaretta Singer, Princesse de Polignac* (University of Rochester Press, 2003). On Singer's relationship with Smyth, see Cossart, *The Food of Love*, 86–88; Kahan, *Music's Modern Muse*, 133–35, 155–56, 161.

57 Kahan, *Music's Modern Muse*, 110. The Polignacs became enamored with their Venice home during lunch at the Curtises' home in 1900. The prince looked out the window of Palazzo Barbaro, saw Palazzo Contarini-Montecuccoli on the other side of the Grand Canal, and said he would like to live there. His wife then purchased it for him as a birthday gift.

58 In order of purchase: *Champ de Tulipes, Hollande* (1886, Musée d'Orsay, Paris), Wildenstein, *Monet or the Triumph of Impressionism*, 3:403; *L'Église de Varengeville à Contre-jour* (1882, Barber Institute of Fine Arts, Birmingham, UK), Wildenstein, *Monet or the Triumph of Impressionism*, 2:271; *En Norvégienne* (1887, Musée d'Orsay, Paris), Wildenstein, *Monet or the Triumph of Impressionism*, 3:435–36; *Les Dindons* (1877, Musée d'Orsay, Paris), Wildenstein, *Monet or the Triumph of Impressionism*, 2:169–70; Kahan, *Music's Modern Muse*, 45. In 1889, Winnaretta Singer made the single largest donation (2,000 francs) to the funds Monet was collecting to purchase the painting *Olympia* by Édouard Manet and donate it to the Louvre. Kahan, *Music's Modern Muse*, 142, reports that Singer also owned three Monet paintings (*Pommiers en Fleurs*, *Les Bords de la Seine*, and *La Lecture sous les Arbres*), though this is not confirmed by Wildenstein's catalogue raisonné. For details on acquisition of the paintings: *Champ de Tulipes, Hollande*: Kahan, *Music's Modern Muse*, 72; *Les Dindons:* Cossart, *The Food of Love*, 47, and Kahan, *Music's Modern Muse*, 142; *En Norvégienne*: Kahan, *Music's Modern Muse*, 45–46 and note 50, which reports that Sargent acted as the broker for the purchase the same zyear he did his portrait of Singer, known at the time as Princess Louis de Scey-Montbéliard.

59 Kahan, *Music's Modern Muse*, 111–12; Louis Duchesne, *Correspondance avec Madame Bulteau (1902–1922)* (École Française de Rome, 2009); Jean de Tinan, *Lettres à Madame Bulteau* (Honoré Champion, 2019); Tom Stammers, "Rooms of their own — the female collectors who reshaped French society," *Apollo*, November 29, 2020. Palazzo Dario was owned by Isabelle Crombez, Countess de la Baume-Pluvinel, who purchased it in 1898.

60 Augustine Bulteau's circle included Anna de Noailles and her sister Hélène, Princess de Caraman-Chimay, as well as Winnaretta Singer. Ethel Smyth was admired and supported by the entire group of women, whom she had met in Paris in 1903. When Palazzo Dario was filled with guests, Countess de la Baume made Palazzo Venier de' Leoni, today the Collezione Peggy Guggenheim, available to others; Régnier, *L'Altana*, 184.

61 Ethel Smyth, *Quatre Mélodies pour Voix et Orchestre de Chambre* (1907) *sur des Poèmes de Régnier* ("Odelette," "La Danse," "Chrysilla," and "Ode Anacréontique").

62 Cecilia Riva, "Austen Henry Layard, Collector and Amateur: Diplomacy, Art History and Collecting in 19th Century Europe" (PhD diss., Università Ca' Foscari, 2019), 126–266; Stefania Ermidoro and Cecilia Riva, *Rethinking Layard 1817–2017* (Istituto Veneto di Scienze Lettere e Arti,

2020), 137–54, 205–20.

63 Enid Layard's Guestbook, British Library, Western Manuscript Collection, MS 50149.

64 Lady Layard's Journal, Baylor University, October 12, 1908.

65 Régnier, *L'Altana*, 212.

66 October 4, 1908.

67 F. T. Marinetti, Umberto Boccioni, Carlo Carra, and Luigi Russolo, "Against Passéist Venice," in *Futurism: An Anthology*, ed. Lawrence Rainey, Christine Poggi, and Laura Wittman (Yale University Press, 2009), 67–70. Jennifer Scappettone, *Killing the Moonlight: Modernism in Venice* (Columbia University Press, 2014), 137–95.

68 Gregori, *Palace of Wonders*, 79 and note 80. Monet was in room 105—now room 1101—on the first floor of guestrooms in Palazzo Badoer Tiepolo Zucchelli. The window where Monet sat to paint was indicated by Alice Monet in the illustrated salutation of a letter to Germaine Salerou dated October 17, 1908.

69 Gregori, *Palace of Wonders*, 74–88. On November 12, 1887, the city voted to give Walther's company a ten-year contract to provide electric light to private parties. Mario Baldin, *La Illuminazione Pubblica a Venezia: Il nuovo Impianto* (Premiata Tipografia di San Lazzaro, 1928), 29–30. In 1889, Walther and Edison di Milano formed the Società Anonima per la Illuminazione Elettrica di Venezia, headquartered in San Luca.

70 Piguet, *Monet et Venise*, 57 note 29; Wildenstein, *Claude Monet*: Biographie et Catalogue Raisonné 54 notes 496 and 497. Electricity was installed at Giverny in 1907. Wildenstein reports that on November 28, 1907, installation of a new electric streetlamp in front of Monet's house was approved.

71 Claire Joyes, *Claude Monet et Giverny* (Chêne, 1985), 94.

72 October 22, 1908.

73 Sarah Quill, "Lighting Up the Darkness: The National Gallery, London," in *From Darkness to Light*, 167–76. For example, the National Gallery in London did not have electric lighting until 1935, and it was the subject of lengthy debate. Reticence about installing electric light in museums was based on a variety of reasons: preference for an "aesthetic of darkness" (Rosella Mamoli Zorzi, "John Ruskin and Henry James in the Enchanting Darkness of the Scuola Grande di San Rocco," in *From Darkness to Light*, 53–70). The quality of artificial light was no match for natural light (David E. Nye, "The Artificial Lighting Available to European and American Museums, 1800–1915," in *From Darkness to Light*, 39); there were economic concerns, including the cost of installing the system and the cost of extending hours of operation beyond sunset (*From Darkness to Light*, 39). There were also safety concerns, like the risk of fire (Tonini, "The Light in the Venice Ducal Palace," 84).

74 Tonini, "The Light in the Venice Ducal Palace," 79–86. The innovation initially was limited to only some parts of the building. Antonio Vendrasco, "La Luce Elettrica nel Palazzo Ducale," *L'Adriatico*, July 13, 1896, quoted in Tonini, "The Light in the Venice Ducal Palace," 84–85. *L'Adriatico* howled at the desecration, lamenting that the installation of electric light "distorts the real nature and cancels the character of the most superb building in the art world."

75 Giuliano Pavon, *La Nascita dell'Energia Elettrica a Venezia*, 1866–1904 (Cartotecnica Veneziana, 2001); Baldin, *La Illuminazione Pubblica*, 28–30. At a city council meeting on January 8, 1886, Count Francesco Donà requested that an electric lighting grid be installed. In August, a trial plan for Giudecca was approved. In 1888, the municipality began to keep the public gardens open until midnight, as they were illuminated with electric lighting. In 1887, the Municipal Office approved Walther's project, and in 1889, Walther and Edison instituted the Società Anonima per l'Illuminazione Elettrica di Venezia. In 1925, it was decided that a new plant for the city would be funded.

76 "Le Luci di Venezia," 38.

77 Filippo Grimani, *Il Gazzettino*, December 28, 1907, quoted in "Le Luci di Venezia," 38.

78 Baldin, *La Illuminazione Pubblica*, 26.

79 "Le Luci di Venezia," 38.

80 "Felici Esperimenti di Illuminazione in Piazza San Marco: Dalla Luce Verde alla Luce Rossa," *Il Gazzettino*, September 18, 1909.

81 Nye, "The Artificial Lighting Available," 25–40.

ANDRÉ DOMBROWSKI, pp 137–45

1 Georges Besson, "Exposition Claude Monet (Galerie Bernheim-Jeune)," *La Phalange*, June 20, 1912; and Louis Vauxelles, "La 'Venise' de Claude Monet," *Gil Blas*, May 29, 1912.

2 On the Impressionist instant and period time technologies, see André Dombrowski, *Monet's Minutes: Impressionism and the Industrialization of Time* (Yale University Press, 2023).

3 Claude Monet to Gustave Geffroy, October 7, 1890, in Daniel Wildenstein, *Claude Monet: Biographie et Catalogue Raisonné*, vols 1–5 (Wildenstein Institute and La Bibliothèque des Arts, 1974–1991). All subsequent references to Claude Monet's letters come from this source unless otherwise cited. This translation from Claude Monet, *Monet by Himself: Paintings, Drawings, Pastels, Letters*, ed. Richard Kendall (Barnes & Noble, 2004), 120.

4 Gustave Geffroy, "La Venise de Claude Monet," *La Dépêche*, May 30, 1912.

5 Henry James, *Italian Hours* (Houghton Mifflin, 1909), 44.

6 Richard Thomson, *Monet & Architecture* (National Gallery, 2018), 207.

7 Geffroy, "La Venise de Claude Monet"; see also Camille Mauclair, "Les 'Venise' de Claude Monet," *La Semaine Littéraire*, June 15, 1912, 281–83.

8 Parisiana, "Art et Chiffon," *L'Art et la Mode*, June 15, 1912; Arsène Alexandre, "Venise, Monet et la Peinture de Paysage," *Comoedia*, June 1, 1912.

9 Intérim, "Expositions Impressionnistes: Exposition d'Ensemble (Hôtel des 'Arts'); Les Portraits de Renoir (Galerie Durand-Ruel); La 'Venise' de Claude Monet (Galerie Bernheim)," *La Chronique des Arts et de la Curiosité*, June 15, 1912. Jean Variot, "Les 'Venise' de Claude Monet," *L'Univers*, June 21, 1912.

10 Joachim Pissarro, *Monet and the Mediterranean* (Rizzoli, 1997), 179. On Monet's painting schedule in Venice, see also Philippe Piguet, *Monet et Venise* (Éditions Herscher, 1986), 60.

11 Alice Monet to Germaine Salerou, October 12, 1908, in *Monet et Venise*. All subsequent references to Alice Monet's letters come from this source unless otherwise cited, and all of Alice Monet's letters are written to Germaine Salerou unless otherwise cited. The letters containing the schedule were first quoted in Jacqueline Guillaud and Maurice Guillaud, *Claude Monet at the Time of Giverny* (Centre Culturel du Marais, 1983), 139.

12 October 17, 1908.

13 Pissarro, *Monet and the Mediterranean*, 50.

14 Wildenstein, *Claude Monet*, vol. 4, 236.

15 Pissarro, *Monet and the Mediterranean*, 50.

16 Paul Hayes Tucker, *Monet in the 20th Century* (Yale University Press, 1998), 57.

17 Paul Joanne, *Italie: Collection des Guides-Joanne* (Hachette, 1901), 87–88 (italics in the original). Monet purchased the 1907 edition; see Ségolène Le Men et al., *La Bibliothèque de Monet* (Citadelles & Mazenod, 2013), 247. Richard Thomson has interestingly made the guidebooks that Monet read in preparation for his trip key to an interpretation of the paintings; see Thomson, *Monet & Architecture*, 191–207.

18 Pierre Gusman, *Venise* (Renouard, H. Laurens, 1907), 62, cited in Thomson, *Monet & Architecture*, 196.

19 Geffroy, "La Venise de Claude Monet."

20 James, *Italian Hours*, 26.

21 James, *Italian Hours*, 30; see also 39.

22 September 29, October 1, and December 5, 1908.

23 Joanne, *Italie*, 41; and Gregorio Gattinoni, *Il Campanile di San Marco in Venezia: Monografia Storica* (Zuanne Fabbris, 1910). See also, among others, Carlo M. Cipolla, *Le Macchine del Tempo: L'Orologio e la Società, 1300–1700* (Il Mulino, 1981).

24 I take the term from historian Vanessa Ogle, *The Global Transformation of Time*, 1870–1950 (Harvard University Press, 2015), 9.

25 Robert Schram, *Adria-Zeit* (published by the author, 1889). See also Ogle, *Global Transformation of Time*, 27–28.

26 Michael Downing, *Spring Forward: The Annual Madness of Daylight Saving Time* (Shoemaker & Hoard, 2005).

27 Gustav Bilfinger, *Der Bürgerliche Tag: Untersuchungen über den Beginn des Kalendertages im Classischen Altertum und im Christlichen Mittelalter* (W. Kohlhammer, 1888); and Bilfinger, *Die Mittelalterlichen Horen und die Modernen Stunden: Ein Beitrag zur Kulturgeschichte* (W. Kohlhammer, 1892). I doubt Monet read Bilfinger himself, but the existence of this literature points to a substantive interest in the topic during Monet's life.

28 Pissarro, *Monet and the Mediterranean*, 146.

29 Pissarro, *Monet and the Mediterranean*, 51.

30 Georges Clemenceau, "Révolution des Cathédrales," *La Justice*, May 20, 1895.

31 Marc Elder, *À Giverny, Chez Claude Monet* (Bernheim-Jeune, 1924), 9.

32 Monet to Gustave Geffroy, December 20, 1908.

JONATHAN P. RIBNER, pp 147–53

This essay was developed from Jonathan Ribner, "The Poetics of Pollution," in Katharine Lochnan et al., *Turner Whistler Monet: Impressionist Visions* (Art Gallery of Ontario/Tate, 2004), 51–63, 236–38. I am grateful to Anna Lea Albright, Melissa Buron, Natalie Danford, Elena Marchetti, Karen Serres, Richard Slovak, and Lisa Small for their contributions, whether informational or editorial.

1 For recent commentary on the products of those campaigns, see Karen Serres, ed., *Monet and London: Views of the Thames* (Paul Holberton Publishing, 2024). For the London paintings, see also Richard Thomson's excellent *Monet & Architecture* (National Gallery, 2018), 171–89.

2 For Monet's Venice paintings, see Thomson, *Monet & Architecture*, 191–207. Elena Marchetti alerted me that Monet's visit coincided with the Veneto's fog season (late October and November). Foggy views of Venice were painted by John Singer Sargent (*Venice in Grey Weather*, 1880–81, private collection) and Pierre-Auguste Renoir (*Fog in Venice*, 1881, private collection), discussed and reproduced in Hugh Honour and John Fleming, *The Venetian Hours of Henry James, Whistler and Sargent* (Bulfinch Press, 1991), 57–59. For an evocative, personal discussion of Venetian and London fog by a fog connoisseur, see Laura Pashby, *Chasing Fog: Finding Enchantment in a Cloud* (Simon & Schuster, 2024), chapters 8 and 9.

3 Guillaume Apollinaire, "La Vie Artistique: Claude Monet," *L'Intransigeant*, May 31, 1912.

4 For a discussion of the *enveloppe*, see John House, *Monet: Nature into Art* (Yale University Press, 1986), 220–25. House indicates that the term had become commonplace in French art discourse by the late 1880s. See also John House, "Monet: The Last Impressionist," in Paul Hayes Tucker, *Monet in the 20th Century* (Yale University Press, 1998), 9; and Evan R. Firestone, *Mist and Fog in British and European Painting: Fuseli, Friedrich, Turner, Monet and Their Contemporaries* (Lund Humphries, 2023), chapter 4.

5 Anna Lea Albright and Peter Huybers, "Paintings by Turner and Monet Depict Trends in 19th Century Air Pollution," *PNAS (Proceedings of the National Academy of Sciences)* 120, no. 6 (January 31, 2023), accessed August 17, 2024, doi.org/10.1073/pnas.2219118120. Paintings by Whistler (six), Gustave Caillebotte (seven), Camille Pissarro (four), and Berthe Morisot (one) are also considered. For critiques of these claims, see

Sebastian Smee, "Art History, Not Air Pollution, Explains Changes in Monet's Paintings," *Washington Post*, February 1, 2023;
and Michael F. Marmor, "Most Paintings by Turner and Monet Show Stylistic Evolution, Not Changes in Pollution," *PNAS* 120, no. 16 (April 10, 2023), accessed August 17, 2024, doi.org/10.1073/pnas.2302177120. In response, see Albright and Huybers, "Reply to Marmor: Multiple Perspectives for Appreciating the Meaning and Beauty of Turner and Monet Paintings," *PNAS* 120, no. 16 (April 10, 2023), accessed August 17, 2024, pnas.org/doi/abs/10.1073/pnas.2303372120; and in support of Albright and Huybers, see John E. Thornes, "Polluted Realism in the Art of Turner and Monet," *PNAS* 120, no. 10 (March 1, 2023), accessed August 17, 2024, pnas.org/doi/10.1073/pnas.2300462120.

6 See Jonathan Ribner, "The Poetics of Pollution," in Lochnan et al., *Turner Whistler Monet*. For recent additions to this line of research, see Frances Fowle, "Painting Pollution: Industrialism, Impressionism and Monet's Thames Series," in Serres, *Monet and London*, 87–101; and Michael Lobel, *Van Gogh and the End of Nature* (Yale University Press, 2024). That the visual effects in Monet's London paintings were conditioned by fog polluted with coal smoke is indicated in Paul Hayes Tucker, "The Revolution in the Garden: Monet in the Twentieth Century," in Tucker, *Monet in the 20th Century*, 27 and 286 note 56; and in George T. M. Shackelford and MaryAnne Stevens, "Catalogue," in Tucker, *Monet in the 20th Century*, 128.

7 For Monet's claim to an innocent eye, see the recollection of his advice during a painting lesson, published by Boston artist Lilla Cabot Perry in 1927 (she met Monet in 1889), in Linda Nochlin, ed., *Impressionism and Post-Impressionism, 1874–1904*, Sources & Documents in the History of Art (Prentice-Hall, 1966), 35–36.

8 William C. Seitz, *Claude Monet* (Abrams, 1960), 10.

9 Claude Monet to Gustave Geffroy, December 7, 1908, in Daniel Wildenstein, *Claude Monet: Biographie et Catalogue Raisonné*, vols 1–5 (Wildenstein Institute and La Bibliothèque des Arts, 1974–1991). All subsequent references to Claude Monet's letters come from this source unless otherwise cited.

10 For the Molino Stucky, see Dennis Romano, *Venice: The Remarkable History of the Lagoon City* (Oxford University Press, 2024), chapter 18; *Venezia, Città Industriale: Gli Insediamenti Produttivi del 19o Secolo* (Assessorato alla Cultura e alle Belle Arti, 1980), 107–9, including a photograph (post-1897) of the mill with dark smoke billowing from two chimneys (fig. 25d); Richard J. Goy, *Venice: An Architectural Guide* (Yale University Press, 2010), 430; and Margaret Plant, *Venice, Fragile City, 1797–1997* (Yale University Press, 2002), 173–74, 430. For the mill's architecture, see Giandomenico Romanelli, "Alla Ricerca di un Linguaggio," in *Venezia, Città Industriale*, 30. The Molino Stucky replaced a smaller, steam-powered Stucky mill complex, which had begun operating in 1884 on the same site, formerly occupied by the church of Santi Biagio e Cataldo, secularized by Napoleon and demolished in 1882.

11 Anna Lea Albright kindly shared data pertaining to sulfur dioxide emissions in nineteenth-century Venice. For Venetian industry, see Romano, *Venice*, chapter 18; and *Venezia, Città Industriale*. For air quality, see Michael Stolberg, *Wolken über der Serenissima: Eine Kleine Geschichte der Luftverschmutzung in Venedig* (Centro Tedesco di Studi Veneziani, 1996). For a descriptive list of Venetian industrial sites, see Nicola Randolfi, "Industrie e Attività a Venezia agli Inizi del '900," in *Quaderni: Documenti sulla Manutenzione Urbana di Venezia* 11, no. 4 (September 2000): 34–40, accessed August 17. 2024, insula.it/images/pdf/resource/quadernipdf/Q04-05.pdf.

12 Smoke rising from industrial sites on Giudecca is visible in two pastels and an etching by Whistler dating from his sojourn in Venice (September 1879–November 1880). See Alastair Grieve, *Whistler's Venice* (Yale University Press, 2000), 114–16.

13 For the San Girolamo mill, see Adolfo Bernardello, "Il Molino a Vapore di S. Girolamo a Venezia (1840–1870)," *Atti dell'Istituto Veneto di Scienze, Lettere ed Arti, Classe di Scienze Morali, Lettere, ed Arti* 154, no. 2 (1995–96): 257–90, and 257 note 1 for the quotation from Ruskin from *The Complete Works of John Ruskin* (J. Wanamaker, n.d.), 357. Ruskin's mention of "smog" predates common use of the term. For the mill, see also Romano, *Venice*, chapter 17 and chapter 17 note 103. The abandoned church was converted to a mill (closed in 1870) at the initiative of a Bavarian entrepreneur, Friedrich Christian Oexle, who purchased the property in 1840.

14 *"Ten O'Clock," a Lecture by James A. McNeill Whistler* (Thomas Bird Mosher, 1920), 13. Regarding this famous passage, Honour and Fleming wonder, "Was he thinking of Venice or of London, or of both?" *Venetian Hours*, 39.

15 Light intensity is distinct from color (i.e., hue) intensity, also known as saturation or chroma, which corresponds to a color's purity. Hue intensity is diminished by tinting (the addition of white), which has a dulling effect.

16 Gustave Geffroy, "La Venise de Claude Monet," *La Dépêche*, May 30, 1912.

17 The figures are from Anthony S. Wohl, *Endangered Lives: Public Health in Victorian Britain* (Harvard University Press, 1983), 21. See also Peter Brimblecombe, *The Big Smoke: A History of Air Pollution in London since Medieval Times* (Methuen, 1987).

18 René Gimpel, *Diary of an Art Dealer*, trans. John Rosenberg (Farrar, Straus and Giroux, 1966), 73. For a rich study of response to London fog by writers and artists, see Christine L. Corton, *London Fog: The Biography* (Belknap Press of Harvard University Press, 2015).

19 O'Rell indicates that, although pea-soupers were not as frequent as his compatriots believe, fog is always present in London. Max O'Rell, *John Bull et son Île: Moeurs Anglaises Contemporaines* (Calmann Lévy, 1883), 87.

20 Camille Mauclair, "Les 'Venise' de Claude Monet," *La Semaine Littéraire*, June 15, 1912, 282.

21 Robert L. Herbert, *Monet on the Normandy Coast: Tourism and Painting, 1867–1886* (Yale University Press, 1994), 6.

22 For Monet's growing affluence, see Michael J. Call, *Claude Monet, Free Thinker: Radical Republicanism, Darwin's Science, and the Evolution of Impressionist Aesthetics* (Peter Lang, 2015), 123; and Virginia Spate, *Claude Monet: The Color of Time* (Thames and Hudson, 1992), 201.

23 For the purchase of the Venice paintings by the Bernheim-Jeune brothers (December 18, 1908), see Jackie Wullschläger, *Monet: The Restless Vision* (Allen Lane, 2023), 384.

24 For Monet's competitive travel to locations with tourist appeal previously represented by other painters, see Richard Thomson, "Monet and Other People's Places: Travel, Tourism, and Competition," in *Claude Monet: The Truth of Nature*, ed. Angelica Daneo et al. (Prestel, 2019), 60–67.

25 For Anglophobe French opinion regarding London's fog and darkness, see Jonathan P. Ribner, "The London Sublime," *British Art Journal* 16, no. 2 (Autumn 2015): 83, 88 notes 79 and 80.

26 See John House, "The Impressionist Vision of London," in *Victorian Artists and the City: A Collection of Critical Essays*, ed. Ira Bruce Nadel and F. S. Schwarzbach (Pergamon, 1980), 85.

27 Claude Monet to Alice Monet, March 4, 1900.

28 Mauclair, "Les 'Venise' de Claude Monet," 282.

29 André Michel, "Promenades aux Salons," *Journal des Débats Politiques et Littéraires*, June 5, 1912.

30 Geffroy, "La Venise de Claude Monet." Geffroy's point was echoed by Honour and Fleming, who characterized the Venetian paintings as "a peculiar synthesis of observation and recollection—evocations, suffused with the warm glow of memory but veiled as if they were a distant souvenir." Honour and Fleming, *Venetian Hours*, 157.

31 Evan Charteris, *John Sargent* (William Heinemann, 1927), 171, quoted in Honour and Fleming, *Venetian Hours*, 159.

32 Henry James, "Venice," in *Italian Hours*, ed. John Auchard (Pennsylvania State University Press, 1992), 12; originally published in *Century Magazine* 25 (November 1882): 3–23.

33 In 1540, Venice's historic center counted 129,971 inhabitants; as of June 30, 2015, the population had decreased to 56,072. Salvatore Settis, *If Venice Dies*, trans. André Naffis-Sahely (New Vessel Press, 2016), 8–11; originally published in Italian as *Se Venezia Muore* in 2014.

34 Octave Mirbeau, *Venise* (Bernheim-Jeune, 1912), n.p.

35 Mirbeau, *Venise*, n.p.

36 Mirbeau, *Venise*, n.p.

37 Mirbeau's "rose veil" is interpreted as referring to the mist enshrouding Venice, in Sylvie Patin, "The Last Act: Turner, Whistler and Monet in Venice," in Lochnan et al., *Turner Whistler Monet*, 205.

38 Mirbeau, *Venise*, n.p.

39 Octave Mirbeau, "Claude Monet," *Le Figaro*, March 10, 1889.

40 See the catalogue entry by Sylvie Patin in Lochnan et al., *Turner Whistler Monet*, 230, no. 106.

41 For the caricatures, see "Oscar Monet, Caricaturist," in James A. Ganz and Richard Kendall, *The Unknown Monet: Pastels and Drawings* (Clark Art Institute, 2007), 33–53.

42 The relationship of the caricatures to Monet's painting is addressed by Ann Cannon in "Distorted Impressions and the Art of Exaggeration: Monet's Caricatures" (MA scholarly paper, Boston University, 2018).

43 Monet's claim that he wished to have been born blind was recorded by Lilla Cabot Perry, as cited in note 7 above. In the eighteenth century, Britons on the Grand Tour arrived in Venice nursing a priori assumptions: "The milordi who stopped there on the way to or from Rome went to see what they had already imagined—and the fantasies through which the city was filtered came not from reality but from a potent set of pre-existing myths." Bruce Redford, *Venice & the Grand Tour* (Yale University Press, 1996), 51.

44 James, "Venice," 7.

45 Henry James, "Venice: An Early Impression," dated by James 1872, originally published 1873, in *Italian Hours*, 52.

FÉLICIE FAIZAND DE MAUPEOU, pp 155–61
(translated by Mark Polizzotti)

1 Octave Mirbeau, *Venise* (Bernheim-Jeune, 1912), n.p.

2 Philippe Piguet, *Monet et Venise* (Éditions Herscher, 1986), 19.

3 This correspondence was published by Daniel Wildenstein in *Claude Monet: Biographie et Catalogue Raisonné*, vols. 1–5 (Wildenstein Institute and La Bibliothèque des Arts, 1974–1991).

4 Claude Monet to Gaston Bernheim-Jeune, October 25, 1908, in Wildenstein, *Claude Monet: Biographie et Catalogue Raisonné*. All subsequent references to Claude Monet's letters come from this source unless otherwise cited.

5 November 4, 1908.

6 December 29, 1908.

7 December 10, 1885. In writing "had I refused," Monet is alluding to the conditions Georges Petit set regarding the artist's participation in his exhibition: not to show any paintings belonging to Durand-Ruel and not to participate in the Impressionist group show (which proved to be the last one).

8 François Thiébault-Sisson, "Claude Monet: Les Années d'Épreuve," *Le Temps*, November 26, 1900.

9 December 30, 1908. Apparently, the contract mentioned canvases brought back from Italy in general, not only from Venice. This contract is not at the Musée Marmottan Monet, which holds the artist's papers and archives that remained at Giverny. Despite requests to

the Bernheim archives, I was not allowed to consult the document, or even confirm that it is housed there.

10 February 1, 1912. "Still, I do not wish to cause you any inconvenience, should you no longer find our agreement beneficial."

11 March 29, 1912.

12 April 8, 1912.

13 To Gaston and Joseph Bernheim-Jeune, April 12, 1912.

14 To Paul Durand-Ruel, April 15, 1912.

15 To Paul Durand-Ruel, May 10, 1912.

16 To Joseph Bernheim-Jeune, April 18, 1912.

17 To Paul Durand-Ruel, May 10, 1912.

18 Adolphe Tabarant, "Venise: L'Exposition Claude Monet," *Paris Midi*, May 29, 1912.

19 Georges Lecomte, "Un Radieux Poème à la Gloire de Venise," *Le Matin*, June 3, 1912.

20 Notably in the *Chronique des Arts*, June 15, 1912: "After a wait of four years, Claude Monet is exhibiting his series of Venice paintings (1908)."

21 To the Bernheim-Jeune brothers, April 8, 1912.

22 "It might seem surprising that Monet, coming after so many others, and especially after the beautiful paintings by Le Sidaner from five years ago, did not seek out less familiar subjects than the banal Rio, Palazzo seen from the water, and Contarini that everyone has done. Perhaps he didn't stay long enough, troubled by too many memories to try to penetrate further into Venice." Camille Mauclair, "Les 'Venise' de Claude Monet," *La Semaine Littéraire*, June 15, 1912, 283.

23 André Michel, *Le Journal des Débats Politiques*, June 5, 1912. "Regardless, his Venice is wholly his own. Faithful to his usual practice, he selected, from among the traditional repertoire of subjects that the 'poor old Lido' offers its painters, several themes whose banality we might have thought would dissuade him ... But what does the pretext matter? The monuments of Venice are of no interest to him. He shows them to us so wobbly and unstable that it looks as if their rotting pilings are about to give way and crumble forever. Before they can disappear, however, the great magician has viewed them, between sky and water, in a mirage of opal, mauve, violet, and orange incantations; he has evoked and orchestrated around these evanescent phantoms the richest and subtlest harmonies, and the Venice of Claude Monet, more fleeting than any other, nonetheless exists from now on."

24 Parisiana, "Art et Chiffon," *L'Art et la Mode*, June 15, 1912. The writer added that Monet instead depicted "the one true Venice of those who love it and cherish its sunsets, with their soft and infinitely melancholy light, or its dawns, translucent as pure opal."

25 Max Goth, *Les Hommes du Jour*, June 15, 1912. Before his words about the vision Monet provides, Goth wrote, "Even yesterday, when we attempted to 'think about' Venice, outmoded clichés, left to us by the likes of Ziem, Baedeker, traveling salesmen, snobs, newlyweds, novels, and romances, clouded our vision. We all knew, obscurely, that we needed the purifying flame of a genius to cleanse that away. Claude Monet understood this and has restored to us, in its full splendor, the Venice of calm monuments reflecting, in the languid flow of its waterways, their immutable stone facades in which history inscribes, in wide, deep strokes, the entire soul of its people: at once fierce and humble, mystical and pagan, proud and tender."

26 Louis Vauxcelles, "La 'Venise' de Claude Monet," *Gil Blas*, May 29, 1912. "I know that he is and remains the master of light. . . . Still, I can't help thinking of the architecture of Canaletto's Venetian palazzos."

27 Mauclair, "Les 'Venise' de Claude Monet," p. 282. "Painters of monuments, from Guardi to Corot, knew this; the Impressionists don't care."

28 Parisiana, "Art et Chiffon." "Monet has given us the beautiful and noble Venice beloved of da Vinci and Tiepolo, Titian and Carpaccio!"

29 Raymond Bouyer, *Bulletin de l'Art Ancien et Moderne*, June 8, 1912. "It's the evanescent, slightly faded, already outmoded formula of vague, cursory Impressionism, which has imperceptibly turned decorative; it shall not erase, in the endless series of painters of Venice, the dreams of a Turner or the precision of a Guardi."

30 "To all those who know the city of lagoons only through the dazzling interpretations of Ziem and his imitators, Monet's views of Venice must seem rather pale and highly disconcerting. Nor do they look like the depictions by Guardi or Canaletto, in which the buildings are rendered with marvelous precision." François Thiébault-Sisson, "An Enchantment of Light and Colour. Venice as Seen by Claude Monet," *Le Temps*, June 11, 1912.

31 "Monet . . . follows in the wake of so many others, in particular the fine Le Sidaner of five years ago . . . [Monet] does not forget Guardi or Whistler, who brought an indispensable concern for drawing to their evocation of Venice." Mauclair, "Les 'Venise' de Claude Monet," 283.

32 Unattributed review in *Chronique des Arts et de la Curiosité*, June 15, 1912. Arsène Alexandre, "La Vie Artistique: Claude Monet et Venise," *Le Figaro*, May 29, 1912, also draws a parallel with music: "It's like a paraphrase of Beethoven's great *molto vivace* 'Durch Leiden Freude, Joy at the Cost of Suffering.'"

33 Tabarant, "Venise: L'Exposition Claude Monet."

34 "It wasn't long before I asked for your friendship, for a preface to the catalogue." To Geffroy, May 2, 1912.

35 Gustave Geffroy, "La Venise de Claude Monet," *La Dépêche*, May 30, 1912. "So it is for all the pages of this poem, in which the reality of things is magnified by another reality, which is that of air and light. Claude Monet is a poet."

36 June 7, 1912.

37 Sixteen at 12,000 francs, equivalent to around 1,500 U.S. dollars at that time and 48,500 U.S. dollars today (nos. 1–5, 7, 14–18, 21, 24, 25, 27, and 29); ten at 10,000 francs, equivalent to 1,200 U.S. dollars in 1912 and 39,000 U.S. dollars today (nos. 9–13, 19, 20, 22, 23, and 26); two at 14,000 (nos. 6 and 28) equivalent to 55,000 current U.S. dollars and 1,700 U.S. dollars in 1912; and one at 15,000, equivalent to 1,800 U.S. dollars in 1912 and now around 60,000 U.S. dollars (no. 8). Prices provided by the Durand-Ruel archives, which I'd like to thank for its help with my research.

38 To Paul Durand-Ruel, March 30, 1908. "As for doing this on the terms you offer, I flatly refuse. I'm no beginner willing to hold a trial exhibition or bow to such demands. And if you want this exhibition to take place this year, these are my conditions: firm purchase of at least 15 or 16 canvases, at the prices indicated, paid half up front, the other half in six months. These canvases are to be selected before the exhibition opening."

39 Since the correspondence between these two dealers cannot be consulted, this hypothesis remains unverifiable.

40 Letter 158, Camille Pissarro to Claude Monet, June 12, 1883, *Correspondance de Camille Pissarro*, vol. 1 (Valhermeil, 2003).

41 See *Monet and Boston: Lasting Impression* (Museum of Fine Arts, Boston, 2021).

42 I contacted the archives of Durand-Ruel, Bernheim-Jeune (Dauberville), the Museum of Fine Arts, Boston, the Getty Museum, and the Wildenstein Institute. I have also corresponded with fellow art historians and organizers of this exhibition André Dombrowski and Géraldine Lefebvre, whom I would like to thank here.

43 The Wildenstein catalogue raisonné mentions numbers 1740, 1749, 1751, 1757, 1761, 1765, and 1767 and gives the title of the exhibition in French.

44 Félicie Faizand de Maupeou, *Claude Monet et l'Exposition: Une Stratégie de Carrière à l'Avènement du Marché de l'Art* (Presses Universitaires de Rouen et du Havre, 2018).

45 He was nonetheless involved in the framing, and he asked for the paintings to remain framed as he wished.

46 The May 29, 1912, issue of *Le Gaulois* published an account of the opening.

47 *The Grand Canal* was bought by Mr. and Mrs. H. Croker from Hillsborough, North Carolina; *The Palazzo da Mula* by E. Faust from Saint Louis; and *The Palazzo Contarini* by Arthur Meeker from Chicago. Research failed to turn up any specific information about these buyers.

48 *Illustrated Catalogue of Highly Important Old and Modern Paintings of Sterling Artistic Distinction Belonging to Mr. Arthur B. Emmons, Newport, to the Estate of the Late Thatcher M. Adams, New York, to the Private Collector Mr. Joseph F. Flanagan, Boston, Collections of the late Mr. Henry Sayles, Boston and Mr. Harris B. Dick, New York . . . : to be Sold at Unrestricted Public Sale in the Grand Ballroom of the Hotel Plaza* (American Art Association, 1920).

49 The painting was one of the works sold by Monet to the dealer in May 1912. Nevertheless, the work was eventually returned to Monet in June 1912. The painting remained in Giverny in the collection of Michel Monet before being sold in the 1960s.

DONATO ESPOSITO, pp 165–73

1 Paul Leroi, "Francesco Guardi," *L'Art* 12 (1878): 103–106.

2 Leroi, "Francesco Guardi," 106.

3 The Musée Jacquemart-André and the Musée Cognacq-Jay, both with superb Canalettos of Venice, did not open until 1913 and 1929, respectively.

4 W. G. Constable, *Canaletto: Giovanni Antonio Canal, 1697–1768*, 2nd ed., rev. by J. G. Links, vol. 2 (Clarendon Press, 1989), 267, no. 169 (as Canaletto). The French title of the painting is *L'Entrée du Grand Canal et l'Église de la Salute à Venise*.

5 Patrick Noon, *Richard Parkes Bonington: The Complete Paintings* (Paul Mellon Centre for Studies in British Art, 2008), 290–91, no. 229.

6 Leroi, "Francesco Guardi," 106.

7 Hôtel Drouot, Paris, April 17–20, 1882.

8 Paul Leroi, "Alexis Febvre," *L'Art* 28 (1882): 216–17, 235–37, 256–57. Paul Leroi, "Alexis Febvre," *L'Art* 29 (1882): 15–16.

9 Hôtel Drouot, Paris, April 17–20, 1882, lots 56 *Piazza San Marco* (etched by Pierre Teyssonnières); 57 *La Piazzetta* (etched by Léon Gaucherel); 58 *San Giorgio Maggiore* (etched by Auguste Boulard); 59 *Santa Maria della Salute* (etched by Gustave Greux). Each painting measured 70 × 95 cm. In addition to this quartet of works, there were three other (likely more minor) Venetian subjects by Guardi in the same sale (lots 60 *La Place Saint-Marc*, 61 *Vue de la Piazzetta, à Venise*, and 62 *Autre Vue de la Piazzetta*).

10 The collection formed by Gustave Rothan and sold in 1890 (Hôtel Drouot, Paris, May 29–31, 1890) also had several Venetian works in it, including *Le Môle, Vu du Bassin de San Marco* by Canaletto (Musée du Louvre) and one by Guardi (illustrated in *L'Art* 12 [1878], opposite page 106).

11 Galerie Sedelmeyer, Paris, March 25, 1892, lots 27 (68 × 101 cm) and 28 (62 × 98 cm), respectively.

12 Musée du Louvre (RF 1961 33).

13 Martin Butlin and Evelyn Joll, *The Paintings of J. M. W. Turner* (Paul Mellon Centre for Studies in British Art, 1977), 216–17, no. 387.

14 Galerie Georges Petit, Paris, May 17, 1904, lots 58 *La Piazzetta* by Canaletto (54 × 84 cm); 59 *Vue du Grand Canal, à Venise* by Canaletto (54 × 83 cm); 62 *La Place Saint-Marc, à Venise* by Guardi (46 × 76 cm); 63 *Le Grand Canal* by Guardi (46 × 76 cm). Only lot 59 is traced and listed in Constable, *Canaletto*, 308–9, no. 244, as a copy.

15 Hôtel Drouot, Paris, May 16, 1904, lots 6 (72 × 95 cm) and 14 (63 × 78 cm), respectively.

16 Hôtel Drouot, Paris, March 25, 1908, lot 32 (no size given).

17 Today at the Museum of Fine Arts, Boston (19.173), and the Clark Art Institute, Williamstown (1955.596), respectively.

18 T. C., "Holiday Rambles (by Our Paris Correspondent): Venice," *Illustrated London News*, August 6, 1887.

19 Ziem's *Vue de Venise*, exhibited at the Paris Salon in 1852, won him a first-class medal and was immediately bought by the French state. It was on view at the Musée du Luxembourg from 1853 to 1929. The following decade another of his

Venetian subjects, *Venise, Vue du Palais des Doges*, from 1864, was bought by the state.

20 For example, Ziem's first painting from 1852 was translated into an etching, *Vue de Venise*, by Léon Gaucherel, and published in *L'Art* 14 (1878), opposite page 326.

21 Léa Saint-Raymond, "Ziem, un Virtuose du Marché," in *Félix Ziem (1821–1911): Saisir la Lumière* (Silvana Editoriale, 2023), 43.

22 "The French Turner," *Illustrated London News*, June 16, 1906.

23 The Wallace Collection, London (P366).

24 Isabelle Collet, "Un Brevet d'Immortalité. Histoire d'Une Donation," in *Félix Ziem (1821–1911)*, 22–27.

25 The donation was one of the cornerstones of the young collection; others were the large groups of work by the painter Fernand Pelez and the sculptors Jules Dalou and Jean Carriès that dominated the institution until 1945. Department store magnate Alfred Chauchard bequeathed many more depictions of Venice by Ziem to the French national collection, but this postdates Monet's trip in 1908.

26 Petit Palais, Paris (PPP247).

27 For example, *Ancient Italy—Ovid Banished from Rome* (private collection; Butlin and Joll, *The Paintings of J. M. W. Turner*, 205–6, no. 375) was on view at Galerie Sedelmeyer in Paris in 1894.

28 Butlin and Joll, *The Paintings of J. M. W. Turner*, 267–68, no. 509 (Musée du Louvre, Paris: RF1967.2). This canvas was in Paris by 1890 and may have been exhibited there in 1894.

29 Butlin and Joll, *The Paintings of J. M. W. Turner*, 220–21, no. 393.

30 Frederick Wedmore, "The New Turner Drawings," *The Standard*, October 21, 1890.

31 "Art Notes," *Liverpool Mercury*, October 27, 1890.

32 "The Chronicle of Art: Art in November: The New Turners at the National Gallery," *Magazine of Art*, December 1890, v.

33 Butlin and Joll, *The Paintings of J. M. W. Turner*, 239, no. 418.

34 The original group had numbers N00458 to N00562.

35 In 1901 (numbers N01857 to N01890) and 1905 (numbers N01980 to N02068).

36 Butlin and Joll, *The Paintings of J. M. W. Turner*, 182–83, no. 349.

37 Vernon also donated Turner's beautiful *The Dogano, San Giorgio, Citella, from the Steps of the Europa* (Butlin and Joll, *The Paintings of J. M. W. Turner*, 222–23, no. 396). Here the white forms of the city's landmarks have been manipulated and placed as though it were an artificial stage set. The gondolas and other craft provide the only accents of color against an otherwise muted pale tonality. Monet may have directly referenced this work in his own *San Giorgio Maggiore at Dusk*.

38 Frances Spalding, *The Tate: A History* (Tate Gallery Publishing, 1998), 10–11.

39 "The Turner Drawings at the National Gallery," *The Standard*, June 24, 1879.

40 "Turner Drawings."

41 Noon, *Richard Parkes Bonington: The Complete Paintings*, 296–97, no. 231. This painting is also known as *View of the Piazzetta near the Square of St. Mark, Venice*.

42 The Canalettos owned by the Musée Cognacq-Jay in Paris were not publicly accessible until 1929.

43 The Metropolitan Museum of Art, New York (59.188.1).

44 Léon Rosenthal, *Venise, Reine de la Couleur* (Bibliothèque de la Vie Moderne, 1899), 5.

45 Rosenthal, *Venise*, 5–6.

46 Andrew McLaren Young et al., *The Paintings of James McNeill Whistler* (Paul Mellon Centre for Studies in British Art, 1980), 123–24, no. 213.

47 Young et al., *The Paintings of James McNeill Whistler*, 123, no. 212.

48 In mid-1899 the Guildhall Art Gallery staged a large loan exhibition, *Turner and Some of His Contemporaries*. Included was the crowded luminous painting *The Grand Canal: Scene—A Street in Venice* (The Huntington, San Marino, California, (22.52; Butlin and Joll, *The Paintings of J. M. W. Turner*, 198–99, no. 368). Unfortunately, Monet was not in London at the time.

49 Christie's, London, May 6, 1899, lot 79; Butlin and Joll, *The Paintings of J. M. W. Turner*, 228–29, no. 403. National Gallery of Art, Washington, DC (1961.2.3).

50 "The Fowler Collection," *The Times*, May 8, 1899.

51 "Twenty Masterpieces of the English School," *Pall Mall Gazette*, November 20, 1899. See also Frank Rinder, "English Pictures—New and Old," *The Art Journal*, January 1900, 27.

52 Christie's, London, May 21–23, 1908, lot 49 (17.5 inches in diameter).

53 *Venice: Moonlight* was lent by Humphrey Roberts, and *The Grand Canal, Venice* and *The Colleoni Statue, Venice* were both lent by Stephen George Holland.

54 "Winter Exhibition at Burlington House," *The Times*, January 5, 1901.

55 The 1841 painting is in a private collection. Butlin and Joll, *The Paintings of J. M. W. Turner*, 219, no. 391. The canvas is identified here for the first time as having been exhibited in 1901 (*Winter Exhibition*, Royal Academy of Arts, London, 1901, no. 5, as *Venice*), that exhibition history having been overlooked in the catalogue raisonné by Butlin and Joll and all subsequent literature, including for its sale at Christie's, New York, April 6, 2006, lot 97.

56 Tate, London (N01780).

RICHARD THOMSON, pp 175–93

1 James Buzard, *The Beaten Track: European Tourism, Literature, and the Ways to "Culture," 1800–1918* (Oxford University Press, 1993), 41–42, 44.

2 Isabelle de Lannoy, *J.-J. Henner: Catalogue Raisonné*, vol. 1 (printed by the author, 2008), nos. B.127–34, 147.

3 Geneviève Lacambre, "Chronologie," in *Gustave Moreau: Between Epic and Dream* (Réunion des Musées Nationaux, 1999), 263, 273.

4 Edgar Degas to Gustave Moreau, September 21, 1858, in *The Letters of Edgar Degas*, ed. Theodore Reff, vol. 3 (Wildenstein Plattner Institute, 2020), 9–10.

5 Marie-Liesse Boquien, "James Tissot (1836–1902)—Bio-chronologie," in *James Tissot: L'Ambigu Moderne* (Réunion des Musées Nationaux, 2020), 268. Tissot purchased one of the two canvases from his friend.

6 *Carolus-Duran, 1837–1917* (Réunion des Museés Nationaux, 2003), 202–5, 207.

7 Auguste Rodin to Rose Beuret, *Correspondance de Rodin: 1860–1899*, vol. 1, ed. Alain Beausire and Hélène Pinet (Musée Rodin, 1985), 34.

8 Auguste Rodin to President of the National Art Collections Fund, *Correspondance de Rodin: 1908–1912*, vol. 3, 224.

9 Hayem owned Monet's *Les Déchargeurs de Charbon (The Coal-Heavers)*, 1875, Musée d'Orsay, Paris (W.364).

10 Jean Lorrain, "Venezia Bella. Les Artistes Mystérieux," *L'Echo de Paris*, June 2, 1893, quoted in *Chroniques d'Art, 1887–1904* (H. Champion, 2007), 194.

11 Yann Farinaux-Le Sidaner, "Edmond Aman-Jean, Sa Vie, Son Oeuvre," in *Aman-Jean, 1858–1936. Songes de Femmes* (Le Capucin, 2003), 67.

12 Lorrain, "Venezia Bella," quoted in *Chroniques*, 194.

13 Karen Serres, ed., *Monet and London: Views of the Thames* (Paul Holberton Publishing, 2025).

14 Mark Twain, *The Innocents Abroad* 1869; (Penguin Classics, 2002), 156–57.

15 Mark Twain, *A Tramp Abroad* 1880; (Penguin Classics, 1997), 363.

16 Guy de Maupassant, "Venise," *Gil Blas*, May 5, 1885.

17 Henry Havard, *Amsterdam et Venise* (Plon, 1876), 9.

18 Stephen Ongpin, *Drawing Inspiration: Sketches and Sketchbook Pages of the 19th and 20th Centuries* (Stephen Ongpin Fine Art, 2016). He gave the watercolor to his mistress Elizabeth Bezanson, who became his second wife in July 1889. The painting is in the Musée d'Orsay, RF1246.

19 Marie-Madeleine Aubrun, *Jules Bastien-Lepage, 1848–1884: Catalogue Raisonné de l'Oeuvre* (publisher unknown, 1985), nos. 332 and 336-39.

20 Ruth Berson, *The New Painting: Impressionism 1874–1886* (Fine Arts Museums of San Francisco, 1996), 251.

21 Henry Havard, "La Peinture Indépendante: Huitième Exposition des Impressionnistes," *Le Siècle*, May 17, 1886, quoted in Berson, *The New Painting*, 453.

22 Daniel Wildenstein, *Claude Monet: Biographie et Catalogue Raisonné*, vol. 4 (Wildenstein Institute and La Bibliothèque des Arts, 1974–1991), nos. 1761–3 and 1771.

23 Diane de Blacas, *Lansyer: Le Maître du Luminisme* (Concept-Image, 2004), 154, 156.

24 Georges Lafenestre, "Les Salons de 1893. I. La Peinture au Salon des Champs-Élysées," *Revue des Deux Mondes* 3, vol. 117 (June 1, 1893): 671.

25 *Eugène Boudin: L'Atelier de la Lumière* (Réunion des Musées Nationaux, 2016), 229.

26 Salon de la Société Nationale des Beaux-Arts, *Exposition de 1897. Catalogue des Ouvrages de Peinture, Sculpture, Dessins, Gravure, Architecture et Objets d'Art Exposés au Champ-de-Mars* (C. Hérissey, 1897), no. 147.

27 Susan Morris, *The Father of Impressionism: Eugène Boudin and His Circle* (Richard Green, 2016).

28 Laurent Guillaut, "Catalogue," in *Henri Martin (1860–1943): Du Rêve au Quotidien* (Silvana Editoriale, 2008), 137.

29 *Société Nationale des Beaux-Arts. Exposition de 1897*, nos. 1144–52. *Salon Nationale des Beaux-Arts. Exposition de 1898. Catalogue des Ouvrages de Peinture, Sculpture, Dessins, Gravure, Architecture et Objets d'Art Exposés au Champ-de-Mars*, nos. 1137–48.

30 *Alfred Smith, 1854–1936: Un Regard sur la Vie Moderne* (Musée des Beaux-Arts, 2007), 160, 164, 170.

31 Achille Segard, "Henri Martin," in *Peintres d'Aujourd'hui: Les Décorateurs*, vol. 2 (Librairie Paul Ollendorff, 1914), 44.

32 Maurice Barrès, *Un Homme Libre*, quoted in *L'Oeuvre de Maurice Barrès*, ed. Philippe Barrès (Club de l'Honnête Homme, 1965), 234; Jean-Paul Goujon, *Pierre Louÿs: Une Vie Sécrète* (1870–1925) (Fayard, 2002), 69.

33 Gustave Soulier, "Lévy-Dhurmer," *Art et Décoration*, January–June 1898, 7.

34 Yann Farinaux-Le Sidaner, *Le Sidaner: L'Oeuvre Peint et Gravé* (Éditions André Sauret,1989), 26, 30.

35 Maurice Denis to André Gide, December 12, 1907, in *André Gide Maurice Denis Correspondance, 1892–1945*, eds. Pierre Masson and Carina Schäfer (Gallimard, 2006), 268–69.

36 Gustave Kahn, "Chez Bernheim-Jeune une Série de Monet sur Venise," *Mercure de France*, June 16, 1912.

37 George D. Painter, *Marcel Proust: A Biography* (Chatto and Windus, 1959), 268–69.

38 Boni de Castellane, *De l'Art d'Être Pauvre* (Tallandier, 2009), 283–84.

39 "Les Carnets d'Henri-Edmond Cross. III," *Bulletin de la Vie Artistique* 13 (July 1, 1922): 303–4.

40 Françoise Cachin, *Signac: Catalogue Raisonné de l'Oeuvre Peint* (Gallimard, 2000), nos. 406–21.

41 Marianne Mathieu and Dominique Lobstein, *Monet Collectionneur* (Hazan, 2017), 278.

LISA SMALL, pp 195–237

1 Alice Monet to Germaine Salerou, October 3, 1908, in Philippe Piguet, *Monet et Venise* (Éditions Herscher, 1986).

2 Marc Elder, *À Giverny*, *Chez Claude Monet* (Bernheim-Jeune, 1924), 53. See also a letter Alice sent to Germaine in which she reported that Monet found paintings by El Greco to be "amazing," in Jacqueline Guillaud and Maurice Guillaud, *Claude Monet at the Time of Giverny* (Centre Culturel du Marais, 1983), 267.

3 See Virginia Spate et al., *Monet and Japan* (Gardners Books, 2004).

4 Claude Monet to Alice Monet, February 1, 1883, in Daniel Wildenstein, *Claude Monet: Biographie et Catalogue Raisonné*, vols. 1–5 (Wildenstein Institute and La Bibliothèque des Arts, 1974–1991).

5 Harmon Siegel, *Painting with Monet* (Princeton University Press, 2024), 94.

6 When Corot died in 1875, the critic Philippe Burty wrote, "Some of these studies, very personal works and marked

by the delicacy of drawing and the keenness of the overall structure, are famous in the studios. Corot lent them willingly, and they have had a happy influence on the contemporary school." Quoted in Peter Galassi, *Corot in Italy: Open-Air Painting and the Classical-Landscape Tradition* (Yale University Press, 1991), 3. The author thanks Eric Weider for this citation.

7 Gary Tinterow, *Corot* (Metropolitan Museum of Art, 1996), xiv. See also Paul Hayes Tucker, *Monet in the '90s: The Series Paintings* (Museum of Fine Arts , Boston, and Yale University Press, 1989), 232–33.

8 Siegel, *Painting with Monet*, 62.

9 *Eugène Boudin* (Musée Jacquemart-André, 2013), 210, quoted in Sotheby's, "Impressionist & Modern Day Art Sale," sothebys.com/en/auctions/ecatalogue/2019/impressionist-modern-art-day-n10148/lot.109.html.

10 In his article "Le Pèlerinage de Giverny," *Revue de l'Art Ancien et Moderne*, January 1, 1927, 50, Édouard Mortier, Duke of Treviso, recounts an anecdote about Monet and Renoir at the Louvre standing in front of a Canaletto in which Monet disparagingly claims, "Look, he does not even put in the reflections of the boats!"

11 Philippe Monnier, *Venice in the Eighteenth Century* (The Gorham Press, 1910), 125.

12 Liana Amanda Bellon, "Souvenirs of Venice: Reproduced Views, Tourism, and City Spaces" (PhD diss. McGill University, 2016), 34.

13 Tucker, *Monet in the '90s*, 136–37.

14 Louis Gillet, *Trois Variations sur Claude Monet* (Plon, 1927), 16. Canaletto likely used a camera obscura to help create some of his compositions. See Philip Steadman, *Canaletto's Camera* (UCL Press, 2025).

15 "Art et Curiosité: Une Féerie de Lumière et de Couleur. Venise Vue par Claude Monet," *Le Temps*, June 11, 1912. In his lukewarm review of the *Venise* exhibition ("Les 'Venise' de Claude Monet," *La Semaine Littéraire*, June 15, 1912, 281–83), Camille Mauclair complained that Monet's lack of detail made it impossible to distinguish Palazzo Contarini from any other palazzo.

16 Gustave Geffroy, "La Venise de Claude Monet," *La Dépêche*, May 30, 1912.

17 Quoted in Paul Hayes Tucker, *Monet in the 20th Century* (Yale University Press, 1998), 30. For Turner's engagement with the city, see Ian Warrell, *Turner and Venice* (Tate, 2004).

18 Albert Besnard quoted in Karen Serres, ed., *Monet and London: Views of the Thames* (Paul Holberton Publishing, 2024), 57; Gustave Kahn quoted in Tucker, *Monet in the 20th Century*, 32.

19 Quoted in Sylvie Patin, "The Last Act: Turner, Whistler, and Monet in Venice," in Katharine Lochnan et al., *Turner Whistler Monet: Impressionist Visions* (Art Gallery of Ontario/Tate, 2004), 203.

20 This painting by Turner was on view in Paris in 1900 at the Exposition Universelle, where Monet may have seen it.

21 Turner's subject here references Venice's rich artistic legacy—the very tradition with which Monet himself was grappling. See Christie's, "Visionary: The Paul G. Allen Collection Part I," christies.com/auction/visionary-the-paul-g-allen-collection-part-i-22010-nyr.

22 A visitor to Giverny recounted asking the artist if he ever considered painting the Thames at night, to which Monet replied, "It would be difficult in the wake of Whistler, without falling into the trap of imitation. But maybe I will do it one day." *Monet and London*, 45. For more on Whistler's Venice work see Margaret F. MacDonald, *Palaces in the Night: Whistler in Venice* (University of California Press, 2001).

23 J. A. M. Whistler, *Ten O'Clock* (Houghton, Mifflin and Company, 1896), 15.

24 See Lochnan et al., *Turner Whistler Monet*. For the prints belonging to each of the two sets, see University of Glasgow, "The 'First Venice Set,'" etchings.arts.gla.ac.uk/catalogue/sets_texts/?eid=venice1 and University of Glasgow, "The 'Second Venice Set,'" etchings.arts.gla.ac.uk/catalogue/sets_texts/?eid=venice2.

25 Charles Merrill Mount, *Monet: A Biography* (Simon & Schuster, 1966), 379. Mount claims that Sargent encouraged the president of the Brooklyn Museum to purchase Monet's *The Palazzo Ducale*, but this author has found no evidence to confirm this.

26 For Sargent's Venetian work and his relationship with Monet, see Warren Adelson and Richard Ormond, *Sargent's Venice* (Yale University Press, 2006); Richard Ormond and Elaine Kilmurray, *John Singer Sargent: Complete Paintings*, vol. VI (Paul Mellon Centre for Studies in British Art, 2006); and Warren Adelson and Elaine Kilmurray, *Sargent and Impressionism* (Adelson Galleries, 2010).

27 See Elaine Kilmurray, "Sargent, Monet . . . and Manet," in *Sargent and Impressionism*, n.p.

28 John Singer Sargent to Claude Monet, undated [probably 1894], and December 28, 1894, quoted in Kilmurray, "Sargent, Monet . . . and Manet," n.p.

29 April 12, 1909, quoted in Guillaud and Guillaud, *Claude Monet at the Time of Giverny*, 279.

30 Sargent offered this painting as a gift to the Curtises, but Ariana so disliked the way the artist portrayed her and her son that she refused to accept it. In 1899, Sargent instead presented it to the Royal Academy as his admission piece.

31 The Brooklyn Museum's Sargent watercolors were acquired in 1909. See Teresa A. Carbone and Erica E. Hirshler, *John Singer Sargent Watercolors* (Museum of Fine Arts, Boston, 2012).

32 Quoted in John Leighton, "Claude Monet," in *Manet and the Sea*, ed. Juliet Wilson-Bareau and David Degener (Philadelphia Museum of Art, 2004), 206.

33 *Manet: 1832–1883* (Metropolitan Museum of Art, 1983), 373–75.

34 Quoted in John House, catalogue entry for *Venice, The Doge's Palace*, in *Nineteenth-Century European Paintings at the Sterling and Francine Clark Art Institute* vol. 2, ed. Sarah Lees (Clark Art Institute, 2012), 669–71. Alice Monet would make a similar observation about the location's popularity with artists (see Lisa Small's other essay in this volume).

35 Paul Leroi quoted in catalogue entry for *Venice, The Doge's Palace*, in *Nineteenth-Century European Paintings*, 669–71.

36 See Marina Ferretti-Bocquillon et al., *Signac, 1863–1935: Master Neo-Impressionist* (Metropolitan Museum of Art, 2001).

37 *Signac, 1863–1935*, 71.

38 The author wishes to thank Sylvie Patin for confirming that although a reproduction of the photograph of the Monets in Venice has now been placed on view at Giverny, we can only speculate on whether a print of it hung there during in his lifetime.

NILES LUTHER, pp 239–42

1 Théodore Duret, *Manet and the French Impressionists*, trans. J. E. Crawford Flitch (J. B. Lippincott Company, 1910), 146. Although the paintings were not exhibited in Paris until 1912, Duret was able to see them in Monet's Giverny studio.

2 Anthony Grafton et al., eds., *The Classical Tradition* (Belknap Press of Harvard University Press, 2010), 291.

3 "Art Music" refers to a specific genre I'm defining in my work, distinct from the general musicological term "art music," which describes music of high phonoaesthetic value. My conceptualization represents a new categorical framework with its own specific meaning and scope.

4 Ottorino Respighi (1879–1936) was an Italian composer known for his orchestrations of early music and his symphonic tone poems. His *Ancient Airs & Dances, Suite III* (1932) reinterprets sixteenth- and seventeenth-century Italian lute pieces for modern orchestra. The suite consists of four movements: "Italiana" (anonymous lute piece, late sixteenth century), "Arie di Corte" (lute songs by Jean-Baptiste Besard, sixteenth century), "Siciliana" (anonymous lute piece, late sixteenth century), and "Passacaglia" (Baroque guitar piece by Ludovico Roncalli, 1692), with additional material drawn from works by Santino Garsi da Parma.

5 Carl Friedrich Abel (1723–1787) was a German composer who was one of the last virtuosos of the viola da gamba. His Suite in D Minor: I. Arpeggiata comes from his collection *27 Pieces for Bass Viol*, composed in the eighteenth century. The "Arpeggiata" movement draws on Baroque improvisational practices wherein composers would notate simple chord progressions and leave the specific arpeggiation patterns to the performer's discretion (similar to figured bass). This approach showcases the viola da gamba's capacity to render harmonically rich textures through broken chords while honoring the instrument's historical performance practices. Abel represents a bridge between late Baroque and early Classical styles, preserving the viola da gamba's traditions even as the instrument was falling from favor in European courts.

6 Claude Debussy (1862–1918) was a leading French Impressionist composer whose works broke from traditional harmonic structures; "Clair de Lune" (1890), the famous third movement from his *Suite Bergamasque*, is written in D major in 9/8 time and marked "andante très expressif." Its title ("Moonlight") comes from Paul Verlaine's Symbolist poem of the same name, reflecting Debussy's deep connection to the French literary Symbolist movement. "La Fille aux Cheveux de Lin" is specifically the eighth piece from his first book of *Préludes* (1909–10), exemplifying his atmospheric, coloristic approach to composition that paralleled Impressionist painting techniques.

7 Frédéric Chopin (1810–1849), though Polish by birth, spent most of his adult life in Paris; his 21 Nocturnes (1827–46) are considered among the most significant solo piano works in the classical repertoire. Chopin built upon the nocturne form pioneered by the Irish composer John Field, infusing it with the expressive bel canto vocal techniques of Italian opera—particularly works by Vincenzo Bellini and Gaetano Donizetti. His innovative approach is evident in the long, ornate melodic lines that mimic the human voice while the left hand creates a harmonic foundation reminiscent of an orchestral accompaniment.

8 Maurice Ravel (1875–1937) combined impressionistic elements with classical form and precision; his "Pavane pour une Infante Défunte" (1899) demonstrates his gift for subtle orchestration and melodic grace. Originally composed as a piano piece and later orchestrated in 1910, the work showcases Ravel's meticulous craftsmanship and his ability to evoke nostalgia through carefully constructed harmonies. Ravel is often compared to Debussy, but Ravel maintained a stronger connection to traditional forms while still exploring innovative harmonic language and timbral colors that bridged late Romanticism and early twentieth-century modernism.

9 Samuel Barber (1910–1981) was an American composer who maintained a lyrical, expressive style during an era dominated by experimental modernism. His Violin Concerto, Op. 14 (1939) combines romantic melodicism with modernist elements, particularly in its contemplative second movement, which opens with a hauntingly expressive oboe solo before the violin enters with a contrasting rhapsodic theme. The Adagio for Strings, Op. 11 (1936), originally the second movement of his String Quartet, Op. 11, and later arranged for string orchestra, has become one of the most recognizable pieces of twentieth-century American classical music. Its gradual build to an emotional climax through long-breathed phrases exemplifies Barber's gift for creating profound emotional impact through seemingly simple means, establishing a distinctly American voice that honors European classical traditions while speaking with direct emotional clarity.

MELISSA BURON joined the Victoria and Albert Museum in 2024 as director of collections and chief curator. Previously, she held curatorial positions in European art at the Fine Arts Museums of San Francisco, where most recently she was the director of curatorial affairs. Her curatorial contributions have supported more than twenty special exhibitions on subjects from the fifteenth to the nineteenth century. Her prior original exhibitions include *Truth and Beauty: The Pre-Raphaelites and the Old Masters* (2018) and *James Tissot: Fashion & Faith* (2019–20), which was co-organized with the Musée d'Orsay.

LISA SMALL has been a curator at the Brooklyn Museum since 2011, becoming senior curator of European art in 2017. She has organized numerous permanent collection installations and special exhibitions, including *Monet to Morisot: The Real and Imagined in European Art* (2022–23); *Jacques-Louis David Meets Kehinde Wiley* (2020); *Rembrandt to Picasso: Five Centuries of European Works on Paper* (2019); *The Brooklyn Della Robbia* (2018–present); *Rodin: The Body in Bronze* (2017); and the touring exhibition *French Moderns: Monet to Matisse, 1850–1950* (2017–21, 2023–27).

ANDRÉ DOMBROWSKI teaches in the department of the history of art at the University of Pennsylvania, where he is the is the Frances Shapiro-Weitzenhoffer Professor of 19th Century European Art. He is the author of *Cézanne, Murder, and Modern Life* (2013), which is winner of the Phillips Book Prize, and *Monet's Minutes: Impressionism and the Industrialization of Time* (2023). He is also the editor of the 2021 Wiley Blackwell *Companion to Impressionism*.

DONATO ESPOSITO is a freelance art historian and curator specializing in British art from the eighteenth and nineteenth centuries. He has published on artists as diverse as Sir Joshua Reynolds, James Tissot, and John Atkinson Grimshaw. Recently, he cocurated the exhibition *Reframing Reynolds: A Celebration* for the Box, Plymouth.

FÉLICIE FAIZAND DE MAUPEOU is a specialist in late nineteenth-century painting, specifically Impressionism. She has contributed widely to journals and has published or edited several books on the subject, including *Claude Monet and the Exhibition: A Career Strategy in the Advent of the Art Market* (2020) and *Collecting Impressionism: A Reappraisal of the Role of Collectors in the History of the Movement* (2022). A researcher in art history at the University of Paris Nanterre, she coordinates two research programs there: one on artists' libraries and the other on Impressionism.

NILES LUTHER, a New York based composer and cellist, is a pioneer of Art Music—compositions that transform visual art through bespoke sonic experiences. He earned a bachelor's degree in classical cello performance from the Manhattan School of Music in 2019. From 2019 to 2021, as musical director of the Kehinde Wiley Studio, he composed, orchestrated, and installed scores for art films exhibited in galleries across New York, London, and Paris. In 2022 and 2023, he served as principal cellist for the national Broadway tour of *Les Misérables*. Supported by the Ford Foundation, Luther became the first-ever composer-in-residence (2023–25) at the Brooklyn Museum.

ELENA MARCHETTI is an art historian and curator specializing in nineteenth-century French paintings and Venetian art and architecture. She holds a Ph.D. in history of art from the University of Bologna and currently serves as a curator at the Palazzo Ducale and at the Museo Correr in Venice, under the Fondazione Musei Civici di Venezia. Marchetti's scholarly work on a range of topics has been published in exhibition catalogues, journal articles, and essays.

JONATHAN P. RIBNER is an associate professor in the department of the history of art and architecture at Boston University. He specializes in late eighteenth- and nineteenth-century French painting and sculpture and has also published on Victorian visual culture. Author of *Loss in French Romantic Art, Literature, and Politics* (2022), he has contributed book and exhibition reviews to to numerous academic journals and magazines. His essay "The Poetics of Pollution" in the 2004 exhibition catalogue *Turner Whistler Monet* considers the impact of air quality on Monet's London paintings and Whistler's work in Venice. Currently, he is working on a general-audience book intended to enhance the reader's capacity to take pleasure in art.

RICHARD THOMSON was Watson Gordon Professor of Fine Art at the University of Edinburgh (1996–2018), to which he remains attached in active retirement. A specialist in late nineteenth-century French art, he has published widely, both monographs—on Toulouse-Lautrec (1977), Seurat (1985), Degas (1988, 1995)—and sociocultural volumes—*The Troubled Republic* (2004), *Art of the Actual* (2012), and *The Presence of the Past* (2021). He has curated or cocurated many exhibitions in leading international museums, including three on Monet: *Monet: The Seine and the Sea* (2003), *Monet* (2010–11), and *Monet & Architecture* (2018). His next exhibition will be *Monet: The Wild and the Tamed* for the Munch museum, Oslo (2027), and he is preparing a book on Monet's drawings and sketchbooks.

WORKS IN THE EXHIBITION

Works listed in approximate exhibition order.

(Dimensions are unframed or sheet dimensions).

John Singer Sargent
An Interior in Venice, 1899
Oil on canvas, 26 × 32 9/10 in.
Royal Academy of Arts

Claude Monet
Venice, Palazzo Dario, 1908
Oil on canvas, 26 1/16 × 32 3/16 in.
The Art Institute of Chicago, Mr. and Mrs. Lewis Larned Coburn Memorial Collection

Claude Monet
The Red House, 1908
Oil on canvas, 25⅔ in. × 31⅘ in.
Collection Galerie Larock-Granoff

Unknown artist
Palazzo Dario on the Grand Canal, Venice, Italy, 1860–1880
Photograph, 20 11/16 × 14⅜ in.
Victoria and Albert Museum, Given by S. E. Bunney

Georges Allié
Claude Monet's Salon-Studio in Giverny, c. 1920
Photograph, 6⅓ × 8 1/10 in.
© Collection Philippe Piguet

Unknown artist
Palais Vénitien
Postcard, 9⅔ × 7½ in.
Musée Marmottan Monet, Given by Michel Monet, 1966

Unknown artist
Venice, Grand Canal
Postcard sent to Blanche Hoschedé, 3½ × 5½ in.
Musée Marmottan Monet, Given by Michel Monet, 1966

Unknown artist
Venice, Grand Canal and Palazzo Franchetti
Postcard, 7⅔ × 9⅔ in.
Musée Marmottan Monet, Given by Michel Monet, 1966

Unknown artist
Venice, Piazza San Marco from the Ducal Palace
Postcard, 7¾ × 10 in.
Musée Marmottan Monet, Given by Michel Monet, 1966

Unknown artist
Venice, Piazzetta San Marco—da Mare
Postcard, 10 × 7½ in.
Musée Marmottan Monet, Given by Michel Monet, 1966

Unknown artist
Venice, Fishing Boat
Postcard, 5½ × 3½ in.
Musée Marmottan Monet, Given by Michel Monet, 1966

Unknown artist
Venice, Panorama of San Giorgio and Gondola
Postcard, 7½ × 10 in.
Musée Marmottan Monet, Given by Michel Monet, 1966

Unknown artist
Venice, Grand Canal with Regatta—Panorama
Postcard, 7½ × 10 in.
Musée Marmottan Monet, Given by Michel Monet, 1966

Unknown artist
Palazzo Ducale of Venice. Exterior Loggia of the Palazzo Ducale and Island of San Giorgio
Postcard, 3½ × 5½ in.
Musée Marmottan Monet, Given by Michel Monet, 1966.

Unknown artist
Venice, the Rialto Bridge on the Grand Canal
Postcard sent by Alice Monet to her granddaughter Alice Butler, October 7, 1908, 3½ × 5⅓ in.
© Collection Philippe Piguet

Unknown artist
Venice, View from the Dock on the Piazzetta
Postcard sent by Alice Monet to her granddaughter Alice Butler, October 25, 1908, 3½ × 5⅓ in.
© Collection Philippe Piguet

Unknown artist
Venice, a Procession on the Grand Canal
Postcard sent by Alice Monet to her granddaughter Alice Butler, November 27, 1908, 3½ × 5⅓ in.
© Collection Philippe Piguet

Unknown artist
Venice, Grand Hotel Britannia
Postcard sent by Alice Monet to her granddaughter Alice Butler, November 25, 1908, 3½ × 5½ in.
© Collection Philippe Piguet

Unknown artist
Venice, Grand Canal, Palazzo Barbaro
Postcard sent by Alice Monet to Simone Salerou, October 10, 1908, 8½ × 5⅓ in.
© Collection Philippe Piguet

Venice, Letter from Alice Monet to Germaine Salerou,
October 17, 1908
Letterhead of the Grand Hotel Britannia, 8½ × 5⅓ in.
© Collection Philippe Piguet

Unknown artist
Alice Monet Surrounded by Pigeons, Piazza San Marco, Venice, early October 1908
Silver print in the form of a postcard, 5½ × 3½ in.
© Collection Philippe Piguet

Catalogue for the 1912 *Venise* exhibition, (Bernheim-Jeune, 1912)
Bound book, 8¾ × 11⅜ in.
Collection of Paul Hayes Tucker, lent in honor of Robert L. Herbert

Pierre Gusman
Venise (Renouard, H. Laurens, 1904)
Bound book, 10¼ × 7¾ in
Brooklyn Museum
(Exhibited only in Brooklyn)

John Ruskin
Le Repos de Saint-Marc (Hachette, 1908)
Bound book, 7¼ × 5 in.
Brooklyn Museum
(Exhibited only in Brooklyn)

John Ruskin
The Stones of Venice (1885)
Bound book, 10¼ × 7¼ in.
Brooklyn Museum Libraries and Archives
(Exhibited only in Brooklyn)

Venice and *Venice, Piazzetta di San Marco* from *Italian Scenery*, a book of engravings based on drawings by Elizabeth Frances Batty, 1820
Engraving, 10⅓ × 6⅓ in. each
Fine Arts Museums of San Francisco, Achenbach Foundation for Graphic Arts

Samuel Prout
S. M. della Salute, Venice, Pl. No. 20 in *Sketches in France, Switzerland and Italy* (Hodgson & Graves, c. 1840)
Lithograph, 10 9/16 × 14½ in.
Fine Arts Museums of San Francisco, Achenbach Foundation for Graphic Arts

Frederick de Wit
View of Venice, c. late 17th c.
Engraving, 16 × 40 in.
Victoria and Albert Museum

Attributed to Alessandro dalla Via
Regatta on the Venetian Grand Canal Honoring Ernest Augustus IV of Hanover, Duke of Brunswick-Lüneburg, Presented in 1685 to His Local and Foreign Guests, 1686
Engraving, 20½ × 36¾ in.
Fine Arts Museums of San Francisco, Gift of William Eddelman

Carlo Naya
Venezia, mid-19th c.
Album of albumen silver prints, 10 9/16 × 13 13/16 in.
Fine Arts Museums of San Francisco, Gift of Elizabeth D. Moyer, PhD, and Michael C. Powanda, PhD, in Honor of Robert Flynn Johnson and James Ganz

Michele Marieschi
from the series *Magnificentiores Selectioresque Urbis Venetiarum Prospectus*, 1741
Etchings, approximately 12 × 18 in. each
Fine Arts Museums of San Francisco, Achenbach Foundation for Graphic Arts, unless otherwise indicated

Frontispiece
The Piazzetta and Ducal Palace, Pl. No. 1
Santa Maria Formosa, Pl. No. 2
The Gates of the Arsenal, Pl. No. 3
The Basin of St. Mark's, Pl. No. 4
The Bridge and Market of the Rialto, Pl. No. 5
Santa Chiara, Pl. No. 6
Palazzo Pesaro, Pl. No. 7
Piazza S. Marco, Pl. No. 8
Santa Maria della Salute, Pl. No. 9
The Piazzetta, Pl. No. 10
Courtyard of the Ducal Palace, Pl. No. 11
Campo SS. Giovanni e Paolo, Pl. No. 12
Piazzetta S. Basso, Pl. No. 13
Cannaregio, Pl. No. 14
Canal Grande, Pl. No. 15
Fine Arts Museums of San Francisco, Museum Collection
Campo San Rocco, Pl. No. 16
Fine Arts Museums of San Francisco, Museum Collection
Rialto, Pl. No. 17
The Molo and S. Maria della Salute, Pl. No. 18
Piazza and Piazzetta, Pl. No. 19
Campo dei Friari, Pl. No. 20
The Regatta, Pl. No. 21

Claude Monet
The Grand Canal, Venice, 1908
Oil on canvas, 28 13/16 × 35 5/16 in.
Fine Arts Museums of San Francisco, Gift of Osgood Hooker

Claude Monet
The Palazzo Ducale, 1908
Oil on canvas, 32 × 39 in.
Brooklyn Museum, Gift of A. Augustus Healy

Canaletto
The Bucintoro at the Molo on Ascension Day, c. 1745
Oil on canvas, 45¼ × 64 inches
Philadelphia Museum of Art, The William L. Elkins Collection

Canaletto
Venice, the Grand Canal Looking East with Santa Maria della Salute, 1749–50
Oil on canvas, 52 × 64⅞ in.
Fine Arts Museums of San Francisco, Museum Purchase, Gift of Diane B. Wilsey in Celebration of the Legion of Honor Centennial and in Memory of Ann Getty

Studio of Canaletto
Venetian Scene, mid-18th c.
Oil on canvas, 27½ × 49½ in.
Fine Arts Museums of San Francisco, Gift of Mrs. Clarence Sterling Postley
(Exhibited only in San Francisco)

Claude Monet
Rising Tide at Pourville, 1882
Oil on canvas, 26 × 32 in.
Brooklyn Museum, Gift of Mrs. Horace O. Havemeyer

Claude Monet
Waves Breaking, 1881
Oil on canvas, 23½ × 32 in.
Fine Arts Museums of San Francisco, Gift of Prentis Cobb Hale
(Exhibited only in Brooklyn)

Charles-François Daubigny
Le Bateau-Atelier from the album *Voyage en Bateau*, 1861
Etching, 5 1/16 × 7 in.
Fine Arts Museums of San Francisco, Achenbach Foundation for Graphic Arts

Claude Monet
Sailboats on the Seine at Petit-Gennevilliers, 1874
Oil on canvas, 21¼ × 25¾ in.
Fine Arts Museums of San Francisco, Gift of Bruno and Sadie Adriani

Claude Monet
Banks of the Seine at Lavacourt, 1879
Oil on canvas, 22⅞ × 31½ in.
The Frick Pittsburgh

Claude Monet
Japanese Footbridge, Giverny, 1895
Oil on canvas, 31 × 38½ inches
Philadelphia Museum of Art, Gift of F. Otto Haas, Reserving the Life Interest of His Wife Carole Haas Gravagno

Claude Monet
The Seine near Giverny, 1885
Oil on canvas, 25 × 36¼ in.
Frederic C. Hamilton Collection, Bequeathed to the Denver Art Museum

Claude Monet
Waterloo Bridge: Effect of Sunlight in the Fog, 1903
Oil on canvas, 29 × 39½ in.
National Gallery of Canada

Claude Monet
Houses of Parliament, Sunlight Effect, 1903
Oil on canvas, 32×36¼ in.
Brooklyn Museum, Bequest of Grace Underwood Barton

Claude Monet
San Giorgio Maggiore, Twilight, 1908
Oil on canvas, 25×36 in.
Amgueddfa Cymru–Museum Wales

Claude Monet
The Palazzo Ducale, Seen from San Giorgio Maggiore, 1908
Oil on canvas, $25\frac{9}{16}$×$39\frac{9}{16}$ in.
Solomon R. Guggenheim Museum, Thannhauser Collection, Bequest, Hilde Thannhauser

Claude Monet
Low Tide at Pourville, near Dieppe, 1882
Oil on fabric, $23\frac{9}{16}$×32 in.
Cleveland Museum of Art, Gift of Mrs. Henry White Cannon

Claude Monet
A Cliff at Pourville in the Morning, 1897
Oil on canvas, 26×39½ in.
Montreal Museum of Fine Arts, purchase, John W. Tempest Fund

Claude Monet
The Break-up of the Ice, 1880
Oil on canvas, 23¾×39¼ in.
University of Michigan Museum of Art, Acquired through the Generosity of Russell B. Stearns (LS&A, 1916), and His Wife, Andree B. Stearns

Lucien Lévy-Dhurmer
Venice: The Grand Canal at Night, c. 1895
Pastel on paper, 23×32 in.
Collection of Celia Morrissette/Keith Johnson
(Exhibited only in Brooklyn)

J. M. W. Turner
San Giorgio Maggiore, c. 1835
Gouache on gray paper, 5×8⅔ in.
Victoria and Albert Museum

J. M. W. Turner
The Grand Canal, Venice, near the Accademia, with Santa Maria della Salute in the Distance, c. 1840
Gouache, graphite, and watercolor on paper, 7½×11⅛ in.
Tate Britain, Accepted by the Nation as Part of the Turner Bequest 1856

J. M. W. Turner
The Piazzetta, Palazzo Ducale (Doge's Palace) and New Prisons from the Bacino, Venice, with Moored Boats, 1840
Watercolor on paper, 9⅝×$12\frac{3}{16}$ in.
Tate Britain, Accepted by the Nation as Part of the Turner Bequest 1856

J. M. W. Turner
The Grand Canal, Venice, with the Palazzo Balbi and the Mocenigo Palaces, and the Rialto Bridge in the Distance, 1840
Graphite and watercolor on paper, 8¾×$12\frac{15}{16}$ in.
Tate Britain, Accepted by the Nation as Part of the Turner Bequest 1856

J. M. W. Turner
The Dogana and Santa Maria della Salute, Venice, across the Grand Canal from the Hotel Europa (Palazzo Giustinian) at Twilight, 1840
Graphite, watercolor, and pen and ink on paper, 7⅝×11 in.
Tate Britain, Accepted by the Nation as Part of the Turner Bequest 1856

J. M. W. Turner
Boats at the Entrance to the Canale della Giudecca, Venice, off Santa Maria della Salute and the Dogana, c. 1840
Graphite, watercolor, bodycolor, and pen and ink on paper, 7½×$11\frac{1}{16}$ in.
Tate Britain, Accepted by the Nation as Part of the Turner Bequest 1856

J. M. W. Turner
The Campanile and Piazza of San Marco (St Mark's Square), Venice, with the Pilastri Acritani beside the Basilica, from the Porta della Carta of the Palazzo Ducale (Doge's Palace), 1840
Gouache, graphite and watercolor on paper, 11⅛×7½ in.
Tate Britain, Accepted by the Nation as Part of the Turner Bequest 1856

Thomas Moran
Sunset Santa Maria and the Ducal Palace, Venice, 1902
Oil on canvas, 20¼ × 30 in.
Promised gift of Bernard and Barbro Osher, Fine Arts Museums of San Francisco

Jean-Baptiste-Camille Corot
Vue de Venise (Santa Maria della Salute from Campo della Carita), 1828
Oil on paper laid down on canvas, 9⅜×12⅝ in.
Gallery 19C

Jean-Baptiste-Camille Corot
Venise—Vue du Campo della Carita en Regardent le Dôme de la Salute, 1834
Oil on paper laid down on canvas, 10½×15 in.
Gallery 19C

Edward Steichen
Camera Work, No. 42/43 (April/July, 1913)
Photograph, bound volume, 12¼×8⅛ in.
Brooklyn Museum Libraries and Archives
(Exhibited only in Brooklyn)

Alvin Coburn
Camera Work, No. 21 (January, 1908)
Photograph, bound volume, 13⅜×9 ½ in.
Brooklyn Museum Libraries and Archives
(Exhibited only in Brooklyn)

Francis Frith
Untitled Photograph of Piazza San Marco, 1850s–70s
Whole-plate albumen print from wet collodion glass negative, 6½×8 in.
Victoria and Albert Museum, Acquired from F. Frith and Company, 1954

Francis Frith
Untitled Photograph of Venice from San Giorgio, 1850s–70s
Whole-plate albumen print from wet collodion glass negative, 6½×8 in.
Victoria and Albert Museum, Acquired from F. Frith and Company, 1954

Francis Frith
Untitled Photograph of Island of San Giorgio, 1850s–70s
Whole-plate albumen print from wet collodion glass negative, 6½×8 in.
Victoria and Albert Museum, acquired from F. Frith and Company, 1954

Francis Frith
Untitled Photograph of Foscari Palace, 1850s–70s
Whole-plate albumen print from wet collodion glass negative, 6½×8 in.
Victoria and Albert Museum, acquired from F. Frith and Company, 1954
(Exhibited only in San Francisco)

Francis Frith
Untitled Photograph of Grand Canal, Venice, 1850s–70s
Whole-plate albumen print from wet collodion glass negative, 6 ½×8 in.
Victoria and Albert Museum, acquired from F. Frith and Company, 1954
(Exhibited only in San Francisco)

Francis Frith
Untitled Photograph of Venice, Palazzo Ducale, 1850s–70s
Whole-plate albumen print from wet collodion glass negative, 6½×8 in.
Victoria and Albert Museum, acquired from F. Frith and Company, 1954
(Exhibited only in San Francisco)

Francis Frith
Untitled Photograph of Venice, Palazzo Ducale, 1850s–70s
Whole-plate albumen print from wet collodion glass negative, 6½×8 in. Victoria and Albert Museum, acquired from F. Frith and Company, 1954
(Exhibited only in San Francisco)

Carlo Ponti
Venezia, Piazza San Marco, c. 1860–70
Albumen silver print, $10\frac{9}{16}$×13¾ in.
Fine Arts Museums of San Francisco
(Exhibited only in San Francisco)

Carlo Ponti
Venezia, Chiesa Salute, c. 1860–70
Albumen silver print, 13½×10½ in.
Fine Arts Museums of San Francisco
(Exhibited only in San Francisco)

Carlo Ponti
Venezia, Basilica San Marco, c. 1860–70
Albumen silver print, $10\frac{9}{16}$×13¾ in.
Fine Arts Museums of San Francisco
(Exhibited only in San Francisco)

Henri Le Sidaner
Le Palais des Doges, Venice, c. 1906
Oil on panel, 5⅝×7⅞ in.
La Salle University Art Museum, Gift of Richard M. Thune

Robert Blum
Venetian Gondoliers, c. 1880–89
Oil on canvas, 18⅜×28⅝ in.
Promised gift of Bernard and Barbro Osher, Fine Arts Museums of San Francisco

Jane Emmet de Glehn
Canal View, Venice, early 20th c.
Oil on canvas, 16×19 in.
Collection of Mary McClean
(Exhibited only in Brooklyn)

Paul Signac
Venice or, The Gondolas, 1908
Black chalk and watercolor on paper, 7½×9⅘ in.
Musée Marmottan Monet

Paul Signac
The Lagoon of Saint Mark, Venice, 1905
Oil on canvas, 51×64 in.
Chrysler Museum of Art, Gift of Walter P. Chrysler, Jr.

John Singer Sargent
The Church of San Stae, Venice, c. 1907
Oil on canvas, 22×28 in.
Private collection
(Exhibited only in Brooklyn)

John Singer Sargent
La Riva, c. 1903–04
Opaque and translucent watercolor with graphite underdrawing, 14×$20\frac{1}{16}$ in.
Brooklyn Museum, Purchased by Special Subscription
(Exhibited only in Brooklyn)

John Singer Sargent
The Bridge of Sighs, c. 1903–04
Translucent and opaque watercolor with graphite and red-pigmented underdrawing, 10×14 in.
Brooklyn Museum, Purchased by Special Subscription
(Exhibited only in Brooklyn)

John Singer Sargent
Venetian Boats, c. 1903–08
Watercolor on paper, $9\frac{15}{16}$×$13\frac{13}{16}$ in.
Brooklyn Museum, Purchased by Special Subscription
(Exhibited only in Brooklyn)

John Singer Sargent
The Giudecca, c. 1904
Translucent watercolor and touches of opaque watercolor and graphite, with graphite underdrawing, 10×14 in.
Brooklyn Museum, Purchased by Special Subscription
(Exhibited only in Brooklyn)

John Singer Sargent
Santa Maria della Salute, 1904
Translucent and opaque watercolor and graphite, with graphite underdrawing, $18\frac{3}{16}$×$22\frac{15}{16}$ in.
Brooklyn Museum, Purchased by Special Subscription
(Exhibited only in San Francisco)

John Singer Sargent
From the Gondola, c. 1903–04
Translucent watercolor and touches of opaque watercolor and graphite, with graphite underdrawing, 10×14 in.
Brooklyn Museum, Purchased by Special Subscription
(Exhibited only in San Francisco)

John Singer Sargent
All' Ave Maria, c. 1902–04
Translucent watercolor and touches of opaque watercolor, 10×14 1/16 in.
Brooklyn Museum, Purchased by Special Subscription
(Exhibited only in San Francisco)

John Singer Sargent
Santa Maria Della Salute, Venice, c. 1904–09
Watercolor on paper, 18×12 in.
Victoria and Albert Museum, Given by Mrs. Ormond and Miss Sargent in Memory of Their Brother

Emily Sargent
Interior of the Frari, 1885
Pencil and watercolor, 12 × 9⅜ in.
Brooklyn Museum, Anonymous Gift
(Exhibited only in Brooklyn)

William Merritt Chase
The Antiquary Shop, 1879
Oil on canvas, 26½×33 15/16 in.
Brooklyn Museum, Gift of Mrs. Carll H. de Silver in Memory of Her Husband
(Exhibited only in Brooklyn)

Emma Ciardi
La Scala dei Giganti, 1911
Oil on beaverboard, 14×11½ in.
Brooklyn Museum, Gift of the Estate of Emil Fuchs
(Exhibited only in Brooklyn)

William Bell Scott
Upper Portion of the Facade of St. Mark's, Venice, 1862
Watercolor on paper, 13 9/10×9 9/10 in.
Victoria and Albert Museum

James McNeill Whistler
The Mast, 1880
Etching on paper, 13½×6 7/16 in.
Brooklyn Museum, Gift of Mrs. Charles Pratt
(Exhibited only in Brooklyn)

James McNeill Whistler
The Beggars, 1880
Etching on paper, 2⅛×8¼ in.
Brooklyn Museum, Gift of Mrs. Charles Pratt
(Exhibited only in Brooklyn)

James McNeill Whistler
The Beggars, 1879–80
Etching, 12×8¼ in.
Fine Arts Museums of San Francisco, Bequest of Lucie Stern
(Exhibited only in San Francisco)

James McNeill Whistler
Bead Stringers, 1886
Etching, 8 15/16×6 in.
Brooklyn Museum, Gift of Mrs. Charles Pratt
(Exhibited only in Brooklyn)

James McNeill Whistler
Nocturne: Furnace from the portfolio *A Set of Twenty-Six Etchings*, 1878–80
Etching, 6 9/16×9 1/16 in.
Fine Arts Museums of San Francisco, Gift of Osgood Hooker
(Exhibited only in Brooklyn)

James McNeill Whistler
Nocturne, 1879–80
Etching printed in brown ink, 7 15/16×11 9/16 in.
Fine Arts Museums of San Francisco, Museum purchase, William H. Noble Bequest Fund

James McNeill Whistler
Nocturne, 1879–80
Etching, 7 15/16×11 9/16 in.
Fine Arts Museums of San Francisco, Bequest of Lucie Stern

James McNeill Whistler
The Palaces, c. 1880
Etching and drypoint on paper, 10 1/16×14 in.
Brooklyn Museum, Gift of Mrs. Charles Pratt
(Exhibited only in Brooklyn)

James McNeill Whistler
The Palaces, 1879
Etching, 9⅞×14⅛ in.
Fine Arts Museums of San Francisco, Gift of Osgood Hooker
(Exhibited only in San Francisco)

James McNeill Whistler
The Doorway, 1880
Etching and drypoint on paper, 11 9/16×7 15/16 in.
Brooklyn Museum, Gift of Mrs. Charles Pratt
(Exhibited only in Brooklyn)

James McNeill Whistler
The Doorway, 1879–80
Etching and drypoint with roulette printed in brown, 11½×7⅞ in.
Fine Arts Museums of San Francisco, Bequest of Lucie Stern
(Exhibited only in San Francisco)

James McNeill Whistler
Fruit Stall, 1886
Etching, 8⅞×5⅞ in.
Brooklyn Museum, Gift of Mrs. Charles Pratt
(Exhibited only in Brooklyn)

James McNeill Whistler
The Riva, No. 1, 1879–80
Etching and drypoint, 7 15/16×11¾ in.
Fine Arts Museums of San Francisco, Gift of Osgood Hooker
(Exhibited only in San Francisco)

James McNeill Whistler
Long Lagoon, ca. 1879–80
Etching printed in brown ink, 6⅛×9 in.
Fine Arts Museums of San Francisco, Victor and Lorraine Honig Collection
(Exhibited only in San Francisco)

James McNeill Whistler
San Biagio, from the portfolio *A Set of Twenty-Six Etchings*, 1879–80
Etching and drypoint printed in brown-black, 8 3/16×11 13/16 in.
Fine Arts Museums of San Francisco, Gift of Mr. and Mrs. Robert F. Gill through the Patrons of Art and Music
(Exhibited only in San Francisco)

John Ruskin
The Sound Side of the Basilica of St. Mark, from the Loggia of the Doge's Palace, Venice, c. 1850–52
Watercolor over pencil on paper, heightened with bodycolor, 38×18 in.
Private collection

Claude Monet
Water Lilies, 1914–17
Oil on canvas, 65⅜×56 in.
Fine Arts Museums of San Francisco, Museum Purchase, Mildred Anna Williams Collection

Claude Monet
Water Lilies, 1907
Oil on canvas, 37⅜×28¾ in.
Musée Marmottan Monet

Claude Monet
Water Lilies, 1914–17
Oil on canvas, 67×48 in.
Collection of Diane B. Wilsey

Claude Monet
Water Lilies, 1907
Oil on canvas, 36¼×31 15/16 in.
Museum of Fine Arts, Houston, Gift of Mrs. Harry C. Hanszen, 68.31
(Exhibited only in San Francisco)

Claude Monet
Self-portrait on the Surface of the Lily Pond (Autoportrait à la Surface du Bassin aux Nymphéas), c. 1905
Photograph, 4⅓×5¾ in.
© Collection Philippe Piguet

Claude Monet
The Palazzo Ducale, 1908
Oil on canvas, 22⅖×36¼ in.
Hasso Plattner Collection, Museum Barberini, Potsdam

Claude Monet
The Rio della Salute, 1908
Oil on canvas, 31 9/10×25⅔ in.
Hasso Plattner Collection, Museum Barberini, Potsdam

Claude Monet
The Palazzo Contarini, 1908
Oil on canvas, 28¾×36¼ in.
Hasso Plattner Collection, Museum Barberini, Potsdam

Claude Monet
The Palazzo Contarini, 1908
Oil on canvas, 36¼×31 9/10 in.
Kunstmuseum St. Gallen, Ernst Schürpf Foundation

Claude Monet
The Ducal Palace Seen from San Giorgio Maggiore, 1908
Oil on canvas, 25⅗×39⅓ in.
Kunsthaus Zürich, Donated by Walter Haefner
(Exhibited only in Brooklyn)

Claude Monet
The Grand Canal, Venice, 1908
Oil on canvas, 29×36⅜ in.
Museum of Fine Arts, Boston, Bequest of Alexander Cochrane
(Exhibited only in San Francisco)

Claude Monet
The Church of San Giorgio Maggiore, Venice, 1908
Oil on canvas, 26⅛×36⅞ in.
Indianapolis Museum of Art at Newfields, The Lockton Collection

Claude Monet
The Palazzo Ducale Seen from San Giorgio Maggiore, 1908
Oil on canvas, 25¾×36½ in.
The Metropolitan Museum of Art, Gift of Mr. and Mrs. Charles S. McVeigh

Claude Monet
San Giorgio Maggiore, 1908
Oil on canvas, 23×32 in.
Amgueddfa Cymru

Claude Monet
The Grand Canal, 1908
Oil on canvas, 32⅛×36 7/16 in.
Private collection

Claude Monet
The Palazzo da Mula, 1908
Oil on canvas, 26⅛×36¾ in.
Private collection

Claude Monet
San Giorgio Maggiore, 1908
Oil on canvas, 23⅔×28¾ in.
Private collection

Claude Monet
San Giorgio Maggiore, 1908
Oil on canvas, 23⅔×28¾ in.
Private collection, Courtesy of Alon Zakaim Fine Art, London

Claude Monet
The Palazzo Ducale Seen from San Giorgio Maggiore, 1908
Oil on canvas, 25⅞×36¼×⅞ in.
Private collection

MONET'S 37 VENICE PAINTINGS

The twenty-nine paintings Monet made of Venice are reproduced here in the order they were listed in the catalogue for the 1912 *Venise* exhibition at Galerie Bernheim-Jeune. The eight paintings that were not exhibited follow. Each listing includes the title and date of the artwork and its number in Daniel Wildenstein's *Claude Monet: Biographie et Catalogue Raisonné*. That is followed by the month and year that each was purchased from Monet by Bernheim-Jeune and Durand-Ruel. Paintings included in an exhibition at the Brooks Reed Gallery in Boston in 1912 are indicated. The initial ownership of each painting before Monet's death in 1926 is noted next, and last is its current location. Félicie Faizand de Maupeou provided key assistance in compiling this information. See her essay in this volume for more on the exhibition and initial purchasers of the paintings.

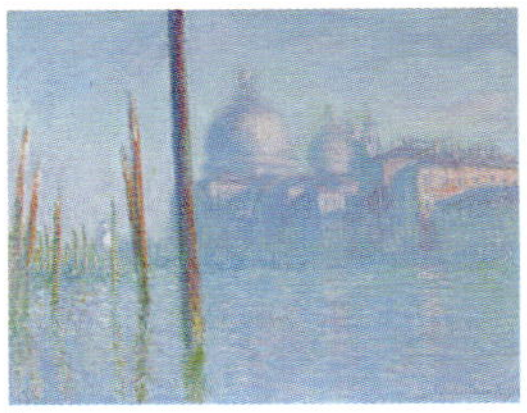

1
The Grand Canal, Venice, 1908 (W.1736)
March 1912
October 1912 acquired by the Davies sisters
Fine Arts Museums of San Francisco

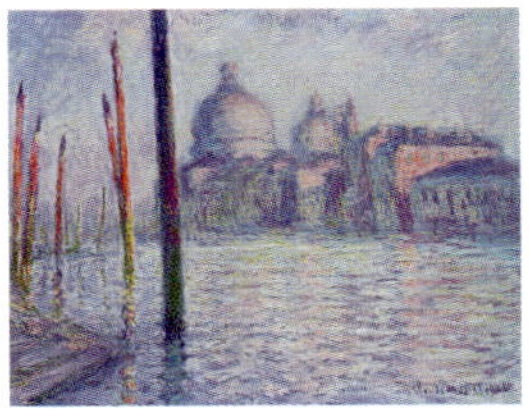

2
The Grand Canal, 1908 (W.1737)
March 1912
June 1912 acquired by Jacques Doucet
Location unknown

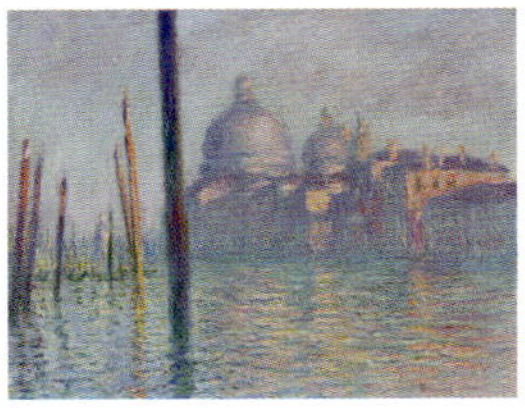

3
The Grand Canal, Venice, 1908 (W.1738)
March 1912
November 1912 acquired by
Alexander Cochrane
Museum of Fine Arts, Boston

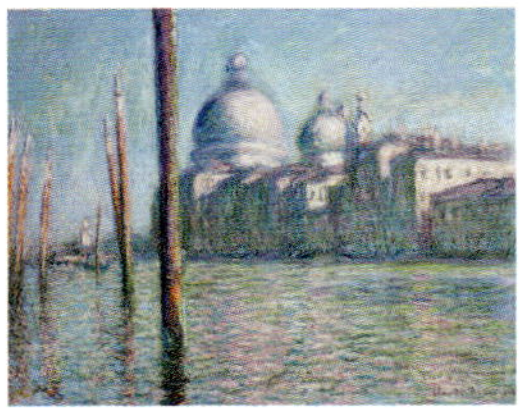

4
The Grand Canal, 1908 (W.1739)
May 1912
October 1913 acquired by
Hunt Henderson
Private collection

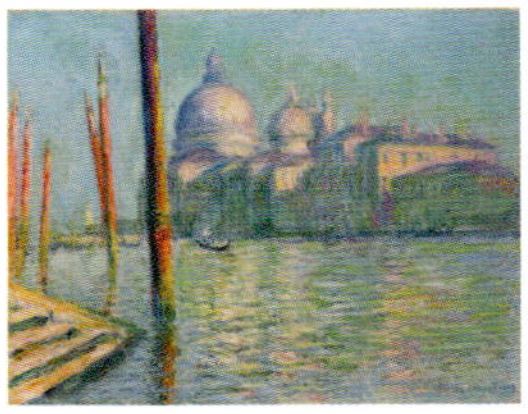

5
The Grand Canal and Santa Maria Della Salute, 1908 (W.1740)
May 1912
1912 Brooks Reed exhibition
October 1912 acquired by
Joseph F. Flanagan
Private collection

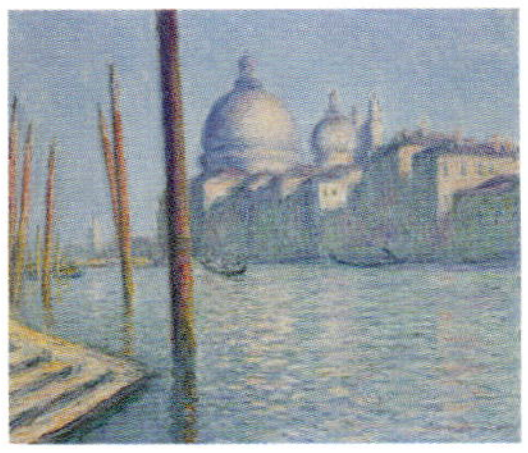

6
The Grand Canal, 1908 (W.1741)
May 1912
January 1913 acquired by
Mr. and Mrs. H. Crocker
Private collection

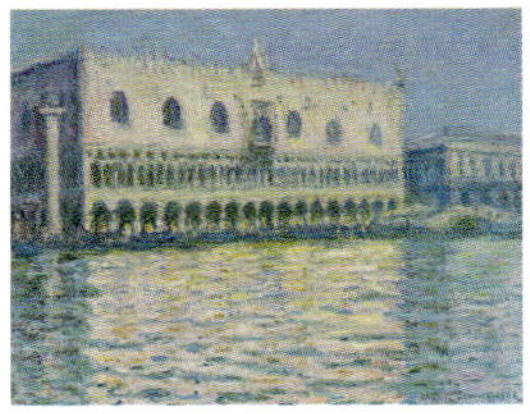

7
The Palazzo Ducale, 1908 (W.1742)
May 1912
1917 acquired by
Pierre Dubied
Private collection

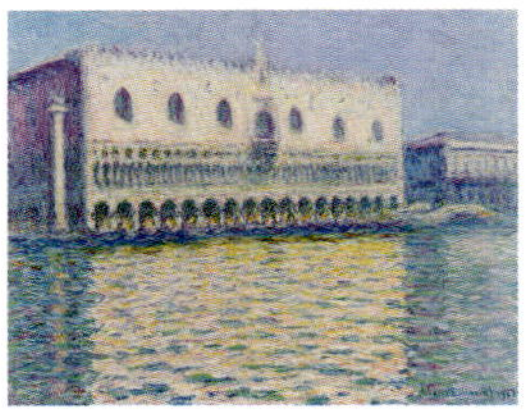

8
The Palazzo Ducale, 1908 (W.1743)
May 1912
December 1913 acquired by
Arthur B. Emmons
Brooklyn Museum

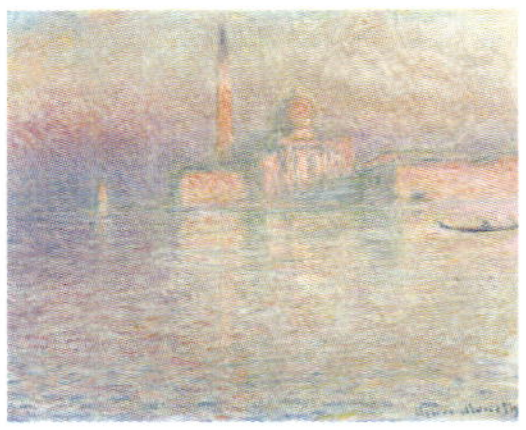

9
San Giorgio Maggiore, 1908 (W.1745)
March 1912
July 1912 acquired by
Alexander Cochrane
Private collection

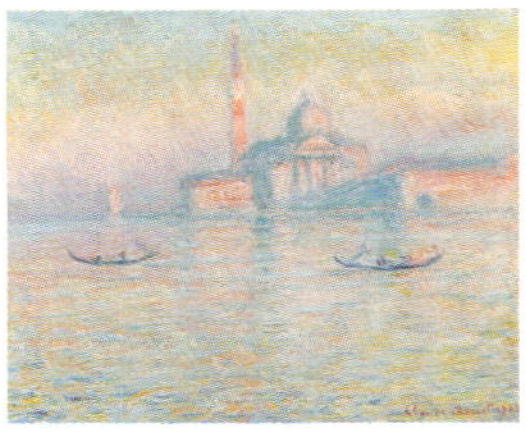

10
San Giorgio Maggiore, 1908 (W.1746)
March 1912
1925 acquired by
Henri Canonne
Private collection

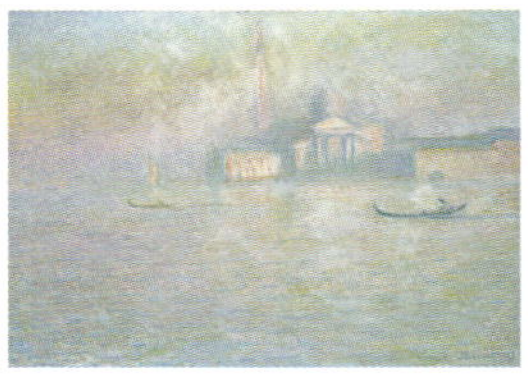

11
San Giorgio Maggiore, 1908 (W.1747)
March 1912
October 1912 acquired by
the Davies sisters
Amgueddfa Cymru

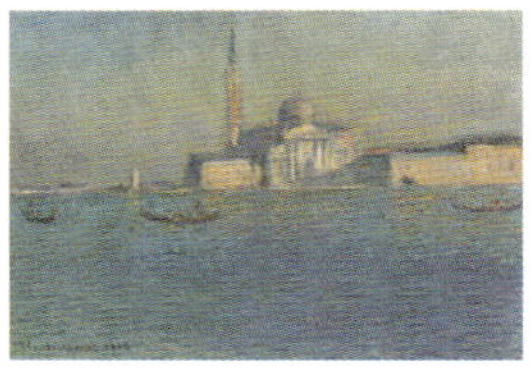

12
San Giorgio Maggiore, 1908 (W.1748)
March 1912
December 1915 acquired by
Martin A. Ryerson
Private collection

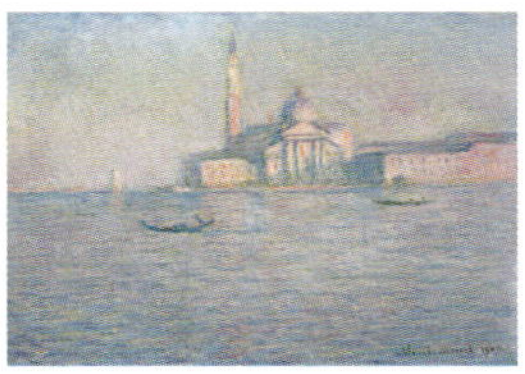

13
The Church of San Giorgio Maggiore, Venice, 1908 (W.1749)
March 1912
1912 Brooks Reed exhibition
November 1912 acquired by
Mrs. Breckenridge Long
Indianapolis Museum of Art at Newfields

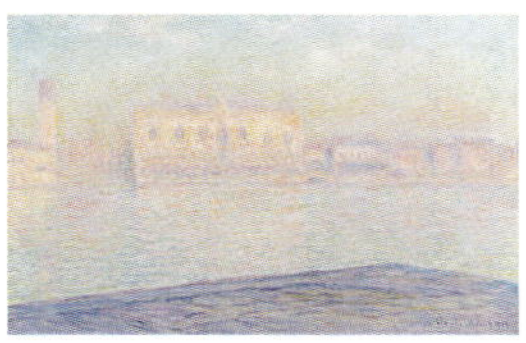

14
The Palazzo Ducale Seen from San Giorgio Maggiore, 1908 (W.1751)
May 1912
1912 Brooks Reed exhibition
December 1912 acquired by
Grace M. Edwards
Kunsthaus Zürich

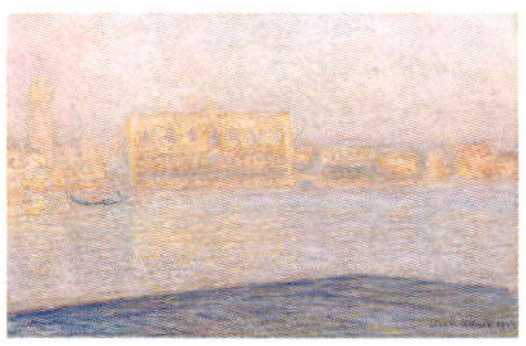

15
The Palazzo Ducale Seen from San Giorgio Maggiore, 1908 (W.1752)
May 1912
1912 acquired by
Durand-Ruel
Private collection

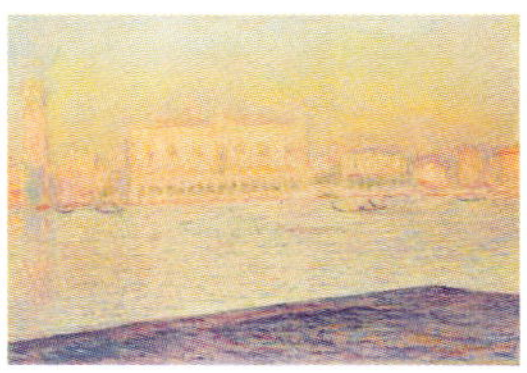

16
The Palazzo Ducale Seen from San Giorgio Maggiore, 1908 (W.1753)
May 1912
June 1912 acquired by
Durand-Ruel
Location unknown

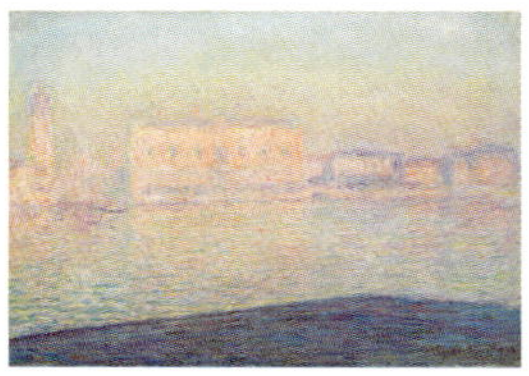

17
The Palazzo Ducale Seen from San Giorgio Maggiore, 1908 (W.1754)
May 1912
May 1913 acquired by
Arthur B. Emmons
Private collection

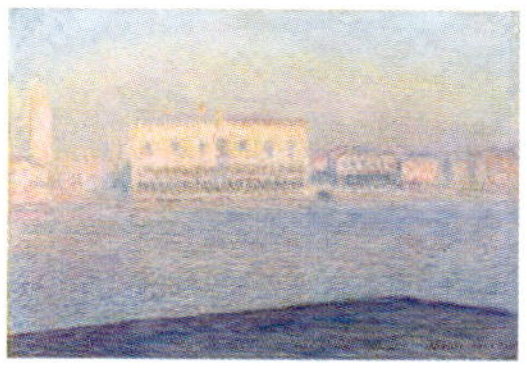

18
The Palazzo Ducale Seen from
San Giorgio Maggiore, 1908 (W.1755)
May 1912
1912 Bernheum-Jeune and Durand-Ruel
The Metropolitan Museum of Art

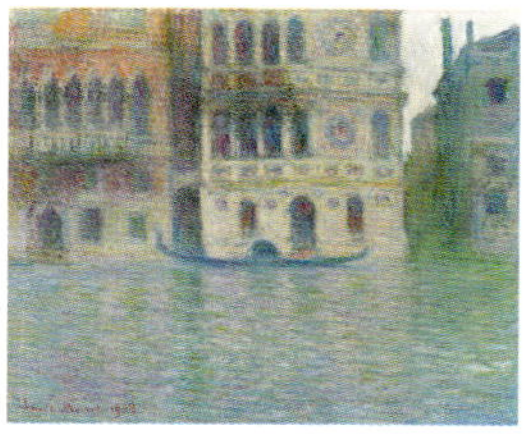

19
Venice, Palazzo Dario, 1908 (W.1757)
May 1912
1912 Brooks Reed exhibition
December 1912 acquired by
Arthur B. Emmons
The Art Institute of Chicago

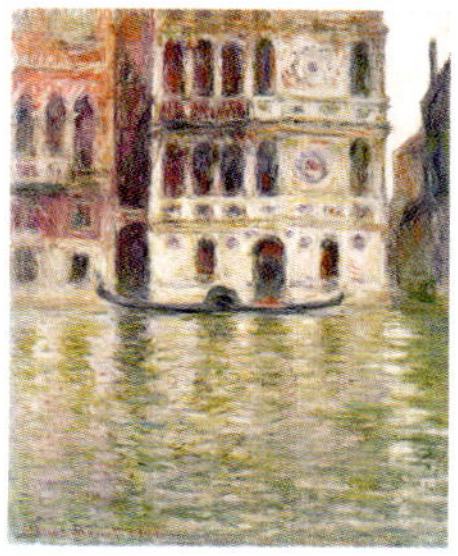

20
The Palazzo Dario, 1908 (W.1758)
May 1912
June 1912 acquired by
Claude Monet
Private collection

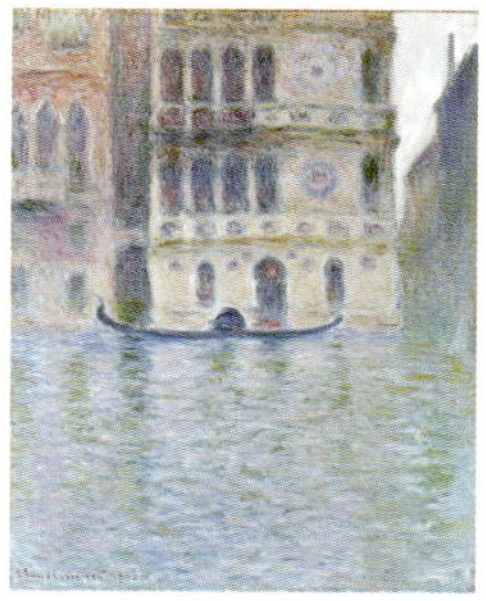

21
The Palazzo Dario, 1908 (W.1759)
May 1912
July 1913 acquired by
Margaret Davies
Amgueddfa Cymru

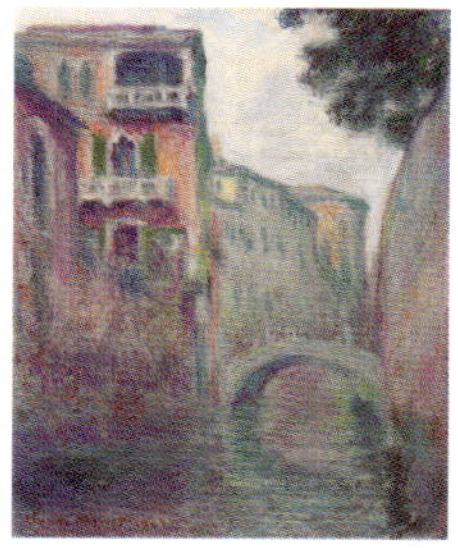

22
The Rio della Salute, 1908 (W.1761)
March 1912
1912 Brooks Reed exhibition
November 1912 acquired by
Miss E. H. Henderson
Private collection

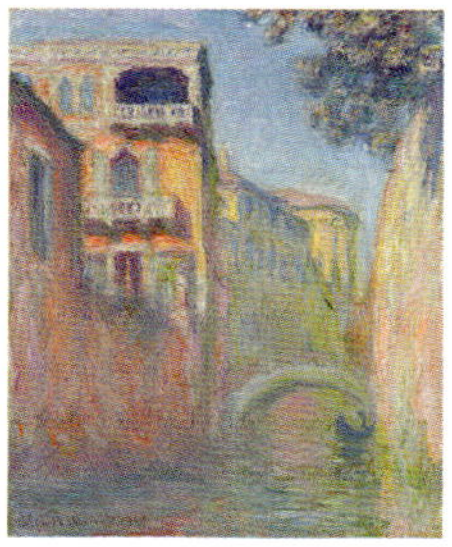

23
The Rio della Salute,1908 (W.1762)
March 1912
June 1912 acquired by Durand-Ruel
Hasso Plattner Collection

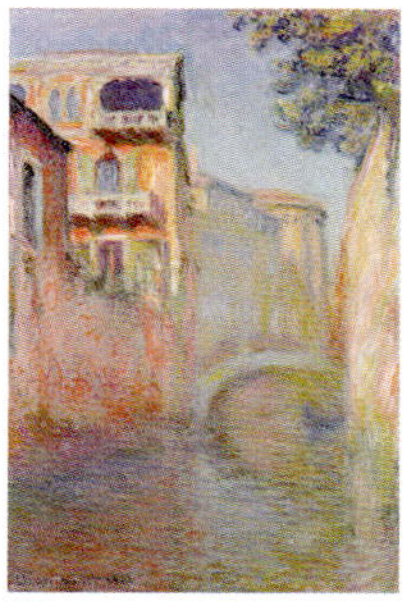

24
The Rio della Salute, 1908 (W.1763)
March 1912
January 1924 acquired by Henri Canonne
Pola Museum of Art

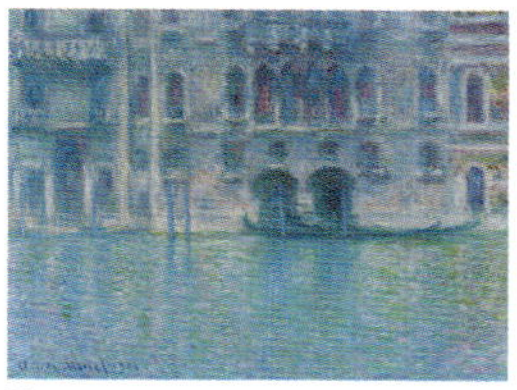

25
The Palazzo da Mula, Venice, 1908
(W.1764)
May 1912
May 1913 acquired by Arthur B. Emmons
National Gallery of Art

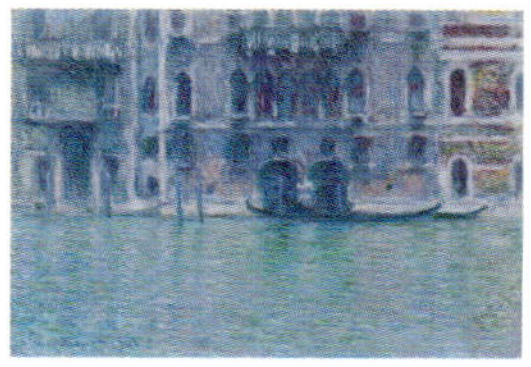

26
The Palazzo da Mula, 1908 (W.1765)
March 1912
1912 Brooks Reed show
January 1913 acquired by E. Faust
Private collection

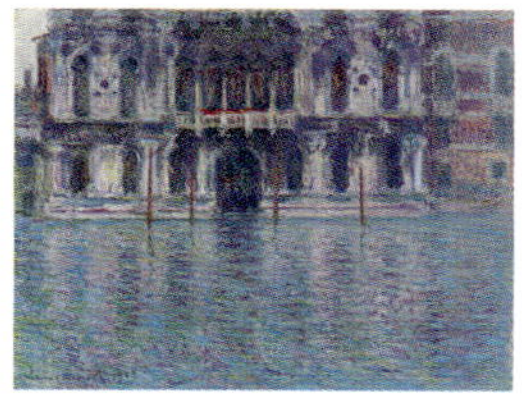

27
The Palazzo Contarini, 1908 (W.1766)
May 1912
January 1917 acquired by
Adolph Lewisohn
Hasso Plattner Collection

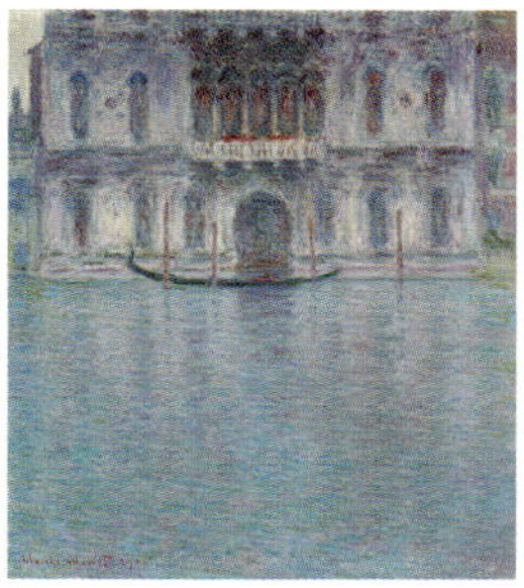

28
The Palazzo Contarini, 1908 (W.1767)
May 1912
1912 Brooks Reed exhibition
December 1912 acquired by
Arthur Meeker
Kunstmuseum St. Gallen

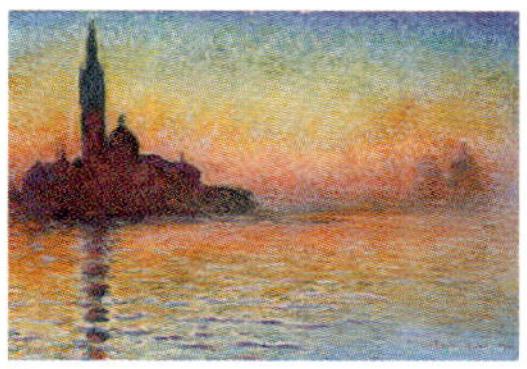

29
San Giorgio Maggiore at Dusk, 1908
(W.1768)
March 1912
May 1912 acquired by the Davies sisters
Amgueddfa Cymru

PAINTINGS 30–37 WERE NOT IN THE 1912 *VENISE* EXHIBITION

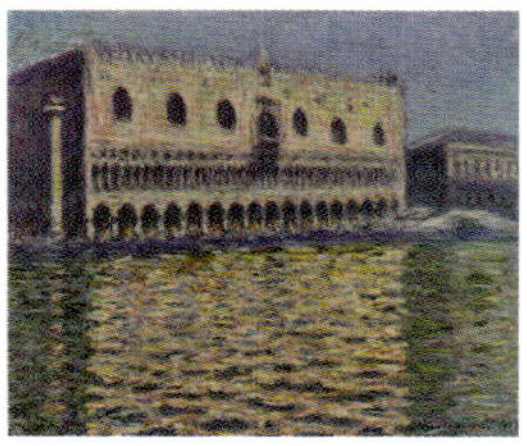

30
The Palazzo Ducale, 1908 (W.1744)
March 1913 acquired by Bernheim-Jeune
and Durand-Ruel
1914 acquired by Paul Cassirer
Private collection

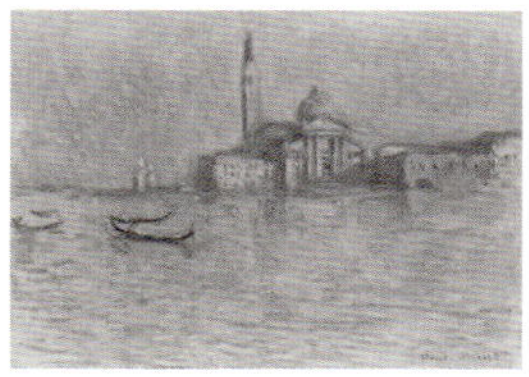

31
San Giorgio Maggiore,1908 (W.1750)
C. before 1920, given by Monet to
Mary Hunter
Private collection

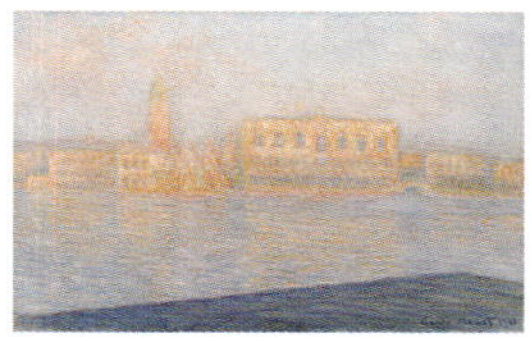

32
The Palazzo Ducale, Seen from
San Giorgio Maggiore, 1908 (W.1756)
After 1926 acquired by
Justin K. Thannhauser
Solomon R. Guggenheim Museum

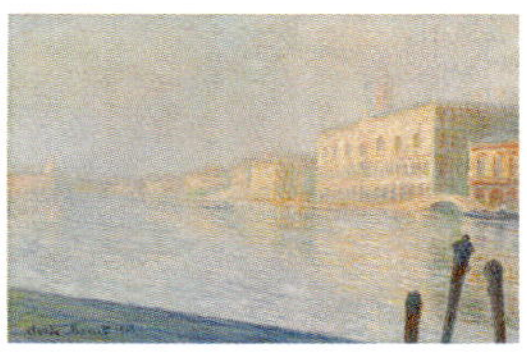

33
The Palazzo Ducale, 1908 (W.1770)
C. 1912–13 probably acquired by
Bernheim-Jeune
C. before 1926 acquired by
Dr. Hans Wendland
Hasso Plattner Collection

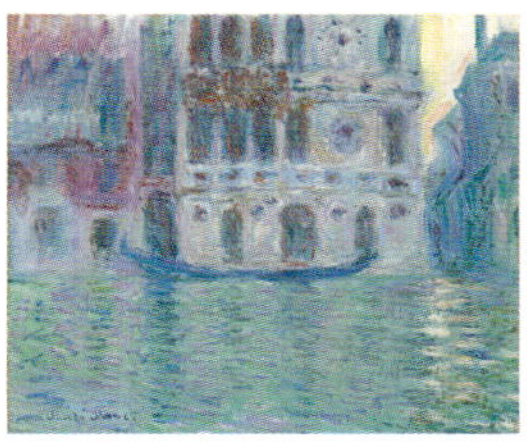

34
The Palazzo Dario, 1908 (W.1760)
After 1926 acquired by
Gaston Bernheim-Jeune
Private collection

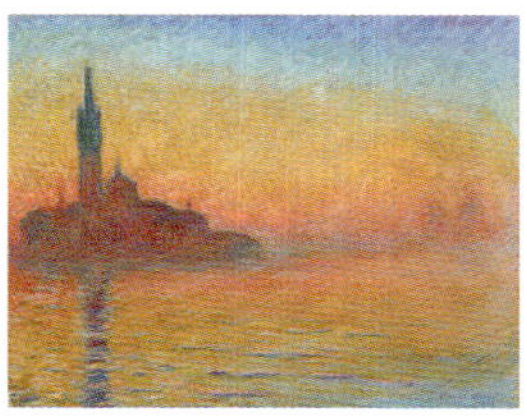

35
Twilight, Venice, 1908 (W.1769)
1925 sold by Monet to
Shojiro Ishibashi
Artizon Museum

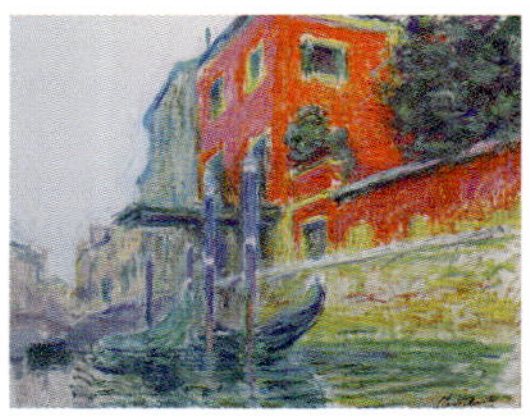

36
The Red House, 1908 (W.1771)
Sold after 1926
Collection Galerie Larock-Granoff

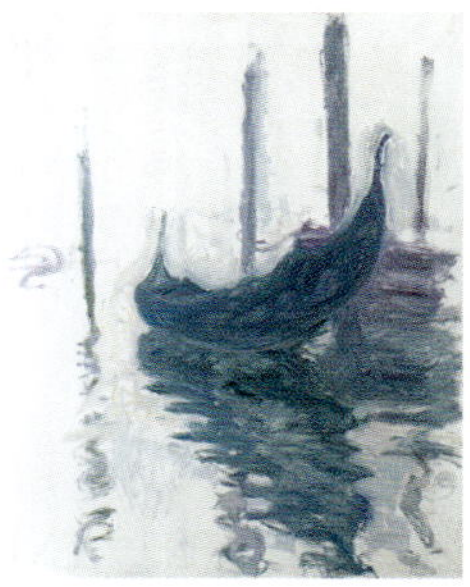

37
Gondola in Venice, 1908 (W.1772)
C. before 1926 given by Monet to
Georges Clemenceau
Musée d'Arts de Nantes

SELECTED BIBLIOGRAPHY

Adelson, Warren, and Richard Ormond. *Sargent's Venice*. Yale University Press, 2006.

Adelson Galleries. *Sargent and Impressionism*. Adelson Galleries, 2010.

Albright, Anna Lea, and Peter Huybers, "Paintings by Turner and Monet Depict Trends in 19th Century Air Pollution." *PNAS* (*Proceedings of the National Academy of Sciences*) 120, no. 6 (January 31, 2023).

Alexandre, Arsène. *Claude Monet*. Bernheim-Jeune, 1921.

Ambrosini, Lynne, et al. *Daubigny Monet Van Gogh: Impressions of Landscape*. Taft Museum of Art, 2015.

Amiot-Saulnier, Emmanuelle. *Monet's Garden: Masterpieces from the Musée Marmottan Monet*. Sakiip Sabanci Museum, 2012.

Art Institute of Chicago. "Monet Paintings and Drawings at the Art Institute of Chicago." publications.artic.edu/monet/reader/paintingsanddrawings/section/135470.

Aurisch, Helga, and Tanya Paul. *Monet and the Seine: Impressions of a River*. Museum of Fine Arts, Houston, 2014.

Bellon, Liana Amanda. "Souvenirs of Venice: Reproduced Views, Tourism, and City Spaces." PhD thesis, McGill University, 2016.

Bettagno, Alessandro. *Venezia da Stato a Mito*. Marsilio, 1997.

Brettell, Richard. *Monet in Normandy*. Rizzoli, 2006.

Clarke, David. *Water and Art*. Reaktion, 2010.

Cogeval, Guy, et al. *Claude Monet, 1840–1926*. Réunion des Musées Nationaux, 2010.

Davis, Robert C., and Garry R. Marvin. *Venice, the Tourist Maze: A Cultural Critique of the World's Most Touristed City*. University of California Press, 2004.

Distel, Anne, and Hélène Adhémar, eds. *Hommage à Claude Monet*. Réunion des Musées Nationaux, 1980.

Dombrowski, André. *Monet's Minutes: Impressionism and the Industrialization of Time*. Yale University Press, 2023.

Duret, Théodore. *Les Peintres Impressionnistes: Claude Monet*. Harvard University Press, 1878.

Duret, Théodore. *Manet and the French Impressionists*. J. B. Lippincott, 1910.

Eisenman, Stephen F. "Death and Tourism: Claude Monet's Paintings of Venice." In *Value, Art, Politics: Criticism, Meaning and Interpretation after Postmodernism*, edited by Jonathan Harris. Liverpool University Press, 2007.

Eisenman, Stephen F. *From Corot to Monet: The Ecology of Impressionism*. Rizzoli, 2010.

Elder, Marc. *À Giverny, Chez Claude Monet*. Bernheim-Jeune, 1924.

Faizand de Maupeou, Félicie. "An Unprecedented Artistic Gesture: The Exhibition of Monet's *Water Lilies* at the Orangerie des Tuileries." *exposure* 3, no. 17 (2017).

Fels, Marthe de. *La Vie de Claude Monet*. Librairie Gallimard, 1929.

Geffroy, Gustave. *Claude Monet: Sa Vie, Son Temps, Son Oeuvre*. G. Crès et Cie, 1922.

Geffroy, Gustave. *Claude Monet: Sa Vie, Son Temps, Son Oeuvre. Neuf Reproductions hors Texte*. G. Crès et Cie, 1924.

Gillet, Louis, *Trois Variations sur Claude Monet*. Plon, 1927.

Gregori, Elsa. *Palace of Wonders Venice: History of the Palaces, Families and Events That Shaped the Insula of St. Moisè*. Supernova, 2020.

Guillaud, Jacqueline, and Maurice Guillaud. *Claude Monet at the Time of Giverny*. Centre Culturel du Marais, 1983.

Halsby, Julian. *Venice: The Artist's Vision: A Guide to British and American Painters*. Trafalgar Square, 1992.

Haynes, Deborah. "Answers First, Questions Later: A Bakhtinian Interpretation of Monet's Mediterranean Paintings." *Semiotic Inquiry* 19, nos. 1–2 (1998): 217–30.

Herbert, Robert L. *Monet on the Normandy Coast: Tourism and Painting, 1867–1886*. Yale University Press, 1994.

House, John. *Monet: Nature into Art*. Yale University Press, 1988.

James, Henry. *Italian Hours*. Ecco Press, 1909.

Joyes, Claire. *Claude Monet et Giverny*. Chêne, 1985.

Joyeux-Prunel, Béatrice. "Monet au Risque d'une Cartographie: Du Territoire à sa Dilution." In *Impressionnisme: Du Plein Air au Territoire*, edited by Frédéric Cousinié. Presses Universitaires de Rouen et du Havre, 2013.

Kelly, Simon. "How Monet Became a Millionaire: The Importance of the Artist's Account Books." *Journal of Cultural Economics*, no. 47 (2023): 437–60. https://doi.org/10.1007/s10824-023-09473-y.

Kendall, Richard, ed. *Monet by Himself: Paintings, Drawings, Pastels, Letters*. Barnes & Noble, 2004.

Kilmurray, Elaine, and Richard Ormond. "Venetian Figures and Landscapes 1898–1913." In *John Singer Sargent: Complete Paintings*, volume 6. Paul Mellon Centre for Studies in British Art, 2006.

King, Ross. *Mad Enchantment: Claude Monet and the Painting of the Water Lilies*. Bloomsbury, 2016.

Koja, Stephan. *Monet*. Österreichische Galerie Belvedere, 1996.

Kuster, Ulf. *Monet: Light, Shadow, and Reflection*. Fondation Beyeler, 2017.

Le Men, Ségolène, et al. *La Bibliothèque de Monet*. Citadelles & Mazenod, 2013.

Lemonedes, Heather, et al. *Monet in Normandy*. Rizzoli, 2006.

Levine, Steven Z. *Monet and His Critics*. Garland, 1976.

Levine, Steven Z. *Monet, Narcissus, and Self-Reflection: The Modernist Myth of the Self*. University of Chicago Press, 1995.

Lochnan, Katharine, et al. *Turner Whistler Monet: Impressionist Visions*. Art Gallery of Ontario/Tate, 2004.

Lovell, Margaretta M. *A Visitable Past: Views of Venice by American Artists, 1860–1915*. University of Chicago Press, 1989.

McCauley, Elizabeth Anne, et al., eds., *Gondola Days: Isabella Stewart Gardner and the Palazzo Barbaro Circle*. Isabella Stewart Gardner Museum, 2004.

Mount, Charles Merrill. *Monet: A Biography*. Simon & Schuster, 1966.

Mirbeau, Octave. *Venise*. Bernheim-Jeune, 1912.

O'Neill, Michael, et al. *Venice and the Cultural Imagination: "This Strange Dream upon the Water."* Routledge, 2016.

Piguet, Philippe. *Monet et Venise*. Éditions Herscher, 1986.

Pissarro, Joachim. *Monet and the Mediterranean*. Rizzoli, 1997.

Plant, Margaret. *Venice, Fragile City: 1797–1997*. Yale University Press, 2022.

Portulese, Anthony. "*A Phenomenology of Display*: Monet's L'Orangerie, the Panorama Rotunda, and the History of Proto-Installation Art." *Rutgers Art Review* 37 (2021): 64–92.

Romano, Dennis. *Venice: The Remarkable History of the Lagoon City*. Oxford University Press, 2024.

Rubin, James H. *Why Monet Matters: Meanings Among the Lily Pads*. Penn State University Press, 2021.

Schwander, Martin. *Venice: From Canaletto and Turner to Monet*. Fondation Beyeler, 2008.

Scappettone, Jennifer. *Killing the Moonlight: Modernism in Venice*. New York: Columbia University Press, 2014.

Seitz, William C. *Claude Monet: Seasons and Moments*. The Museum of Modern Art, 1960.

Seitz, William C. *Claude Monet*. Abrams, 1960.

Serres, Karen, ed. *Monet and London: Views of the Thames*. Paul Holberton Publishing, 2024.

Shackelford, George T. M. *Monet: The Late Years*. Kimbell Art Museum, 2019.

Shackelford, George T. M. "Monet and the Mediterranean: Fort Worth and New York." *The Burlington Magazine* 139, no. 1135 (1997): 716–19.

Siegel, Harmon. *Painting with Monet*. Princeton University Press, 2024.

Spate, Virginia. *Claude Monet: The Colour of Time*. BCA, 1992.

Spate, Virginia, et al. *Monet and Japan*. Gardners Books, 2004.

Stuckey, Charles. *Claude Monet 1840–1926*. Thames and Hudson/Art Institute of Chicago, 1995.

Stuckey, Charles. *Monet: A Retrospective*. Hugh Lauter Levin Associates, 1985.

Stuckey, Charles. "The Predications and Implications of Monet's Series," from *The Repeating Image*. The Walters Art Museum, 2007.

Tanner, Tony. *Venice Desired*. Harvard University Press, 1992.

Thomson, Richard. *Monet & Architecture*. National Gallery, 2018.

Thomson, Richard. *Monet: The Seine and the Sea*. National Galleries of Scotland, 2003.

Tucker, Paul Hayes. *Claude Monet: Late Work*. Rizzoli, 2010.

Tucker, Paul Hayes. *Claude Monet: Life and Art*. New Haven: Yale University Press, 1995.

Tucker, Paul Hayes. *Monet in the '90s: The Series Paintings*. Museum of Fine Arts, Boston/Yale University Press, 1989.

Tucker, Paul Hayes, et al. *Monet in the 20th Century*. Yale University Press, 1998.

Westheider, Ortrud, et al. *Claude Monet: The Truth of Nature*. Prestel, 2019.

Westheider, Ortrud. *Impressionism: The Hasso Plattner Collection*. Prestel, 2021.

Westheider, Orthud, and Michael Philipp, eds. *Impressionism: The Art of Landscape*. Prestel, 2017.

Wildenstein, Daniel. *Monet: Biographie et Catalogue Raisonné*, volumes 1–5. Wildenstein Institute and La Bibliothèque des Arts, 1974–1991.

Wildenstein, Daniel. *Monet or the Triumph of Impressionism*. Taschen, 2015.

Wullschläger, Jackie. *Monet: The Restless Vision*. Penguin Random House UK, 2023.

Selected reviews of *Claude Monet: Venise* at Galerie Bernheim-Jeune (1912)

Alexandre, Arsène. "La Vie Artistique: Claude Monet et Venise." *Le Figaro,* May 29, 1912.

Apollinaire, Guillaume. "Claude Monet." *L'Intransigeant*, May 31, 1912.

"Art et Curiosité: Une Féerie de Lumière et de Couleur. Venise Vue par Claude Monet." *Le Temps*, June 11, 1912.

"Beaux-Arts et Curiosité: Venise Vue par Claude Monet." *Le Temps,* June 11, 1912.

Besson, Georges. "Exposition Claude Monet (Galerie Bernheim-Jeune)." *La Phalange*, June 20, 1912.

Bouyer, Raymond. "Venise par Claude Monet." *Le Bulletin de l'Art Ancien et Moderne,* June 8, 1912.

Geffroy, Gustave. "Claude Monet." *La Vie*, June 1, 1912.

Geffroy, Gustave. "La Venise de Claude Monet." *La Dépêche*, May 30, 1912.

Genet, Henri. "Beaux-Arts et Curiosité: Les 'Venise' de Claude Monet." *L'Opinion*, June 1, 1912.

Ghéon, Henri. "Exposition Claude Monet (Galerie Bernheim-Jeune)." *L'Art Décoratif*, June 20, 1912.

Goth, Max. *Les Hommes du Jour*, June 15, 1912.

Guillemot, Maurice. "De Venise à Giverny." *Le Siècle,* May 27, 1912.

Intérim, "La 'Venise' de Claude Monet." *La Chronique des Arts et de la Curiosité,* June 15, 1912.

Kahn, Gustave. "Chez Bernheim-Jeune, une Série de Monet sur Venise." *Mercure de France*, June 16, 1912.

Lecomte, Georges. "Un Radieux Poème à la Gloire de Venise." *Le Matin,* June 3, 1912.

"Les Arts: Claude Monet," *Paris Journal*, June 12, 1912.

Mauclair, Camille. "Les 'Venise' de Claude Monet." *La Semaine Littéraire,* June 15, 1912.

Michel, André. "Promenades aux Salons VI." *Journal des Débats*, June 5, 1912.

Parisiana. "Art et Chiffon. *L'Art et la Mode*, June 15, 1912.

Tabarant, Adolphe. "Venise: L'Exposition de Claude Monet," *Paris-Midi*, May 29, 1912.

Variot, Jean. "Les 'Venises' de Claude Monet." *L'Univers*, June 6, 1912.

Vauxcelles, Louis. "La 'Venise' de Claude Monet." *Gil Blas*, May 29, 1912.

"Venise." *Gil Blas*, May 27, 1912.

"Vision d'Art: Venise par Claude Monet." *Le Gaulois*, June 14, 1912.

Note: Page numbers in italic type indicate illustrations.

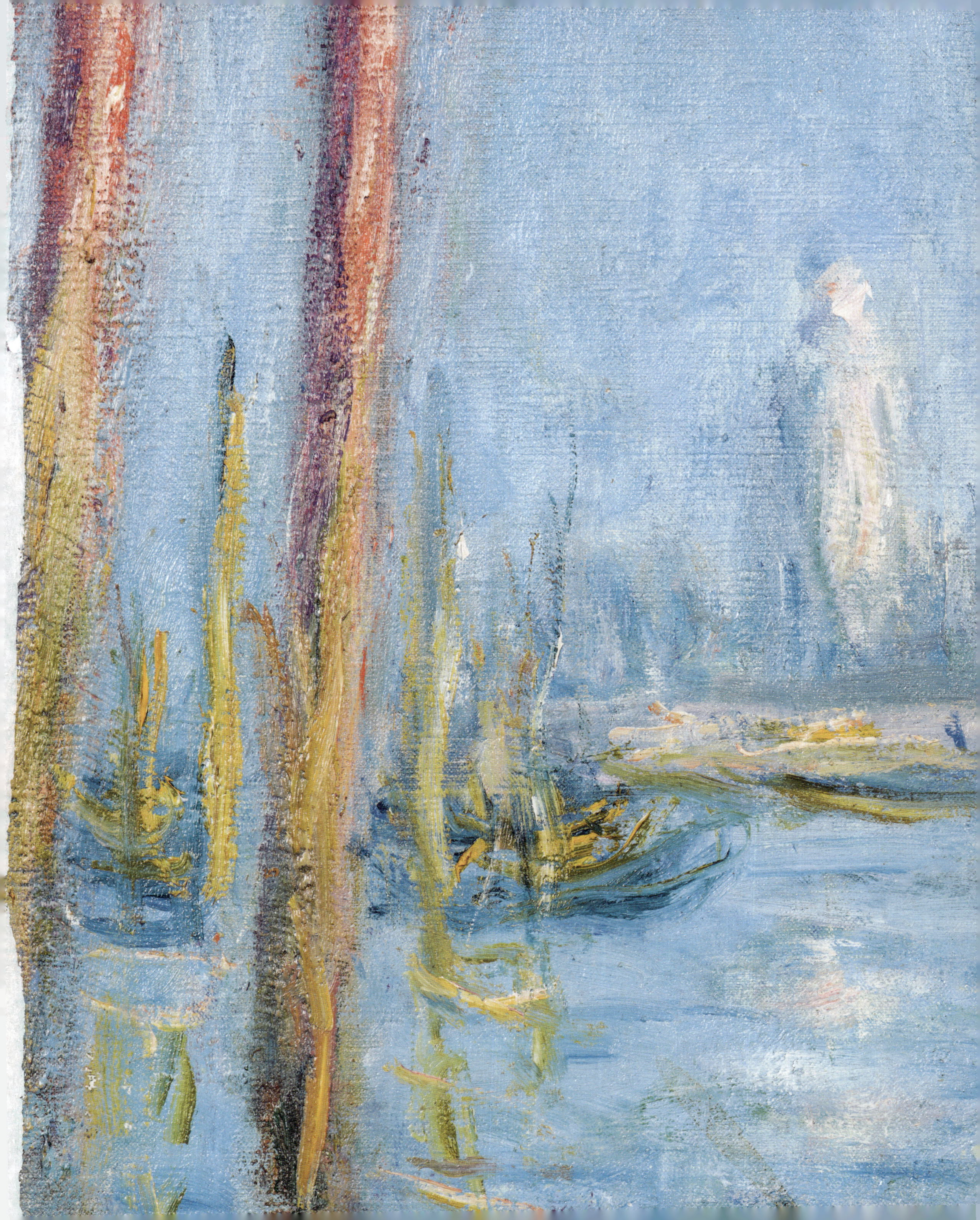

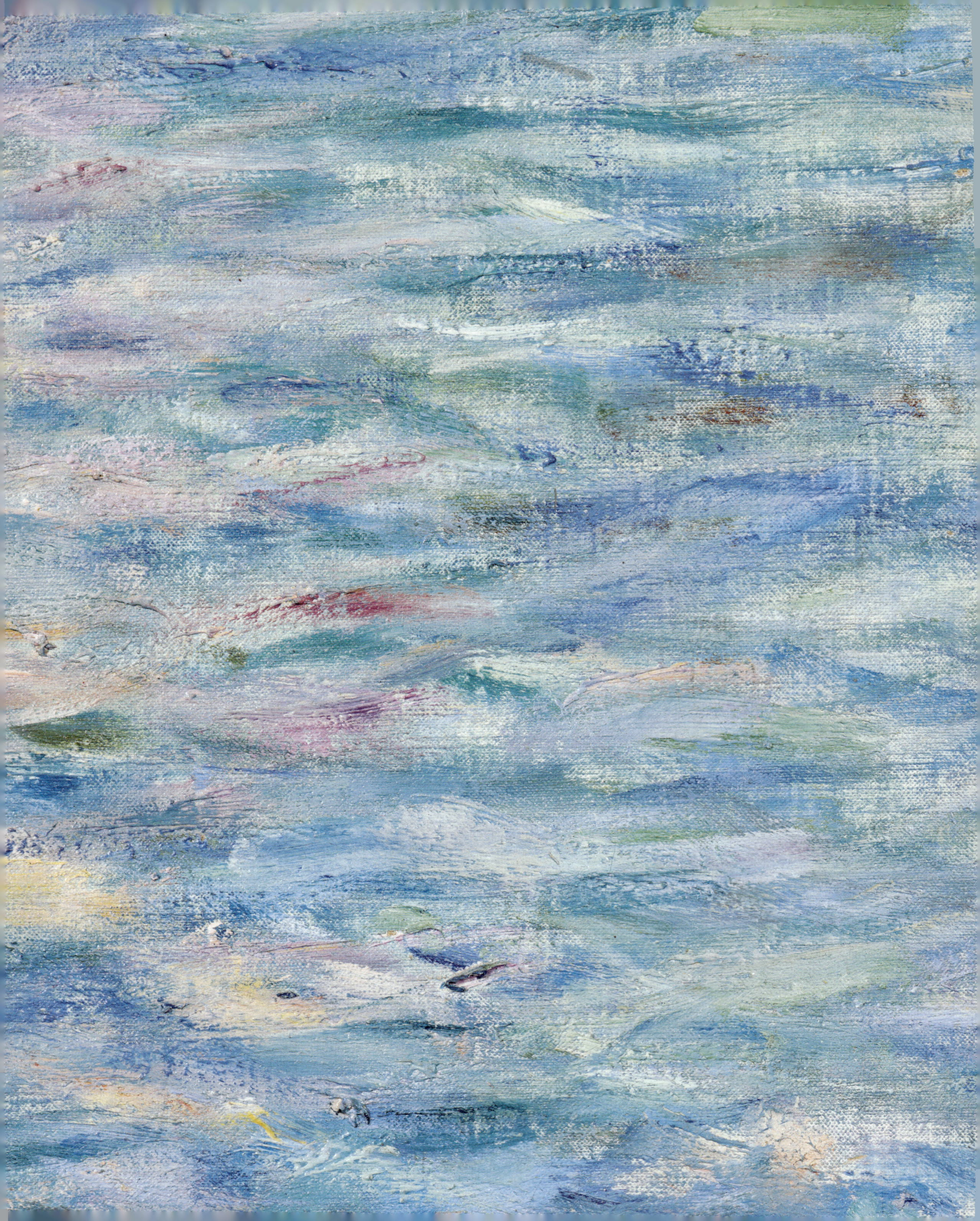